APPLYING PSYCHOLOGY

APPLYING PSYCHOLOGY

Second Edition

Virginia Nichols Quinn
Northern Virginia Community College

McGraw-Hill Publishing Company
New York St. Louis San Francisco Auckland Bogotá Caracas
Hamburg Lisbon London Madrid Mexico Milan Montreal
New Delhi Oklahoma City Paris San Juan São Paulo
Singapore Sydney Tokyo Toronto

APPLYING PSYCHOLOGY

1 2 3 4 5 6 7 8 9 0   DOC DOC   8 9 4 3 2 1 0 9

ISBN 0-07-051073-3

This book was set in Times Roman by the College Composition Unit
in cooperation with Monotype Composition Company.
The editors were James D. Anker, Michael Morales, and James R. Belser;
the production supervisor was Leroy A. Young.
The cover was designed by Rafael Hernandez.
New drawings were done by Hadel Studio.
R. R. Donnelley & Sons Company was printer and binder.

See Acknowledgments on pages 507-513.
Copyrights included on this page by reference.

Library of Congress Cataloging-in-Publication Data

Quinn, Virginia Nichols.
    Applying psychology / Virginia Nichols Quinn.—2nd ed.
        p.   cm.
    Bibliography: p.
        Includes index.
    ISBN 0-07-051073-3
    1. Psychology.   2. Psychology, Applied.   I. Title.
BF121.Q56   1990
    158—dc20   89-12113

ABOUT THE AUTHOR

Virginia Nichols Quinn has been a professor of psychology at Northern Virginia Community College for more than sixteen years. She received her bachelor's degree from Hunter College where she majored in psychology and minored in mathematics and education. She completed her master's degree and coursework for her doctorate in psychometrics at Harvard University. Her professional experiences in applying psychology include teaching children with behavioral problems, working as a consultant in decision making and problem solving for the United States Department of Defense, and serving as the director of psychology at a children's rehabilitation hospital. In addition, she has applied psychological principles to politics in her successful campaign for mayor of Round Hill, Virginia and her role as a member of school boards and planning commissions. Her strongest concern is to make psychology understandable, practical, and useful to students; she is the author of numerous study guides and test banks to accompany psychology texts.

CONTENTS IN BRIEF

CONTENTS

PREFACE

In preparing the preface for the first edition of this text, I recalled my father's annoyance when I decided to continue studying for a doctorate at Harvard. He pounded his fist on the kitchen table and warned, "Virginia, you're going to educate yourself right out of humanity; no one will be able to talk to you!" He feared that I would bury myself in textbooks and lose my sense of reality. I hope the first edition proved that even after a lengthy education I can still talk with most people and remain an active member of humanity.

I also hope that this text demonstrates that books (or at least this text-book) can be closely connected to reality, even useful. A good text should not be only for the elite. This text is designed for beginning students who have little or no knowledge of psychology. The tone of the text is conversational and should read as easily as a newspaper or magazine article. Students should be able to enjoy the content and concentrate on the topics without struggling to understand what they are reading.

The content includes basic topics in psychology and describes their application across a broad range of everyday experiences, including—but not limited to—work, education, consumer concerns, community and civic programs, social and environmental interests, sports, mental health, human relations, forensics, and a variety of vocational interests. Cartoons, illustrations, photos, and clippings from newspapers and magazines are used to spark interest and show the relevance and importance of psychology. The intent of this text is not only to maintain the integrity of traditional psychology by acknowledging the basic research required but also to make psychology useful so students will be enticed into continuing their study either formally or informally.

For many decades psychologists have known that students learn more when they read actively rather than passively. Psychologists have also confirmed that practice and feedback are critical to learning. *Applying Psychology* does just this by putting these basic principles in psychology to use. As a result, this is not an ordinary text that can be read passively. This book has been designed for students to use, write in, and personalize with their own notes. Each chapter has several unique features including:

Chapter Outline At the beginning of each chapter an outline previews the major topics to be included.

Exhibits A variety of newspaper and magazine articles and other information are highlighted to show the relevance and application of psychological principles.

Exercises After each new concept is discussed, the student has the opportunity to interact with the material and demonstrate an ability to apply the newly acquired knowledge.

Feedback This section of the chapter either provides reinforcement for material that was learned correctly or alerts the student to the need for further review of the text.

Checkpoints Each chapter is broken into readable units based on the length of the average attention span. After reading about one-third of a chapter and completing the required exercises, the student reaches a checkpoint with review questions. Answers can be checked at the end of the chapter.

Running Glossary All key terms are defined in the margin where they first appear.

Chapter Inventory This list of specific learning objectives appears at the conclusion of each chapter. Students can use these objectives as a checklist for review and exam preparation.

Among the important new features in this edition are the outlines at the beginning of each chapter and the running glossary in the margins. The text size has increased from fourteen to sixteen chapters with more comprehensive coverage in every chapter. Memory, thinking, and problem solving are now covered in two chapters rather than only one. A new chapter on "Identifying Problem Behavior" has been added. Throughout the book numerous sections have been revised and updated.

It would be impossible to list the names of the thousands of students who studied the manuscript and the first edition of this text and offered comments for making this edition more useful and explicit. But to each and every student, I am most grateful. Many ideas in the text came from reviewers for the first edition: Alice Brown, Southwest Virginia Community College; James D'Amato, Rockland Community College; Jim Eison, Roane Community College; Eugene Fichter, Northern Virginia Community College; Norman Halls, Westfield State College; Donald Murdock, Suffolk County Community College; Marlene Polkovich, Special Intermediate Vocational School, Wisconsin District No. 916; Robert Rea, Charles County Community College; Robert Sands, State University of New York, Agricultural and Technical College at Alfred.

I am grateful for the comments, suggestions, and intelligent criticisms offered by the reviewers for the second edition: Thomas Bond, Thomas Nelson Community College; Ronald Caldwell, Blue Mountain Community College; James Dailey, Vincennes University; Nancy Dash, C. S. Mott Community College; Pauline Gillette, Northern Virginia Community College; Harriette B. Ritchie, American River College; Mary A. Rogers, Inver Hills Community

College; Caroline Roth, Northern Virginia Community College; Linda Truesdale, Midlands Technical College; Everette K. Wagner, San Antonio College.

A special tribute must be paid to my husband, Paul, and my children, Dana and Stephen, who were supportive and encouraging in spite of my grumpy moods as deadlines approached. Finally, thanks must go to my father who, by pounding his fist, left me with something to prove persistently!

Virginia Nichols Quinn

APPLYING
PSYCHOLOGY

CHAPTER 1

EXAMINING THE METHODS OF PSYCHOLOGY

The proper study of mankind is man.

Alexander Pope

psychology Scientific
study of human
behavior and
thought processes

How can you properly study mankind? It sounds like a tall order! Suppose you are wandering college halls in search of ways to learn about yourself as well as other people. You could probably get help from professors of history, anthropology, sociology, literature, art, political science, and many other disciplines. Many subjects focus on people's behavior. History records behavior, sociology observes behavior, and literature, art, and political science inform you about behavior. But only one discipline attempts to use scientific methods to explain why people behave the way they do—*psychology*. The viewpoints of psychologists and the methods they use to learn about human behavior are the subjects of this chapter.

The chapter begins by examining the five main views of psychology. Each view has a slightly different emphasis on what the focus of psychology should be. The possible specializations in psychology are listed and discussed briefly. The next section emphasizes the importance of proper methodology and interpretation. After the description of each method, a caution note is added. Finally, the ethical requirements of psychologists are considered.

WHAT IS APPLIED PSYCHOLOGY?

applied psychology
Approach involving
practical uses of
the study of behavior
and thoughts

Psychology is the scientific study of human behavior and thought processes. *Applied psychology,* as the name suggests, emphasizes the practical uses of psychology rather than its history and theories. Applied psychology gained importance in the late 1960s.

In an often-quoted speech before the American Psychological Association, Miller (1969) recommended:

> The secrets of our trade need not be reserved for highly trained specialists. Psychological facts should be passed out freely to all who need and can use them.... There are simply not enough psychologists, including non-professionals, to meet every need for psychological services. The people at large will have to be their own psychologists, and make their own applications of established principles.

Unfortunately, applying psychology is not as simple as many people believe. Some people have a mistaken notion that psychologists can analyze and understand the causes and nature of behavior with minimal effort. Indeed, several popular paperbacks promise to resolve your every problem and bring instant happiness after an hour of reading. Book advertisements promise to control pain, relieve grief, and remove stress. They also pledge to increase sexual desire and performance and improve popularity. However, such promises are not likely to be fulfilled. Learning to apply psychology is complex. First, you must recognize the basic principles of psychology. You also need to understand the methods of psychology and their limitations. Finally, you need to know when to apply the principles and methods.

Even skilled psychologists have been sharply criticized for not taking the required time in applying psychology. Several radio and television stations around the United States offer call-in therapy. A listener calls the station and reports a problem on the air to a psychologist. The psychologist usually probes the listener and offers advice within two to five minutes. Since the conversation between the psychologist and the caller is broadcast, listeners can apply the advice to themselves or be informed or entertained by the predicaments of other people. Several of the problems that radio and television psychologists face are described in Exhibit 1-1.

EXHIBIT 1-1

3
EXAMINING THE
METHODS OF
PSYCHOLOGY

Would-Be Stars, Beware
Cameras Never Blink

Media psychology has come a long way since Joyce Brothers first scandalized many of her colleagues by going public, says Sonya Friedman, but there are still plenty of personal and professional pitfalls for those who enter the glare of the spotlight...

Friedman, author of "Men Are Just Desserts," "Smart Cookies Don't Crumble," and "A Hero is More Than Just a Sandwich," columnist for *The Ladies Home Journal* and *The Detroit Free Press,* and host of a daily television show and weekly radio program, said her 15 years working in the media have given her the chance "to make every single mistake" there is.

Walking the tightrope between the caring profession of psychology and a commercial endeavor like hosting a radio program or offering advice in a newspaper column is far from easy, Friedman said.

What is easy, she lamented, is "to fail to maintain professionalism when people dangle money and fame in front of you." Her watchword is "credibility," she said, and her credo is "do no harm."

A basic rule in the electronic media is that the time constraints of on-air advice shows must be followed, she said. "You are not practicing therapy on the air."

Nevertheless, she believes that even within five minutes of air time, a psychologist can do a lot of good: to offer a glimmer of hope to someone with a problem, and point out a direction for a resolution. "You have a chance to open a window." After such shows, Friedman said she returns calls to those who seem seriously troubled.

Far from endeavoring to dispel apprehension about entering the mine-strewn field of television, Friedman warned: "When you screw up on air, 20,000 people just heard you...."

Source: Landers, S. (1987, November). Would-be stars, beware: Cameras never blink. *APA Monitor.*

Some psychologists maintain that the radio method is effective in educating masses of people about the applications of psychology. Other psychologists feel that call-in psychology is harmful because the advice is hasty and can be misinterpreted and misapplied.

Exercise 1-1

Check five items on the following list that are important to the study of applied psychology.

☐ Reading history

☐ Practical uses

☐ Everyday behavior

☐ Analyzing theory

☐ Using principles of psychology

☐ Finding quick, simple solutions

☐ Reading how-to pop psychology books

☐ Using the methods of psychology

☐ Learning when to use the methods and principles of psychology

☐ Entertaining an audience

You may compare your answers to those in the Feedback section at the end of the chapter.

Views of Psychology

Although most psychologists agree that all aspects of human behavior must be studied, they disagree on which aspects are of greatest importance. The disagreement is friendly. There are five major views of behavior: behaviorist, gestalt, psychoanalytic, humanist, and cognitive. Many psychologists do not adhere to a single view but are eclectic in their approach, choosing a view to fit a particular situation.

behaviorism Belief that psychology should be scientific and based on observable events

Behaviorism. *Behaviorism* began in the United States about seventy-five years ago with John Watson. Watson felt that psychology should be scientific and based on observable events that two or more people agree upon. According to the behaviorist view, only behaviors that can be observed and agreed upon are worthy of interest in psychology. People's inner thoughts and feelings are only of importance if they are expressed in overt actions or affect their behavior in some way. Behaviorists hold that, except for a few reflexes, all behavior is learned. People learn to respond to certain stimuli. Skinner (1938), a current leader in the behaviorist perspective, maintains that behavior is shaped by consequences. Behaviors that are rewarded increase in frequency, and those that are punished decrease. For example, if you received $100 every time you said "psychology," you might find yourself repeating the word constantly. On the other hand, if you were whipped for using the word, you would probably cease to use it. Applications of the behaviorist perspective are discussed in detail in Chapter 3.

gestalt School of psychology that emphasizes patterns of organization in behavior

Gestalt psychology. Around the same time that the behaviorist movement began in the United States, the *gestalt* perspective emerged in Germany. The German word "gestalt" does not have an exact English equivalent. It is translated as a form, shape, pattern, or organized whole. The basic belief of the gestaltists is that the whole is greater than the sum of its parts. Clearly, this is the opposite of everything you learned in geometry!

But the gestaltists compare behavior to music rather than mathematics. Think of your favorite tune. If you looked at each note individually, you could never create the melody. However, you could change every note and still play the melody in a different key. The pattern or organization of the notes is of prime importance. According to the gestalt view, human behavior loses its meaning if it is broken into components. They argue with behaviorists that the organization of behavior is more important than outward actions. Psychology, in the gestalt view, should focus on sensory, perceptual, and insight processes. Chapter 2 considers sensory and perceptual gestalt applications. Insight and problem solving are discussed in Chapter 5.

psychoanalysis View that psychology should focus on unconscious feelings

Psychoanalysis. *Psychoanalysis* is the oldest of the five perspectives, tracing its beginnings to the writings of Sigmund Freud about 100 years ago. According to the psychoanalytic view, people are controlled by impulses buried in their unconscious. We are unaware of most of our motives and feelings. Our outward behavior is like the tip of an iceberg; beneath our conscious outward behavior is a vast unconscious.

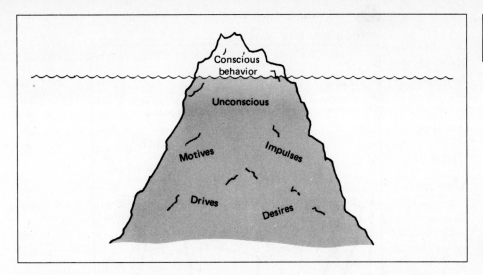

Figure 1-1
Psychoanalytic Iceberg

The psychoanalytic view has been called the third great blow for humans. First, Galileo stated that the earth is not the center of the universe. Next, Darwin announced that humans and apes had a common ancestor. And Freud delivered the final blow by stating that humans are controlled by unconscious impulses. Since we are unaware of our unconscious, we must be psychoanalyzed to learn of these inner unknown feelings. Many of our unknown feelings are sexual and aggressive urges. Methods used in psychoanalysis are covered in Chapter 11.

Humanistic psychology. *positive aspect Humanistic psychology* began in the 1950s with the works of Carl Rogers and Abraham Maslow. Humanists believe that people are constantly growing, changing, and struggling to become. They maintain that psychologists should focus on the importance of self-direction. Free will and the ability to make choices independently are critical to humanists. The real world is what *you* believe it to be. You are unique. Since no one else fully comprehends your world, you must make your own choices. Chapter 11 discusses the methods used by humanists in counseling sessions.

humanistic psychology
View that emphasizes
the importance of
self-direction and
personal growth

Cognitive psychology. your thinking makes you act a certain way. The *cognitive* view is the most recent development and emphasizes the processes that our minds use. Cognitive psychologists are interested in how we think, remember, solve problems, create mental images, and form our beliefs. The development of computers promoted a greater interest in cognitive psychology. As scientists became more interested in how computers solve problems, psychologists began to use more scientific approaches to study how people solve problems. Currently, cognitive psychology is expanding to include dreaming, hypnosis, meditation, and the effects of drugs on thinking. in order to change behaviour you have to change your thinking.

cognitive psychology
View that focuses
on how the mind
processes information

The eclectic view. *Eclectic* psychologists choose among behaviorist, gestalt, psychoanalytic, humanist, and cognitive methods, according to the problem they are facing. Most psychologists are eclectic, accepting and respecting the work of all five views. drawing on all views

eclectic view Belief that
psychology should
select among
appropriate findings of
behavioral, gestalt,
psychoanalytic,
humanist, cognitive,
and other views

"I try to present the facts, not as I see them, but as they are."

Figure 1-2
This politician is clearly
not a humanist.

Exercise 1-2

Read the following play and decide which viewpoint each character is demonstrating: *behaviorist, gestalt, psychoanalytic, humanist, cognitive,* or *eclectic.* State the reason for your choice.

Scene: It is 8 P.M. in the bedroom of a 2-year-old boy. The boy is standing by his bed surrounded by his mother, father, grandfather, Uncle Gordon, and Aunt Rachel, all psychologists.

Boy *(Crying):* I won't go to bed by myself. I want to sleep in someone else's bed. I'm scared of the dark.

Mother: Poor child, he doesn't even know why he's afraid. Probably something horrible happened to him in the dark when he was a newborn in the hospital. Now he will never stay alone in a dark room. Someday I'll have to work with him to get this problem out of his unconscious.

Uncle Gordon: Don't waste your time! Just put some cookies by his bed. If he eats his favorite oatmeal cookies in the dark, he won't mind staying here.

Aunt Rachel: Oh, Gordon, you're always trying to look at the petty aspect of behavior. This poor child may have trouble understanding what darkness is. Maybe his eyes don't adapt easily.

Grandfather: Let me have a chat with the boy and find out how he is thinking.

Father: I agree that cookies aren't the answer. But let me ask you, son, what happens when the room is dark?

Boy: Terrible dreams come out of the closet.

Father: Do you want me to close the door so the dreams can't come out?

Boy: Sure, but ask Uncle Gordon to bring me the cookies and Aunt Rachel to check my eyes, and I'd like to talk to Mom about when I was a baby, and have a chat with Grandpa about how I think.

a. Mother: PSYCHOANAlytic   Reason: getting the problem out of his unconcious.

b. Father: humanist   Reason: telling the boy that he'll shut the door.

c. Uncle Gordon: behaviorist   Reason: giving him something he likes for a certain way he reacts.

d. Aunt Rachel: Gestalt   Reason: saying his eyes don't adapt easily (sensory)

e. Grandfather: Cognitive   Reason: wanting to find out how he thinks.

f. Boy: Eclectic   Reason: wanting to try all views.

You may check your answers in the Feedback section.

Subspecialties of Psychology

If you browse through a college catalog, you will notice many offerings in the psychology department (see Exhibit 1-2). Undergraduate students study in a number of different fields of psychology. However, if training in psychology continues in graduate school, students must usually choose an area of specialization. Exhibit 1-3 lists brief descriptions of common subspecialties. Psychologists who specialize in graduate school are not necessarily locked into a subfield. As their interests change, they sometimes take up new specializations.

EXHIBIT 1-2

Undergraduate Psychology Courses Offered at the University of Colorado at Boulder

Special

Psychology of contemporary American women

Laboratory computers in psychology

Psycholinguistics

Language development

Women and mental health

General

General psychology

Statistics and research methods in psychology

Independent study

Honors seminar

Senior thesis

Teaching of psychology

History of psychology

Special topics in psychology

Practicum in peer advising

Biological

Clinical neuroscience and behavioral medicine

Introduction to biopsychology

Nutrition and behavior

Physiological psychology

Hormones and behavior

Behavioral genetics

Quantitative genetics

Drugs and the nervous system

Gerontology: A multidisciplinary perspective

Principles of developmental psychobiology

Clinical

Psychology of adjustment

Child and adolescent psychology

Child psychology practicum

Abnormal psychology

Psychopathology

Survey of clinical psychology

Community psychology and mental health

Principles of psychological testing

Developmental

Developmental psychology

Experimental

Cognitive psychology

Psychology of perception

Introduction to cognitive simulation

Psychology of learning

Ethnology and comparative psychology

Behavior of zoo animals

Social

Social psychology of ethnic groups

Social psychology of social problems

Social psychology

Human judgment and social policy

Psychology of personality

Women in cross-cultural perspective

Cross-cultural psychology

Psychotherapists

Psychologists are sometimes confused with other professionals who work closely with people who have emotional problems. A psychotherapist is a professional with special training in managing or treating emotional problems and mental illnesses. Psychotherapists include psychologists, psychiatrists, and psychiatric social workers. Perhaps you have wondered about the differences in training among these three types of professionals. Although their functions sometimes overlap, there are some clear contrasts in both the education and roles of each of the three general types of psychotherapists.

Psychiatrists. Psychiatrists are medical doctors who have special training in psychological disorders. They are the only type of therapist who can prescribe medications. Since most forms of psychosis and psychosomatic illness require medication along with psychological treatment, psychiatrists usually supervise the management of these disorders. Severe forms of anxiety and any emotional problem that has a medical element will require the assistance of a psychiatrist.

Psychologists. Many psychologists have medical training but few have a medical degree. The most advanced degree in psychology is a Ph.D. Not all psychologists are psychotherapists; some specialize in research or in other areas and applications. Specific course requirements vary in each state. There are two specialties in psychology that focus on therapy: clinical psychology and counseling psychology. Most states require licenses to practice in either of these two areas. Clinical psychologists specialize in psychological testing and in methods for performing therapy. Counseling psychologists focus more on educational and vocational aspects of adjustment. However, often they are also concerned with personal, social, and emotional problems. Counseling psychologists may have either an Ed.D. or a Ph.D.; some have only an M.A. or Ed.M. in counseling.

Psychiatric social worker. Psychiatric social workers may have either a master's degree or a doctorate in social services or social work and must be licensed for private practice as therapists. Most often they deal with people who need social services. They refer people to appropriate agencies and help.

The terms psychiatrist, psychologist, and psychiatric social worker are regulated by state laws. Only persons with appropriate education and experience are licensed to use the titles. What about a woman who calls herself a "mental counselor" or a man who lists his titles as "mind therapist" and "psychohealer"? Chances are they are both quacks, persons who are neither trained nor qualified in psychology or psychiatry. Lists of members of the American Psychiatric Association and the American Psychological Associa-

EXHIBIT 1-3

Subspecialties in Psychology

Clinical psychologist Performs therapy and handles emotional problems

Comparative psychologist Works with lower animals such as rats, mice, pigeons, or monkeys; uses experimental procedures in a laboratory setting

Consumer psychologist Studies and evaluates emotional appeals, marketing, packaging, and advertising methods

Counselor Tests, advises, and suggests resources for additional assistance

Developmental psychologist Studies changes that occur with each age, from prenatal stages through old age

Educational psychologist Improves methods of teaching, studying, learning, and testing

Engineering psychologist Develops improvements in equipment design

Environmental psychologist Assists in planning communities and buildings, emphasizing human needs

Experimental psychologist Develops scientific methods to find causes of behavior

Forensic psychologist Studies crime prevention and motivation and causes of crime

Health psychologist Helps people develop healthier lifestyles and avoid illness

Industrial and organizational psychologist Organizes job selection and working conditions for optimal production

Personality psychologist Assesses individual differences and tests patterns of behavior

Physiological psychologist Studies the biological causes of behavior

Psychometrician Constructs tests to measure intelligence, achievement, aptitude, and personality; designs experiments and applies statistics

School psychologist Evaluates students to diagnose learning or emotional problems that may interfere with success in school

Social psychologist Studies attitudes, prejudices, group interactions, and leadership

tion are available at most public libraries. Qualifications can be checked by looking up a therapist's name in one of the indexes.

Exercise 1-3

Briefly describe the type of training you would expect each of the following therapists to have had.

a. Clinical psychologist: _specializes in psychological testing and in methods for performing therapy._ PhD

b. Psychiatrist: _medical Doctors who have special training in psychological disorders._

Engineering
psychologists are
involved in the design
of complex air
traffic-control
equipment. (*Joel
Gordon*)

c. Psychiatric social worker: MASters degree or a doctorate in social services or social work and must be licensed.

d. Mind therapist: no training. people who call themselves this are probably Quacks.

e. Counseling psychologist: vocational and educational Aspects of Adjustments. MA EDM EDA PhD

Please check your descriptions against those found in the Feedback section.

Checkpoint
Use the following questions to check your understanding of this portion of the chapter. Choose and mark the one correct response to each question.

1. What is the purpose of applied psychology?
   a. To expose the history of psychology
   b. To study the theories of psychology
   (c.) To use the discoveries of psychology
   d. To use the findings of history, sociology, and other disciplines
2. What does psychology study?
   (a.) Human behavior
   b. Animal thinking
   c. Unconscious thoughts
   d. Human perception

3. Who is most likely to state, "The whole is more than the sum of its parts"?
   a. A behavioral psychologist
   b. A psychoanalyst
   c. A gestalt psychologist
   d. A humanist

4. Suppose you wanted a young woman to wear her red sweater. If you held a behavioral view, what might you do?
   a. Discuss her perception of the color red.
   b. Give her a reward for wearing the sweater.
   c. Point out her unconscious need to wear red.
   d. Let her discuss her attitudes and associations with red.

5. Which view of psychology is primarily concerned with behavior that can be observed and agreed upon?
   a. The behaviorist view
   b. The gestalt view
   c. The psychoanalytic view
   d. The humanist view

6. Bing's psychologist told him that he should not blame himself for being aggressive. He is controlled by unconscious impulses. What view does his psychologist probably hold?
   a. A behavioral view
   b. A gestalt view
   c. A psychoanalytic view
   d. A humanist view

7. What would a humanist psychologist emphasize?
   a. Organization
   b. Impulses
   c. Rewards
   d. Choices

8. Which type of psychologist is most interested in how your mind processes information?
   a. Behavioral
   b. Cognitive
   c. Psychoanalytic
   d. Humanistic

9. Which of the following professionals is likely to accept and practice more than one view of psychology?
   a. A psychoanalyst
   b. A behaviorist
   c. A gestalt psychologist
   d. An eclectic psychologist

10. At what stage do most psychologists specialize?
    a. In high school
    b. As undergraduate students in college
    c. As graduate students and thereafter
    d. Never

11. Which of the following therapists is a physician?
    a. Psychiatric social worker
    b. Clinical psychologist
    c. Psychiatrist
    d. Mind therapist
12. What is a psychotherapist?
    a. A therapist who focuses on the unconscious
    b. A person who specializes in vocational interests
    c. A professional who treats emotional problems or disorders
    d. A physician who works with children
13. Which types of psychologists are psychotherapists?
    a. Clinical and counseling
    b. Environmental and forensic
    c. School and social
    d. Educational and developmental
14. Which of the following professions is not governed by state licensing?
    a. Psychologists
    b. Psychiatrists
    c. Psychiatric social workers
    d. Mind therapists

Check your responses against the Checkpoint Answer Key at the end of the chapter. If you had difficulty with any question, reread the text. If you had little or no difficulty answering the questions or have resolved problems that you might have had, you are ready to continue with the next portion of the chapter.

METHODS OF PSYCHOLOGY

You may have heard that psychology is just "common sense." Sometimes the findings do make sense; however, they must be based on evidence. Psychologists of all types use a variety of different techniques to gather their evidence. Psychology is considered a borderline science. Every attempt is made to use scientific methods, but, as you can imagine, it is difficult to measure human behavior accurately. Natural sciences measure weights of materials and components of chemicals, while psychologists are faced with the difficult task of measuring humor, motivation, adjustments, and changes in people. Methods used in psychology have limitations, so read the cautions carefully.

Observation

Observation requires watching people and recording what happens. The psychologist does not meddle or interfere with what people are doing. Sometimes a one-way mirror is used because people often change their behavior when they believe they are being watched.

  Recording of observations must be factual. Psychologists note what happens without making any interpretations or inferences. For example, if someone laughs, the psychologist records the laughter. No inference is made about the cause of the laughter. Whether the laughter was caused by something

observation Research method that requires watching and recording behavior without interference or interpretation

funny, a joyous feeling, nervousness, or an attempt to cover up fears cannot be determined through observation alone.

Caution! Beware of insinuations based on observation. Since inferences should not be made from observations, behavior cannot be explained. For example, suppose you observed that there were a large number of bearded men in a particular town. All you can conclude is that the town has a large number of bearded men. There are innumerable reasons for their beards. Perhaps beards are in vogue, or women prefer men with beards, or razor blades are expensive. Maybe the men are trying out for Santa Claus roles. The list of possible causes could be as long as this book. Suppose you saw a woman lift up papers and stare around the desk surface beneath them. Next she rubbed the desk with the palm of her hand. What can you conclude? Is she looking for a small object, brushing dust, or wiping a spot? If you are a cautious observer, you will not conclude anything. You will simply record her behavior.

Exercise 1-4

Have you heard the joke about the psychologist and the frog? It seems the psychologist was observing a frog's response to a bell. The psychologist rang a bell. The frog jumped. The psychologist immediately wrote down that the frog jumped. The psychologist cut off one of the frog's legs and again rang the bell. The frog jumped. The psychologist noted that the frog jumped. A second leg was cut from the frog and the bell was rung. The psychologist again recorded her observation of the frog jumping. She then cut off the frog's third leg. The frog once again jumped in response to the ringing bell. The psychologist noted

Figure 1-3
It would be difficult to avoid making an incorrect interpretation of this observation.

"That means that about 5 percent of our applicants will get a loan."

the behavior. Finally, the psychologist cut off the frog's fourth leg and rang the bell. The frog did not move. The psychologist wrote in her notes, "When frog's fourth leg is cut, frog becomes hard of hearing."

From what you know about the technique of observation, criticize the psychologist's conclusion.

She assumed that the frog did not jump because he was hard of hearing. She shouldn't have assumed anything. She should have just recorded that he did not jump after 4th leg was cut off.

Please turn to the Feedback section to check your criticism.

Case Study

The *case-study* method is used primarily by clinical psychologists working with troubled persons. A case study is an in-depth examination of one individual. The purpose is to learn as much as possible about the person's problems. The technique is expensive and takes several sessions for completion.

Psychologists usually begin by acquiring biographical information that relates to the problem. In the case of a child, psychologists usually interview parents and request reports from teachers and other significant people who know the youngster. They then interview the troubled person and begin extensive testing. Depending on the type of problem, intelligence, aptitude, achievement, perception, and personality tests may be administered. Based on the results of the tests, biographical information, and interviews, recommendations are made to alleviate the problems. Such recommendations may include therapy, a change in classes or jobs, a new direction in leisure activities, or improved communication with authorities and family members.

case study In-depth study of one individual, usually including tests, biographical and family histories, and interviews

Survey

Have you ever received a call asking you which television program you were watching? Or perhaps you have received a questionnaire enclosed with an appliance or some equipment that you purchased. The questionnaire might have asked unusual questions, from the number of bathrooms in your house to how much time you spend vacationing. In both instances, someone was conducting a *survey*. Think back on how you responded—or if you responded.

The purpose of a psychological survey is to determine the attitudes and behaviors of a large group of people. Usually everyone in the group cannot be questioned; thus, psychologists choose only a sample of the group. The sample might include half the group or as little as 5 or 10 percent of the group.

If only a small percentage of people is chosen for the sample, they must be selected carefully. Caution must be taken to be sure that the sample has the same important attributes as the population they represent. For example, suppose the officials of a college wanted to determine whether students felt that instructors were giving them higher grades than they deserved. They only want to survey 10 percent of the students. If the college is half male and half female, their sample should reflect that. Similarly, the sample should include the same distribution of subject majors and age groups as the total college pop-

survey Poll to determine attitudes and behaviors of a group of people

"*Now think carefully. The answer
you give will represent the opinion of
millions of Americans.*"

Figure 1-4
Hopefully this woman
is part of a carefully
selected sample.

normal curve
Bell-shaped
frequency distribution

ulation. Even more important, the sample's grades should reflect the distribution of the total college population.

Suppose grades were distributed on a *normal curve* as shown in Figure 1-5. Indeed it would be unusual to have such a perfect assortment of grades, but assume for convenience that most students in the college have grades between 60 and 80. An equal number have grades between 80 and 90 and 50 and 60. Very few have grades above 90 or below 50. The sample must show the same distribution of grades if it is to represent everyone in the college (see Figure 1-6).

After carefully selecting the sample, the college administrators would need to be accurate in wording their questions. Students may honestly feel that they are graded too leniently. However, they may fear their grades will drop if they admit their true feelings to college officials. Researchers have found that people do not always respond honestly to surveys (see Exhibits 1-4 and 1-5).

Often questions are worded in a general way to draw out one response. For example, most people are in favor of such general concepts as peace and education and are opposed to violence and pollution. If asked, "Are you in favor of world peace?" most would reply, "Yes." However responses might vary considerably if people were asked how world peace could be achieved. Good questions should bring out a variety of responses.

Now that the questions are written and a list of names has been carefully selected for a sample, how can you get the questions to the people in the sample? The cheapest method is the telephone. But you will be limited to people

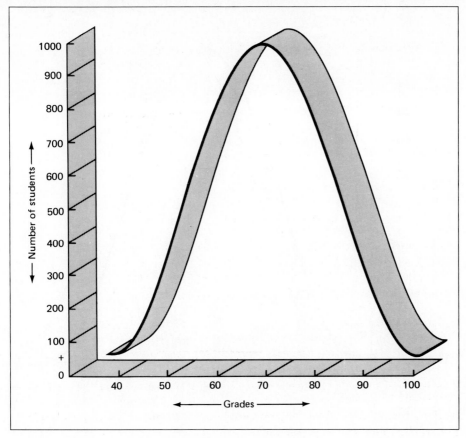

Figure 1-5
Grade Distribution,
Total College
Population

who have telephones and listed numbers; people without phones or with un-listed numbers will be left out. To be sure, they may have different attitudes from the rest of your sample. You cannot assume that their thinking would be the same as the rest of the group.

Another alternative is to mail the questionnaires. Think about question-naires you have received in the mail. If you are like most people, you neither completed nor returned them. Usually, less than 10 percent of the people re-turn questionnaires received by mail. A 15 percent return is considered high by psychologists. Unfortunately, evidence from such a small percentage of a sam-ple cannot be of much use. Those who took the time to answer questions are not necessarily typical of the people who chose not to respond.

The most accurate method for conducting surveys is through personal in-terviews. However, it is also the most time-consuming and costly method. As a result, surveys using the interview method are either overwhelmingly expen-sive or derived from samples that are too small to permit conclusions.

Caution! When reading the results of a survey, first note when the survey was taken. World events change! People do modify their thinking and change their minds. American attitudes toward Iran were relatively neutral until hostages

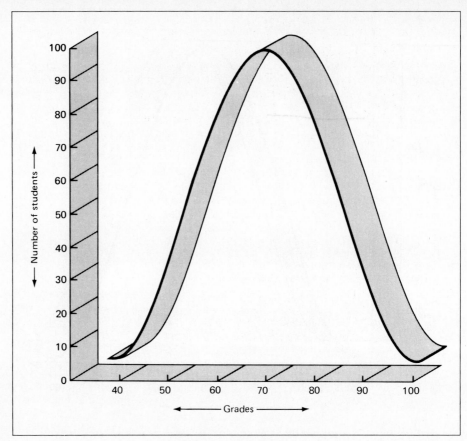

Figure 1-6
Grade Distribution,
Sample

EXHIBIT 1-4

Seat Belt Statistics
Most drivers say they wear their seat belts, but once they get in their cars it's a different story, according to a federally sponsored survey in suburban Atlanta, Ga.
Researchers from the national Centers for Disease Control, the Georgia Department of Human Resources and the Department of Health in DeKalb County, a county east of the city, conducted two surveys on seat belt use in the county last July.
Of 337 drivers interviewed by phone, just 127, or 38 percent, said they never, seldom, or only sometimes used their seat belts.
But when researchers went to 48 randomly selected intersections and peeked into 2,157 cars stopped at the lights, 70 percent of the drivers weren't buckled up, the CDC reported.
The difference could be attributable in part to variances between the random phone survey and the observation survey, says CDC researcher Dr. Scott Wetterhall.
But he says previous studies have shown people simply don't always behave as they say they do.
Seat belt use was lower among men, among drivers under 30 or over 60, and among non-white drivers.

Source: Associated
Press. (1987,
December 4). Seat
belt statistics.
Arlington Journal.

EXHIBIT 1-5

19

EXAMINING THE
METHODS OF
PSYCHOLOGY

VCR's: No Family Affair

Ask your average owner of a videocassette recorder what's so wonderful about having a VCR and he or she may well say that it's a great way for the family to spend time together. But watch that same family in action and you're likely to find quite a different story: VCR use is, by and large, a solitary sport.

In Great Britain, where VCR ownership resembles that in the United States, more than 40 percent of all houses have VCR's. In those with children, that figure rises to more than 50 percent. Psychologist Barrie Gunter of England's Independent Broadcasting Authority and sociologist Mark R. Levy of the University of Maryland surveyed more than 400 households in four regions of England to find out who watches what with whom.

Almost three-quarters of the respondents agreed with the statement, "Watching video is often an enjoyable way for my family to spend some time together." But video-use diaries painted a different picture. Almost 60 percent of the videotapes played during a two-week period were watched alone. Only 22 percent were viewed with adults from the same household and a mere 6 percent were viewed with children from that household.

By comparison, broadcast-television viewing was far more sociable: Only 24 percent of TV programs viewed directly off the air were viewed alone; 42 percent were watched in the company of other adults and another 17 percent with both adults and children from the same household.

Source: Grant, E. (1988, January). VCR's: No family affair. *Psychology Today.*

"Excuse me, sir. Are you interested in going to Heaven?"

Figure 1-7
An example of a general question designed to bring forth an obvious response...

were taken. Similarly, attitudes toward fashions, education, activities, and relationships constantly sway.

Judge the wording of the questions used. Were the questions worded to bring out only one response? The choice of words in the question should be neutral and not show any bias.

Read the results of surveys conscientiously. Check the size and representatives of the sample. If they are not stated, chances are good that the poll is hiding something. The conclusion that "three out of four housewives surveyed recommended Slowpoke baking powder" could mean that only four housewives were surveyed. All four housewives may be major stockholders in the Slowpoke Company. Conclusions should be based on a large representative sample.

As the article in Exhibit 1-6 warns, survey conclusions can be worded to convey totally different impressions. It is usually best to read survey results directly rather than accept another person's interpretation. As in observation, facts are important and inferences should be avoided.

Exercise 1-5

State the main difference between the case-study method and the survey method.

Case study is an indepth examination of one person, whereas the survey method involves a large group of people.

Exercise 1-6

A librarian has been campaigning to have more city funds allocated to buying books. He decided to prove that most of the people in the city felt there were not enough books in the library. He conducted a survey by asking people who checked out books, "Would you like more books in the library?" Ten people were asked and nine responded yes. The tenth person was uncertain. The librarian concluded: "Ninety percent of the people in our city want more funds allocated for library books. No one opposes additional funding for the library." Criticize the librarian's survey method in each of the following areas:

a. Selection of the sample: *only people who check out books.*

b. Size of sample: *only ten people? (90 percent) making believe a larger # of people were asked*

c. Wording of the question: *not very accurate*

d. Conclusion: *did not ask for more funds in his survey. Did not state size or selection.*

Please turn to the Feedback section to check your answers.

EXHIBIT 1-6

21

EXAMINING THE
METHODS OF
PSYCHOLOGY

Religion in America: A Rashomon Result

One more set of statistics that can be read several ways comes from a new survey of American attitudes and values. The official version is below at left; at right, an alternate—equally accurate—reading, based on the same data, by Carin Rubenstein, a social psychologist and associate editor of *Psychology Today.*

- "Forty-nine percent of Americans say they have made a personal commitment to Christ which they feel has changed their lives."

- More than half of Americans (51 percent) say they have not made an important commitment to Christ.

- "Twenty-six percent of the American public over the age of 14, representing more than 45 million people, are highly religious."

- Fifty percent of the American public over the age of 14, representing more than 87 million people, have low religious commitment.

- "Blacks are far more likely to be highly religious than whites....Women are more inclined than men to be highly religious....Those with lower, rather than higher, incomes [and]...levels of education are more likely to be highly religious....There is a steady increase in religious involvement of Americans as they grow older."

- In general, underprivileged groups and minorities—blacks, women, the poor, the uneducated, and the elderly—are the most religious.

- According to a press release, "The ...report detects a religious current sweeping the United States today, finding America is a nation of people committed to religious beliefs."

- An alternate release might read: "The report detects strong religious faith only among underprivileged Americans, finding privileged America a nation of people largely indifferent to religion."

Source: Rubenstein, C. (1981, July). Religion in America: A Rashomon result. *Psychology Today.*

Correlation Method

Suppose you want to find out whether high school students who travel tend to get higher grades. Look at the roster in Exhibit 1-7 and imagine these were your results. There appears to be a clear relationship or *correlation* between the number of miles traveled during the past year and the grade-point average of students. What can you conclude? Does travel improve ability or knowledge? Do good students yearn to travel? Or do students from enriched homes travel and do well in school? All could be true. There is simply not enough information to prove a cause.

Suppose a psychologist found a correlation between the number of churches in a community and the amount of alcohol consumed. It is not likely that the people are drinking in church. Nor is it probable that after drinking, people build churches. One factor does not necessarily cause the other, although it might. In this case, there is most likely an underlying factor related to both the amount of alcohol consumed and the number of churches—namely, the population of the community.

Rather than simply inspecting a roster of numbers, psychologists use statistical formulas to compute correlations. Correlations can be positive or negative. A *positive correlation* means that as one variable increases, so does the

correlation
Relationship between scores on two variables

positive correlation
When one variable increases, the other also increases

EXHIBIT 1-7

Name	Greatest Distance Traveled during Past Year	Grade-Point Average
	Distance Traveled and Grade-Point Average	
Jim B.	850 miles	4.0
Karen J.	740 miles	3.9
Sarah L.	720 miles	3.8
Louie A.	550 miles	3.5
Clyde R.	400 miles	3.2
John C.	360 miles	3.0
Nora H.	300 miles	2.7
Mike B.	220 miles	2.4
Harry T.	200 miles	2.2
Irene Y.	160 miles	2.0
Bill B.	140 miles	1.6
Leslie C.	110 miles	1.4
Cork C.	60 miles	1.0
Justine G.	50 miles	0.8
Ed C.	30 miles	0.6

negative correlation When one variable increases, the other decreases

other. The example of grade-point average and distance traveled was a positive correlation. *Negative correlations* are equally important. In a negative correlation, as one factor increases, the other decreases. For example, there is a negative correlation between the amount of alcohol consumed and the ability to drive a car. As the amount of alcohol people drink increases, their scores on driving tests will decrease. While correlation is a useful method for studying many relationships, it does have limitations. The article in Exhibit 1-8 reports on the danger of using a correlation study on child abuse. The researchers comment on the importance of finding the true causes of child abuse.

Caution! Correlation is *not* causation. Too often when a strong relationship is found between two variables, readers or listeners conclude that one factor causes the other. There can be many other possible explanations for the relationship. For example, suppose there is a positive relationship between the number of peaches eaten and the number of cases of poison ivy. There is no evidence that peaches cause poison ivy. Nor can you conclude that poison ivy causes a craving for peaches. In all probability, peaches and poison ivy grow during the same season.

experiment Research technique using controls to find causes of specific behaviors

hypothesis Educated guess that gives a tentative explanation and a basis for research

The Experiment

The *experiment* is the only method that can determine whether one factor **causes** another. Although other methods can reveal relationships, they cannot provide any information on the cause of the relationship. In a psychological experiment conditions are "controlled" so that causes can be discovered. The psychologist begins with an *hypothesis,* or educated guess about a relationship. The hypothesis may be formed after checking the results of a survey or a correlation study.

EXHIBIT 1-8

23

EXAMINING THE
METHODS OF
PSYCHOLOGY

The Family
Does Abuse Beget Abuse?

"Adults who were maltreated [as children] have been told so many times that they will abuse their children that for some it has become a self-fulfilling prophecy," say graduate student Joan Kaufman and psychologist Edward Zigler. Even when some people manage to break the cycle, the researchers say, they "are left feeling like walking time bombs."

Many people believe that child abuse inexorably repeats itself in successive generations, and a large body of research appears to support their belief. However, after a close look at the evidence, Kaufman and Zigler conclude that for a variety of methodological reasons, many of these studies severely overestimate the risks of repeated abuse.

Kaufman and Zigler's analysis of the child-abuse literature suggests that while the vicious cycle certainly occurs, and is cause for concern, it's the exception, not the rule; only about 30 percent of people who are abused as children complete the cycle with their own offspring. The researchers note, however, that this rate is six times higher than the rate of child abuse in the general population.

Kaufman and Zigler stress that it's time researchers stop asking, "Do abused children become abusive parents?" and start asking, "Under what conditions is the transmission of abuse most likely to occur?" Two of the studies they reviewed provide clues to the answers. They show that the cycle is less likely to repeat in people who, as children, had the loving support of a parent or foster parent, and in those who, as adults, have a loving, supportive relationship with a spouse or lover and have relatively few stressful events in their lives. An additional brake on the cycle includes being aware of having a history of abuse and consciously resolving not to repeat it.

"Being maltreated as a child puts one at risk for becoming abusive," Kaufman and Zigler conclude, "but the path between these two points is far from direct or inevitable."

Source: Rosenfeld, A. (1987, August). The family: Does abuse beget abuse? *Psychology Today*.

Suppose a survey checked children's school grades and vitamin-pill consumption. If a strong positive correlation was found, a psychologist might wish to determine whether vitamin pills cause improved achievement. The hypothesis would be, "Children who take vitamin pills are more successful in school than children who do not." Success in school will be measured by achievement tests.

The psychologist needs two groups: an *experimental group* and a *control group*. Both groups are equal in school achievement at the beginning of the experiment and are alike in every way. Students are randomly assigned to either the experimental group or the control group but are not told which group they are in.

The psychologist then gives the experimental group a vitamin pill every morning. The control group receives a pill that looks and tastes like a vitamin pill but is only a *placebo*, an inert substance. If the control group did not receive anything, the psychologist could not be certain that vitamins alone were causing success. It is possible that simply receiving a free pill every morning could make students work better. All conditions must be exactly the same for both groups, except for the content of the pills.

Just believing they received vitamins could affect students' work. Beecher (1959) reported experiments that found a placebo injection (saline solution)

experimental group Group that receives treatment being investigated in an experiment

control group Group of research participants that are the same as the experimental group with the exception of the variable being studied

placebo Inert substance or fake treatment often used on a control group in an experiment

was 70 percent as effective as morphine for reducing pain. People who believe they took something often feel better and work harder. Thus, it is important that people in the control group believe they are taking something too.

At the end of the experiment both groups would again be administered achievement tests. Their scores on the tests would be compared. A mathematical formula can be used to decide whether the differences between the two groups' scores are large enough to be statistically significant, that is, not just the result of chance. If all other conditions were carefully controlled and the differences are statistically significant, the psychologist can conclude that the differences are probably caused by the vitamins.

Caution! Control is a key factor in experiments. All factors other than the condition being tested must be controlled. It is critical that subjects not know whether they are in an experimental or control group. Often the novelty of participating in an experiment can produce exceptional results!

When reading experiments, check to be sure a control group was used. Without a control group, you cannot be certain of a cause-and-effect relationship. For example, consider the experiment described. An improvement in achievement scores among students who took vitamin pills for a month would not prove that vitamin pills caused the achievement. Possibly all children improve their achievement scores within a month! Their success on the test could be attributed to variables other than vitamins.

Exercise 1-7
State the key difference between the conclusions that can be reached after a correlation study and after a controlled experiment.

Correlation if a relationship does exist or not

Experiment whether or not something is causing cause or not

Exercise 1-8
List five steps needed in a controlled experiment.

a. *Hypothesis*
b. *experimental group or controlled group*
c. *All conditions must be exactly the same*
d. *Control all conditions except factor being tested*
e. *check for differences.*

You may check your answers in the Feedback section.

ETHICS

Although there are federal regulations for scientific research, the American Psychological Association established additional ethical guidelines to protect the records and welfare of persons who are being studied or are participating in research. Psychologists are expected to:

• Respect the dignity and welfare of participants and protect them from both physical and mental harm.

• Get voluntary consent from people participating in experiments.

• Allow participants to withdraw from an experiment at any time.

• Avoid deception and inform participants of the purpose and procedures immediately following their involvement.

• Keep records confidential and guarantee the participants' right to privacy.

Checkpoint

Use the following questions to check your understanding of this final portion of the chapter. Choose and mark the one correct response to each question.

15. What does a cautious observer do?
    a. Interfere with behavior
    b. Infer causes
    c. Record behavior
    d. Draw cause-and-effect conclusions
16. Which type of psychologist is most likely to use a case-study method?
    a. A clinical psychologist
    b. An experimental psychologist
    c. A comparative psychologist
    d. A consumer psychologist
17. What is included in a case study?
    a. An experiment, a survey, and tests
    b. A case history, interviews, and tests
    c. A survey, observation, and an experiment
    d. A correlation, tests, and a survey
18. A company decides to take a telephone poll of how people will vote in a coming election. What is wrong with this survey technique?
    a. The sample is not representative.
    b. The sample will be too large.
    c. The technique is too costly.
    d. The technique is too time-consuming.
19. Assume you want to survey a small representative sample from a tiny town of 100 people. One-quarter of the town residents are over 65. What percentage of your sample should be over 65?
    a. 5 percent
    b. 10 percent
    c. 12½ percent
    d. 25 percent
20. What is the main disadvantage of mailing questionnaires?
    a. People are more dishonest on questionnaires received in the mail.
    b. Only a small percentage of people return the questionnaire.
    c. It is a time-consuming and costly method.
    d. Many people do not receive their mail.
21. The results of a study reported that 80 percent of the doctors surveyed recommend soaking your feet in Relaxy Solutions. What can you conclude?
    a. A large number of doctors were surveyed.
    b. A small number of doctors were surveyed.

    c. The pollster is not revealing the number of doctors surveyed.

    d. No doctors were surveyed.

22. A study reported that the number of windows in men's houses correlates with the number of neckties they own. What conclusion can be reached?

    a. Owning neckties causes men to buy houses with many windows.

    b. Living in a house with many windows causes men to purchase neckties.

    c. People give neckties to men who live in houses with many windows.

    d. No cause-and-effect conclusion can be reached.

23. Which of the following methods can determine causes?

    a. The survey

    b. Observation

    c. Correlation

    d. The experiment

24. A psychologist gave children an arithmetic test. She gave them lollipops for a month and then retested them. Their scores on the test improved. What does her experiment lack?

    a. Observation

    b. Adequate testing

    c. A survey

    d. A control group

25. According to the ethical regulations of the American Psychological Association, what must psychologists tell subjects in their experiments?

    a. Whether they are in the experimental group or control group

    b. The theories behind the experimental hypothesis

    c. The purpose and methods of the experiment

    d. The names of other subjects in the experiment

Check your responses against the Checkpoint Answer Key at the end of the chapter. If you had difficulty with any question, reread the text. If you had little or no difficulty answering the questions or have resolved problems that you might have had, you are ready to check yourself against the chapter inventory that follows.

CHAPTER INVENTORY

Use this list of objectives as a review checklist. You should be able to do each task outlined in the objectives. If you can, you may feel confident that you have mastered the material in this chapter.

1. Describe the nature of applied psychology.
2. Distinguish among the views of psychology: the behaviorist view, the gestalt view, the psychoanalytic view, the humanist view, and the cognitive view.
3. Recognize that most psychologists are eclectic and define the term.
4. Distinguish among psychologists, psychiatrists, and psychiatric social workers.
5. Briefly describe the subspecialties of psychology.
6. Identify psychology as a borderline science, and recognize the need for scientific methods.

7. Describe the procedure used in observation, and specify the cautions and limitations.
8. Identify the purpose of case studies, and describe the procedures used.
9. Explain the procedure required in a survey, and recognize the importance of sample selection and sample size.
10. State the limitations and cautions associated with the survey method.
11. Distinguish between correlation and causation.
12. Recognize the experiment as the only method that determines causes.
13. List the steps required in an experiment, and explain the need for control groups.
14. List five ethical guidelines established by the American Psychological Association.

Feedback

The correct answers to the exercises follow. If you did not answer an exercise correctly, review the preceding pages and return to the exercise to correctly complete it.

1-1. You should have checked the following:
   ☑ Practical uses
   ☑ Everyday behavior
   ☑ Using principles of psychology
   ☑ Using the methods of psychology
   ☑ Learning when to use the methods and principles of psychology

1-2. a. Psychoanalytic: concerned with past events buried in his unconscious
   b. Humanist: accepts the view that dreams are in the closet
   c. Behavioral: wants to reward desired behavior
   d. Gestalt: concerned with perception and understanding
   e. Cognitive: concerned with the process of the mind
   f. Eclectic: accepted all the views

1-3. a. A Ph.D., specializing in testing and therapy
   b. An M.D., with additional training and an internship in psychological disorders
   c. A master's or doctorate, specializing in family and marital problems and community social services
   d. Probably a quack!
   e. An M.A., an Ed.M., Ed.D., or a Ph.D. in counseling, specializing in educational and vocational adjustment

1-4. The psychologist was recording observations correctly until the end of the experiment. The correct observation should have been "When frog's fourth leg is cut, frog does not jump." (Admittedly, the psychologist's conclusion was funnier!)

1-5. The case-study method examines one person in depth, while the survey method samples the attitudes of many people.

1-6. a. The sample was not carefully selected to represent everyone in the city. People who do not use the library were excluded.

    b. Only ten people were questioned. Although the population of the city was not stated, chances are the sample was only a fraction of the percentage of the entire population—too small to be accurate.

    c. The question did not include anything about allocating money in the city budget.

    d. The conclusion did not state the size of the sample or the selection method used. The librarian inferred that people wanted more city money, although the question made no reference to funding. The conclusion should be factual rather than inferential.

1-7. After a correlation study, one can only conclude that a relationship does or does not exist. After an experiment, one can conclude whether or not one factor is causing another.

1-8.   *a.* Formulate an hypothesis.

    b. Assign subjects to experimental and control groups.

    c. Check to be sure the two groups are similar.

    d. Control all conditions except the factor being tested.

    e. Test both groups to see if there are significant differences.

Checkpoint Answer Key

1. *c*	**8.** *b*	**14.** *d*	**20.** *b*
2. *a*	**9.** *d*	**15.** *c*	**21.** *c*
3. *c*	**10.** *c*	**16.** *a*	**22.** *d*
4. *b*	**11.** *c*	**17.** *b*	**23.** *d*
5. *a*	**12.** *c*	**18.** *a*	**24.** *d*
6. *c*	**13.** *a*	**19.** *d*	**25.** *c*
7. *d*			

CHAPTER 2

PERCEIVING

Genius, in truth, means little more than the faculty of perceiving in an unhabitual way.

William James

Imagine you are out walking and hear a buzz in the sky. A friend looks skyward and shouts excitedly, ''Wow! It's a Boeing 757!'' You look up and see a mere airplane and cannot tell how it differs from every other plane. After your friend explains that 757s have quiet engines and a long body, you begin to notice these details.

Or suppose you are starving and you start eating a juicy steak, only to have someone complain that the cook used a heavy hand on the salt. The steak tasted delicious at first. But as you continue eating, you begin to detect a terribly salty flavor.

Obviously no ingredients were added to your steak, nor did the plane change form. Why did your perception of the airplane and the steak change? In this chapter you will learn about conditions that affect your perception and methods you can use to improve your perception.

Senses are the only source of information from the outside world. In the first portion of this chapter, the differences between internal and external sensation will be examined. The relationship between attention and perception will be considered, and some common attention-getting techniques will be described. In the next portion of the chapter you will investigate some of the conditions that influence the interpretive aspect of perception, and you will also look at some common illusions. Finally, methods for improving perception and evidence on topics such as sensory bombardment, sensory deprivation, and extrasensory perception will be reviewed.

WHAT IS PERCEPTION?

perception Process that combines both sensing and interpreting

sensation Bringing stimuli from the outside world into the nervous system

interpretation Inferring meaning from what is sensed by comparing it with previously stored information

Perception is a process that combines both sensing and interpreting. Information from the outside world comes through our senses. The information is then interpreted, and this interpretation gives meaning to what is sensed. For example, when you hear your alarm clock ring, the actual sound you hear is the **sensation**. How you construe the meaning of the alarm is your **interpretation**. If it is 7 A.M. on a weekday, you would probably interpret the alarm as a signal to get moving and begin the day. However, the same alarm may have a different meaning on a holiday. You might perceive yourself as absurd for setting the alarm, or you might snicker at the alarm and roll over. In both instances, the sensation (the ring) was the same, but your interpretation changed because of other factors.

Exercise 2-1

a. Imagine you are driving along a road and notice a red hexagonal sign. You read the word ''Stop.'' You immediately take your foot off the gas pedal and begin to apply the brakes. Which part of your experience involved sensation, and which involved interpretation?

Sensation: _taking foot off the gas And Applying brakes._

Interpretation: _noticing the red stop Sign._

b. How might your interpretation have changed if you were walking along the same road and saw the same sign? _____Standing Still_____

~~instead~~

Check your responses in the Feedback section at the end of the chapter.

External Senses

Usually the sources of information from the outside world are thought of as the senses of seeing, hearing, smelling, tasting, and touching. Improving each of these senses—perhaps with contact lenses, hearing aids, or sinus surgery— could involve physiological changes. But even after all these corrections and improvements, our senses would still be limited. For example, look at the frame in Figure 2-1. You can probably see three or, possibly, four dots.

Actually there are eight dots in the frame. Several dots are so small that you are not consciously aware of them. Similarly, you probably have neither heard nor smelled a flea. Their sounds and odors are beneath our sensory **thresholds**, and we cannot perceive them consciously. A threshold is the smallest amount of a stimulus that we are aware of sensing: the tiniest image, the softest sound, the faintest scent, or the blandest taste and texture. To find your hearing threshold, turn down your radio or stereo to the point where you can just barely detect the sound. If you lower the volume any further, the sound will seem to disappear. The level of sound you can just barely hear is your threshold.

threshold Smallest amount of stimuli that a person is aware of; stimulus a person can barely sense

Subliminal Stimuli

What about the radio or stereo sounds beneath your threshold? Some believe that you hear them unconsciously, even though the sound seems inaudible to you. The sounds, sights, and other stimuli beneath your threshold are considered **subliminal**. Research on hypnosis has confirmed that unconscious influences are possible.

subliminal Stimulus beneath a person's sensory threshold

The article in Exhibit 2-1 suggests that even patients in comas may have some awareness. Further, as reported in Exhibit 2-2, people under anesthesia may be influenced by audio tapes. Might we also be unconsciously influenced by subliminal information? Wolfe (1983) found that we can see things without conscious awareness. But it is not clear whether subliminal messages can definitely change our behavior.

A few studies during the 1950s implied that people could easily be influenced by subliminal suggestions and be totally unaware of them. Movie houses experimented with subliminal flashes of "Buy popcorn" in their films; some claimed major increases in popcorn sales. The implications were alarming. However,

Figure 2-1
How many dots do you see?

EXHIBIT 2-1

Doctors Urged to Talk to Comatose Patients

Doctors may feel foolish talking to patients who are comatose, but their words could benefit the patients and the physicians as well, a medical consultant said last week.

"We should talk to comatose patients because they may hear, because some comatose patients may get better and because we are caring professionals," Dr. John La Puma and his colleagues wrote in an article in January's *Archives of Neurology,* a publication of the American Medical Association.

"We're not advising doctors to do absurd things like talk to them about the [Chicago] Cubs or the Bears," La Puma said in a telephone interview. "We're talking about relating to patients, about being courteous."

La Puma conducted the study with David Schiedermayer, Ann Gulyas and Mark Siegler, all of the University of Chicago's Center for Clinical Medical Ethics.

They informally sampled the views of staff doctors at the University of Chicago Hospitals and Clinics in 1986 on the idea of talking to comatose patients.

The first response they got was laughter, La Puma said.

"But once we got past that, we got into deeper feelings," he said.

"Physicians are, by nature, people who want to help others. They feel very frustrated when they can't do that."

La Puma said he had no direct contact with any patient who had recovered from a coma as a result of a doctor's words. But he said research has shown the issue is worth more study.

Auditory stimulation such as a loud click has led to changes in patients' heart and respiratory rates even though it has failed to arouse them, he said.

The article cites an account of a comatose patient who recovered and remembered things that were said during her coma. She also remembered thinking, "We know each other, doctor, but you never say hello to me. Why do you act as if I'm not here?"

Source: (1988, January 19). Doctors urged to talk to comatose patients. *Washington Post Health.*

these experiments were not carefully controlled. The increased sales could have been attributed to weather conditions, the type of audience attracted to particular films, changes in refreshment displays, or many other possible factors. As you read about the results of subliminal experiments, check to be sure that the experimenters used proper controls. Controlled laboratory studies have not shown evidence that subliminal advertising is effective.

EXHIBIT 2-2

Pep Talks Help Patients

Patients under anesthesia who are reassured in the operating room that their surgeries are progressing nicely are likely to experience faster and better recoveries than those who are not. Even though such patients are unconscious and have no post-surgical recollection of having heard the encouraging pep talks by their physicians or nurses or on recorded tapes, their recuperation goes well. Doctors theorize that the subliminal message of optimism somehow gets through and is reactivated during the recovery time.

In a recent issue of *The Lancet,* the British medical weekly, doctors at St. Thomas' Hospital in London report that women recovering from hysterectomies suffered relatively less pain, discomfort and nausea because of the cheery message played to them while under anesthesia.

Source: Shearer, L. (1988, October 16). Pep talks help patients. *Parade Magazine.*

The study of subliminal stimuli continues. During the 1980s there was a suspicion that devil messages were recorded backwards on music albums. Many were frightened that these subliminal messages could change people. However, Vokey and Reed (1985) found no evidence that these messages could affect attitudes or behavior. To date there simply is not enough evidence to decide whether or not subliminal cues affect people.

Exercise 2-2

A rather dull-witted psychology instructor wants to find out whether students respond to subliminal suggestion. After a long monotonous lecture, he writes on the blackboard in ¼-inch letters "What time is it?" He observes several students checking their watches and proclaims, "Aha! You reacted to the subliminal message!"

a. From what you know about the meaning of the word "subliminal," what is wrong with this experiment? _the ¼ inch letters was not beneath the threshold._

b. What other factors might make you question the instructor's conclusion? _Long and boring lecture leads to students very willing to check their watches._

Check your answers in the Feedback section.

Internal Senses

The senses of hearing, seeing, smelling, touching, and tasting give information about the external world. There are also senses that provide internal information. Do you want to get in touch with some of your internal senses? Turn off a few of your external senses. Close your eyes and cover your ears. Saunter around the room for a few minutes. (If you are on a busy street, on a cliff, or in a crowded area, wait until later.) Without visual or sound cues, you will have to rely on internal senses. Take time out. Do your strolling now and come back to complete the next two exercises.

Exercise 2-3

Record your experiences from your perceptual stroll by answering the following questions about your internal senses.

a. Were you more aware of your steps and movements? _yes_

b. Did you go astray or veer to the left or right when you were trying to walk a straight path? _yes_

c. What problems did you have in maintaining your balance or equilibrium? _I really didn't have a problem._

d. Could you tell if there was an obstacle near you or if you were going through a doorway or narrow space? _not really, relied on memory mostly._

e. How much time did you spend strolling? Did the time pass slowly or quickly? *time seemed to go slower than usual.*

Exercise 2-4

Each of the questions in Exercise 2-3 related to one internal sense. Based on your experiences and responses to these questions, list five internal senses.

a. *movement*   d. *nearness*

b. *direction*   e. *time*

c. *balance*

You may check your answers in the Feedback section.

Perception and Attention

Perception is strongly influenced by attention. Unfortunately, if you daydream during a lecture little or nothing will reach your brain. Attending is not always easy, so so you take notes and make conscious efforts to remain alert. Did you notice an error in the last sentence? You probably were concentrating on the content and although your eyes saw the word "so" repeated, you ignored it. Likewise you were probably not focusing any attention on your thumb until you read this sentence. You simply cannot attend to every stimulus around you, so only certain things are selected. Have you ever driven down a highway with your gas needle nearing "empty"? Chances are you became preoccupied with the location of gas stations. Another day when your tank is full but your stomach is empty, the gas stations might be overlooked, but every diner and restaurant will catch your eye. Attention is usually focused on needed things. If you are hungry or thirsty right now, you might have a problem keeping your attention focused on the reading rather than on the refrigerator.

Advertisers often appeal to needs and interests as a sure way to attract attention. They insinuate that popularity will increase because houses are cleaner or teeth are brighter. But since advertisers are not always certain of the needs of their audience, they have to draw on other principles to gain attention. Their most common techniques will be considered.

Contrasts. Perhaps the most basic way to invite interest is to create some sort of change. Contrasts in color, shape, size, movement, and mood are usually effective attention-getters. A small red barn in the midst of white limestone skyscrapers would be apt to catch your eye. A lecturer is more likely to hold your attention when she frantically waves her arms and hops around than when she stands motionless behind a lectern. Creating contrasts is as old as vaudeville. A good program would never feature a number of slapstick comedians followed immediately by several comic monologues. We need a variety of moods to hold our attention. You may want to check how often television commercials use the principle of change and variation to hold your attention. Look for color contrasts and changes in settings, moods, and movements.

Changes in intensity. Another way to win attention is through changes in intensity. Ever notice that radio and television commercials tend to be louder than the rest of the program? Flashing lights on movie marquees and neon signs also exploit our interest in contrasting intensities.

Figure 2-2
National and
international affairs
apparently have
less importance...

Repetition. Repetition is another key to attention. A friend who accepts your invitation with a "yes, yes, yes," will attract more notice than someone who merely responds, "yes." Candidates for political office pass out bumper stickers and buttons in hopes that the repetition of their names will hold your attention. Likewise, advertising slogans and product names are frequently repeated many times in magazine ads and commercials. But if repetition is overdone, it can become monotonous and boring, and attention will be lost to a more interesting stimulus.

Figure 2-3
Advertisers know how
to appeal to needs
and interests.

"I'd like a word with you about your work station."

Figure 2-4
It appears this worker's
use of "contrast" is
gaining attention.

Novelty. One sure way to divert your interest is through novelty. If, as you continue your reading, a large purple blob crossed the room ringing a fire siren, your interest would undoubtedly stray from this book. Commercials frequently appeal to an attraction to novelty. Rabbits that seek breakfast cereal, cats that do Latin-American dances, and elves with baking abilities are only a few.

Figure 2-5
The man with the
novel label will surely
attract more attention
than Ed, Nancy, Bill,
John, or Ted.

Social insinuations. Social insinuations can also attract our interest. If everyone else appears interested in something, we assume it worthy of our attention. Perhaps as a child you and your friends were involved in a prank of putting your ears to the sidewalk as if there were some unusual sounds emerging. Soon others would join you in response to the insinuation that there was something worth hearing under the sidewalk. Similarly, ads frequently suggest that products are popular or praised and approved by famous people.

Exercise 2-5

Assume you have been selected as campaign manager for a woman who is running for mayor. The woman is not well known in the community, and your immediate goal is to have her gain the attention of voters. Based on your knowledge of techniques for attracting attention, indicate which of the following alternatives would be preferable and why.

a. Have her appear at social occasions wearing (1) neutral colors and conservative dress or (2) bright colors and striking clothes.

Alternative: _Bright colors and striking clothes._

Reason: _these would draw more attention_
then the more subtle colors
and conservative clothes.
(Drawing Attention)

b. Hang (1) conventional rectangular posters on walls or (2) hexagonal posters from wires.

Alternative: _hexagonal posters from wires._

Reason: _different shape & different_
way of putting then so people
can see them. (novelty)

c. In the local paper place (1) half-page ads in three locations or (2) a single full-page.

Alternative: _half-page adds in three locations._

Reason: _the more you see it the more_
you'll think this person is
important. (Repidition)

d. Have her make a short promotional speech (1) on a local music program or (2) on a local talk show.

Alternative: _local talk show music_

Reason: _reach more people more Attention._

_____

_____

_____

_____

e. Either (1) surround her with people who appear intrigued and ask her questions, or (2) have her travel alone.

Alternative _Surround her with people_

Reason: _if other people notice that_
the people are asking her questions
they would probably do the same.
(Social insinuation)

Compare your choices and reasons with those given in the Feedback section.

Distraction and Pain Control

Sometimes it is desirable to be distracted from stimuli. Pain is one example. Although it is important to feel pain so that you know if you have a sore throat or an infected toe or tooth, there are times when you want to turn off some of the pain experience. In experiments psychologists have shown that people can experience relief from pain when distracted. Some considerate and imaginative dentists have used this advice and supply stereophonic headphones or small television sets. Others are more conventional and hand out magazines. Distraction is an important factor in natural childbirth. Attention is diverted to concerns with breathing and monitoring the progress of the labor. The mother is so concerned with her role in delivery that she is less aware of the pain she is experiencing.

Both Olshan (1980) and Beers and Karoly (1979) found that pain can be relieved through mental exercises. If you are suffering from severe stomach discomfort, you might pretend your pain is caused by running furiously up Mount Everest. Imagine the fame, the crowds, and the awards awaiting you, the fastest person to climb Mount Everest! Perhaps a little farfetched, but it may help. Next time you have a nagging headache or sore muscles, try to focus your attention on something fascinating and see if you perceive less pain.

Checkpoint

Use the following questions to check your understanding of this portion of the chapter. Choose and mark the one correct response to each question.

1. Which two processes are always involved in perception?
   a. Attention and subliminal stimuli
   b. Subliminal stimuli and sensation
   c. Sensation and interpretation
   d. Internal sensation and distraction
2. Which of the following stimuli would be beneath your sensory threshold?
   a. A bright light bulb that almost blinds you
   b. The odor of a grain of salt

    c. The low-pitched tones of a bass
    d. A lecture that you are ignoring
3. What does current research on subliminal stimuli suggest?
    a. Almost everyone is constantly influenced by subliminals.
    b. Only visual subliminal stimuli affect behavior.
    c. There is not enough evidence to determine the influence of subliminal stimuli.
    d. People cannot be affected by subliminal stimuli.
4. Which of the following contain three internal senses?
    a. Senses of balance, nearness, and time
    b. Senses of balance, touch, and smell
    c. Senses of vision, hearing, and touch
    d. Senses of hearing, time, and taste
5. A woman is engrossed in her work. She suddenly looks at the clock and realizes she has worked through her lunch hour. Which of the following reasons best explains why she had not noticed the time?
    a. Her attention was focused on her work rather than on the clock.
    b. The clock's ticking was only a subliminal cue.
    c. There are social insinuations about clock watching.
    d. Her work may have been painful.

Listed on the left are techniques for winning attention. Match the statement on the right that provides the best example of each technique.

6. __D__ Repetition   *a.* A woman paints a white stripe on her black car.

7. __E__ Novelty   *b.* A teacher raises his voice and screams, "Quiet!"

8. __B__ Changes in intensity   *c.* The crowd around a store bargain table grows constantly.

9. __C__ Social insinuations   *d.* A mother nags constantly, "Don't forget to clean your room."

10. __A__ Contrasts in color, shape, or size   *e.* A man squirts everyone he sees with a water pistol.

Use the Checkpoint Answer Key at the end of the chapter to verify your responses. If you had any difficulty with a question, carefully reread the text. If you had little or no difficulty answering the questions or have resolved any problems that you might have had, you are ready to continue with the next portion of this chapter.

FACTORS AFFECTING INTERPRETATION

Having discussed sensation and attention, we can move on to the interpretation of perception. Interpretation implies that meaning is inferred from what is sensed. Because each person has had different experiences, needs, and emotions, no two people interpret reality in quite the same way. Have you ever looked at a priceless modern painting and found it absurd and senseless? Apparently it had meaning for at least one other person and probably for many others. Individual differences in perception are important. It would be a boring world if everyone viewed reality in exactly the same way. But sometimes these differences can present problems. Ask any police officer who has tried to determine what occurred at a traffic accident! Sometimes there will be as many perceptions as there are observers. This section of the chapter will investigate some of the main factors that cause varying interpretations in perception: expectation, and needs, motivations, and emotions. It will also examine some common illusions.

Expectation

F. Scott Fitzgerald stated, "We do not first see and then define; we first define and then see." Past experience and learning often point out what should be expected. For example, if you were in a card game with some people who had cheated you before, you would be on guard for deceptive actions. Simple coughs or foot tapping might be interpreted as trickery. Previous experience has a strong influence on perception. The story told in Exhibit 2-3 reminds us that even the "world's smartest man" can err based on a mistaken expectation. Previous plane rides probably did not include boy scouts with backpacks.

People have some idea of what exists out there, and to some extent this determines what is perceived. Ask one of your professors to check your grade on a "jest." Based on past experience the teacher will probably assume you said "test." It is doubtful that anyone had ever before expressed concern over a score on a "jest."

Past knowledge also provides a frame of reference. If a boss is accustomed to a secretary who makes at least five errors on every page typed, a replacement who makes only two errors on each page would be perceived as a good typist. However, the replacement secretary would be rated far lower when compared with more efficient coworkers in the organization. The appraisal of the secretary's competency changes when the frame of reference shifts. Likewise, how you judge a film will depend on whether you compare it with one that won an Oscar or an old rerun of a B movie. The frame of reference will make an impressive difference.

EXHIBIT 2-3

Source: Comer, P.
(1988, January/
February). World's
smartest man.
*Saturday Evening
Post.*

The World's Smartest Man

A small private plane developed engine trouble while still many miles from a suitable landing strip. The pilot, realizing there was nothing he could do to keep the plane in the air, rushed back to where his three passengers sat and explained the predicament. He added, "I am a married man with two small children. I regret to tell you there are only three parachutes aboard." And with that, he grabbed one of the parachutes and bailed out.

One of the passengers reacted quickly to the pilot's exit. "I am a brilliant scientist!" he announced. "I am the world's smartest man! The world cannot do without me!" And with that, he too bailed out.

The other two passengers, an elderly priest and a boy scout, were quiet for a moment. "Son," the priest said finally, "I am old and have lived a full life. I am ready to meet my Maker."

"You'll have to cancel it, Father," the boy scout answered, smiling. "The world's smartest man just bailed out with my backpack!"

Two horticulturists are presented with the same species of a tiger lily and asked to comment. One describes the bloom as small and slightly misshapen. The other reports that the bloom is lavish and perfect in form. Both agree that the color is vibrant and brilliant. Using the concept of *frame of reference,* describe the possible causes of agreement and disagreement between the horticulturists.

Comparing the flower to a larger one
Comparing the flower to ones that are
smaller and Almost the same shape.

You may check your description of the causes with those in the Feedback section.

Sometimes you are told what to expect. Your own past experiences and frame of reference will have less importance. Look at the professor in Figure 2-6. You expect to see a man, and you probably do. Take another look. Could it be a mouse? The figure will switch from man to mouse depending on what you expect to see.

In one experiment two groups of subjects were shown the same stimulus figure shown in Figure 2-7a. One group was told it was the number ''7'' and the other group was told it was the number ''4.'' When the two groups were asked to reproduce the figures, their drawings resembled those in Figure 2-7b. Being told what to expect had a clear impact on what was perceived.

Many initiation rituals are based on telling people what to perceive. One gimmick involves passing around a pair of peeled grapes to blindfolded initiates. The initiates are told they are feeling the eyes of a dead person. Even if you have never experienced this type of ritual, you can probably imagine the horror that accompanies the resulting perception. Although the participants are touching ordinary grapes, the expectation of something horrible changes their perception.

Figure 2-6
Professor Ahman Oramouz

Uniforms have been used to influence our expectations and perceptions. As the excerpt in Exhibit 2-4 reports, we have specific expectations from people in uniforms. If you met a woman dressed as a nun, you probably would expect her to be holy and somewhat reserved. As a result, you would most likely see her as religious and self-controlled, rather than as a rowdy materialist.

Exercise 2-7

A psychologist, named Sirpola (1935), told one group of subjects that he would present words related to boats. He then presented the stimulus words: "sael," "dack," and "wharl." The group interpreted the words as "sail," "deck," and "wharf."

He presented the same stimulus words to a second group of subjects. This time he said the words would be related to animals.

a. Give an educated guess on how the words were interpreted.

"sael": _SEAL_

"dack": _DUCK_

"wharl": _Whale_

Figure 2-7a
Stimulus figure

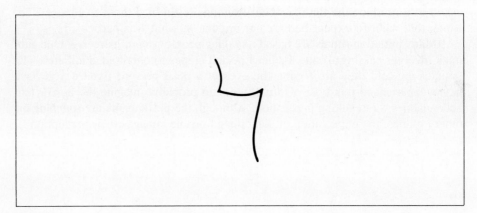

Figure 2-7b
Reproduced figures

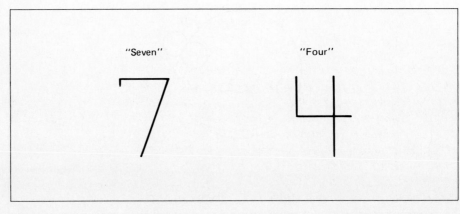

EXHIBIT 2-4

43
PERCEIVING

Standard Issue

…One function of service apparel is to communicate a company's selling points, whether it be cleanliness, professionalism, safety or just plain good taste. Thus, like a chameleon, service apparel assumes the properties of the group it represents. It embodies the group's ideals and attributes, allowing its wearer to transmit the dominant values of the company or organization. Effective uniforms can go a long way toward establishing a desirable impression: the hygienic nurse, the brave soldier, the law-and-order police officer.

Uniforms help to boost customers' confidence in an organization or business. Since many services (such as an airplane flight) cannot be inspected before they are bought, consumers are reluctant to take a chance on an unknown provider. By contributing to a recognizable and familiar image, uniforms enhance company credibility and lessen consumers' hesitancy.

Lynn Shostack, a services-marketing consultant based in New York, has proposed that the more abstract the service, the greater the consumer's need for tangible evidence of its quality. As Harvard marketing professor Theodore Levitt has observed, in the extreme case the marketer must essentially create a physical surrogate for the product. For example, while airline customers are actually buying a ride from point A to point B, their choice of a carrier is often based upon such things as food quality, the attentiveness of flight attendants and perhaps even the feelings evoked by the airline's color scheme.

As people deal with a service business over time, they are likely to be served by several individuals in the same roles. For example, a hotel guest may encounter different employees on various shifts during the course of a stay. The continuity of uniform can smooth over fluctuations in service quality and personnel by providing a consistent picture of the provider, regardless of who happens to represent the organization at any given time. The very presence of a uniform implies coherent group structure—someone who wears the uniform and a superior who authorizes that person to wear it…

Source: Solomon, M. (1987, December). Standard issue. *Psychology Today.*

b. Why did the two groups give such different responses?

Because the psychologist gave two different presentations of the group of words

Check your answers in the Feedback section.

In another investigation, a psychology professor introduced the same male guest lecturer to two different classes. The first class was told to expect a rather cold, dull, uninteresting person. The second class was told to expect a warm, intelligent, friendly lecturer. The lecturer presented identical information in the same manner to both groups. The groups perceived him differently and according to their expectations: The first group found his lecture boring and did not ask questions; the second group found him warm and stimulating and asked many questions. This experiment has been replicated successfully many times. The results suggest that telling someone what to perceive in another person will influence what is experienced.

Exercise 2-8

A party is moving rather slowly, and there are many awkward silences and pauses. The host corners you in the kitchen and pleads for help. You agree to assist with the introductions. From what you know about expectations and perceptions, suggest the type of introductions that might help get the party going.

introducing the people you know
with common interests or subjects,

Compare your suggestion with the one in the Feedback section.

Needs, Motivations, and Emotions

Earlier in this chapter, needs and motivations were mentioned as factors affecting attention. Needs and motivations constantly interact and create emotions. It is difficult to separate the roles of these three factors, but there has been considerable research on how they work together to affect perception.

One group of psychologists studied how financial needs affect the perception of coin size. Middle-class college students were asked to adjust the size of a light to approximate the sizes of a penny, a nickel, a dime, and a quarter. The students were then hypnotized and told they had a history of poverty. The hypnotist suggested they lacked even the basic necessities. While still under hypnosis the students were again asked to adjust the size of the light to the size of the same four coins. They adjusted the light to sizes significantly larger than each coin. During a second hypnosis session, the same students were told they had wealthy backgrounds and enjoyed many sumptuous luxuries. This time they adjusted the light to a smaller size than they had in their normal condition. Figure 2-8 shows the results of the experiment. Although it is impossible to separate the roles of needs, motivations, and emotions in the perception of the subjects, it is clear that all three factors interacted to change the perception of coin size.

The old adage "love is blind" illustrates how emotions affect perception. Even unattractive people seem incredibly beautiful when you feel deep emotions for them. And when you feel this sense of love, warmth, and well-being, you usually have a more favorable perception of the whole world. Each type of emotion influences perception differently. If you are fearfully walking through a dark alley, you are apt to perceive every sound and shadow as looming danger. Because of your fearful state, you interpret even ordinary stimuli as potential threats to your safety.

Psychologists use perceptions to learn more about underlying emotional states and to analyze personalities. They use ambiguous pictures or inkblots and ask for a description of what is seen. Each person's perception is considered an expression of personal emotions, motivations, and needs. Chapter 9 will discuss this method of personality assessment in more detail.

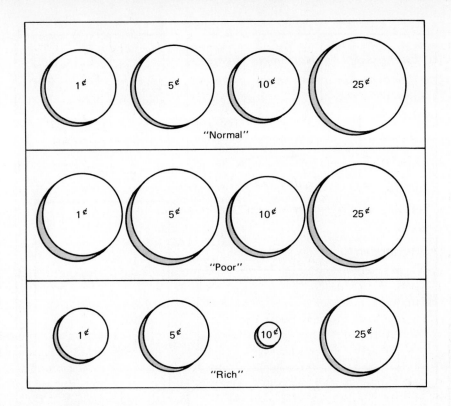

Figure 2-8
Average size of light
spots judged equal to
coin size.

Exercise 2-9

Two women, Mrs. S. and Ms. T., belong to the same recreation club. They
were given an outline of the club and were asked to draw a plan of how the
facilities were arranged. Examine the correct plan of the club and the sketches
made by Mrs. S. and Ms. T. (see Figures 2-9, 2-10, and 2-11 on pages 46, 47,
and 48). Based on their perceptions of the club, see what you can learn about
the needs and motivations of each woman.

a. Which areas of the club are emphasized by both women? _LAP pool_
& pro shop

b. Which areas of the club were emphasized only by Mrs. S.? _Kids pool_
LArge Pool, picnic AreA, & snAck BAR

c. Which areas of the club were emphasized only by Ms. T.? _womens SAUNA,_
exercise room, lockers, & tennis courts

d. Which areas did both women minimize or forget? _men's lockers_
& sAunA.

e. What are some possible reasons for the differences in their perception of
the club? _Different needs to be met_
And different interests.

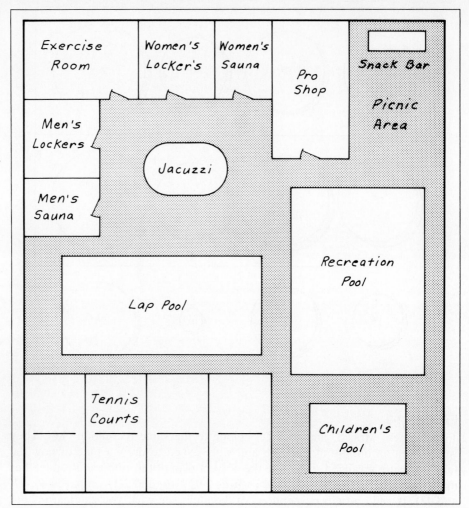

Figure 2-9
Correct club plan

Illusions

Illusions are misinterpretations or errors in perception. Look at two common visual or optical illusions in Figure 2-12. In both the Muller-Lyer and Ponzo illusions the horizontal lines are the same length. In the Muller-Lyer illusion the bottom line appears longer, and in the Ponzo illusion the upper line looks longer. If all but the horizontal lines were removed from the drawings, it would be obvious that the two lines are equal. The other lines in the drawing cause you to misinterpret their size.

Illusions can be bothersome and problematic. Pilots who rely solely on their own senses can misinterpret their altitudes or flight attitude. This would be a dangerous situation were it not for aircraft instruments. Pilots are taught to use instruments in situations where visual illusions are likely.

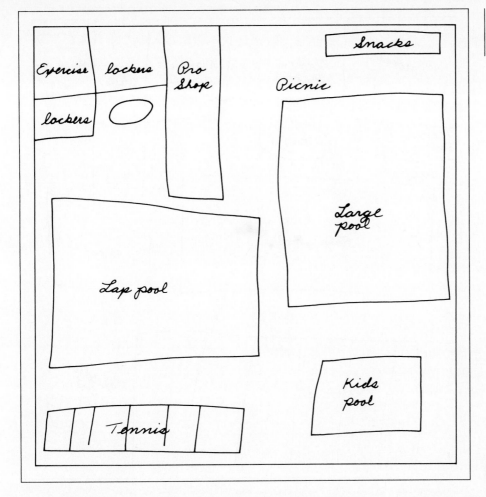

Figure 2-10
Mrs. S. sketch

Beauty experts, clothing designers, and interior decorators all use their knowledge of illusion to improve appearances. Eye shadow is used to create the illusion of deep-set eyes; obese men wear suits with vertical stripes to appear slimmer; and rooms are painted white and equipped with small-scale furniture to appear more spacious. Examine your friends and your environment more closely, and you will probably find many examples of illusions.

Checkpoint

Use the following questions to check your understanding of this portion of the chapter. Choose the one best response to each question.

11. Perception includes sensation and interpretation. What does interpretation involve?
    a. Giving meaning to what is sensed
    b. Finding the cause of sensation

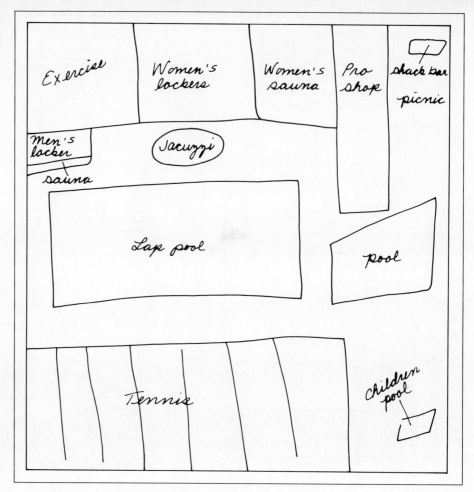

Figure 2-11
Ms. T. sketch

    c. Knowing what to expect
    d. Correcting illusions
12. After hearing a local choral group sing, a woman exclaims, "They are the best singing group in the world!" What is her probable frame of reference?
    a. All the singing groups in the world
    b. Singing groups she has heard before
    c. The orchestra that accompanied the group
    d. Her mood on the day she heard the group
13. Which of the following explanations would best account for a man hearing ghost footsteps in his attic?
    a. He has heard ghost footsteps in other attics.
    b. He believes in ghosts and expects to hear footsteps.
    c. The Muller-Lyer illusion has distorted his perception.
    d. His financial needs have distorted his perception.
14. If you were told that a certain new job was fun, how would your perception of the job be affected?
    a. You would find the job more difficult.
    b. You would view the job as disappointing.

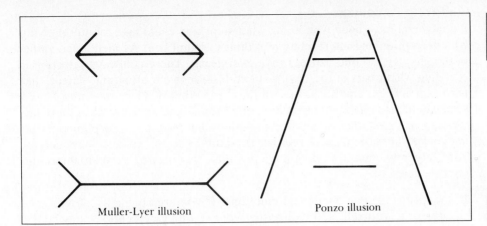

Muller-Lyer illusion

Ponzo illusion

Figure 2-12
Muller-Lyer illusion
Ponzo illusion

> *c.* You would find the job boring.
> *d.* You would find the job enjoyable.

15. In a study of middle-class college students, a group of psychologists had the students adjust the size of a light to approximate the sizes of coins. What did the results of this study suggest?
    a. Expectation affects perception.
    b. Expectation does not affect perception.
    c. Needs and emotions affect perception.
    d. Needs and emotions do not affect perception
16. What is an illusion?
    a. An error in sensation
    b. An error in interpretation
    c. An incorrect frame of reference
    d. An error caused by needs
17. Which of the following is the best example of an illusion?
    a. A student is tense about an exam and views everything negatively.
    b. A poor girl sees money as more important than grades.
    c. A fat man appears thinner when he wears oversized clothes.
    d. A man who is late for work tries to sneak by his employer's desk.

Check your responses against the Checkpoint Answer Key at the end of the chapter. If you had difficulty with any question, reread the text. If you had little or no difficulty answering the questions or have resolved problems that you might have had, you are ready to continue with the final portion of this chapter.

PERCEPTION IN ACTION

Having looked at the basic principles of sensation, attention, and perception, you will now have an opportunity to actively apply some of these ideas to improve your own perception. In this portion of the chapter you will be considering steps you can take to improve your own sensitivity, awareness, and perception. You will also examine some common and not-so-common problems: perceptual impairment, perceptual bombardment, and perceptual deprivation. The chapter will conclude by defining types of extrasensory perception and checking the evidence from studies of ESP.

Improving Perception

Perhaps you have been wondering what steps you could take to improve your own perception and interpretation of things around you. As mentioned earlier in the chapter, no one can perceive everything. There is always selection in choosing which part of the environment deserves your attention. Factors like past experiences, emotions, motivations, and what other people infer have a strong influence on the interpretation of surroundings. In many ways these factors can also limit and restrict interpretations and resulting perceptions. By using your awareness of these restricting factors, you can enhance and increase your perceptual abilities. Here are a few hints that may be useful in improving your perception:

1. Identify your own needs and emotions. If you are having a "down" day, admit it to yourself, and realize that your resulting perceptions may be distorted.
2. Acknowledge your own frame of reference, and concede that others may be using different frames of reference.
3. Try to broaden your view by taking a different perspective. Exchanging positions with another person can create a totally new perception.
4. Differentiate between what you are sensing and what you are interpreting or inferring. There is often a great difference between what is observed and what is inferred.
5. Be suspicious when you are told what to perceive. Search for other possibilities.
6. Recognize techniques that are used to attract your attention, and try to maintain control over undesirable distractions.
7. Remember that you can be fooled by illusions.

Exercise 2-10

Now check your ability to use these hints. In each of the following examples a person is demonstrating a problem in perceiving accurately. Using the hints listed above, explain what each person should do to improve perception.

a. Jim told Bob that their new office building had a faulty heating system. Bob felt chilly as soon as he entered the building, even though the temperature was 72° (5) _____

_____

b. Claire woke up with a hangover and a severe headache. She looked in the mirror and saw a face full of wrinkles. Actually Claire was an extremely attractive and youthful-looking person. _Since she felt_ (1) _Bad she expected herself to look Bad._

c. Marsha drove through a red light. She said she had trouble concentrating on her driving because of all the blinking lights from nightclubs and casinos. (6) _Maintain control over undesirable distractions._

d. Sidney, a chain smoker, cannot understand why nonsmokers are so finicky about sitting near smoke. (3) _____

_____

e. When Bill saw Meg in a slinky black dress, he was sure she had lost 10 pounds. Actually Meg's weight was the same. (5) _____

_____

_____

f. Harry's boss gave him a poor evaluation because she noticed that Harry spent time staring out the window or off into space. She felt Harry was a daydreamer. Harry had been having difficulty with eyestrain, and his doctor told him to look into the distance periodically to relax his eyes. (4) _____

_____

_____

You may check your responses in the Feedback section.

Sensory and Perceptual Impairments

Thus far, the discussion of perception has focused on the problems and limitations of people with normal sensory and perceptual abilities. As you know, there are many individuals who have perceptual impairments. Three of the more common types of impairments are blindness, deafness, and dyslexia. People who suffer from these defects have specific limitations and must learn ways to compensate for their deficiencies.

Blindness. Perhaps you have thought of blind individuals as being able to read braille or walk around with the aid of a cane or seeing-eye dog. Surprisingly, less than 20 percent of the blind can read braille, and only about 10 percent can make their way around with canes and seeing-eye dogs. Blindness is a sensory impairment. Blind people must rely heavily on their other external senses and on their internal senses. Remember the blindfolded stroll you took while reading the first part of this chapter? Just as you were more aware of your other senses when you were blindfolded, blind persons constantly depend on these other senses. Many blind people show an unusual ability to picture their surroundings through the use of other senses.

There is some hope that total blindness may be eliminated in the near future. Efforts are being made to develop a system that will allow a blind person to see through a glass eye. The glass eye will contain a tiny camera. Wires from the camera will go to a miniature computer placed in an eyeglass frame. The picture messages from the computer will be sent to electrodes that are permanently placed in the brain. Although this system probably will not provide normal vision, it may help to give some visual information to the blind.

Deafness. Deafness is another sensory impairment and can become a severe problem in babies and young children because it is difficult to detect. Many parents are not aware that their child has hearing limitations until it is time for the child to speak. Often deafness is not discovered until the child is almost 2 years old. By then the child is already handicapped in the development of language abilities. If found early enough, many types of hearing loss are correctable with either medication, hearing aids, or surgery. But not all deafness is congenital. Hearing losses can occur from working in a noisy environment. Although after the age of 30 everyone becomes progressively deaf to the higher frequencies, people who work in noisy settings will show a more rapid rate of hearing loss.

Just as modern technology is giving hope to the blind, there is also hope for the deaf. The article in Exhibit 2-5 promises an electronic implant that will help the deaf and blind. Scientists are currently working on microphones that can send electrical signals to electrodes implanted in the brain. With the aid of these electronic systems it may be possible to bring hearing to the deaf.

dyslexia Perceptual impairment that results in reading problems; reversed, scrambled, or confused message is sent to the brain

Dyslexia. *Dyslexia* is a type of perceptual impairment that affects the ability to read. The dyslexic person reads a scrambled or reversed message. For example, "was" might be read as "saw," "517" could be interpreted as "751," and the concepts of "hot" and "cold" might be confused. The errors in perception involve reversals, mirror images, or some other type of confusion. Although there continues to be much research, the exact cause of dyslexia is uncertain. Studies have shown that people with dyslexia are usually average or above in intelligence and have no clear evidence of brain damage. Nelson Rockefeller, Woodrow Wilson, and Albert Einstein were among the famous dyslexics. Although the cause dyslexia has not been determined, effective programs have been developed to help individuals adjust to their perceptual distortions. Research on the cause of dyslexia continues (see Exhibit 2-6).

EXHIBIT 2-5

Repair Shop: Body

The blind will see, the deaf hear, and the paralyzed walk. The messianic promise from the Old Testament book of Isaiah may just be fulfilled by the next millennium due to the work of scientists at several major medical centers. The reason: a new kind of computer microchip that can be implanted in the body to repair or replace the lost functions of damaged nerves.

...one chip can carry as many as 40 microscopic gold wires that press against the surfaces of single nerves. The more wires on a chip, the better the communication between brain and cell. Each wire picks up one nerve's electrical activity like a wiretap stealing one conversation from a telephone cable. Engineers will use the chips to build artificial eyes and ears....

Most researchers in the field agree that practical implants will be available within the decade. Gerald Loeb surely believes so. After 14 years at the National Institute of Neurological and Communicative Disorders and Stroke, he is leaving to set up his own engineering laboratory. He intends to build an artificial eye that will feed images from a TV camera into a microchip implanted in the visual centers of the brain. "It will take ten years to develop," he says. "The technology we need is now available. I don't see any reason we can't build a device that will bring eyesight to the blind."

Source: Davies, O. (1987, November). Repair shop: Body. *Omni.*

EXHIBIT 2-6

53
PERCEIVING

Dyslexia: Reading Both Ends against the Middle

Seeing is not the problem for dyslexics learning to read, but interpreting what they see is. Recent research seems to suggest that the problem may lie in a peculiar advantage dyslexics have over normal readers: They are better at recognizing letters presented in their peripheral field of vision than they are at identifying those presented in their foveal, or central, field of vision.

Physiologists Gad Geiger and Jerome Lettvin tested the peripheral vision of 10 university students. Five were normal readers; the other five were described as residual dyslexics who had improved their reading ability through tutoring.

In the first part of their study, Geiger and Lettvin had each student sit in front of a blank screen. A dot was projected onto the screen to provide each student with a "fixation point," that is, a place on which to focus their eyes. A second projector then flashed a pair of letters onto the screen, one at the fixation point and the other at varying horizontal distances from it.

Previous research has shown that the greater the distance from the fixation point, the harder it is for normal readers to identify the letters correctly. Geiger and Lettvin found that the normal readers usually outscored the dyslexics in correctly identifying the letters presented at closer distances but, as expected, their scores sharply declined as the letters were projected farther from the fixation point. Surprisingly, the reverse occurred for the students with residual dyslexia. They were actually better at identifying letters in the periphery.

In the second part of their study, Geiger and Lettvin had the students undergo the same test, this time flashing strings of three letters at varying distances from the students' fixation point. Previous research has shown that as this distance increases, normal readers have a harder time correctly identifying the letter in the center of the string because it becomes "masked" by the flanking letters.

Geiger and Lettvin found that this "masking effect" did occur for the normal readers as expected. But for the dyslexics "the 'masking effect' was relatively larger near the center of the gaze and relatively smaller at greater" distances.

Their findings, the researchers say, are a clue to the difficulty dyslexics have with reading, and also point to education strategies to help them improve it. As further evidence, they cite the case of one 25-year-old man described as a severe dyslexic. When tested, his reading ability was on the third-grade level, but he showed the same advantage as the residual dyslexics in recognizing letters presented in his peripheral field of vision. However, he was given reading exercises designed to encourage use of his peripheral vision, and when tested four months later, his reading ability was up to the 10th-grade level.

"While normal readers generally learn to read in the foveal field," the researchers conclude, "dyslexics learn to read outside the foveal field. It is commonly assumed that reading is a foveal art. In education, this assumption reinforces dyslexia. Our preliminary findings provide evidence that an alternative reading strategy can be learned."

Source: Greene, C. (1987, November). Dyslexia: Reading both ends against the middle. *Psychology Today.*

Exercise 2-11

Consider three of the more common forms of perceptual impairment: blindness, deafness, and dyslexia. In your own words, describe the steps that a person with each of these impairments can now take to adapt.

a. Blindness: _____

b. Deafness: _____

c. Dyslexia: _____

Exercise 2-12

Now take a look into the future. What steps might be taken to alleviate each of the disorders discussed in Exercise 2-11.

a. Blindness: _____

b. Deafness: _____

c. Dyslexia: _____

You may compare your responses with those in the Feedback section.

Sensory Deprivation

Have you ever wondered what would happen if you were taken hostage and put in solitary confinement? Solitary confinement provides little or no stimulation, and you would probably have nothing to see, hear, or smell. Psychologists have been interested in how people are affected when their senses are deprived of stimulation and they experience *sensory deprivation*.

In a study during the 1950s student volunteers were paid $20 a day to stay in an isolation room. They had to lie on a bed wearing a blindfold, ear plugs, gloves, and cardboard cuffs. Most of the students could not bear the isolation and quit within one or two days. Many of those who did stay reported hallucinations, including voices, vivid pictures, or strange smells. In all cases, the isolation was considered an unpleasant experience. A more recent study found that males from urban areas were more likely to hallucinate than males from rural areas. Most of the rural men thought about work on their farms. The city men were more accustomed to stimulation and found it difficult to do any coherent thinking without it.

Most people never have to spend time in solitary confinement or in a lonely research post at the north pole. But many people are subjected to low levels of stimulation or boredom. There are many situations when there is limited opportunity for stimulation. Monotonous jobs that require repeating the same action over and over can create boredom. For example, folding pillowcases all day long requires little intellectual effort and could become a monotonous routine. When you are given such a boring job, your performance usually deteriorates and your perceptual abilities may show some impairment. And, as you probably suspected, you will find the experience unpleasant.

Sensory Bombardment

Although there has been much research on sensory deprivation, there has been relatively little evidence collected on sensory overload or bombardment. The best-known form of *sensory bombardment* is light shows. Bright lights are flashed in rapid, wild patterns to the accompaniment of loud rock music. The purpose of the bombardment is to produce "psychedelic experiences." A psychedelic experience usually involves perceptual distortions, including a confusion of the sense of time, a loss of control, and strange

sensory deprivation
Removal or reduction of sensory stimuli from the environment

sensory bombardment
Overloading the senses with stimuli

sensations. In one study on sensory bombardment, 24 percent of the subjects who were exposed to a sensory overload of light and sound had psychedelic experiences. Other studies (Goldberger, 1982; Kaminoff & Proshansky, 1982; and Tyhurst, 1951) have shown that high levels of sensory overload may cause irritability, tension, nervousness, reading problems, and hearing and judgment impairments.

Exercise 2-13
Based on the evidence from psychological studies of sensory deprivation and sensory bombardment, explain why each of the following situations could occur:

a. A college student, who is the oldest of twelve lively children, finds it difficult to concentrate in a quiet library. She prefers a noisy cafeteria. _____
Used to noise

b. A stodgy old man attends a light show and finds himself frantically waving his arms and moving around. _____

_____

c. An astronaut who was alone in a space capsule for three days claims he saw a Martian flying in space. _____

_____

You may check your explanations in the Feedback section at the end of the chapter.

Extrasensory Perception

Many psychologists believe that people have the ability to perceive or influence objects and events without the normal use of the senses. This ability is called "extrasensory perception." The study of ESP is relatively new to the field of psychology and is included in the field of **parapsychology**. Parapsychology studies behavior that cannot be explained by either physics or physiology. These behaviors are labeled "psi events." The main psi events of interest in parapsychology are:

Telepathy *Telepathy* is another word for mind reading and has been a central theme in many fantasies and science-fiction stories. People communicate without speaking or seeing each other. Each knows what the other person is thinking. In some cases, identical twins have claimed telepathic ability between themselves.

Clairvoyance *Clairvoyance* is an ability to perceive objects or events that are beyond the reach of the normal senses. A clairvoyant person might be able to describe a traffic jam more than 100 miles away.

Precognition *Precognition* is the ability to foresee the future and know what is going to happen. Jeanne Dixon became famous for this ability when she predicted the assassination of President Kennedy. You may have experienced a weak version of precognition in the form of a premonition—possibly a vague feeling that something was going to happen to a close friend

extrasensory perception (ESP) Ability to perceive and/or influence objects without using external senses

parapsychology Field of psychology that focuses on extrasensory perception

telepathy Ability to understand what another person is thinking without the use of the senses; mind reading

clairvoyance Ability to perceive objects or events that are not within the reach of the senses

precognition Ability to foresee future events

psychokinesis (PK)
Ability of the mind to
manipulate physical
objects without any
physical contact

or relative. Perhaps it was nothing definite, but if the person did get sick you may have taken this as proof of your precognitive ability.

Psychokinesis *Psychokinesis* is the ability of a mind to manipulate physical objects. In a PK demonstration a person may bend forks and spoons or make clocks and watches begin to tick.

Do these abilities really exist? Although remarkable phenomena have been demonstrated in nightclubs and on television, the evidence from laboratory experiments is less convincing. Individuals who seem to have outstanding ESP one day will have no such ability the next day. People who claim ESP abilities state they cannot function normally in a sterile laboratory environment.

Most psychologists doubt the existence of psi events, but evidence is still being collected. Watch for their findings, and check your own ESP! As suggested in Exhibit 2-7, the debate continues.

Checkpoint

Use the following questions to check your understanding of the final portion of this chapter. Choose the one best response to each question.

EXHIBIT 2-7

Psi Shrinks

Psychologist Jeffrey Munson of the Durham, North Carolina–based Foundation for Research on the Nature of Man (FRNM) received several phone calls after the space shuttle *Challenger* exploded in 1986. The callers, all of them distraught, claimed they had foreseen the tragedy—and done nothing. "They said they had premonitions or dreamed about it," he recalls. "They felt terribly guilty that they had received this information and not used it to help in some way."

Munson relates that the FRNM (a nonprofit organization that studies paranormal phenomena) receives hundreds of phone calls a year from people who are similarly disturbed about psychic experiences. "They are sometimes confused or depressed," he explains. "Suddenly the normal rules of living don't apply anymore and it can be frightening."

Munson says that many of these people recognize they have a problem dealing with their experiences. "But they are often hesitant to contact a psychiatrist or psychologist because they fear being branded 'crazy'."

In order to help these people, the FRNM is putting together a referral list of psychiatrists, psychologists, and counselors who claim expertise in the paranormal. So far the directory contains the names of more than 50 mental-health professionals around the country with an interest in psi. "I hope to use the directory to refer people to professionals who will give them legitimate psychological help—without the threat of an opinion that works against them from the start," Munson states. "Some people who call us may or may not have psychic experiences, and some of them may even be deluded or even have some kind of organic disease. But they shouldn't be labeled disturbed automatically because they're claiming paranormal experiences."

Psychologist James Alcock of York University in Toronto, however, isn't impressed with the idea of a directory of psi-inclined counselors. "If a person with a delusion that he can read minds is told by his therapist, 'That's ESP,' it may make the patient feel better in the short term," he notes. "But if this is the beginning of schizophrenia, it could keep the person from getting the treatment he really needs."

Source: Baker, S. (1988, January). Psi shrinks. *Omni.*

18. You see a man shuffling through papers on his desk. You do not want to confuse observation and inference. What would be your observation?

a. A man has misplaced a paper.
b. A man is shuffling through papers.
c. A man is looking for a missing paper.
d. A man is annoyed with his carelessness.

19. What are three of the more common perceptual impairments?

a. Blindness, deafness, and dyslexia
b. Deafness, dyslexia, and illusion
c. Blindness, sensory deprivation, and sensory bombardment
d. Dyslexia, clairvoyance, and sensory deprivation

20. How do blind people know that they are going through doorways?

a. They rely on their internal and other external senses.
b. They use extrasensory perception.
c. They use computer-brain implants.
d. They have psychedelic experiences.

21. What do studies on sensory deprivation suggest?

a. Isolation is a pleasant experience.
b. Isolation is a relaxing experience.
c. Isolation is a stimulating experience.
d. Isolation is an unpleasant experience.

Match the term on the left with one phrase from the list on the right. Only one phrase can be correctly related to each term.

22. ___D___ Dyslexia
23. ___I___ Psychedelic experience
24. ___F___ Psychokinesis
25. ___e___ Parapsychology
26. ___H___ Clairvoyance
27. ___A___ Precognition
28. ___B___ Telepathy
29. ___G___ Illusion
30. ___C___ Sensory bombardment

a. Ability to foresee the future
b. Reading the thoughts of another person
c. Sensory overloads in light shows
d. Receiving scrambled or reversed messages
e. A field of psychology that includes ESP
f. Ability to manipulate objects through the use of the mind
g. An error in interpretation
h. Ability to see something beyond the range of normal vision
i. Characterized by a loss of control, confusion of time, and strange feelings

Check your responses against the Checkpoint Answer Key at the end of the chapter. If you had difficulty with any question, reread the text. If you had little or no difficulty answering the questions or have resolved problems that you might have had, you are ready to check yourself against the chapter inventory that follows.

CHAPTER INVENTORY

Use this list of objectives as a review checklist. You should be able to do each of the tasks outlined in the objectives and apply them to everyday examples. If you can, you may feel confident that you have mastered the material in this chapter.

1. Define perception.
2. Distinguish between sensation and interpretation.
3. Identify the limitations of the senses.
4. Provide examples of thresholds and subliminal stimuli.
5. Summarize the problems encountered in the study of subliminal stimuli.
6. Distinguish between internal and external senses and identify five internal senses.
7. Explain five ways to gain attention.
8. Describe the role of distraction in pain control.
9. Explain how expectation influences interpretation.
10. Describe how needs, motivations, and emotions influence interpretation.
11. Define illusions and give three examples.
12. Identify seven ways to check and improve perception.
13. Consider three types of perceptual impairment, and recognize possible ways to improve these conditions.
14. Explain the results of studies on sensory deprivation and sensory bombardment.
15. Categorize the study of ESP as a field in parapsychology.
16. Identify and explain four areas of study in parapsychology.
17. Recognize problems encountered in the study of extrasensory perception.

Feedback

The correct answers to the exercises follow. If you did not answer an exercise correctly, review the preceding pages and return to the exercise to complete it correctly.

2-1. *a.* The color, shape, and letters on the sign that you saw would be your sensation. The meaning that you gave the sign, "Stop your car," involved interpretation.

   b. If you were walking you probably would not stop, since your interpretation would be different. You would not interpret the sign as applying to you.

2-2. *a.* Subliminal stimuli are beneath the threshold. Letters of ¼ inch would probably be above the visual threshold for students in front seats. Likewise, students may have been able to guess the letters being written if they saw his hand movements.

   b. The instructor did not control a number of factors. Check to see how many you identified:

   1 His lecture was long and monotonous; perhaps this caused the students to check their watches.
   2 It is also possible that students normally check their watches toward the end of a lecture.

    3 The instructor's behavior is not reported; perhaps he checked his watch.

    4 Likewise, if one or more students who were able to read the message began checking the time, this may have influenced other students.

    5 The term "several students" is vague; this may have been a small percentage of the class.

2-3. Some typical responses to a blindfolded stroll follow:

    a. "I noticed every step I took." "I put my foot down carefully each time to be sure there wasn't a step or something in front of me." "I was really conscious of every move I made."

    b. "I thought I was walking straight, but I found myself in the middle of the room." "I kept moving toward the left; once I was almost against the wall." "I had trouble figuring out which way was straight ahead; I was veering to the right."

    c. "I was afraid I'd lose my balance, so I kept my arms outstretched." "I started to get dizzy." "I didn't have any trouble with balance."

    d. "Even though I couldn't see anything, I could tell when I was going through a doorway." "I could tell when I moved from a big room into a narrow hall." "I didn't know what it was, but I knew there was something big in front of me."

    e. "I was sure I had been walking for at least ten minutes, but it was less than four minutes." "Time sure passed slowly; I was aware of every second."

2-4. Each experience related to one of the following internal senses:

    a. Sense of movement

    b. Sense of direction

    c. Sense of balance

    d. Sense of nearness

    e. Sense of time

2-5. *a.* Alternative 2: Bright colors and striking clothes will make her stand out in the group and draw attention in her direction.

    b. Alternative 2: Hexagonal posters suspended from wires might attract more attention because of their novelty.

    c. Alternative 1: Repetition is a useful technique in gaining attention.

    d. Alternative 1: The contrast from music to speaking would attract more attention.

    e. Alternative 1: An atmosphere of intrigued and interested people would create a social insinuation that she was an interesting and popular candidate.

2-6. It appears that the two horticulturists are using differing frames of reference. The first is probably comparing the lily with larger flowers of a different shape. The second horticulturist most likely has had experience with smaller flowers of a similar shape. Their frame of reference for color is probably similar, and as a result they are in agreement.

2-7. *a.* Seal, duck, and whale.

    b. The subjects were told what to expect and this influenced their perception.

2-8. Introductions suggesting that each guest is an exciting person would probably help get the party moving. For example: "Sam, meet Bob Taylor. Bob had me in hysterics the last time we met. He's a super story teller. Some of the pranks his kids have pulled are really incredible. Tell Sam about the time your daughter ended up on top of a flagpole." Or "Jane, don't tell me you haven't met Angela. Angela has just returned from a fascinating vacation. She went to a resort that gave dancing instruction. Now she's an expert on the Wiggle Waggle."

2-9.
a. Both women emphasized the pro shop and the lap pool.
b. Mrs. S. emphasized the snack bar, picnic area, large pool, and children's pool.
c. Ms. T. emphasized the exercise room, women's sauna and locker area, and the tennis courts.
d. The men's lockers and sauna were minimized or forgotten.
e. Personal emotions, needs, and motivations probably are the key reasons for the inaccuracies in the perception of the club. It is likely that Mrs. S. has children and uses the pools, snack area, and shop. Ms. T. probably plays tennis, swims laps, and uses the exercise and locker facilities.

2-10.
a. Bob needs to be suspicious of what he has been told to perceive.
b. Claire should identify her own needs and emotions. She should admit that she is having a bad day and that her perceptions may be distorted.
c. Marsha needs to recognize the techniques that are used to attract attention and try to maintain control over undesirable distractions.
d. Sidney might try to broaden his perspective by sitting in a smoking area without lighting a cigarette.
e. Bill should remember that illusions can be deceiving.
f. Harry's boss must learn to differentiate between observation and inference.

2-11.
a. A blind person can adapt to the impairment by using other external and internal senses more fully. Learning braille and using a cane or seeing-eye dog are other possibilities.
b. A deaf person must also rely on other senses. Medication, hearing aids, and surgery might be helpful.
c. A dyslexic person would benefit from a special program designed to help with adjustment to distorted perception and peripheral vision.

2-12.
a. In the future, blind people will be aided by the use of an electronic camera that is wired to the brain and electronic microchips.
b. Deaf individuals will be aided by an electronic microphone wired to the brain and electronic microchips.
c. The exact cause of dyslexia may be determined in the future, and possibly there will be a cure.

2-13.
a. This college student, like the city men in the study of sensory deprivation, is accustomed to a noisy environment. She finds the lack of stimulation in a quiet library distracting and has difficulty concentrating.

b. This man may be having a psychedelic experience from the light show. Psychedelic experiences can cause a loss of control and unusual reactions.

c. Remaining in isolation for a long period of time can cause hallucinations. It is possible that the astronaut hallucinated because of the lack of stimulation in his space capsule.

Checkpoint Answer Key

1. *c*	9. *c*	17. *c*	25. *e*
2. *b*	10. *a*	18. *b*	26. *h*
3. *c*	11. *a*	19. *a*	27. *a*
4. *a*	12. *b*	20. *a*	28. *b*
5. *a*	13. *b*	21. *d*	29. *g*
6. *d*	14. *d*	22. *d*	30. *c*
7. *e*	15. *c*	23. *i*	
8. *b*	16. *b*	24. *f*	

CHAPTER 3

LEARNING AND CHANGING BEHAVIOR

Give me a dozen healthy infants, well-formed, and my own specified world to bring them up in and I'll guarantee to take any one at random and train him to become any type of specialist I might select—doctor, lawyer, artist, merchant chief, and yes, even beggarman and thief, regardless of his talents, penchants, tendencies, abilities, vocations, and the race of his ancestors.

John Watson

Have you ever wondered why your behavior changes when you are with different individuals or groups? Perhaps you have been in some situations where you tend to joke and see humor in everything. Yet other people see only your serious side. Sometimes you act shy or bashful, and at other times you are outspoken and friendly. Why do you keep changing? Psychologists would say that it has something to do with your learning.

If you are at a party and everyone is laughing merrily at your stories and jokes, you are apt to tell a few more. Your history teacher, however, might scowl when you try to introduce some humor into the class discussion. Only your sober and serious comments will be encouraged. Or perhaps you have been around people you thought to be much smarter than you. You probably felt a bit uneasy and were afraid to say something that might make you sound stupid or foolish. You appeared shy and bashful. But, since you are accepted pretty well among your close friends, you have no such fears and concerns. You are more likely to say what you think.

Learning is constantly influencing your behavior. Somehow learning is usually associated with classroom instruction. In reality, most learning occurs elsewhere. Almost everything you do involves some learning. Whether you are eating ice cream with a spoon, choosing a fishing rod, knitting an afghan, or playing poker, your behavior involves learning. In this chapter you will take a closer look at learning and consider its relationship with performance. You will examine more closely the reasons why behavior changes and how you can influence other people as well as change your own behavior. Two major forms of learning, classical conditioning and instrumental or operant conditioning, will be described and applied to many different kinds of situations. You will also weigh the ethical problems in using conditioning.

WHAT IS LEARNING?

If almost everything you do involves *learning*, you may wonder how to differentiate between learned and unlearned behavior. Other than a few basic reflexes and some haphazard actions, almost everything you do has been learned in some way. Learning happens internally. It cannot be seen or touched. In fact, it cannot even be measured accurately. Psychologists usually measure learning by looking for a change in performance. If performance shows a relatively lasting change, then they infer that learning occurred.

learning Relatively lasting changes in behavior that are caused by experience or practice

Suppose that last year a boy was introduced to the water for the first time. The child showed some random movements of his arms and legs and then nearly sank. This year you see the child at the beach swimming a strong crawl for about 20 feet. You could rightly assume that the boy had learned to swim. Even though you did not see the learning, you assume it occurred, because the child's performance has changed. It is likely that the child had some experiences in the water since you saw him a year ago. It was during these experiences and practice that learning happened. Now, every time the boy jumps in the water he is able to swim. His new ability is lasting or relatively permanent.

Now imagine that you go to a bowling alley with a woman who has never bowled before and who admits to be lacking in athletic talent. You manage to push her fingers into the holes in the bowling ball. Suddenly she drops the ball on the floor. The ball rolls down the alley, and she has a strike. Was her strike the result of learning? Clearly it does not sound as if she has learned much about the sport, other than how to get her fingers out of the ball. Psychologists look for more permanent changes in performance before assuming that learning has occurred. If she could bowl a strike with some consistency, you could conclude that she had learned. Such chance behaviors do not provide enough evidence to pass judgment on learning.

In judging whether a situation involves learning, look for two important conditions: (1) a relatively permanent change in behavior, and (2) some experience or practice that caused the change. Experiences could include observing other people and reading as well as practice. The woman in the bowling-alley example had an experience, but it is doubtful that it caused a lasting change in behavior.

Learning is not necessarily positive. People learn to steal, cheat, lie, and swindle. In each of these cases, both requirements for learning are present. Similarly, people can learn to litter, pollute, waste natural resources, and spoil the environment.

Performance as a Measure of Learning

When there is a lasting change in performance, you can infer that learning has occurred. But learning is only one factor; in reality many other factors may also influence performance. Even if you studied endlessly for a midterm exam and felt that you had thoroughly mastered the subject matter, a sleepless night or fever and nausea could affect your performance on the test. Or suppose during the test you had an attack of hiccups or the person next to you had a sneezing fit. A low grade would not necessarily mean you had not learned much. Performance is used as a measure of learning, because learning itself is not observable or measurable. It is important to remember that such factors as motivation, distraction, and health can also affect performance.

Exercise 3-1

A middle-aged automobile mechanic has been taking accounting courses evenings. He is now considering changing his career. Although he was always respected as a mechanic, his mind has recently been distracted from his work (see Figure 3-1). He spends time planning and thinking about his new career. In breaking in a new employee he was unable to think of the names of even simple parts of the engine. In your own words describe why this man's present performance may not be a good measure of what he has learned about automobile repair.

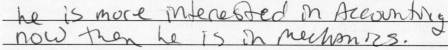

he is more interested in Accounting now then he is in mechanizs.

You may check your answer in the Feedback section at the end of this chapter.

CLASSICAL CONDITIONING

Since performance is observable and can be measured, behavioral psychologists limit their measurement of learning to measurement of changes in performance. They have identified two techniques that cause changes in performance. Behavioral psychologists believe that classical conditioning and

Figure 3-1

instrumental or operant conditioning are responsible for almost all learning. *Classical conditioning,* an approach that uses associations and relationships, will be considered first. Reflexes and emotional respondents play the key roles in classical conditioning.

Reflexes

There are many behaviors that occur in all people whenever special stimuli are presented. For example, if someone were to slip a pickle in your mouth, you would begin to salivate. Likewise, if this book caught fire and suddenly burned your fingers, you would pull your hands away from it. Because these behaviors always occur in all people and do not require any learning, they are called "reflexes."

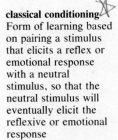

classical conditioning
Form of learning based on pairing a stimulus that elicits a reflex or emotional response with a neutral stimulus, so that the neutral stimulus will eventually elicit the reflexive or emotional response

reflex Response that is always elicited after a given stimulus and does not require learning

Figure 3-2
Perhaps an exaggerated example of the common knee-jerk reflex...

"*Reflexes...amazing!*"

You are probably familiar with several common reflexes. If you hit someone in the center of the knee, you are likely to be kicked with a knee-jerk reflex. Or if you are walking along the beach and a gust of wind blows some sand in your eyes, you will experience an eye-blink reflex. A whiff of pepper will make you sneeze. If someone tickles the sole of your foot, you will scrunch your toes. Medical books have recorded many such reflexes in humans.

Emotional Respondents

emotional respondent
Emotion that is
always elicited
by a given stimulus
and does not
require learning; an
emotional reflex

An *emotional respondent* is an emotional reflex or a feeling that always results from a certain stimulus. Fear is a common emotional respondent. Normal people find pain unpleasant and become fearful. Fear is the normal response to pain, and no learning is required. Anger is another common emotional respondent. Love and joy, more positive feelings, are also considered emotional respondents. If you have ever been infatuated with someone, you probably have experienced some positive emotional respondents. Joy and bliss are possibilities. Each emotional reaction is felt internally in response to some specific type of stimulus. The outward expression of the emotion may vary according to your learning and past experience. But whether you ran up and hugged the person or simply stood and giggled, you experienced the same internal feeling. Similarly, if someone held a knife against your back, you would undoubtedly experience fear as an emotional respondent. How you expressed the fear would vary according to your cultural background and previous learning experience.

Both reflexes and emotional respondents happen automatically in response to specific stimuli. Whenever something is thrown in your eye, you blink. If an electric shock is sent through the seat of your chair, you rise. A painful experience causes fear and anxiety, and a pleasurable encounter causes joy and happiness.

Exercise 3-2

The following scenario includes three reflexes and five emotional respondents. Draw one line under each reflex and two lines under each emotional respondent.

Clyde, whose union is on strike, has become addicted to watching an afternoon soap opera. This afternoon he notices that it is time for his series to begin and gets himself a cold beer. As he opens the bottle, it fizzes and squirts in his eye. He blinks and becomes annoyed. He then carries his beer over to his favorite chair and settles down to a half-hour of feeling comfortable. The program begins. The charming, innocent heroine is being threatened by a surly, vicious woman. Clyde grows tense. He nervously picks up a cigarette and burns his finger. He pulls his hand away and wraps it around the cold beer. He turns his attention back to the television screen. The evil woman is choking the lovely heroine and kills her. Clyde watches the heroine fall and feels overwhelmed with sadness. He attempts to turn off the television set. But there is a short in the switch, and Clyde gets a sharp electric shock. He pulls his hand away and feels afraid to touch the set again.

You may compare your answers to those in the Feedback section.

The Process of Classical Conditioning

Through classical conditioning you can learn to blink your eye, even when something is not thrown into it. You can automatically rise from your chair without the use of an electric shock. Similarly, people can have fears and anxieties without undergoing a painful experience. The reflex responses and emotional respondents will occur with associations.

Suppose a woman is sitting in a chair wired so that electric shocks can be passed into the seat. A psychologist is trying to use classical conditioning to make her rise from the chair every time he scratches his head. (Psychologists sometimes perform strange experiments!) He has observed that she reflexively rises from the chair whenever an electric shock is sent to her seat.

Figure 3-3

Now when he administers the electric shock, he simultaneously scratches his head.

Figure 3-4

Soon she will associate the head scratching with the electric shock. When she sees him scratch, she will anticipate the shock and rise from her chair. Eventually she will rise from the chair whenever he scratches his head, even if the shock is not administered.

Figure 3-5

Imagine how ridiculous she might feel rising from a chair just because a man scratched his head!

The classical-conditioning process has three stages:

1. A reflex is observed, and the stimulus that causes the reflex is identified. In the example the reflex was withdrawal or rising from the chair. The stimulus that caused the reflex was the electric shock.
2. Another stimulus is paired with the stimulus that causes the reflex. The psychologist scratched his head at the same time he administered the electric shock. This pairing is repeated many times.
3. The new stimulus causes a reflexive response, even when the original stimulus is removed. The woman rose when the psychologist scratched his head, even when the electric shock was not put through her chair.

Exercise 3-3

A psychologist wishes to use the knee-jerk reflex to make a man kick his leg in response to a whistle. In your own words, specify what should occur in each stage of classical conditioning.

a. Stage 1: _striking the knee to make leg kick._

b. Stage 2: _Blowing a whistle whenever striking the knee_

c. Stage 3: _Blowing the whistle and making the leg kick without striking_

You may check your description in the Feedback section.

The process of classical conditioning follows the same pattern when emotional respondents are used in place of reflex reactions. In the first step, a stimulus that elicits an emotional response is identified. For example, most people would respond to the stimulus of having a gun pointed at them with fear and fright. In the second stage, this stimulus (the pointed gun) is paired with another stimulus that does not usually cause a fearful reaction—perhaps an old sneaker. This pairing is repeated many times. Each time you are handed an old sneaker, a gun is pointed at your head. Eventually you will become frightened when handed the sneaker, even if the gun does not appear. Although this is hardly a common example, there are many instances where such classically conditioned fears occur. Someone who on four different occasions had been fired from a job on Tuesday may develop a fear of going to work on Tuesdays. Or a person who has had a number of different painful experiences in a dentist's office may have an unpleasant sensation when detecting the smell of the dentist's cologne. Think of your own fears. Can you trace the causes?

Checkpoint

Use the following questions to check your understanding of this portion of the chapter. Choose and mark the one correct response to each question.

1. How do psychologists measure learning?
   a. By reaction time of basic reflexes
   b. By relatively permanent changes in performance
   c. By quantity and quality of practice
   d. By motivation and interest
2. Which of the following is an example of learning?
   a. A boy falls down when he is pushed.
   b. A woman feels pain when she smashes her finger in the car door.
   c. A girl throws a candy wrapper in a trash basket.
   d. A man sneezes whenever he inhales snuff.
3. How is learning related to performance?
   a. Learning and performance are always the same.
   b. Learning is the opposite of performance.
   c. Learning is one of many factors that affects performance.
   d. Learning is measurable, and performance is inferred.
4. Some behaviors happen automatically and without learning. What are these behaviors called?
   a. Reflexes
   b. Associations
   c. Experiences
   d. Reactions
5. Which of the following is the best example of an emotional respondent?
   a. You blink whenever your grapefruit squirts you in the eye.
   b. You always ask for advice when you are lost.
   c. You do your homework at the same time every night.
   d. You become frightened whenever you feel pain.
6. How are reflexes and emotional respondents alike?
   a. They occur automatically and can be used in classical conditioning.
   b. They require learning and practice and are influenced by motivation.

c. They involve fears and can be removed through classical conditioning.

d. They involve pleasurable experiences and should be increased by using classical conditioning.

7. A doctor who gives painful shots to children always wears a white coat. Through classical conditioning the children learn to associate the white coat with the painful needle. How will these children probably react when they see a barber who wears a white coat?

a. They will be frightened.

b. They will be relieved.

c. They will feel confused.

d. They will suffer from bed-wetting.

8. What is the first step in classical conditioning?

a. Removing a stimulus

b. Identifying a reflex or emotional respondent

c. Pairing a stimulus with a reflex or emotional respondent

d. Pairing a reflex with an emotional respondent

Use the Checkpoint Answer Key to verify your responses. If you had any difficulty with a question, carefully reread the text. If you had little or no difficulty answering the questions or have resolved any problems that you might have had, you are ready to continue with the next portion of this chapter.

USING CLASSICAL CONDITIONING

You are probably now aware of the importance of classical conditioning in forming some of your fears, attitudes, and superstitions. Next you will look at how you can use classical conditioning to help yourself, whether you are acting, pretending, or trying to overcome some fear or anxiety. The uses of classical conditioning in controlling undesirable behavior will also be examined.

Acting and Pretending

Actors frequently use classical conditioning to make themselves feel emotions so they can portray them in a more convincing way. One technique taught in many acting schools requires potential actors and actresses to think of experiences in their lives that caused strong emotions. The loss of a close relative or an unhappy love affair might be used to bring on feelings of sadness and some honest tears. If a play involved a crying scene, dwelling on these past experiences and associating them with the scene could help an actor again be moved to tears. Likewise, a scene requiring a frightened reaction might require the actor to envision the approach of a poisonous snake. Actors and actresses who use this technique feel that it helps them to appear less phony in portraying feelings, since they are actually experiencing the emotions.

You have probably been in situations where you wanted to hide your true feelings. Watching an extremely large person try to squeeze into a small seat on a bus might strike you as amusing, but undoubtedly you would not want to embarrass the person. Taking a hint from acting schools, you might find it profitable to dwell on a serious experience, like a final exam. Your sincere, serious expression would certainly cover your amusement.

Figure 3-6
Classical conditioning
is useful in some jobs.

Exercise 3-4

A close friend has invited you and his boss to a Sunday brunch. Your friend is anxious to make a good impression and wants the boss to enjoy herself. You are finding the boss to be a complete bore, telling old "moron" jokes. When she asks, "Why did the moron throw his clock out the window?" you pretend not to know, since you want to be polite to your friend. When she finishes with "He wanted to see time fly," you manage a courteous laugh. The dull boss is continuing her monologue of moron jokes. How might you use the principles of classical conditioning to make yourself appear honestly amused by her supposed wit?

think of something that was funny to you in the past.

Compare your response with the answer given in the Feedback section.

Controlling Fears and Anxieties

Most fears are acquired through classical conditioning. A boy is bitten by a nasty little dog and develops a fear of all dogs. Even though the dogs do not bite him and may even appear friendly, the boy fears the sight of them. The appearance of any dog is associated with the pain a dog once caused. As the boy grows older, the fear may become bothersome and embarrassing.

Classical conditioning techniques could help him control his fear. A psychologist would want to remove the emotional respondent of fear and replace it with a more pleasant emotional respondent. Sitting on his mother's lap and being hugged would probably bring a feeling of relaxation and joy. At first he could be shown a picture of a dog while being hugged. Perhaps he could then progress to a toy dog and finally to a real one, using the same pleasant association. If the psychologist achieves the desired goal, eventually the appearance of the dog will be a pleasant emotional experience rather than a painful one.

desensitization
Therapeutic approach
that uses a gradual
method of classical
conditioning to
remove fears

This gradual method for removing fearful associations is sometimes referred to as "desensitization." Exhibit 3-1 describes how desensitization has been used to reduce fear of flying. The same technique has been successful in removing fear of heights and of crowds.

Exercise 3-5

A 35-year-old woman dropped out of high school 20 years ago because of failing grades. She felt humiliated everytime a test was returned to her because she usually had the lowest grade in the class. She is now taking a psychology class at her local community college and has an intense fear of taking exams. Her instructor announced that the first test will be next week. She has begun to panic!

Her psychology instructor, Professor Allheart, knows she has become an expert on baseball trivia during the past 20 years. First the good professor asks her several true-false questions about baseball facts. Her responses are perfect, and she feels pleased and proud. Next she is given a short written test on baseball, and again she feels successful. As a final step the woman is given an exam of baseball questions interspersed with psychology questions.

a. What method is the professor using? _de sensitization_

b. Why might this method help remove the woman's anxieties and fear of exams? _gradually she will fell less anxiety about tests times._

EXHIBIT 3-1

Grounding the Fear of Flying

The behavior modification technique of desensitization has been reported successful with at least part of the sweaty-palm, white-knuckle group of airplane travelers. Desensitization involves a step-by-step exposure of the person to progressively fearful situations connected with the phobia. In successful cases, the phobic situation gradually becomes associated with positive, relaxed feelings rather than with anxious or hysterical ones.

Researchers at the New Jersey Medical School in Newark have developed an audio-visual therapy program—using film clips and tapes—to help persons with a fear of flying. In their initial study, the investigators reported that 78 percent of 51 people who had previously refused to fly were able to fly after treatment. In addition, the subjects underwent significant attitude changes about flying and, in some cases, about other fears and phobias, as well.

Check your responses in the Feedback section.

Unwanted Behavior

The principles of classical conditioning have been used by psychologists to help people rid themselves of such undesirable behavior as bed-wetting (enuresis) and drug and alcohol addiction. Recent studies have shown that bed-wetting can usually be cured through classical conditioning, except in rare cases where the lack of control is complicated by emotional and physiological problems. Bed-wetting occurs when a child does not awaken when the bladder is full. As a result, the child wets the bed. A psychologist invented a device that consists of a wired sheet that detects urine. As soon as it begins to flow, an alarm rings to awaken the child. The training routine follows the standard procedures of classical conditioning. The sound of an alarm causes a reflex response of waking up. The alarm is paired with the initial flow of urine, a sign that the bladder is full. At first the child will awaken when the alarm rings and will begin to associate the ringing of the alarm with a full bladder. After several nights the child will awaken to a full bladder, whether or not the alarm rings. A similar device for snoring is described in Exhibit 3-2.

Controlling alcohol and drug addiction involves a slightly different procedure. One technique that has been used with some success involves lacing drinks with a substance that causes vomiting. If a person drinks such a substance (called an "emetic"), the normal reflex response is to throw up. If the substance is mixed and paired with alcoholic beverages, the association can become so strong that the alcoholic will feel nausea at the sight of a drink. There is one serious limitation in this technique: It is extremely difficult to have an alcoholic agree to take the treatment.

emetic Substance that causes vomiting

EXHIBIT 3-2

Antisnore Device

Man's eternal quest for a truly effective way to prevent snoring has led him over the centuries to any number of ingenious, if often impractical, devices, some merely useless, some ridiculous, others downright painful.

One of the earliest was a chin strap that held the snorer's jaw shut. Another triggered a piercing wail whenever the hapless sleeper lost control of his mandible. Next was a device that violently shook his pillow at the faintest sound, followed by a web of wires that broadcast antisnoring propaganda via an earplug.

None of these Rube Goldberg cures proved popular, either with the snorer or with his or her bedmate. Too often the devices woke up the wrong person or incorrectly activated themselves because they couldn't tell the difference, say, between a snore and the sound of passing traffic.

So it remained for one Anthony R. Dowling, an Australian inventor from the Sydney suburb of Vaucluse, to develop a compact, self-contained electronic mechanism worn in the outer ear. It will detect snoring via the vibrations it causes in the head and auditory canal, then emit a buzzing sound that is inaudible to a sleeping partner. Gradually this behavior modifier—complete with a combination microphone/speaker—will break a snorer's habit, according to patent documents Dowling has filed.

Source: Nobbe, G. (1987, November). Antisnore device. *Omni.*

Exercise 3-6

Briefly describe how each of the following individuals could use classical conditioning.

a. An actress who must pretend she is nauseated: _thinking about something that has made her very sick_

b. A girl who is afraid of the sight of blood and wants to become a physician: _gradually associating blood with things that are not involved with fear_

c. A boy with enuresis: _setting an alarm whenever the boys bladder is full._

You may compare your descriptions with those given in the Feedback section.

OPERANT CONDITIONING

Although classical conditioning accounts for many of your fears and attitudes, most behavioral psychologists believe your actions are influenced by the feedback you receive. Suppose you are blindfolded and told to throw a ball at a target. You keep throwing the ball but no one tells you when or if you are close to the target. Without feedback, or knowledge of your success, you cannot improve your skill. You need to hear such comments on "Good throw" or "Really close" or even some negative information such as "Way off" in order to improve. You will try to win favorable comments and avoid the derogatory remarks. You learn to do things that may result in rewards and avoid behavior that may result in punishment. For example, handing in work assignments on time might result in a few words of praise from your boss. You might even eventually earn a bonus, raise, or promotion. In contrast, sleeping at your desk could bring complaints and cost you your job. If you want to have an income, you behave in ways that will allow it to continue. Having an income might be considered a reward, losing your job a punishment.

The type of learning that occurs because of rewards and punishments is labeled either "operant conditioning" or "instrumental conditioning." Both terms refer to the same technique, a method of conditioning based on rewards, or positive reinforcers, and punishments, or other negative reinforcers. In classical conditioning association is the significant feature. In operant conditioning reinforcers and punishments are the key. Reinforcers and punishments provide feedback.

operant (instrumental) conditioning Type of learning that occurs because of positive or negative reinforcements

Positive Reinforcement

Suppose someone asked you to sit on top of a flagpole for 12 hours and promised you a reward. The reward was a stick of gum. Would you be likely to repeat the flagpole-sitting behavior? Chances are you would not unless there was a severe gum shortage and you craved gum. Although the gum was a reward, it would not serve as a *positive reinforcement*. The purpose of a positive reinforcement is to increase the same behavior. What would it take to make you climb up and sit on top of the flagpole again? Perhaps a good positive re-

positive reinforcement Rewards that increase the likelihood of a behavior

inforcer for you would be a new car, or a headline in the newspaper, or a screen test from a movie studio. If these did not serve as reinforcers, maybe you would sit there for an invitation to the White House or a tour of the Greek islands. Perhaps just smiles of approval from your friends would work. For a positive reinforcement to be effective and increase behavior, it must be appropriate. Finding the right reinforcer can be difficult. Some can be rewarded with money, others seek only attention and approval.

Behavioral psychologists believe your entire personality is shaped by reinforcers. If you are talkative, your parents and friends have probably found appropriate ways to reinforce your conversation. Simply paying attention and listening is a way of showing approval and is a positive reinforcement. You may have learned some successful flirting techniques or ways of hedging an answer when you are uncertain. Again, approval was the likely reinforcer.

For a reinforcement to be effective, it should occur immediately or as soon as possible following the desired behavior. If a man is training his dog to beg and delays the dog-biscuit reward for an hour after the begging behavior, the pet will not recognize the biscuit as a reward for begging. Instead, the dog may connect the biscuit with more recent behaviors that may have included barking, chewing the furniture, or chasing a cat.

Exercise 3-7

A man serves his wife breakfast in bed, complete with a good French champagne and fresh strawberries. His wife consumes her breakfast with little conversation or comment. Two weeks later when she reads about positive reinforcements in her psychology class, she decides that she would like her husband to serve breakfast in bed more frequently. When she goes home she gives him a penny.

List two things wrong with her positive reinforcement.

a. _No conversation or even a compliment._

b. _giving him a penny would make the husband think that what he did wasn't worth much._

Compare your answers with those in the Feedback section.

Figure 3-7 The positive reinforcement certainly is effective in increasing asking behavior.

negative reinforcement
Removal of an
unpleasant stimulus
to increase the
likelihood of a
behavior

punishment An
unpleasant stimulus
that decreases
the likelihood of
a behavior

Negative Reinforcement

Like positive reinforcements, *negative reinforcements* are used to increase behavior. However, while positive reinforcements present pleasant stimuli when
you behave as desired, negative reinforcements remove unpleasant stimuli when
you behave as desired. For example, suppose your roommate constantly nags
you to pick up your messy clothes and clean the room. If you keep your area tidy,
the nagging stops. Nagging, the negative reinforcer, is increasing the likelihood
of your cleanup behavior. You want to escape from the nagging, so you pick up your
clothes and maintain a neat room. In many instances, negative reinforcement is
indeed effective in increasing specific behaviors that will permit an escape.

Punishment

The purpose of *punishment* is to weaken a behavior or lessen its likelihood.
Punishment can be effective. A study by Sherman and Berk (1984) found that
men who were arrested for wife-beating were less likely to beat their wives
during the next six months than men who were not arrested. The experiment
was carefully controlled and the men were only arrested for twenty-four hours.

However, many other studies have found disadvantages and problems
with punishment. Generally punishment will suppress a response only for a
short time. In most cases the undesired response will reappear later. If your
kid brother annoys you by tapping his foot all through dinner, you might decide that an appropriate reaction would be a swift kick under the table. Your
"punishment" might eliminate the behavior for the present, but chances are
his undesired foot-tapping behavior will reappear. Similarly, a mother who
washes her daughter's mouth with soap to clean up her language may find that
the cleaning will not last very long, particularly if the mother is not around.
Unfortunately, people often punish others when they are angry and upset. As
a result the punishment seems unreasonable and little is learned.

Guidelines for Punishment

Effective punishment can help eliminate an undesirable behavior. However, if
the punishment is not chosen carefully, there can be unexpected side effects.

Sometimes a punishment can have elements of positive reinforcement. A
teacher may believe she is punishing a 6-year-old boy when she shouts, "Mike,
don't tell me you are out of your seat again. You never sit still!" In reality, Mike
is gaining the attention he is seeking. Classmates turn and notice him and the
teacher becomes totally preoccupied with his problem. What she thought was a
punishment turns out to be a positive reinforcement. The next time Mike feels a
need for attention, he will know that getting out of his seat and walking around the
classroom will win the notice he wants. Similarly, a hockey player put in the pen-
alty box for a clash and fight often gets cheers from the crowd. His rowdy behavior may well increase because of the attention of the crowd.

Psychologists have developed several guidelines for punishment. Four important rules are:

- Avoid combining rewards with punishments.

- Punish immediately or reinstate the situation that caused the need for punishment.

- Avoid inadequate punishment.
- The punishment should suit the crime.

Exercise 3-8

Imagine that the town council of your community has been considering ways of dealing with the litter problem in the parks and streets. After several public hearings on the matter, four ordinances are proposed. Based on the recommended guidelines for punishment, which ordinance would you recommend and why?

a. Any individual who litters or in any way disturbs the beauty of the town's parks and streets will be fined the sum of $1. The fine must be paid within two years of the offense.

b. Any individual who litters or in any way disturbs the beauty of the town's parks and streets will be fined a sum of no less than $2000. The fine must be paid within one hour of the offense.

c. Any individual who litters or in any way disturbs the beauty of the town's parks and streets will be fined a sum of $20 and given a work assignment of two hours with the town's sanitation crew to be completed within seven days of the offense.

d. Any individual who litters or in any way disturbs the beauty of the town's parks and streets will be given a work assignment of one hour with the town's sanitation crew. Those attending the town's schools will be excused from class in order to complete the work assignment.

C. Being fined the $20 Along with a work assignment can show the person what he did wrong and why and hopefully not do it again.

Check your choice and reason in the Feedback section.

Types of Punishment

Several categories or types of punishment have been identified. Coopersmith (1967) described three types.

Corporal punishment. *Corporal* refers to the body, and corporal punishment involves inflicting bodily harm when a person behaves in an undesirable way. A spanking, a whipping with a switch, a slap across the face, and a punch in the nose would all qualify as corporal punishments.

corporal punishment
Inflicting bodily harm to decrease undesirable behavior

Withdrawal of love and approval. Parents sometimes reprimand their children for misbehavior by threatening to remove their love. Statements like "If you go outside the yard again, I won't love you anymore" or "I hate you because you just spilled your juice" are examples. If this technique is used persistently the child will feel that the parents' love is weak and undependable. The child is given the impression that love and affection have to be earned. As a result the child may become anxious and show such symptoms as nail-biting, bed-wetting, or thumb-sucking.

management
Conditioning method
that allows a person to
choose alternatives of
reward or punishment

Management. *Management* permits the person to escape the punishment and gain a reward. A parent who states, "If you don't eat your spinach, you may not have dessert" is permitting the reward of dessert for a desired behavior (eating spinach) and a punishment of no dessert for the undesired behavior (not eating spinach). Of the three techniques Coopersmith found this to be the most effective.

Checkpoint

Use the following questions to check your understanding of this portion of the chapter. Choose and mark the one correct response to each question.

9. A psychologist is using the technique of desensitization to help a person overcome a fear of thunder. What will the psychologist do?
   a. Be sure that the person never hears thunder.
   b. Have the person associate the thunder with an eye-blink reflex.
   c. Gradually increase the loudness of thunder while associating it with a pleasant stimulus.
   d. Give the person drugs that will cause emotional confusion whenever exposed to thunder.

10. How is classical conditioning used in controlling bed-wetting?
    a. An electric shock is given as punishment for bed-wetting.
    b. A special antidepressant drug is associated with an alarm.
    c. An emetic is given whenever the child wets the bed.
    d. An alarm is rung whenever the bed is wet, so that the child learns to awaken to a full bladder.

11. Which of the following is a key element in operant conditioning?
    a. Reflexes
    b. Emotional respondents
    c. Reinforcements
    d. Fears

12. A young boy polished his father's shoes. The father gave his son a book in the hope that he would repeat the shoe-shining behavior. The boy has not shined a shoe since. Which of the following best describes the role of the book?
    a. A reward and a positive reinforcement
    b. A reward but not a positive reinforcement
    c. A positive reinforcement but not a reward
    d. A punishment and a positive reinforcement

13. What are the two most important characteristics of a good positive reinforcer?
    a. Appropriate and immediate
    b. Emotional and immediate
    c. Appropriate and emotional
    d. Sensitive and emotional

14. What is the relationship between punishment and negative reinforcement?
    a. Negative reinforcement decreases behavior and punishment increases behavior.
    b. Punishment decreases behavior and negative reinforcement increases behavior.

    c. Negative reinforcement requires corporal punishment.

    d. Punishment and negative reinforcement are the same.

15. Which of the following is considered the most effective method of punishment?

    a. Corporal punishment

    b. Withdrawal of love

    c. Withdrawal of approval

    (d.) Management

16. Kathy is tired of having her young sister, Jane, monopolize the telephone for hours. What should Kathy do to help cut down on Jane's telephone talking?

    a. Kick Jane whenever she talks on the phone.

    b. Refuse to talk to Jane if she spends more than ten minutes on the phone.

    (c.) Promise Jane unlimited use of the phone if she can limit her calls to five minutes—otherwise, no phone use for a week.

    d. Tell Jane that if she spends more than five minutes on each phone call she will be despised by the rest of the family.

Check your responses against the Checkpoint Answer Key at the end of the chapter. If you had little or no difficulty answering the questions or have resolved problems that you might have had, you are ready to continue with the final portion of this chapter.

Reinforcements versus Punishments

You are probably familiar with the conflicting adages, "Spare the rod and spoil the child" and "You can catch more flies with honey than with vinegar." Which should you believe? Will you spoil a child by not using punishments, or is it better to stick with rewards? Most psychological research concludes that a child disciplined with rewards will show better emotional adjustment than one disciplined with punishments. If a child is punished harshly by parents and teachers, an aversion or dislike for them is likely to develop. In addition the child will tend to avoid activities associated with the parents and teachers. Family activities and school studies could become unpopular.

    Further, since punishment is generally either painful or frustrating, it can lead to aggression. A study by Bandura (1959) found that boys who were severely punished for aggression at home tended to be overly aggressive in school. Punishment is most effective and least damaging when a rewarding alternative is offered. If a father scolds his daughter for not completing her homework, he should also praise her when she does complete her assignments. Unfortunately, repeated corporal punishments can result in child abuse. Parents who use punishments rather than rewards may cause serious problems for preschool children, as described in Exhibit 3-3.

    As mentioned in the previous section, a punishment that draws attention to a person can serve more as a positive than as a negative reinforcement. One way the teacher could avoid this dilemma is to put more emphasis on Mike's positive behavior. Remarks such as "Look at how nicely Mike is sitting in his seat. I wish everyone would sit and work like that" would give Mike a rewarding alternative. Punishment would be still more effective if she offered an al-

EXHIBIT 3-3

> ### Chronic Pain Traced to Abuse
>
> When preschoolers complain of abdominal, head or chest pain that seems to have no physical cause, it may mean that they are depressed as the result of abuse, say Javad Kashani, professor of psychiatry at the University of Missouri at Columbia, and Gabrielle Carison, a professor of psychiatry at the University of New York at Stony Brook.
>
> With a team of mental health and education professionals, they studied 1000 preschoolers referred to a child development unit over a five-year period beginning in 1981.
>
> Nine children, six boys and three girls ages 3–6, were diagnosed as having a major depressive disorder. All nine expressed somatic complaints while none of the control group, chosen from the original pool of 1000, complained of physical pain.
>
> The depressed preschoolers also were much more likely to report feelings of sadness, suffer sleep changes and fatigue and loss of appetite. All of the depressed children had been abused or severely neglected, versus 22 percent of the control subjects.
>
> Complaints of bodily pain decreased as the children got older, according to the researchers.
>
> In describing their study in the March issue of *The American Journal of Psychiatry,* they comment, "We hypothesize that the helplessness, fear, and frustration experienced by abused preschoolers by virtue of their small size, limited abilities, and immature defenses may increase their vulnerability to depression."

Source: Landers, S. (1987, June). Chronic pain traced to abuse. *APA Monitor.*

ternative directly; "If you stay in your seat, you can play a special game. If you walk around, you will not play the game."

Punishment situations arise far beyond the classroom and home. Prisons are a prime example of attempts at punishments that sometimes work and sometimes do not. Statistics on repeat offenders are alarming. Again it seems that punishment is more effective when it is combined with a positive experience or alternative.

Exercise 3-9

A father is shopping at a supermarket with his 2-year-old son. His son persistently tries to gain his attention with chatter, but the father is preoccupied with his shopping list. The boy then looks at his surroundings and begins pointing to items on the shelves. He screams that he wants cookies, candies, strange cereals, and other impractical items. His father becomes embarrassed by the sudden outburst and begins scolding him. His child continues to scream, now even louder. To keep peace his father reaches for the nearest bag of lollipops and stuffs one in the boy's mouth. Even this does not satisfy the boy and his loud crying continues.

From what you have read about rewards and punishments, suggest how this father might avoid a similar episode the next time he brings his son to the supermarket.

try to pay more attention and give the child a choice for good behaviour or Bad.

Compare your suggestion with the ones given in the Feedback section.

Shaping

A mother might complain that she would indeed love to reward her teenage son for keeping his room clean, but she never has the opportunity. It would be a long wait for a neat room. Consequently, she may resort to punishment for his untidiness. What sort of alternatives does this mother have? One possibility is *shaping,* sometimes referred to as a "method of approximations." Shaping requires a series of steps. The first thing to do is to define your objective or the target behavior. In this case the target behavior would be having her son completely clean his room. However, any small step that her son takes in the direction of the target behavior will be rewarded. When her son picks up his sneakers to wear them, the mother notices how much better the floor looks without his tennis shoes. She rewards her son with an extra half hour before curfew. The next step might require her son to pick up his wet towels as well before he is permitted the added time at night. After he has mastered picking up his sneakers and wet towels, he will also need to pick up his dirty socks and underwear for the reward. Finally, her son will be rewarded with added curfew time only if his room is totally tidy and spotless.

shaping Rewarding each behavior in a sequence that will eventually lead to a target behavior

Shaping is based on the principles of operant conditioning and is widely used by psychologists. There are two basic methods of shaping. The first type was described in the example of the teenager learning to keep his room orderly. The mother rewarded a sequence of behaviors beginning with very simple steps and finally arriving at the target behavior. Schools use this type of shaping. In first grade you were promoted if you could recognize the letters of the alphabet and sound them out in simple words. In second grade your reward of promotion would only be given if you could read simple sentences and perform some basic addition and subtraction. Each reward was a reinforcement that would help lead to your target behavior of being an informed, literate person, skilled in language, mathematics, science, and the humanities. You certainly could not expect your twelfth-grade teacher to reward you for achievements on the first-grade level. Likewise your first-grade teacher would not be giving many rewards if she was waiting for twelfth-grade abilities. This method has also been used by clinical psychologists working with withdrawn children. Many of these children will not even approach another person. Initial rewards are given when the child sits in a chair near the psychologist. Next the child will be rewarded only if eye contact with the psychologist is achieved. Eventually these children will be expected to converse with the psychologist before receiving their rewards.

The second type of shaping is the reverse of the first type; it permits a person to perform the final step of behavior and be rewarded. This approach is frequently used in teaching an infant self-feeding. The mother or father puts food on a spoon, then places the spoon in the baby's hand and helps the baby aim the spoon toward the mouth. The final step of putting the food in the mouth is done by the baby, usually accompanied by cheers of enthusiasm from the proud parents. On subsequent trials the baby will do its own aiming for the mouth. Eventually filling the spoon, aiming, and inserting in the mouth will be required before the parents cheer and the baby receives the reward of food. Most ski instructors now use a technique called "graduated length methods" or GLM. This is really a shaping technique that permits a beginner to accomplish the target behavior of skiing down a slope, even though the person is on very short skis. Gradually the task is made more difficult by increasing the length of the skis. The more traditional methods for teaching skiing used the first type of shaping. The beginner was kept on a relatively flat surface until some basic skills could be demonstrated. Then the person could be taken to a slight incline until snowplow turns and stops were accomplished. Only after the necessary components were mastered could a person be taken up a lift to complete the target behavior of skiing down the slope.

Exercise 3-10

Two methods of shaping have been described. One breaks the target behavior into component steps. The other allows the person to perform the target behavior with some help, gradually removing the help. Assume you have been assigned as a swimming instructor at a summer camp. You want to find out which method of shaping is more effective in teaching swimming to 10-year-old

Many ski schools use shaping. Students first learn to master techniques on short skis. Once they are successful, they gradually move on to longer and longer skiis. (*Alan Carey/The Image Works*)

children. You are assigned two groups of children. Each group will be instructed with only one shaping technique. Describe how you would instruct each group.

Group a: _breaking the target behavior into_
steps; starting off in shallow water, breathing
exercises, immersing head underwater, movement of arms & legs.

Group b:
helping the beginner physically to swim. Holding (supporting)
them while they are in a swimming position and gradually decreasing help.

You may check your instructional techniques in the Feedback section.

Behavior Modification

Behavior modification techniques are an application of shaping. Again, the first step is to identify a target behavior. Then each progressive step toward the target behavior is rewarded. Careful records are kept to show progress toward the target behavior. Behavior may be used either to help others or for self-help.

Nord (1970) reported an interesting use of behavior modification by a hardware company. The business was having problems with employees being late and absent from work. To reward the employees who came to work on time every day, they had a monthly drawing for home appliances. Employees who had been late or absent during the month were not eligible. At the end of six months, the company held a special drawing for a color television set. Only those employees who had been to work on time every day for six months could participate. They found that employees with colds or mild problems were coming to work rather than staying at home as they had done in the past. After the program was in effect for one year, absenteeism and lateness had been reduced by 75 percent.

Recently behavior modification has been used in pain-control clinics. Here the concern has been with patients who become so totally preoccupied with their pain that they cannot take an interest in anything else. In most cases these patients have not been able to receive help in any other way. They are usually the worst cases. The staff members of pain clinics are instructed to walk away from any patient who begins to talk or complain about pain. The only time a patient is permitted to discuss pain is during an appointment with a physician who asks about the location and extent of the pain. Only "well" behaviors are rewarded. Staff members give special attention to patients who talk about subjects other than pain or who become involved in other activities. Patients are encouraged to keep busy and show an interest in a variety of subjects. The success of this type of behavior-modification program has varied. But usually more than half of the patients will be helped.

In a sense absenteeism, tardiness, and complaining could be considered bad habits. These bad habits have been controlled through behavior modification. Would you care to use the same method to control your own bad habits? Perhaps you bite your nails, overeat, or lose your temper too easily. Or per-

behavior modification
Technique that uses principles of conditioning to reach a desirable goal

haps you want to improve yourself in some way. You might want to study more, get more exercise, or be more sociable. You can use the same behavioral approaches to control your bad habits and improve yourself by using the five steps of behavior modification.

1. Identify a target behavior, such as losing 25 pounds, jogging 2 miles, or controlling your temper. This is your ultimate goal.
2. Establish a baseline. Record your present status. This means you must write down your present weight, the distance you now jog, or the number of times you lose your temper each day.
3. Identify a suitable reinforcer. Find a reward that will motivate you. It can be something simple, such as a bubble bath, a cold beverage, or a half-hour of listening to favorite records. Or it can be a night on the town, a new outfit, or a canoe trip. Make a list of your favorite things and then find the ones that will be most appropriate for you.
4. Set subgoals, or steps toward the target. Your subgoals might be losing 2 pounds each week or jogging a ¼ mile, then a ½ mile, then 1 mile, and finally 2 miles.
5. Write down your weight loss, your jogging distance, or the number of temper outbursts.

Exercise 3-11

Ken is a compulsive overspender. If he has a plastic credit card in his pocket, he feels he can buy anything, whether or not he can afford it. He has been lured into buying such frivolous items as a monogrammed leather case for his tennis racket and a sterling-silver toothpick. His bills are mounting. Last month he charged more than $880. He could pay his present bills within six months if he could prevent himself from continuing his useless spending.

Sailing is Ken's favorite sport, but he never seems to have enough money to sail with his friends. One group is planning some inexpensive weekend sailing trips at a local lake. They are also arranging a magnificent voyage up the inland waterway of the Atlantic coast next year.

Ken wants to change his spendthrift behavior. List what he might do to help himself by using the five steps of behavior modification.

a. _Setting a spending limit on ~~his~~ or his Credit Card_
b. _Record At present how much he is indebt._
c. _Using weekend sailing with Frrends As reinforcer_
d. _gradually cutting down on spending_
e. _Record how much less you are spending_

Compare your list with the one found in the Feedback section.

Imitation and Modeling

modeling Learning that occurs by imitating others

Many of your present skills and attitudes were acquired by imitating other people. This type of learning is labeled "modeling" or "observational learning." If you see another person rewarded for a behavior, you tend to imitate it. If they are punished, you would probably avoid similar behaviors, at least for the present. Many childhood behaviors are based on modeling. Children learn to walk, talk, and use facial expressions similar to their parents. Unfortunately they even imitate some negative behaviors. A mother who fakes a headache whenever she is criticized is likely to find that her daughter will claim a similar malady whenever she is scolded.

Several studies have shown that children can even learn aggression from their parents. Parents who show hostile actions and use physical punishments tend to have more aggressive children than parents who use verbal punishments and control. In one experiment (Bandura, Ross, & Ross, 1963) children watched a film of adult actors hitting a clown doll with a hammer. After the film the children were given a similar doll. Interestingly, they also struck it and behaved aggressively. Children who had not seen the film played peacefully with the clown doll.

Modeling techniques have also been used to help people overcome phobias. In Bandura's (1969) study, adults who had a strong fear of snakes viewed a film showing people playing with snakes. At the beginning of the film a plastic snake was used. As the film progressed a real snake was introduced, and contact became closer and more daring. The phobic viewers could stop the film whenever it became too upsetting and restart with a less frightening scene. People with snake phobias have also been helped by watching live models handling snakes. In fact, the live models have been even more successful than films in helping individuals conquer their phobias.

85

LEARNING AND
CHANGING BEHAVIOR

"Now this time, watch!"

Figure 3-8
An unusual example of
using modeling...

Most exercise, dance,
and yoga classes learn
through modeling.
(*Susan Lapides*)

Exercise 3-12

A 5-year-old girl hits her 3-year-old sister. Her mother scolds, "Don't ever hit your little sister!" and spanks the 5-year-old. Why might this spanking increase hitting behavior in her children? _Because her punishment is with hitting therefore the 5-year-old see's that bad behavior receives hitting._

Check your response in the Feedback section.

Extinction

Since some learning results in undesirable behavior, sometimes a behavior needs to be unlearned or extinguished. For example, suppose a baby girl finds her tongue and sticks it out. Her parents laugh and applaud. She enjoys their attention and amusement. However, when the girl is 3 or 4 years old, this behavior will no longer be amusing. It is more likely to be deemed rude and annoying. How can the behavior be extinguished? If parents and friends discontinue their laughter and applause whenever the tongue appears, *extinction* will probably occur.

The first step in extinction is determining what is reinforcing the behavior. If the reinforcer is repeatedly and consistently withheld, the undesirable act will probably not continue. Assume you were kind enough to bring a woman at

extinction Weakening or diminishing of a response; removal of the positive reinforcer to decrease the likelihood of a behavior

work a cup of coffee every morning for a week. If she neither drank it nor thanked you, you probably would not continue to bring coffee. Without any reinforcement your coffee-serving behavior would cease.

Perhaps you are wondering about using punishment to extinguish behavior. Punishment is usually not an effective method in extinction if the original positive reinforcer is not removed. A girl who is punished for fighting, but always gets what she wants when she fights for it, is likely to continue to show fighting behavior. The general rule for extinction is to remove the positive reinforcer.

Exercise 3-13

Jim brings his girlfriend, Barbara, a bouquet of dandelions and hollyhocks every Saturday night. To be polite she always thanks him and puts them in a vase. Barbara hates both dandelions and hollyhocks and dislikes most flowers. What could she do to extinguish Jim's flower-bearing behavior?

gently tell him she is Allergic to most flowers. Stop thanking him.

Check your suggestion in the Feedback section.

ETHICAL CONCERNS

As psychologists come closer to learning how to control their fellow human beings through conditioning techniques, there has been an increasing debate about the ethics of controlling another person's behavior. Many psychologists feel that such control could limit and restrain personal freedom. Others claim conditioning could create a better world by eliminating undesirable and selfish behavior. They see behavior modification as an important advance in the treatment of psychological problems (Hill, 1985). Think about the many uses and possible abuses of conditioning. Is society moving closer to a better world or merely restricting freedom?

Checkpoint

Use the following questions to check your understanding of the final portion of this chapter. Choose the one best response to each question.

17. Which of the following methods of discipline leads to better emotional adjustment in children?
    a. Positive reinforcement of appropriate behavior
    b. Negative reinforcement of inappropriate behavior
    c. Corporal punishment for inappropriate behavior
    d. Extinction of appropriate behavior
18. Why is scolding not always an effective form of negative reinforcement?
    a. There is no corporal punishment.
    b. It creates attention—a powerful positive reinforcement.
    c. It tends to extinguish behavior.
    d. It is not easily imitated and modeled.

19. Initially a father rewards his son for pulling on his socks. Next the son is rewarded only if he puts on both his shoes and socks. Eventually he only rewards his son when he fully dresses himself. What technique is the father using?

  a. Negative reinforcement

  b. Modeling

  c. Extinction

  d. Shaping

20. What is the first step in behavior modification?

  a. Identify the goal.

  b. Extinguish old behaviors.

  c. Record progress.

  d. Imitate a model.

21. What is the purpose of behavior modification?

  a. To increase motivation

  b. To change behavior

  c. To model desirable behavior

  d. To model undesirable behavior

22. Which of the following is the best example of modeling?

  a. You read about a man who won $1000 for holding his breath for three minutes. You practice holding your breath.

  b. You kick your friend whenever he lights an unpleasant-smelling cigar.

  c. You ignore a woman whenever she uses foul language.

  d. You are pleasant only to people who punish you.

23. What is the best method for extinguishing behavior?

  a. Present a negative reinforcer.

  b. Present a positive reinforcer.

  c. Remove the negative reinforcer.

  d. Remove the positive reinforcer.

24. Why are psychologists concerned about the use of conditioning methods?

  a. They believe that they are often ineffective.

  b. They believe that they could restrict freedom.

  c. They believe that they do not use sufficient negative reinforcement.

  d. They feel there is no difference between positive and negative reinforcement.

Check your responses against the Checkpoint Answer Key at the end of the chapter. If you had difficulty with any question, reread the text. If you had little or no difficulty answering the questions or have resolved problems that you might have had, you are ready to check yourself against the chapter inventory that follows.

CHAPTER INVENTORY

Use this list of objectives as a review checklist. You should be able to do each of the tasks outlined in the objectives and apply them to everyday examples. If you can, you may feel confident that you have mastered the material in this chapter.

  1. Define learning.

  2. Distinguish between learning and performance.

3. Describe the roles of reflexes and emotional respondents in classical conditioning.
4. List three stages in the process of classical conditioning.
5. Explain how classical conditioning can be used in acting, controlling fears, and eliminating unwanted behavior.
6. Describe operant conditioning.
7. Define positive reinforcement and specify two important conditions.
8. Distinguish between negative reinforcement and punishment.
9. Identify four guidelines for punishment and describe three categories of punishment.
10. Identify the strengths and weaknesses of positive and negative reinforcements.
11. Recognize attention as a positive reinforcer.
12. Explain and give examples of two types of shaping.
13. Describe the uses of behavior modification.
14. Outline five steps in the behavior-modification process.
15. Describe how learning occurs through modeling.
16. State the necessary conditions for extinction.
17. Discuss the controversy of the ethics of conditioning.

Feedback

The correct answers to the exercises follow. If you did not answer an exercise correctly, review the preceding pages and return to the exercise to correctly complete it.

3-1. The automobile mechanic is no longer motivated to work on engines. His interest in accounting is undoubtedly distracting him from his work.

3-2. The three reflexes were: "He blinks"; "He pulls his hand away"; "He pulls his hand away." The five emotional respondents were: "becomes annoyed"; "feeling comfortable"; "Clyde grows tense"; "feels overwhelmed"; "feels afraid."

3-3. *a.* Stage 1: Striking a man on the center of his knee will cause him to kick.
   b. Stage 2: Each time you strike the man in the center of his knee, blow a whistle. Repeat this many times.
   c. Stage 3: Blow the whistle but do not strike the man's knee. Watch him kick.

3-4. You might try thinking about some hysterically funny situation or joke. Perhaps a favorite cartoon or old comedy film would get you through the situation.

3-5. *a.* Desensitization
   b. Through the gradual approach, the woman will begin to feel successful when she takes exams. It should help to remove some of her anxiety.

3-6. *a.* She could think about how she felt the last time she had the flu or a virus. Associating someone or an object from the set with a disgusting or distasteful food would also help.
   b. She could listen to her favorite relaxing music while looking at pictures of blood cells. She might then progress toward a finger with a

tiny drop of blood. Again she would need a pleasant association. Gradually she might progress until her fear is removed.

  c. He would profit from an alarm device based on classical conditioning. Whenever urine flows an alarm would awaken him. He would associate the alarm with his full bladder and eventually awaken even without the alarm.

3-7. *a*. The reinforcement was not immediate. It came far too late.

  b. The reinforcement was not appropriate. One penny hardly seems an adequate reward for such service!

3-8. Ordinance *c* should have been the one you favored. It provides for adequate punishment, appropriate for the offense. Although the punishment is not immediate, it occurs within a reasonably short time of the offense. It also provides a reinstatement of the circumstances by forcing the person to return to the scene. Each of the other ordinances violated at least one guideline.

3-9. It would help if the father paid some attention to his son when he was behaving appropriately. When they are about to go on a shopping expedition he could offer the boy a choice: If the boy behaves nicely, they could spend time together on a favorite activity; if he misbehaves, he will be by himself.

3-10. Group *a:* This group could be taught the components of swimming. They might begin by learning to put their heads in the water. Next they will be expected to take arm strokes with their heads in the water before they are praised. Kicking techniques might come next. Finally they would only be praised if they could coordinate arm strokes, kicks, and breathing.

Group *b:* This group would start out swimming with assistance. Gradually the assistance would be removed. They might begin by learning to swim on a paddleboard or with water wings. Next they would swim while you held one hand beneath their stomachs. You would gradually use less strength holding them until they were swimming on their own.

3-11. *a*. The target behavior is not to put any charges on his accounts.

  b. He presently spends $880 in one month.

  c. Sailing seems a suitable reinforcer.

  d. If Ken can go for a full week without charging any items, he should reward himself with a weekend sailing trip. If he can keep it up for a year, he should allow himself to go on the inland-waterway voyage.

  e. He should note what he charges each week.

3-12. The mother is showing her daughter that authority is established by spanking or hitting. The next time the little girl wants to show her authority, she may imitate her mother's behavior.

3-13. If Barbara removes her positive reinforcement of thanking Jim and putting the flowers in a vase, she could extinguish his behavior. She might say nothing and simply let the flowers wither on a table or on the floor.

Checkpoint Answer Key

1. *b*	7. *a*	13. *a*	19. *d*
2. *c*	8. *b*	14. *b*	20. *a*
3. *c*	9. *c*	15. *d*	21. *b*
4. *a*	10. *d*	16. *c*	22. *a*
5. *d*	11. *c*	17. *a*	23. *d*
6. *a*	12. *b*	18. *b*	24. *b*

CHAPTER 4

IMPROVING MEMORY

Hide not your talents; they for use were made. What's a sun-dial in the shade!

Benjamin Franklin

Where were you on the evening of last October 25th? Unless that date was your birthday, anniversary, or other significant occasion, it is doubtful that you can recall your whereabouts. Yet if you were given a few clues, or even a choice of two or three possibilities, you might have less difficulty remembering.

How can you improve abilities like memory? Without memory, learning would be impossible. In this chapter you will look at three stages of memory and consider why memory sometimes succeeds and sometimes fails. With a better understanding of the memory process, you should be able to improve your study skills, your ability to score well on tests, your performance at work, and your ability to recall people and events. This chapter will help you learn ways to sharpen your memory and minimize forgetting.

MEMORY

Take a moment and imagine what it would be like not to have a memory. You would not know who you are, where you are, or what day it is. You would be incapable of speaking, reading, writing, eating with a fork, or taking a shower. Even if someone told you your name you could not remember it. But you would not realize that you were lacking a memory, since you would be unaware that you ever possessed the capacity to retain anything.

Now that the importance of memory has been established, take another moment and consider the many things you do remember. In addition to factual information, such as dates in history and mathematical truths learned in school, you are capable of remembering an enormous assortment of trivial information. Right this minute, you can probably state which drawer is used to store your socks, the number of windows in your bedroom, and whether you have milk in the refrigerator and gas in your car.

Many psychologists have compared the human memory to a filing cabinet. The analogy suggests that you pick out special information from the environment and store it in your brain. If you file it correctly, you will be able to retrieve it easily from your brain file. But if you misfile it or forget where it is filed, you will have trouble retrieving or remembering the information.

Exactly where is this file? It is difficult to envision a huge file cabinet in every human brain. Certainly memories are not stored in file folders. But the analogy is not totally ridiculous. There has been some evidence that memories may leave a *trace* or impression in the brain. Just which portion of the brain stores the memory traces has been a subject of some controversy.

trace A memory impression stored in the brain

Although there is uncertainty about the location of memory, there is agreement about the human brain's capacity. People use only a tiny portion of their memory potential. Are you wondering how you can make more efficient use of your memory capacity? Certainly, increasing memory is an extremely noble goal. The first step is to examine the process or stages involved and check where improvement can be made.

The Stages of Memory

Most views of memory describe three stages: sensory register, short-term memory, and long-term memory. Each stage is part of the memory process. The main difference between each stage is the length of time involved. The sensory register is the first step in the memory process and lasts only a few milliseconds. It is difficult to imagine such a fleeting time span. The next phase is short-term retention, lasting only a few seconds. Long-term retention, the final stage in memory, can last a lifetime. Figure 4-1 shows the relationship between the three stages of memory. Read on to find out why there is such a difference in your capacity at each stage.

Sensory register. As you see, hear, feel, or experience anything from the external world, it first enters the senses and the *sensory register* of your brain. The sensory register records everything that you sense. Information in the sensory register decays rapidly. The record lasts less than a second and is usually lost. Only a fractional percentage of sensations are passed along into short-term memory. As you are sitting and reading this chapter, a sizable amount of information is entering your sensory register. Hopefully the words you are reading and the concepts they present will be passed along to short-term and long-term retention. Among the stimuli that will probably be lost are such things as a horn honking or a bird chirping outside your window. Your sensory register takes in far more information than can be processed, so most inputs will be lost.

sensory register
The first stage of memory when information that is sensed is briefly recorded and rapidly decays if not passed along to short-term memory

short-term memory
The second stage of memory when information is stored for less than thirty seconds

Short-term memory. *Short-term memory* is similar to attention span. If you looked up the telephone number of a local restaurant, you could probably retain it just long enough to dial the number. If a friend asked you to repeat the number an hour later, you would have to return to the phone directory. Short-term memory has both a limited duration and a limited capacity. Although there are individual

Figure 4-1 Stages of memory

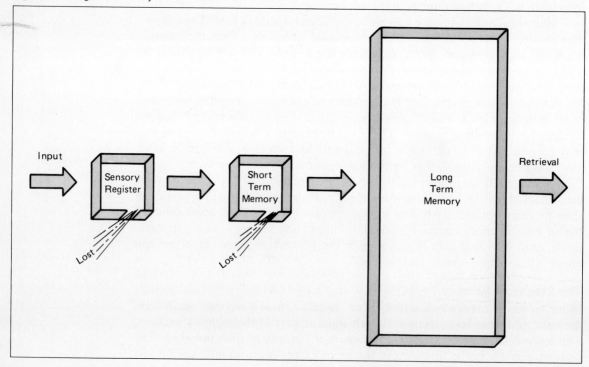

differences, for most people only about seven items can be manipulated at a time. Your short-term memory can probably handle a telephone number within your dialing area, but if the area code is added, you may have a problem.

Since items can be stored either individually or in chunks, many people find it profitable to group information or items. For example if you wish to remember the phone number "627-4357," it will consume the seven spaces in the average short-term retention. However, if you convert the numbers to letters and meaningful words, you could translate the number to "NAP-HELP." Now you need to retain only two words and would have room for five additional items. Grouping individual items together to allow for additional short-term retention is called "chunking." According to Chase and Simon (1973), chess masters use chunking. When they glance at a board, they see patterns rather than individual chess pieces. After a quick peek at a board that lasts only two or three seconds, a chess master can reproduce the entire arrangement on the board perfectly. It would clearly be beyond the capacity of the average short-term memory to handle the location of thirty-two chess pieces.

A recent study of verbal memory reported in Exhibit 4-1 found that memory experts use smaller chunks than other people. Experts are also aware of the importance of intonation and rhythm as they memorize. Have you ever noticed how easily you remember musical lyrics?

Short-term retention is usually most efficient during the first few seconds. Efficiency begins to diminish in about twelve seconds and after twenty seconds items will fade away unless they are passed along to long-term memory. Practice and rehearsal help to maintain items in short-term memory. If you repeat a phone number over and over again to yourself, you are more likely to remember it if you hear a busy signal the first time you dial. On the other hand, if you are distracted or need to retain some new information in your short-term memory, chances are you will find yourself with your finger poised to dial and no idea which numbers should be struck. Rote rehearsal has been found to be an effective method in increasing retention.

Klatzky (1975) reports that by talking to yourself and repeating information either silently or aloud, a memory can endure almost indefinitely. There has also been some evidence that what you hear can be retained longer than what you see. If you want to remember the name of someone you just met, use the name as you are talking with the person. The repetition of the name will act as a rehearsal, and you will be hearing your own voice. Next time you look up a phone number or fill your tank with gas, try saying the number out loud or calling out the cost of the gasoline. Then, if there is a delay in reaching the number or in paying your gas bill, you will impress everyone with your outstanding short-term memory.

Long-term memory. *Long-term memory,* as the term implies, lasts much longer than short-term memory. Most studies have suggested that anything that is remembered more than five minutes is considered to be in long-term memory. Memories can last hours, days, months, years, or a lifetime. With so many memories lasting for such long durations, long-term memory must have a vast capacity. The exact capacity has never been determined, but even after 100 years of memories, new material can still be stored. You need to sort

chunking Grouping individual items together into units to increase short-term retention

long-term memory The third stage of memory; items remembered more than five minutes are likely to be stored there indefinitely

EXHIBIT 4-1

Memory, Chunk-Style

Can you recite the second sentence of the Pledge of Allegiance? Most people say, "Of course," and then think through the entire pledge before realizing that it consists of a single sentence.

People often memorize the pledge, as well as passages such as the Gettysburg Address, as a chunk, verbatim. Although most prose does not lend itself to this kind of memorization, some people, such as actors, can easily learn and recall substantial, albeit unremarkable, tracts. Among their tricks: Experts break passages into smaller chunks than novices do and use specific words from the text as cues to help them remember the rest.

Researchers selected eight expert memorizers from the Indiana University drama department and compared their abilities with those of eight novices. Initially, people had 20 minutes to learn each of two three-paragraph passages. Later in the week their recall of the passages was tested at least six times. The researchers, Indiana University psychologist Margaret Jean Intons-Peterson and psychologist Mary M. Smyth of the University of Lancaster, England, used word-for-word transcriptions to analyze their rehearsal strategies.

Even the novices were able to remember substantial tracts of prose, Intons-Peterson and Smyth report (*Journal of Experimental Psychology: Learning, Memory, and Cognition*, Vol. 13, pp. 490–500). Verbatim recall was high, approaching 85 percent even after four days. The researchers found, however, that experts learned and recalled the material more quickly.

Why? Experts included fewer words per chunk as they memorized than the novices did. They also focused more on specific words—for example, initial words of sentences and paragraphs—to help jog their memory.

The experts also consciously searched for a certain intonation while memorizing the passages, experimenting until they found the "correct" one. When trying to recall the passage they often made brief, preliminary efforts, continuing only when they remembered the preferred intonation and cadence.

Nonprofessionals can copy some of the experts' techniques, says Intons-Peterson: "Alter intonation, use numbers and bits of humor as retrieval cues and pay special attention to beginnings of paragraphs and sentences."

Source: Simon, C. (1988, March). Memory, chunk-style. *Psychology Today.*

---

through an immense supply of information to find a correct response in long-term memory. As a result, retrieval or recall from long-term memory is generally slower and more difficult than recall from short-term memory.

Exercise 4-1

Indicate whether each description is an example of sensory register, short-term memory, or long-term memory.

a. A woman recognizes a man she met at a party the previous night. _____
_____ Long term_____

b. A baby feels a breeze come across his face. _____ Sensory _____

c. An old man reminisces about his childhood. _____ Long term _____

d. A waitress at a fast-food chain takes an order for three hamburgers, two french fries, and five milkshakes. _____ Short term _____

Check your answers in the Feedback section.

Improving Long-Term Memory

You probably have seen advertisements for books and lectures that promised to improve your memory. There are a number of tricks and gimmicks that have been successful in increasing the efficiency of long-term retention. Most techniques focus on one of two aspects of memory: depositing or retrieving information.

Improving Depositing

Most of the systems for improving the deposit of memories in the brain use *mnemonics*. Mnemonics or mnemonic devices give meaning and organization to help memory. "Thirty days hath September..." is without doubt the best-known mnemonic in the English language. If you have ever studied music, you are familiar with the mnemonic for remembering the notes associated with the five lines of the treble clef, *"Every Good Boy Does Fine."*

mnemonics A method that gives meaning and organization to help memory

Mnemonics are not limited to use by children. Mathematics students who want to memorize the first fifteen digits in the decimal expansion of π use the expression "How I want a drink, alcoholic of course, after the heavy lectures involving quantum mechanics." By counting the number of letters in each word, they can recite the extended value of π as 3.14159265358979. Engineering students could use the mnemonic *"Brave boys rescue our young girls by victory garden walls"* to remember the colors *b*lack, *b*rown, *r*ed, *o*range, *y*ellow, *g*reen, *b*lue, *v*iolet, *g*ray, and *w*hite as the colors used to represent the numbers 0, 1, 2, 3, 4, 5, 6, 7, 8, and 9 on electrical transistors.

Psychologists have identified several formal mnemonic systems for remembering lists. The pegword system and the method of loci have been used with success in a variety of situations. If you have a list of things to remember, try these procedures to see which works most successfully for you.

Pegword. First memorize and practice reciting the following poem. Keep repeating it even after you think you have memorized it perfectly. Extensive studying enhances long-term retention.

pegword A method for improving memory, using a poem to attach mental image associations with items on a list that is to be retained

1 is a bun	6 is sticks
2 is a shoe	7 is heaven
3 is a tree	8 is a gate
4 is a door	9 is a lion
5 is a hive	10 is a hen

Next create as vivid an image as possible for each item—bun, shoe, tree, etc. The poem can help you learn ten unrelated items by using mental images. For example, if you want to remember to purchase ten or less items on your way home one evening, you could associate each item with a number from the poem and conjure some sort of image in your mind. Figure 4-2 shows a possible set of images that could help a person remember to bring home a number of unrelated items. Any item can be hooked onto each peg, and ridiculous images will be remembered even more easily than sensible ones. One advantage to the system is that you can usually recall items backwards as well as forwards. The main disadvantage is that you are limited to ten items. Some systems extend the pegs up to twenty and thirty, but they have been less successful than the ten-pegword method.

poem	list	image
1 is a bun	soda	
2 is a shoe	peanut butter	
3 is a tree	birthday candles	
4 is a door	thumb tacks	
5 is a hive	razor	
6 is sticks	cough drops	
7 is heaven	shampoo	
8 is a gate	flash cubes	
9 is a lion	oil	
10 is a hen	light bulb	

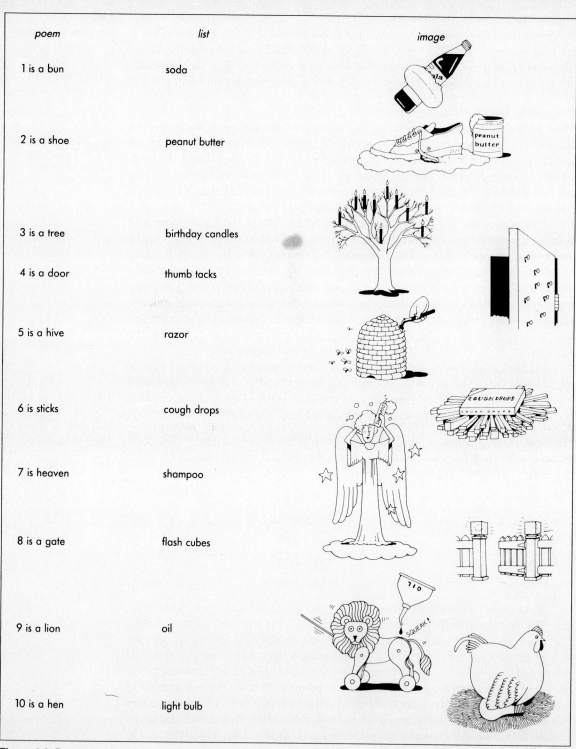

Figure 4-2 Pegword method

Loci. This method is sometimes referred to as the "house method." The first step is to walk through your house, apartment, or other familiar location and assign a number to each piece of furniture or fixture that you pass. Most individuals can be successful with about twenty items. After mastering twenty locations you can gradually increase the number. Once the list of locations is established, you need to overlearn the locations, as in the pegword method.

Again, as in the pegword method, the next step is to associate each item on the list to be memorized with a location. Assume that as you enter the front door of your home the first thing you see is an umbrella stand. This would be number 1 on your loci list. You would then continue with each item as you come to it. Perhaps an easy chair, an ottoman, a coffee table, a planter, a sofa, a stereo, a rocker, an end table, a bar stool, a wood stove, and a log bin could be items 2 through 12. Using the previous list, your associations could be an umbrella stand filled with soda, your easy chair smeared with peanut butter, the ottoman set with birthday candles, and thumb tacks nailed into your coffee table. Your list could continue throughout your house, using as many locations as you wished.

The method is surprisingly effective. Bower (1973) found that students using the method of loci could recall two or three times more than students using traditional rote-memory methods. The method of loci also helped the students keep the list in correct order. Students were given five lists with twenty words on each. Subjects using the loci method recalled an average of 72 percent of the items while the control group, using traditional memory methods, recalled an average of only 28 percent.

loci A mnemonic device that associates locations along a familiar path with items to be remembered

Exercise 4-2

In the early days of Rome, orators never read their speeches; they had to recite them from memory. History books state that the great Roman orator, Cicero, memorized his speeches by using a mnemonic technique. Supposedly he walked through his garden and numbered each part that he passed. He then associated each topic that he wished to address in his speech with a location in his garden. When it was time to deliver his oration, he simply thought of the images of his garden and was able to recite his speech perfectly.

a. What mnemonic device was Cicero using? _____ *Loci method*

b. What other method might have been useful to Cicero? _____ *peg word method*

c. Why was Cicero's method better than the alternative? *Because he had to learn a speech not a list*

Compare your responses with the answers given in the Feedback section.

There are a variety of other techniques for improving the deposit of material into long-term retention. Psychologists have advised that organizing information into meaningful units will assist memory. If you had a long grocery list, it would be helpful if you divided the list into vegetables, meats, dairy products, canned goods, paper products, and cleaning materials. Thorndike (1977) demonstrated the importance of organization and meaningfulness by showing the following passage to two groups of subjects.

A farmer wanted his mule to go into the barn. The mule would not go in, so he asked his dog to bark and scare it in. The dog refused to bark, so the farmer asked his cat to scratch the dog to make it bark. The cat would not scratch the dog unless it got some milk, so the farmer asked the cow to provide some milk. The cow gave the farmer the milk, the farmer gave the milk to the cat, the cat scratched the dog, whereupon the dog barked and scared the mule into the barn.

One group of subjects was shown the passage as it appears above. A second group was shown the passage with the first two sentences at the end. Recall was much better when the first two sentences were at the beginning so that subjects were aware of the purpose of the animal activity. When the sentences were at the end, recall was not as good.

It is easier to remember meaningful information. Undoubtedly you would have less trouble memorizing a speech written in English than one written in Russian or an unfamiliar language. The purpose of mnemonics is to give meaning through associations. These strategies coupled with concentration and overlearning can usually improve the depositing of memories.

Exercise 4-3

A spelling teacher has given the following list of words to his students: psychiatry, neighbor, seize, lieutenant, psalm, retrieve, psychology, reign, brief, psychotherapy.

a. Show how the students can organize the words into three groups so they will be better able to remember the correct spelling.

Group 1	Group 2	Group 3
psalm	seize	lieutenant
psychology	neighbor	retrieve
psychiatry	reign	brief
psychotherapy		

b. Why will this grouping help students remember the correct spelling?

each group has similar spellings. It will improve the depositing into long term memory

You may compare your responses in the Feedback section.

Improving Retrieval

Have you ever had an answer or a name "on the tip of your tongue"? This expression is often used to describe a failure to retrieve information that you once deposited. Although the deposit was successful, you are experiencing a problem in locating and picking up the memory. Everyone has had the experience of seeing an actor or famous person and not being able to recall the name, although they are certain they know it. Frequently, after some sorting and associating, the correct name emerges.

Free association is considered an effective method for improving retrieval. Klatzky (1980) reports that it helps to tap into areas that are associ-

free association
Following a sequence of associated spontaneous personal thoughts

ated. For example, if you misplaced an assignment, it would probably help to retrace your steps. Go back to your desk and walk through the rooms and places you had been. The reenactment will jar your memory. The more similarity between the present cues and those that existed when the information was deposited in your memory, the better your chance of accurate retrieval. An old photo will often elicit old memories that would not ordinarily be retrieved.

On the other hand, slight changes in appearance can make retrieval difficult. If you met a coworker at the beach or on a hike, she would most likely be dressed differently. The change in appearance would make it more difficult to recognize her. One system that usually helps with the recall of names is the alphabetic system. There is some evidence that words beginning with the same letter are associated in memory. A quick run through each letter of the alphabet will sometimes help you recall the first letter of her name. Once you have the first initial, the name is considerably easier to recall.

Checkpoint

Use the following questions to check your understanding of this portion of the chapter. Choose and mark the one correct response to each question.

1. It is believed that memories leave impressions on the brain. What are these impressions called?
   a. Memory images
   b. Memory traces

Figure 4-3
Wouldn't you love to know which technique Mr. Total Recall uses?

    c. Files

    d. Memory potentials

2. Which stage of memory has the shortest duration?

    a. Sensory register

    b. Short-term memory

    c. Long-term memory

    d. Retrieval

3. Imagine your boss called you and asked you to come into her office immediately with three pencils, a ball-point pen, two paper clips, an eraser, and six rubber bands. Which of the following methods would be most effective for assuring that you remember all the items?

    a. Change your setting so that you will not be bored.

    b. Cover your eyes so that you will not be distracted.

    c. Repeat the list to yourself over and over again.

    d. Go through the alphabet until you come to the letter of each item.

4. How many items or "chunks" can your short-term memory handle?

    a. About three

    b. Exactly five

    c. About seven

    d. Exactly ten

5. Which of the following techniques are favored by memory experts?

    a. Using large chunks and distraction

    b. Using large chunks and rhythm

    c. Using small chunks and distraction

    d. Using small chunks and rhythm

6. Which of the following is the best example of long-term memory?

    a. Looking at the page numbers as you turn the pages

    b. Feeling an itch at the end of your nose

    c. Blinking your eyes when dust blows

    d. Giving the answers to checkpoint questions

7. A man uses the name "Roy G. Biv" to help him recall the colors of the spectrum as *r*ed, *o*range, *y*ellow, *g*reen, *b*lue, *i*ndigo, and *v*iolet. Which technique is he using?

    a. A mnemonic device

    b. The method of loci

    c. The pegword method

    d. Overlearning

8. In which situation would the pegword method be most effective?

    a. You want to remember people's faces.

    b. You want to remember people's names.

    c. You want to remember a list of ten items.

    d. You want to remember a list of fifty items.

9. If you wanted to use the method of loci to help you remember a list, what would be your first step?

    a. Memorize the poem "1 is a bun..."

    b. Walk through your home and identify each location you pass.

    c. Divide the list into meaningful groups of items.

    d. Repeat the list of items over and over again aloud.

10. Assume that you need to memorize fifty words. Which type of words would be easiest to remember?
    a. Words in a foreign, unfamiliar language
    b. Words that are part of a meaningless passage
    c. Words that are part of a meaningless passage written in a foreign language
    d. Words that are part of a meaningful passage
11. A woman has forgotten where she put her keys. She last remembers seeing them in the ignition of her car as she drove home from work. Which of the following suggestions would probably be the most useful in helping her locate the keys?
    a. Use the method of loci.
    b. Use the pegword method.
    c. Go through the alphabet.
    d. Retrace her steps from the car.

Check your responses against the Checkpoint Answer Key at the end of the chapter. If you had difficulty with any question, reread the text. If you had little or no difficulty answering the questions or have resolved problems that you might have had, you are ready to continue with the next portion of this chapter.

FORGETTING

Forgetting can be embarrassing, inconvenient, and unpleasant. Why do you forget? There are several possibilities. First, it is possible that you are not aware that the event occurred. Your sensory register may not have received the input. This type of problem is not usually referred to as forgetting, since you never really experienced or learned the information. Second, although you experienced something, you never processed it into short-term and long-term memory. As you saw in Figure 4-1, many memories of events are transitory and fleeting and are not stored in either short-term or long-term memory. The third possibility has been of greatest concern to psychologists. Items or events have been stored in long-term memory but are now difficult to retrieve. Several explanations have been given to describe why this type of retrieval problem occurs. Among the reasons offered are repression, amnesia, disuse, distortion, interference, and drugs.

Exercise 4-4

There are three possible reasons for forgetting something: (1) you never sensed it; (2) you sensed it and processed it for a fleeting moment, but did not store it in your long-term memory; (3) you stored it in long-term memory but are unable to retrieve it. For each of the following examples of forgetting, indicate whether the cause is (1), (2), or (3).

a. Jim memorized a poem last night and now cannot remember the third line. __3__

b. Gladys watched the weather forecast on the news last night but was daydreaming about her summer vacation. She cannot remember whether showers were forecast for today. __2__

c. Mabel was so excited when she heard she won the Irish Sweepstakes that she forgot she was brewing coffee. She burned the bottom of the pot. _3_

d. Everyone laughed when Bill forgot to wear a tie to the party. No one told him it was a formal occasion. _1_

Compare your answers to those in the Feedback section.

Repression

repression Forgetting that is caused by an unconscious blocking of thoughts or events that are threatening or frightening

One possible explanation for being unable to retrieve memories is *repression*. Repression is unconsciously motivated forgetting. It is an unconscious blocking of things that are frightening or threatening. Traumatic events and anxiety-provoking people and situations can be painful if they are retrieved from long-term memory. Everyone has encountered some form of repression. Any time you refuse to talk or think about an unpleasant happening, you are experiencing a type of repression. According to Freud, it is a way of protecting yourself from remembering things that are distressing. These unbearable thoughts remain buried in the unconscious and can be revealed only through hypnosis or dreams.

Although repression can account for some forgetting, it is a limited explanation. Repression only applies to highly unpleasant emotional experiences. People often forget pleasant or neutral experiences as well. Further, most examples of repression are based on observations of patients in clinical settings. There has been little experimental evidence.

Suppression

suppression Consciously and intentionally avoiding unpleasant thoughts and memories

Have you ever wanted to forget something? Perhaps you did something embarrassing or foolish and wanted to suppress the memory. *Suppression* is a conscious effort to avoid thinking about an event. Since you are aware of the event, suppression is different from repression. As a result, as pointed out in Exhibit 4-2, forgetting is more difficult.

Amnesia

amnesia A loss of memory or a memory gap that includes forgetting personal information that would normally be recalled

Amnesia is a disorder that displays the most extreme form of repression. Because of the dramatic effect, amnesia patients have been used as the subjects of novels, films, and soap operas. The symptoms include a loss of personal information. Amnesia victims forget who they are, where they are from, and almost all other personal information. Interestingly, they retain basic memories. They remember how to add, subtract, read, write, dress, and cook.

hysterical amnesia Amnesia that has no organic or physical cause; usually occurs after a trauma and is temporary

There are several forms of amnesia. The best-known and most often popularized form is *hysterical amnesia*. In this type of amnesia, there is no organic or physical reason for the problem. Hysterical amnesia usually occurs after a traumatic event and is generally temporary.

organic amnesia Amnesia that has physiological causes

Amnesia can have physiological causes. Alcoholism, drug abuse, disease, injuries, nutritional deficiencies, and brain damage are possible contributors. Amnesia from physiological causes can be either temporary or permanent and is labeled ''organic amnesia.''

global demential amnesia A type of amnesia characterized by an absent-mindedness about present events

A third type of amnesia, called ''global demential amnesia,'' is characterized by an absentmindedness about the present. This form is common in older, senile patients who have excellent recall about their past lives but have difficulty keeping apprised of the present. Most often this form of amnesia is permanent.

EXHIBIT 4-2

105

IMPROVING MEMORY

Suppress Now, Obsess Later

How do you get rid of an unwanted thought? Psychologist Daniel M. Wegner has found that the usual strategy—trying hard not to think about it—can backfire: The more we try to suppress unwanted thoughts the more likely we are to become preoccupied with them.

Wegner and his colleagues told a group of college students not to think about white bears and then asked them to dictate their ongoing thoughts into a tape recorder and ring a bell each time a white bear came to mind.

Not thinking about white bears proved difficult for the students: They rang the bell or mentioned the bear more than once a minute during a five-minute session. In other words, actively trying to suppress an idea paradoxically makes us think about it.

Why is it so difficult to get rid of unwanted thoughts? In trying not to think about a white bear, the researchers explain, we must first think about it.

What's a worrier to do? The researchers repeated the experiment, but this time told another group of students to think about a red Volkswagen if they happened to think of a white bear. Using a single distracting thought did the trick; it helped the students to avoid thinking of the dreaded white bear.

This strategy, the researchers suggest, may prove useful in the treatment of obsessive thinking as well as in the treatment of addictions, such as smoking. But they admit that more work needs to be done before we fully understand thought suppression. "In the meantime," they say, "it seems clear that there is little to be gained in trying not to think about it."

Source: Neath, J. (1987, December.) Suppress now, obsess later. *Psychology Today.*

Like repression, amnesia is a limited explanation of why forgetting occurs. It is not nearly as common as the media suggest and can only account for a tiny percentage of forgetting.

Exercise 4-5

A Princeton student reported that he met Albert Einstein while strolling across campus one day. They stopped and chatted for a few minutes, and the student invited Einstein to join him for lunch. Albert Einstein asked in which direction he had been walking when he came upon the student. When the student indicated the direction, Einstein stated that he had already eaten. He politely thanked the student for the invitation.

Which type of amnesia was Einstein experiencing? _global_
demential

You may check your answer in the Feedback section.

Fading and Distortion

There has been some evidence that memories will fade with time if they are not used. This is possibly an accurate explanation of forgetting in short-term retention. However, fading does not provide a complete explanation for long-term forgetting. Strangely, people often forget valuable information and remember things that are totally useless.

However, several experiments (Loftus, 1975; Loftus et al., 1978) have shown that memories can become distorted with time. New material changes to conform with information that was previously learned. As additional material is learned, old information becomes incorporated. Experimental subjects have watched slides and films of accidents involving cars striking either a pedestrian or another vehicle. In one situation slides showed a *green* car passing. The experimenter asked the subjects if the *blue* car passing had a ski rack. When asked the color of the passing vehicle, most of the subjects recalled it as blue rather than green. Control subjects were not given the color blue when asked about the passing vehicle. They remembered the car as green.

In another situation subjects were asked to estimate the speed of the car when it ''smashed'' into another vehicle. These subjects overestimated the speed considerably. Control subjects who were asked to estimate the speed when the car ''hit'' the other vehicle gave fairly accurate estimates.

Exercise 4-6

From what you know about distortion of memories, why might the warning ''Beware eyewitness testimony!'' be accurate?

distort memory & change response

You may compare your answer with the one given in the Feedback section.

Interference

Interference is the most popular explanation for why forgetting occurs. It is similar to the distortion explanation but gives clearer details. You forget because other information interferes with your remembering. According to the interference description of forgetting, there are two types of obstructions to remembering: proactive interference and retroactive interference.

The details of this accident will probably become distorted with time. (*Dan Chidester/The Image Works*)

Proactive interference. Proactive means "acting forward." *Proactive interference* refers to instances when previous memories block the recall of more recent learnings. If you have trouble learning the French phrase for "good-bye" because you keep thinking of the German phrase that you previously learned, you are experiencing a proactive interference: You have difficulty remembering "au revoir" because you keep remembering the old "auf wiedersehn." Or suppose you meet a new psychology instructor named Professor Kassel, who reminds you of your old girlfriend Flora Belle. You may have difficulty remembering the professor's correct name and want to call her Flora Belle. In proactive interference, earlier learning interferes with new learning.

Retroactive interference. Retroactive means "acting backward." *Retroactive interference* refers to instances where recent learning blocks the recall of previous memories. If after finally learning the French phrase "au revoir" you have trouble remembering the German phrase "auf wiedersehn," you are experiencing retroactive interference. New learning interferes with your ability to recall something from the past. If the next time you meet your old girlfriend Flora Belle, you have difficulty remembering her name and have an urge to call her "Professor," retroactive inhibition will be contributing to your forgetting. Fig. 4-4 shows how proactive and retroactive interference can cause forgetting.

Exercise 4-7
Indicate whether each of the following is an example of proactive or retroactive interference.

a. You have difficulty learning the metric system because you keep thinking of inches, feet, and yards. __Pro__
b. You have trouble learning the scissor kick with your sidestroke swimming and keep going back to your old flutter kick. __PRO__
c. After reading the book *Gone with the Wind,* you want to see the movie. Now you have trouble remembering what was in the book and keep thinking of the film. __Retro__
d. When you first learned to drive, you used a car with a standard shift. For the past five years you have been driving a car with automatic transmission. You are asked to drive a car with a standard transmission and find yourself forgetting to use the clutch and treating the car as if it were automatic. __Retro__

Check your responses against those given in the Feedback section.

Positions

Are you familiar with a poem that begins "Twas the night before Christmas...?" Chances are you can recall the first few lines. But if you were asked to continue, you would have difficulty. It is also likely that you can recall the closing lines "Merry Christmas to all and to all a good night!" Similarly, young children usually have no difficulty singing the first line of the alphabet song "A, B, C, D," and enjoy ending with a robust "X, Y, Z." It is the middle part that creates confusion.

Psychologists have reasoned that you have little difficulty remembering the first part because of a *primacy effect.* It is the first thing you learn, and you will not be bothered by any proactive interference. Most people can remember

proactive interference
Forgetting that occurs because of confusion with previously learned material

retroactive interference
Forgetting that occurs because of confusion with newly learned material

primacy effect An explanation of why the first things learned are easier to remember

Figure 4-4 Proactive and retroactive interference

the first few bars of any tune they hear, the picture on the cover of a magazine, and their first date. The last items learned are also easier to remember. They are fresh in your mind and not bothered by retroactive interference. This is called a "recency effect."

recency effect An explanation of why the last things learned are easier to remember

Think about the last party you attended. If you remember the first people you met when you entered and the last few people you spoke with before leaving, you experienced primacy and recency effects. Most students find that they have little difficulty remembering the first part of their assigned reading.

The end of the chapter is also easier to recall. It is the middle section that is most difficult. It has no primacy and recency advantages. Unfortunately, the middle portion is affected by both proactive and retroactive interference. Students usually need to apportion more time to the middle section, since it will be more difficult to remember.

Exercise 4-8

Assume you have been asked to give an address to a local civic group. Several friends have come to your aid and have helped write an outstanding five-page speech. Now you need to memorize the talk so that it will sound as if it is your own. Based on what you have learned about interference and positions, describe a strategy for remembering the speech. Keep in mind the sections that are likely to be easy or difficult to learn.

go over middle part repeatedly or break speech into small units.

You may compare your strategy with the ones described in the Feedback section.

Drugs

Recent studies have shown that certain drugs given in carefully controlled doses can help people remember. McGaugh (1983) reported that the hormones epinephrine and norepinephrine enhance memory. There has also been evidence (McGaugh, 1970) that some more common drugs, such as nicotine and caffeine, will speed up the incorporation of information in long-term memory. However, if the dosage of even these ordinary drugs is not carefully controlled, memory can be disrupted and poisoning is possible.

Most drugs impede memory. For example, tranquilizers have a strong negative impact on memory. A recent study (see Exhibit 4-3) found that the tranquilizer diazepam actually blocks memory for up to six hours.

Many studies (Birnbaum et al., 1978; Darley et al., 1973; Miller et al., 1978; Nahas, 1979; Peterson, 1984; Relman, 1982; Wetzel et al., 1982) have concluded that both marijuana and alcohol have a detrimental effect on memory. The greatest impairment is the ability to transfer information from short-term to long-term memory. People who have had several drinks or have been smoking marijuana can usually carry on a conversation, recalling and retrieving information from the past. They can also remember new things for a few seconds. The usual problem is in forming lasting memories. After an evening of being high at a party, many individuals will have difficulty the next morning recalling their own behavior at the celebration.

If you have been drinking or smoking marijuana, intake of information will be more difficult than retrieval. Experiments have shown that sober subjects can recall information from the past both when intoxicated or sober. But if a

Tranquil Daze

The millions of people who quiet their anxiety with daily doses of diazepam (brand name: Valium) may be blocking out more than their discomfort. The tranquilizer, also used as a sleeping aid and muscle relaxant, appears to interfere with memory formation for up to six hours after a normal dose is taken.

Diazepam does not hinder retrieval of information locked into memory before the drug was taken, nor does it inhibit short-term memory while one is under its influence, says psychologist Steven Mewaldt of Marshall University. Diazepam does, however, appear to interrupt formation of permanent or "long-term" memory. Mewaldt reported these findings at the most recent meeting of the American Psychological Association.

"If the formation of memory can be described as a chain of events," Mewaldt says, "then diazepam appears to break that chain at one point." Although Mewaldt has not yet pinpointed exactly where the break occurs, he has narrowed it down.

In a series of studies, Mewaldt and his colleagues tested diazepam's effects, having people recall word lists or series of numbers they memorized either before taking the drug or while under its influence. The scientists had them rehearse the material out loud, to capture potential effects on their memorization strategies.

Mewaldt and his colleagues found that diazepam's memory-blocking action was not a result of people being too "laid back" to care about rehearsing the material they had been asked to memorize. "We did not find differences in intensity or type of rehearsal between the two groups, but we found huge differences in recall," Mewaldt says.

Mewaldt believes that diazepam acts at the biochemical heart of memory. Other researchers have found that it interferes with the normal function of GABA, a neurotransmitter thought to be involved in memory formation.

Mewaldt notes that the memory-blocking impact of the drug, for which 23 million prescriptions were written in 1985, depends on the frequency, dose and time of day that it is taken. "If people are taking diazepam as a sleeping aid, it will probably be gone by the time they wake up in the morning," he says. "But if they are taking it during their daily activities, that presents more of a concern."

Mewaldt urges caution for those who take the drug without serious medical need. "I have had students admit to taking diazepam in order to calm down so they can study for an exam," he says. "That's certainly counterproductive."

Source: Chollar, S. (1988, January). Tranquil daze. *Psychology Today.*

subject is intoxicated when learning information, recall will diminish when the subject is sober (Parker, Birnbaum, & Noble, 1976). The subject will actually recall better if intoxicated. This situation is sometimes referred to as "state dependence." Recall is best if you are in the same state as you were when you learned the information. A student who likes to have a few beers while studying will probably perform better on an exam if he is sipping some brew. But, keep in mind that memory is best when you have not been drinking or smoking marijuana at all. About 10 percent of people who seek help for alcohol problems have serious brain damage and memory problems (NIAA, 1982).

Checkpoint

Use the following questions to check your understanding of this portion of the chapter. Choose and mark the one correct response to each question.

12. Which of the following reasons for forgetting has been of greatest concern to psychologists?
    a. Failure to sense information
    b. Failure to process material in short-term memory
    c. Inability to retrieve material from long-term memory
    d. Inability to retrieve material from short-term memory
13. What is repression?
    a. An unconscious blocking of painful memories
    b. A conscious retrieval of pleasant memories
    c. A hypnotic method for recalling dreams
    d. A clinical technique for observing amnesia patients
14. How are suppression and repression related?
    a. Both are unconscious.
    b. Both are conscious.
    c. Suppression is conscious and repression is unconscious.
    d. Repression is conscious and suppression is unconscious.
15. When is hysterical amnesia most likely to occur?
    a. After brain damage
    b. After excessive alcoholic consumption
    c. After a traumatic experience
    d. With senility
16. Which of the following provides the most popular explanation of forgetting?
    a. Repression
    b. Amnesia
    c. Fading
    d. Interference
17. A student just read her assignment in sociology. Now she is studying psychology. She is having difficulty reading her psychology assignment because she keeps thinking of her sociology. What is she experiencing?
    a. Proactive interference
    b. Retroactive interference
    c. A primacy effect
    d. A recency effect
18. A tap dancer claims he finds it easy to remember the first few steps of any dance routine but becomes confused as he gets further along. Why does he have less difficulty with the first part?
    a. There is a recency effect.
    b. There is a primacy effect.
    c. There is less repression.
    d. There is a state dependence.
19. Shelley took a Valium to help her relax during her history exam. What is likely to happen?
    a. She will be relaxed and remember the material she learned.
    b. She will be relaxed but her memory will be blocked.
    c. She will not be relaxed but her memory will be enhanced.
    d. She will not be relaxed and will feel a need for alcohol.

20. Wally had seven martinis and met an attractive girl, Ellen. The next day he could recall neither her name nor her address. In which of the following situations would Wally be most likely to remember Ellen?
    a. After sleeping
    b. After drinking seven martinis
    c. After drinking several cups of coffee
    d. After smoking marijuana

Check your responses against the Checkpoint Answer Key at the end of the chapter. If you had difficulty with any question, reread the text. If you had little or no difficulty answering the questions or have resolved problems that you might have had, you are ready to continue with the next portion of this chapter.

IMPROVING STUDY METHODS

In all probability you are wondering how to use your knowledge of memory and forgetting to improve your own study skills. There is no uniform set of study habits that works for everyone. Diverse study systems seem to benefit different individuals. However, there are a few general suggestions that psychologists have found profitable for most people. Several methods have been discovered that can improve concentration, apportionment of time, and test preparation.

Improving Time Schedules

One of the most important skills that you can learn in college is how to plan your time to study successfully. The best students are not necessarily the most intelligent. Often they are students who have learned how to organize their time and use self-discipline. Most of us have experienced the stress of feeling that there is too much to do and too little time. In truth, there rarely is enough time to do everything. But if you set your priorities and plan your time carefully, you will experience less stress and your grades will probably improve.

One system for planning your time for a semester suggests three types of calendars (Quinn & Daughtry, 1988). The first calendar is used for long-range plans, for an entire term. The second calendar sets your short-term plans on a weekly basis. The final calendar sets your immediate plans or daily list of activities.

Long-range plans. Buy or make a calendar that has a large space for each day of the entire term. This calendar will be used to plot the entire semester. First mark vacations and holidays so blocks of free time will be obvious. Next, fill in days with work, family, or other responsibilities. As soon as you receive course outlines from your instructors, fill in key dates for tests, midterms, deadlines for assignments or papers, and final examinations. Next add major social events, perhaps concerts, dances, or sports events.

Then add deadlines that you set for yourself. Remember the importance of breaking long assignments into sections. When setting deadlines for yourself, give yourself some space before the official deadline. This will help you avoid the stress of time pressures. Use some method for distinguishing fixed dates from deadlines that you have assigned yourself; perhaps different colored inks or print for fixed deadlines and script for personal deadlines. A typical term calendar is shown in Figure 4-5.

By actually writing a schedule for yourself, you can avoid procrastination. If a term paper is due in ten weeks, you can break the assignment into weekly tasks. You might use the first week to research several possible topics. The following week you could select the topic. Then give yourself two weeks to read and take notes. By week five you could begin your outline. This would give you four weeks for writing and a week to edit and revise the paper.

A completed term calendar shows a clear picture of the entire semester. Hang this calendar in a conspicuous place, such as over your desk or on your closet door.

Figure 4-5 A term calendar

Short-range plans. Once your term calendar is completed, you are in a good position to plan each week. For most people, Sunday is a good day to develop a weekly plan. Again, it is best to begin by filling in fixed obligations: work hours, class times, and commuting time. It's a good idea to enter these in the manner you have chosen to indicate fixed deadlines.

As you begin to fill in study times, consider the time of day when you are most efficient. Many people find that they work best at a particular time of day. Some feel more efficient in the morning, while others reach a peak during the afternoon or evening hours. Still others perform evenly throughout the day. It is always helpful to study during your peak time.

Figure 4-5 *Continued*

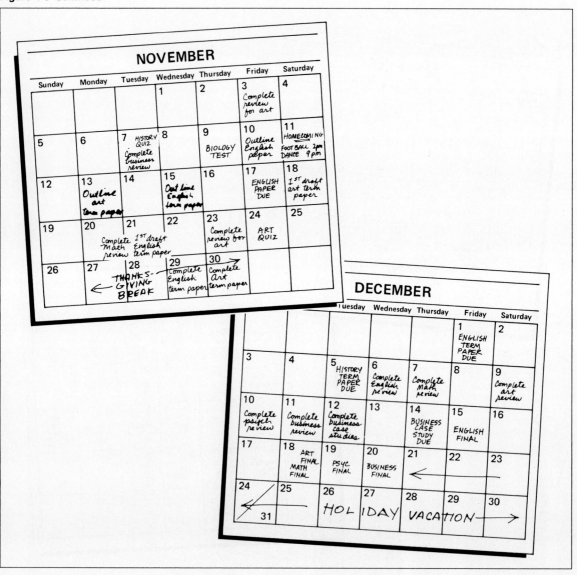

There are several important general principles to remember in planning a study schedule. To avoid interference, it is best to study just before and just after class. In most cases distributed practice is more efficient than massed practice, so it is better to study for thirty minutes a day over a ten-day period than to study for five hours on one day (see Exhibit 4-4). This is particularly true if you find the subject dull and boring. If the material is stimulating and exciting, spacing is less important.

Schedule times for your most difficult subjects first. Be sure to include some fun and leave some free time. Figure 4-6 shows the schedule of a student taking sixteen credit hours, commuting fifteen minutes each way, and working six hours each week.

Immediate plans. If you function well at night, you may want to take ten or fifteen minutes to plan the next day; otherwise save the planning until morning. Make a daily list of accomplishments or a simple checklist of what you want to do. Again you may separate necessary from unnecessary (but desirable) items by using print and cursive script or different colored inks. Figure 4-7 shows a typical daily list.

Exercise 4-9

Mrs. L. is a working parent who is also taking two courses at a community college. Lately she has been feeling stressful because two term papers and two final exams are scheduled for completion within three days. Although it may be too late to correct her current problems, describe three types of calendars that Mrs. L. could use to help her use her time more efficiently.

EXHIBIT 4-4

Spaced-Out Memory

Remember the old grade-school maxim: "Say a new word ten times quickly and it's yours"? Now the results of a long-term study by a pair of psychologists may turn that bromide into an old wives' tale. In fact, say Harry Bahrick of Ohio Wesleyan University in Delaware, Ohio, and Elizabeth Phelps of Princeton University in New Jersey, if you want a new word to stick in your brain for the long haul, it's best to space out the initial repetitions over a much longer period of time.

Beginning in 1979, Bahrick and Phelps had a group of students learn the Spanish equivalents of 50 English words. Some of the students learned the Spanish words in "forced feedings," with many repetitions of the word in a single day. Others learned them at a much slower rate, in some cases receiving repetitions only after intervals of 30 days. Eight years later, the students were tested for long-term recall. Those who had learned the words in one-day "cram sessions" recalled only 6 percent, while those who learned them over 30-day intervals remembered as many as 25 percent.

Would the "spaced-out" method work for learning more complex knowledge systems like music or math? Although its effectiveness is difficult to determine scientifically without special teaching methods and specific long-term tests, Bahrick's hunch is that "the principles will apply to almost any subject you'd learn in school—music, mathematics, even what you know about baseball."

Source: Lawren, B. (1988, February). Spaced-out memory. *Omni.*

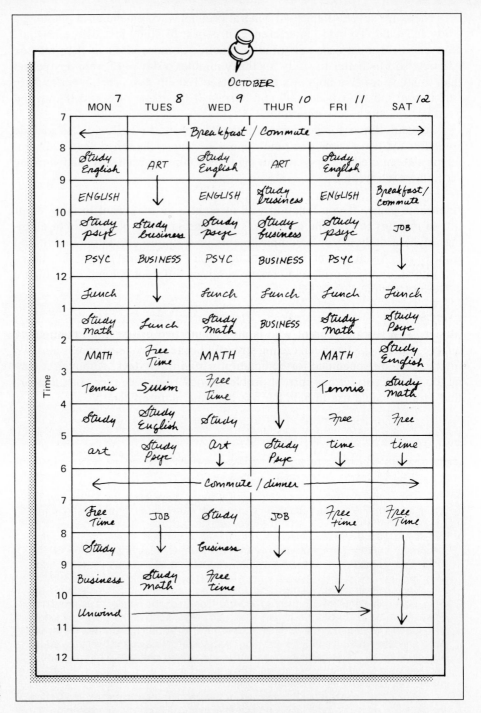

Figure 4-6
A weekly calendar

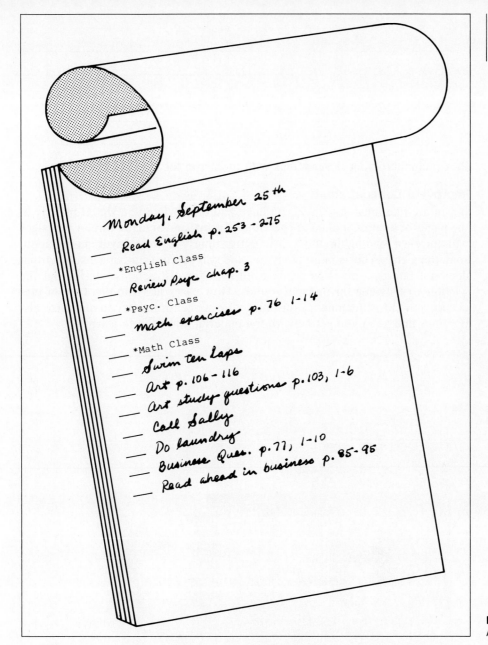

Monday, September 25th
___ Read English p. 253 - 275
___ *English Class
___ Review Psyc chap. 3
___ *Psyc. Class
___ Math exercises p. 76 1-14
___ *Math Class
___ Swim ten laps
___ Art p. 106 - 116
___ Art study questions p. 103, 1-6
___ Call Sally
___ Do laundry
___ Business Ques. p. 77, 1-10
___ Read ahead in business p. 85-95

Figure 4-7
A daily list of activities

a. _____

_____

_____

b. _____

_____

_____

c. _____

_____

Please compare your descriptions with the list in the Feedback section.

Improving Concentration

If you are like most students, you have had days when you stared blankly at the pages of a book, looked at each line of print, and actually turned the pages without ever reading anything. The entire time you were daydreaming about something else. This is more likely to happen if you are studying a subject that does not interest you. You might even look for distractions, staring out the window or listening for unusual sounds. How can you avoid this type of preoccupation? Most techniques for improving concentration try to minimize distractions and keep you active with the material you need to learn.

Clearly these students have not chosen a work area that will improve their concentration. (*David S. Strickler/The Picture Cube*)

One important factor in minimizing distractions is the location of the study area. There has been evidence that study sessions are more productive when a special area is set aside for work. When distracting thoughts occur, it is best to leave the work area. Return again only when studying will continue. It is also considered important to keep your study area free of photographs or other items that may cause your mind to wander. Sitting in an upright position is preferable to relaxing on a sofa or easy chair. Although there are individual differences, many students find that soft music will block out intermittent sounds and noises that would be more distracting (Lapp, 1987).

Keeping your mind focused on your studies is usually easier if you are actively involved with the material to be learned. Students find it useful to underline important points or use highlighters, ink pens that brighten words. Others prefer to outline or write notes in the margin. These techniques, along with making flash cards of important terms and concepts and making up exams, all seem to work equally well. The important factor is to keep alert and involved with the subject. Studies have shown that active study results in more learning than passive study.

One procedure for keeping active that has had exceptional success is labeled the *SQ3R method,* a mnemonic for "*S*urvey, *q*uestion, *r*ead, *r*ecite, and *r*eview. The first step is to survey the assignment by checking the major headings and gaining a general impression about the subject you will be studying. After checking the headings, make up a general question for each topic. Next begin reading, but as you read search for the answers to your questions. Then recite the answers to your questions. It is preferable to recite aloud so that you get additional sensory input. The final step is to review, emphasizing the areas where you had difficulty answering your own questions. An important asset of this method is that you receive feedback and find out whether you have mastered the subject or need to spend more time studying.

SQ3R A mnemonic for survey, question, read, recite, and review; a successful approach to studying

This student has chosen a special area for studying that has minimum distractions. (*Joel Gordon*)

Exercise 4-10

Read the following scenario and list four ways that Heathcliff could improve his study habits.

Heathcliff curled up on the sofa to begin reading his economics assignments. The midterm was the next morning, and he had postponed the reading until the night before so that the material would be fresh in his mind. He hated economics and decided to turn on the television to keep himself awake. As he began the reading, his mind drifted toward the program he was half watching. He closed his eyes and began daydreaming. He began to realize how tired he was and soon dozed off into a sound sleep.

a. _____

b. _____

c. _____

d. _____

Compare your list with the one given in the Feedback section.

Preparing for Tests

Memory is usually measured through one of three methods: recall, recognition, or relearning. Most instructors use either the recall method (essay questions), or the recognition method (multiple-choice tests). Only rarely will relearning be used as a measure.

Essay tests measure memory through ability to recall information and are graded subjectively. Although teachers usually expect specific answers, they are often influenced by the appearance and organization of a response. When written neatly with pen rather than pencil and put in correct grammatical form, the same content tends to receive a higher grade. Although this tip will not improve your ability, it could improve your test score.

On multiple-choice tests, you must recognize a correct answer imbedded among several wrong alternatives. Recognition is a more sensitive measure than recall. Multiple-choice tests can detect learning that might not be picked up on a recall test. For example, although you may not be able to name every country in Europe, you probably could select the European nations from a list of countries throughout the world. A common problem with multiple-choice questions is guessing. Many instructors penalize wrong responses. It is usually wise to determine whether points will be deducted for guessing.

While cramming for tests is never recommended, it is extremely popular. Everyone is occasionally caught in a situation where cramming is necessary. If you must cram, the excerpt in Exhibit 4-5 presents some useful suggestions.

In taking any test, it is best to answer the easy questions first. This will leave additional time for the more difficult items. When you come to troublesome questions, it sometimes helps to jog your memory by using free association. Jot down anything that comes into your mind. Free association can help retrieval. But never waste too much time on one question. By budgeting your time, you can have a few minutes at the end to reread the test.

EXHIBIT 4-5

121

IMPROVING MEMORY

How to Cram

...it doesn't take a psychologist to explain why cramming often fails. "You throw things into your mind, knowing that you're going to spit them out in a couple of hours and forget them. It's not a good way to learn at all," says NYU journalism senior David Reilly....

But if you're forced into a late-night, last-minute study session, the results don't have to be disastrous. Here's some advice to help make the morning after less anxious than the night before:

- **Find out what kind of test you're in for.** If you cram, you're likely to fare better on multiple-choice and fill-in-the-blank tests because they jog your memory with cues.

- **Compose a scene that you can recreate during the exam.** If you can, study at the desk or in the room where you'll take the test, or do something while you study that you can do again when you take the test. For example, Dansereau suggests that you chew grape gum. "The flavor acts as a cueing device," he explains.

- **Build your concentration.** Spend 10 minutes warming up with a novel or magazine before you tackle a tough chapter....

- **Watch what you eat and drink.** Avoid heavy meals and alcohol. Both could make you drowsy, cautions Lapp. If you need a cup of coffee to perk up, fine. But putting too much caffeine in your system can make you jittery and break your concentration.

- **Mark your book.** Even if you only have time to read the chapter once, it helps to highlight important terms and sections....

- **Spend time repeating or discussing facts out loud.** Recitation promotes faster learning because it's more active than reading or listening....Discussion groups are helpful for this reason.

- **Take short breaks at least every few hours.** They'll help you beat fatigue, which takes a heavy toll on learning. Two hourlong sittings separated by a 15-minute break are more productive than one two-hour session in which your mind wanders throughout the second half. It doesn't matter what you do during those breaks; just take them.

- **Experiment with memory techniques.** They impose structure on new information, making it easier to remember at test time. The "house" method is one of the oldest. Let's say you want to remember a list of sequential events for a history exam. Try to imagine the events taking place in separate but connected rooms of your house. When the test asks you to recall the events, take a mental amble through the rooms.

  Another simple technique involves acronyms. You may have learned the names of the Great Lakes (Huron, Ontario, Michigan, Erie, and Superior) with this one: HOMES.

- **Try some proven learning strategies.** Richard Yates, a counselor and time-management expert at Cleveland State University, recommends the SQ3R method: survey, question, read, recite, review. Survey the material to formulate a general impression; rephrase titles and headings into questions; read through the material quickly to find the main points and the answers to your questions; recite those main ideas, taking brief notes; and review. Even when you're pressed for time, the strategy can help. "It may take a little longer," says Yates, "but it's worth the effort."

- **Get some sleep.** UF's Schank quit all-nighters after his freshman year. "I'd go into a final and be so wired from staying up all night that I'd lose my concentration," he says. "I'd miss questions that I knew I wouldn't miss if I were in a good frame of mind." Now he crams until about 3 A.M., sleeps for about four hours, and hits the books again at 8 A.M.

Source: Miller, J.Y.
(1987, Fall). How to
cram. *Campus Voice.*

Psychologists and memory researchers can't specify how much sleep you need—everyone has his or her own threshold—but they do stress its importance. Says Lapp, "You're better off getting some sleep so that your mind is rested for the exam than you are cramming the whole night."

...Unless you've got back-to-back exams, don't cram and then do something else for a few hours before a test. Freshly learned material is remembered much better after a period of sleep than after an equal period of daytime activity.

• **Relax.** It may sound simplistic, but it's [the] key to good test performance....

Cramming is like going to the dentist; if you have to do it, you want it to be as painless and as productive as it can be. After all, no one goes to college to take a semester-long class and promptly forget all the new information that's been taught....

Many people suffer from test anxiety. Perhaps you have walked into exam rooms with sweaty palms, butterflies in your stomach, and a dry mouth. These are only some of the symptoms. Unfortunately, another symptom is difficulty in retrieving memories. Your mind goes blank and you cannot think of any answers while completing the test. As soon as the exam is handed in and you leave the room, your anxiety ends. The correct responses become apparent to you—but it is too late.

A moderate amount of anxiety seems to help test performance. You are alert and eager to do well. But a high level of anxiety is detrimental. Psychologists have suggested three techniques for helping individuals overcome test anxiety. By writing out answers and imagining a test situation when you are completely relaxed, you can help to make yourself less sensitive. This *desensitization* technique for removing anxieties and fears is discussed in Chapter 3. The second suggestion is to *overlearn*. Even when you think you understand and know the information completely, keep studying. This will increase your confidence and keep the answers more available when anxiety strikes. The third technique is to put yourself into a *relaxed state* before entering the examination room. Panic exchanges with classmates can intensify test anxiety. Think of something soothing, perhaps the sound of waves splashing on the shore as you sit on the sand soaking up sunshine, or maybe a quiet snowfall while you nap by a fire. This method is only useful if you tend toward high anxiety. Seek the help of a professionally trained psychologist or counselor if the problem is sufficiently distressful and self-help measures have failed. Remember, moderate anxiety is helpful. You do not want to doze off during the test.

Checkpoint
Use the following questions to check your understanding of this portion of the chapter. Choose and mark the one correct response to each question.

21. Which type of calendar should you develop first?
a. Long-range
b. Weekly
c. Daily
d. Hourly

22. Jim has a term paper due next month. What advice would you give him?
    a. Be sure to be free the night before the paper is due.
    b. Procrastinate; most teachers accept late papers.
    c. Try to pace yourself so that the paper will be ready early.
    d. Relax and enjoy yourself now, so you will be rested when you have to work.
23. Alicia finds history boring. How should she plan to study?
    a. Cram before the final.
    b. Study in short blocks of time.
    c. Study in long blocks of time.
    d. Avoid studying and wait until an interest develops.
24. What is the first step in the SQ3R method?
    a. Study
    b. Select
    c. Speculate
    d. Survey
25. What do techniques for improving concentration stress?
    a. Keeping actively involved with the material to be learned
    b. Keeping yourself comfortable while you are studying
    c. Surrounding yourself with items of interest
    d. Cramming and massed practice
26. Jan walked into her final exam in math and felt jittery. Her mouth was dry, her palms were sweaty, and her stomach felt nervous. Suddenly she could not remember a single formula. What was Jan experiencing?
    a. Global demential amnesia
    b. Organic amnesia
    c. Test anxiety
    d. Fading
27. Which of the following would be most useful in increasing the confidence of a person who usually experiences test anxiety?
    a. Taking new responsibilities
    b. Avoiding active study
    c. Underlearning
    d. Overlearning

Check your responses against the Checkpoint Answer Key at the end of the chapter. If you had difficulty with any question, reread the text. If you had little or no difficulty answering the questions or have resolved problems that you might have had, you are ready to check yourself against the chapter inventory that follows.

CHAPTER INVENTORY

Use this list of objectives as a review checklist. You should be able to do each of the tasks outlined in the objectives and apply them to everyday examples. If you can, you may feel confident that you have mastered the material in this chapter.

1. Name the three stages of memory, and describe what occurs during each.
2. Outline one way to improve short-term memory.
3. Distinguish between the two aspects of long-term memory, depositing and retrieving.
4. Describe how mnemonics, the pegword system, the method of loci, meaningfulness, and organization can improve depositing.
5. Explain the importance of association and alphabetics in retrieval.
6. List three possible reasons for forgetting, and identify the possibility of greatest interest to psychologists.
7. Describe repression, suppression, fading, and distortion, and recognize their limitations as explanations of forgetting.
8. Specify three types of amnesia.
9. Define and give examples of proactive and retroactive interference and primacy and recency effects.
10. Explain how drugs can affect memory.
11. Identify ways to improve time schedules using long-range, short-range, and immediate plans.
12. Explain how active studying can improve concentration.
13. Specify three methods used to measure memory.
14. Describe how to prepare for tests and avoid test anxiety.

Feedback

The correct answers to the exercises follow. If you did not answer an exercise correctly, review the preceding pages and return to the exercise to correctly complete it.

4-1. *a.* Long-term memory
  b. Sensory register
  c. Long-term memory
  d. Short-term memory
4-2. *a.* The method of loci
  b. The pegword method
  c. By using the method of loci, Cicero could make his speech as long as he wished; the pegword method would have limited the length.
4-3. *a.*

Group 1	**Group 2**	**Group 3**
psychiatry	neighbor	lieutenant
psalm	seize	retrieve
psychology	reign	brief
psychotherapy		

  b. This grouping will help students learn the correct spelling because the lists are organized according to similar spellings. This will improve the depositing of the spelling of each word in long-term memory.
4-4. *a.* 3
  b. 2
  c. 3
  d. 1
4-5. Global demential amnesia

4-6. Psychological experiments have shown that eyewitness testimony can be distorted. The type of question asked from the witness could distort a memory and change a response.

4-7. *a*. Proactive interference
   b. Proactive interference
   c. Retroactive interference
   d. Retroactive interference

4-8. Since the middle portion will be more difficult to learn than the first portion and the end, it will take more time to learn it. You could simply apportion more time to the center section. Or you might break the speech into smaller units and begin with a different unit each time you begin to work on memorizing the speech. In this way different sections would be benefiting from primacy and recency effects.

4-9. *a*. Term calendar with key dates for assignments, dates for major work projects and family responsibilities
   b. Weekly calendar with class times, work hours, and parenting responsibilities
   c. Daily checklist of activities to be completed

4-10. a. Heathcliff should sit in a straight-backed chair rather than a sofa.
   b. He should space his studying rather than cramming the night before an exam, particularly when he dislikes a subject.
   c. He should not allow distractions to creep in when he is studying. The television program is apt to take his mind off his work.
   d. When he begins to notice that he is not attending to his studies, Heathcliff should leave the area and return only when he is ready to resume his work.

Checkpoint Answer Key

1. *b*	**8.** *c*	**15.** *c*	**22.** *c*
2. *a*	**9.** *b*	**16.** *d*	**23.** *b*
3. *c*	**10.** *d*	**17.** *a*	**24.** *d*
4. *c*	**11.** *d*	**18.** *b*	**25.** *a*
5. *d*	**12.** *c*	**19.** *b*	**26.** *c*
6. *d*	**13.** *a*	**20.** *b*	**27.** *d*
7. *a*	**14.** *c*	**21.** *a*	

CHAPTER 5

THINKING AND PROBLEM SOLVING

There is no more miserable human being than one in whom nothing is habitual but indecision.

W. James

Have you ever considered how many problems you solve during the course of a day? No doubt some problems are simple, such as choosing what to wear or what to eat for breakfast. Others, however, may be more complicated. Perhaps you must find a way to make a deposit in your overdrawn checking account, or find a way to study when you have out-of-town guests. The solutions you choose for some problems can have an important impact on your life. Your choice of a major in college or a first job will most likely influence your entire career in some way.

This chapter will consider ways to improve your problem-solving abilities. Thinking, the basis of problem solving, will be considered first. Next, the focus will be on the steps involved in problem solving and how to use creative approaches. Finally, you will learn how psychologists measure thinking and problem-solving abilities.

THINKING

Whether you are remembering about your childhood, daydreaming about television stardom, trying to fix a leaky faucet, or painting a mural, you are thinking. The term "thinking" is very broad and complex. It includes processes from preoccupation and daydreaming to complex problem solving and creating new ideas. Psychologists often refer to the thinking process as "cognition." *Cognition* refers to any mental activity, whether conscious or unconscious.

cognition Mental or thought process

Thoughts come in various forms. Sometimes you think in images. For example, if asked to come up with a scheme for rearranging your living room furniture to make room for a new piano, you would undoubtedly think in images. On the other hand, if asked to explain your position on a new increase in electric rates, you may rely more on words. Some thoughts are in the form of neither words nor images. Ideas such as peace, kindness, and coldness are concepts. Concepts are formed from experiences. Most thoughts involve a combination of images, words, and concepts. It is not always easy to distinguish among them. Think about your last vacation. Can you separate the images, words, and concepts in your thoughts? Thinking seems so natural that most of us are unaware of the complexity of our thought processes.

Scripts

Often we do some impressive thinking without realizing it. Schank and Abelson (1983) noted that a great amount of thought is often required to understand even the simplest very boring little story or script. A *script* is very short and we automatically fill in details. Consider the script:

script A brief story that requires you to fill in information

> Jane threw a bridal shower for Cathy. Cathy received fifteen irons and fifteen mixers. She went to the returns department the next day.

This script is indeed a very boring little story. However, think of all the blanks you had to fill in to understand even this simple story. If you were an alien from another planet, the script would be very difficult to understand. First, you need to know what it means to "throw a bridal shower" and the purpose of a bridal shower. You also need to know what irons and mixers are and that most people only need one of each. You also have to fill in the fact that these items were gifts that were purchased at a store and could be returned. Fortunately, most of this thinking happens automatically!

"*You're right, it does look suspicious.*"

Figure 5-1
It appears the wardens
are filling in the details
of this script.

Exercise 5-1

Read the following script from Minsky (1983) and indicate three things you had
to fill in to understand the story.

> Jane was invited to Jack's birthday party. She wondered if he would like a kite.
> She went to her room and shook her piggy bank. It made no sound.

a. _____

b. _____

c. _____

Please check your list in the Feedback section at the end of the chapter.

Logical Thinking

Whether or not you have ever taken a formal course in logic, chances are you
use logical thought many times every day. However, you may not be aware of
the sequence of steps in your logical thought process. Logical thought consists
of two beliefs and a conclusion based on the two beliefs. The first belief is
called the "major premise" and the second belief is labeled the "minor
premise." Logically enough, the conclusion is called the "conclusion."

premise A belief

Consider the sequence of logical thought:

Major premise If the traffic light is red, I must stop my car.

Minor premise The traffic light is red.

Conclusion Therefore, I must stop my car.

This logical sequence is reasoned by millions of individuals many times each day. In most cases the thought process is unconscious, and people are not even aware that they have thought logically. Most decisions require logical thought. When judging whether you are sick enough to stay home from work, you might reason:

Major premise If I have a fever, I should not go to work.

Minor premise I have a fever.

Conclusion Therefore, I should not go to work.

Conversely,

Major premise If I do not have a fever, I should go to work.

Minor premise I do not have a fever.

Conclusion Therefore, I should go to work.

Assuming that your premises are true, if you follow a logical thought sequence, you will reach a valid conclusion. Unfortunately, sometimes people base their thinking on false premises. For example, the major premise: "If I do not have a fever, I should go to work" would not be true if it is Sunday and you only work on weekdays. Even though your logic is correct, your conclusion would be false.

Predicate Thinking

The thought process is not always logical. Freud identified a type of nonlogical thought process that he labeled "predicate thinking." Predicate thinking is based on sentence structures. When two sentences have the same predicates or endings, people unconsciously associate the subjects or beginnings. Advertisements often appeal to predicate thinking. Advertisers might make statements like "Distinguished men drink Boozy brand liquor" or "Good mothers buy Sticky brand cake mix." They hope you will use nonlogical thought and reason:

predicate thinking Nonlogical thought that unconsciously associates subjects of sentences that have the same predicates or endings

- Distinguished men drink Boozy brand liquor.
- I drink Boozy brand liquor.
- Therefore, I am a distinguished man.

or

- Good mothers buy Sticky brand cake mix.
- I buy Sticky brand cake mix.
- Therefore, I am a good mother.

Exercise 5-2

Read each of the following thought sequences. If it is possible to reach a logical conclusion, write the correct conclusion. If the sequence is an example of predicate thinking and is not logical, simply put an "X" on the final line.

a. If there is a blizzard, the college will be closed.
There is a blizzard.

b. Young women wear modern hairstyles.
Matilda wears modern hairstyles.

_____

c. A smart person reads Genius magazine.
Ichabod reads Genius magazine.

_____

d. Whenever I am in the bathtub, the telephone will ring.
I am in the bathtub.

_____

Compare your conclusions with the ones in the Feedback section.

Critical Thinking

Distinguishing between logical and predicate thought requires critical thinking. You must evaluate the statements and make judgments based on reason. Recently, educators have stressed concern about developing critical thinking skills in children. In the past, children who argued were often considered rebellious. Currently, children are being encouraged to challenge the prevailing opinion. Critical thinking is becoming a stronger part of the education curriculum.

Without critical thinking skills, we can easily be misled by propaganda and deceptive advertising. Ennis (1985) and Paul (1984) identified several guidelines for critical thinking:

• Separate logical ideas from emotional arguments.

• Try to see both sides, for and against what is being proposed.

• Don't be afraid to question a weak-sounding argument.

• Look for inconsistencies in statements.

• Wait for enough evidence and don't rush to conclusions.

If we use these guidelines we will be less susceptible to hoaxes.

Exercise 5-3

For each of the following claims, indicate which of the above guidelines for critical thinking would help you make a proper evaluation.

a. There are eight good reasons why you should chew Gummy gum.

_____

b. I'm in favor of increasing spending on government services and salaries and reducing taxes.

_____

c. I can't stand small children, so there's no way I'd vote for a new school in this community.

_____

d. We need to expand the highway for more bicycle space and anyone who questions it must be pretty stupid.

You may check your responses in the Feedback section at the end of the chapter.

Problem Solving

Although logical thinking can be an important aspect of problem solving, there are also other factors involved. Many problems are solved by trial and error. There is no system; you just take chance guesses. This process drags on and is not efficient.

Psychologists have suggested a more practical series of steps for solving problems.

Define the problem. Before solving a problem, someone needs to admit that a problem exists. Short people are familiar with the problem shown in Figure 5-2. Unfortunately few store managers have recognized and defined the problem, so tall customers and sales people continue to reach for items or allow short persons to leave without purchases.

Find the facts. Often the facts will make the solution obvious. The comedian Norm Crosby gave a humorous example of ignoring some facts.

> I have a friend who went through a harrowing experience recently. He locked his car with the keys in the ignition. He stood there for two hours with a wire coat hanger trying unsuccessfully to fish out the keys through a narrow opening in the window. It was awful. His wife sat inside the car crying her heart out.

Look for possible solutions. Once you understand the problem and have gathered all the facts, it is time to search for possible solutions. Most people will base their selection of possible solutions on past experiences. The article in Exhibit 5-1 reports the merits of knowing a solution. If a solution once worked on a similar problem, chances are it will be successful once again. The difficulty with such an approach is that it tends to limit your thinking and view.

EXHIBIT 5-1

Squarely on the Head

A key and highly complex machine in a factory mysteriously stopped. Machinists and engineers who tried to locate the problem and correct it all failed. As a result, production was suspended, and an expert was called in. Upon arrival, the examiner looked the machine over briefly and tapped here and there with a hammer; soon the all-important machine was humming again.

When the expert later submitted his bill for $200, the plant manager turned white. "All you did was tap the machine a few times," he wrote back. "Please itemize your bill."

Back from the expert came this reply, written on the bottom of the bill:

Tapping machine with hammer	$1.00
Knowing where to tap	$199.00

Source: Curnane, J. (1987, December). Squarely on the head. *Saturday Evening Post.*

Figure 5-2
A tall person may not
recognize this problem.

mental set A limited
view of possible
solutions and a
tendency to respond
in the same way
regardless of the
problem

functional fixedness
Using objects only for
their known purposes
and being unable to
think of other possible
uses to solve problems

This difficulty is referred to as a "mental set," or an inability to get out of a rut. Check your own mental set by solving the problems in Exhibit 5-2.

One variation of mental set that can restrain thinking is called "functional fixedness." Functional fixedness involves the use of objects. The more you use an object for one purpose, the less likely you are to think of other possible uses. For example, suppose ice has formed on your car windshield and you are without a scraper. What else could you use to scrape the ice? Credit cards in your wallet or a spatula from your kitchen might do the job. Of course the usual function of a credit card or a spatula is not ice scraping. If you can think beyond the usual purposes of objects, you can often come up with alternative solutions to your problem. Anyone who has used a coin to tighten a screw or a newspaper as a shield from the rain has, in a sense, overcome functional fixedness.

Choose a solution and evaluate the effectiveness. After reviewing possible solutions, select what appears to be the best alternative. Then test this solution to be sure it works. If the solution is useful, your problem is solved. If the solution does not work, you must again study the alternative answers and make a selection. The process will continue until an effective solution emerges.

Exercise 5-4
Martin has a problem. He needs $200 for books within the next three weeks. He decided to use a systematic approach to find a solution to his problem:

a. Define the problem.
b. Find the facts.

EXHIBIT 5-2

133

THINKING AND
PROBLEM SOLVING

Mental Set

a. The word "premise" can be used in several ways. Sometimes it refers to a belief. For example, a person might say, "He acted on the premise that no police protection was available." Another common meaning of premise is property. Perhaps you have read signs stating "Keep off the premises."

Now think about logical thought. What is the final statement called? If you said "premise" you were in a mental set. The final statement is called the "conclusion."

b. How many squares do you see?

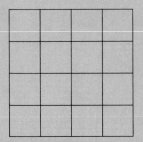

Answer: 30 squares. Once you saw beyond the obvious answer 16, or perhaps 17 (if you counted the square that contains the smaller ones), you were on your way to solving the problem. There are squares within squares. After counting the squares, you need to keep looking and consider how small squares could be used as parts of larger units.

Source: Raudsepp, E. (1980). *More creative growth games.* New York: Perigee Books.

c. Consider possible solutions.
d. Choose a solution and evaluate its effectiveness.

The flow diagram in Figure 5-4 shows the actual steps he took. Divide the diagram into four sections. Label each section to show which step in his systematic approach is being used. The first section has been done for you.

Artificial Intelligence

Artificial intelligence (AI) is a term that describes computer programs that solve problems by "thinking" the way people do. Most of these programs are based on sets of rules similar to logical thinking. One AI program, MYCIN, was designed to diagnose infectious diseases and is about as efficient as most doctors (Mason, 1985). In fields such as geology, insurance, and engineering, AI programs have solved problems far more quickly than people could.

One of the most exciting aspects of AI research is the knowledge we have gained about the human thought process. Researchers must break down the thought process into steps in order to write programs. As a result we have gained far more appreciation for the human mind's abilities in evaluating scripts, using common sense, and even recognizing a friend (Schank & Hunter, 1985).

artificial intelligence
Computer programs
that solve problems

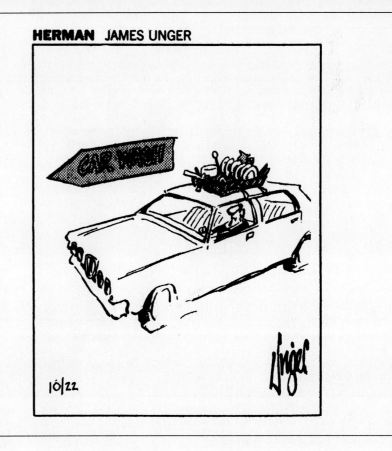

HERMAN JAMES UNGER

Figure 5-3
A man overcoming
functional fixedness at
a car wash...

Checkpoint

Use the following matching questions to check your understanding of this portion of the chapter. Listed on the left are ten important terms. Match each term with one phrase from the list on the right.

1. ____ Cognition
2. ____ Script
3. ____ Logical thinking
4. ____ Premise
5. ____ Predicate thinking
6. ____ Critical thinking
7. ____ Trial and error
8. ____ Mental set
9. ____ Functional fixedness
10. ____ Artificial intelligence

a. A belief
b. The inability to use an object for a new purpose
c. The thinking process
d. Random guessing at answers
e. Associating subjects of sentences
f. Thinking in a rut
g. Computer programs that solve problems
h. Used for valid conclusions
i. Little story that requires filling details
j. Making judgments based on reason

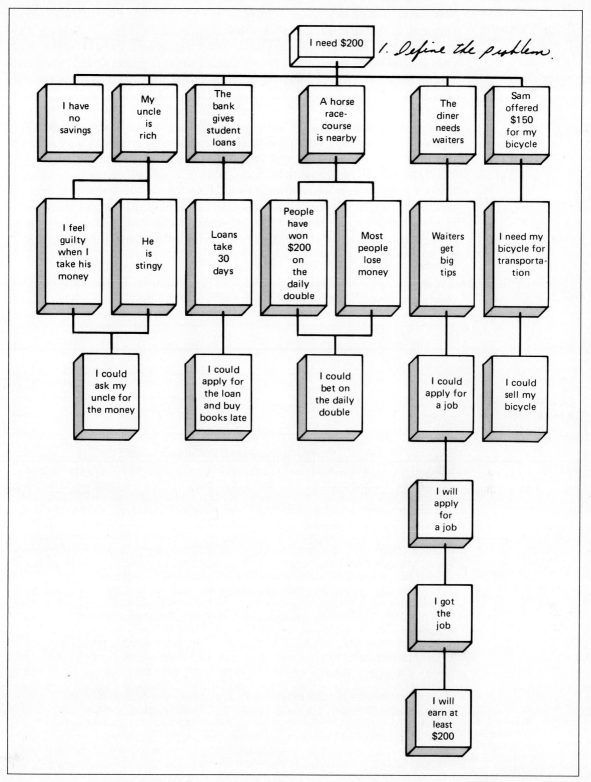

1. Define the problem.

Figure 5-4

creativity Ability to
see things in a new
way and come up with
unusual solutions

CREATIVE THINKING

One area of thinking that computers have not invaded is creative thinking. Psychologists have difficulty agreeing on the exact definition of *creativity*. However, most psychologists view creativity as an ability to see things in a new and unusual way and to come up with unique solutions to problems. Creativity is the opposite of mental set. It provides an original path from humdrum ideas and dull, routine views. Creative thinking lends excitement and helps find new solutions to old problems. Psychologists agree that creativity is not the same as intelligence. Often highly intelligent people are not at all creative. Likewise creative ability seems to stay intact even when intellectual ability diminishes (see Exhibit 5-3).

Some researchers base their evaluations of creativity on the production of a result or an accomplishment. They look for such socially valued products as inventions, art, or musical works as signs of creativity. Although there is some relationship between creative ability and accomplishments, according to Barron and Harrington (1981), this relationship is very low.

Exercise 5-5
The man in Figure 5-5 seems pleased with his invention. Would most psychologists consider his invention creative? Why or why not? _____

_____

_____

_____

_____

EXHIBIT 5-3

Piano Playing Preserved in Dementia

When Alzheimer-like dementia wastes a mind, can oases of cognitive functions, such as artistic abilities, survive? According to psychologist William W. Beatty and his colleagues at North Dakota State University in Fargo, there have been anecdotal reports suggesting that demented patients can remain proficient at music or painting. But few researchers have probed the cognitive landscape of these individuals in any detail.

Beatty's group recently ran a battery of tests on a demented 81-year-old woman, who once taught music at the college level. Beatty found, for example, that she cannot identify pictures of famous people, say where she lives, or perform simple motor skills on command such as waving.

But she can still play the piano, albeit not superbly. Musical judges rank her playing (which is also impaired by trembling of her hands) somewhere between that of a young, rusty amateur and that of an elderly, once accomplished pianist who has arthritis.

According to Beatty, the woman has also been able to transfer her piano skills to an unfamiliar instrument, the xylophone. "We think in some sense she's retained the concept of how to play," he says. "It's not just an overlearned motor act that she's spitting out." Only her learned motor responses related to music are preserved. "It's consistent with her inability to do simpler things, like wave goodbye."

Beatty says he's not sure whether his study will have any implications in treating dementia. But it is possible, he says, that "you might be able to use the patient's preserved skills to get at some other memories that aren't normally accessible." For example, his patient could play songs, requested by title, that she could not name when they were played for her.

Source: Weisburd, S. (1987, October 31). Behavior: Piano playing preserved in dementia. *Science News.*

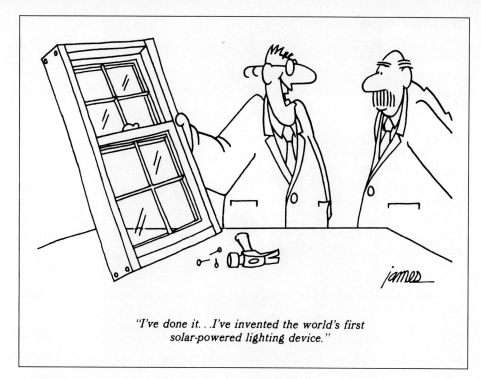

*"I've done it. . .I've invented the world's first
solar-powered lighting device."*

Figure 5-5

You may check your answer in the Feedback section.

Characteristics of Creative Thinkers

Do you view creative people as wild, imaginative, and different? The article in Exhibit 5-4 suggests that creative people may have more emotional mood swings than other people. Most people who have made creative contributions are considered nonconforming, independent, confident, and moody.

But apparently creativity also requires hard work. Madigan and Elwood (1984) stressed the importance of curiosity and persistence. They described the story of the invention of Velcro by the creative Swiss inventor, George de Mestral. While hunting, George and his dog became covered with burrs. As he struggled to remove the burrs, George became curious about why the burrs stuck so well to his clothes. He studied the burrs under his microscope and discovered hundreds of tiny hooks on each burr. He spent years of persistence trying to find a way to attach these types of hooks to tape. The final result was Velcro.

Other creative persons report similar experiences. Beethoven labored long hours writing, tearing up, and rewriting his works. The Nobel prize winner Thomas Mann claimed he struggled to make himself write three pages each day.

Exercise 5-6

Read the following list of adjectives and check those which describe common characteristics of creative thinkers.

☐ Conforming

☐ Confident

Interpretive dancing
often permits a high
level of creativity.
(*Jaye R. Phillips/The
Picture Cube*)

☐ Independent

☐ Boring

☐ Moody

☐ Intelligent

☐ Curious

☐ Persistent

Compare your checks in the Feedback section at the end of the chapter.

Improving Creativity

How can you become more creative? Many psychologists suggest jotting down every idea that occurs to you, whether good or bad. Avoid the "idea killers" listed in Exhibit 5-5! Trying to think of only good ideas can be both stifling and frustrating. Give yourself plenty of time. Some psychologists suggest acting out and drawing diagrams to help you visualize problems. They recommend talking to yourself out loud and walking through the problem as you act it out. It is always useful to follow in the steps of well-known creative thinkers and be persistent. The excerpt in Exhibit 5-6 provides some excellent ideas on how to improve your creativity.

EXHIBIT 5-4

139

THINKING AND
PROBLEM SOLVING

Mood Swings and Creativity: New Clues

For centuries there has been speculation that creativity is somehow linked to "insanity" or mental illness, although scientific studies of the suspected connection are sparse. Nancy C. Andreasen of the University of Iowa College of Medicine in Iowa City now reports that, at least among a small group of creative writers, there is a close association between creativity and "affective disorders" such as depression and manic depression.

Reasons for this relationship remain unclear. "Nevertheless," says Andreasen in the October *American Journal of Psychiatry,* "affective disorder may produce some cultural advantages for society as a whole, in spite of the individual pain and suffering that it also causes."

During the past 15 years, Andreasen interviewed 30 faculty members at the University of Iowa Writer's Workshop, one of the best-known creative writing programs in the country. She also interviewed 30 control subjects of comparable age, sex and education, whose occupations included hospital administration, law, and social work.

Andreasen found that 80 percent of the writers had had an episode of either severe depression or manic depression—either with a pronounced mania characterized by euphoria, increased energy and poor judgment, or a milder "hypomania"—at some time in their lives. Schizophrenia, marked by severe thought disorders, was absent in the sample, but 30 percent of the writers were diagnosed as alcoholic. Depression or manic depression occurred among 30 percent of the controls, and 7 percent were alcoholic. None of the controls was schizophrenic.

The writers also reported significantly more first-degree relatives with creative achievements in a variety of fields, including literature, art and music. The breadth of creativity in these families suggests that a "general factor" predisposing to creative success may be genetically transmitted, says Andreasen. Average intelligence, as measured by several IQ tests, was virtually the same for writers and controls.

Andreasen's report follows a 1983 study by Washington, D.C., psychologist Kay Jamison of 47 top British artists and writers. More than one-third reported having sought treatment for depression or manic depression. Poets and playwrights in the study were most likely to have severe mood disorders or dramatic mood swings.

Twenty artists in France, including writers, painters, sculptors and musicians, are being examined by Kareen and Hagop Akiskal of the University of Tennessee in Memphis and psychiatrists at the University of Paris. The ongoing study consists of extensive interviews and includes 20 comparison subjects in other occupations.

"So far, the most striking aspect of the artists is their temperament, not the presence of major psychiatric disorders," says Hagop Akiskal. "Since their teens and 20s, they've been moody people with emotional ups and downs."

Nearly 70 percent of the artists have some type of affective disorder, notes Akiskal. The most common diagnoses are a moderate form of manic depression or even milder, intermittent periods of mood swings. More severe mood disorders, he says, probably disrupt an artist's career.

Furthermore, a recent study of 750 psychiatric patients in Memphis conducted by the Akiskals found that those with mild manic depression or mood swings were more likely to be creative artists. But the same diagnoses also appeared in excess among people who were successful in business and leadership positions, says Hagop Akiskal. Studies of creativity and affective disorders need to consider distinguished people who are not artists, he points out.

Source: Bower, B. (1987, October 24). Mood swings and creativity: New clues. *Science News.*

EXHIBIT 5-5

Certifiable Idea Killers

"It would cost too much."

"It's been done before."

"The last guy who thought that way isn't here any more."

"Haven't you heard? There's a recession!"

"It will never track."

"The front office will table it."

"The computers would have to be reprogrammed."

"It doesn't fit our corporate image."

"It's politically not feasible."

"It'll put more people out of work."

"It will make the rich richer and the poor poorer."

"Middle America won't like it."

"It won't appeal to the youth-oriented market."

"It's a Band-Aid solution."

Source: Curnane, J. (1987, December). Certifiable idea killers. *Saturday Evening Post.*

Exercise 5-7

Mr. C wants to increase creativity in his toy manufacturing company. He has developed a list of ideas. Place a + sign beside each idea that is likely to improve creativity and a − sign beside each idea that might hamper creativity.

_____ Avoid ideas that our computer can't handle.

_____ Take your time and come up with plenty of ideas.

_____ Feel free to be unconventional.

_____ Talk out your ideas.

_____ Eliminate ideas that might be expensive.

_____ Stick with the toy company's image.

_____ Think of unconventional ways to use our equipment.

Compare your responses in the Feedback section.

Teaching Creativity

Many courses have been developed to teach creative thinking. However, according to Mayer (1983), creativity improves only on the specific tasks being taught. The creative skills learned do not seem to work in other situations. Perhaps we need more creative approaches to teaching creativity!

Checkpoint

Use the following questions to check your understanding of this portion of the chapter. Choose and mark the one correct response to each question.

11. Which of the following types of thinking is found in humans but not in computers?
    a. Logical
    b. Mathematical
    c. Creative
    d. All of the above

EXHIBIT 5-6

141
THINKING AND
PROBLEM SOLVING

How to Be More Creative

How Can You Do It Better?

- Try consciously to be original, to come up with new ideas.

- Don't worry about looking foolish if you say or suggest something unusual or if you come up with the wrong answer.

- Eliminate cultural taboos in your thinking (such as gender stereotyping) that might interfere with your ability to come up with a novel solution.

- Try to be right the first time, but if you're not, explore as many alternatives as you need to.

- Keep an open mind. If your initial approach doesn't work, ask whether you made assumptions that might not be true.

- If you get stuck on one approach, try to get to the solution by another route.

- Be alert to odd or puzzling facts. If you can explain them, your solution may be at hand.

- Think of unconventional ways to use objects and the environment. Look at familiar things as if you've never seen them before.

- Consider taking a detour that delays your goal but eventually leads to it.

- Discard habitual ways of doing things and force yourself to figure out new ways.

- Do some brainstorming with one or more other people. This involves trying to produce as many new and original ideas as possible, without evaluating any of them until the end of the session.

- Strive for objectivity. Evaluate your own ideas as you would those of a stranger.

Source: Papalia D. & Olds, S. (1988). *Psychology.* New York: McGraw-Hill.

12. Which of the following is the opposite of creativity?
    a. Intelligence
    b. Mental set
    c. Persistence
    d. Scripts

13. Bill invented an exercise machine. What characteristic must it have to be considered creative?
    a. New and original
    b. Conforming and acceptable
    c. Working condition and inexpensive
    d. Humdrum and expensive

14. What is the relationship between creative ability and creative achievement?
    a. There is a high relationship.
    b. There is a high negative relationship.
    c. There is a slight relationship.
    d. There is no relationship.

15. Which mental illness has been linked to creativity?
    a. Schizophrenia
    b. Paranoia
    c. Cocaine addiction
    d. Manic depression

16. What are two common characteristics of creative persons?
  a. Humor and conformity
  b. Curiosity and persistence
  c. Impulsiveness and dependence
  d. Acceptance and timidity

17. Which of the following statements is likely to kill creative ideas?
  a. Take your time.
  b. Talk to yourself.
  c. Come up with lots of different ideas.
  d. That's not the way the boss usually does it.

18. Peter just completed a course in creative poetry writing. What is likely to happen?
  a. His poetry writing will become more creative.
  b. His poetry writing will become less creative.
  c. His poetry writing will not change.
  d. All of his creative skills will improve.

Check your responses against the Checkpoint Answer Key at the end of the chapter. If you had difficulty with any question, reread the text. If you had little or no difficulty answering the questions or have resolved problems that you might have had, you are ready to continue with the next portion of the chapter.

MEASURING THINKING ABILITIES

Along with a set of physical characteristics, each person has a unique pattern of abilities and talents. In discussing thinking abilities, the emphasis thus far has been on general characteristics that can be applied to most people. At this point you may be wondering how you compare with other people. Psychologists have a number of testing instruments that can be used to measure and compare talents and abilities. You are probably most familiar with intelligence and achievement tests, since they are used more often than other instruments. It is difficult to attend school without taking a number of standardized intelligence and achievement tests. *Standardized* means that the test has been tried on a large population and your score may be compared with the scores of other individuals and groups. But other types of standardized tests are also available—from tests of neurological and motor abilities to tests of creative, artistic, and musical talent.

standardized test Test that has a uniform set of instructions for administration and scoring; the results can be compared with the scores of a larger population

intelligence Ability to learn or adapt

Intelligence Tests

Psychologists do not completely agree on the definition of the concept of *intelligence*. However, most of their explanations infer an ability to learn and adapt in a very broad sense. Many psychologists have jokingly defined intelligence as "what intelligence tests measure." Attempts to measure intelligence have been far from perfect, and clearly many intelligence tests are available that measure something far removed from an ability to learn.

One major problem in measuring intelligence is the number of elements that can contribute to the ability to learn. Some have argued that intelligence is innate; you are born with certain abilities and capacities. But factors like cultural exposure, health, and nutrition have been found to influence intelligence.

Intelligence tests have not been successful in measuring innate abilities. However, results of individual intelligence tests are helpful in planning educational programs.

Individual tests of intelligence. There are two common types of intelligence tests: individual tests and group tests. For the most part, psychologists prefer individual tests. This means that the individual works alone with the psychologist in answering questions and performing tasks. During the testing session the psychologist can observe the person's behavior, along with any specific difficulties that are encountered. Many psychologists prefer the Wechsler scales because they reveal patterns of abilities. The strengths and weaknesses of each person are made clear. The results of Wechsler tests can be used to prescribe special methods of instruction based on the person's pattern of abilities.

Group tests of intelligence. In a group test there is more opportunity for error. Group tests are often administered by classroom teachers, clerks, secretaries, and other individuals who may not have been trained in testing. Behavior is not noted, and there is more room for misjudgments. An individual who misunderstood the directions could lose credit for an entire section of the test. Likewise a good guesser or cheater could achieve a high score. People who do not read well generally score poorly on group tests. Group tests are less expensive, but they are also less accurate.

Exercise 5-8

When Ted was in grade 2, he took a group intelligence test with his class. He remembers the day because he had a heavy cold and neither a tissue nor a handkerchief. He kept sniffing and looking around to borrow a tissue. The teacher who was administering the test thought he was cheating and made him start over. He was too upset to explain. He had to complete the test in the remaining ten minutes and never even saw the last page.

a. List five reasons why Ted's resulting IQ score of 82 may not be accurate.

1. _____

2. _____

3. _____

4. _____

5. _____

b. Suggest a way for Ted to find more accurate information about his ability to learn. _____

_____

Please check your responses in the Feedback section.

Classification. Intelligence tests measure your "intelligence quotient" or IQ. The IQ classification system is based on the scores obtained on individual tests, but most group tests have adopted the same labels.

Score	Classification
0–29	Untrainable
30–49	Trainable
50–69	Educable
70–79	Borderline
80–89	Dull normal
90–109	Average
110–119	Bright normal
120–129	Superior
130 and above	Very superior

The use of classification and labeling based on IQ scores has been sharply criticized. Even the best test of intelligence can have errors of five to ten IQ points. Also, because cultural factors contribute to IQ scores, disadvantaged children can be mislabeled. A teacher who identifies a child as dull normal or borderline is not likely to seek challenging tasks to stimulate the child. Many schools use track systems that separate children into educational channels according to their scores on group tests. Children in the lower tracks usually are given fewer opportunities. These children often are from families or school systems that have less stimulating activities.

Limitations. Several psychologists have argued that current intelligence testing has an extremely narrow focus. Gardner (1983) pointed out that traditional IQ tests really only measure three things: language ability, mathematical/logical reasoning, and spatial/perceptual skills. Gardner believes there are other aspects of intelligence. He includes musical ability, bodily ability, intrapersonal ability (self-understanding), and interpersonal ability (understanding of others). Gardner (1985) found that intelligence tests correlate well only with schoolwork. They do not correlate well with later growth and accomplishments. As the article in Exhibit 5-7 points out, improvement in IQ scores does not necessarily bring improvements to society.

Wagner and Sternberg (1985) argued that intelligence tests do not measure practical skills. They contend that there are nonacademic skills that are not taught but are closely related to business success. Such skills include:

- The ability to adapt to new or unexpected situations
- The ability to have sudden insights when solving problems
- The ability to size things up and learn from examples rather than instruction

The article in Exhibit 5-8 shows the difference between standard IQ test questions and the type of questions suggested by Sternberg.

Exercise 5-9
Imagine that Gardner and Sternberg decided to write a new IQ test together. They both agree that they want to expand the scope of questions beyond the usual questions on language ability, logical reasoning, and perceptual skills. List seven additional areas that they would test.

a. _____

b. _____

EXHIBIT 5-7

145
THINKING AND
PROBLEM SOLVING

IQ Gains: A Rational Revolution?

The interpretation of IQ scores is a notoriously controversial business. And the results of a new study are likely to add to the debate.

James R. Flynn, a New Zealand political scientist, surveyed data from 14 countries—including the United States, the Netherlands, France, Canada, Japan, and Great Britain—to see whether intelligence-test scores changed from one generation to the next. Flynn found "massive" increases: The gain averaged the equivalent of 15 IQ points in a single generation (30 years).

What are the consequences of this new generation gap? Flynn says that if the traditional view of IQ is correct, "a generation with a massive IQ gain should radically outperform its predecessors."

But nothing of the kind has been seen. For example, the Netherlands today has almost 60 times more "potential geniuses" (people with IQ's greater than 150) than it did in 1952, yet a recent study found no dramatic increase in scientific discovery there. Indeed, the number of patents granted each year has decreased by one-third.

The increase in IQ scores calls into question the significance of the tests. While the tests do measure abstract problem-solving ability, Flynn concludes that the skills needed to answer IQ-test questions "can diverge over time from the real-world problem-solving ability called intelligence."

Though the cause of the score increases is not yet understood, the "cultural distance" between two generations must be [the] key. However, similar gaps separate the cultures of different racial or socioeconomic groups within a single generation. Flynn argues that the reported IQ differences between such groups do not imply meaningful differences in intelligence.

Source: Rubin, J. (1987, November). IQ gains: A rational revolution? *Psychology Today.*

c. _____

d. _____

e. _____

f. _____

g. _____

Check your list in the Feedback section.

Other Standardized Tests

Other than IQ, most standardized tests measure either achievement or specific aptitudes. *Achievement tests* are designed to measure academic success. Your score on a standardized achievement test may be compared with the average scores of other students. Most achievement tests give a *grade-level score*. This means that your score was roughly the same as the average student with a certain number of years schooling. A girl with a reading grade level of 10.0 reads at about the same level as most 10th-grade students who took the test.

Aptitude tests are supposed to differ from achievement tests. Aptitude indicates potential, while achievement suggests specific accomplishments. However, in truth, most aptitude tests measure accomplishments. One of the best predictors of future performance is your present achievement. Have you ever taken the Scholastic Aptitude Test (SAT) or American College Testing program (ACT)? Both are aptitude tests used to predict aca-

achievement test Test designed to measure past accomplishments, particularly in academic subjects

aptitude test Test of potential used to predict future success

EXHIBIT 5-8

A Different Sort of I.Q. Test

Standard I.Q. tests measure, in the main, two varieties of intelligence—verbal and logical-mathematical. But according to critics like Robert Sternberg, a Yale psychologist, tests should measure other key elements of intelligence, such as insight. The first two questions on this quiz, which is taken from Dr. Sternberg's book "Intelligence Applied," are standard I.Q. questions that he says rely for their answers on specific skills a child learns in school. But the other questions, he says, measure the sort of intelligence not found on standard I.Q. tests and depend for answers on such mental skills as insight, thinking in novel ways and detecting fallacies. The answers appear below.

Standard I.Q. Questions:
1 TENNIS is to RACQUET as BASE-BALL is to:
   a. Club
   b. Strike
   c. Bat
   d. Home run
2 In the following series what number comes next? 3, 7, 12, 18
   a. 24
   b. 25
   c. 26
   d. 27

Insight Questions
3 Aeronautical engineers have made it possible for a supersonic jet fighter to catch up with the bullets fired from its own guns with sufficient speed to shoot itself down. If a plane, flying at 1000 miles an hour, fires a burst, the rounds leave the plane with an initial velocity of about 3000 miles an hour. Why won't a plane that continues to fly straight ahead overtake and fly into its own bullets?
4 If you have black socks and brown socks in your drawer, mixed in a ratio of 4 to 5, how many socks will you have to take out to make sure of having a pair of the same color?
5 In the Thompson family, there are five brothers, and each brother has one sister. If you count Mrs. Thompson, how many females are there in the Thompson family?

Novel Thinking Questions
In solving the following analogies, assume that the statement given before the analogy is true, whether it actually is true or not, and use that assumption to solve the analogy.

6 LAKES are dry.
   TRAIL is to HIKE as LAKE is to:
   a. Swim
   b. Dust
   c. Water
   d. Walk
7 DEER attack tigers.
   LION is to COURAGEOUS as DEER is to:
   a. Timid
   b. Aggressive
   c. Cougar
   d. Elk
8 DIAMONDS are fruits.
   PEARL is to OYSTER as DIAMOND is to:
   a. Mine
   b. Tree
   c. Ring
   d. Pie

Inference Questions
The following problems require detecting the relationship between the first two items, and finding a parallel relationship between the second two. In answering, explain what those relationships are.

9 VANILLA is to BEAN as TEA is to LEAF.
10 ATOM is to MOLECULE as CELL is to ORGANISM.
11 UNICORN is to SINGLE as DUET is to BICYCLE.
12 NOON is to EVE as 12:21 is to 10:01.

Answers
1 c
2 b
3 Gravity pulls the bullets down; thus unless a pilot consciously dives to run into the bullets, they will not hit the plane.
4 Three.
5 Two. The only females in the family are the mother and her daughter, who is the sister to each of her brothers.

6	*d*	11	A unicorn and a single both refer to one of something, a duet and a bicycle both refer to two of something.
7	*b*		
8	*b*		
9	Vanilla comes from a bean, and tea from a leaf.	12	Each of the terms of the analogy is the same forward and backward.
10	Atoms combine to form a molecule, cells combine to form an organism.		

Source: Goleman, D. (1986, Nov. 9). A different sort of IQ test. *New York Times.*

demic success in higher education. However, both include tests of reading comprehension, general knowledge, and other skills associated with academic accomplishments.

Aptitude tests have a broader latitude than measurement of academic potential. Psychologists have developed tests of psychomotor abilities, athletic potential, mechanical ability, musical and artistic talent, and creativity. In most cases these aptitude tests are based on skills and attributes possessed by accomplished people in the specific field.

The development of the computer has clearly increased interest in problem solving and the process of thinking. Further, the computer has eased the development and scoring of tests, making evaluations less expensive and more available. Recent improvements in medical technology have also provided strong insights into how the brain functions as we think (see Exhibit 5-9). Perhaps future abilities testing will be done by electronic devices!

Checkpoint

Use the following questions to check your understanding of this final portion of the chapter. Choose and mark the one correct response to each question.

EXHIBIT 5-9

Thinking Too Much Might Not Be Smart

Figures of speech describing the process of problem-solving often use energy-intensive imagery in which our brains are kept busy "cranking out answers," "grinding away at problems," and "crunching numbers." But new research suggests that mental performance need not be so trying.

Richard Haier of the University of California at Irvine has preliminary data showing a relationship between higher scores on intelligence tests and lower rates of metabolism in the brain's cortical areas. One interpretation of the research, he says, is that people who perform better on intelligence tests may have more energy-efficient neural circuitry.

Haier had his subjects perform the Raven's Advanced Progressive Matrices test, a difficult, standardized, nonverbal test of abstract reasoning, while he performed positron emission tomography (PET) scans on their brains. The test requires that subjects recognize a pattern within a matrix of abstract designs and then select another design that completes the pattern. PET scans allow direct measurement of brain function by graphically depicting areas with higher glucose metabolism.

"Although one might assume that a good performer's brain would 'work harder' than that of a subject who did poorly," says Haier, "our data suggest that the opposite is true."

Source: (1988, February 27). Thinking too much may not be smart. *Science News.*

19. Mrs. T claims the test she is using is standardized. What can you assume?
    a. It is an achievement test.
    b. It is an intelligence test.
    c. It has never been used before.
    d. It was tried on a large population.

20. Which of the following factors is a problem in measuring intelligence?
    a. People will not take intelligence tests.
    b. Many factors influence intelligence.
    c. There is no classification system for intelligence.
    d. There are no tests that show strengths and weaknesses.

21. What is the advantage of individual intelligence tests over group tests?
    a. Psychologists can observe behavior.
    b. Individual tests are shorter.
    c. Individual tests are cheaper.
    d. All of the above

22. Why are the Wechsler scales considered the most useful individual tests?
    a. They measure creative and artistic abilities.
    b. They show patterns of strengths and weaknesses.
    c. They do not require the presence of a psychologist.
    d. They can be connected to electronic devices.

23. What is one disadvantage of group tests?
    a. They are more expensive.
    b. They require many psychologists.
    c. They are difficult to score.
    d. They are less accurate.

24. What is one problem that often arises from the current classification system for IQ scores?
    a. Standardization
    b. Functional fixedness
    c. Mislabeling
    d. Predicate thinking

25. Why are the current IQ tests being criticized?
    a. They are too narrow in focus.
    b. They are too broad in focus.
    c. They are used too often.
    d. They are not used enough.

26. Which of the following areas is not measured on traditional IQ tests?
    a. Verbal ability
    b. Insight
    c. Reasoning
    d. Perceptual skills

27. Millie, a first grader, has a reading grade-level score of 3.0. What does this mean?
    a. Millie has the reading ability of a 3-year-old.
    b. Millie is in the bottom 3 percent of her class.
    c. Millie reads at the level of most third graders.
    d. Millie is in the top 3 percent of her class.

28. Which area is supposed to be measured by the SAT and ACT?

    a. Intelligence

    b. Achievement

    c. Insight

    d. Aptitude

Check your responses against the Checkpoint Answer Key at the end of the chapter. If you had difficulty with any question, reread the text. If you had little or no difficulty answering the questions or have resolved problems that you might have had, you are ready to check yourself against the chapter inventory that follows.

CHAPTER INVENTORY

Use this list of objectives as a review checklist. You should be able to do each of the tasks outlined in the objectives and apply them to everyday examples. If you can, you may feel confident that you have mastered the material in this chapter.

1. Define cognition and differentiate among three forms of thought.
2. Explain how scripts are used.
3. State the sequence of logical thought, and distinguish between logical and predicate thought.
4. Describe critical thinking.
5. Isolate four steps involved in problem solving.
6. Explain how mental set and functional fixedness can impair problem solving.
7. Define artificial intelligence.
8. Describe creativity and identify the characteristics of creative thinkers.
9. Identify ways to improve creativity.
10. Specify the limitations of teaching creativity.
11. Describe the purpose of intelligence tests.
12. Explain the limitations of group intelligence tests.
13. Identify the narrow focus of traditional intelligence tests.
14. Explain the difference between aptitude and achievement.

Feedback

The correct answers to the exercises follow. If you did not answer an exercise correctly, review the preceding pages and return to the exercise to correctly complete it.

5-1. You might have listed any three of the following:

    a. People bring gifts to birthday parties.

    b. A kite is a possible gift.

    c. Kites cost money.

    d. Money is kept in piggy banks.

    e. Money in piggy banks makes a sound.

    f. Piggy banks with no money make no sound.

5-2. *a.* Therefore, the college will be closed.

    b. X

  c. X

  d. Therefore, the telephone will ring. (Assuming that the premises are really true...)

5-3. a. Try to see both sides. (Are there reasons why you should not chew it?)

  b. Look for inconsistencies in statements.

  c. Separate logical ideas from emotional arguments.

  d. Don't be afraid to question a weak-sounding argument.

5-4. See Figure 5-6.

5-5. Most psychologists would not consider his invention creative. Windows are not unusual and he has not developed a new solution.

5-6. ☑ Confident

  ☑ Independent

  ☑ Moody

  ☑ Persistent

5-7. − Avoid ideas that our computer can't handle

  + Take your time and come up with plenty of ideas.

  + Feel free to be unconventional.

  + Talk out your ideas.

  − Eliminate ideas that might be expensive.

  − Stick with the toy company's image.

  + Think of unconventional ways to use our equipment.

5-8. a. 1 Ted was sick.

  2 He was distracted by his need for a tissue.

  3 The teacher who was administering the test was not aware of the problem.

  4 He became upset when he was accused of cheating. This compounded his difficulties.

  5 He did not have enough time to complete the test.

  b. Ted could take an individual intelligence test, administered by a psychologist.

5-9. a. Musical ability

  b. Bodily ability

  c. Self-understanding

  d. Understanding of others

  e. Ability to adapt to new situations

  f. Insight ability

  g. Ability to size things up

Checkpoint Answer Key

1. c	**8.** f	**15.** d	**22.** b
2. i	**9.** b	**16.** b	**23.** d
3. h	**10.** g	**17.** d	**24.** c
4. a	**11.** c	**18.** a	**25.** a
5. e	**12.** b	**19.** d	**26.** b
6. j	**13.** a	**20.** b	**27.** c
7. d	**14.** c	**21.** a	**28.** d

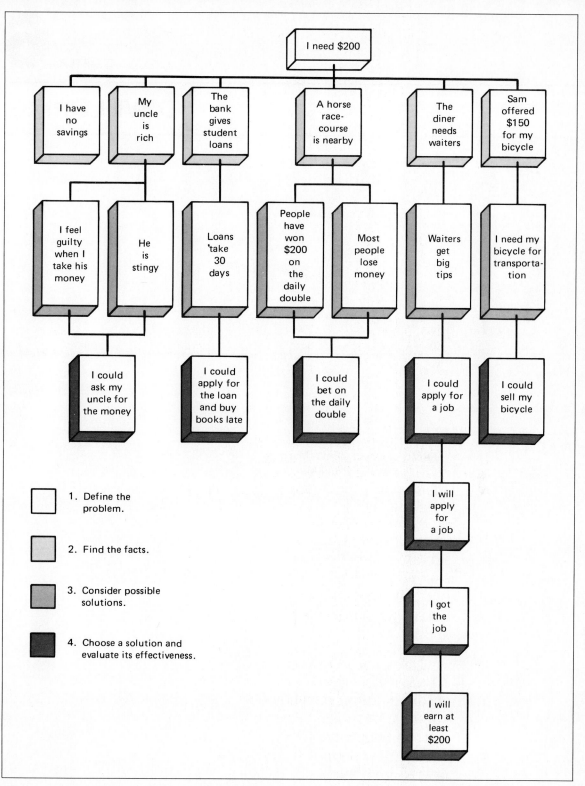

Figure 5-6

CHAPTER 6

DEVELOPING

Age only matters when one is aging. Now that I have arrived at a great age, I might as well be 20.

Pablo Picasso (at 80)

How far back can you remember? Can you recall events from the first year of your life? The second or third years? Chances are you have a few blurry memories of your early childhood. Yet undoubtedly many incidents back from that period affected the type of person you are today. Such factors as far past as your mother's health during her pregnancy, the absence or presence of your father, and the type of discipline that your parents used had strong impacts on your development.

Your recall of school-age events is probably a bit sharper. Here, teachers and peers became major influences. Peers became even more significant during your adolescence. In this chapter you will not only consider these earlier stages of development, but you will also focus on the responsibilities of adult life and the changes and adjustments required in your continued development through middle and old age.

The process of development begins with conception. As incredible as it may seem, every human began with the uniting of two cells. How people grow, change, and face adjustments is the focus of developmental psychology. In this chapter you will begin by reviewing the importance of a decision to become a parent and the responsibilities and knowledge required. Next you will look at each stage of development, from conception through old age, and consider the characteristics and problems encountered.

PARENTHOOD

Although it is best if parenthood is the result of a carefully considered decision, many individuals become parents accidentally. Numerous unwanted babies are born. A steadily increasing number of babies are born out of wedlock to teenage mothers. Although some are welcomed, most are not. Current estimates suggest that there are more than 1 million abortions in the United States each year. These abortions are the result of unwanted and unplanned pregnancies.

Since parenting requires considerable responsibility and commitment, psychologists feel that it is best to learn about child rearing prior to pregnancy. As the child develops, parents tend to become involved in current problems and adjustments, and they have less time to learn. Although there have been rumors claiming the existence of a maternal instinct that permits any woman to rear children perfectly, there has been no support for this claim. Women are no more talented than men in rearing children. There is neither a maternal nor a paternal instinct. Both mothers and fathers need to learn about child development to be effective parents.

In addition to an understanding of the nature of human development, it is also useful for both parents to understand how children are likely to affect their marriage. It is important for parents to consider and agree upon a desirable family size, their roles as parents, and the type of discipline preferred. By sharing ideas and reaching agreement about child-rearing methods, parents are more likely to be consistent and relaxed in caring for children.

Effects of Children on a Marriage

Occasionally couples who are having difficulties with their marriage will decide to have a child, believing the baby will bring them closer together. This decision usually results in a broken marriage. It is indeed rare for a child to save a marriage that is floundering. The presence of a new baby usually has a strong emotional impact on both mother and father. There is very little time for transition in adjusting to a new baby. The infant is suddenly there, so husband and wife must abruptly shift to roles of father and mother. Both the transition and commitment are more immediate than in marriage.

There is an additional responsibility, since parents realize that they cannot divorce their children. Spitz (1965) noted that the presence of a child often exposes problems and jealousies that were previously unnoticed. A husband who was insecure about his relationship with his wife will often be jealous of the attention that she focuses on their offspring. Husbands and wives who are immature may find the responsibility of caring for a child burdensome. The child will then become the subject of arguments over duties and obligations.

Even in mature relationships, the presence of an infant may be expected to cause some disruptions. But parents who are happy with each other and with the newborn infant are willing to make the required adjustments.

Family Size and Planning

Quite often family size does not result from choice. In the past decade there has been an apparent increase in infertility among married couples in the United States. If you were given a choice, would you prefer to be an only child, a member of a large family, or one of two siblings? Each of these family sizes has advantages and disadvantages. Although only children generally gain more materially and have more adult attention, many complain of loneliness and more pressure from their parents. Members of larger families are rarely lonely. Some complain of a lack of privacy, where others grumble about not having enough attention from their parents. There is often competition among brothers and sisters. This competition within the family has been labeled ''sibling rivalry'' by psychologists. Sibling rivalry is common even in families where there are only two or three children. Although lack of sibling rivalry may be considered an advantage of being an only child, the only child may feel competitive and have difficulty sharing when interacting with other children.

sibling rivalry
Competition among
brothers and sisters
in a family

Exercise 6-1

Each of the following statements was made by a misinformed individual. Help set the person straight by supplying correct information.

a. ''Why bother with child psychology? All women have a maternal instinct and know exactly how to raise children.''
nobody knows exactly how to raise their children plus it would put them more at ease knowing what to expect.

b. ''My wife and I are not getting along. We argue constantly. We have decided to start a family so we can have a common interest.'' _starting a family will not resolve the problem but make it worse_

c. ''When and if I ever meet someone I want to marry, I plan to have at least ten children. Children in large families are always happier.'' _untrue_

d. "I would never have more than one child. Only children have every advantage and no disadvantages." ___untrue_____

You may compare your responses with the ones given in the Feedback section.

Parental Roles

Traditionally, child care, emotional support, and housework were part of the roles of mothers and wives. Fathers set rules and provided authority in the family. They were also the source of financial support and contact with the community. Although the traditional roles may still be encountered in some homes, more often the father exhibits less authority and participates more in household duties and child care. According to the article in Exhibit 6-1, this shifting of roles has presented some problems for marriages.

Many fathers-to-be begin adjusting to their new roles during their wife's pregnancy. Although the woman plays the primary role in carrying the child, the expectant father plays a significant role in providing emotional support. Women who share their feelings and concerns with their husbands during pregnancy can usually deepen their relationships. Women who turn their feelings inward and do not communicate their feelings often find their husbands feel

EXHIBIT 6-1

Married with Child

Parents of young children beware! Your children are surviving day-care centers, but your marriage may not be surviving the shared child-care responsibilities.

With more women entering the work force, more men are entering the child-care force. Picking Johnny up from day-care, feeding him dinner and giving him a bath has become Dad's job as well as Mom's. And as the free hours in the day disappear, the marriage may begin to suffer, observe Ann C. Crouter, an associate professor of human development at Pennsylvania State University, and her colleagues.

Crouter's group compared the role of the father in two types of families. In one, the father was the sole supporter; in the other, both parents were employed. The researchers found that fathers whose wives were employed spent more time caring for the children than did those who supported the family alone. Unfortunately, spending more time with the children did not bring more harmony to the family.

Among men whose wives were employed, the greater their involvement with their children the greater their unhappiness with their marriage. The other men did not experience the same frustrations.

Why are fathers who share the provider role less happy? Crouter and colleagues suggest that with both parents at work during the day the remaining hours are quickly filled with child-care and other household responsibilities. Mom and Dad have little time or energy left to enjoy being together without the children around. Additionally, some men may resent their increased share of household chores.

Not all men whose wives are employed were unhappy with their marriages, the researchers report (*Developmental Psychology,* Vol. 23, pp. 431–440). And by no means are employed wives bad for the family. They do point out, however, that dual-income couples should recognize the additional burdens they carry and would do well to set aside time to be together—alone.

Source: Berfein, J. (1988, February). Married with child. *Psychology Today.*

neglected. Interestingly, several studies have reported that expectant fathers have even more anxiety about the well-being of the baby than their wives (Lamb, 1979; Greenberg & Morris, 1974; Lynn, 1974). Chapter 12 covers male and female roles in marriages in greater detail.

Child-Rearing Styles

Psychologist Diana Baumrind (1967, 1970) differentiates among three styles of child rearing. Think about your own childhood. How did your parents discipline you? Discipline is a way of regulating behavior. Did they use a set of rigid rules? If you were told what to do without any reasons or explanations, your parents were using an *authoritarian approach*. In an authoritarian environment, a parent might tell a child to wear mittens. If the child asks "Why?" the parent would reply "Because I said so!" If the child does not comply, the mittens are forced on and the child is spanked for not adhering to the rule. The parents would use the same method to be certain the child ate balanced meals, went to bed on time, shared toys, and completed chores. The child would not be given choices. In an authoritarian home, parents make the decisions and use external force and punishment to be sure that rules are kept.

Perhaps your home atmosphere was far looser and less structured. In a *permissive approach,* little or no discipline is used. If your parents chose this rearing style, you had few rules, limits, or boundaries. A child raised by permissive parents would be asked, "Would you like to wear mittens today?" and would be allowed to wear them or not wear them regardless of the weather. Similarly, the child would choose meals and bedtime and participate with other children and family activities as desired. This style of child rearing is sometimes chosen by parents who were raised in an authoritarian atmosphere. They resent the approach used on them and select a permissive style in protest

authoritarian discipline
Regulating the behavior of others by rigid rules

permissive approach
Method using little or no discipline

In a permissive approach to child rearing, there are few boundaries and rules. (*Mark Antman/The Image Works*)

against their own parents' methods. Some parents are afraid to confront their children. Others believe that children must learn by their own mistakes. Such parents, as well as those who are too busy or disinterested, will often choose a permissive approach.

Both the authoritarian and permissive styles of child rearing are extremes. Most parents choose a middle ground. Chances are you were reared in a more *democratic environment*. In a democratic home, children are given rules and restrictions, but the rules are usually accompanied by an explanation. A child might be cautioned to wear mittens because the weather is cold or to go to bed because everyone feels better after a good rest. If the child can give a good reason for not keeping a rule, parents will listen and perhaps grant an exception. The aim in a democratic approach to discipline is to have children learn to control their own behavior.

democratic approach Method using explanations and reasoning for rules

Most psychologists feel that democratic methods of discipline are preferable. Children reared in either authoritarian or permissive homes usually experience problems in adjusting to different school environments. However, children reared in democratic homes can usually adjust to either permissive or authoritarian environments with little difficulty.

Exercise 6-2

Indicate what type of discipline each of the following examples illustrates: authoritarian, permissive, or democratic.

a. Joan's usual bedtime is 8 P.M. She told her mother that she wanted to stay up later tonight to watch a special Halloween program on television. Her mother agreed to let her stay up a half-hour later, since Joan could sleep later the next morning. _~~permissive~~ Demo_

b. Gary is expected to study every evening from 7 P.M. until 9 P.M. He is not permitted to make or receive phone calls during study time. Last night he called a friend during study time to check on the pages required in his social studies assignment. His father fined him $1 and told Gary he would not listen to excuses. _Author,_

c. Nelson wants to have a friend over for dinner tonight. His mother explained that she only had enough pork chops for members of the family. She suggested that Nelson invite his friend the next night when his father would be preparing a large batch of spaghetti. _Demo_

d. Julie throws toys all around her house. Her parents often trip and have difficulty walking from room to room. They believe that Julie will decide if the toys need to be picked up. _perm._

You may check your responses in the Feedback section.

PRENATAL CONCERNS

The first stage of development begins with conception. The greatest percentage of a person's growth occurs between conception and birth. The importance of prenatal care cannot be overemphasized. The health of the mother during pregnancy will have a marked influence on the life of the child she is carrying. Illnesses such as rubella (German measles), syphilis, tuberculosis, and certain types of influenza can affect the fetus adversely. A mother who has the virus for acquired immune deficiency syndrome (AIDS) can infect her fetus. Infants infected with AIDS have had head and facial abnormalities (Marion, Wiznia, Hutcheon, & Rubinstein, 1986).

Drillien and Ellis (1964) pointed to evidence that women with adequate diets were more likely to have healthy babies and uncomplicated births than malnourished women. The National Center for Health Statistics (1986) recommends a weight gain of about 26 to 35 pounds. Women who gain less weight are more likely to miscarry, have a stillborn baby, or a baby under 5 pounds. Women who gain more than 35 pounds put their fetus at risk. A pregnant woman's use of drugs, alcohol, tobacco, and caffeine can have noticeable effects on her unborn child. Perhaps the most severe problems occur from addictive drugs. The unborn child becomes addicted and must go through a narcotic withdrawal at birth. The detrimental effects of cocaine are described in Exhibit 6-2.

Engstrom et al. (1964) confirmed that women who are tense and unhappy about their pregnancy have more problems in the prenatal stage and more difficult deliveries at birth. The investigators also found that children of anxious pregnant women are generally less well adjusted throughout their development.

Sometimes expectant parents are concerned about the possibility of their child inheriting an illness present in either or both of their families. Genetic counselors can usually provide mathematical odds but cannot be certain. A technique called "amniocentesis" is generally a better predictor. A physician takes a sample of the fluid the fetus is floating in. There is a very slight risk of hurting the fetus, but the procedure permits the detection of Down's syndrome, Turner's syndrome, sickle cell anemia, Rh disease, and other possible birth defects.

amniocentesis
Procedure involving the removal of fluid samples from the uterus of an expectant mother to detect possible disease or genetic defects

THE BIRTH PROCESS: APPROACHES AND ORIENTATIONS

In recent years there has been an increasing concern about the conditions that surround the birth of an infant. Many American mothers receive an anesthetic just prior to the birth of the baby. Some receive a general anesthetic, so they are completely unconscious at the time of birth. Others receive regional anesthetics, so they are awake but not aware of pain. In both situations the drugs they receive are passed into the infant's bloodstream. Haire (1972) found that babies of mothers who had received anesthetics had a greater chance of birth injury and respiratory problems. Brazelton (1970) noted that the drugs affected the motor activities and muscular responses of the baby during its first week of life. Their findings have been substantiated by many other studies during the past decade. As a result, there has been a recent increase in the number of drugless childbirths.

Lamaze method A preparation for active and conscious participation in the birth process

The most popular form of drugless childbirth is the *Lamaze method*. This method is often referred to as "prepared childbirth," since the expectant mother must begin preparing for the birth several months before the baby is due. She learns to use breathing and muscular reactions in response to uterine contractions. She feels less pain because she is distracted by her need to control her breathing and muscles. (Chapter 2 describes the relationship between

EXHIBIT 6-2

159

DEVELOPING

Crack Comes to the Nursery

More and More Cocaine-Using Mothers Are Bearing Afflicted Infants

When reports surfaced in the early 1980s that cocaine use by pregnant women could cause serious physical and mental impairment to their newborns, it was another warning that the snowy white drug was not as harmless as some believed. Doctors found that cocaine, like heroin and alcohol, could be passed from the user-mother to the fetus with disastrous results. Since then the epidemic of cocaine-afflicted babies has only become worse. The main reason: growing numbers of women are using crack, the cheap and readily available purified form of cocaine that plagues America's inner cities and has spread into middle-class suburbs. Says Dr. Richard Fulroth, a Stanford University neonatologist: "The women have tears streaming down their cheeks when they tell me, 'In the back of my mind I knew I was hurting my baby, but in the front of it, I needed more rocks.'"

...As doctors see more and more crack-damaged infants—many of them premature—a clearer picture of the effects of the drug on the fetus is emerging. It is not a pretty one. Because a mother's crack binge triggers spasms in the baby's blood vessels, the vital flow of oxygen and nutrients can be severely restricted for long periods. Fetal growth, including head and brain size, may be impaired, strokes and seizures may occur, and malformations of the kidneys, genitals, intestines, and spinal cord may develop. If the cocaine dose is large enough, the blood supply can be cut so sharply that the placenta may tear loose from the uterus, putting the mother in danger and killing the fetus. The horrid litany is not just the result of binges. Even one "hit" of crack can irreparably damage a fetus or breast-fed baby.

At birth the babies display obvious signs of crack exposure—tremors, irritability and lethargy—that may belie the seriousness of the harm done. These symptoms may disappear in a week or more, but the underlying damage remains. While the long-term effects of crack are unknown. Stanford's Fulroth points out that children born with small heads often have lower than normal I.Q. levels by ages three to six.

Because there is no specific treatment for cocaine babies, therapists must work with the mothers. Parenting programs are teaching women how to handle the babies' long bouts of inconsolable crying and unresponsiveness. But such programs are usually designed for motivated women with some financial resources. Says Dr. Robert Cefalo, of the University of North Carolina School of Medicine: "We should be reaching these women before they conceive."

Two often, that is difficult to do. Crack mothers who show up at hospitals have often smoked up to the last stages of labor. Many are so high they do not notice when labor begins. Says Fulroth: "The crack cocaine mothers are the sickest you're going to see. They come in right when they're ready to deliver, and you just hold your breath waiting to see what you're gonna get." The message is clear: for expectant mothers—and their babies—crack is a nightmare.

Source: Langone, J. (1988, September 19). Crack comes to the nursery. *Time.*

distraction and pain.) The baby benefits, since the mother does not usually need drugs. As an added benefit, the mother is awake and alert and can enjoy the birth experience. Often, the father assists and plays a supporting role.

A more controversial approach to childbirth has been suggested by Leboyer (1975). In an attempt to minimize the shock of birth, Leboyer advised that delivery rooms should be dimly lit and the baby handled gently. In the *Leboyer method*, the baby is not slapped. Rather the infant is placed in a warm

Leboyer method
Childbirth method that attempts to minimize shock to the newborn infant

bath and then laid on the mother's belly. Among the criticisms hurled against this technique are concerns about exposing the baby to germs from the water and the mother's body, and worries that the physician may not see problems because of the poor lighting. The article in Exhibit 6-3 describes the controversy over the relative merits of using the Leboyer method.

Exercise 6-3

Anita, who is one month pregnant, has several bad habits. She has three cups of coffee with breakfast and is a constant gum chewer. She swears, smokes at least twenty cigarettes each day, and sips cola beverages all afternoon. At about 5 P.M. Anita switches to bourbon. She usually has one or two drinks and then eats an enormous dinner. She is excited about becoming a mother and wants to do the right things for her baby. Her friends have told her that it is best to have a general anesthetic at delivery. She believes that she will be more relaxed if she does not feel the pain.

EXHIBIT 6-3

Leboyer Method Challenged

In *Birth Without Violence* (Alfred A. Knopf, 1975), Frederick Leboyer advocated ways to make birth a more humane process. Specifically, he advised that infants be delivered in a dark, quiet, warm room, not in a harshly lit, noisy, cold one; that infants not be given the traditional slap on the rear and immediately severed from the umbilical cord, but be placed on their mothers' abdomens and kept attached to the cord for about five minutes; and that infants not be put on a cold scale but in a warm bath....

A study supporting the advantages of the Leboyer delivery over a more conventional one was published in 1976 by Danièle Rappoport of the French National Center for Scientific Research. Rappoport found that children born by the Leboyer approach seemed protected from the colic and shortness of breath sometimes seen during the first months of life, showed marked ambidexterity, began walking at an earlier age than average, displayed less than the normal amount of trouble in self-feeding and toilet training and had a higher-than-average IQ...A drawback of the study, however, was that no control subjects were used.

Now an investigation that fails to find the Leboyer method superior to a more conventional delivery is reported

...by Nancy M. Nelson and colleagues at McMaster University Medical Center in Hamilton, Ontario. Like the earlier study, though, it has some weaknesses.

Nelson and her co-workers randomly assigned 56 women to either a Leboyer delivery or a more conventional delivery, but one in which newborns were treated gently and encouraged to interact with their parents. For instance, infants in the latter group didn't get a slap on the rear, but were delivered in a room lit by fluorescent lights, were severed from the umbilical cord within a minute after delivery and did not get a warm bath. The researchers then used a variety of clinical and behavioral tests to assess the outcome of the infants in both groups. As they report, no statistically significant differences between the two groups could be found in newborn deaths, or in infant behavior during the first hour of life, at 24 to 72 hours after birth, or at eight months of age. In fact, a number of newborns in the Leboyer group reacted to the warm bath with irritation and crying, not pleasure. These results, Nelson and her colleagues conclude, suggest that the Leboyer procedure is no more beneficial to children than a more conventional, gentle delivery is.

Source: (1980, April 8). Leboyer method challenged. *Science News.*

Anita is now asking for your advice. Which of her bad habits should be eliminated? Do you agree with her friends about the use of a general anesthetic? *She should eliminate drinking coffee & sodas, smoking, alcohol, not eat enormous amts of food. She needs to be calm and not swear or get irritated. She should not have a general anesthetic. If all these bad habits she has acquired*

You may compare your advice with that given in the Feedback section. *cont. the baby is already at risk. a general anest. will put the baby under even more risk.*

PATTERNS OF DEVELOPMENT

Development is a continuous process that begins at conception. Once infants are born they begin to experience complex changes physically, intellectually, and emotionally. The changes are gradual and occur throughout the lifespan. As a convenience, psychologists have separated the lifespan into stages and identified specific changes that may be expected during each period. When you are considering changes and adjustments at each stage, remember that the transition from each stage to the next is gradual rather than sudden. A child does not awaken on a third birthday with an abrupt change from babyhood to early childhood. Similarly the age groups assigned to each are general. There are vast individual differences. One person may progress to young adulthood at 16, while another will still be battling adolescent problems at 24.

Age	Stage
Birth–3 years	Babyhood
3–6 years	Early childhood
6–12	Later childhood
12–18	Adolescence
18–40	Young adulthood
40–65	Mature adulthood
Over 65	Aging adult

Checkpoint

Use the following questions to check your understanding of this portion of the chapter. Indicate whether each statement is true or false.

1. __F__ Women have a natural ability to rear children because of their maternal instinct.
2. __F__ The birth of a child will usually strengthen a weak marriage.
3. __F__ Only children often feel lonely.
4. __T__ Competition among brothers and sisters is called "sibling rivalry."
5. __F__ Childbearing is a woman's task; the expectant father has no role.
6. __T__ Authoritarian parents do not give their children choices.
7. __F__ In a permissive home, children are restricted but are given explanations.
8. __T__ Most psychologists prefer democratic methods of discipline.
9. __T__ The greatest percentage of growth occurs during the prenatal period.

10. <u>F</u> The diet of a pregnant woman rarely affects her unborn child.

11. <u>T</u> Anxious women tend to have problems delivering their babies.

12. <u>T</u> Amniocentesis is a technique for detecting some genetic abnormalities in an unborn infant.

13. <u>F</u> Mothers who receive anesthetics during childbirth tend to have healthier babies.

14. <u>F</u> The Lamaze method of childbirth is natural and does not require any preparation.

15. <u>F</u> Each stage of development is distinct, with sudden changes occurring between stages.

Use the Checkpoint Answer Key to verify your responses. If you had any difficulty with a question, carefully reread the text. If you had little or no difficulty answering the questions or have resolved any problems that you might have had, you are ready to continue with the next portion of this chapter.

BABYHOOD

The firstborn baby is often a shock to new parents. The newborn rarely resembles babies seen in advertisements. Since advertisers are aware of the shortcomings of a newborn's appearance, they use babies between 6 and 12 months old. Infants are called "neonates" during their first two weeks of life. They usually have wrinkled, blotchy red skin and large heads that may be misshapen. Their necks are impossible to find beneath folds of skin. Nonetheless parents are usually so overjoyed with their offspring that they see beauty in the appearance.

neonate Newborn infant, usually less than two weeks old

Most neonates sleep two-thirds of the time, about sixteen hours each day. They follow a pattern of awakening when hungry and crying until fed. After feedings they remain alert and active a few minutes, then sleep for two or three hours until hunger strikes again. Some neonates experience difficulty sleeping and spend more time crying. Birns et al. (1966) found crying neonates can be soothed by rocking gently, humming in low tones, or speaking in a soothing manner. Some neonates are easier to comfort than others. There is also considerable variation in which method will be most effective. There are vast individual differences in neonate irritability. Unfortunately many parents fear they might spoil their new baby if they show attention. In reality, it is impossible to *spoil* neonates. They are totally reliant on others for survival. Affection and handling comfort them and help to relieve irritability. Unhappy neonates who are not shown attention tend to become more agitated and restless. Fathers can play an important role in relieving their infant's discomforts, since neonates usually respond to the lower frequencies of male voices.

What can neonates do? There is evidence of neonates' ability to recognize the voice of their mothers. There has been extensive evidence that learning begins at or before birth. The average neonate can see best at distances of about 8 inches, although others see best at spans from 7 to 15 inches. According to Pick and Pick (1970), other distances appear blurred.

Exercise 6-4

Assume you are babysitting for a 10-day-old baby girl. The mother fed her and has left. The baby was awake and moving her hands and feet for five minutes.

She then began crying. Her crying is growing louder. List three things you
could do to soothe the baby.

a. ___Rock the baby___

b. ___humming in low tones___

c. ___Speak in a soothing manner___

Turn to the Feedback section to check your list.

As the infant progresses from the neonate period through the babyhood
stage, the need for affection remains powerful. A baby who feels accepted and
loved by parents will feel worthy and lovable and will develop a positive self-
concept. By consistently satisfying their baby's needs, parents can help their
infant develop a sense of trust. By the end of their first year, most babies can
differentiate between strangers and familiar persons. Babies who have developed a sense of trust will feel secure with people they know, but they may be
skeptical of strangers.

One area of concern for many parents is how and when to feed the baby.
Common questions are, "Is it better to bottle-feed or breast-feed our baby?" and
"Should we use a feeding schedule or feed the baby on demand?" In response to
the first question, there are some advantages to breast-feeding infants. The infant
is provided with natural immunities passed through the mother's milk. The
mother is not burdened with the task of sterilizing bottles and keeping formula
available. However, the mother's freedom is somewhat restricted, and if she is
feeling depressed, burdened, or tied down by the baby, breast-feeding may tire
her and increase her despondency. According to Mussen et al. (1978) the attitude
and affection of the parent at feeding time are more important than whether the
bottle or breast is used. If the parent is affectionate, talking to and touching the
baby, the style of feeding will not matter.

The answer to the second question, whether to adhere to a feeding schedule, will depend on the lifestyle of the parents. Studies have shown that babies
who are fed on demand are at least as healthy as those fed on strict schedules.
Keeping in mind that feedings should be relaxed and happy times for the infant, the comfort and convenience of the parents are a prime concern. Parents
who awaken at precisely 7 A.M., have breakfast at 7:30 A.M., lunch at noon,
and dinner at exactly 7 P.M. will probably be more at ease if their baby is on a
schedule. In contrast, parents who awaken sometime between 6 and 10 A.M.,
sometimes skip breakfast and opt for a late brunch, nibble during the afternoon, and have dinner when they feel hungry will probably be more comfortable with a demand schedule. If the feedings are accompanied by warmth and
affection the baby will eventually adjust to either method.

In addition to affection, the baby also needs stimulation. Even during the
first months of life, babies prefer new and novel things (Fantz, 1958). Infants
enjoy mobiles and having their cribs moved to vary their view. Babies are usually fascinated when they enter a new room and surroundings. They need to
explore and manipulate objects. Touching, smelling, and listening are important. Once babies begin to crawl, their curiosity becomes heightened. Although playpens are safe places, babies also need time to investigate their en-

vironment. Children need to see new areas. Walks through the neighborhood and visits to stores and other people's homes will keep them stimulated.

During their first two years, babies play alone. They explore their surroundings, handle toys, and engage in make-believe. They often talk to themselves while playing. Language begins with babbling and cooing. Although most 1-year-olds can understand simple conversation, they usually can only speak a few words. Between one and two years, most babies learn to utter some word combinations. Words are usually mispronounced; for example, a blanket might be called a ''blah-blah.'' You are probably familiar with this type of baby talk. Should baby talk be corrected? Most psychologists would suggest that it not be corrected, since it might frustrate the child. However, parents should not repeat the baby-talk mispronunciation. Rather, they should enunciate the word correctly. Otherwise the child could be subject to future ridicule by other children.

Two-year-olds usually have some problems communicating. Because they lack vocabulary, they will try to make themselves understood by repeating their statements in louder voices. A child may ask, ''Cookie?'' If the father answers ''No,'' the child will say in a louder voice ''Cookie!'' as if the father did not hear or understand the first request. It usually helps if the parent informs the child that the request or message is understood. If the father responds ''I know you want a cookie right now, but I would rather you ate your lunch first. Finish your lunch and then have a cookie. If you want your cookie,

Figure 6-1
Thanks to the store manager, the children will be able to explore their environment!

"Sorry, Mrs. Martin . . . we let you, then everybody would want to do it."

eat some lunch.'' Two-year-olds need to be addressed in explicit terms. Often they are confused and frightened by idioms and expressions that they interpret literally. Figure 6-2 illustrates some common misunderstandings.

Dreams create another area of confusion. Many 2-year-olds believe that dreams come in through the window or the closet. Young children often fear the darkness of their rooms and have difficulty verbalizing and talking about these worries. Simple rituals such as pulling shades, closing closet doors, and using a night light can help allay these fears.

The most important accomplishment of babyhood is the development of independence. From newborns who are totally dependent on parents, babies

Tommy grew up overnight.

He plays the piano by ear.

It's raining cats and dogs.

He's the spitting image of his father.

I'm all thumbs.

I was tied up at work.

CANEVARI

Figure 6-2
Interpretations

gradually learn to understand, speak, walk, feed themselves, become toilet-trained, and partially dress themselves by the time they are 3. They should be encouraged to try things on their own. As babies become more accomplished, they also try to assert their independence. You have probably heard the expression, "the terrible two's." Two-year-olds are pleased with their skills and want to be recognized as individuals. "No" becomes a popular word in these youngsters' vocabularies. They have their own ideas and are unwilling to accept adult rules as readily as they did the previous year.

Exercise 6-5

In each of the following instances, a couple is expressing disagreement about their baby. Assume you have been asked to help them resolve their differences. For each of the following conflicts, indicate the person with whom you agree.

a. **George:** There is something wrong with Chester; he doesn't like strangers. Whenever a strange person picks him up, he cries.
Helen: Chester is normal. Now that he is almost 1 year old, he knows the difference between friends and strangers. He trusts people he knows, so he is perfectly normal.

George _____ or Helen __✔__

b. **Marsha:** We shouldn't put Lalla in a crib by herself to drink her bottle. We should talk to her and let her know we care while she is being fed.
Otto: Nonsense! We shouldn't distract her while she is drinking. She needs to be more independent now that she is 6 months old.

Marsha __✔__ or Otto _____

c. **Karla:** Now that we have a baby, we'll have to be far more organized. Babies have to eat every four hours. I'm going to be a nervous wreck trying to stick to a schedule, but I guess it's best for little Elliot.

Figure 6-3
Babies can be trying as they develop independence in feeding themselves.

Henry: I think little Elliot will get along just fine without a set schedule. Why don't we just feed him when he acts hungry? We always eat when we're hungry.

Karla _____ or Henry __✓__

d. **Patrick:** Let's keep our little baby Priscilla in her crib most of the time. If she stays in the same spot, she'll be more secure. If you move her around, she will become confused.
Michelle: I think we should let Priscilla see different things. She needs more stimulation than just the view from her crib.

Patrick _____ or Michelle __✓__

e. **Sidney:** Little Alicia always calls cookies "kakaks." I think we should call a cookie "cookie" so she learns the right word.
Diane: Oh, Alicia is so cute with her baby talk. Let's not spoil it by letting her hear the right word.

Sidney __✓__ or Diane _____

f. **Nellie:** I think that something is wrong with Larry. All of a sudden he is afraid to go to bed at night. He cries and claims he is scared. I'll bet it's just a big act to get attention. We probably should punish him for crying.
Bob: Larry is only 2 and maybe is afraid at night. Lots of 2-year-olds have fears. Don't punish him. Maybe we can figure out what's bothering him.

Nellie _____ or Bob __✓__

Turn to the Feedback section to check your choices.

EARLY CHILDHOOD

Early childhood has traditionally been referred to as the "preschool" period. However, today an increasing number of children between the ages of 3 and 6 are attending some sort of nursery school or day-care program. Most programs at these schools and facilities focus more on structured playing than on academic learning. Academic gains in kindergarten do not seem to be retained (see Exhibit 6-4).

Playing is an important occupation in early childhood. Through play activities the young child can often let out aggressive feelings and other emotions. A child who is frustrated by the demands of older brothers and sisters can release feelings by throwing a doll or stuffed animal against the wall or punishing it in some way. Positive emotions can also be expressed. Hugging and showing affection to dolls and stuffed animals are common in young children.

But play provides far more than emotional expression. The preschool child learns primarily through play activities (Piaget, 1952). Until age 2 or 3 most children play alone or parallel to other children. Even if several 2-year-olds are sitting on the floor together, each is usually playing independently. Each watches and copies the other children. By the time a child is 3, social play usually begins. Children play socially with each other and must learn to understand and talk to each other. In the process of learning to share and take turns, quarrels should be expected. Social play is considered the most important activity of preschool children. If other children are not available for inter-

EXHIBIT 6-4

Kindergarten Days: Too Much, Too Soon?

If a half day of kindergarten is good for kids, a whole day should be better. Following this line of thought, New York City instituted all-day kindergarten classes for the 1983–84 school year. At the end of the year, the children were tested and compared with those who had continued to attend half-day classes. The hoped-for results were found. All-day students, especially those whose first language was not English, made significantly greater gains than students in half-day classes did.

Those gains, however, were short-lived. Reading and mathematics tests administered at the end of second grade showed no measurable differences between children with half-day and full-day kindergarten experience, says educator Carolyn H. Jarvis of New York City's Board of Education. She reported her findings at the annual meeting of the American Psychological Association.

Source: Trotter, R. (1988, January). Kindergarten days: Too much, too soon? *Psychology Today.*

action, the preschool child's development will suffer. Children who live in isolated areas or do not have playmates should be brought to places where they can meet other children and learn to play happily and successfully.

Play activities also help young children develop motor coordination. Running and skipping games, block building, and seesaw and slide activities all help to develop gross motor coordination. Coloring, cutting, pasting, and doing simple jigsaw puzzles aid in the development of fine motor skills. These activities are generally included in nursery school programs. If a child is not exposed to an organized preschool program, parents should give their child opportunities to learn and benefit from such play activities.

Many children who do not have playmates spend considerable time watching television. Unfortunately these children are not learning important social skills and developing crucial motor skills. Not only should parents monitor the types of programs being watched but they should also take heed of the advertisements.

The advertisements that seemed to influence children most recommended low-nutrition foods. Young children's eating habits are a source of frustration for most parents. Because the growth rate slows down during early childhood, there is less interest in food. As a result, early childhood is a period of picky eating. As suggested in the humorous clipping in Exhibit 6-5, mealtime is often a continuation of play activities. Since appetites are diminished, parents have the difficult task of being certain that nutritious foods are eaten.

How can parents enforce rules about eating? Further, what is the best way to discipline a preschool child? According to Kohlberg (1969, 1976), most young children base their morality and sense of right and wrong on rewards and punishments. Actions that are punished are presumed to be bad. Rewarded actions are considered good. Young children base their values on the attitude of their parents and other people they care for. Ginott (1969) warned parents to criticize and scold *actions* rather than their children's personalities. For example, a young boy who clutters his toys on the kitchen floor should not be personally accused of being "sloppy" or "stupid." Instead, the punishment should be focused on the disarray of the toys. An appropriate scolding might be, "When you throw your toys all over the kitchen floor, I get annoyed. The

EXHIBIT 6-5

169
DEVELOPING

How to Eat Like a Child and Other Lessons in Not Being a Grown-Up

Peas: Mash and flatten into thin sheet on plate. Press the back of the fork into the peas. Hold fork vertically, prongs up, and lick off peas.

Mashed potatoes: Pat mashed potatoes flat on top. Dig several little depressions. Think of them as ponds or pools. Fill the pools with gravy. With your fork, sculpt rivers between pools and watch the gravy flow between them. Decorate with peas. Do not eat.

Alternative method: Make a large hole in center of mashed potatoes.

Pour in ketchup. Stir until potatoes turn pink. Eat as you would peas.

Spinach: Divide into little piles. Rearrange into new piles. After five or six maneuvers, sit back and say you are full.

French fries: Wave one French fry in air for emphasis while you talk. Pretend to conduct orchestra. Then place four fries in your mouth at once and chew. Turn to your sister, open your mouth, and stick out your tongue coated with potatoes. Close mouth and swallow. Smile.

Source: Ephron, D. (1979, June). How to eat like a child. *Saturday Evening Post.*

---

room looks sloppy and someone could get hurt." Ginott feels strongly that positive alternatives should be offered. A parent might add, "The room will look tidy if you put your toys in the bin. Then it will be safe for us." By following Ginott's advice, parents can help their children develop a better understanding of values, along with a positive self-image.

Exercise 6-6

Assume that you must help develop a set of guidelines for a new day-care center for children ages 3 to 6. For each heading make some suggestions for the program. The first has been done for you.

a. Social play: Allow time for the children to interact with each other. Play group games and have activities that require sharing and taking turns.

b. Gross motor activities: _____

_____

_____

c. Fine motor skills: _____

_____

_____

d. Television: _____

_____

_____

e. Meals: _____

_____

_____

f. Discipline: _____

_____

_____

You may check your answers in the Feedback section.

LATER CHILDHOOD

Later childhood, the period from age 6 to the onset of puberty, brings many changes. Although physical growth is initially slow, there is vast intellectual, moral, and social expansion. But school-age children still need time to play to improve their health and motor coordination. The absence of exercise can make children more prone to heart disease in later years. Ismail and Gruber (1967) found that physical exercise in school-age children also improves academic achievement.

According to Piaget (1952), around age 7 most children make several major advances in intellectual development. Memory improves and becomes more organized. Children are suddenly capable of solving more difficult problems and become more aware of their achievement. They distinguish between make-believe and reality. As the article in Exhibit 6-6 reports, the struggle about the existence of Santa is usually resolved. They compare themselves with their friends and make judgments about school performance as well as athletic and social skills.

During the elementary school years, children become more aware of their own sex. They tend to select playmates of the same sex and play together in groups. This is often referred to as the "gang age." By puberty, most narrow their friendships to one or two close companions.

EXHIBIT 6-6

Santa Lives

Santa Claus has been laying a gift on children we never really knew about: an important early intellectual struggle over whether or not he really exists.

There's no reason to hurry to tell kids the truth, say psychologists Cyndy Scheibe and John Condry. And parents who try to prolong a child's wide-eyed innocence may be surprised to learn that their children believe in old St. Nick several years longer than they think they do.

To see when kids quit believing, the researchers interviewed 172 children in grades one to five and gave questionnaires to 361 sixth-graders. "Children begin to have doubts about Santa Claus at about 5 years of age, and most children stop believing between ages 7 and 8," Scheibe and Condry say. Although about 70 percent of first-graders are firm believers, only about 10 percent of their parents believe their children are still that naïve.

Children aren't eager to give up on Santa. "Rather than merely accepting the idea that Santa Claus is really their parents the first time someone tells them, children seem to go through a relatively complex process of weighing the evidence...before coming to the correct conclusion," the researchers say. However, despite the struggle, "the process does not seem to be harmful to children," Scheibe and Condry say. "Rather, it seems to be a useful experience in learning how to decide what is 'true.' "

Source: Bozzi, V. (1987, December). Santa lives *Psychology Today*.

Moral development proceeds as the children accept the standards and rules of their friends and teachers. They have a better understanding of the meaning of rules and base their morality on whether accepted rules are kept or broken (Kohlberg, 1976). This is indeed an improvement over early childhood when morality was strictly based on rewards and punishments.

Checkpoint

Use the following questions to check your understanding of this portion of the chapter. Choose and mark the one correct response to each question.

16. What is a neonate?
    a. A premature baby
    b. A newborn baby
    c. An irritable baby
    d. An unloved baby
17. What have psychologists found to be the best technique for feeding babies?
    a. Breast feeding
    b. Bottle feeding
    c. Some breast feeding and some bottle feeding
    d. Either breast or bottle feeding accompanied by affection
18. According to psychologists what type of feeding schedule should parents follow for their babies?
    a. A fixed four-hour schedule
    b. A fixed three-hour schedule
    c. A demand schedule
    d. A schedule they feel comfortable with
19. In addition to affection, what else do babies need?
    a. Rules
    b. Standards
    c. Stimulation
    d. Interaction with other babies
20. How should parents handle a little girl who uses baby talk?
    a. Permit her to use baby talk and use the same pronunciation so she will feel she is correct.
    b. Permit her to use baby talk but use the correct pronunciation so she can hear the right sounds.
    c. Criticize her and make her say the word correctly.
    d. Punish her for baby talk and listen only when she speaks correctly.
21. What is the most important activity of a preschool child?
    a. Social play
    b. Reading
    c. Watching television
    d. Keeping rules
22. Don is an 8-year-old boy. What type of friends would you expect him to associate with?
    a. A group of 8-year-old boys
    b. A group of 8-year-old girls

  c. One or two 8-year-old boys
  d. One or two 8-year-old boys and one or two 8-year-old girls
23. During which stage do most children learn to accept rules and standards of morality?
  a. The neonate stage
  b. Babyhood
  c. Early childhood
  d. Later childhood

Use the Checkpoint Answer Key to verify your responses. If you had any difficulty with a question, carefully reread the text. If you had little or no difficulty answering the questions or have resolved any problems that you might have had, you are ready to continue with the final portion of this chapter.

ADOLESCENCE

Clearly massive change occurred between conception and age 12. From a microscopic organism, a grown child finally emerges. Now through physical, social, and mental changes the child must develop into an adult. The period of shifting from a child to an adult is termed "adolescence."

Levinson (1986) views the onset of adolescence as the continuation of the preadulthood stage (stage 0). It is a time when young people gain independence as they separate from their parents both physically and emotionally. By the end of adolescence, there is a sense of independence and an urge to get away from the family (Levinson's stage 1).

Physical Changes

Toward the end of later childhood, sexual change or puberty begins. Secondary sexual characteristics develop: enlarged hips and breast development in girls, and muscular development and voice changes in boys. Both sexes begin to grow pubic hair. Puberty is completed when primary sexual functioning occurs. Girls menstruate and boys develop a larger penis with potential for ejaculation. The ages for pubertal changes vary widely. Generally girls undergo puberty about two years before boys.

Social Changes

Adolescence is often viewed as a stormy period, a time of critical changes that have lasting effects. Recently psychologists have advised that adolescence may not be as turbulent as had been forecast in the past. When you recall your own teenage years, you probably remember some of your worries and fears. If you were like most adolescents, you had a clique, or a group of friends that you preferred. The clique might have been a formal group such as a club, sorority, or fraternity. But more likely, it was an informal group. Within the clique you probably had one or two best friends. Undoubtedly you worried about what your friends thought of you.

Most adolescents have deep concerns about what their peers think. They are conformists within their cliques. They dress alike and use the same language expressions. Adolescents of the 1950s used terms like "neat" and "spiffy"; the 1960s brought "cool" and "groovy"; while the 1970s introduced "funky" and "funkadelic"; and youths in the 1980s "bad." Most adolescents prefer peers who are similar to themselves. The majority choose friends of the same race, economic group, and opinions. They constantly pressure each other to conform to the standards of the clique. Often teenagers develop social fears. Shyness is common, and such tasks as speaking before a class are often dreaded.

Although most adolescents prefer to be with their friends, they also need time for themselves. Adolescence is sometimes referred to as a time of identity crises, or a period when each individual must assert independence. Most fluctuate between dependence on parents and attempts to assert independence. Rebellion against parents is common in adolescence. It usually takes the form of questioning, arguments, and unwillingness to adhere to family rules. Although teenagers want to assert their freedom, they still depend upon the natural affection of their parents. Parent abuse can result from adolescent rebellion that is not handled properly.

Adolescent suicides have created a growing concern. The national suicide rate for adolescents has increased by 200 percent since 1950. Wealthy areas have experienced an even greater increase in adolescent suicides.

Drugs are another common problem. If their parents use drugs, adolescents are more likely to follow. But generally peers are even more influential than parents. Although there is evidence of a general slowdown in drug use nationwide, urban and affluent areas are still battling the problem.

"We're just pleased he can still get into the Christmas spirit."

Figure 6-4
One adolescent's independent approach to the holiday spirit...

Intellectual Development

As each child converts into an adult during the adolescent period, an expansion in mental activity is needed. Fortunately, comprehension and ability to handle abstract concepts increase. The adolescent begins to understand individual human rights and dignity. With this understanding, a sense of justice and conscience develops. According to Rogers (1972) the adolescent also has a better ability to plan for the future. The average 15- or 16-year-old can think about what is likely to occur in ten or twenty years and plan for the changes.

Exercise 6-7

Listed below are examples of changes that occur during adolescence. Indicate whether each change is physical, social, or mental.

a. _S𝑚_ Fourteen-year-old Bill is an excellent pianist. He used to love to show off before groups. Lately he cringes and blushes when his parents ask him to play a tune for their friends.

b. _S𝑚_ Fifteen-year-old Ida stormed out of the house when her parents asked her to remove the dishes from the dishwasher. She shouted, "Everyone tells me what to do. I never have time to myself."

c. ___𝑚___ Peter seems more understanding now that he is 16. He had been annoyed that his father never attended religious services with the family. Yesterday he told his father that people must act according to their own conscience.

d. ___P___ Poor 13-year-old Ned! The instructor asked him to withdraw from choir. He had been a boy soprano, but now he can never be certain of the note he will sing.

e. ___S___ Now that Gail is 13 she refuses to wear half of her clothes. She will only wear jeans with a certain label and shirts with an insignia. She claims, "That's what all my friends wear, and I don't want to look strange!"

You may check your answers in the Feedback section.

STAGES IN ADULT DEVELOPMENT

The study of adult development is recent. Levinson (1986) maintains that all adults go through the same basic sequence of stages. After interviewing adults in a research project, he concluded that throughout our adult life, we are creating a *life structure* or pattern. Sometimes we build on the structure and sometimes we change the structure. Levinson's stages are listed in Exhibit 6-7.

life structure The basic pattern of a person's life

YOUNG ADULTHOOD

There is no set age when adolescence is completed. Many people in their thirties still show some adolescent problems. But usually some adult responsibilities are accepted during the late teens. Individuals who remain in school for an extended time or remain at home with parents mature more slowly. A young man who completes a bachelor's degree, continues for a master's, then a doctorate is apt to be associating with younger people. If he writes home for checks and avoids work and social responsibility, he is likely to prolong his adolescence. Acceptance of adult responsibility requires important decisions. Among the most crucial are choosing a marriage partner and a career (see Chapters 12 and 16). The young adult years usually a begin with goals and

EXHIBIT 6-7

Levinson's Developmental Periods		
Stage	Description	Ages
0	Preadulthood	Conception to age 22
1	Early adult transition	17–22
2	Entry life structure for early adulthood	22–28
3	Age 30 transition	28–33
4	Culminating life structure for early adulthood	33–40
5	Midlife transition	40–45
6	Age 50 transition	50–55
7	Culminating life structure for middle adulthood	55–60
8	Late adult transition	60–65

Note: Stages 6, 7, and 8 are proposed.

hopes. Both Sheehy (1976) and Gould (1975) sampled individuals in their twenties and described them as ambitious and striving. Sheehy labeled the stage "the trying twenties." Levinson (1986) viewed the twenties as the "entry life structure for early adulthood." It is a time when we have chosen a lifestyle and are totally independent.

Sheehy (1976), Gould (1975), and Levinson (1986) also sampled young adults in their thirties, and described the early thirties as a time of reassessing (Levinson, stage 3). There was a yearning to fill in missing features. Childless couples began to think of raising children. Women who had been at home began to explore possible careers. Couples married for seven or more years were becoming discontent with marriage and were "looking around." By the late thirties adults settle down and become more satisfied (Levinson, stage 4). Sheehy labeled this contentment "rooting."

The twenties and thirties are a period of many changes. Although immaturities are common in the early twenties, by the completion of the young-adult stage, a mature person is expected to emerge. How can you tell if you are a mature person?

Most psychologists believe that a mature person accepts responsibility and some specific personal characteristics. Take inventory and see how you rate on this list of attributes of maturity.

- Ability to think for yourself. If you are mature, you can make up your own mind based on your own values. You may seek other opinions, but the final decision will be your own.

- Willingness to accept responsibility for decisions. If you make a mistake, you can recognize your weakness and accept the blame.

- Control of fear and anger. Although you still have worries and irritations, you have better control. You no longer panic and fly into a rage or burst into tears.

- Willingness to work. Rather than shirk responsibility you want to contribute to society and become financially independent. You prefer not to rely on parents and relatives for money.

• Capacity for sexual love and lasting relationships. You are able to show your inner feelings and accept the feelings of another person in a deep and intimate relationship.

Exercise 6-8

In the following scenario, draw one line under each sign of immaturity and two lines under each indication of maturity.

Natalie is 28 and works as a hairstylist at a local shop. She enjoys her work, but her employer is considering firing her. She tends to lose her temper and become abusive when customers do not care for the way she styles their hair. Yesterday she told a man that no one could ever style his horrible hair well—his hair was just too thin and wispy. Her boss told her she could continue only if she could learn to control her temper.

Natalie has a very close boyfriend and discussed her problem with him. He listened and was sensitive to her concerns. But Natalie is having trouble deciding whether to change careers. She plans to call her mother tonight and find out what she should do.

Check your responses in the Feedback section.

MATURE ADULTHOOD

After settling down in the late thirties and enjoying what Sheehy labeled ''rooting,'' most people experience an ''uprooting'' or sense of dissatisfaction sometime during their forties. Physical deterioration becomes obvious. The forties usually bring face wrinkles, thickening waistlines, and gray or thinning hair. However, men and women who have been pleased with their lifestyle and accomplishments tend to experience fewer problems in coping with the changes of middle age.

The changes that occur during mature adulthood have inspired a variety of expressions such as ''middle-age revolt,'' ''midcareer crisis,'' and ''middle-age slump.'' All refer to the recognition of losing youth and accepting the coming of old age. Levinson (1986) labeled this period, stage 5, the ''midlife transition.'' It is a time when we question our values and assess our accomplishments, realizing that time is limited. The first part of life is over.

In addition to facing their own problems, most mature adults must also care for aging parents. Some need to face the death of one or both parents. There is often a sense of loneliness during this period. Children are growing up and leaving or planning to leave the home. Husbands and wives now must relate to each other as spouses rather than as parents.

In the past considerable emphasis was directed at women's adjustments to menopause during middle age. Recently psychologists have found that many beliefs about menopause cannot be proved. For example, depression is not necessarily associated with the hormonal changes of menopause. The symptoms of depression are brought on by psychological reasons. Also, interest and enjoyment of sex do not diminish with menopause. More often, sex life improves because there is less anxiety about pregnancy. Women who work generally adjust better to middle age than women who have remained at home.

This suggests that social and psychological factors tend to be at least as important as the physical changes in women during mature adulthood.

Depression during middle ages is equally common among both men and women. Men who have been doing heavy physical work are often upset by their diminishing strength. Although there is no decline in their efficiency, men who work in offices or in production begin to realize that their fruitful working years may be ending.

Mature adulthood is not necessarily a depressing period. Men and women who have been pleased with their relationships and accomplishments usually enjoy these years and make excellent adjustments. According to Levinson, during this time we go through stages 6, 7, and 8. We have a stronger sense of ourselves and our lifestyles. Ideally, this stage will bring a stronger acceptance of oneself and one's lifestyle.

Exercise 6-9

Lewis and Maureen are both 40. They have been married twenty years and have an 18-year-old daughter. Lewis works on the docks as a longshoreman loading and unloading ships. Maureen has never worked and is wondering whether to look for a job. Assume they have asked for your help in planning for mature adulthood. Tell them what to expect and how to make a better adjustment.

a. Lewis: _____

_____

_____

_____

_____

b. Maureen: _____

_____

_____

_____

_____

Turn to the Feedback section to compare your advice.

OLDER ADULTHOOD

In past years developmental psychologists focused only on the early stages of development. Few ventured beyond the adolescent years. Recently there has been an increasing interest in gerontology, the study of old age. Aging causes some loss of vitality. As a result, the aging adult usually spends more time visiting doctors and thinking about death (Kalish & Reynolds, 1976). Taking precautions about physical health, diet, and exercise can create a healthier old age. Eubie Blake, the famous jazz piano player and composer, joked at age 96, "If I had known I was going to last this long, I would have taken better care of myself."

Retirement probably has the most severe impact on aging adults, particularly if they have not planned for it. In addition to financial planning, aging adults should plan to develop their interests. Travel, reading, hobbies, school, volunteer work, or even beginning a new career are all possibilities. Unfortunately, retirement is sometimes very sudden. The U.S. Bureau of Labor reported that the suicide rate after forced retirement is 12 times more than normal. Often suicide results because people feel unnecessary and have lost their sense of meaningfulness in life.

In the past, families included aging parents and grandparents in their homes. Currently, there has been an increase in the number of aging adults in retirement communities, nursing homes, and residences for the aged. Efforts are made to help improve their attitudes about the enjoyment and importance of life. The poet Kenneth Koch (1977) visited nursing homes and taught elderly people to write poems. One woman expressed the meaningfulness she found in the experience:

> *Motherless, fatherless, sisterless*
> *All gone and no more*
> *I felt so lonely*
> *Yet within me I felt a joy of joyfulness*
> *When I read poems relating to things around me*
> *Like the sun in the skies*
> *It gives me hope for the future*
>
> Mary Zahorjko (age 94)

This 79-year-old runner is confirming Neugarten's belief that age is irrelevant. (*Susan Lapides*)

Neugarten (1980) has raised hopes that people may be changing their attitudes about aging. She feels that age is becoming more irrelevant. There are many young-old persons who are vigorous and healthy. Age itself is a poor predictor of lifestyle. Fewer young-old people are willing to adhere to the traditional and formal elderly role. An increasing number of aging adults are working, involved in community affairs, and generally enjoying their lives. As Neugarten joked, "Aging is 'in.' " The excerpt in Exhibit 6-8 describes contributions that are made by the elderly.

Exercise 6-10
By planning ahead you can make better adjustments when you are an aging adult. For each area listed, mention one way planning could improve your adjustment.

a. Physical: _____

b. Financial: _____

c. Interests: _____

d. Attitudes: _____

You may check your answers in the Feedback section.

DEATH AND DYING

Have you ever noticed that people avoid using the word "death"? Rather than say a woman died, friends and relatives will say, "She passed away" or "She is no longer with us." Even doctors and nurses will say, "The patient expired." Perhaps you have even wondered why death insurance is called "life insurance."

Until recently death had been a taboo subject, a topic to be avoided. Even when people were dying of a fatal disease, friends and relatives would reassure them and hint that they could live. Weisman (1972) called it a conspiracy of silence. The dying person never heard honest reactions and responses. Kübler-Ross (1969) helped to make death a more comfortable subject. After spending time with patients who were dying, she identified five stages in their reactions.

Denial At first patients insist that it was a mistake. They are certain the diagnosis is wrong or something has been overlooked.

Anger Patients then ask, "Why me?" and become annoyed with God or fate or whoever is responsible. It is not unusual for patients to blame their doctors.

Depression There is a loss of interest and a sense of hopelessness and despair.

Bargaining Patients make promises in exchange for a longer life. Some promise their doctors to give up smoking, alcohol, or sugar, if they can be helped to survive. Others promise God they will lead a better life.

Acceptance During the last stage, patients become void of feelings. Although not joyful, they develop an inner peace and finally accept death.

EXHIBIT 6-8

Elderly Help Themselves by Changing Environments

...M. Powell Lawton...described research...done on elderly people and their environments, and gave examples of those who actively challenged the stereotype of an isolated, failing old age.

Lawton, editor of the APA journal *Psychology and Aging,* has conducted numerous studies since 1970 on the dynamic relationship between aging and the environment.

Not only is this relationship reciprocal, he said, but "like the chemical combination of two elements, both person and environment change with the transaction."

Depending upon older people's physical and mental capabilities, they can alter their home environments, blocks, or even communities to positively affect their lives, he said.

His favorite example of people modifying their homes involved 50 "very impaired older people" living alone who used in-home service agencies.

Lawton found they had arranged the area where they spent most of their time to make everything they needed accessible: a chair or wheelchair in the living room that gave them a good view out the window and easy access to the front door; a television and radio in immediate reach; and surfaces on each side of the chair for articles such as food, medicine, photos of loved ones or reading matter.

These people rarely left home, and if they went upstairs, did so only to sleep. "The control was achieved by maximizing the amount of incoming information and the readiness of access to a small number of top-priority resources," he said.

With somewhat more physical and mental stamina, older people can also change the blocks they live on.

One notable example was the Sunset District project in San Francisco. Highly competent older people were made "'block captains." Each was responsible for knowing every older neighbor on the block and checking on his or her needs.

Senior citizens can also help initiate crime watches, control litter, maintain grassy areas or bus stops, monitor the outside appearance of their own and their neighbors' homes, and can participate in various other volunteer activities, Lawton said.

And those healthy and interested enough to do so can promote change at the more complex neighborhood and community levels, suggested Lawton, citing the Gray Panthers as a group that has taken its concerns to high-level political officials on many occasions.

By becoming involved in town councils and planning commissions, elderly people can achieve such things as limiting traffic on certain streets, regulating land use for shopping and other amenities, and establishing community priorities for health and social services.

Although many of his examples were of people assuming leadership positions, Lawton acknowledged that many changes occur through "secondary proactivity," or activity resulting from initiation by other people, such as a younger professional....

Source: De Angelis, T. (1987, November). Elderly help themselves by changing environments. *APA Monitor.*

Kübler-Ross's stages were criticized by Kastenbaum and Costa (1977). They argued that not all dying patients experience every stage. Further, the stages do not always occur in the same order. They were also concerned that friends and relatives who are familiar with the five stages would be less understanding and empathetic toward the dying. They could assume an attitude that "it's just a stage."

hospice Place for terminally ill patients where understanding, feelings, and dignity are primary concerns, along with health care.

The recent interest and concern about death and dying has encouraged the hospice movement in the United States. A *hospice* is a place for dying patients.

Understanding and the dignity of death are of prime importance. Patients and their families are encouraged to share their feelings, talk about death, and even plan their funerals. As a result dying patients develop a healthier attitude toward death and emotional, moral, and practical issues are resolved.

Checkpoint

Use the following questions to check your understanding of the final portion of this chapter. Match each term on the left with the expression on the right that provides the best example.

24. ___C___ Adolescence
25. ___ae___ Secondary sexual characteristics
26. ___h___ Primary sexual functioning
27. ___aA___ Clique
28. ___d___ Peers
29. ___B___ Identity crisis
30. ___I___ Trying twenties
31. ___G___ Rooting
32. ___K___ Midlife transition
33. ___J___ Gerontology
34. ___f___ Hospice

a. A group of friends, "the crowd"
b. Rebelling against parents and finding yourself
c. Period of change from a child to an adult
d. Friends in the same age group
e. Enlarged hips, breast development, voice change
f. A comfortable place for the dying
g. Contentment that occurs in the late thirties
h. Onset of menstruation
i. A period of ambition and striving
j. The study of aging
k. Changes that occur in the forties and fifties

Check your responses against the Checkpoint Answer Key at the end of the chapter. If you had difficulty with any question, reread the text. If you had little or no difficulty answering the questions or have resolved problems that you might have had, you are ready to check yourself against the chapter inventory that follows.

CHAPTER INVENTORY

Use this list of objectives as a review checklist. You should be able to do each of the tasks outlined in the objectives and apply them to everyday examples. If you can, you may feel confident that you have mastered the material in this chapter.

1. Outline the focus of developmental psychology.
2. Explain the importance of parenting decisions.
3. Describe how children affect marriages.
4. Describe the factors involved in parental decisions on family size, parental roles, and type of discipline.
5. Identify concerns during the prenatal stage.
6. Describe three approaches to childbirth.
7. List seven stages of development.
8. Describe the lifestyle of a neonate.
9. Identify three needs during babyhood.
10. Identify the needs and problems of early and later childhood.
11. List and describe Levinson's developmental periods.

12. Distinguish among the physical, social, and mental changes in adolescence.
13. Outline common problems encountered during young adulthood.
14. Define maturity and list five attributes.
15. Recognize the changes and characteristics of mature adulthood.
16. Describe recent changes in the study of problems of the aged.
17. Specify the five stages of death identified by Kübler-Ross and three areas of criticism.

Feedback

The correct answers to the exercises follow. If you did not answer an exercise correctly, review the preceding pages and return to the exercise to correctly complete it.

6-1. *a.* Women do not have a maternal instinct. Everyone must learn about development and child rearing.
   b. Children rarely, if ever, help a shaky marriage. If anything the pressures of raising children will worsen the problems that presently exist.
   c. It is best if both partners agree on family size. Children in large families are not necessarily happier. Many feel they lack parental attention and must compete with many brothers and sisters.
   d. Although only children do have advantages, they often suffer from loneliness and can have problems adjusting to other children.

6-2. *a.* Democratic
   b. Authoritarian
   c. Democratic
   d. Permissive

6-3. Anita should not drink coffee, cola beverages, or bourbon. She should give up smoking and ignore the advice of her friends. The anesthetic could have a harmful effect on her baby.

6-4. *a.* Rock the baby.
   b. Speak in soft, soothing tones.
   c. Hum in a low voice.

6-5. *a.* Helen
   b. Marsha
   c. Henry
   d. Michelle
   e. Sidney
   f. Bob

6-6. *b.* Organize some running and jumping games. Allow the children to make buildings with wooden or styrofoam blocks. If possible, visit a park with swings, slides, and seesaws.
   c. Arrange cutting and pasting activities, along with coloring and painting. Have simple jigsaw puzzles available.
   d. Although there may be a few educational television programs that would be beneficial, television time should be limited. The children should spend most of their time in active play.

    e. Meals should be as nutritious as possible, but you should realize that children in this age group often have limited appetites.

    f. Children should be rewarded for desirable behavior. When children misbehave they should understand that they are being punished for their actions. They should be helped to understand the proper way to act.

6-7. *a.* Social

    b. Social

    c. Mental

    d. Physical

    e. Social

6-8. Signs of immaturity include: "She tends to lose her temper"; "She told a man that no one could ever style his horrible hair well"; and "She plans to call her mother tonight and find out what she should do." Signs of maturity include: "works as a hairstylist"; "enjoys her work"; and "has a very close boyfriend."

6-9. *a.* Lewis should realize that his physical strength may be diminishing. He might want to investigate activities that do not require the strength of his present job. He should also realize that his relationship with his wife may change when his daughter leaves the home.

    b. Maureen will probably have a sense of loneliness when her daughter leaves. She will probably make a better adjustment if she has a job or an outside interest. She should prepare herself for a closer relationship with her husband.

6-10. *a.* Through proper diet, exercise, and health care you can enter the aging years as a healthier person.

    b. If you face the reality of retirement you can make plans for a retirement fund or income.

    c. Since you will have more leisure time, you can plan areas of interest to pursue.

    d. If you keep active and alive with interests and ideas, you will find more enjoyment.

Checkpoint Answer Key

1. *F*	**10.** *F*	**19.** *c*	**28.** *d*
2. *F*	**11.** *T*	**20.** *b*	**29.** *b*
3. *T*	**12.** *T*	**21.** *a*	**30.** *i*
4. *T*	**13.** *F*	**22.** *a*	**31.** *g*
5. *F*	**14.** *F*	**23.** *d*	**32.** *k*
6. *T*	**15.** *F*	**24.** *c*	**33.** *j*
7. *F*	**16.** *b*	**25.** *e*	**34.** *f*
8. *T*	**17.** *d*	**26.** *h*	
9. *T*	**18.** *d*	**27.** *a*	

MOTIVATION

The last temptation is the greatest treason:
To do the right thing but for the wrong reason.

T. S. Eliot

Twenty-seven passengers step off a bus at a terminal in Chicago. Eight rush for restrooms. Four run with outstretched arms to people who have been waiting for them. Another four stroll into a snack bar. One young woman carefully checks to be sure the locks on her luggage are secure. She slowly inspects each surface for scratches. Two men, who apparently met on the bus, ask for directions to the nearest bar. A teenage girl looks around nervously and appears confused. Three elderly women head for the terminal exit door and gaze skyward at the tall buildings. Two middle-aged men seat themselves in the lobby. One reads a newspaper, while the other stares into space. A woman with a crying 2-year-old boy angrily warns him to be quiet.

What causes such different behaviors? Perhaps you have wondered why people in similar settings behave so differently from one another. Unfortunately, you can never be certain that you are guessing the correct causes of behavior. The reasons for behavior are studied by psychologists interested in motivation. In this chapter, you will learn more about *motivation*—why people behave the way they do.

motivation The needs and incentives that cause people to behave as they do

Psychologists interested in motivation examine factors that cause behavior. These may include thinking, feeling, acting, or any possible combination of the three. Motivation for behavior is an immensely complex subject. Sometimes you can identify your motivation, but often you cannot. Whether you are aware of it or not, sometimes your motivation is based on physiological needs such as hunger, thirst, and a need for rest. At other times your motivation will reflect such psychological needs as desire for approval or a craving for love. In this chapter you will examine our basic needs and higher goals. You will also consider how incentives and outside influences can increase your motivation.

WHAT IS MOTIVATION?

Perhaps, as you turned to this chapter, you had an inkling that motivation is closely related to achievement and success. Indeed, there is a sharp relationship between motivation and success. However, motivation can also cause many behaviors besides achievement and success. It can cause eating, drinking, sleeping, driving a car, and even cutting a college class. A person who is not motivated is either dead or in an intensely deep coma. Motivation is based on internal needs that push and drive you. If you can determine your needs, you can explain why you behave the way you do. You can identify your motivation.

Conscious and Unconscious Motivation

Uncovering needs and identifying motivation are not always easy. People often become puzzled when asked to explain their behavior. Finding excuses for displeasing behaviors can be particularly thorny. The comedian Flip Wilson has managed to keep his motivation cloaked with his joke, "The devil made me do it." Supposedly, Flip is totally unaware of how he could possibly do anything evil intentionally. Many psychologists would agree with him and assume that he was unconsciously motivated.

Have you ever found it difficult to explain your own behavior? It is usually relatively simple to reason that you ate a big dinner because you were hungry. Or you might be able to explain that you are working hard so that you can get a raise or a good grade. These are examples of conscious motivation. But people also do

unconscious motivation
Motives, feelings, and impulses that are not in a person's awareness but nonetheless may influence the individual's behavior

repression Forgetting that is caused by unconscious blocking of thoughts that are threatening or frightening

things they cannot explain. Maybe you have occasionally found yourself walking around aimlessly. Or possibly you have sat in the driver's seat of your car without your car keys. Freudian psychologists believe that much human behavior is caused by *unconscious motivation.* As a result most people are often not conscious or aware of what causes their behavior. For example, some people are constantly late for appointments and meetings. Even though they make a conscious effort to get an early start, nonetheless they end up being late. Freudian psychologists would blame their tardiness on unconscious motivation, maybe an unconscious desire to make an entrance and be noticed.

Another type of unconscious motivation is *repression,* described in detail in Chapter 4. Repression is motivated forgetting. A student who failed a midterm and must appear for a conference with the instructor might forget to keep the appointment. The student is being truthful and honestly forgets! The thought of being shamed by a teacher is too distressing to think about consciously. As a result, the student is unconsciously motivated to get rid of any thoughts of the embarrassing meeting. Unconscious motivation helps remove personal guilt for behavior, since your actions or lack of actions are labeled unintentional.

Exercise 7-1

For each of the following examples, indicate whether the motivation appears to be *conscious* or *unconscious.*

a. Meg has a boring ecomonics professor who drones on during class in a dull monotone. Meg makes a special effort to take notes so she will keep herself alert during his lectures. ____Con____

b. George notices that a ladder is extended across the sidewalk where he is walking. George scoffs at superstitions and ridiculous people who think walking under ladders will bring bad luck. Yet he walks out into the street to avoid stepping under the ladder. ____uncon____

c. Jill keeps a special "birthday book" and prides herself in remembering to send cards and notes to friends and relatives on their special days. Although her younger sister's birthday is recorded in the book, Jill has forgotten to send her a birthday card for the past four years. ____uncon____

d. The last few times Tim wore his wild red-striped ski hat on the slopes, several attractive girls seemed to notice him. Jim plans to wear his wild ski hat on his next trip to Aspen. ____Con____

Turn to the Feedback section to check your answers.

Needs and Incentives

incentive Reward that motivates behavior

Needs and *incentives* are the pushes and pulls of motivation. Some of our motivations are biologically or emotionally based and they push us. These pushing forces such as hunger, thirst, and curiousity are considered needs. Other motivations result when we are pulled by an incentive, perhaps a slice of cheesecake, a frosty lemonade, or a sensuous member of the opposite sex. Consider someone at a pie-eating contest, gulping his tenth pie. It is unlikely that a hunger need has anything to do with his continued eating. It is far more likely that he is being pulled by an incentive, perhaps a cash prize, a ribbon, or the attention given a winner.

As you probably suspected, most of our motivations result from a combination of pushes and pulls. We lack something such as food, sleep, approval, or respect and we are driven to satisfy these needs. We push ourselves. In addition to this pushing, we sometimes experience some pulling. Even if our need is only slight, we often can be pulled by an enticing incentive.

Whether their motivation is conscious or unconscious, people have a broad range of needs. Some needs are shared by everyone. For example, everyone is motivated to stay alive and survive. Food, rest, oxygen, and other necessities for life are common to all people. Other needs vary from one person to the next. For example, some people need to drive a fancy sports car and wear designer clothes. Others may need to travel to far-off lands and live among different cultures. Undoubtedly, you have heard of individuals who had a need to climb high mountains or do missionary work in underdeveloped countries. Strangely, some people even feel a need to write psychology books!

Exercise 7-2
Suppose some neighborhood children set up a lemonade stand on a hot summer day. You are out cutting grass and doing yard work. After an hour you need to quench your thirst and you buy a large glass of lemonade. The children are thrilled when you buy a second glass and they explain that you are their first customer. Although you are no longer thirsty, you buy a third glass because you know this will please them.

How were the first two glasses motivated by a need and the third motivated by an incentive? How were you "pushed"? How were you "pulled"? _____

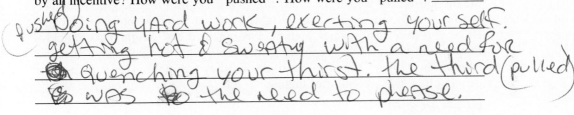

(handwritten) push Doing yard work, exerting yourself. getting hot & sweaty with a need for Quenching your thirst. the third (pulled) was the need to please.

Figure 7-1 It appears a dental plan would be an enticing incentive that would take care of his needs.

Survival Needs

Most Americans experience only a mild form of survival need. Survival needs are biological necessities required to continue living. You may have believed yourself starving or dying of thirst. But chances are your needs were minimal when compared with people who had beyond doubt been without water or food for days.

Keys et al. (1950) studied men who had been fed just enough to stay alive during World War II. They found that the men became preoccupied with food thoughts and fantasies. The men delighted in reading cookbooks and exchanging favorite recipes. They forgot about wives, girlfriends, and sex. They became apathetic, dispirited, and irritable.

There has been considerable evidence that thirst needs are even stronger than hunger needs. When any physiological needs are not satisfied, personality changes generally result. Persons who have been without sleep for extended periods have been known to become anxious and hallucinate. Have you ever been in steady, persistent pain for a prolonged time? You probably noticed your own personality change. In all likelihood, you were easily irked and had difficulty concentrating. Your interest and motivation were concentrated on how to relieve yourself of some pain and become more comfortable.

homeostasis Ability of vital functions to maintain a stable condition

The human body constantly tries to keep a balanced, stable condition. The maintaining of this balanced condition is called "homeostasis." Homeostasis acts like a thermostat in regulating your body temperature. You sweat when your body is too hot and shiver (produce heat) when you are too cold. Or you might remove or put on a sweater. Similarly, you feel hungry and eat and stop eating when you feel satisfied or full.

set point Mechanism that maintains a person's usual weight

Why do some people eat more than others? Some researchers believe that the thermostat for weight, or "fatostat," varies in different people. Each person has a different *set point* for weight. Your set point is your usual weight. Have you ever lost several pounds and regained the weight very quickly? Bennet and Gurin (1982) reported that people who diet fall below their set points. Their bodies then feel deprived and they eat more. This explains why people often gain weight after dieting.

Exercise 7-3

Several studies have suggested that children who eat a good nutritious breakfast tend to perform better in school. From what you have learned about problems encountered by men who had hunger needs in Keys's study, explain why a school breakfast program could help undernourished children.

_____

_____

Compare your response with the one given in the Feedback section.

Curiosity and Arousal

Most people seek a moderate amount of stimulation or arousal. They avoid boredom but also avoid too much stimulation. If you are alone with nothing to do, you may turn on your stereo or television, or pick up a magazine. Likewise, if you are at a crowded party with blaring music and loud chatter, you might seek some fresh air and quiet.

There are, however, large individual differences in the amount of stimulation that people need. Farley (1986) described two extremes of arousal needs, *type T* (capital T) and *type t* (lower case t). Type T individuals are thrill-seekers. They need more risks and adventures than other people to get revved up. As a result they like to experiment, prefer novelty, and enjoy conflicts and excitement. At the opposite end of the spectrum are the type t's (little t's). These people like certainty, stability, and a sense of peace. Most people fall in the middle of the type T ← - → type t spectrum and seek a moderate amount of stimulation.

type T personality
High thrill seeking

type t personality Low
thrill seeking

Exercise 7-4
How would Farley describe Edgar (Figure 7-2)? Why? _____ *type t personality (low thrill seeking) He seems to require a low Amount of stimulation.*

Safety and Security Needs

Chances are you take many precautions to be certain you are safe and secure. You live in some type of shelter, whether it be an apartment, a house, a tee-pee, or a barn. This shelter protects you from rain, snow, and other unfavorable elements. But undoubtedly, your motivations and concerns for safety and security extend well beyond your need for shelter. Do you have locks on your doors and windows? How about flashlights and hurricane lanterns? If you keep a spare tire in your car and maintain health and auto insurance, you are responding to your motivation to satisfy safety and security needs. Our country supports a national military force; towns and cities have police and fire departments. These groups all attest to our needs for safety and security.

Figure 7-2

"Edgar's need for entertainment is at a bare minimum."

According to Farley, this man has a type T personality and needs a high level of risk and adventure. (*Galen Rowell/Peter Arnold, Inc.*)

Checkpoint

Use the following questions to check your understanding of this portion of the chapter. Choose and mark the one correct response to each question.

1. What do psychologists interested in motivation study?
   a. Actions and overt behavior
   b. Factors that cause behavior
   c. Achievement and success
   d. Repression

2. What is the difference between conscious motivation and unconscious motivation?
   a. Unconscious motivation causes guilt and conscious motivation does not.
   b. Conscious motivation is repressed and unconscious motivation is not.
   c. People are aware of unconscious motivation but unaware of conscious motivation.
   d. People are aware of conscious motivation but unaware of unconscious motivation.

3. Which of the following is an example of an incentive?
   a. Food
   b. Hunger
   c. Thirst
   d. Curiosity

4. Which of the following is the strongest need?
   a. Hunger
   b. Thirst

Figure 7-3
Some safety and
security needs can be
intense!

   c. Safety
   d. Stimulation
5. What is the purpose of homeostasis?
   a. To increase your arousal
   b. To keep your body in stable condition
   c. To meet safety and security needs
   d. To identify unconscious motivation
6. Ted is described as a type T. Which activity would he probably prefer?
   a. Sitting by a plant
   b. Reading a book
   c. Riding a roller coaster
   d. Sleeping

Use the Checkpoint Answer Key to verify your responses. If you had any difficulty with a question, carefully reread the text. If you had little or no difficulty answering the questions or have resolved any difficulty you might have had, you are ready to continue with the next portion of this chapter.

THE NEED TO AFFILIATE

The needs for love and belongingness are sometimes called "affiliation needs." If you have ever felt lonely or isolated, you have experienced a need to affiliate. Affiliation is not limited to romantic or parental love. You also need friends who accept you. There are immense differences in affiliation needs. Some people are satisfied with one or two close, deep friendships. Others crave superficial relationships with large groups. Some fluctuate between group and individual friend-

affiliation need
Motivation to belong
and associate with
other people and
feel loved

ships. Selection of friends usually changes with development. People look for ways to please others and win their approval. Most are selective, seeking acceptance from only certain friends and associates. It would clearly be impossible to win everyone's approval!

Clubs such as Alcoholics Anonymous and Weight Watchers are designed to motivate people through their need for affiliation and social approval. Many individuals drink or eat because they feel unwanted or lonely. Although eating and drinking are physiological needs, they are often also associated with affiliation. Whether enjoying a formal dinner party or a few beers with some friends, the purpose is not solely satisfying hunger and thirst needs. Alcoholics Anonymous and Weight Watchers recognize the social implications of eating and drinking. The groups were formed to approve refraining from alcohol and excessive food. To win acceptance from the groups, you must keep sober and thin.

Just as there are differences in the type and number of friends needed, there are also wide variations in the intensity and strength of the need to belong and be accepted by others. Crowne and Marlowe (1964) developed a test to measure the need for social approval. They then used subjects who had either extremely high or extremely low scores on their tests. Next, the high and low scorers were asked to do a chore. They were told to put twelve spools in a box, lifting only one at a time. When the box was full, they had to empty it and repeat placing each spool back in the box. Sound like fun? Interestingly, the subjects who had high scores on the need-for-approval test claimed they enjoyed the task. They were also far more enthusiastic about the scientific usefulness of the experiment than were the low scorers. High scorers even stated they had learned something from the experiment. Evidently the low scorers had less need to be approved and could recognize a dull chore!

High needs for approval and affiliation can also be identified through clothes. Sorority and fraternity pins, team or club windbreakers, and dressing alike are ways of demonstrating a need to belong. Adolescents often show remarkable conformity in their dress. Men and women who frequent singles bars or attend every mixer and dance usually have strong affiliation needs.

Advertisers capitalize on the need for love and belongingness. Many ads begin with a negative appeal. Jim is lonely and disapproved of by everyone. He has either dandruff, messy hair, bald spots, bad breath, a bad odor, or ill-fitting underwear. However, after using the advertised product, his problem is solved and he gains popularity. The advertisers are appealing to your need for approval. They hope you will believe their product will gain you the same popularity as Jim. Check magazines, newspapers, and your television for this type of ad.

Exercise 7-5

Read the following scenario and check each sentence that demonstrates a need for affiliation and approval.

Helen, a 20-year-old college junior, is tired of living alone. Next Tuesday she will move into an apartment with three other girls. Right now she is planning a "moving-out" party. She plans to invite everyone she knows. Helen had never had a party in her apartment before because she was afraid it might annoy her landlord.

Tonight she is going to a friend's party and intends to invite every new person she meets. She wants everyone to think she has many friends. A big moving-out party will prove she is popular!

You may check your checks in the Feedback section.

THE NEED TO ACHIEVE

achievement need
Motivation to accomplish tasks and be a success

Achievements can be any accomplishment, from getting an office with a view or a personal secretary to maintaining the clearest complexion on campus. An achievement is a demonstration of success. Think of some achievements that you felt gave you status among others. Did you ever receive the highest grade on an exam or earn enough money for a car or an unusual vacation? Perhaps you have won a contest!

Some contests require an accomplishment while others are based strictly on luck. Often people feel a sense of achievement in winning contests based more on chance than on actual accomplishments. Bingo and sweepstake addicts delight in the possibility of winning huge sums of money easily. Studies have shown that only rarely are these individuals strong achievers at work. Strong achievers usually want to feel personally responsible for their own success.

Games of chance do not require individual efforts. According to McClelland (1961), people with strong needs for achievement like to use their own skills and want to improve themselves. They prefer tasks that require some effort but are not impossible. If they have control of their jobs and can set their own goals, they feel more satisfied with themselves. A high achiever would prefer a game of chess to a game of poker.

Achievers usually set goals for themselves that everyone else will believe is a symbol or sign of success. They want to do well and enjoy getting positive feedback from others. Men and women with strong needs for achievement like to get pats on the back. Feedback from others is more important than money. Adams and Stone (1977) reported that high achievers will even spend their leisure time in activities that will reflect achievement.

Why do some people have strong needs for achievement? McClelland found that the need for achievement is related to parent attitudes. Parents who are high achievers themselves usually demand independence from their children. The children must become self-reliant at a relatively early age. As a result, the children develop a sense of confidence and find enjoyment in their own achievements (Feshbach & Weiner, 1982).

On the other hand, parents who have low needs for achievement are more protective of their children. They help their children perform everyday tasks such as dressing and feeding far more than necessary. Their children have less freedom and usually have low achievement needs.

Exercise 7-6

From what you have learned about people's needs for achievement, indicate whether each of the following is apt to be a *high achiever* or a *low achiever*. State the characteristic of a high or low achiever that the person is demonstrating.

Figure 7-4
Howard looks like a
man with a high need
to achieve.

"It just seems to me, Howard, that you're missing the whole point of having a terrace in the city."

a. Jill was furious when she learned that her new office would not have a carpet. _____ high _____

_____

b. Reverend Williams always studies the face of her congregation when she gives a sermon. She wants to be sure she is inspiring her audience. _____

_____ high _____

c. Claude can only work if he has a midmorning break. He needs some relaxation to concentrate for a full morning. _____ low _____

_____

d. When Mark learned he would not be paid for his overtime, he said, "Forget it. I won't work for free!" _____ ~~high~~ low _____

_____

e. Ted has been practicing basketball skills at every opportunity. He wants to be able to score a basket from every possible angle. _____ high _____

_____

f. Laura's boss asked her to develop a project that she would enjoy performing. Laura became upset and announced that she hated to define her own work. She would rather just follow orders. _____ *Low*

_____

g. Joshua never walks to his junior high school alone. His mother accompanies him to be sure he will not be harmed by other children or traffic.

_____ *Low*

h. Wanda spends half her salary on sweepstakes and raffle tickets. _ *Low*

_____

You may check your answers in the Feedback section.

Workaholics. Workaholism results when the need to achieve runs wild. *Workaholics* develop a passion for their work. Some are driven to work as much as twelve or fifteen hours every day, including weekends. The term "workaholic," generally used by lay people rather than psychologists, is based on "alcoholic," a word that implies a negative excess. However, unlike alcoholics, workaholics are usually respected. They love their jobs and are having fun. They are successful and enjoy themselves. Former senator William Proxmire, an admitted workaholic, revealed "The less I work, the less I enjoy it." The article in Exhibit 7-1 describes a few other workaholics.

workaholic Person who prefers work to socializing and relaxing

    Although workaholics are usually respected by coworkers and friends, their families tend to be less enthusiastic. It is not uncommon for workaholics to skip meals, limit their social conversation, and even work their way through holidays.

    Perhaps you are wondering about yourself. Undoubtedly, you have worked during a lunch hour. Possibly, you have stayed up all night completing a term paper or project. But for the workaholic, these are routine events. Almost every night there is some project or task that requires their concentration. Whether the job be fine-tuning the engine of a car, writing an article for the newspaper, or keeping a spotless kitchen, workaholics cannot pull themselves away. No job is too menial or unimportant. Are you generally inclined to shout "Thank God it's Monday" rather than join the usual chorus of "T.G.I.F."? If so, you might want to check yourself on the quiz in Exhibit 7-2. Although this quiz is not a scientific analysis, it does allow you to compare yourself with people who have been termed workaholics.

Exercise 7-7
In your own words, describe one positive aspect and one negative of workaholism.

a. Positive: _get more work done, looked on with respect from co-workers high feelings of Accomplishment_

b. Negative: _never have enough time for yourself or friends._

EXHIBIT 7-1

Source: Machlowitz, M. (1980, July/August). Workaholism: What is it? *Saturday Evening Post.*

Workaholism: What Is It?

Even New York City's 1977 blackout couldn't keep workaholics at home. Several hundreds of people went to work despite the knowledge that buildings would be locked and businesses closed. I found them pacing impatiently outside their offices, demanding to be allowed to enter, even if reaching their desks would require climbing 30 flights of stairs. Others went about their business on the street. One vice president of Booz, Allen & Hamilton, a leading management consulting firm, sat on the steps outside 245 Park Avenue working with a hand-held calculator. His only concern was that the calculator's batteries might require recharging before electricity was restored. Quite a few others conducted impromptu conferences while perched on their briefcases all along the sidewalks or, as a concession to the day's 100 degrees F. heat, inside airconditioned cars. One such conferring pair, seated at a Park Avenue plaza, concluded, "We probably got more done out here." When I asked a senior Pan Am executive why he bothered commuting at all or why he didn't just go home, he told me, "I have too much to do to stay home."

One elderly attorney toiled away while his office building burned down around him. He ignored the warnings, sirens, and screams until he was finally forcibly ejected by firefighters. A pregnant publicist I know was enjoying the rare luxury of a leisurely lunch when she felt her first labor pains. She rushed from the restaurant to her obstetrician's office. When he assured her that delivery was still hours away, she went back to work.

EXHIBIT 7-2

Quiz: Are You a Workaholic?

Who are work addicts and what makes them tick? What's wrong with being a workaholic, and more importantly, what's right about it? Despite disparate circumstances, most workaholics share common characteristics. In order to identify workaholics, I've developed a quiz based on these characteristics. If you wonder whether you're a workaholic—or if you think you might be working or living with one—take this test and see.

yes   no

 ☐ **1.** *Do you get up early, no matter how late you go to bed?*
As one management consultant confessed, "I'd get home and work until [about] 2 A.M. and then get up at 5 A.M. and think, 'Gee, aren't I terrific!'"

 ☐ **2.** *If you are eating lunch alone, do you read or work while you eat?*
Robert Moses, New York's long-time Parks Commissioner, reportedly considered lunches a bore and a bother because he couldn't bear to interrupt work. He used a large table as a desk so lunch could be served right there.

☐ **3.** *Do you make daily lists of things to do?*
Ever-present appointment books and cluttered calendars are a hallmark of workaholics. Indeed, their main way of wasting time, admits Dr. Elizabeth Whelan, a Harvard University epidemiologist, may be looking for lost lists!

yes no

4. *Do you find it difficult to "do nothing?"*
It was claimed that David Mahoney, the handsome, hard-working chairman of Norton Simon, Inc., abandoned transcendental meditation because he found it impossible to sit still for 20 minutes.

5. *Are you energetic and competitive?*
President Johnson once asked Doris Kearns, then a White House Fellow, if she were energetic. Kearns replied, "I hear you need only five hours of sleep, but I need only four so it stands to reason that I've got even more energy than you."

6. *Do you work on weekends and holidays?*
In *Working,* author Studs Terkel related that the president of a Chicago radio station confessed that he regularly works in his home on weekends. But, he added, "when I do this on holidays, like Christmas, New Year's, and Thanksgiving, I have to sneak a bit so the family doesn't know what I'm doing."

7. *Can you work anytime and anywhere?*
Two associates at Cravath, Swaine and Moore, one of Manhattan's most prestigious law firms, were said to have bet about who could bill the most hours in a day. One worked around the clock, billed 24 and felt assured of victory. His compet-

itor, however, having flown to California in the course of the day, worked on the plane and billed 27.

8. *Do you find vacations "hard to take"?*
George Lois, the art director who heads Lois Pitts Gershon, an advertising agency, had to think a while when I asked him when he had taken his last vacation. Finally, he recalled when it was: 1964—almost 14 years before!

9. *Do you dread retirement?*
After retiring from the ad agency where she had created such classic slogans as Clairol's "Does she…or doesn't she?" Shirley Polykoff started her own advertising agency. As president of Shirley Polykoff Advertising in New York, she still—some six years later—has no plans to slow up or step down. She says, "I'm doing more now than I've ever done. I don't know how you retire if you're still healthy and exuberant about living. They'll have to carry me out in a box!"

10. *Do you really enjoy your work?*
As Joyce Carol Oates, the Canadian novelist, once told *The New York Times,* "I am not conscious of working especially hard, or of 'working' at all.…Writing and teaching have always been, for me, so richly rewarding that I do not think of them as work in the usual sense of the word."

If you answered "Yes" to eight or more questions, you, too, may be a workaholic.

Source: Machlowitz, M. (1980, July/August). Are you a workaholic? *Saturday Evening Post.*

Check your descriptions in the Feedback section.

Fear of success. What about people who are afraid to achieve? Psychologists believe the fear of success is usually related to a lower need, the need for love and belongingness. They are afraid they will lose valued friendships and affection if they become successful.

Horner (1969) was a pioneer in the study of fear of success in women. She gave college students one sentence and asked them to complete an essay. Male students were given the sentence: "After first-term finals, John finds himself at the top of his medical school class." Female students were given the same sentence, with the name "Ann" substituted for "John." The men had a positive attitude toward "John." Only about 10 percent of the male students had any negative comments. Interestingly, almost two-thirds of the women had negative attitudes toward "Ann." They described her as either unpopular and rejected, or a guilty cheat, or a hoax. Studies by Maccoby and Jacklin (1974) and Monahan and Shaver (1974) have supported Horner's findings.

Although fear of success had been more common among women, more recent studies have found that men are also becoming susceptible. Pike and Kahill (1983) used Horner's descriptions of "John" and "Ann" and found that male physicians showed a higher fear of success than female physicians. Many men feel insecure about achieving at the expense of personal friendships and health.

Need for power. Some people constantly try to dominate and control others. They are motivated by a *need for power*. People with a strong need for power tend to argue and dominate conversations. Competitive sports like tennis are popular with them. They also accumulate such prestige symbols as gold and platinum credit cards and expensive cars. If they cannot demonstrate their power, they often suffer from chronic high blood pressure and illness (McClelland et al., 1980).

power need Motivation to dominate and rule others

Checkpoint

Use the following questions to check your understanding of this portion of the chapter. Choose and mark the one correct response to each question.

Figure 7-5
Could Sally be suffering from fear of success?

"Sally, I'd like to talk to you about your attitude."

7. Which of the following describes an individual trying to fulfill a need for love and belongingness?

a. Jim always tries to locate a policeman when he walks through a lonely park in the dark.
   b. Jill spends all her spare time reading about people from other cultures.
   c. Kyle is new in town and just joined the local teen club.
   d. Marge is working nights and weekends to be sure she gets a promotion.

What is an affiliation need?
   a. A need to belong
   b. A need to achieve
   c. A physiological need
   d. A curiosity need

9. Assume that you asked two groups of individuals to scrub a floor with a toothbrush. Group A had a high need for social approval and group B had a low need for social approval. Based on the results of the study by Crowne and Marlowe, how would you expect the groups to react?
   a. Both groups would enjoy the task.
   b. Group A would enjoy the task more than group B.
   c. Group A would enjoy the task less than group B.
   d. Both groups would refuse to do the task.

10. An advertisement shows a couple in an empty room. No one has showed up at their party because they serve the wrong brand of pretzels. In the next scene they announce that they are switching to a superior brand. Suddenly crowds of people come swarming to their party! To which need is the advertiser appealing?
   a. Physiological
   b. Curiosity
   c. Love and belongingness
   d. Achievement

11. How can esteem and self-esteem needs best be met?
   a. Through achievements
   b. Through affiliation
   c. Through curiosity
   d. Through failures

12. Which of the following families are most likely to have children with a high need for achievement?
   a. The Marshalls, who are extremely protective of their children
   b. The Potters, who encourage their children to be independent
   c. The Bakers, who keep their children surrounded by friends
   d. The Haskells, who limit their children's friendships

13. Which of the following individuals could be described as a workaholic?
   a. Bill likes to drink beer when he works.
   b. Todd waits until the night before exams and then crams.
   c. Karen rarely has a meal without studying or making a list at the same time.
   d. Linda prefers to work when there are other people around.

14. Which need is most closely related to the fear of success?
   a. Curiosity
   b. Achievement

MOTIVATION

c. Esteem
d. Love and belonging

Use the Checkpoint Answer Key to verify your responses. If you had any difficulty with a question, carefully reread the text. If you had little or no difficulty answering the questions or have resolved any problems that you might have had, you are ready to continue with the final portion of this chapter.

MASLOW'S HIERARCHY OF NEEDS

Trying to sort and organize every possible need seems like a monstrous task. Yet Abraham Maslow (1970), one of the most important contributors to the field of motivation, managed to classify human needs or motivations into a pyramidlike hierarchy. In order to progress upward to the top of the pyramid, you need to satisfy each need along the way.

At the base of his pyramid, Maslow placed everyday *physiological needs* required for survival—needs for food, drink, rest, elimination, etc. On the next level, Maslow put *need for stimulation* and escape from boredom. The need to explore and satisfy curiosity would be included on this second level. *Safety and security needs* follow. As you continue up his pyramid, you develop a *need for love and a sense of belonging*. At this fourth level, friendships become important. As you move to the upper levels of the hierarchy, you *need to feel respected by others*. The final level is reached by very few people. It involves carrying out one's total potential. Maslow labeled the top step of his hierarchy *self-actualization*.

Maslow felt that people move up and down this pyramid throughout their lives. Indeed, people can move to different steps or needs on the pyramid

self-actualization
Highest need on
Maslow's hierarchy;
need to grow and
fulfill potential

Figure 7-6
Maslow's hierarchy
of needs.

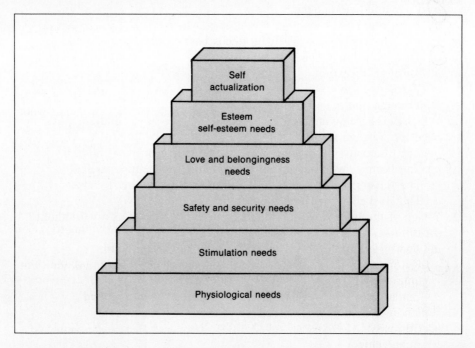

within a single day. His pyramid is like a ladder you climb throughout your life. You must step on each rung to reach the next. But suppose a person is on a high rung. For example, a woman may have progressed to the point where she is looking for approval and self-esteem. Suddenly, a man points a gun in her back. She will abruptly descend the hierarchy to satisfy her need for safety and security. Whenever a rung in the hierarchy "breaks," the person must return down to that level to satisfy the need. However, usually their progress back up to the higher level will occur rapidly.

Maslow's hierarchy has met criticism. Some argue that people often experience several needs at the same time. Further, there are wide individual differences. Maslow's hierarchy cannot explain why people will starve or be tortured rather than give up their personal beliefs.

Exercise 7-8

Max has stayed awake for two days and two nights preparing a design project for his drafting class. He wanted to impress his instructor and classmates with his planning ability. Suddenly he no longer cares about his project. He just wants to go to bed. Explain what has happened to Max's motivation, according to Maslow's hierarchy of needs.

Esteem needs very high, he has gotten tired so it seems less important (physiologic needs) motivation has lowered.

You may check your response in the Feedback section.

SELF-ACTUALIZATION

Maslow himself had difficulty finding a precise definition for self-actualization. He felt that all people have some inner talents or abilities that they want to use or actualize. If all lower needs are met, people can grow and develop by using these abilities. This growth is a continuous process that allows individuals to find self-fulfillment and realize their full potential.

In his attempt to identify some characteristics of people who have reached the level of self-actualization, Maslow studied the lives of forty-nine people whom he believed to be self-actualizers. Among those studied were Albert Einstein, Eleanor Roosevelt, Abraham Lincoln, Thomas Jefferson, William James, and Jane Addams. Among the common characteristics of self-actualizers were:

Honesty They have an ability to be objective and do not show selfish interest.

Creativity They are spontaneous and natural and enjoy trying new approaches.

Acceptance They have total acceptance of themselves and are willing to accept others for what they are.

Appreciation They possess an ability to become fully absorbed, enjoying even simple and basic experiences.

Sense of humor They can recognize cleverness and whimsy and will laugh easily.

Sensitivity They experience a deep feeling of sympathy for other people.

201
MOTIVATION

peak experience Brief
sense of overwhelming
total fulfillment that
approximates self-
actualization

According to Maslow, self-actualization is extremely rare. He screened about 3000 students and found only one self-actualized person. Although self-actualization is slightly more likely among older individuals, it is far from common. Most people never move above the level of esteem. They never reach self-actualization and fully develop their potential.

Slightly more common than self-actualization are what Maslow called "peak experiences." A peak experience is an extremely brief, momentary sense of total happiness or fulfillment. For a few seconds or perhaps a minute, you have a sense of self-actualization. This feeling could come from such experiences as watching a spectacular sunset, holding a baby, running a marathon, creating a sculpture, or greeting a returned love. Peak experiences give the same feeling of aliveness and wholeness that self-actualizers encounter. However, the feeling ends abruptly.

Exercise 7-9

The article in Exhibit 7-3 quotes Louise Nevelson, the famous sculptor. Each of her sayings reflects one or more characteristics found in self-actualizers:

EXHIBIT 7-3

The Sayings of Mrs. N.

The self-construction of the Nevelson persona has as much to do with words as with Paisley scarves or triple-layered eyelashes. In memoirs, lectures and interviews, the artist has built up a sort of collage of comments—often repeated, but often to good effect—on art, life, love and other themes. A sampling:

On the Appeal of Black It is the most beautiful color. It really is. You take, for instance, any material, and when you convert it into black—I don't even mean wood or a sculpture, I mean anything, for instance, a house—it's so distinguished.

On Advising Younger Artists I only know this—you can't give advice to an artist. Could I tell Caruso that he's got to sing or that he's got to take lessons? Caruso was born with a voice. Then of course he cultivated it. Without equipment you can give advice until doomsday and it's no good. To the persons that feel—and they have a right to fulfill that—that they want to give their life to what they are doing, I say, sure, go to work, just work, and the work will invite you to move.

On Independence It's a hell of a thing to be born, and if you're born, you're at least entitled to yourself.

On Moral Obligation If you don't live up to your greatest potential, then you are cheating God.

On Influences A white lace curtain on the window was for me as important as a great work of art. This gossamer quality, the reflection, the form, the movement, I learned more about art from that than I did in school.

On Generosity When you have a center you can help everybody. From that place you throw the ball of generosity. That is where I move from. Everything I do, more or less, comes from that place.

Source: Mrs. N (1981, January 12). The sayings of *Time*.

---

honesty, creativity, acceptance, appreciation, sense of humor, and sensitivity.
Identify which characteristic(s) each saying reflects.

a. On the appeal of black: _____Appreciation_____

b. On advising younger artists: _____Acceptance_____

c. On independence: _____honesty_____

d. On moral obligation: _____Creative_____

e. On influences: _____Creativity_____ _____Appreciation_____

f. On generosity: _____Sensitivity_____

Please check your answers in the Feedback section.

INTRINSIC AND EXTRINSIC MOTIVATION

Absolutely everything you do is caused by either intrinsic or extrinsic motivation. If you are *intrinsically* motivated, you are performing the activity because
you enjoy it. The activity is rewarding in itself. For example, assume you like
to watch football games on Sunday afternoons. Just watching the game brings
good feelings. A friend who finds football games uninteresting would not have
this intrinsic motivation.

Now, assume you want this friend to join you. You might have to provide
an *extrinsic* motivator. An extrinsic motivator supplies an outside reward. Perhaps you could offer your friend some tasty snacks or concert tickets or cash
for watching the game with you. These external rewards would provide extrinsic motivation for sitting through a boring experience.

Although you and your friend would be doing the same thing, namely,
watching the football game, your motivations would be different. As a result,
you would be likely to watch a football game the following Sunday. However,
if there are neither snacks, nor concert tickets, nor cash, your friend is not
likely to be by your side.

Think of some things that motivate you intrinsically. You probably need
no external rewards for eating a tasty meal or sleeping in a cozy bed. But what
about studying? If you enjoy learning in itself, you are intrinsically motivated.
On the other hand, if you are studying strictly to earn course credits and an
eventual degree or certificate, you are extrinsically motivated. Perhaps you
have both types of motivation in studying. If you enjoy learning but also look
forward to a good grade, a degree, and maybe a well-paid job, you qualify for
both intrinsic and extrinsic motivation.

Psychologists have been interested in the effects of extrinsic motivation
on intrinsic motivation. They found that when extrinsic motivation is introduced, intrinsic motivation tends to decrease. Among the evidence are experiments by Deci (1972, 1975). For one experiment, Deci found subjects who enjoyed doing puzzles and were intrinsically motivated. He divided the subjects
into two groups. One group was told they would receive $1 for each correct
puzzle solution. The second group received no external reward. After this experience, he allowed each subject to be alone and choose an activity. The sub-

intrinsic motivation
Performing activities
because they are
rewarding and
enjoyable in
themselves

extrinsic motivation
Performing activities
only for an outside or
external reward

jects who were paid spent far less time on puzzles than those who were not paid. Deci concluded that the money had shifted their interest to external benefits. As a result, intrinsic motivation was reduced.

Deci (1971) found only one type of external reward that could increase intrinsic motivation. Verbal praise was effective in enhancing intrinsic interest. Although material rewards caused subjects to lose intrinsic motivation, praise and social approval intensified intrinsic attraction.

Exercise 7-10

Ted, a 14-year-old boy, always loved to chop and split wood. It gave him a sense of power and strength to see the wood break into segments. Several neighbors noticed how well he performed this task and offered to pay him $5 an hour to prepare wood for their fireplaces. Ted's parents are concerned. He no longer has any interest in cutting wood for them. He will only do it for a fee.

a. From what you have learned about intrinsic and extrinsic motivation, explain why Ted lost much of his interest in chopping and splitting wood.

he was not being appreciated for his power and strength *money became more important, the pleasure he felt diminished with the onset of people paying him to do it. Why do it for free?*

b. How might Ted's intrinsic interest be restored?

if he stops being paid for the job and instead gets praise for it, then his intrinsic motivation may return.

You may compare your answers with those in the Feedback section.

Job Satisfaction

Both intrinsic and extrinsic factors affect job satisfaction. Herzberg (1968) referred to intrinsic motivation as a *growth factor* and extrinsic motivation as a *hygiene factor*. According to Herzberg, people can be satisfied in one of these areas and dissatisfied in the other.

The growth aspect of a job provides a person with a sense of achievement and recognition. If the work itself is enjoyable and gratifying, a person will be happy and satisfied. Performing tasks will allow personal growth and a feeling of accomplishment. The person will be intrinsically motivated to work.

The hygiene area involves extrinsic motivators, namely working conditions and benefits. Administration, salary, fringe benefits, and job security are a part of the hygiene factor. The article in Exhibit 7-4 notes a current trend toward increased interest in hygiene factors.

But even if the salary and working conditions are terrific, you can still dislike your job. As the article in Exhibit 7-5 points out, people who take jobs solely for money or external rewards can become extremely unhappy. Hygiene factors can keep you from being dissatisfied, but they can never make you like your job. Clearly, money can increase productivity. However, neither money nor any other external factor can make you enjoy your work and feel

EXHIBIT 7-4

205
MOTIVATION

For Love or Money?

All of us who work make choices about what criteria are most important in a job. Rewarding work and career advancement have traditionally outweighed simply earning a high income for many people. But since the early 1970s, earning money has become more important to many workers than intrinsic rewards.

Management consultant Charles N. Weaver and psychologist Michael D. Matthews compared workers' responses to surveys conducted in the early 1970s and the early 1980s by the National Opinion Research Center. At both times, men chose what they considered to be the most important aspect of a job from five possible criteria.

In the early 1970s, 53 percent listed interesting and meaningful work as their preference. The next most popular choice was a job offering opportunities for advancement. Providing a high income only ranked third, followed by job security and short work hours.

When the researchers analyzed the responses of working men to the same questions in the early 1980s, they found that although a rewarding job was still the most popular choice, fewer than half of those questioned listed it as their most important requirement. High income, on the other hand, rose in importance, ousting career advancement for second place, Weaver and Matthews report (*Personnel,* Vol. 64, pp. 62–65).

The increasing preference for high-paying jobs rather than intrinsically rewarding ones may be only a temporary response to inflation, say Weaver, of St. Mary's College in San Antonio, Texas, and Matthews, of Drury College in Springfield, Missouri. But they fear it is part of a fundamental shift in attitudes during the past 10 or 15 years toward greater materialism and individualism. Although the researchers did not break workers down by age, they suspect much of this trend is due to the influx of younger workers with more hedonistic values.

Source: Stark, E. (1988, February). For love or money? *Psychology Today.*

satisfied. Any happiness attained from hygiene factors is at best temporary. If you were given a substantial raise, you would undoubtedly be thrilled. However, your joy would only be short-lived. Soon you would be looking for another raise.

Since external and hygiene factors can bring only brief and fleeting satisfaction, psychologists have focused most of their attention on growth and in-

EXHIBIT 7-5

Why People Take the Wrong Job

We all like and need money and have some healthy needs for status and recognition as well. But because in our Western society having these things implies that one is a "good" person, we sometimes put too much value on them. As a result, many people end up doing what will bring rewards rather than what fits them. They are seen as good members of society but don't feel good about themselves.

Executives we spoke with often justified accepting jobs they didn't really want on the ground that the material rewards the jobs provided were essential to realizing a fulfilling private life. They fail to realize (except in hindsight) that no matter how much they earn, no matter how much status is attached to the position, their private lives will suffer through emotional spillover if the job doesn't fit them.

Source: Bartolome, F., & Evans, P. A. Lee. (1980, March/April). Must success cost so much? *Harvard Business Review.*

flex-time Program that permits employees to schedule their own hours of work

trinsic motivation. They have investigated ways to improve morale and job satisfaction through job enrichment. Job enrichment implies increasing responsibility and freedom and allowing more variety.

One type of enrichment that is gaining popularity is *flex-time*. Each employee is permitted to work hours that fit in with their tasks and projects as well as with other needs. Employees are responsible for writing their own schedules. For example, if a particular job requires working late on Monday night, a person could choose to sleep late one morning or leave early on Friday. Four-day workweeks are as feasible as six-day workweeks. Workers may decide when they prefer to do their jobs and work at a time when they are most motivated.

Another form of enrichment was tried at a Volvo automobile plant. Each person at the plant was given added responsibilities. Their jobs were made more diverse, and they were permitted to make more decisions. Gyllenhammer (1977) found that this approach not only improved morale but also increased productivity. Currently, five Volvo plants have adopted this type of job enrichment.

management by objectives (MBO) System that requires managers to set goals and employees to develop their own strategies to accomplish the goals

Management by objectives (MBO) is undoubtedly the most famous of the many attempts at job enrichment. MBO is a system that requires the employer to set goals. Each employee then decides on personal strategies or objectives to help reach the goals. In a sense, employees design their own jobs. They are then held individually responsible for accomplishing their own goals.

For example, assume that a woman works for a community recreation center. Her employer sets a goal of attracting more teenagers to the center. The woman may set any objectives she wishes to help reach her employer's goal. Her list of objectives could include booking a rock concert, scheduling teen dances and hayrides, or creating a competitive sports program. Since she is selecting her own strategies, presumably her intrinsic motivation for their accomplishment will be increased. She has a greater sense of responsibility for achieving her own objectives.

Although MBO makes sense as a theory, it is not always an effective way to increase intrinsic motivation and growth. First, not all jobs are conducive to this approach. How can a tollbooth worker or a short-order cook possibly set their own objectives? In addition, MBO has sometimes created problems. Both the employer and the employee must fully understand each other. This often requires exceptional communication skills. If there is any misunderstanding, pressures and tension will usually result.

Exercise 7-11

Imagine you are job hunting. You want to be certain you will be satisfied with both the hygiene and growth aspects of your new job. List three hygiene and three growth conditions that would help you feel satisfied with the job.

Hygiene	Growth
Salary	A sense of Acheivment
Fringe Benefits	& Accomplishments
Job Security	recognition.
Administration	

You may check your lists in the Feedback section.

Opposing Incentives

Sometimes incentives can pull you in opposite directions. You like the hours and location of one job, but prefer the salary of another. The stronger incentive will usually pull you.

Dieting is an example of opposing incentives. On the one hand you are pulled by the appeal of food, and on the other hand you are drawn toward a slimmer appearance. Usually the food is a stronger incentive and the diet fails. Some recent research has shown that spouses can help strengthen incentives toward a slimmer appearance by lending their encouragement and support.

But according to Stuart and Davis (1972) some husbands have difficulty helping their wives lose weight. Stuart studied a group of women who had difficulty losing weight. He found their husbands were strengthening the food incentive. Although they knew their wives were trying to diet, they constantly tempted them with appealing refreshments. The men had a variety of reasons for wanting to keep their wives obese. Some liked to use their wives' weight as a tactic in arguments, calling their wives "fat slobs." Others used their wives' fatness as an excuse for extramarital affairs. Still others preferred to keep their wives unattractive, fearing that if they were slimmer, they might become unfaithful. Clearly, none of these men could encourage their wives' dieting and provide the required incentives.

Next time you diet, plan to keep your kitchen free of food incentives. If you can find a mate who will encourage slimness, you will be more likely to lose weight!

Does this man appear to be pulled by a food incentive? Unfortunately, food is often a stronger incentive than the desire to lose weight. (*Joel Gordon*)

Checkpoint

Use the following questions to check your understanding of this final portion of the chapter. Indicate whether each statement is true or false.

15. __F__ According to Maslow higher needs must be met before lower needs.
16. __T__ Maslow's hierarchy cannot explain some human behaviors.
17. __F__ Most people self-actualize by the time they reach college.
18. __T__ People who reach the level of self-actualization can enjoy very simple experiences.
19. __T__ Peak experiences are usually brief.
20. __F__ An artist who is paid for his paintings is likely to have increased intrinsic motivation.
21. __F__ Social approval tends to diminish intrinsic motivation.
22. __T__ An improvement in health benefits will make the hygiene aspect of a job more satisfying.
23. __F__ If the hygiene aspect of a job is satisfying, you will have increased intrinsic motivation at work.
24. __T__ Job enrichment helps to improve intrinsic motivation and growth.
25. __T__ Management by objectives is a form of job enrichment.
26. __F__ Employee morale will improve if the employer makes more decisions.

Check your responses against the Checkpoint Answer Key at the end of the chapter. If you had difficulty with any question, reread the text. If you had little or no difficulty answering questions or have resolved problems that you might have had, you are ready to check yourself against the chapter inventory that follows.

CHAPTER INVENTORY

Use this list of objectives as a review checklist. You should be able to do each of the tasks outlined in the objectives and apply them to everyday examples. If you can, you may feel confident that you have mastered the material in this chapter.

1. Define motivation.
2. Distinguish between conscious and unconscious motivation.
3. Describe the role of needs and incentives in motivation.
4. Explain why physiological needs must be met.
5. Identify and describe stimulation and safety and security needs.
6. Recognize love and belongingness as affiliation needs and provide examples.
7. Specify how advertisers exploit the need for love and belongingness.
8. Distinguish between the characteristics of individuals with high and low needs to achieve.
9. Describe the characteristics of workaholism.
10. Describe the need for power.
11. Explain how fear of success can interfere with achievement.
12. Identify the order of the steps on Maslow's hierarchy of needs.

13. Explain the relationship between Maslow's hierarchy of needs and individual motivation.
14. List and explain the characteristics of individuals who have reached self-actualization.
15. Distinguish between intrinsic and extrinsic motivation and describe their relationship.
16. Describe how growth and hygiene factors affect job satisfaction.
17. Identify three types of job enrichment.
18. Define incentive and provide one example of how incentives affect motivation in dieting.

Feedback

The correct answers to the exercises follow. If you did not answer an exercise correctly, review the preceding pages and return to the exercise to correctly complete it.

7-1. *a.* Conscious
   b. Unconscious
   c. Unconscious
   d. Conscious

7-2. You were "pushed" to buy the first two glasses because you had been deprived of fluid and were motivated by your thirst need. You were "pulled" to ask for the third glass of lemonade by the incentive of pleasing the children.

7-3. A child who is undernourished will be preoccupied with a need for food. If the child is well-fed with a good breakfast, he or she will be able to progress to higher needs in Maslow's hierarchy.

7-4. Edgar is a type t. There is little or no risk or excitement in watching a plant. Edgar seems to enjoy certainty and stability.

7-5. Every sentence described affiliation and approval needs and should have been checked.

7-6. *a.* High achiever: The carpet would give her a higher status. High achievers are conscious of status.
   b. High achiever: High achievers enjoy getting positive feedback from others.
   c. Low achiever: A high achiever would prefer an activity that reflected achievement.
   d. Low achiever: High achievers are motivated more by a sense of accomplishment than by money.
   e. High achiever: High achievers like to improve their personal skills.
   f. Low achiever: High achievers prefer to be independent and set their own goals.
   g. Low achiever: Low achievers usually have overprotective parents.
   h. Low achiever: Low achievers prefer games of chance to games of skill.

7-7. *a.* Workaholics are successful, enjoy themselves, and are respected.
   b. It is difficult to socialize with workaholics.

7-8. Max had been working at the esteem, self-esteem level. A lower need arose. Max fell back to his physiological need for sleep.

7-9. *a.* Appreciation
   b. Sensitivity, acceptance, honesty
   c. Acceptance, sense of humor, honesty
   d. Creativity
   e. Appreciation, honesty
   f. Sensitivity

7-10. *a.* Ted had an intrinsic motivation to chop wood. When external rewards (extrinsic motivation) in the form of money were introduced, Ted's intrinsic motivation diminished. Extrinsic motivation tends to diminish intrinsic motivation.
   b. If Ted is not paid for chopping and splitting wood but is praised for his fine work, his intrinsic motivation might be restored.

7-11.

Hygiene	**Growth**
Good administration	Flex-time
Good salary and fringe benefits	A job with responsibility
Good job security	Management by objectives

Checkpoint Answer Key

1. *b*	**8.** *a*	**15.** *false*	**22.** *true*
2. *d*	**9.** *b*	**16.** *true*	**23.** *false*
3. *a*	**10.** *c*	**17.** *false*	**24.** *true*
4. *b*	**11.** *a*	**18.** *true*	**25.** *true*
5. *b*	**12.** *b*	**19.** *true*	**26.** *false*
6. *c*	**13.** *c*	**20.** *false*	
7. *c*	**14.** *d*	**21.** *false*	

CHAPTER 8

UNDERSTANDING EMOTIONS

The main thing in life is not to be afraid to be human.

Pablo Casals

Have you ever played a game with a computer and felt like a complete loser? Whether you were losing a game of soccer, football, or chess or were not able to follow computer-generated notes, you might have found yourself becoming angry and frustrated. Undoubtedly you have also experienced a few wins over a computer. Recall the sense of satisfaction and glee you felt. Your opponent, the computer, can never sense or feel these emotions.

Emotions are one area where humans are clearly superior to machines. But unfortunately emotions are not always helpful; sometimes they can interfere with intellectual abilities. When you felt upset about losing to a computer, you might have been dwelling on your feelings rather than on better strategies for winning. Similarly, you might have felt so proud of your victories that your concentration was broken. In this chapter you will learn ways to improve your understanding, expression, and handling of emotions.

Emotions separate humans from machines. However, it is extremely difficult to define and measure specific human emotions. Most psychologists rely on self-reports and bodily, facial, and physiological changes to estimate likely emotions. In this chapter you will learn how each of these measures is used. You will also become acquainted with some basic human emotions: anger, fear, and joy. Attention will be focused on conflicts that lead to frustration and the stress that emotions can cause.

WHAT ARE EMOTIONS?

emotion Feeling that
arouses an individual
to act or change

Emotions are internal feelings that arouse people to act or to change within themselves. These feelings can be pleasant, unpleasant, or mixed. Emotions are rarely pure. Consider the case of a father waiting for his 15-year-old daughter to come home from a Saturday-night party. The clock strikes 1 A.M. The father paces the floor. The phone rings. It is his daughter. She announces she is about to leave the party and will be home in twenty minutes. This poor father is feeling a variety of emotions. He is pleased that his daughter was considerate and called him. He is relieved that she is safe. But he is also angry that he is being deprived of his sleep because of her late hours. It is likely he also has some concerns and fears about her trip home. Is the driver of her car sober? Are the other drivers on the road lucid enough to be cautious? Perhaps he becomes angry with himself for worrying about her. It would be difficult to describe the many emotions he is experiencing. Most psychologists would say he is feeling a form of all three of the basic emotions: joy, anger, and fear.

Identifying this man's emotions was simplified because his situation was described. But suppose you stopped in to visit him without knowing his daughter was out. (Admittedly, 1 A.M. would be a strange hour for a casual visit!) How could you assess his emotions? You might ask him to *describe* how he felt. But his feelings were so mixed, he might have trouble sorting and recognizing each of them. And even if he were able to separate his different emotions, he might prefer not to disclose one or more of them to you.

As an alternative you could choose to *observe* him. Perhaps you could detect a worried expression or a face flushed with anger. But could you be certain that anger was causing the flushing? Maybe his flushing results from embarrassment. It is 1 A.M. and he may feel awkward if you learn that his daughter is still out. You watch him pace the floor. But again you cannot be certain whether he is angry, fearful, or joyfully exercising. Observation provides awareness that emotions are being experienced, but we need additional information before we can determine precisely which emotion.

So you open a bag filled with stethoscopes, blood-pressure gauges, and an assortment of other devices that *measure physiological changes*. But all you learn is that indeed he is experiencing physiological changes. You conclude that he is feeling some intense emotions. But which emotions and how intense?

Clearly the techniques currently available for measuring and determining emotions are less than adequate. However, each can in some way help give a better understanding of the emotional changes humans experience.

Exercise 8-1

Based on the example of the father awaiting his daughter, identify three methods used to infer types of emotions being experienced. Explain one shortcoming of each method.

a. _describing the emotions (may leave out one or two feelings that the person does not want you know about_

b. _observing the person (cannot be absolutely sure in pinpointing the emotions._

c. _measuring physiological changes, (all you learn is that the person is feeling but cannot tell which emotions or how intense they are._

Check your answers in the Feedback section.

Subjective Reports of Emotions

Suppose a psychologist approached you and asked you to describe your present emotions. Do you feel happy? fearful? guilty? embarrassed? annoyed? None of these terms describing emotions has a clear or precise definition. All require subjective opinions. Your ideas of happiness may differ widely from the ideas of the person next to you. There are significant individual differences in the interpretation of personal emotions.

If you are like most people, you feel inhibited about discussing emotions openly with a stranger. You could probably best assist the psychologist by describing some recent events in your life and your feelings about them. You may have been experiencing some subtle emotions that are difficult to recognize. Knowledge of a situation often aids in surmising emotions. It is easy to imagine the emotions of a person walking into a surprise party or of someone being handed back a paper graded "A." Similarly, psychologists can infer emotions when events are described.

One technique that has been used to help people recognize and express their emotions is *sensitivity training* in groups which are sometimes referred to

sensitivity training
Form of group therapy
that requires total
honesty and trust
among members

as encounter groups, training groups, or T-groups. Usually a group of ten to twenty people come together for a session. A psychologist or trainer is with the group but does not lead them.

According to Carl Rogers (1970), the group goes through several stages. Initially the group expects the trainer to lead them. When they realize the trainer is not directing their session, there is a general sense of confusion. Group members feel frustrated and annoyed. They resist exposing their own feelings. Soon one or two individuals begin to express past feelings, perhaps old arguments with close friends or their problems in choosing a college. Next members begin to express their unhappiness with the lack of structure and direction within the group. They begin to attack each other and make negative remarks. Rogers believes these negative comments are a way of testing the reactions of other members of the group. Once it is established that the group can accept true feelings, a trusting attitude develops. Finally, deeper emotions are described. The atmosphere becomes open, and personal defenses are broken down. Members are expected to express their feelings honestly. They confront anyone who is dishonest or hides behind a mask.

Clearly, encounter groups provide an intense emotional exchange. Those who have benefited from the sessions claim a greater awareness of their own emotions as well as an increased sensitivity to the feelings of other people. But although some persons profit from the experience, others remain unaffected. Unfortunately, still others may be harmed. Total openness can be painful, particularly when group members are severely critical. Hartley et al. (1976) studied the effects of participating in encounter sessions. The damage rate ranged from less than 1 percent to almost half the group!

Exercise 8-2

Recently, Lucy was dismissed from college for poor grades. Yesterday she lost her job as a salesclerk because a customer complained about her attitude. Lucy is upset and confused about her emotions. She is considering signing up for a T-group session with a local psychologist.

a. How might Lucy benefit from the session? *She may gain a better understanding of her feelings. She may also profit from an honest exchange and acceptance from the group.*

b. Why might Lucy become further upset by the session? *She may have difficulty accepting criticism from the group. It could be painful for her.*

You may compare your responses with those in the Feedback section.

Observing Facial Expressions and Body Language

Studies of facial expressions date back over 100 years. Early studies focused on muscle changes and were performed by anatomists rather than psychologists. Anatomists focus on structural and physical changes rather than emotions. Because of the extensive research of Paul Ekman and his colleagues (Ekman, 1980, 1982; Ekman & Friesen, 1978; Ekman et al., 1980) psychologists have been directing more attention to facial expressions as a measure of emotion.

Ekman developed a system for mapping facial muscle changes, called *Facial Action Coding System*, or FACS. He then used this system to identify facial changes that people can use to express emotions. He found more than 7000 possible combinations of muscle changes. But most of these changes were not associated with any specific emotion. Ekman and his colleague Friesen practiced in front of mirrors and learned to control their own facial muscles. This gave them an awareness of precise muscle changes that accompany different emotions. They then developed a guide for using their FACS system to identify each emotion.

Ekman points out the difference between *spontaneous* and *deliberate* changes in facial expressions. Spontaneous changes occur immediately and are not planned. You hear a hysterically funny joke and break into a wide grin. On the other hand actors and actresses must learn to use facial changes and gestures to express emotions. Their actions are deliberate. Have you ever pretended to be surprised at a gift you really expected? To show surprise, you raised your eyebrows, wrinkled your forehead, and opened your eyes and mouth widely. You may have observed others in the past who expressed surprise spontaneously, or you may have recalled your facial changes from a previous experience. You deliberately imitated a facial expression. The article in Exhibit 8-1 describes some subtle differences between spontaneous and delib-

EXHIBIT 8-1

Anatomy of a Lying Smile

A smile can be deceiving, but can you tell the difference between a decoy and the real McCoy? According to psychologists at the University of California at San Francisco, there are subtle differences between smiles when people are truthful and when they lie about experiencing pleasant feelings.

Smiles that reflect actual enjoyment (See Figure 8-1, left) include the activity of the outer muscle that circles the eye more often than when enjoyment is feigned, report Paul Ekman and his colleagues in the March *Journal of Personality and Social Psychology*. Smiles intended to conceal strong negative emotions frequently include muscular action around the lips and eyes linked to disgust (right), fear, contempt or sadness.

The investigators studied videotapes of 31 student nurses. First, each subject was told to describe her feelings to an interviewer after seeing a pleasant nature film. Then they saw a film showing amputations and burns and were told to convince the interviewer they had seen a pleasant film. Descriptions of the young womens' facial muscle actions, such as pulling the brows together and wrinkling the nose, were made by two observers experienced in using a facial measurement technique developed by Ekman and his co-workers.

Although deceptive interviews produced significantly more "masking" smiles across the entire group, on an individual basis the face provided clues to deceit in fewer than half of the subjects. The researchers are now looking at how other behavioral signs, including body posture and speech content, may operate as clues to deceit in different people.

The spectrum of smiles that provide various social signals remains to be determined, add the scientists. For example, "phony" smiles that occur when nothing much is felt were not considered in their study.

Source: (1988, March 15). Anatomy of a lying smile. *Science News.*

Figure 8-1
(Picture Credit: Paul Ekman)

erate facial expressions. Trying to camouflage true feelings results in a different use of facial muscles.

Psychologists are also interested in distinguishing between expressions of emotion common to all people and those that vary from culture to culture. Most of the evidence suggests that facial expressions are universal. Smiles, tightened lips, and frowns express the same emotions in New York, Hong Kong, and Santiago. However, the frequency and intensity of these expressions vary according to culture. According to Morris et al. (1979), culture has a stronger influence on body language than on facial expressions. Body language is a way of showing feelings without using words. Waving a fist, applauding, kissing, and embracing are examples of body language. Most body language is cultural and varies from one society to the next. For example, clapping hands means appreciation and applause in one culture, and worry and anxiety in another.

Some societies discourage open displays of emotions, particularly unpleasant ones. A person who shows sadness or anger is not respected. The stories and novels in these cultures usually relate tales of heroes and heroines who can hold in emotions with exceptional control. Other groups expect emotions to be expressed openly. They use more gestures, movements, and voice changes. Psychologists have found that body language as a method of expressing emotions is usually similar within families. Some families tend to show emotional outbursts. They jump up and down, cheer loudly at games, and wave their arms frantically when angry. Others are more stoic: They applaud politely and hold in their anger. One study found that married couples grow to look alike as a result of using similar facial expressions (see Exhibit 8-2).

Think about the methods members of your family use to express emotions. Do you use some of the same body language?

Exercise 8-3

Mr. Clarke, a senior personnel manager, is interested in hiring someone for a dangerous international job. He is interviewing people from several different countries. As he describes the frightening aspects of the assignment, he watches their facial expressions. (He is an expert at FACS.) Only those applicants who show no signs of fear in the use of their facial muscles are considered for the job.

His assistant, Mr. Lewis, prefers to focus on body language. He notices whether the candidates pace the floor, shift their weight from foot to foot, or twiddle their thumbs as the dangerous job is described.

a. Whose method do you prefer, Mr. Clarke's or Mr. Lewis's? Why? _Mr. Lewis's Because even though they can hide their emotions their body language tells a story in itself. Mr. Clarks is more reliable_

EXHIBIT 8-2

217

UNDERSTANDING
EMOTIONS

Wedded Faces

As is commonly believed, husbands and wives do grow to look alike, reports psychologist Robert B. Zajonc.

With several of his graduate students, Zajonc collected facial photographs from husbands and wives in 12 Midwestern couples. Half the photos were taken when the couples first married, half about 25 years later. College undergraduates rated youthful and older pairs of these faces for either their resemblance to one another or for the likelihood that the individuals depicted were married.

With younger faces, students did no better than chance would predict at identifying the husbands and wives. However, "after 25 years the two spouses [were] perceived as more similar in appearance...and more likely to be married to each other."

Why should married people look more alike with time? Earlier studies suggest that people in close proximity tend to mimic one another's facial expressions, the researchers say. Daily mimicry among spouses, they write, "would leave wrinkles around the mouth and eyes, alter the bearing of the head, and the overall expression. Eventually [it] would produce...changes that make spouses appear more similar than they originally were."

Not only do emotions influence our facial expressions, but in a controversial theory Zajonc has proposed that facial expressions also help produce emotions. Tensing or relaxing facial muscles, he says, can alter the flow of blood to the brain, in turn regulating the release of various neurochemicals that may influence our moods. In this way, mimicked facial expressions may aid spouses in empathizing with one another, since such imitation could lead to shared emotions.

If empathy is gained from facial mimicry, couples who have grown more alike in appearance should have better marriages. In fact the researchers found that the greater the resemblance between spouses, the greater their happiness with their marriage.

The researchers believe that their results may also explain similarities in appearance between other family members. As with married partners, sons and daughters also share a close environment and are vulnerable to the effects of mimicry. Resemblance among family members "may be more than a matter of common genes," the researchers say.

Source: Hall, H. (1987, December). Wedded faces. *Psychology Today.*

b. What is the weakness of both techniques? *distinguishing No Spontaneous or Deliberate Behavior. They could be Acting just to get the job.*

Compare your responses to those in the Feedback section.

Physiological Changes with Emotion

None other than Hippocrates, the father of modern medicine, once wrote, "It is more important to know what kind of person has a disease, than to know what kind of a disease a person has." Hippocrates recognized that emotional factors are crucial to the understanding of internal bodily changes. For many years, as modern medicine progressed, Hippocrates' ideas were lost. There was a stricter emphasis on medical, surgical, and technological methods. However, current estimates suggest that approximately 80 percent of all physiological and medical problems have emotional components. Hippocrates had a valid point!

Undoubtedly, you are aware of some physiological changes that accompany your own emotions. Think of how your body reacts when you experience stress. Stress can be caused by an overabundance of any emotion. Although fear and anger are most commonly associated with stress, excessive joy can likewise be a cause.

Perhaps you have had butterflies in your stomach, a dryness in your mouth, or a pounding heart. All three are common reactions to stress. Other body reactions that you may have noticed in intense emotion include faster breathing, sweating, facial flushing, dilation of eye pupils, and a tightening of muscles. There are also other changes that can only be measured by technical instruments. In times of stress there are many increases in body functions. Blood pressure, heart rate, the amount of blood discharged to muscles, the rate and depth of breathing, the flow of adrenalin, and the electric resistance of the skin all increase.

There has also been research to determine whether such different emotions can produce a specific or unique change. Presently there is little or no conclusive evidence to suggest that different emotions produce unique changes. The same physiological changes can result from a variety of different emotions. Intense fear, anger, or joy can cause the same internal bodily changes.

Exercise 8-4
Assuming Mr. Herkimer (Figure 8-2) is experiencing some intense emotions, list three reactions his body may be encountering.

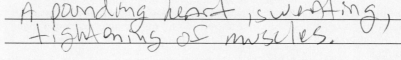

A pounding heart, sweating, tightening of muscles.

Figure 8-2

"Have a seat, Mr. Herkimer, and I'll get your file."

The Pros and Cons of Physical Responses to Emotions

Generally your body's response to stress helps you. With the many increases in functioning, you are better prepared for emergencies. Because of increases in blood flow and adrenalin, you have additional strength. You can run faster and have more energy. You have probably heard tales of little old ladies who were able to lift cars in order to save loved ones. Perhaps you have even had a burst of strength yourself when you felt emotional stress. A drowning person often finds additional stamina and manages to swim. Similarly, athletes often surpass all of their previous achievements at an important contest. They feel intense emotion when the big event occurs. Remember the Olympic hockey game in 1980? No one imagined the American team had a chance of winning!

Unfortunately, physiological reactions that accompany emotions do not always cause pleasant results. Continuous stress can make physical problems more likely. Dry coughs, ulcers, headaches, high blood pressure, strokes, and heart attacks can result from prolonged physiological changes. In studying voodoo deaths, Seligman (1974) reported that people can die from fear. A person who believes a voodoo threat will undoubtedly experience intense fear. At times of intense fear, heart rate increases rapidly. After a prolonged increase in rate, the heart begins to compensate by slowing down. Occasionally the heart overcompensates, slowing down to a halt, causing death.

Exercise 8-5

In your own words, describe one example of how emotions can cause physical changes that are helpful and two examples of changes that are harmful.

a. Helpful: _Duest of Stength & Additional Stamina_

b. Harmful: _Continuous stress and fear._

_____

_____

_____

You may compare your examples to those in the Feedback section.

Measuring Physical Changes in Emotion

The best-known device for measuring physical changes that result from emotions is the *polygraph,* more commonly known as a lie detector, since it is frequently used to check truthfulness. The polygraph or lie detector is a machine that measures heartbeat, blood pressure, breathing, digestive activities, and electric resistance on the surface of the skin. A number of electrode plates are attached to the body of the person being checked. The plates are then connected to a machine that will record physical changes on a sheet of printout. The assumption is that lying causes intense emotion. Since intense emotion results in physiological changes, the machine should record noticeable variation whenever a person lies. Conversely, there should be little or no physiological change when a person is truthful.

polygraph Instrument commonly known as a lie detector that measures changes in heart beat, blood pressure, breathing, digestive activity, and electric resistance on the skin surface

Imagine you are hooked up to a polygraph machine. In the usual procedure, you would be asked a number of neutral questions that would not arouse any emotion. Neutral questions might include, "What is your name?" or "What did you have for breakfast this morning?" Since these questions do not usually arouse emotions, it would be assumed that your heart rate, blood pressure, and other physiological functions were at their normal levels. These levels would be recorded as your "baseline." Next you would be asked critical questions such as, "Were you with Louis the night he was murdered?" or "Where did you hide the stolen car?" Any variation from your baseline on the printout would make the examiner suspicious that you were emotionally aroused.

But does this emotional arousal mean that you are lying? The accuracy of polygraphs as lie detectors has been disputed. Just being strapped to a machine and being questioned can arouse emotions. Also there are immense individual differences in emotional arousal when lying. Some people can lie easily, while others feel intense emotion with even a mild uncertainty. Cheating on polygraphs is not uncommon. Subjects can tense their muscles and dwell on upsetting thoughts when the examiner is asking neutral questions. Since physical stress can provide the same changes as emotional stress, lie detector cheaters can bite the corner of their tongues or press their foot against a nail in their shoe on neutral questions. This will produce a high baseline. When critical questions are asked, little change will be detected. Unfortunately, as shown in Exhibit 8-3, polygraphs have been wrong!

Psychologists agree that no single method is effective for measuring emotions. Even the combinations of verbal reports, facial expression, body language, and polygraphs do not always give accurate results. However, if a variety of measures are used, mistakes are less likely.

Checkpoint

Use the following questions to check your understanding of this portion of the chapter. Choose and mark the one correct response to each question.

1. Emotions are feelings that arouse a person. What type of feelings are they?
   a. Internal feelings
   b. Pleasant feelings
   c. Unpleasant feelings
   d. Pure feelings
2. Assume you want to assess the current emotions of another person. The person is giving you a verbal description of present feelings. Which of the following would be most useful in your assessment of the person's emotions?
   a. An understanding of the person's inhibitions
   b. An understanding of the person's frustrations
   c. An understanding of the situation that aroused the emotions
   d. An understanding of the people who were present when the emotion was aroused
3. What is the purpose of sensitivity training?
   a. To permit people to understand the physiological changes that accompany emotions
   b. To help people interpret the facial expressions and body language of others

EXHIBIT 8-3

221
UNDERSTANDING
EMOTIONS

> ### The Search for Truth
>
> An Ohio man who spent two years in jail for a murder he didn't commit says he plans to work to outlaw lie detector tests which contributed to his own conviction. "I'm not angry at the jury or the prosecutors," said Floyd Fay, who was cleared of the crime last week. "But that polygraph examiner hasn't seen the last of me." Court officials said two polygraph examiners who said Fay was lying about the murder of a store owner had interpreted Fay's results backwards. "I want to somehow effectively use the facts of my case," said Fay, "to help prevent someone else from getting in the same situation." Fay claims any criminal who knows how to beat a polygraph can beat it. Two other men were arrested for the crime last week.

Source: (1980, November 2). The search for truth. *Washington Star.*

    c. To allow people to change their own facial expressions by practicing in front of mirrors
    d. To help people understand and express their emotions openly

4. Which of the following is most likely to be affected by a person's cultural experiences?
    a. Facial expression
    b. Body language
    c. Physiological changes
    d. Inner feelings

5. Which of the following gives the best description of the cause of stress?
    a. Fear and anger
    b. Mild feelings of emotion
    c. Intense emotion
    d. Unpleasant experiences

6. Many studies have attempted to associate each emotion with specific physiological changes. What have these studies concluded?
    a. Each emotion produces a different and unique physiological change.
    b. Anger produces unique physiological changes.
    c. Fear produces unique physiological changes.
    d. Different emotions can produce the same physiological changes.

7. What happens to your energy level at times of stress?
    a. It remains constant.
    b. It increases.
    c. It decreases.
    d. It decreases then increases.

8. According to Seligman, what is the cause of voodoo deaths?
    a. Inhibitions about expressing emotions
    b. A lack of understanding of facial expression
    c. Inappropriate body language
    d. Bodily reactions to fear

9. What is the purpose of a polygraph machine?
    a. To determine which emotion a person is experiencing
    b. To determine why a person is lying
    c. To measure physiological changes
    d. To determine whether a person has criminal tendencies

10. Why is the polygraph not always an effective lie detector?
    a. It is difficult to measure heart rate and blood pressure.
    b. Many intense emotions are not accompanied by physiological changes.
    c. Emotions can be aroused for reasons other than lying.
    d. The machine cannot measure physiological changes.
11. What is the best method for measuring emotions?
    a. Verbal reports
    b. Facial expression and body language
    c. Polygraphs
    d. A combination of the above

Use the Checkpoint Answer Key to verify your responses. If you had any difficulty with a question, carefully reread the text. If you had little or no difficulty answering the questions or have resolved any difficulty you might have had, you are ready to continue with the next portion of this chapter.

TYPES OF EMOTIONS

Many psychologists believe there are only three basic emotions: anger, fear, and joy. All other emotions are considered variations on one or more of these three emotions. For example, hatred, rage, and hostility are forms of anger. Jealousy and guilt are based on fear. Love and happiness are fundamentally feelings of joy. Sadness is likely to be a combination of fear and anger.

Have you ever wondered why you become angry or fearful or joyful? Anger, joy, and fear have separate and distinct causes. After studying the causes of each of these three basic emotions, you will look at possible ways to handle and control them.

Anger

frustration Feeling that results whenever you cannot reach a desired goal

Anger is indeed an unpleasant emotion. Think of the last time you felt angry with yourself or with someone else. Anger usually is aroused by *frustration*, associated with a situation that is beyond your control. For example, assume you had a long, hard day at work and are anxious to get home at a reasonable hour. Your car engine will not turn over. You have no idea what is wrong and there is nothing you can do about it. You feel frustrated and your frustration leads to anger. Frustration occurs whenever you cannot reach a desired goal. Psychologists have found that frustration often results in some form of anger or resentment. If you become irritated and kick the car, your behavior is fairly normal.

There are many possible reasons why you cannot reach a desired goal. Sometimes you simply lack the ability. For example, in the case of your car failing to start you were unable to diagnose the problem and correct it. In addition to feeling irritation toward the car, you may have been annoyed with yourself for not learning ways to troubleshoot engine problems. Often people aspire to goals far beyond their abilities. A shy man may wish to be a super-salesman or a woman with limited finances and intelligence may wish to become a nuclear physicist.

Frustration can also result from confusion about goals. Sometimes people feel pulls in more than one direction. Kurt Lewin (1935) specified three types of goal confusion or conflict that people experience. Each of these three types of conflicts leads to a feeling of frustration.

Approach-approach conflicts. Of the three types of conflicts, these are the least frustrating. In an *approach-approach conflict* there are two desirable goals. But you cannot possibly reach both of them at the same time. Maybe there are two good parties in different parts of town at the exact same time on the same night. You must miss one, but which one? Or assume a rich aunt hands you $50,000 to buy yourself a new car. Both a Mercedes and a Porsche look appealing. You must make a choice, but indeed it is a pleasant dilemma. In an approach-approach conflict, you always win, even if you must lose another appealing alternative. As a result, approach-approach conflicts are only mildly frustrating.

Avoidance-avoidance conflicts. These are the most frustrating of the three types of conflicts. You must choose between two undesirable goals. Did your mother ever tell you to clean your messy closet or go to bed? Assuming you disliked cleaning closets and were not tired, you experienced an *avoidance-avoidance conflict*. The thought of wasting hours cleaning a cluttered closet was dreadful, but the notion of suffering hours of boredom was also unappealing. The usual reaction to an avoidance-avoidance conflict is to attempt to escape. Perhaps you threatened to run away from home. When no escape is possible, facing the conflict is inevitable. The result is being forced to make an unpleasant choice. The choice is accompanied by intense frustration and anger.

Approach-avoidance conflicts. These are the most common of the three types of conflicts. Usually a goal has both positive and negative aspects. Eating a piece of chocolate fudge will provide a delicious taste. But it will also cause tooth decay and, perhaps, unwanted pounds. Studying for an exam will result in a better grade, but it will require an evening away from friends.

A student choosing a college is often involved in a complicated *approach-avoidance conflict*. Perhaps the college with the best program is expensive or

approach-approach conflict Conflict that results from choosing between two desirable goals

avoidance-avoidance conflict Conflict that results from being forced to choose between two undesirable goals

approach-avoidance conflict Conflict that results from weighing the positive and negative aspects of a single goal

Figure 8-3
Approach-approach conflict

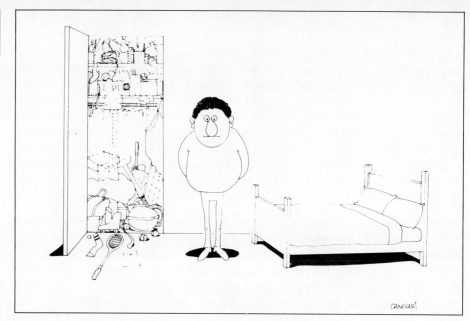

Figure 8-4
Avoidance-avoidance
conflict

a long way from home. A nearby college is good but only has a few specialized courses. On the other hand, the student could skip college and take a full-time job. The job will provide more money now, but future income will be limited. When the positive and negative aspects of more than one goal are judged, a multiple approach-avoidance conflict is being faced. Most people constantly face multiple approach-avoidance conflicts. Beginning with deciding what to wear and choosing a breakfast, you are repeatedly weighing the pros and cons of your alternatives. However, clothing and breakfast choices rarely cause severe frustration. Major decisions on colleges, jobs, marriages, and divorces create far more anxiety.

In approach-avoidance conflicts, the approach tendency is usually stronger at first. Consider a woman who accepts a leading role in a play. She looks forward to the applause on opening night and has an approach tendency. But she knows she feels nervous when performing before groups and has a slight feeling of avoidance. As the goal comes closer, the avoidance tendency increases. By opening night she has butterflies in her stomach and intense stage fright. Think about some of your own approach-avoidance conflicts. Have you ever backed out of an event at the last minute because of an increasing avoidance tendency?

Exercise 8-6

Indicate whether each of the following persons is experiencing an approach-approach conflict, an avoidance-avoidance conflict, or an approach-avoidance conflict.

a. Kim wants to take roller-disco lessons but is afraid she will fall and make a fool of herself.

AP — AV

Figure 8-5
Approach-avoidance
conflict

b. Mike cannot decide whether to order a delicious, juicy steak or luscious lobster Newburg.

AP—AP

c. Josh hates going to Spanish class but will fail the course if he cuts another class.

AV—AV

d. Barry is having trouble deciding whether to vacation at a mountain resort or at the ocean.

AP—AP

e. Eve is having fun at the beach but is afraid she will suffer a severe sunburn if she remains much longer.

AP—AV

f. Irene is looking forward to entertaining her friends at a dinner party but dreads having to cook for an entire day.

_____ AP — AV _____

Exercise 8-7

a. Which individual will probably experience the most frustration and anger? ___Josh___

_____

b. Which persons will probably feel the least frustration and anger? _____

_____ mike & Barry _____

Turn to the Feedback section to check your answers.

Anger and Aggression

Regardless of the type of conflict, the outcome is frustration. Reactions to frustration differ. Sometimes escape is attempted, but often anger results. Some people can tolerate more frustration than others. People use a variety of methods to express their anger. *Aggression* is one of the most common means. Aggression includes a wide range of behaviors from petty quarreling to extreme physical violence. The goal in aggression is to hurt or destroy another person or object either verbally or physically.

aggression Behavior that hurts or destroys another person, either verbally or physically, or both

There are immense differences in aggressive tendencies among people. Some people just withdraw from situations when they sense frustration and anger. Others express their anger violently and become aggressive. Psychologists differ in their explanations of why such variations occur. Whether aggressive tendencies are inherited or learned remains a controversial issue. However, most psychologists are now leaning toward a learning explanation.

Psychologists have found that people rely on past experiences. If in the past aggressive behavior gave a successful outlet for frustration and anger, aggression will be tried again. Research by Bandura and Walters (1963) concluded that aggressive behavior can also be learned from others. They found that children raised by aggressive adults tended to be more aggressive than children reared by adults who emphasized cooperation and peaceful behavior. Berkowitz (1968) noted that normally only certain stimuli or cues will lead to aggression.

Since aggressive behavior can be learned, psychologists have questioned whether films and television programs featuring aggression influence the behavior of viewers. Experiments with children have had mixed results. Although some studies found that children who watched violent television programs behaved more aggressively, others found the young viewers to behave less aggressively. Apparently individual children react differently to seeing violence on a screen. Some psychologists argue that violent programs can provide a healthy outlet for aggressive feelings. Watching a hero whack a villain may help a viewer release personal anger that has been pent up. The article in Exhibit 8-4 reports the results of research in prisons. Aggressive films do not appear to cause an increase in prison violence. Whether violence can actually be controlled through films is the subject of present research.

EXHIBIT 8-4

227

UNDERSTANDING
EMOTIONS

Conflicks Do Not Make Conflicts

Prison wardens sometimes refuse to show movies rather than run the risk that films with violent, sexual, or racial themes will encourage riots and assaults. Their fears, according to a recent survey, may be exaggerated.

David Agresti, an instructor in criminal justice at the University of South Florida in Tampa, and student researchers Linda Getz and Pete Collins asked recreation supervisors in 50 state, federal, and territorial prisons which movies they had shown during a three-month period. Most were regularly screening the strong stuff: in correctional institutions for men, 50 percent of the films were rated R and another 3 percent were rated X. Women inmates saw 38 percent R's and 1 percent X's. The reason, Agresti found, is that most institutions rent films with money from inmate canteens selling cigarettes, supplies, and food: "Because it's inmate money, usually it's inmates and some staff members who choose the films."

The recreation supervisors may have been trying to justify their policies, but they reported no appreciable increases in inmate violence or sexual assaults during or after screenings. Indeed, Agresti argues that prisoners enjoying a film may actually be less prone to violence than those who stay in their cells. If this is so, violent, sexy films may actually promote prison peace, since Agresti found that attendance is directly proportional to the aggressiveness and sex in the films [R- and X-rated movies generally drew 98 percent of the prisoners].

Source: Thomas, P. (1980, June). Conflicks do not make conflicts. *Psychology Today.*

Exercise 8-8

Little Victor's parents often have violent fights. His mother throws pots and pans, and his father has broken vases and windows. Victor is frequently spanked and beaten for misbehaving. In an attempt to control Victor's aggression, his parents do not permit him to watch television programs or movies that show violence.

Little David's parents quarrel occasionally but generally are calm and cooperative. Although they limit the amount of time David may watch television, they allow him to view whatever programs he wishes. David often chooses aggressive shows and films.

Which child is more likely to show aggressive and violent behavior?

Why? *Victor, because he has learned from his parents that aggression & violence is the "way" to handle certain situations plus he has no outlet (like watching violent TV shows) to release his own A & V. Beh.*

Turn to the Feedback section to check your choice and reason.

Handling Anger

There are several options in handling anger. First, you can express your feelings *directly*. If a woman annoys you, you can tell her so in an angry voice or shake your fist at her. If your car will not start, you can kick it. If your boss chastises you, you could empty your wastebasket on his head. Direct anger allows you to vent your feelings. It also helps others to know and understand your feelings. However, obviously there are times when it is not the best option.

A second alternative is to express anger *indirectly*. Sometimes you cannot or should not show anger toward the person or object responsible for your frustration. Instead you place your anger or aggression on a person or object that is less threatening to you. Since your anger changes places from one object to another, indirect anger is often labeled "displacement." Have you ever had a teacher who seemed to pick on you? You probably were wise if you avoided a direct expression of your anger. Direct anger may have increased the friction. If you acted in a friendly manner toward the teacher but slammed down your books or became irritable with a loyal friend, you were displacing your anger. Although this alternative allows you to release your anger, it is definitely unfair to whoever receives the brunt of your emotions. Figure 8-6 shows the classic example. A man is harassed by his boss. The man takes his anger out on his wife who, in turn, scolds her child. The child vents anger on the family pet.

A third option is to hold in or *internalize* anger. Rather than express anger openly, you hold it inside yourself. Averill (1976) found that anger is often considered a negative or "bad" emotion. As a result people try to hide their anger and bottle it within themselves. This attitude toward anger can be unhealthy. As anger builds up and becomes more intense, stress results. As mentioned earlier in the chapter, stress causes physiological changes that can be unpleasant and harmful to general health. People who internalize their feelings of anger are more likely to suffer a number of possible physical disorders.

A final alternative is to *control* the onset of the feeling of anger. The first step in controlling anger is to find the cause. Sometimes the cause of anger can be avoided. If a coworker's lunchtime bragging irritates you, a different table in the lunchroom may be your answer. Unfortunately the solution is rarely that simple. More often people find themselves in situations that are unavoidable. But preparation and planning can help.

Psychologists have developed a number of suggestions for controlling anger. Talking to yourself in a positive way can be beneficial. Likewise a sense of humor can often break intense anger. By finding something amusing in the situation, you can make tension crumble. Physical exercises have also been effective in controlling anger. Using the added physical strength that intense emotions produce can help to release some pressure. Jogging, racquetball, hitting punching bags, and lifting weights are effective ways to use up physical energy.

Relaxation exercises have also been beneficial in controlling anger. One type of relaxation exercise stresses tensing and relaxing muscles in various parts of your body: your arms, your legs, your feet, and even your nose and tongue. Another relaxation exercise emphasizes deep breathing.

Exercise 8-9

Judy spent the past two months working diligently on her psychology term paper. Her professor refused to grade it because it was submitted one hour late. Judy felt her face flush with anger and her heart pound.

Indicate how Judy might behave if she handles her anger directly, indirectly, and internally.

The Saturday Evening
POST
March 20, 1954 - *15¢*

New York's Communist Cop
By CRAIG THOMPSON

THIS IS ON ME
By Bob Hope

*For 25 years a professor of psychiatry has used this painting
to teach students about frustration and projected hostility.*

Figure 8-6
A classic example of
indirect anger or
displacement

a. Direct anger: _letting her professor know how she feels about his decision._

b. Indirect anger: _she may take her anger out on her friends or a close family member_

c. Internalized anger: _holding her anger in and becoming stressed._

Exercise 8-10

Describe three possible methods Judy could use to control her anger.

a. _having a sense of humor about the situation._

b. _talking to herself in a positive way._

c. _physical exercise._

You may check your responses in the Feedback section.

Joy

Joy, clearly the most pleasant of the three basic emotions, is the most difficult to define. Joy has been vaguely described as an active positive feeling of exhilaration and pleasure. Joy is a transient emotion and can last a few seconds, minutes, or hours. Joy that lasts and endures longer has been labeled happiness. Happiness, however, requires more than the active pleasure of joy. In his research on happiness, Freedman (1978) found that joy can only last when a person also has a sense of contentment and inner peace. A lottery winner will experience an immediate emotion of joy when the winning number is called and again when the money is awarded. However, whether this joy will endure and lead to happiness is another question. Psychological research has found that lottery winners rarely experience lasting joy or happiness from their winnings.

Freedman surveyed 100,000 people to find out the relationship between lifestyles and happiness. He found that married couples tend to be happier than both couples who are living together and single individuals. Money did not help procure happiness. Once a basic standard of living is met, increases in income did not cause increases in happiness. Age and religion did not influence happiness either. Freedman concluded that social relationships had the strongest bearing on joy and happiness.

Happiness is indeed a desirable state. Not only does it provide positive personal feelings, but it can also have other beneficial outcomes. Happiness is good for your health, and can even enhance learning.

Exercise 8-11

Professor Bliss is working on a formula for happiness. Student assistants have made six suggestions for components of happiness: joy, social relationships, money, age, religion, and inner peace. According to Freedman's research, which of the suggested six components should be included in his formula?

You may check your response in the Feedback section.

Fear

Fear involves a sense of danger. The most common reaction is to attempt to escape from the fearful situation. Fears may be either realistic or unrealistic. Some realistic fears are essential and are necessary for survival. Vicious dogs, moving cars, poisonous snakes, burning buildings, contagious diseases, and toxic foods should be feared and avoided. Realistic fears are specific. Not all dogs are feared, only those that are threatening. If you have realistic fears, an affectionate puppy that jumps on your lap will not precipitate a fear reaction. Normally parked cars, gartersnakes, campfires, common headcolds, or healthy breakfasts would not arouse realistic fears.

Have you ever feared failing an exam? Your grade probably reflected whether your fear was realistic or unrealistic. If you scored a D or an F, you undoubtedly had a realistic fear.

Advertisers capitalize on realistic fears. They feature such scenes as a lone woman stranded out in a frigid snowstorm by a car that will not start. If you have ever feared this type of situation, you are a perfect target for their new battery. You are probably also familiar with ads that show a family being forced to move from their attractive home and begin an impoverished lifestyle. Someone lacked an appropriate life insurance policy. Scare tactics are common in commercials and letters advertising smoke detectors, burglar alarms, and automobile and theft insurance. The ads threaten an unpleasant, fearful outcome if their product is not purchased.

Checkpoint

Use the following questions to check your understanding of this portion of the chapter. Match the term on the left with the correct phrase from the list on the right.

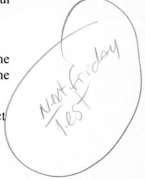

12. __c__ Anger
13. __d__ Frustration
14. __e__ Approach-approach conflict
15. __h__ Avoidance-avoidance conflict
16. __i__ Approach-avoidance conflict
17. __A__ Aggression
18. __f__ Displacement
19. __b__ Internalized anger
20. __G__ Relaxation exercises
21. __m__ Social relationships
22. __K__ Joy
23. __L__ Escape
24. __J__ Realistic fears

a. Hurting another person or object
b. An unhealthy approach
c. An unpleasant basic emotion
d. Caused by a blocking or confusion of goals
e. Least frustrating conflict
f. Indirect anger
g. Method for controlling anger
h. Most frustrating conflict
i. Most common conflict
j. Basis for scare tactics used in ads
k. Most pleasant emotion
l. Most common reaction to fear
m. Important for happiness

Check your responses against the Checkpoint Answer Key at the end of the chapter. If you had difficulty with any question, reread the text. If you had little or no difficulty answering the questions or have resolved problems that you might have had, you are ready to continue with the next portion of this chapter.

EMOTIONAL STRESS

As mentioned earlier in the chapter, *stress* is caused by intense emotion. Whether intense anger, fear, joy, or a combination of all three, the result will be stress. Stress creates physiological changes that can be dangerous. If you are feeling emotional stress, you are more likely to drive your car carelessly. You also might either go on an eating binge or have difficulty eating. Stressful people often drink or smoke more than usual.

stress Tension caused by intense emotion

Sources of Stress

Holmes and Rahe (1967) suggested that major events are the prime cause of stress. They published a list that identifies a number of important experiences that produce intense emotion. Items are ranked from the most stressful to the least stressful. A quick glance at Exhibit 8-5 will reveal that both happy and unhappy experiences can produce stress. Research has found that people who experience stress are more susceptible to a number of diseases and physical problems.

EXHIBIT 8-5

Social Readjustment Rating Scale

Life Event	Answer	Point Value
Death of spouse	yes	100
Divorce	yes	73
Marital separation	yes	65
Jail term	yes	63
Death of close family member	yes	63
Personal injury or illness	yes	53
Marriage	yes	50
Fired from work	yes	47
Marital reconciliation	yes	45
Retirement	yes	45
Change in family member's health	yes	44
Pregnancy	yes	40
Sex difficulties	yes	39
Addition to family	yes	39
Business readjustment	yes	39
Change in financial status	yes	38
Death of close friend	yes	37
Change to different line of work	yes	36
Change in number of marital arguments	yes	33
Mortgage or loan over $10,000	yes	31
Foreclosure of mortgage or loan	yes	30
Change in work responsibilities	yes	29
Son or daughter leaving home	yes	29
Trouble with in-laws	yes	29
Outstanding personal achievement	yes	28
Spouse begins or stops work	yes	26
Starting or finishing school	yes	26
Change in living conditions	yes	25
Revision of personal habits	yes	24
Trouble with boss	yes	23
Change in work hours, conditions	yes	20
Change in residence	yes	20
Change in schools	yes	20
Change in recreational habits	yes	19
Change in church activities	yes	19
Change in social activities	yes	18
Mortgage or loan under $10,000	yes	17
Change in sleeping habits	yes	16
Change in number of family gatherings	yes	15
Change in eating habits	yes	15
Vacation	yes	13
Christmas	yes	12
Minor violation of the law	yes	11

Source: Holmes, T. H., & Rahe, R. H. (1967). The social readjustment rating scale. *Journal of Psychosomatic Research, 2,* 213–218.

Chance of illness within 2 years depends on score: 150 or less, 30% chance, 151 to 299, 50% chance; 300 or above, 80% chance.

Most people face an assortment of daily stresses that do not appear on the list. Whether you are late for class or lose your wallet or receive a huge bill in the mail, you are likely to experience intense emotion. Some psychologists argue that these daily hassles are more stressful than major events (DeLongis et al., 1982; Kanner et al., 1981). They claim that we are prepared for major problems and usually handle them well. However, everyday irritations can bog us down and make us more susceptible to physical problems. Some researchers have identified uplifts or positive events that can increase our resistance to physical problems (Cohen & Hoberman, 1983). A list of typical hassles and typical uplifts is shown in Exhibit 8-6.

Exercise 8-12
Read the following list of events that happened to a college student one day. Identify each event as a *major event*, a *hassle*, or an *uplift*.

a. Favorite song is played on the radio ___uplift___

b. Can't find the car keys ___hassle___

Standing in airport lines and lugging baggage are little hassles that can cause weariness and stress.

EXHIBIT 8-6

"Hassles" and "Uplifts"	
Typical Hassles	**Typical Uplifts**
1. Too many responsibilities	1. Relating well with your spouse or lover
2. Concerns about physical appearance	2. Having enough time to do what you want
3. Being lonely	3. Being visited, phoned, or sent a letter
4. Not enough personal energy	4. Having enough money for entertainment and recreation
5. Concerns about getting ahead	5. Being with children
6. Not enough time for entertainment and recreation	6. Free time
7. Job dissatisfactions	7. Music
8. Concerns about the meaning of life	8. Getting unexpected money
9. Fear of rejection	9. Spending time with family
10. Too many things to do	10. Sex

Source: Adapted from Kanner, Coyne, Schaefer, & Lazarus. (1981).

c. Stuck in heavy traffic on the way to class _____ hassle

d. Closest friend attempted suicide _____ major

e. Receives notice of election to Phi Beta Kappa honor society _____ uplift major

f. Uncle sends check for $50 _____ uplift

Handling Stress

Whether our problems are major events or minor hassles, we must find a way to handle the stress or cope. Coping requires a constant effort to manage the demands that make us feel stressful. Shaver and O'Connor (1986) identified three categories of successful coping:

1. Attacking your problem
2. Rethinking your problem
3. Accepting your problem but lessening the physical effects of the stress it causes

When you *attack* a problem, you confront it directly. You define your problem, consider your options, and choose one or more options as your solution. Imagine you received the stressful news that your grade-point average is too low to permit you to continue in college. First, you would define your problem as being dismissed from of college. Next, you would consider your options. You could consider other colleges, perhaps institutions that are less difficult and competitive. You might also consider working or trying a different career. Another option might be to appeal your case to an academic dean. Your final step would be to choose your best option. According to Pearlin and Schooler (1978), people who attack problems have an increased feeling of control and effectiveness.

Rethinking a problem involves changing your initial judgment. You decide that the situation is not a problem after all. You might see a negative situation as building character. After being dropped by a college, a student might be grateful to be free of academic and money pressures. Often people can see humor in stressful situations. The man in Figure 8-7 is clearly rethinking the traffic problem!

The final approach to coping involves *accepting* a problem and taking steps to avoid any physical effects. If you feel stressed and upset, you might take time out to enjoy some recreation. This approach is useful when problems can be neither avoided nor solved. A mother of several active preschool children will clearly need to arrange for some personal time for fun and rest.

Exercise 8-13

Each of the following persons is coping with stress. Indicate whether the coping strategy involves *attacking* the problem, *rethinking* the problem, or *accepting* the problem (but lessening the physical effects).

a. Ms. A suffered a neck injury in a car accident. She claims the incident has helped her to better understand people who have constant pain. _~~Accepting~~ Rethinking_

b. Mr. N. is with a new date and has been waiting more than thirty minutes for service in a restaurant. He begins to crack jokes about the slow service and decides the delay is permitting extra conversation time. _Rethinking_

c. Mr. W. was given a poor evaluation by his boss. He considered quitting, transferring to another department, and appealing his evaluation. He decided to file an appeal. _Attacking_

"Hey, is this great traffic, or what?"

Figure 8-7
An example of rethinking a problem

d. Mrs. H. works in an office next to a woman with a loud, high-pitched voice. Mrs. H. plans a quiet jog through the park every lunch hour to relieve her tension. _____*Accepting*_____

Stress and the Immune System

Research has provided strong evidence that stressful experiences can weaken our immune systems. The article in Exhibit 8-7 cites studies showing a link between stress and herpes. Maier and Laudenslager (1985) reported that past stressful experiences weaken our present immune systems. Perhaps you have found that after a period of being under pressure, you become ill. After long hours of stressful studying for finals, students often suffer from colds and viruses during exam week. The article in Exhibit 8-8 points out that even minor mood swings can affect our immune systems.

EXHIBIT 8-7

Worried Sick: Hassles and Herpes

A growing number of studies are finding links between psychological states—particularly stress—and immune function. The emerging facts have given birth to a new discipline, psychoneuroimmunology, which seeks to understand the links between psychological status, central nervous system activity, endocrine function and immune response.

In trying to understand this complex relationship, neurobiologists and physicians have found it useful to study people with herpesvirus infections. The virus spends most of its time in a latent, or inactive, phase, residing in the cell bodies of certain peripheral nerves. Occasionally it becomes active, reproduces and is transported down the nerve-cell axons to the skin, where it may cause the formation of blisters or "cold sores." Anecdotal evidence has linked herpes reactivation to psychological stress, but only recently have controlled studies confirmed that link.

New research by Susan Kennedy and her colleagues at Ohio State University's College of Medicine in Columbus took psychological and immunological data from married men and compared them to separated or divorced men matched for age and education; all the subjects had herpes. Separated and divorced men were more anxious, depressed and lonely than their married counterparts—and had higher levels of herpesvirus antibodies. Since antibody levels go up during periods of viral reactivation, higher antibody levels are believed to reflect a depressed immune system incapable of keeping the viral infection under control.

Among married men, marital quality had its correlates with immune function as well. Poorer marital quality was related to higher viral antibody levels, and lower ratios of helper T cells to suppressor cells—another measure of immune suppression.

Other researchers are finding that immune function may be linked not only to personal stress, but also to the perception that others nearby are experiencing stress. Jill Irwin at Queen's University in Kingston, Canada, and her colleagues at the University of Rochester (N.Y.) measured the activity of natural killer cells in mice exposed to foot shocks, and compared those measures to unstressed mice. Unstressed mice not in the vicinity of the stressed mice showed no suppression of normal immunity as measured by killer cell activity. But unstressed mice kept in cages close enough to hear and smell their stressed neighbors showed significant drops in killer cell activity.

The researchers suggest that cues associated with a nearby stressful experience may provoke changes in immune function, perhaps as a result of an increase in sympathetic nervous activity. Such activity—the so-called fight or flight response—has been shown to suppress immunity.

Source: (1987, December 7). Worried sick: Hassles and herpes *Science News*.

EXHIBIT 8-8

237

UNDERSTANDING
EMOTIONS

Moody Immunity

Research has repeatedly shown that extreme stress and depression can weaken the body's ability to fight off potential invaders, but now it seems that even daily ups and downs may toughen the task of the immune system.

To gauge the effect minor stress has on immunity, psychologist Arthur A. Stone and colleagues traced the moods and immune responses of 30 dental students. The researchers gave these men an unfamiliar but harmless protein for a little more than two months and tracked the levels of antibodies their bodies produced against it. (Immunization against a virus works the same way.) The students also reported on their moods three times a week.

Stone and colleagues found that bad moods and relatively low antibody production occurred on the same days, presumably giving the students less "protection" against the foreign protein. Good moods corresponded to a bolstered immune response, better enabling the body to "reject" the substance.

The findings strongly suggest that "minor, daily mood fluctuations are associated with immune functioning," the researchers say. Although previous research had mainly established a link between stress and subsequent sickness, the researchers note their study provides evidence that happiness may play a part in keeping people healthy.

Source: Roberts, M. (1987, November). Moody immunity. *Psychology Today.*

Stress and Illness

While stress can make you more prone to illness, being ill often introduces new stressors. You fall behind in your work. You must consume unappetizing medicines. You worry about whether the medicine will succeed. You might wonder if you should call your doctor or get another opinion. Indeed, illness presents much additional stress.

How you cope with the stress of an illness can affect your recovery (see Exhibit 8-9). Although most research has focused on heart disease, there has been some research on emotional control of cancer (Angell, 1985; Sklar & Anisman, 1981; Taylor et al., 1984). At present there is insufficient data to prove that cancer can be controlled through emotions. However, research and experimentation are continuing.

Checkpoint

Use the following questions to check your understanding of the final portion of the chapter. Choose and mark the one correct response to each question.

25. Which type(s) of intense emotion can cause stress?
    a. Only anger
    b. Both anger and fear
    c. Both fear and joy
    d. Anger, fear, or joy
26. According to Holmes and Rahe, which events are stressful?
    a. Happy experiences
    b. Unhappy experiences
    c. Both happy and unhappy experiences
    d. Minor problems

"Nurse, please show Mr. Fillmond to a larger
room so we can use the big needle."

Figure 8-8
Another stress of
being ill...

27. Some psychologists argue that daily hassles are more stressful than major events. According to research, what can increase our resistance to the stress of these hassles?
    a. Uplifts
    b. Major problems
    c. Illness
    d. Other hassles

28. Bill is making a constant effort to manage the demands that make him feel stressful. What is he doing?
    a. Relaxing
    b. Coping
    c. Lowering his immunity
    d. Resisting

29. Ms. P. has defined a problem, considered her options, and chosen a solution. Which method of coping did she use?
    a. Attacking the problem
    b. Rethinking the problem
    c. Accepting the problem
    d. All of the above

EXHIBIT 8-9

239

UNDERSTANDING
EMOTIONS

Ill-Fated Denial

How well a person deals with the immense stress of life-threatening illness can strongly affect the chances of recovery. For many people, denying their condition's gravity and danger forms a crucial part of coping, a strategy that helps initially but that can have serious health consequences later on.

Most hospitalized heart patients deny their illness to some extent, say Yale University psychologist Jacob Levine and colleagues, who studied 45 male coronary patients after their heart attack, bypass surgery or both. The researchers interviewed the patients within days of their transfer from intensive care to a regular hospital ward and assessed their level of denial. They also tracked the men's health and their compliance with their physicians' orders to quit smoking, attend exercise classes and the like for one year after they left the hospital.

The patients' denial took several forms. Some men used it to shield themselves during the early days of extreme danger. Others continued to reject the reality of their condition long after they had left the coronary ward.

Deniers did better in the short run, spending less time in the hospital and suffering fewer adverse symptoms while there. But facing facts paid off in the long run in fewer rehospitalizations and better, more lasting recovery, the researchers report (*Psychosomatic Medicine,* Vol. 49, pp. 109–117).

Denial has two sides, Levine and colleagues explain. By reducing fear, depression and anxiety, it may keep the resulting physical stresses in check, thus reducing the risk of short-term complications. In the long run, however, denial discourages patients from taking steps to improve their chances of recovery.

Source: Benderly, B. L. (1988, March). Ill-fated denial. *Psychology Today.*

30. What conclusion can presently be reached concerning emotional control of cancer?
    a. Cancer can be controlled by emotions.
    b. Cancer cannot be controlled by emotions.
    c. Emotional factors are more important than medical treatment of cancer.
    d. Emotional factors may play a role in the treatment of cancer.

Check your responses against the Checkpoint Answer Key at the end of the chapter. If you had difficulty with any question, reread the text. If you had little or no difficulty or have resolved problems that you might have had, you are ready to check yourself against the chapter inventory that follows.

CHAPTER INVENTORY

Use this list of objectives as a review checklist. You should be able to do each of the tasks outlined in the objectives and apply them to everyday examples. If you can, you may feel confident that you have mastered the material in this chapter.

1. Define emotions.
2. Identify three methods for measuring emotions and describe the limitations of each.
3. Explain the nature and purpose of sensitivity training.
4. Summarize the role of facial expression and body language in the expression of emotions.

5. Identify physiological changes that accompany emotions.
6. Criticize the use of the polygraph as a lie detector.
7. Identify three basic emotions.
8. Recognize frustration as a cause of anger.
9. Provide examples of three types of conflict that can cause frustration.
10. Describe the role of learning in the development of aggression.
11. Specify four options in handling anger.
12. Explain the relationship between joy and happiness.
13. Distinguish between realistic and unrealistic fears.
14. State the causes of stress and recognize examples of stressful events.
15. Identify methods of handling stress and insomnia.
16. Discuss the relationship among stress, illness, and the immune system.

Feedback

The correct answers to the exercises follow. If you did not answer an exercise correctly, review the preceding pages and return to the exercise to complete it correctly.

8-1. *a.* Verbal descriptions: People are not always aware of their own emotions. Even if they are aware, they are not always willing to share their feelings with others.

b. Observation: Observation does not allow you to distinguish between emotions. The same behavior can represent several different emotions.

c. Measuring physical change: Physical changes do not allow you to distinguish between emotions. Several different emotions can cause the same physical changes.

8-2. *a.* Lucy may gain a better understanding of her feelings. She may also profit from an honest exchange and acceptance from the group.

b. Lucy may have difficulty accepting sharp criticism from the group. It could be painful for her.

8-3. *a.* Mr. Clarke's observation of facial expression is probably more reliable. Facial expression is less influenced by past environment and is likely to be more consistent in people from different cultures.

b. Neither method distinguishes between spontaneous and deliberate behavior. A candidate could be acting just to get the job.

8-4. Mr. Herkimer may be having stomach butterflies, a dry mouth, a pounding heart, an increase in blood pressure, a change in the amount of blood sent to muscles, breathing changes, a flow of adrenalin, and an increase in skin resistance.

8-5. *a.* Emotions can provide a sudden burst of energy that can be helpful.

b. Continuous high levels of emotions can increase the likelihood of physical problems. Intense emotions can cause extreme changes in heart rate and even death.

8-6. *a.* Approach-avoidance

b. Approach-approach

c. Avoidance-avoidance

d. Approach-approach

      e. Approach-avoidance

      f. Approach-avoidance

8-7. *a.* Josh

     b. Mike and Barry

8-8. Victor is more likely to show aggressive and violent behavior. A child's behavior is more likely to be influenced by the behavior of parents than by television.

8-9. *a.* Judy would confront the professor directly. She might express the unreasonableness of not accepting the paper or ask if the professor always submitted work on time.

     b. Judy would displace her anger onto someone or something else. She might throw a book against the wall or start an argument with an unsuspecting friend.

     c. Judy would not express her anger but would keep it inside. She might begin to feel nauseated, her throat might become dry, or she might feel physically uncomfortable.

8-10. *a.* She could convince herself that the paper was not that important. She might even try to say something amusing to break the tension.

      b. She could try to get some physical exercise. Jogging or a fast-paced game of tennis might help her consume some of her emotional energy.

      c. She could try to relax either by taking deep breaths or by alternately tensing and relaxing muscles in her body.

8-11. Joy, social relationships, and inner peace

8-12. *a.* Uplift

      b. Hassle

      c. Hassle

      d. Major event

      e. Major event

      f. Uplift

8-13. *a.* Rethinking the problem

      b. Rethinking the problem

      c. Attacking the problem

      d. Accepting the problem

Checkpoint Answer Key

1. *a*	**9.** *c*	**17.** *a*	**25.** *d*
2. *c*	**10.** *c*	**18.** *f*	**26.** *c*
3. *d*	**11.** *d*	**19.** *b*	**27.** *a*
4. *b*	**12.** *c*	**20.** *g*	**28.** *b*
5. *c*	**13.** *d*	**21.** *m*	**29.** *a*
6. *d*	**14.** *e*	**22.** *k*	**30.** *d*
7. *b*	**15.** *h*	**23.** *l*	
8. *d*	**16.** *i*	**24.** *j*	

CHAPTER 9

ADJUSTING

You cannot care for others unless you care for yourself first.

Lilladee Ballenger

Imagine you are at a carnival. There are exciting sideshows and booths with games all around you. Your attention is suddenly drawn to a sign reading, "Gelda the Great, Fortune Teller—Learn your future for only $8." You walk over to Gelda's tent and see another poster: "Gelda knows your past and everything about you." Intrigued and curious you pay the $8 and enter Gelda's mysterious, dark tent.

Gelda is sitting at a round table in the midst of candles, a crystal ball, and zodiac posters. As you seat yourself across from her, Gelda begins to prove she knows you well. "Gelda knows all. You are a sensitive person, but other people do not fully understand you. You care for others and worry about what they think of you. You have a good sense of humor and enjoy laughing and being amused. You have a tendency to put off things that you do not like to do. Then you feel guilty."

Amazing! Gelda quickly described your personality and some of your adjustment problems rather well. But she also summarized a few characteristics that are common to almost all humans. Fortune tellers often use similar generalizations. These general attributes are found in most people. Psychologists have devised some more efficient ways to evaluate individual personalities and adjustments. In this chapter you will study common adjustment problems as well as some better methods than Gelda's for assessing adjustment and personality.

Your adjustments are based on your self-concept or how you view yourself. Methods that you use to protect your self-concept will be explored. You will review several methods psychologists use to measure personality and consider the shortcomings of each technique. A variety of adjustment problems will be described. Finally, you will learn a few ways to maintain a healthy personality.

WHAT IS ADJUSTMENT?

You are probably not aware of the many simple adjustments you make routinely. Have you ever told a joke and no one laughed? You immediately adapted to the silence either by repeating the punch line, explaining the joke, or excusing the silence with a statement like, "I guess you had to be there!" Or perhaps you have gone to a party in casual clothes only to find everyone in their fanciest attire. Here, you might have excused your appearance with continued explanations that you had not realized the party was semiformal, or jokes about going fishing after the festivities. In each of these situations you had to make adjustments in your thinking and behavior.

Not all adjustments are simple. Marriages, deaths, new jobs, and new friends require some major changes in thinking and behaving. Adjustment is the continuing process of adapting and fitting yourself to your surroundings and meeting the needs of the moment. You must adapt to constant demands and stresses.

Adjustments require both *internal* and *external* changes. Changes in the individual's attitudes, feelings, emotions, and motivation are internal adjustments. External changes are observable behaviors that are based on internal adjustments. Because of new attitudes and feelings, adjustments in outward behavior are made. External changes include such social changes as new roles and relationships.

Suppose a woman tries on last year's summer clothes and notices they are a bit snug. She wants to look better and become more physically fit. She decides to sign up for an aerobic dance class. Her internal attitude about her weight and shape required an adjustment when she noticed the change in her appearance since last summer. This internal adjustment provoked another internal change, a motivation to change her appearance. As a result of her internal adjustments, the woman made an external adjustment, namely a new role as a participant in an aerobic dance class. External adjustments are caused by internal changes. Internal changes result from changes in self-concept or attitudes about yourself.

Exercise 9-1

Assuming that the gentleman in Figure 9-1 is prepared to make some adjustments, describe one internal adjustment and one external adjustment that would be appropriate.

a. Internal: _need to Adjust Attitude ABut importance At work. He wasnt missed._

b. External: _may need to interact with other people more make A few calls or write notes._

Please compare your answers with those in the Feedback section.

Figure 9-1

Self-Concept

Your *self-concept* is your own image or picture of yourself. Your opinions of your health, appearance, disposition, influence on others, abilities, and weaknesses are part of your self-concept. A self-concept is a collection of beliefs based on your judgment of yourself; it is not necessarily accurate. *Self-esteem* is another way of viewing self-concept: A person with high self-esteem has a positive self-concept, while a person with low self-esteem has a negative self-concept.

Most people have a strong need to check themselves and their appearances. Even homes without radios, televisions, dishes, sofas, or tables have at least one and probably several mirrors. Few people can pass a mirror without at least a brief glance at themselves. The appearance aspect of a self-concept is easy to check. However, attitudes toward appearance can vary.

Your opinions about yourself are usually based on the attitudes of other people toward you. The process of developing a self-concept begins with parents. The name that is chosen for a child often reflects the parents' attitude. For example, Reginald Randolph Wallingford III may be expected to become sophisticated. In a study of attitudes toward names, Marcus (1976) found that John was expected to be kind and trustworthy; Ann would not be aggressive; Agnes would be old, while Robin would be young and bright; and Tony would be sociable.

Often parents select names that reflect their hopes and expectations for their child's adjustment and personality. However, regardless of the chosen name, encouragement, love, praise, and interest from parents have been found to aid the development of positive self-concepts or high self-esteem in babies and children. Children who are constantly scolded and rarely shown affection are likely to develop poor self-concepts or low self-esteem. Children with low self-esteem have less self-confidence and develop feelings of inferiority. They are likely to have difficulty interacting with other children and becoming accepted by them. As a result children with poor self-concepts often develop behavior problems that elicit negative attitudes from peers, teachers, team coaches, and other group leaders. This further corrodes self-esteem. Problems in self-concept that occur as early as first grade have been found to affect a child's entire future.

As children develop, they begin to compare themselves with others, silently asking such questions as "Am I as nice as Sally?" "Am I as good-looking as Dana?" or "Can I work as hard as Leslie?" The opinions of friends become critical and far more important than the views of parents as adolescence approaches. Apparently teenagers think highly of each other. A study by David Myers (1980) found that most high school seniors have high self-esteem.

Each person has an *ideal self,* a glamorous or dream self. The ideal self is a goal, the way a person would like to be. Usually an ideal self is based on attributes that are likely to be respected by parents, peers, teachers, and significant people. Your ideal self may change in different social situations. At a party you may want to appear as an attractive flirt, but at a town meeting you might hope to have people view you as a competent leader. In a job interview you may want to impress your potential employer with your efficiency and knowledge, but you probably want your old friends to see you as a warm, relaxed person. Some people are more adept at changing their image than others. If your actual performance meets or comes close to your ideal, you will have high self-esteem.

self-concept Collection of beliefs that a person has about his or her own self-image

self-esteem Personal regard that people have for their own worth

ideal self Person's goal or dream self

*"So the prince and the princess lowered
their expectations and lived reasonably
contentedly forever after."*

Figure 9-2
The prince and the
princess may have
been trying to improve
their self-esteem.

Studies by Levanway (1955) and Wylie (1957) concluded that people with good self-concepts tend to be more accepting of others. They are also more accepting of their own failures. However, they fail less, since they tend to be better achievers than people with low self-esteem. High self-esteem is also related to independence and open-mindedness. People with positive self-images will rely on themselves rather than on others and will be more willing to accept criticism and suggestions.

On the other hand, persons with low self-esteem are sensitive to criticism and blame themselves whenever things go wrong. Because they lack confidence, they will succumb to pressure and can usually be manipulated easily. Flattery is sought and others are criticized to boost their own self-images. Most persons with low self-esteem prefer to work on easy tasks where they can be certain of success. Children with poor self-images are often found playing with friends much younger than themselves. Several studies have shown that low self-esteem is a factor in cheating, drug use, and many forms of delinquency.

What can be done to boost self-esteem? Reassurance, positive comments, and sincere caring play important roles. Rosenbaum (1980) provided a list of techniques to be used by engineering managers to bolster the self-esteem of their employees (see Exhibit 9-1, page 248). Since persons with high self-esteem tend to achieve and accomplish more, boosting self-esteem is beneficial to managers and businesses as well as to each individual's self-image.

Exercise 9-2

Indicate whether each characteristic listed below suggests high self-esteem (a good self-concept) or low self-esteem (a poor self-concept).

a. Is self-confident: _high_

b. Communicates and interacts with others: _high_

Figure 9-3
Clearly, the "little
engine" has high
self-esteem.

c. Experiences wide differences between ideal self and actual behavior:
_____ *Low* _____

d. Is highly critical of others: ___ *Low* _____

e. Is independent: ___ *high* _____

f. Is easily manipulated: ___ *how* _____

g. Is open-minded: ___ *high* _____

h. Is self-reliant: ___ *high* _____

i. Prefers easy tasks: ___ *Low* _____

j. Seeks flattery: ___ *Low* _____

k. Is willing to accept criticism: ___ *high* _____

You may check your answers in the Feedback section.

Self-Concept and Personality

Even if a person has a good self-concept, proper adjustments do not necessarily occur. However, a person with a good self-concept is likely to make better adjustments than someone with a poor self-concept. It is difficult to find criteria that will describe good adjustments and a well-adjusted person. Most often, psychologists look for behaviors that are appropriate for a culture and for the particular situation that a person is confronting.

EXHIBIT 9-1

Promoting Self-Esteem

The following is a list of specific ways to inspire motivation by enhancing self-esteem. At first glance, some of these may seem superficial or trite. Nevertheless, if they are used consistently, the accumulation of them will have a positive impact on motivation.

1. Praise a specific task/job.
2. Give a special assignment.
3. Give an "OK" when you agree with someone.
4. Listen actively.
5. Write down others' ideas, and take them seriously.
6. Accept others' opinions and feelings.
7. Accept differences in others.
8. Express your feelings.
9. Give tangible rewards.
10. Arrange for the boss to acknowledge good work.
11. Spend time with others.
12. Support others' actions.
13. Ask for opinions on how to solve problems.
14. Delegate work.
15. Ask for help.
16. Share experiences.
17. Admit it when you are wrong.
18. Repeat compliments from others.
19. Show constructive concern about work problems.
20. Invite someone to join you for coffee.
21. Inquire (with empathy) about someone's family problems.
22. Ask a person to lead all or part of a meeting.
23. Establish and keep follow-up dates.
24. Give complete reasons for directions.

Source: Rosenbaum, B. L. (1980, September 22). Self-esteem gets the job done. *Chemical Engineering.*

Methods and styles of adjusting differ according to both cultures and situations. Patterns of adjusting within an individual form part of a person's personality. Although there are many definitions of personality, most emphasize adjustment to the environment. Personality is a total picture of patterns of behavior and includes thoughts, feelings, and motives that cannot be observed. Some behaviors and feelings are repeated frequently, while others occur only rarely.

As you face new stresses and demands, you must make adjustments. Your self-concept and personality are constantly changing as you make these adjustments. In the next section of this chapter, you will look at some methods people use to adjust and protect their self-concepts.

Checkpoint

Use the following questions to check your understanding of this portion of the chapter. Choose and mark the one correct response to each question.

1. Which of the following individuals is making an external adjustment?
   a. A man who has developed a poor self-concept
   b. A boy who feels unhappy about his appearance
   c. A girl who is satisfied with her grades in school
   d. A woman who applies for a new job

2. How are self-concept and self-esteem related?
   a. A person with a good self-concept has high self-esteem.
   b. A person with a poor self-concept has high self-esteem.
   c. A person with a good self-concept rarely has high self-esteem.
   d. A person with a poor self-concept rarely has low self-esteem.
3. When does development of a self-concept begin?
   a. In babyhood
   b. In first grade
   c. At adolescence
   d. At maturity
4. What is your ideal self?
   a. A high level of self-esteem
   b. A good self-concept
   c. The way you would like to be
   d. Your patterns of adjustment
5. Rucker wants to appear calm and peaceful to his neighbors. However, he finds himself becoming aggravated when the people next door burn their smelly garbage. Rucker loses control and pours a bag of trash on his neighbor's front lawn. What did Rucker experience?
   a. A difference in self-esteem and self-concept
   b. A difference in ideal self and self-esteem
   c. A difference in self-esteem and actual performance
   d. A difference in ideal self and actual performance
6. Which of the following persons is likely to have high self-esteem?
   a. Greg, who plays with younger children
   b. Kat, who is independent
   c. Matt, who looks for compliments
   d. Terry, who is easy to push around
7. Which of the following is likely to increase self-esteem?
   a. Criticism
   b. Praise
   c. Pressure
   d. Anger
8. What do most definitions of personality emphasize?
   a. Observable behavior
   b. Thoughts
   c. Adjustments
   d. Independence

Use the Checkpoint Answer Key to verify your responses. If you had any difficulty with a question, carefully reread the text. If you had little or no difficulty answering the questions or have resolved any difficulty you might have had, you are ready to continue with the next portion of this chapter.

DEFENSE MECHANISMS

Maintaining a good self-concept and high self-esteem is not easy. Each day there are many events that could shatter your self-image. If you notice a new blemish or wrinkle on your face, receive a low grade, or are not invited to lunch by the group, you need to take action to protect your self-esteem. The

defense mechanisms
Variety of unconscious techniques used to avoid anxiety and protect self-esteem

methods you use to protect your self-esteem are called "defense mechanisms."

Suppression and Repression

One way to protect your self-esteem is to avoid thinking about your problem. For example, you might intentionally go to a movie to avoid thinking about an argument. This defense mechanism, a deliberate attempt to avoid stressful thoughts, is labeled "suppression." Scarlett O'Hara in *Gone with the Wind* is among the more famous practitioners of suppression. Remember her line, "I'll shall think about it tomorrow"? Scarlett was suppressing her unpleasant thoughts. Have you ever felt lonely and intentionally kept yourself busy with chores, sports, or shopping to avoid thinking about your loneliness? If so, you were using suppression.

Suppression is only useful for minor problems. Usually you can only pretend a problem does not exist for a short period. Thoughts and worries tend to come back and may be even more stressful if they have been bottled up. Suppression requires a conscious and voluntary effort and has limited use as a defense mechanism.

Issues that are deeply wounding to self-esteem may be too painful to reach consciousness. You unconsciously put them out of your mind. Unconsciously motivated forgetting is called "repression." Repression and suppression were described as reasons for forgetting in Chapter 4. Everyone tends to push unpleasant thoughts out of their conscious minds. Since thoughts that are repressed are not conscious, people can only become aware of them through dreams or hypnosis.

Repression is the most basic defense mechanism. Most other defense mechanisms stem from repression. In its simplest form repression is unconscious forgetting. Suppose you forget to contribute money to a going-away gift for a close friend. Unconsciously you wish your friend were not leaving. Forgetting appointments, birthdays, weddings, and other important events can be signs of repression. Have you ever met someone who was rejecting and cruel to you? If you have difficulty recalling any persons or names, you may be repressing them! Usually thoughts and feelings that are repressed bring on other defense mechanisms.

Exercise 9-3

In your own words describe the key difference between suppression and repression.

suppression is conciously avoiding something
repression is unconciously ~~avoiding~~ something
forgetting

You may check your response in the Feedback section.

Other Defense Mechanisms

Assuming the fellow in Figure 9-4 is deeply worried about being rejected, he may repress the situation. As a result he could forget the name of the woman, their entire conversation, what he was drinking, and where he was that evening. Rather than admit his rejection and suffer, he could also use a number of other unconscious defense mechanisms.

"Normally I don't let rejection bother me, but . . ."

Figure 9-4
The rejection stamped on his forehead may also become buried in his unconscious. Time for some defense mechanisms...

Withdrawal. If the man in Figure 9-4 has trouble talking to women in the future, it could be that he unconsciously fears their rejection. *Withdrawal* usually results when people become intensely frightened or frustrated by a situation. People who fear rejection often avoid or withdraw from social situations. Sometimes the result is shyness. Often people fear rejection even when it is unlikely. Many famous and likeable people have suffered from shyness.

    If you have ever tried to escape from an unpleasant situation, you have used a withdrawal defense mechanism. If used cautiously, withdrawal can be a healthy defense mechanism. Often stepping out of a situation can help you gain a better perspective. However, withdrawal can also result in quitting jobs, dropping out of school, separations, and divorces.

withdrawal Defense mechanism that involves escaping and removing oneself from unpleasant situations

Fantasy. Sometimes people withdraw into a make-believe or *fantasy* world. If the rejected man in Figure 9-4 used a fantasy defense mechanism, he might daydream about his successes with women. He could create his own dream world where he would always be accepted, admired, and loved. Used in moderation, daydreaming and fantasy can be healthy and lead to creative thinking. Everyone daydreams as a method of reducing anxiety. Fantasy can bring a healthy escape from boredom and aid mental relaxation. Reading a novel or watching a soap opera can provide fantasy escapes. However, if fantasy is used excessively, it can become an unhealthy substitute for activity.

fantasy Defense mechanism that involves withdrawing to an imaginary world through daydreams

Regression. *Regression* is withdrawal into the past. If the rejected fellow regressed in a childlike way, he would behave as a child. He might burst into

regression Defense mechanism that involves the use of immature and childlike behaviors to cope with problems

mot

tears, or pout, suck his thumb, throw things, scream, and have a tantrum. Regression requires a return to earlier ways of handling problems. It is generally used when a person is deeply upset and cannot cope in a mature manner. Young children who have been toilet-trained and taught to drink from cups often regress and forget their training when a new baby arrives in their home. The older child does not know how to win parental affection in the new situation. Consequently the child must resort to previous methods for gaining attention and love. The result is regression.

rationalization Defense mechanism that distorts truth to provide excuses for a situation that is unacceptable

Rationalization. *Rationalization* is a distortion of the truth to maintain self-esteem. It provides an excuse or explanation for a situation that is really unacceptable. The man in Figure 9-4 might rationalize that the woman was not really his type and that he was delighted to be rid of her so he could arrive home at a reasonable hour. He might even rationalize that he was just having an unlucky day. Failures are often rationalized as being the result of some external factor, but success is deemed the result of personal abilities.

Most people are unaware of how often they rationalize. Although rationalization is indeed a misuse of logic, it can help to reduce anxiety. Have you ever excused yourself from a poor grade by arguing that the test was unfair or that you were feeling sick when you took the test? Rationalization can also allow you to look at the bright side. If an unpleasant event has already occurred, often little or nothing can be done to change it. After losing the 1960 presidential election, Richard Nixon reportedly commented that he would have more time to devote to his family. This was clearly a rationalization but probably aided his acceptance of a painful reality.

projection Defense mechanism based on guilt that involves accusing another of one's own weakness

Projection. *Projection* is based on guilt. Rather than accept personal weaknesses, unacceptable features are projected onto another person. The rejected

Figure 9-5
The skier's wife is helping him to rationalize his accident.

"On the other hand, the daily rate is a lot cheaper than at the ski lodge."

man could project his rejection onto the lady who stamped him. He would then maintain that it was she who was rejected by everyone. Projection permits you to accuse someone else of your weaknesses. Perhaps you have heard complaints from one fraternity that members of another fraternity hated them. They could easily be projecting their own feelings onto the other group. Or maybe you have known a flirt who complained that every male she met flirted with her. Psychologists often use projective tests to uncover problems. It is assumed that individuals will project their own feelings onto the pictures and illustrations in the test material. Projective tests will be discussed later in the chapter.

Displacement. *Displacement* requires finding a target or victim for pent-up feelings. The rejected fellow at the bar might ridicule and chastise the bartender for poor drinks or slow service. Displacement as a form of aggression is discussed in detail in Chapter 8. The chosen victim is usually a safe person, someone who is not likely to deflate self-esteem. Spouses are often selected. As a result husbands and wives often learn to avoid controversial topics when their mate has had a bad day.

displacement
Redirection of feelings to a substitute person or object when the true cause of the feelings is either an unacceptable or unavailable target

Reaction formation. *Reaction formation* is acting out the exact opposite of unacceptable impulses. People who use reaction formation feel so guilty they bend over backwards to deny their feelings. The result is exaggerated behavior. For example, assume the poor man who was rejected developed a strong hatred for women. He feels guilty about his hatred and unconsciously tries to prove that he really likes women. To prove his acceptance of women, he becomes a leader in the women's rights movement, writing feature articles, soliciting contributions for women's causes, carrying placards, and leading marches for women.

Sometimes parents who really resent their responsibility to rear children will become overprotective. Because a dislike of caring for their own children is considered unacceptable, they try to prove that they really do care. The result is exaggerated behavior and overprotectiveness.

reaction formation
Defense mechanism that causes people to behave in a manner opposite to their unacceptable impulses

Figure 9-6 The "born loser" is projecting.

compensation Healthy
defense mechanism
that allows persons
who are inadequate
in one area to turn
to areas where they
can excel

sublimation Healthy
defense mechanism
that channels
unacceptable impulses
into positive,
constructive areas

Compensation. *Compensation* allows a person to make up for inadequacies by doing well in another area. Perhaps the rejected fellow at the bar could go back to work and prove himself an outstanding accountant, attorney, or automobile salesman. Compensation allows you to deemphasize your weaknesses and play up your strengths. A child who is a poor student may try learning clever jokes to become popular. Compensation is a reasonable defense mechanism and usually leads to a healthy adjustment.

Sublimation. *Sublimation* is the most accepted defense mechanism. Unacceptable impulses are channeled into something positive, constructive, or creative. If the man left the bar and wrote a beautiful blues song about rejection and loneliness, he would be sublimating. Some of the finest poetry and folk music have emerged from oppressed groups, an example of their sublimations.

Of the many defense mechanisms, compensation and sublimation are considered the most healthy and acceptable. Since defense mechanisms are unconscious, usually people are completely unaware of them. Think about some of your own behavior. Can you identify the defense mechanisms you choose most often?

Exercise 9-4

Specify which of the following defense mechanisms is used in each of the following examples:

Repression	Reaction formation
Projection	Regression
Withdrawal	Compensation
Displacement	Rationalization
Fantasy	Sublimation

a. Greg did not complete his biology homework. Rather than be embarrassed in front of the class, he claimed he had a headache and put his head down on his desk. _Withdrawal_

b. Prunella's car broke down. Since she does not have enough money for repairs, she must leave an hour earlier to ride her bicycle or walk to work. Prunella commented that she enjoyed the exercise and saving the gas and oil money. _Rationalization_

c. Billy had stopped sucking his thumb by the time he was 4. At age 7 he was told that his parents were divorcing and he would be living with his mother and a "new father." Billy began sucking his thumb again. _Regression_

d. Janet, a soccer star, tore a tendon in her leg during a game. When her doctor told her she could never play soccer again, Janet worked hard to learn techniques for coaching soccer. _Compensation_

e. Eric was cutting wood and injured his hand with his chain saw. While driving to the emergency room of a local hospital he recalled the painful shots he received during his last visit there. He missed the turn to the hospital and had to ask for directions to find it. _Repression_

f. Martin is a big spender. He tips heavily, buys extravagant gifts, and often gambles. When his thrifty wife bought material to make new kitchen curtains, he accused her of squandering money needlessly. He claimed the old, worn curtains were adequate and called her a spendthrift. _Projection_

g. Little Paulette was upset when her mother spanked her. She ran to her toy crib and smacked her doll. _Displacement_

h. Irene has been trying to support her eight children. They live in an old shack that lacks both heat and plumbing. Irene likes to daydream about winning a lottery, traveling, and buying fancy clothes. _Fantasy_

i. Jeremy has always been a problem to his mother. He never keeps rules and argues with her constantly. In choosing a tattoo, he selected a large heart with "Mom" in the center. _Reaction formation_

j. Whenever Elizabeth is angry she heads for her piano. She has composed several outstanding jazz tunes. _Sublimation_

Turn to the Feedback section to check your responses.

1 Suppression
2 Sub.
3 Sub
4 Reaction
5 withdrawal
6 Projection
7 Repression
8 Rationalization
9 Projection
10 Compensation

MEASURING PERSONALITY

The defense mechanisms you use regularly become part of your style of adjustment and therefore part of your personality. But if most defense mechanisms are unconscious, how can you learn what you are really like? As pointed out in Chapter 1, psychoanalysts would suggest hypnosis and dream analysis to learn about your unconscious. Other psychologists would suggest different techniques.

Measuring personality is a complex task because your personality is constantly changing. You may have developed some characteristics or traits that you did not have a few years, or even a few months, ago. Further, there is no single personality test that can ever give a completely accurate picture of what you are presently like. Although no one test or method can give a valid description of your personality, by using a variety of techniques and tests, psychologists can come closer to an accurate assessment.

Techniques for Personality Assessment

Projective tests. The purpose of *projective tests* is to uncover unconscious urges and needs. It is assumed that people use projection as a defense mechanism and project their own unconscious feelings onto other persons or objects. One of the oldest projective tests was originated by Rorschach (1921). It consists of a series of ten cards with inkblots on them. The psychologist presents the subject with each of the ten cards. The person is then encouraged to "free-associate," that is, to say whatever comes to mind, about what he or she sees on each card. The psychologist then interprets the subject's responses according to a standardized scale. The interpretation of Rorschach responses has been refined since the origin of the test. Typical responses of specific disorders such as depression and simple schizophrenia have been found. A newer variation on the Rorschach is the Holtzman Inkblot Technique (Holtzman, 1975), involving a set of forty-five cards.

Another type of projective test uses pictures of people in ambiguous real-life situations. The most famous of this type of projective test is the Thematic Apperception Test (TAT). Pictures in the TAT show such scenes as a person lying on a sofa and another figure standing next to the sofa, or a child staring

projective test
Personality test that uses ambiguous stimuli and is designed to measure unconscious feelings

The Thematic
Apperception Test
(TAT) uses ambiguous
pictures. Persons are
asked to describe each
picture, projecting their
own feelings onto the
characters shown.
(© 1943 by the
President and Fellows
of Harvard College; ©
1971 by Henry A.
Murray)

at a violin. The subject taking the test is expected to project unconscious feelings onto the figures in the pictures. There is a special variation of this test for children called the Children's Apperception Test (CAT).

Another type of projective test is the widely criticized Draw-A-Person Test (DAP). Here the subject is handed a blank paper and crayon or pencil and simply asked to draw a person. Personality is assessed according to the characteristics and features in the sketch. This test is also sometimes expanded to also include separate drawings of a house and a tree. These tests are the least accurate of the projective tests. In his research, Cressen (1978) reported that interpretation of the drawings is strongly influenced by artistic ability.

There are a number of other types of projective tests that allow open responses. In word-association tests the psychologist presents a series of words, and the subject is then expected to call out the first word that comes to mind. Another type of projective test requires the subject to complete such sentences as:

- "I always worry a great deal about _____ ."
- "When I am angry or upset I _____ ."
- "The happiest time _____ ."

The major limitation of all projective tests is the subjective nature of their interpretation. Rules for interpretation are clearer on the Rorschach, Holtzman, and

TAT than on the other types of projective tests. However, in spite of their limitations, many psychologists find projective tests a good opener in testing sessions. At least they permit individuals to begin talking about their problems.

Self-report inventories. Self-report inventories are based on the idea that there are specific personality traits. Each subject is presented with a list of statements about personality characteristics such as "I feel happiest in a group when I am the person in charge," or "I would rather be alone at home than at a lively party." The person must decide whether each statement is true, false, or somewhere in between. The most popular and most famous personality inventory is the Minnesota Multiphasic Personality Inventory (MMPI), a lengthy and thorough test with 550 items. The primary purpose of the MMPI is to separate normal patterns of responses from patterns associated with mental illness. Another inventory, the California Psychological Inventory (CPI), was designed to identify such normal traits as sociability, self-acceptance, sense of well-being, self-control, tolerance, and responsibility. Although primarily a personality inventory, the CPI also includes assessments of intelligence and achievement. Both the MMPI and the CPI have special scales to detect people who are trying to make good impressions by lying about themselves. However, it is possible to conceal some negative characteristics on these tests. Responses on these inventories depend upon your ability to recall your behavior and attitudes. Often people rationalize and do not fully understand their behavior.

Undoubtedly, you have seen personality inventories in popular magazines and newspapers. Although these quick tests are fun and interesting, they are usually highly inaccurate as measures of personality. It is easy to misinterpret the results of magazines and newspaper inventories since these "tests" are rarely standardized; they are designed strictly for amusement.

Observational and situational tests. An interview is probably the most common example of an observational and situational test. The person being interviewed is being carefully observed, with particular attention directed at their adjustment to the interview situation. Styles of interviews vary. Sometimes the setting is totally structured and the interviewee must respond to a specific set of questions. Other times the setting is open and the interviewee leads the direction. There are all sorts of variations between these two extremes. Regardless of the style used in the interview, psychologists cannot be certain that the person being interviewed would behave the same way in a natural setting. Some people can put on an act for an interview.

Sometimes psychologists observe individuals in a natural setting and record the types of behavior that occur. For example, a psychologist may observe two 5-year-old girls in a playroom. Any aggressive behavior such as hitting, kicking, or pushing will be noted. The psychologist may also record crying, teasing, or attempts to embarrass the other girl.

Occasionally psychologists use situational tests, for example, by putting a person in some type of frustrating situation. In one case an individual may be asked to work at length on a boring task, perhaps sorting buttons into boxes. In another case a person may be expected to complete a complex task with time pressures. As the person tries to assemble an elaborate structure, the psychologist keeps reminding the person, "You have only two minutes; one minute; forty-five seconds''; and finally, ''only eight seconds left.'' The psychologist then observes and records the person's reactions to frustration.

A common technique for recording observed behavior is a rating scale. Have you ever been asked to complete a questionnaire on another person? The items may have asked you to indicate on a scale of 1 (''never'') to 5 (''always'') whether a person is truthful, prompt, friendly, aggressive, responsible, and tidy. Based on your observations, you must rate the person's behaviors. One danger in rating scales is the difficulty in getting truly objective assessments. If the person you were asked to rate is a good friend, you probably would want to be helpful, particularly if your observation might mean a good job or acceptance at a college. Similarly, if you like your friend, you probably have a generally favorable view. As a result you would have a tendency to assess each characteristic in a positive manner. Psychologists call this favorable bias a ''halo effect.'' To assure accuracy on a rating scale, as many judges as possible should be used.

halo effect Bias that causes a person to overlook another person's specific deficiencies because of one favorable characteristic

Exercise 9-5

List one limitation for each of the following techniques for assessing personality.

a. Projective tests: _Subjective nature of their Interpretation._

b. Self-report inventories: _rarely standardized, Also often misinterpretive._

c. Interviews: _Some people can put on An Act._

d. Rating scales: _difficulty in getting truly objective Assesments._

Turn to the Feedback section to check your responses.

Exercise 9-6

What could a psychologist do to overcome these limitations? _They should use A variety of the tests._

Check your answers against those listed in the Feedback section.

Cautions in Personality Assessment

Personality assessment by personnel offices is becoming more common. Often only one test or technique is used. Whether this technique is a rating scale sent to former coworkers and friends, a self-reporting inventory, an interview, or a projective test, the results will have limited validity. A variety of techniques must be used to assure any accuracy. Personality tests are designed for clinical diagnosis and counseling. Any assessment of personality without the consent of the person involved could be considered an invasion of privacy.

Use the following questions to check your understanding of this portion of the chapter. Match each defense mechanism on the left with the correct definition on the right.

9. __e__ Suppression
10. __g__ Repression
11. __I__ Withdrawal
12. __A__ Fantasy
13. __C__ Regression
14. __B__ Rationalization
15. __K__ Projection
16. __J__ Displacement
17. __f__ Reaction formation
18. __H__ Compensation
19. __d__ Sublimation

a. Daydreaming and escaping into a make-believe world
b. Distorting the truth to find excuses
c. Using childlike ways to handle upsetting situations
d. Channeling unacceptable urges into constructive and creative areas
e. A conscious and deliberate effort to avoid unpleasant thoughts
f. Doing the exact opposite of your unacceptable impulses
g. Unconscious forgetting
h. Making up for weaknesses in one area by doing well in another area
i. Running from and escaping unpleasant situations
j. Finding a safe victim for your aggression
k. Accusing another of your personal weaknesses

Match each technique on the left with the correct lettered examples listed on the right. There will be more than one example for each technique.

20. __d,c,f__ Projective tests
21. __A,g,G__ Self-report inventories
22. __b,e,e__ Observational and situational tests

a. Minnesota Multiphasic Personality Inventory
b. Rating scales
c. Thematic Apperception Test
d. Rorschach
e. Interviews
f. Draw-a-Person Test
g. CPI

Use the Checkpoint Answer Key to verify your responses. If you had any difficulty with a question, carefully reread the text. If you had little or no difficulty or have resolved any difficulty you might have had, you are ready to continue with the final portion of this chapter.

Personality Types

Although the key purpose of personality tests is to identify problems in adjustment, some psychologists and physicians have become interested in the relationship between personality and physical problems (see Exhibit 9-2). Special tests have been designed to identify personality types that are prone to specific physical disorders. It now appears that personality and adjustment may play a significant role in the two leading causes of adult deaths, heart disease and cancer.

EXHIBIT 9-2

An Ill Nature

People often equate certain illnesses with particular personality types: Worriers get ulcers; workaholics develop heart disease; repressed emotions surface in asthma. Although research has not tied personality and illness together so neatly, University of California psychologists Howard S. Friedman and Stephanie Booth-Kewley found strong links between the two in their analysis of 101 studies conducted from 1945 to 1984.

Friedman and Booth-Kewley looked at five diseases: coronary heart disease, asthma, ulcers, arthritis and headache. The researchers correlated these diseases with different personality traits.

Although no one trait predicted a single disease, the researchers did find several links between them. For all the diseases except ulcers, there were strong associations with depression, anxiety, anger, and hostility. High levels of these traits were especially predictive of heart disease.

Since "particular aspects of personality and...particular diseases" were not linked together, Friedman and Booth-Kewley suggest that such popular notions as the "arthritic personality" or the "coronary-prone personality" are probably incorrect. However, "there may well exist a generic 'disease-prone personality,' " they write in *American Psychologist* (Vol. 42, pp. 539–555). "Personality may function like diet: Imbalances can predispose one to all sorts of diseases."

Source: Berlfein, J. (1988, March). An ill nature. *Psychology Today*.

Two cardiologists, Freedman and Rosenman (1974), found personality type to be a stronger predictor of heart problems than any other single factor. Among the factors that played lesser roles were smoking, obesity, cholesterol level, and lack of exercise. They labeled the personality type that is prone to heart disease as "type A," and the type that is an unlikely candidate for heart problems "type B." *Type A* persons are competitive, impatient, organized, and pressured by time. They lead stressful lives. The excerpt in Exhibit 9-3 provides a checklist to test your Type A characteristics.

type A personality
Behavior characterized by competitiveness and aggression

However, there are benefits to a type A personality. Research by Glass (1977) found that type A people score higher grades and earn more money than type B people of equal intelligence. His findings are supported by Matthews et al. (1981), who noted that type A psychologists produce the best work. Recent research has found that Type A men, although more prone to heart attacks, are more likely to survive (see Exhibit 9-4).

type B personality
Behavior characterized by a relaxed manner

Type B persons, on the other hand, are less ambitious, more patient, and can relax more easily. They also smoke less and have lower cholesterol levels. However, even when these two attributes are factored out, they still have fewer heart attacks. Psychologists have been attempting to help type A persons modify their behavior and become more like type B persons, as a method of preventing heart attacks. Since most psychologists and cardiologists are Type A persons themselves, it is often difficult to find relaxed leaders for therapy sessions. However, once a type B is found to lead a group, significant changes have occurred among members.

Recently evidence has been presented that suggests a possible relationship between personality type and cancer. Here the responsible personality characteristic appears to be a sense of hopelessness and despair. Studies sug-

EXHIBIT 9-3

261

ADJUSTING

Improve Your Health—Change Your Type A Behavior

- Is "hurry up!" one of your most-used phrases?

- Do you look at your watch dozens of times a day?

- Do you think you have to do every job yourself or else it's never going to get done right?

- Do you get equally upset by a lost glove as by your son's flunking English?

- Are you impatient, even hostile, when kept waiting or when delayed by an uncontrollable event, like a traffic jam?

- Do you constantly try to do more and more in less and less time, and then become anxious when it seems you can't meet all the deadlines?

- Do you find it impossible to say no when asked to assume a responsibility you don't want?

- Do you frequently accept social obligations you know you will resent?

- Are you spending less and less time with family and friends or on recreational activities?

- Are you a person with "high ideals" who is repeatedly disappointed when others don't live up to your standards?

- Do you often rush people's speech, finishing their sentences or saying, "Yes, yes," implying, "Get on with it!"?

- Do you get impatient and annoyed when you see people doing things you feel you can do faster or better?

- Do you have a hard time sitting and doing nothing?

- Do you often try to do or think of two or more things at once?

- Do you spend as much time and energy on trivial matters or chores as on important ones?

If you answered yes to more than half a dozen of these questions, then you're probably what psychologists and cardiologists call a "Type A" personality: a perfectionist—an idealistic, impatient, irritable victim of "hurry sickness." Type A people, research has shown, are especially prone to developing heart disease at an early age. But even if heart disease seems a distant or unlikely threat, being a full-fledged Type A personality is probably ruining the quality of your life, not to mention the lives of the people closest to you.

Source: Brody, J. (1985, May/June). Improve your health: Change your type A behavior. *St. Raphael's Better Health.*

EXHIBIT 9-4

Do Type A Men Have a Survival Edge?

Welcome to the paradoxical world of Type A behavior. Nearly 30 years after this personality pattern was first linked to an increased risk of developing heart disease, a study in the Jan. 14 *New England Journal of Medicine* concludes that hard-charging Type A men may be more likely to survive a second heart attack than their easygoing Type B counterparts.

"We struggled considerably with this finding," says epidemiologist David R. Ragland of the University of California at Berkeley, who conducted the study with Berkeley statistician Richard J. Brand. "But I would tend to say that Type A behavior is less likely [than was believed] to be important as a risk factor for dying from coronary heart disease."

In an editorial accompanying the report, psychiatrist and Type A researcher Joel J. Dimsdale of the University of California at San Diego says the findings show that Type A behavior is not linked to coronary heart disease in a simple, consistent way. Still, he notes that "*something* is going on...between personality and heart disease."

Researchers originally characterized Type A individuals as intensely competitive, impatient, controlling and ambitious, often bereft of clear goals. Type Bs, on the other hand, were said to be relaxed, cooperative and content. In the past decade, other aspects of Type A behavior—including hostility, cynicism and depression—have been explored as key promoters of heart disease.

The Berkeley researchers focused on the initial group of Type A and Type B men studied in the 1960s, 257 of whom had developed heart disease by 1969. Equal proportions of Type A and Type B subjects died suddenly of their first heart attack, a surprising finding in itself. But over the next 13 years, the 160 surviving Type As were only 58 percent as likely to die of another heart attack as the 71 surviving Type Bs. The lower mortality rate held for both younger (ages 39 to 54) and older (ages 55 to 70) Type As who survived an initial heart attack.

Ragland and Brand suggest that Type A patients may be more likely to comply with medical treatment or change their behavior after a heart attack. Type As may also pay closer attention to telltale cardiac symptoms and seek medical care earlier than Type Bs, they say.

However, cardiologist Meyer Friedman of Mt. Zion Hospital in San Francisco, co-director of the original Type A research, says the new data may be based on antiquated diagnoses. Many physical signs of Type A behavior, such as facial tics, rapid blinking, rushed speech and fist clenching, were not known when subjects in the study were diagnosed in 1960, says Friedman. The early interviews tested mainly for impatience, but not for hostility, he adds. According to Friedman, all of the men now would be diagnosed as Type As.

"I think [Ragland and Brand's] study is a disservice," he says.

Friedman's follow-up study, reported in 1975, found that over 8½ years, Type A individuals had roughly twice the chance of developing coronary heart disease as Type Bs, regardless of other risk factors such as cigarette smoking. In more recent work, he has found that men who modify their Type A behavior through group counseling are at a reduced risk for developing heart disease....

And Friedman's former collaborator, cardiologist Ray Rosenman of SRI International in Menlo Park, Calif., says the Berkeley researchers are on the right track. Furthermore, he contends that the original interviews picked up hostility as well as impatience, thus making the diagnoses accurate.

"But we only have hypotheses as to why Type As survive better," says Rosenman. It may be, he notes, that Type As are more willing to change after a first heart attack. Possible risks in the more passive, relaxed approach of Type Bs have not been closely examined, he adds....

In the last five years, says Brand, more studies have appeared showing no relation between Type A and heart attack risk. "This," he says, "has become a very confusing area of research."

Source: Bower, B. (1988, January 23). Do type A men have a survival edge? *Science News.*

gest that persons who are prone to cancer lack a purpose in life, are bored, and have given up on themselves (Shekelle et al., 1981). Sometimes these feelings result from loss of a spouse or other loved ones. Therapy is directed toward giving each person a sense of hope and a reason to live.

Exercise 9-7

Based on evidence from research studies, indicate whether each of the following persons has a type A personality, type B personality, or cancer-prone personality.

a. Ulysses is extremely patient. He can work for hours on a tedious, boring task. _Type B_

b. Bertram sleeps extremely late most mornings. He claims he has no reason to get out of bed. There is nothing to do and no reason to do anything.

_____ _Cancer-prone_ _____

c. Valerie is not interested in a promotion. She prefers her present job where she can take long lunch hours and relax with her friends. ___ _B_ ___

d. Evelyn is a compulsive student. She studies during every waking moment, since she wants to be certain she graduates with honors. ___ _A_ ___

e. Claude hates to waste time sitting in traffic. He honks his horn and waves his fist at anyone who holds him up. ___ _A_ ___

You may check your answers in the Feedback section.

Exercise 9-8
Describe how persons with type A and cancer-prone personalities can be helped.

a. Type A personality: _____

_____

b. Cancer-prone personality: _____

_____

Please turn to the Feedback section to check your responses.

ADJUSTMENT PROBLEMS

There are some personality characteristics that do not necessarily lead to physical ailments but nonetheless interfere with daily living and healthy adjustments. Characteristics such as guilt and insomnia present adjustment problems. At best, life will be less than fulfilling and perfectly enjoyable. At worst, guilt and depression can lead to suicide attempts.

Guilt

Everyone has felt guilt. Think of some of your own experiences. Perhaps you have called in sick at work on a day when you were perfectly healthy. Or maybe you left a sick friend home alone while you rushed away to have a good time. When was the last time you telephoned or wrote to a lonely grandparent? Guilt arises from moral anxiety. When you violate your own internalized standards or morals, guilt results.

Guilt is natural, normal, and essential for maintaining moral standards and rules within any society. Why do some people experience more guilt than others? Clearly some people have stronger morals. Rotter (1966) suggested that some people feel more personal responsibility for their actions. He described these people as "internals." Internals believe they control their own fate. Rotter labeled the opposite extreme "externals." Externals believe that they have little or no personal responsibility for what happens to them. They are victims of chance or fate. Phares (1976) found that internals blame themselves for failures and feel more shame and guilt than externals.

Unfortunately guilt can become excessive, unjustified, and harmful. Needless guilt can lower self-esteem and lead to constant fatigue, sexual frigidity, or even suicide. The causes of painful guilt are often repressed. In such cases, professional help is needed to bring the causes to consciousness. Only then can the appropriateness of the guilt be evaluated.

Exercise 9-9

Read each of the following statements and indicate whether each remark was likely to be made by an internal or an external person.

a. I'm lucky I got here on time. _____ *ex* _____

b. If I'd had a decent teacher I would have passed the course. _____ *ex* _____

c. All those years of practice helped me win the tennis title. _____ *in* _____

d. It was stupid of me to forget to use sunblock; now I have a painful sunburn.

_____ *in* _____

Turn to the Feedback section to check your responses.

Insomnia

insomnia Difficulty getting to sleep, staying asleep, or both

Insomnia or inability to sleep is a common adjustment problem, affecting an estimated 25 million Americans. A person suffering from insomnia may be burdened with worries or guilt at night. While lying awake, additional fears are aroused. The person becomes concerned that sleep may never come. This added worry makes sleep even more difficult and less likely. There is general agreement that sleeping pills cannot cure insomnia (National Institutes of Health, 1984). Psychologists recommend a regular schedule that includes daily exercise, a diet free of caffeine (coffee, tea, cola, and chocolate), and a relaxing routine before bed (warm bath, watching television, or listening to music).

Exercise 9-10

Mr. I suffers from insomnia. Check each suggestion that might help cure his problem.

☐ Take sleeping pills.

☐ Eat chocolate.

☒ Avoid coffee.

☒ Exercise every day.

☐ Be active before bedtime.

☒ Take a warm bath before going to bed.

Check your answers against those listed in the Feedback section.

MAINTAINING A HEALTHY PERSONALITY

The term "mental health" has been used to describe the absence of mental illness or adjustment problems. But just as you may be free of physical illness and still not be healthy, the absence of adjustment problems does not assure a healthy personality. Lack of mental disturbance is merely a minimum condition for a healthy personality. Here is a summary of some suggestions for a mature and healthy personality (Allport, 1961; Johnson, 1971; Mahoney, 1971).

Extend yourself: If you become genuinely involved in your job, your family, a cause, or anything important to you, you will feel better about yourself.

Reach out and show concern for others: By showing compassion and warmth, you will develop more tolerance for others as well as yourself. This will enhance your own security and acceptance of your weaknesses.

Focus on positive aspects in your life: Often problems cloud thinking. Pogrebin (1980) suggested setting aside one day to indulge in pleasures. Take a day off from work or school and sleep late. Share a relaxed lunch at a restaurant with someone you enjoy. Then go to a movie, play, or athletic event. You might finish the day with your favorite music and a bubble bath. The goal is to enjoy simple pleasures. As an alternative you might force yourself to jot down five things you like about yourself and your life.

Take responsibility for yourself: Plan ahead and look to the future. Set objectives for yourself and develop skills that can help you reach your goals. Recognize that you are responsible for your own success. As the article in Exhibit 9-5 points out, you must also schedule some personal time.

EXHIBIT 9-5

'80s Adage: Work Smart, Not Harder

Many aspects of modern life conspire to force people to work "harder" when they could work "smarter," Marilyn Machlowitz observes. But there are some signs this may be changing, and...she had some suggestions for speeding that process.

Machlowitz, who holds a Ph.D. in psychology and is president of her own management consultant company, noted that technology is making feasible many things that were once unthinkable. But along with their advantages, portable computers, FAX machines, overnight delivery, calendar organizers and phones that are available everywhere from cars to hotel bathrooms also make it possible to work anytime and anywhere, she said.

"Instead of responding, 'No, I can't get this to you tomorrow,' with overnight couriers we now may knock ourselves out trying to."...

Time management tips designed to reduce this pressure are often unrealistic or at odds with corporate policy.

"I am told that the day after one company sponsored a time management seminar that suggested taking and making phone calls only at certain hours, a memo went around instructing attendees to ignore what they had just been told," she said....

It should be remembered, she said, that efficiency and effectiveness are not always the same thing. People have told her of hand-delivering items that could easily have been distributed by inter-office mail in an effort to make themselves better known. These attempts to increase visibility "are not the speediest of processes, but they can bring broad benefits," she said. But balancing long- and short-term benefits of such strategies is not easy, even for seasoned professionals.

Other suggestions for using time wisely included giving or getting feedback and taking time to listen. For instance, it may seem efficient to open mail and talk on the phone at the same time, but not if you have to ask the caller to repeat everything, Machlowitz pointed out. Hearing what you don't want to hear is important, too: ignoring the evidence can have catastrophic results.

Meshing personal and professional interests is yet another way to ease pressure, she said. In fact, that may be *the* time management issue today. People

Source: Bales, J.
(1987, November).
'80s adage: Work
smart, not harder.
APA Monitor.

don't seem to notice or care how hard they work on pursuits they enjoy, she noted.

Politicians and corporations are paying more attention to the interaction between family and work, as well. She predicted that with the coming "Baby Bust" and the resulting shrinking pool of employees, more employers will try to entice employees through such incentives as flexible hours and day-care. She quoted former Sen. Paul Tsongas (D-Mass), who left politics after learning he had cancer: "No one on his deathbed ever said, 'I wish I'd spent more time on my business.' "

Relax and use your sense of humor. Martin and Lefcourt (1983) found that humor improves moods and helps eliminate stress. People who find humorous aspects of bad news are less likely to feel tense and depressed. The article in Exhibit 9-6 describes the work of humor consultants in improving mental health.

Checkpoint

Use the following questions to check your understanding of the final portion of this chapter. Choose and mark the one correct response to each question.

23. Which of the following quadruplets is in greatest danger of a heart attack?
    a. Fred, who has a type A personality
    b. Ned, who has a type B personality
    c. Ted, who often feels guilty
    d. Zed, who often feels depressed
24. Who is likely to be most ambitious?
    a. A person with a cancer-prone personality
    b. A person with a type A personality
    c. A person with a type B personality
    d. A person chronically attempting suicide
25. What causes guilt?
    a. Depression
    b. Repressed depression
    c. Violation of morals
    d. Atonement for criticism
26. According to Rotter, which of the following persons is likely to believe she is the victim of fate?
    a. Iva, who is an internal person
    b. Edith, who is an external person
    c. Irene, who suffers from insomnia
    d. Gertrude, who feels guilty
27. Which of the following behaviors is associated with insomnia?
    a. Type B behavior
    b. External-type behavior
    c. Worry and guilt
    d. All of the above
28. What should people suffering from insomnia avoid?
    a. Caffeine
    b. Exercise

EXHIBIT 9-6

267

ADJUSTING

Make 'Em Laugh

Swimming or running laps to purge yourself of job-related stress works fine, but you certainly can't run a lap around the reception desk when you feel the pressure build. Cultivating a sense of humor, though, could help lower your blood pressure a notch or two, according to advocates who see a clear link between stress management and humor, which some characterize as "ho-ho-holistic" medicine.

"Humor is the most powerful stress reliever we have," says Dr. Steve Allen, Jr., son of the well-known comedian and a lecturer at corporations nationwide on the benefits of not maintaining a stiff upper lip. When people are convulsed with laughter, Allen says, their heart rate speeds up and their muscles relax. And the tension, he adds, "evaporates."

To stimulate his audience's funnybones, Allen passes pink and orange scarves down the rows and leads a class in a juggling lesson. Originally, Allen passed tennis balls for the audience to juggle, until he realized that the balls created tension and ruined the therapeutic value of his exercises. "All of us remember a failure experience with at least one kind of ball as a child," says Allen, speaking from his office, a medical practice, in Horsehead, New York.

Allen instructs his class to shout, "Yippee-eye-ay" whenever anyone completes a catch. The effect "is of a roomful of people shouting and laughing away their tensions. It's amazing what a couple of props and permission will do for straight-laced people in three-piece suits," he says.

Juggling scarves is used to drive home the point to the executives Allen lectures that laughter is truly the best medicine. When Allen began lecturing on managing stress at Cornell University several years ago, he realized that there were many advocates of stress-reducing strategies like time management and exercise, but few experts who, in his words, "could help people let go, and let them laugh and play." His juggling exercise is but one way to relieve tension, but "any playful activity will work," Allen says. "Be silly," he advises, pointing out that the word silly is derived from the Old English word "saelig," which translated means "happy, prosperous and blessed."

A 1986 study by the Illinois consulting firm Hodge-Cronin & Associates concluded that 98 percent of the 737 CEOs interviewed said they would prefer to hire a candidate with a sense of humor over a candidate with none, all other criteria being equal. J. Mark Pearson, marketing director with C.W. Metcalf & Company in Fort Collins, Colorado, says that friendly-faced managers are more effective than the lock-jawed, man-of-steel types. People who exhibit a sense of humor are perceived as much more "human," Pearson says. A smile says plainly that the manager is "open to communication."

Despite what the term "humor consultant" suggests, C.W. Metcalf does not coach executives on how to deliver a string of side-splitting one-liners; rather, it preaches "the flexibility to roll good-naturedly with change," Pearson says. "Humor is not about jokes. Only one percent of the population can tell a joke well. That's why Bill Cosby is a millionaire."

At corporate seminars, Metcalf encourages its typically dour audiences to throw funny quotations into memoranda, or to resolve conflict by picturing their office rival in diapers. "We teach our audience to take their guard down—literally—and to not take themselves so seriously. It's hard to think of anyone as threatening when they're wearing diapers," Pearson says.

Humor consultants say they don't plan to turn the nation's workforce into a pack of hyenas in pinstripes. But a humorous note sounded periodically, they say, can't hurt.

Source: Handley, A. (1988, January). 8 resolutions for '88. *US AIR*.

c. Regular schedules

d. Relaxation before bedtime

Check your responses against the Checkpoint Answer Key at the end of the chapter. If you had difficulty with any question, reread the text. If you had little or no difficulty answering the questions or have resolved problems that you might have had, you are ready to check yourself against the chapter inventory that follows.

CHAPTER INVENTORY

Use this list of objectives as a review checklist. You should be able to do each of the tasks outlined in the objectives and apply them to everyday examples. If you can, you may feel confident that you have mastered the material in this chapter.

1. Distinguish between internal and external adjustment.
2. Define self-concept, self-esteem, and ideal self.
3. Describe the factors that affect self-esteem, and explain the characteristics of low self-esteem and high self-esteem.
4. Recognize the relationship between adjustment and personality.
5. Define defense mechanisms and explain why they are used.
6. Distinguish between suppression and repression.
7. Define and provide examples of withdrawal, fantasy, repression, rationalization, projection, displacement, reaction formation, compensation, and sublimation.
8. Describe and give examples of projective tests, self-report inventories, and observational and situational tests.
9. Recognize the limitations of each type of personality test, the cautions in personality testing, and the necessity for administering more than one test.
10. Specify three personality types identified by psychologists, and recognize their correlation with specific diseases.
11. Name two general adjustment problems.
12. Describe the characteristics and give examples of guilt and insomnia.
13. List five steps toward maintaining a healthy personality.

Feedback

The correct answers to the exercises follow. If you did not answer an exercise correctly, review the preceding pages and return to the exercise to correctly complete it.

9-1. *a.* He will have to adjust his attitude about his importance at work. Apparently he was not missed. He might realize he needs to interact with other people more frequently.

   b. He could pick up his telephone and make a few calls. Or he might write a few notes.

9-2. *a.* High self-esteem

   b. High self-esteem

   c. Low self-esteem

      d. Low self-esteem
      e. High self-esteem
      f. Low self-esteem
      g. High self-esteem
      h. High self-esteem
      i. Low self-esteem
      j. Low self-esteem
      k. High self-esteem

9-3. Suppression requires a conscious and deliberate effort to avoid thinking about a problem. Repression is unconscious and cannot be controlled consciously.

9-4. *a.* Withdrawal
      b. Rationalization
      c. Regression
      d. Compensation
      e. Repression
      f. Projection
      g. Displacement
      h. Fantasy
      i. Reaction formation
      j. Sublimation

9-5. *a.* In projective tests interpretation of results is subjective and may differ from one examiner to the next.
      b. In self-report inventories people may try to make a good impression and conceal their faults.
      c. In interviews a person could put on an act.
      d. In the case of rating scales, many different judges should be used.

9-6. A psychologist should use as many different techniques as possible.

9-7. *a.* Type B personality
      b. Cancer-prone personality
      c. Type B personality
      d. Type A personality
      e. Type A personality

9-8. *a.* Type A persons can be helped through group therapy. First they must identify their own type A behavior and situations that are likely to cause stress. Then they can help each other control situations and behavior.
      b. Persons with cancer-prone personality can be helped through therapy. Their goals are to realize their own importance and develop a sense of hope and a willingness and drive to continue living.

9-9. *a.* External
      b. External
      c. Internal
      d. Internal

9-10. ☑ Avoid coffee.
      ☑ Exercise every day.
      ☑ Take a warm bath before going to bed.

Checkpoint Answer Key

1. *d*	8. *c*	15. *k*	22. *b, e*
2. *a*	9. *e*	16. *j*	23. *a*
3. *a*	10. *g*	17. *f*	24. *b*
4. *c*	11. *i*	18. *h*	25. *c*
5. *d*	12. *a*	19. *d*	26. *b*
6. *b*	13. *c*	20. *c, d, f*	27. *c*
7. *b*	14. *b*	21. *a, g*	28. *a*

CHAPTER 10

IDENTIFYING PROBLEM BEHAVIOR

Not everything that is faced can be changed; but nothing can be changed until it is faced.

James Baldwin

Mindy is a popular college freshman. She is pretty, extremely talkative, and bright. At parties she chats easily about any subject. She seems lighthearted and fun-loving to others. However, Mindy usually feels that her high spirits are not within her control. Her ideas move quickly and she needs to blurt them. She also has a quick temper and will give a strong tongue lashing to anyone who criticizes her.

There are times when Mindy becomes quiet. She feels overwhelmingly sad and morose. She avoids other people. Her life seems useless and she fears she is losing control. She has serious thoughts of suicide and considers possible methods she could use. On a few occasions, she has begun to write suicide notes. Is Mindy abnormal? Is her behavior a problem?

Problem behavior is not always easy to define. However, in this chapter you will consider some signs of abnormality along with problems in diagnosing disorders. You will learn the common symptoms of a variety of anxiety disorders, mood problems, personality confusions, schizophrenias, and organic illnesses. You will also be able to answer the questions about Mindy!

WHAT IS ABNORMAL BEHAVIOR?

Abnormal means different from normal or average. Abnormal behavior must be strangely or markedly different from average or expected behavior. But being unusual is not the only criterion for being considered abnormal by psychologists. Einstein, Baryshnikov, and Mother Teresa clearly have behaved very differently from the average person. Yet, each has been honored for being different. Their behavior was desirable, if different.

To be considered abnormal, behavior must also be undesirable. Usually people who are workaholics or manage to be active with little or no sleep are considered normal. Only when their behavior upsets or endangers the lives of family and friends or interferes with their own adjustments will they be labeled "abnormal." Usually abnormal behavior causes emotional distress.

Now, you can evaluate Mindy. Her uncontrolled talking and morose feelings are not considered average. Further, threats of suicide are undesirable for herself, her family, and her friends. Finally, Mindy seems to be suffering from emotional distress.

Exercise 10-1

List three criteria for abnormal behavior.

a. _Strongly or markedly different from ave. behav. or exp._
b. _undesirable_
c. _when behavior upsets or endangers others lives._

Compare your list in the Feedback section.

Problems of Diagnosis

George Albee, a past president of the American Psychological Association, pointed out, "Appendicitis, a brain tumor, and chicken pox are the same everywhere, regardless of culture or class; mental conditions, it seems are not." It is not easy to diagnose psychological disorders. Psychologists do not always

agree on which conditions are really abnormal problems. Further, strange behavior is often only temporary. The extent of a problem may change greatly
from time to time. A person may be so mildly depressed that it is difficult to
tell whether the behavior is normal or abnormal. At another time the same person may suffer a deep depression that requires intensive treatment.

DSM III-R

DSM III-R, the revised third edition of the *Diagnostic and Statistical Manual of
Mental Disorders,* was published in 1987 by the American Psychiatric Association. It is currently the most widely accepted standard for diagnosing problem behavior. DSM III-R describes specific criteria for diagnosing problems. By using
DSM III-R clinicians can agree on the diagnoses of the disorders they are treating
and understand each other. DSM III-R contains descriptions and is not concerned
with the causes of disorders. Among the major categories of disorders described
in DSM III-R are anxiety disorders, abnormal behavior that causes physical problems, changes in identity, mood disorders, substance abuse disorders, personality
disorders, schizophrenia, and organic disorders.

Exercise 10-2
Two psychiatrists are discussing a patient's problems. They want to diagnose
the patient and find the cause of the disorder. How can DSM III-R help them?

_____

_____

_____

_____

Check your response in the Feedback section.

ANXIETY DISORDERS

Anxiety is an uncomfortable feeling. A person has a sense of fearfulness but
cannot identify why. The cause of the fear is not immediately present or is
vague. Perhaps you have met someone who aroused your anxiety. You felt
uncomfortable, fretful, and tense with the person for no apparent reason. Or
maybe you have experienced anxiety at the beginning of a new course or job.
You have no specific fears but feel some uncomfortable tension. A person who
has survived an intensely fearful situation may be left with feelings of anxiety
long after the cause of the fear is gone.

Anxiety becomes a major problem or disorder when fears are exaggerated or
unrealistic. A person suffering from *anxiety disorder* often has such physical
symptoms as sweating, shaking, shortness of breath, and a fast heartbeat. Anxiety disorders are somewhat common. About 13 million adult Americans have experienced anxiety disorders (DSM III, 1980). Anxiety disorders include phobias,
eating disorders, obsessive-compulsive disorders, and post-traumatic stress.

anxiety disorder A
continuous state of
tension, stress, and
fearfulness

Phobias

Phobias are the most common form of anxiety disorder. About 11 million
Americans suffer from some form of phobia (Robins et al., 1984). Phobias are

phobia An intense,
exaggerated, and
unrealistic fear

constant unrealistic fears that interfere with normal living. Instead of fearing only threatening animals, a person fears all animals, even those that are docile and friendly. Such exaggerated fears are labeled "phobias." Some phobias are relatively common and do not cause serious negative results. For example, many people feel queasy at the sight of blood or panic at the sight of a harmless snake or mouse. These simple, exaggerated fears rarely interfere with everyday life.

The most severe phobia that clearly interferes with normal living is agoraphobia. *Agoraphobia* is a fear of leaving one's own home. More than half the people who seek treatment for phobias suffer from agoraphobia (Chambless, 1986). These people are unable to go shopping, go to a movie, drive a car, ride a bus, or even walk on a public street. The article in Exhibit 10-1 suggests that agoraphobia may be related to panic attacks.

The list of possible phobias is almost endless. Fifteen of the more common types include:

agoraphobia Most severe phobia, usually accompanied by panic attacks; an inability to go out of the house

Acrophobia Fear of heights

Androphobia Fear of men

Aquaphobia Fear of water

Autophobia Fear of being alone

Cardiophobia Fear of heart disease

Chrematophobia Fear of money

Claustrophobia Fear of closed places

Hemophobia Fear of blood

Necrophobia Fear of corpses

Nyctophobia Fear of the dark

Panophobia Fear of everything

Phobophobia Fear of one's own fear

Pyrophobia Fear of fire

Thanophobia Fear of death

Toxicophobia Fear of poison

Triskaidekaphobia Fear of the number 13

Zoophobia Fear of animals

EXHIBIT 10-1

Prisoners of Panic

For most people, going to the supermarket to pick up a loaf of bread is nothing to worry about. But for victims of agoraphobia—fear of being out in public—such simple, everyday errands become monumental tasks.

Like the proverbial horse and carriage, agoraphobia and panic attacks—short-lived, overpowering feelings of sheer terror—frequently travel together. To see how panic attacks and agoraphobia are related, psychiatrist Alan Breier of the National Institute of Mental Health and colleagues interviewed 60 sufferers of agoraphobia and/or panic attacks, and charted the course of their illness.

Patients who suffered from both disorders almost always had the panic attacks first, and in about 75 percent of the cases, the episodes of agoraphobia began within a year of the first panic attack, Breier and colleagues report (*Archives of General Psychiatry*, Vol. 43, pp. 1029–1036). The researchers speculate that these individuals begin to avoid going out because they fear suffering another panic attack in a public place.

Interestingly, patients who knew that the first attack was anxiety-related developed agoraphobia at a much slower rate than did patients who attributed the symptoms to a life-threatening ailment, such as a heart attack.

Because a realistic understanding of the early panic attacks seems to decrease the probability of developing full-blown agoraphobia, the researchers recommend that health professionals intervene early in the course of the illness to provide sufferers with accurate information about both disorders.

Source: Schanback, M.C. (1988, January). Prisoners of panic. *Psychology Today.*

A complete list would even mention arachibutyrophobia, fear of peanut butter sticking to the roof of the mouth, and Santa Claustrophobia, a fear of being caught in chimneys! Some phobias can be serious and even life-threatening. Methods for treating phobias are discussed in Chapter 11, "Getting Help."

Exercise 10-3

Ms. F. is a nonswimmer. She is concerned about drowning and always wears a life vest when sailing or canoeing. At beaches, she is careful to stay in the water areas that are protected by lifeguards.

Ms. P. is also concerned about drowning. Although she had some swimming lessons as a child, she will no longer go near water. In fact, she refuses to sit in a bathtub, jacuzzi, or water container of any form. She refuses to shower. She even becomes anxious when she is around water fountains.

Explain why Ms. P. is suffering from a phobia and Ms. F. is not.

_____

_____

_____

Please check your explanation in the Feedback section.

Eating Disorders

Anxiety is believed to cause eating disorders. One eating disorder, *anorexia nervosa,* generally begins when young girls grow anxious about becoming overweight. Although they initially do not want to eat, eventually they completely lose their desire for food. They diet continually and cannot stop even when they are so underweight that their lives are threatened. The sight of food makes them nauseated.

anorexia nervosa Prolonged refusal to eat resulting in a severe weight loss

Researchers believe that women are more likely than men to diet to control their weight. Men are more likely to keep their weight down with exercise (see Exhibit 10-2). As a result more women than men suffer from anorexia nervosa. Although most patients only suffer one episode of anorexia nervosa and recover completely, between 15 and 21 percent starve themselves to death (DSM III, 1980).

Bulimia is an eating disorder related to anorexia. But while anorexic patients are usually painfully thin, bulimics are generally of normal weight. The bulimic person goes on an eating binge and then uses laxatives or tries to vomit.

bulimia Binge eating followed by laxatives or self-induced vomiting

Researchers have found that bulimics eat to control their anxiety. On one binge a bulimic person might consume several candy bars, an entire pie, three sandwiches, a large pizza, a jar of peanut butter, two donuts, and three bowls of cereal. Laxatives and self-induced vomiting are used to avoid getting fat. Bulimia is believed to be most common in college-age women. Estimates of the prevalence in this group range from 5 to 67 percent (Hart & Ollendich, 1985; Polivy & Herman, 1985).

Obsessive-Compulsive Disorders

Have you ever been so concerned with a thought that you found it impossible to concentrate on anything else? Whether you were preoccupied by a broken

EXHIBIT 10-2

The Weighting Game: A Male Version

A number of recent studies indicate that women, but not men, tend to see themselves as overweight even if they are not. Dissatisfaction with body weight among women is thought to be a major risk factor for developing eating disorders such as anorexia and bulimia.

Young men, however, are far from content with their weight, according to a survey of 226 college freshmen—98 men and 128 women—in the November/December *Psychosomatic Medicine*. While nearly nine out of 10 normal-weight 18-year-old women said they wanted to be thinner, normal-weight men expressed conflicting views; more than half wanted to lose weight and about one-third wanted to gain weight. The proportion of both men and women who expressed no desire for weight change was about 15 percent.

Men and women who wished to lose weight shared negative perceptions of their bodies, say Adam Drewnowski and Doris K. Yee of the University of Michigan in Ann Arbor. Both groups viewed themselves as overweight and were unhappy with the shape of their bodies. Men were more likely to use daily exercise for weight control, whereas women more often resorted to dieting anywhere from several days to several weeks per month.

It is unclear whether normal-weight males who want to be thinner and see themselves as overweight are at risk for eating disorders, say the researchers. This group reported dieting more than other males in the college sample, but still dieted much less than the women. Dieting, rather than dissatisfaction with body weight, may be a key risk factor for eating disorders, suggest Drewnowski and Yee.

Source: (1988, January 9). The weighting game: A male version. *Science News.*

romance, an illness of a close relative, or your own safety, many people would say you were obsessed with the thought. However, psychologists would argue that these thoughts were not true obsessions. You were dealing with real problems that most likely could be resolved.

obsessions Unwanted but persistent thoughts or ideas

Obsessions are persistent **ideas** or impulses that invade your mind against your will. They cannot be resolved. The ideas seem senseless but you cannot avoid them. One common obsession centers on being contaminated by germs. As a result of this obsession, a person refuses to shake hands or come into contact with other people.

compulsion Repeated and persistent behavior ritual that a person feels compelled to carry out to avoid disaster

Obsessions often lead to *compulsions*. A compulsion is a persistent **behavior**. People who are obsessed with fears of contamination may become compulsive about hand-washing. They would feel they were never clean and constantly wash and wipe their hands.

Compulsions often take the form of rituals. A hand-washing ritual might consist of two washings with soap and hot water, an antiseptic rinse, and waving the hands in circles to air dry them. The ritual would be repeated whenever another person or object was touched. Failure to complete the ritual would cause intense anxiety. The compulsion is more important than any other aspect of life.

Post-Traumatic Stress

post-traumatic stress Anxiety disorder that causes a person to constantly reexperience a traumatic or shocking event

Severe shocks or traumas cause anxiety. Sometimes the anxiety persists and becomes long-lasting. In these cases the person is considered to be suffering from a *post-traumatic stress* disorder. Symptoms include dreaming about the traumatic event, jumpiness, guilt, trouble concentrating, and overreacting to situations that stir memories of the trauma. Although post-traumatic stress can result from experiencing rape, fire, an earthquake, or a bombing, the condition is most common among wounded Vietnam veterans (see Exhibit 10-3).

Exercise 10-4

Read each of the following symptoms and indicate whether the person is likely to be suffering from anorexia nervosa, bulimia, obsessive-compulsive disorder, or post-traumatic stress disorder.

a. A man who survived the Paris bombings in World War II still awakens with nightmares of the horror scenes. _post t.s.d._

b. A woman is so concerned about being on time that she carries an alarm clock and checks the time every five minutes. _ob-comp._

c. A wounded Vietnam veteran is extremely jumpy. He has strong feelings of guilt about surviving while most of his friends were killed. _post.t.s.d._

d. A college student eats twenty-five pancakes, two large coffee cakes, three pounds of bacon, and two dozen blueberry muffins, and then takes a strong laxative. _Bulimia_

e. A teenager is extremely thin but believes she is overweight. She is starving herself. _An. Nerv._

Please check your responses in the Feedback section.

Figure 10-1 His compulsion is stronger than any other need, including the need for silverware.

EXHIBIT 10-3

More Stress Disorder for Wounded Viet Vets

Severe trauma can trigger a number of reactions, such as recurring nightmares, sudden flashbacks and emotional numbing. In 1980, such reactions were combined into an official psychiatric diagnosis, post-traumatic stress disorder. A rare survey of the disorder in the general population now indicates that it is uncommon, except among wounded Vietnam veterans.

Current or previous symptoms meeting the criteria for post-traumatic stress disorder were reported by just 1 percent of the random sample of 2,493 St. Louis residents, say psychiatrist John E. Helzer of Washington University School of Medicine in St. Louis and his colleagues. Among Vietnam veterans who were not wounded and civilians exposed to physical attack, including rape, about 3.5 percent suffered the disorder, compared with 20 percent of veterans wounded in Vietnam....

Although the full-blown diagnosis was unusual, 15 percent of the men and 16 percent of the women interviewed experienced some of the above symptoms—usually one or two—after a trauma, report the researchers in the Dec. 24 *New England Journal of Medicine.* Traumas, which also included experiencing serious accidents, seeing someone hurt or die and surviving a threat or close call, resulted most often in nightmares, jumpiness and trouble sleeping.

For about half of those with post-traumatic stress disorder, symptoms lasted fewer than six months. However, in about one-third of the cases, symptoms persisted for more than three years. The traumas that produced the longest-lasting symptoms were Vietnam combat among men and physical attack among women....

Source: Bower, B. (1988, January 2). More stress disorder for wounded Viet vets. *Science News.*

Abnormal Physical Problems

Occasionally a person will develop physical symptoms and no organic or physical problem can be found. One of the most dramatic (and fortunately, rare) examples is *conversion disorder*. The patient may suddenly lose sensation in an arm or leg, become paralyzed, or lose the sense of smell, hearing, or seeing. No physical findings can be found to explain the problem.

conversion disorder
Anxiety disorder characterized by a loss of sensation without any physical cause

Sometimes people believe they are ill when in fact they are healthy. Have you ever known someone who constantly complained of a variety of ailments, yet physicians could find no problems? The person could be suffering from *hypochondriasis*. Hypochondriacs are totally preoccupied with health problems. They know the symptoms of an amazing assortment of diseases. It is not uncommon for hypochondriacs to believe they have symptoms of leprosy, heart disease, cancer, or other major disorders. A simple headache could be a signal of a heart attack or a brain tumor to a person with hypochondriasis.

hypochondriasis
Anxiety disorder characterized by a total preoccupation with exaggerated health problems

Checkpoint

Use the following questions to check your understanding of this portion of the chapter. Choose and mark the one correct response to each question.

1. Which of the following factors is required for behavior to be considered abnormal?
   a. Rare
   b. Undesirable

    c. Distress

    d. All of the above

2. Mr. W. is a workaholic who lives alone. He stays at his office until 11 P.M. and then brings home additional work. He rarely gets more than four hours sleep. Is his behavior abnormal?

    a. Yes, because it is rare

    b. Yes, because it is undesirable

    c. No, because it is not undesirable

    d. Yes, because most people need more sleep

3. What is the purpose of DSM III-R?

    a. To describe disorders

    b. To determine causes of disorders

    c. To cure disorders

    d. To treat disorders

4. Which of the following classifications of disorders includes phobias, eating disorders, obsessive-compulsive disorders, and post-traumatic stress?

    a. Anxiety

    b. Anorexia nervosa

    c. Hypochondriasis

    d. Conversion disorder

5. What is the most common form of anxiety disorder?

    a. Eating disorders

    b. Phobias

    c. Obsessive-compulsions

    d. Post-traumatic stress

6. What is a phobia?

    a. A realistic fear

    b. A specific fear

    c. An unrealistic fear

    d. An eating disorder

7. Mr. A. suffers from agoraphobia. Which of the following statements is likely to be true?

    a. He is afraid of being stuck in a chimney.

    b. He is afraid of water.

    c. He does not have panic attacks.

    d. He is afraid of leaving his house.

8. Which phobia is considered most severe?

    a. Acrophobia

    b. Agoraphobia

    c. Claustrophobia

    d. Zoophobia

9. What do patients suffering from anorexia nervosa and bulimia have in common?

    a. Both have obsessive-compulsive disorders.

    b. Both have eating disorders.

    c. Both suffer from post-traumatic stress.

    d. Both are normal.

10. Mrs. H. believes her hair is messy and is going to tangle and choke her. As a result she stops what she is doing every ten minutes and begins a hair-brushing ritual. Which of the following problems is she demonstrating?

    a. Post-traumatic stress
    b. Anorexia nervosa
    c. Obsessive-compulsive disorder
    d. Arachibutyrophobia

11. Which of the following persons might suffer from post-traumatic stress?

    a. A rape victim
    b. A woman surviving an earthquake
    c. A Vietnam veteran
    d. All of the above

Check your responses against the Checkpoint Answer Key at the end of the chapter. If you had difficulty with any question, reread the text. If you had little or no difficulty or have resolved the problems that you might have had, you are ready to continue with the second portion of the chapter.

CHANGES IN IDENTITY OR CONSCIOUSNESS

multiple personality A rare disorder in which a person has two or more distinct personalities, each becoming prominent at different times

You are most likely familiar with the famous story of Dr. Jekyll and Mr. Hyde. Dr. Jekyll suffered from *multiple personality*. He had two distinct and quite different personalities. Each personality had its own memories, preferences, voice, and handwriting. Multiple personality is not fiction. Although extremely rare, it is a real disorder.

Figure 10-2
It appears Dr. Jekyll's "other" personality will give the second opinion.

"I warned you not to insist on a second opinion."

The most famous true story of multiple personality was documented in *The Three Faces of Eve* (Thigpen & Cleckly, 1954). Although cases of multiple personality provide dramatic books, films, and news stories, many psychiatrists and psychologists are skeptical about the popularity of the disorder. It is now often used as an argument in legal defense. Prior to 1979, only 200 cases of multiple personality were identified. Since 1979 more than 2500 cases have occurred. Many professionals suspect that knowledge of the disorder has provided criminals with the ability to fake the symptoms. There are many theories about the causes of multiple personality. However, since the disorder had been so rare, research has been limited. The cause of multiple personality remains unknown.

Amnesia, a partial or complete memory loss, is another type of change in identity or consciousness. As explained in Chapter 4, amnesia can result from physical causes. Alcoholism, drug abuse, head injuries, and nutritional deficiencies are among the possible physical causes. Amnesia can also be caused by psychological factors. This form of amnesia is usually brought on by a highly stressful event and generally is only temporary. The duration varies and can be hours, days, or even years. The amount of memory loss also varies from a very specific repression of the traumatic event to a complete loss of identity. People suffering from severe amnesia may forget who they are and totally lose contact with the real world. Schacter (1986) found that it is often

Figure 10-3
Could this Santa be an amnesia victim with a new identity?

"He wants to know why we're throwing away his mail."

difficult to determine whether people who claim a loss of identity are suffering from a severe form of amnesia or merely faking the symptoms.

Exercise 10-5
Describe two ways in which multiple personality and amnesia are alike.

a. _____

b. _____

Turn to the Feedback section to check your answers.

MOOD DISORDERS

Everyone has good moods and bad ones. You probably can recall feeling sad, gloomy, and listless. Perhaps you were terribly disappointed with your grades, had a serious argument with a good friend, or were fired from a job. You may have remained depressed and grumpy for days or even weeks. You were suffering from a mild form of *depression*. There is even a positive aspect to mild depression (see Exhibit 10-4).

depression Mood disorder in which a person feels overwhelming sadness

EXHIBIT 10-4

Sadder but Wiser

People in the throes of severe depression have an unrealistically negative view of themselves and their world. Paradoxically, research also indicates that those suffering from mild depression may actually see the world more clearly than the rest of us do.

Timothy M. Osberg, a psychologist at Niagara University, had a group of students predict which of 75 events—including getting a new job, borrowing money, developing an allergy, falling in love—were most likely to happen to them in the following two months. Before making these predictions, students filled out a questionnaire tapping symptoms of depression. When Osberg compared the events that actually occurred with the students' depression scores he found that depressed students were more accurate than the nondepressed were in predicting the negative events that happened to them. This was still true even after he allowed for the fact that depressed people are more negative anyway.

In a 1980 study, psychologist Peter M. Lewinsohn of the University of Oregon and his colleagues had a group of depressed and nondepressed people assess, for example, how friendly, popular, assertive or attractive they thought themselves to be. In addition, while talking in small groups, these people were assessed by others whose job was to decide just how friendly or popular or assertive they actually were.

The depressed patients tended to mark themselves down, but their self-assessments were quite accurate when compared with the way the outsiders viewed them. In contrast, the nondepressed individuals saw themselves more positively. Their self-image was not only better than that of the depressed patients, it was also better than outsiders saw them.

Lewinsohn's group concludes that nondepressed people have a halo or glow, an "illusory self-enhancement," that lets them see themselves more positively than others see them. And this may have important consequences for mental health. It is tempting to imagine, the Oregon team suggests, that "to feel good about ourselves we may have to judge ourselves more kindly than we are judged."

Source: Wood, C. (1988, January). Sadder but wiser. *Psychology Today.*

You might also recall some of your happier moods. The bliss of falling in love or winning an award may have kept you in an outstanding mood. Most days your moods are likely to be between the high of bliss and the low of gloom.

However, people with mood disorders are almost constantly coping with these severe moods. Their moods are so severe that they do not have control of themselves. Some people suffer only from depression and experience only low moods. Others have both high moods (mania) and low moods (depression). They suffer from bipolar disorder.

Depression

Recall the last time you felt depressed. What brought on your depression? Maybe you were criticized by someone and went through a period of stress. Or perhaps you suffered a sense of personal loss resulting from the death of someone you loved. Depression is expected after the loss of a loved one, whether through death or divorce. Briscoe and Smith (1975) reported that divorced persons suffer even deeper and more extensive depression than the bereaved. Bereaved persons are given an opportunity to mourn their loss with the support of family and friends. Divorced persons are usually expected to adjust without any condolences or help from others. As a result, divorced persons experience greater difficulty in recovering from their depression.

Sometimes depression has no apparent cause. You probably have had a down day and could not identify the reason. Possibly you were repressing the cause. Psychiatrists have also found that depression can occur regardless of outside events. Researchers have noted that certain hormonal and chemical changes can cause depression. Chronic depression, depression which remains without apparent cause, is dangerous.

What are the symptoms of depression? A depressed person feels drained of incentives, tires easily, and lacks energy. Self-esteem is low, and the focus is on negative aspects of life. Somehow all positive features in life are lost. Personal achievements are minimized. Suppose you admired an oil painting by a depressed man. He would probably say it was easy to sketch or he had good brushes or super paints. He would never take personal credit for his achievement.

Because confidence is low, depressed people tend to *catastrophize,* that is, exaggerate things that may go wrong. Assume you want to cheer up a depressed woman. You recall that she once baked a delicious lemon meringue pie. You invite her to a covered-dish party at your home and ask her to bring her wonderful pie. She would probably begin by giving credit to the recipe rather than her cooking talent. Then she would suggest that you bake the pie. After you insist that you do not have her baking talent, she might begin dwelling on all the possible mistakes she could make. Her thoughts might proceed, "I will probably ruin the crust or blow the mixing order. Once I burned the meringue. Nothing I do comes out right. How can I expect people to eat my food? I should not go to the party."

catastrophize A tendency to exaggerate things that may go wrong

Depressed people prefer not to be cheered up and avoid doing anything pleasurable. Tears come easily, and sleeping and daydreaming can become excessive. One of the danger signals in depression is an unwillingness or inability

Figure 10-4
One symptom of
depression is a sense
of hopelessness.

to communicate with others. Sometimes depression brings on a sudden major change in behavior. A quiet person becomes boisterous or an easygoing person becomes antagonistic. The article excerpt in Exhibit 10-5 presents a case of severe depression and describes the problem of increased occurrence. Exhibit 10-6 (page 286) lists the common symptoms of depression.

Since a depressed person does not want to be cheered up, you may be wondering what you can do to help. Although you can give personal support, victims of depression really need professional assistance. Treatment for depression is described in Chapter 11.

Exercise 10-6

Listed below are several symptoms. Put a check beside each symptom that suggests a possibility of depression.

☑ Lowered self-esteem

☑ Catastrophizing

☐ Excessive energy

☑ Irritability

☑ Thoughts of death

☐ Good communication

☐ Strong motivation

☑ Proneness to tears

☑ Insomnia

☑ Hopelessness

You may compare your list to the one in the Feedback section.

EXHIBIT 10-5

285

IDENTIFYING
PROBLEM BEHAVIOR

Depression

It can steal up as insidiously as a November fog, chilling the heart, sapping the will even to get out of bed in the morning. Victims often experience it as a terrifying aloneness, a sense of being strangely "outside" themselves, like ghostly spectators of their own lives, unable to feel any human warmth. For Artie Houston it was a nightmare in slow motion: everything was such an effort. It would take her five minutes just to get the keys out of her bag and start the car. After she lost her job as business director of a Ft. Worth, Texas, blood center, she would sit by a window, weeping and wringing her hands. When her husband came home from work, he would hear only her despairing murmur: "Oh, God. Oh, God." For Eugene Davis,* a 34-year-old Provo, Utah, stockbroker, it was life bereft of the smallest consolation. Day after day there was only the same smothering "heaviness" in things: "It was not possible," he says, "to really laugh, to find joy in life. Think about it: no joy in life."...

So pervasive is depression that it is called "the common cold of mental illness." Yet, although it is almost always treatable, with a combination of antidepressant drugs and psychotherapy, only one in five victims seeks help. Often people don't recognize or acknowledge that they are suffering from a clinical disorder. And the danger is that the longer depression goes untreated, the more likely it is to become chronic and seriously damaging. Victims may lose jobs, friends, spouses. "An awful lot of life is lost to depression," says Joseph Schildkraut, professor of psychiatry at Harvard Medical School.

But the most disturbing news about depression is that it is increasing—and increasing most among the young. According to the National Institute of Mental Health, the average age of first onset of the disease has dropped dramatically since World War II, from late middle age to people in their mid-20s to early 30s. It now occurs most often among 25- to 44-year-olds, a significant shift from the prewar years, when it tended to strike people most often in their 50s. Contrary to stereotypes of the aged, people 60 and over were found to be the least subject to the disorder. (One possible explanation is that they are more resilient and out of the rat race by that age.)

"Agent Blue." But it is the rise in youthful depression that has most impressed researchers, setting them off in quest of a putative "Agent Blue"—some cultural or environmental factor that might account for the change. "Coming to maturity in the period from 1960 to 1975," concluded psychiatrist Gerald L. Klerman, of New York's Cornell University Medical College, in a recent paper, "seems to have had a profound adverse impact on the likelihood of depressive illness." That period, of course, was marked by unprecedented social upheaval, suggesting that it may have sown the seeds of mass emotional disturbance. Suicides, alcoholism and drug addiction among younger people rose in the 1970s. Klerman, who conducted one of the key surveys on which the new figures are based, believes the turmoil signaled a "new age of melancholy," spurred by the disruption of traditional family ties and the loss of faith in social institutions. But these, admittedly, are only reasonable speculations. Klerman and others do not rule out the possibility of biological causes, such as a new virus or changes in nutrition. "We have had broad changes in our population," explains Dr. Theodore Reich, professor of psychiatry at Washington University in St. Louis. "Menarche has gotten younger in girls, people are taller as a result of diet. It doesn't necessarily have to be the way we brought up our children."

Biology, in fact, looms ever larger in the study of depression. For generations the condition was thought to be purely a state of mind, but in recent years there has been significant progress in understanding its causes. Today it is seen as an illness like ulcers or high blood pressure, the result of an interplay of biological and psychological forces. Many doctors now believe that victims of depression carry an innate susceptibility to the disease; the disease itself can then be triggered by external factors or by change in the body's own chemistry....

---

*Not his real name.

Source: Gelman, D. with Doherty, S., Gosnell, M., Raine, G., & Shapiro, D. (1987, May 4). Depression. *Newsweek.*

EXHIBIT 10-6

Common Symptoms of Depression

- Feelings of sadness, hopelessness
- Insomnia, early wakening, difficulty getting up
- Thoughts of suicide and death
- Restlessness, irritability
- Low self-esteem or guilt
- Eating disturbance—usually loss of appetite and weight

- Fatigue, weakness, decreased energy
- Diminished ability to think or concentrate
- Loss of interest and pleasure in activities once enjoyed, such as sex
- Chronic pains that fail to respond to typical treatment

Bipolar Disorder

At the opposite pole from depression is mania. Mania is an abnormally strong feeling of well-being. A manic person is full of energy, ambitions, plans, and power. Rapid speech and jokes are common. Perhaps this sounds like a wonderful state to be in. Actually the manic state is so extreme that behavior becomes irrational. Large sums of money may be spent or given away. Ideas often become outrageous. Hyperactivity is so strong that nothing is accomplished; the individual may not sleep for several days.

Mania almost always has a dark side. While people can experience depression without ever feeling manic, it is rare for a person to experience only mania. People who have manic episodes almost always go through periods of depression. Their problem is labeled "bipolar disorder" because their moods swing from a manic "pole" to a depressed "pole." On the positive side, people with bipolar disorder are likely to be highly creative (see Chapter 5).

bipolar disorder Mood disorder involving mood swings between depression and mania

Exercise 10-7
Reread the first page of this chapter and diagnose Mindy's possible problem.

_____

_____

_____

You may check your response in the Feedback section.

SUBSTANCE ABUSE AND ADDICTION

About 11 million American are alcoholics, costing more than $50 billion each year. More than 35,000 deaths result from drunken driving each year. Alcoholism is the third major cause of death (National Institute on Alcohol Abuse and Alcoholism, 1981). Nathan (1983) reported that 200,000 new cases of alcoholism are diagnosed each year; most are adolescents. The damage caused by alcohol and drugs leads to a steady deterioration of the brain and other organs of the body which will eventually cause death. Coleman (1972) reported both alcoholics and drug users have low self-esteem and lack of confidence.

Worried about failure, they have severe reactions to criticism and need constant praise and reinforcement.

Alcohol is often consumed to reduce anxiety. Williams (1966) found that nonalcoholics can reduce depression with up to 4 ounces of liquor, that is, about two drinks. However, after the third drink, depression is increased. Research by Nathan and O'Brien (1971) concluded that alcoholics become more depressed after their continued drinking. A more recent study by McKinney proposed that alcoholics are reinforced by the initial decrease in depression (see Exhibit 10-7). They continue to consume alcohol in hopes that depression may be reduced, but depression only becomes deeper.

Alcoholics drink until they are completely intoxicated. Speech becomes slurred, coordination is impaired, and behavior and personality change noticeably. Alcoholics often go to work intoxicated and may even continue their drinking at their jobs. Even more unfortunate, driving while intoxicated is common and accidents, injuries, and deaths result. Several studies have suggested a tendency toward alcoholism may be inherited. As you will note from Exhibit 10-8, recent improvements in technology have allowed researchers to learn more about the effects of alcohol on the brain. Methods for controlling alcoholism are discussed in Chapter 11.

Drug use permits an immediate escape from anxiety and depression but clearly does not resolve any problems. Drug users suffer side effects and become addicted, while the original problem persists. Drugs are generally more expensive than alcohol. As a result the addicted drug user must find ways to come up with money to purchase drugs. Frequently, stealing and prostitution are the techniques chosen. Because of their addiction, drug users will use any

Most new cases of alcoholism are adolescents. *(Alan Carey/The Image Works)*

EXHIBIT 10-7

Alcohol Use and Great Expectations

Some people think of alcohol as a kind of magical elixir that replaces unpleasant feelings with a confidence-enhancing "high" and an array of heightened social and physical pleasures. Mix this expectation with alcohol's "two-faced" physical effects—it acts as a stimulant at low doses and a depressant at high doses—and the stage is set for a vicious cycle leading to alcohol addiction, says psychologist G. Alan Marlatt of the University of Washington in Seattle.

"Any short-term relief [from drinking] is quickly dispelled by the delayed negative effects which in turn give rise to another attempt to gain relief," he says. "The expected solution exacerbates the initial problem."

Several studies have shown that low doses of alcohol pump up heart rate, skin conductance and motor and perceptual performance, whereas higher doses depress these measures of physiological arousal. The initial arousal and energy boost provided by alcohol may feed into expectations that its effects will only be for the better, suggests Marlatt. A number of factors influence expectations about alcohol's effects, including cultural beliefs, personal experience with the substance, the setting in which it is consumed and physiological sensitivity and tolerance. Furthermore, explains Marlatt in the Summer *Alcohol Health & Research World,* recent research indicates that heavy drinkers and alcoholics are far more likely to expect alcohol to transform their emotional state in all sorts of positive ways, while light drinkers have limited expectations of how alcohol will affect them.

Marlatt proposes that moderate drinking serves to enhance or maintain a neutral or positive emotional state. One example, he says, is someone at a wedding reception whose good mood is heightened by drinking champagne, even if overindulgence results in fatigue or slight discomfort later on. Addictive use, however, may be an attempt to transform or cope with a negative emotional state. Consider a heavy-drinking businessman, says Marlatt. He may drink before meeting clients to alleviate hangover effects from the past night's drinking and to fortify his confidence. But because of his tolerance for the drug, he needs several drinks before its stimulating effects kick in. Several hours later he feels tired, restless and unable to concentrate. More alcohol is then sought to provide temporary relief, illustrating the vicious cycle of his alcohol craving.

Research on addiction-prone expectations about alcohol's effects may lead to improved alcohol education and prevention programs, notes Marlatt.

Source: (1987, October 3). Alcohol use and great expectations. *Science News.*

method possible, whether legal or not, to keep themselves high. Methods used in drug therapy are described in Chapter 11.

Exercise 10-8

a. How are alcoholics and drug users alike? _____

_____

_____

_____

b. How are they different? _____

_____

_____

Please turn to the Feedback section to check your answers.

EXHIBIT 10-8

289

IDENTIFYING
PROBLEM BEHAVIOR

Why Drunkenness Causes Clumsiness and Mood Changes

Brain researchers say they have discovered, at least in part, how alcohol makes people drunk.

The staggering and other losses of muscle control, they found, are caused by a reduction in blood flow to the cerebellum, the part of the brain that controls muscle coordination.

They also found that the mood shifts typical of drunkenness were linked to imbalances in the rate of metabolic activity in various parts of the brain's cortex, the seat of conscious thinking.

The findings were made in separate studies by Nora Volkow at the Brookhaven National Laboratory in New York and John Metz of the University of Chicago. Nuclear medicine uses atomic nuclei and other subatomic particles and forces to create images of the inside of the body without surgery.

Volkow's and Metz's findings came from a relatively new procedure called positron emission tomography, or PET, scanning. Subjects are injected with a radioactive form of oxygen, carbon dioxide or glucose that emits subatomic particles called positrons. Sensors around the person's body detect the positrons and reconstruct the image of a "slice" through the body....

Metz's mood experiments revealed differences in glucose-based metabolism. He classed the drinkers into two groups: those who usually had positive changes, such as becoming friendly and elated, and those with negative changes such as anxiety and depression.

In those who had positive changes, the PET scan showed higher metabolic rates (more glucose use) in the parietal cortex, or lobe, of the brain and lower rates in the temporal lobes. Those with negative changes had the opposite metabolic pattern. The temporal lobes, one on each side, are just inboard of the ears. The parietal cortex, also on each side, runs from just above the temporals to the midline where the left and right hemispheres meet.

Source: Rensberger, B., & Hilts, P.J. (1988, June 20). Why drunkenness causes clumsiness and mood changes. *Washington Post.*

SUICIDE

Substance abuse can lead to suicide (see Exhibit 10-9). Suicide is more likely among the lonely. Whether aged, divorced, or living alone, the person attempting suicide is often without friends. The suicide rate is highest among the elderly. However, incidence of suicide among adolescents has increased. Acute suicide is the second most frequent cause of death among young people between the ages of 15 and 24. (Accidents are number one.) The suicide rate for these young people has increased by more than 150 percent in the past twenty years (Harvard Medical School, 1986).

Suppose a friend or coworker indicated he was thinking about suicide. Psychologists suggest that any suicide threat should be taken seriously. Usually the person is calling for help. The first step should be to bring him to a physician, psychologist, or psychiatrist. If he refused, it would be advisable to help him express his feelings and to show sincere concern and empathy. You might suggest that there are alternative solutions to his problem. It would be wise to determine whether he has a specific plan; if there is a plan, the situation is even more dangerous. Offer to hold the weapon (gun, razor, pills, or other) for a given time. Encourage your friend to seek help and offer to accompany him. If he is persistent about avoiding professionals, set another meeting time. Meanwhile you can get professional advice before the next

EXHIBIT 10-9

Drugs and Suicide: Link to Recent Loss

The death of a spouse, rejection by a romantic partner, even eviction from an apartment can push someone with a serious alcohol or drug problem to suicide, according to a report in the June *Archives of General Psychiatry*.

Yet people with mood disorders such as severe depression—a group previously found to have an increased risk of suicide—are less likely than substance abusers to kill themselves shortly after these types of stressful events, say psychiatrist Charles L. Rich of the State University of New York in Stony Brook and his colleagues. Substance abusers, suggest the researchers, are more vulnerable to stress caused by "interpersonal losses and conflicts."

The data, based on 283 suicides in San Diego County, Calif., between 1981 and 1983, may not readily apply to all populations, notes psychiatrist George E. Murphy of Washington University School of Medicine in St. Louis. "Nevertheless, interpersonal loss is strongly confirmed as a major and immediate risk factor for suicide in substance abusers," he writes in an editorial following the report.

The researchers made posthumous diagnoses of substance abuse, as well as mood disorders, after interviews with a suicide victim's family, friends, employers and physicians. Other sources included hospital, school and police records.

Murphy and his colleagues had previously linked suicide in 20- to 30-year-olds to depression, alcohol abuse and drug abuse. The new analysis finds that 42 percent of the suicide victims in this age bracket who were substance abusers—either with or without a mood disorder—had undergone a stressful loss or conflict in the six weeks before taking their lives. In a group of suicides over the age of 30 with the same diagnoses, 38 percent suffered an interpersonal disturbance in their last six weeks.

The researchers found significantly fewer instances of recent loss or conflict among suicides of all ages with a mood disorder or depressive symptoms that did not add up to a diagnosis of "major depression."

Nearly 60 percent of all suicides were substance abusers, say the researchers, and 84 percent of those abused both alcohol and other drugs.

Clinicians should pay close attention to the suicidal thoughts of substance abusers and involve the patient's family and friends in treatment, Murphy says. A short stint in the hospital, he adds, "may be needed for a period of protection [after a recent loss] as well as for detoxification."

Source: Bower, B. (1988, June 18). Drugs and suicide: Link to recent loss. *Science News.*

meeting. A person attempting suicide needs assurances about personal worth and importance to others. A friend who is supportive is crucial to survival.

Checkpoint

Use the following questions to check your understanding of this portion of the chapter. Choose and mark the one correct response to each question.

12. From which of the following disorders was Dr. Jekyll suffering?
a. Split personality
b. Multiple personality
c. Bipolar disorder
d. Amnesia

13. Which of the following is a possible psychological cause of amnesia?
a. A traumatic event
b. Alcoholism

    c. A head injury

    d. A vitamin deficiency

14. Which of the following amnesia victims is most likely to have memory restored?

    a. A drug addict

    b. A person who suffered brain damage

    c. A person with a severe nutritional deficiency

    d. A victim of an airplane crash

15. What is one positive aspect of mild depression?

    a. A more realistic view

    b. An increase in incentive

    c. A quick swing to mania

    d. An increase in memory

16. Which of the following persons is likely to experience the most severe depression?

    a. A person whose spouse just died

    b. A person who is suddenly divorced

    c. A person with type A personality

    d. A person with type B personality

17. Assume you have just admired an afghan crocheted by a depressed man. What is he most likely to do?

    a. Become invigorated because of your compliment

    b. Explain the intricacies and difficulties of crocheting

    c. Claim the pattern was so easy anyone could have done it

    d. Feel encouraged and tell you about his other accomplishments

18. What do most manics also experience?

    a. Multiple personality

    b. Amnesia

    c. Alcoholism

    d. Depression

19. Jacqueline came home from work feeling depressed. She decides to have a few cocktails. How many can she have before becoming even more depressed?

    a. One or two

    b. Three or four

    c. Five or six

    d. None

20. Which of the following persons is most likely to steal?

    a. A guilty person

    b. An alcoholic

    c. A depressed person

    d. A drug addict

21. When should a suicide threat be taken seriously?

    a. When the person is elderly

    b. When the person is between 15 and 24

    c. When the person has a plan

    d. Always

Check your responses against the Checkpoint Answer Key at the end of the chapter. If you had difficulty with any question, reread the text. If you had little or no difficulty answering the questions or have resolved problems that you might have had, you are ready to continue with the final portion of this chapter.

PERSONALITY DISORDERS

personality disorder A pattern of negative traits that cause distress and an inability to get along with others; but the traits are not viewed as abnormal by the person exhibiting them

Personality disorders involve long-lasting traits or habits that interfere with relationships with other people. Most of these negative traits show up at an early age and strengthen with time. People with personality disorders do not recognize their problems. They think their behavior is normal and natural. Among the many forms of personality disorder are antisocial personality and borderline personality.

Antisocial Personality

antisocial personality Condition involving hurting others and breaking laws without any guilt

Persons with *antisocial personalities* seem to lack consciences and morals. They seem to feel no guilt when they hurt others or break laws. Most are attractive males with above average intelligence. They manipulate other people and will seem sincerely sorry when they are caught in a lie or a crime. Some are even sociable and charming. As you might suspect, many young prisoners suffer from antisocial personality.

Borderline Personality

borderline personality Personality disorder involving instability, confused self-image, and problems in relationships

People with *borderline personalities* have trouble understanding who they really are. They are unstable and act impulsively. Their behavior is unpredictable and they often feel empty and bored. It has been suggested that Adolf Hitler and Marilyn Monroe were borderline personalities (Sass, 1982).

Figure 10-5
A victim of antisocial personality disorder.

"Crime certainly doesn't pay. With me, it's always been a labor of love."

Borderline personality is often difficult to diagnose. It seems to be close to depression and leads to such self-destructive behavior as drinking, gambling, sexual promiscuity, and even suicide. Although the symptoms usually last for many years, many borderline patients improve and become stable in their mid-thirties (Harvard School of Mental Health Letter, 1986).

Exercise 10-9
Identify the personality disorders suggested by each of the following descriptions.

a. This person is almost entirely indifferent to the concerns of others and breaks laws freely. _Anti-Social_

b. This person has a constant feeling of emptiness and boredom. _Borderline_

c. This person is unstable and unpredictable. _Borderline_

d. This person will pretend to be sorry for a crime just to manipulate others. _Anti_

Turn to the Feedback section to check your responses.

SCHIZOPHRENIA

The word *schizophrenia* literally means "split mind." But schizophrenia should not be confused with the "split" of multiple personality. The schizophrenic does not have two or more distinct personalities. Rather, in schizophrenia the mind has split with reality and has become fragmented. The schizophrenic patient has thought disturbances and may suffer from delusions and hallucinations.

schizophrenia Severe disturbance involving hallucinations, delusions, or thought disturbances

Thought disturbances include odd associations with jumbled ideas. This may result in speech that cannot be understood and is labeled "word salad." Words are left out and often there are no clear sentences. Word salads are often accompanied by bizarre behavior. A schizophrenic might giggle at a sad event or become furious when given joyous news. Some schizophrenics show no emotion at all.

A schizophrenic person who is having a delusion imagines something that is not true. Even when proof is given to the contrary, the person continues imagining. For example, a woman may imagine she is Betsy Ross and insist that she made the first American flag. The dates that Betsy Ross lived, changes in the style and design of flags, Betsy Ross's tombstone, or any other evidence will be ignored. The woman will persist in her delusion.

A schizophrenic person suffering from hallucinations hears voices or sees images that do not exist in reality. A man who is hallucinating believes that he is seeing and hearing real images and voices. He may carry on a conversation and permit space for an imaginary person. Often the imagined voices and visions play a major role in a schizophrenic's experiences.

Symptoms of schizophrenia usually first appear in adolescence or early adulthood. Generally the symptoms become worse with each schizophrenic episode. But sometimes the symptoms come on abruptly and disappear with time. Schizophrenia varies greatly in types of symptoms, seriousness, and the length of the episodes.

"You think you've got problems—this poor guy
next to me thinks he's invisible."

Figure 10-6
Believing that he is
Napoleon is an
example of a delusion.
The "poor guy" in the
empty chair is an
hallucination.

There is evidence that people can inherit a genetic predisposition toward schizophrenia (Faraone & Tsuang, 1985). Researchers have also found that stress can trigger schizophrenic episodes (Warner, 1986). The article in Exhibit 10-10 suggests that prenatal conditions may also be a factor.

Exercise 10-10
Two men have just seen a film about a woman who has two distinct personalities. She has a kind and wholesome personality and a dark, shady personality. She gives herself a different name when she experiences each of her two sides. One of the male viewers insists she is schizophrenic. Is he right?

NO she has multiple personalities

Please compare your response in the Feedback section at the end of the chapter.

Exercise 10-11
List three possible symptoms of schizophrenia. _hallucinations, delusions, & thought disturbances._

You may check your list in the Feedback section.

EXHIBIT 10-10

295

IDENTIFYING
PROBLEM BEHAVIOR

A Viral Assault

Growing evidence suggests that a predisposition to schizophrenia may result from abnormal brain development caused by exposure to environmental threat before birth. One such assault may be a strain of influenza virus, called Type-A2, that swept through the population of Helsinki, Finland, during fall of 1957, infecting up to two-thirds of the population.

Intrigued by earlier findings that complications during pregnancy, including viral infection, increase the risk of schizophrenia, University of Southern California psychologist Sarnoff A. Mednick and his colleagues compared the diagnoses of 216 psychiatric hospital admittees, whose mothers had been pregnant during the 1957 Helsinki epidemic, with the diagnoses of 1565 similar patients born before the virus appeared.

Patients whose mothers were in their second trimester of pregnancy (between four and six months pregnant) during the epidemic were more likely to be diagnosed schizophrenic than those whose mothers were in their first or third trimester or those born before the virus appeared.

The researchers suggest several reasons for the findings. The virus itself may have interfered with brain development during a particularly sensitive period, or high fever or use of over-the-counter or prescription drugs, which were sold in record amounts during the epidemic, may be to blame. "It is not so much the type of stress as it is the timing of stress during gestation which is critical in determining risk for schizophrenia," the researchers say.

Genetic factors exacerbated by traumas experienced during the second trimester may disrupt proper development of the brain's cortex, the researchers say, by preventing cell growth, by destroying nerve cells or by halting the crucial process of cell migration in the developing brain. "It seems likely that a variety of illnesses or physical or psychological stresses at this critical point in gestation can have related effects on brain development," the researchers say.

Source: Chollar, S. (1988, March). A viral assault. *Psychology Today.*

ORGANIC BRAIN DISORDERS

Organic brain disorders have a clear physical cause within brain tissue. Sometimes the problem is temporary as in the case of vitamin deficiencies. A lack of the vitamin niacin can cause the brain disorder pellagra. Pellagra victims suffer from delirium and hallucinations. However, with a proper diet their behavior will become normal. Syphilis, a cause of brain damage, is treatable with penicillin.

However, organic brain disorders are often permanent and worsen steadily, perhaps leading to death. An example is *Alzheimer's disease,* which causes a gradual loss of memory, thinking, and motor ability. Unfortunately, the diagnosis of Alzheimer's is difficult and there is no known cure or treatment. The article in Exhibit 10-11 suggests that Alzheimer's victims may have different types of membranes on blood-clotting cells. Other research suggests that at least some cases of Alzheimer's disease may be caused by a virus infection (Schmeck, 1988; & Stein, 1988). Although research has been extensive, the exact origin of Alzheimer's disease remains unknown.

Alzheimer's disease
Organic brain disorder causing a gradual loss of memory, confusion, and general mental deterioration

Checkpoint

Use the following questions to check your understanding of the final portion of the chapter. Choose and mark the one correct response to each question.

EXHIBIT 10-11

> ### Inherited Membranes Predict Alzheimer's
>
> Isolating the diagnosis of Alzheimer's disease from other forms of dementia can be difficult; a definitive identification still depends on autopsy reports. But a new study suggests that an abnormality of blood-cell membranes found among families with a higher-than-normal incidence of Alzheimer's may help diagnose or even predict the disease. Focusing on the blood-clotting cells called platelets, scientists recently found that—compared to randomly chosen controls—close relatives of Alzheimer patients were 3.2 to 11.5 times more likely to have platelet membranes that were less rigid than normal.
>
> Researchers associated with the University of Pittsburgh, Carnegie-Mellon University in Pittsburgh and Harvard Medical School in Belmont, Mass., report in the Oct. 23 *Science* that this increased fluidity of platelet membranes can be found in a characteristic pattern among families affected by Alzheimer's disease. Earlier studies had shown that the disease begins earlier and progresses more rapidly in patients with increased fluidity of these membranes. Other evidence suggests that the risk of developing Alzheimer's is higher among certain families.
>
> By including first-degree relatives of 38 Alzheimer patients, the current study examined the correlation between these physiological and genetic components. The authors say that the pattern of inheritance associated with the membrane abnormality closely matches that reported with Alzheimer's. If further studies confirm the membrane aberration as a specific biological marker for Alzheimer's, laboratory techniques to measure membrane rigidity may be incorporated into diagnostic strategies, say the scientists....

Source: (1987,
November 7).
Inherited membranes
predict Alzheimer's?
Science News.

22. Martin has a personality disorder. Which of the following statements is most likely to be true?
    - *a.* He is concerned about his problem and has been seeking help.
    - *b.* He does not recognize his problem.
    - *c.* His problem came on suddenly and will probably disappear in a few days.
    - *d.* He suffers from multiple personality.

23. Which of the following persons is likely to feel no guilt or remorse about breaking laws?
    - *a.* Phil, who has an antisocial personality
    - *b.* Nancy, who has a borderline personality
    - *c.* Janet, who is schizophrenic
    - *d.* Barry, who has Alzheimer's disease

24. Hannah has borderline personality. At what age is she most likely to improve?
    - *a.* 16
    - *b.* 25
    - *c.* 35
    - *d.* 65

25. In schizophrenia what is split?
    - *a.* The personality
    - *b.* The brain
    - *c.* The mind and reality
    - *d.* The memory and motor skills

26. A woman talks and listens to a Martian. What is she experiencing?
    a. Delusions
    b. Hallucinations
    c. Personality disorder
    d. Word salad
27. Which of the following persons with organic brain disorders is least likely to be cured by treatment?
    a. A woman with a vitamin deficiency
    b. A man with pellagra
    c. A man with syphilis
    d. A woman with Alzheimer's disease

Check your responses against the Checkpoint Answer Key at the end of this chapter. If you had difficulty with any question, reread the text. If you had little or no difficulty answering the questions or have resolved problems that you might have had, you are ready to check yourself against the chapter inventory that follows.

CHAPTER INVENTORY

Use this list of objectives as a review checklist. You should be able to do each of the tasks outlined in the objectives and apply them to everyday examples. If you can, you may feel confident that you have mastered the material in the chapter.

1. List three criteria for abnormal behavior.
2. Describe the problems in diagnosis and the purpose of DSM III-R.
3. Specify four forms of anxiety disorders.
4. Define phobia and identify the symptoms of common phobias.
5. Describe the symptoms of anorexia nervosa and bulimia.
6. Identify the symptoms of obsessive-compulsive disorders and differentiate between obsessions and compulsions.
7. Specify the likely causes of post-traumatic stress.
8. Describe the symptoms of conversion disorder and hypochondriasis.
9. Describe the similarities and differences in multiple personality and amnesia.
10. Identify the symptoms of depression and bipolar disorder.
11. Describe the behavior of alcoholics and drug users.
12. State the methods that can be used to assist a person threatening suicide.
13. Identify two forms of personality disorder and describe their symptoms.
14. Explain the symptoms and possible causes of schizophrenia.
15. Distinguish between schizophrenia and multiple personality.
16. Describe three types of organic brain disorders.

Feedback

The correct answers to the exercises follow. If you did not answer an exercise correctly, review the preceding pages and return to the exercise to correctly complete it.

10-1. a. Unusual or markedly different from normal
      b. Undesirable
      c. Causes personal emotional stress

10-2. DSM III-R will provide descriptions of disorders that will help them diagnose the patient. It will not help them find the cause of the disorder.

10-3. Ms. P. has unrealistic and exaggerated fears that interfere with a normal life. Ms. F. has realistic fears that do not interfere with her everyday life.

10-4. *a.* Post-traumatic stress disorder
  b. Obsessive-compulsive disorder
  c. Post-traumatic stress disorder
  d. Bulimia
  e. Anorexia nervosa

10-5. Both involve a change in identity or consciousness. Both can be "faked" if convenient for a person.

10-6. ☑ Lowered self-esteem
  ☑ Catastrophizing
  ☑ Irritability
  ☑ Thoughts of death
  ☑ Proneness to tears
  ☑ Insomnia
  ☑ Hopelessness

10-7. Mindy is suffering from bipolar disorder. She is having mood swings from mania to depression.

10-8. *a.* Both are attempting to escape from their problems and/or relieve depression.
  b. Drug users are more likely to behave illegally to support their addiction. Drug use does allow an immediate escape from depression, while the alcohol deepens depression.

10-9. *a.* Antisocial personality
  b. Borderline personality
  c. Borderline personality
  d. Antisocial personality

10-10. No, the woman has multiple personality rather than schizophrenia. In schizophrenia the split is with reality and the personality is shattered.

10-11. Thought disturbances, delusions, and hallucinations

Checkpoint Answer Key

1. *d*	**8.** *b*	**15.** *a*	**22.** *b*
2. *c*	**9.** *b*	**16.** *b*	**23.** *a*
3. *a*	**10.** *c*	**17.** *c*	**24.** *c*
4. *a*	**11.** *d*	**18.** *d*	**25.** *c*
5. *b*	**12.** *b*	**19.** *a*	**26.** *b*
6. *c*	**13.** *a*	**20.** *d*	**27.** *d*
7. *d*	**14.** *d*	**21.** *d*	

CHAPTER 11

GETTING HELP

Neurotics build dream houses; psychotics live in them; and psychiatrists collect the rent.

Fritz Perls

Suppose you are the owner of a small business and want to hire a bookkeeper to help keep your accounts in order. A middle-aged man with twenty years of bookkeeping experience applies for the job. You find him to be qualified and a likable, friendly person. However, during the interview he confesses that he has suffered from depression and is presently receiving help from a psychiatrist. How would you react? Would you want more information about his depression or would you simply want to end the interview and forget about him? You would clearly be in the minority if you looked upon his getting help for mental problems as an asset.

Although it is fashionable in certain upper-class communities to discuss visits to a psychotherapist, for the most part people view mental problems negatively. Many associate mental problems with criminal behavior. Thoughts of raving maniacs and murders are conjured up, and as a result irrational fears develop. Most people feel uncomfortable about visiting mental institutions or psychiatric wards in hospitals. People who are receiving help for mental problems definitely face a social stigma. They are the subject of jokes about crackpots, the nut house or funny farm, and men in white coats. Yet the majority of persons helped by professionals are not mentally ill; they are simply confronting problems that they cannot handle alone. They are wise to realize they need help.

Help comes in many forms but it usually begins with you yourself. You must admit you have a problem. Sometimes you can resolve the problem simply or use a self-help technique. In this chapter you will learn ways to help others as well as yourself. But there are also times when professional assistance is essential and you will examine the types of techniques that they use. Finally, you will consider how community mental health programs can assist people.

SELF-HELP

Down on me, down on me
Looks like everybody in this whole round world
Is down on me.

Janis Joplin

Yesterday all my troubles seemed so far away
Now it looks as though they're here to stay
John Lennon and Paul McCartney

Have you ever listened to these lyrics and felt they were aimed at you? The popularity of these songs suggests that many people have shared your feelings. What do you do when you feel upset by your feelings, your surroundings, or your own behavior? The first step is to admit that you have a problem. For many people the solution is simple: self-help. Rather than seek help from a friend or relative or rush to a professional, often you can take some steps to help yourself.

Biofeedback

Assume that a middle-aged woman, Missy Hauser, has been told her apartment building is being converted into condominiums. Missy has been living there alone and comfortably for more than twenty years. There is less than

$1000 in her savings account and she can afford neither the down payment nor the monthly maintenance fee for a condominium. Although Missy knows she should be searching for a new place to live, tension headaches and hypertension are preventing her from thinking clearly and taking any action. According to her doctor, both her headaches and blood pressure are affected by stress.

What can Missy do to help herself out of this predicament? One beneficial self-help technique that her doctor might recommend is *biofeedback*. There are a number of devices and instruments available to help people monitor their blood pressure and heart rate. As you may recall from the discussion in Chapter 8, physiological changes always accompany emotional changes.

Missy could check her own blood pressure and then find some techniques to help her lower it. For example, she may want to check her blood pressure before and after such activities as a short walk, watching an exciting hockey game, resting quietly, praying or meditating, or thinking about relaxing on a beach. After getting feedback information on how each activity affects her blood pressure, Missy can choose to spend more time in activities that lower her blood pressure and less time in stressful ventures. Chances are Missy may want to use more of her time for meditation and relaxing thoughts.

Many studies have shown that meditation can help relieve hypertension. Simply resting and concentrating on prayer or a relaxing experience can lower blood pressure significantly. Interestingly, blood pressure usually remains lowered long after the meditation experience even if the person is bothered by stresses and strains. Somehow stress becomes less of a burden after a quiet experience. People can help themselves simply by learning how to relax.

Exercise 11-1

Listed below are some steps required to practice biofeedback for self-help. The steps are in a confused order. Specify the correct order.

biofeedback
Technique that provides information on heart rate and blood pressure so that a person can control these internal processes

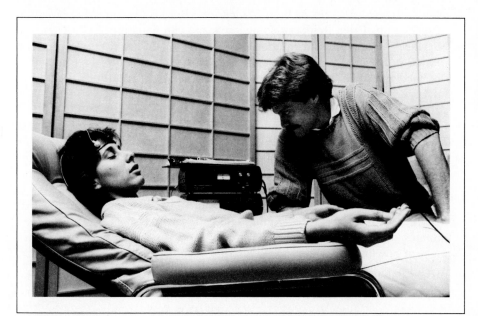

Some biofeedback measures require professional assistance. However, simple measures such as blood pressure and pulse rate can be evaluated by individuals. (*Joel Gordon*)

a. _____ Measure your rate after each activity.

b. _____ Purchase or borrow a device for measuring physiological functions.

c. _____ Choose the activity that lowers your rate the most and repeat the activity as often as possible.

d. _____ Obtain approval from your physician to begin a biofeedback program.

e. _____ Measure your rate before each activity.

f. _____ List a number of activities that you think may help lower your emotional responses.

Please turn to the Feedback section to check your responses.

Self-Control

Undoubtedly you have heard friends complain about lacking self-control. There probably have even been times when you yourself wished you had greater self-restraint. Whether you want to lose weight, stop smoking, hold on to your temper, or overcome your shyness, self-control is a possible solution. As you know, it is not easy to say no to a delicious snack. Likewise watching everyone light cigarettes can make a person trying to kick the habit request one last cigarette. Taking charge of yourself is difficult, but according to psychologists it is possible!

The first step in a self-control program is to find the type of events that trigger your problem. Suppose that a construction worker, Erica, is having trouble controlling her anger whenever her pushy, irksome foreman gives ridiculous orders. Erica could follow the advice of Novaco (1975) and use four steps.

1. _Prepare for the situation._ First Erica acknowledges the fact that her foreman's attitude makes her angry. She thinks about the type of dumb statements her foreman makes that are most aggravating. For example, she may recall her foreman shouting, "Hey, you, keep the plaster off the floor. It belongs on the wall."

2. _Think of ways to confront the provocation._ Before the annoying situation occurs again, Erica thinks of some ways she can handle herself. Then she imagines the actual confrontation or episode. When her foreman shouts a foolish order, Erica might imagine herself just shrugging and replying, "Whatever you say, sir," or "I guess that's why you're a foreman and I'm a laborer." By thinking about the situation beforehand, Erica will be prepared for the confrontation when it occurs.

3. _Cope with arousal and agitation._ When Erica spots her foreman heading in her direction, she will probably notice her heartbeat speeding up, her face flushing with anger, or her palms sweating—all signs of arousal. If she takes a few deep breaths and tries to relax the muscles, she will have a better chance of keeping calm and carrying out her plan.

4. _Reward yourself._ If Erica succeeds in controlling her anger, she rewards herself. Her reward can be anything that she really enjoys, perhaps fifteen minutes of listening to some favorite tapes, a six-pack of beer, an extra night of bowling, or tickets to an opera.

The same four steps could be used to handle many situations. A man who has difficulty getting rid of door-to-door salespersons and a teenage boy who has trouble asking girls to roller-skate could follow the same sequence to help themselves.

However, the sequence is not everyone's answer to self-help. Perhaps you are a smoker or drinker. Although you would prefer to eliminate these habits and be a healthier person, you find smoking or drinking extremely enjoyable and rewarding. Relaxing with a cup of coffee and a cigarette gives comfort and gratification. Similarly, a cocktail, beer, or wine and some lively conversation with friends can bring pleasure and satisfaction. Eliminating habits that are enjoyable is particularly problematic.

Nolan (1968) suggested that smoking could be controlled by removing the pleasurable aspect from the habit. Smoking is only permitted in a smoking chair. The smoking chair should be uncomfortable and located in a boring and inconvenient spot. A garage or basement corner usually qualify as uninteresting and undesirable atmospheres, ideal for a smoking chair. If you wish to smoke, you must go to your chair, sit down, and remain there the entire time you are smoking. You may leave your chair only after you are finished with your cigarettes.

Presumably, Nolan's technique could also be used to help you give up drinking. Drinking alone in a garage or closet does not sound like much fun. Nolan's method is a variation of behavior modification (described in Chapter 3). The loneliness and bleak surroundings of the smoking chair remove the usual positive atmosphere of socializing while smoking (or drinking).

Exercise 11-2

Fred is a police officer in a large city. He has been assigned to a high-crime area where many people are hostile toward police. Whenever people resist arrest and call him names, Fred loses his temper. He shouts back and often gets into physical fights. Because he has difficulty controlling himself, Fred is in danger of losing his job. List four steps Fred could take to control his anger.

a. _____

_____

b. _____

_____

c. _____

_____

d. _____

_____

You may check your responses in the Feedback section.

Exercise 11-3

Allison lives in a dormitory and wants to give up smoking. Her roommate suggested that Allison put an old chair in the corner of the dorm laundry room, facing a blank wall, and use it as a smoking chair.

Why should Allison accept her roommate's recommendation?

_____

_____

Turn to the Feedback section to check your answer.

Self-Help Groups

Jean Nidetch (1962) claimed she was overweight and had trouble sticking to her diet. She invited six overweight friends to chat about their difficulties and successes in dieting. The group then examined ways to help each other. The group expanded and soon became the international business, Weight Watchers. Whether you simply get together with friends who have similar problems or join an international organization, you are relying on a *self-help group*.

The purpose of self-help groups is to give social support to each member. During meetings, participants share their experiences and discuss problems and possible solutions. They socialize and encourage each other. Because of problems related to alcohol, drugs, eating, etc., people often feel isolated. Group meetings provide an opportunity for affiliation and acceptance. Alcoholics Anonymous (AA) is the largest and most famous self-help group. The article in Exhibit 11-1 explains how the formation of an AA group changed the drinking habits of an entire Alaskan community.

EXHIBIT 11-1

After Tragedies, Alaskan Villagers Work Together to Stay Sober

Akhiok, Alaska—For nearly 50 years, Ephraim Agnot was a drunk. He drank whiskey and beer, and when there was no more liquor, he turned to Lysol, hair lotions and after shave. "I had to have alcohol in my gut all the time," he said.

The alcohol helped Agnot forget the deaths it helped cause. His first wife drank, then fell from a boat and drowned. His second wife died after a drunken brawl with him. One of his sons drank too much and suffocated on vomit. A grandson, plagued by alcohol, committed suicide.

But for the past seven months, Agnot has been sober. And so have most of his neighbors, who have joined together to transform this Aleut village of 70 people on Alaska's Kodiak Island.

A year ago, more than 90 percent of Akhiok's 42 adults were chronically drunk. Today, island alcohol counselors report that at least 80 percent of them are sober. "It's very mystical," Agnot said. "I'm very surprised at the people who've been drinking and stopped."

The sobriety movement here began last fall when one couple stopped drinking and started an Alcoholics Anonymous group. It was imbued with urgency in January, when an intoxicated villager shot and killed himself. Since then, it has been reinforced by visits from Kodiak alcohol counselors. Villagers have also met with Elisabeth Kubler-Ross, a psychiatrist and well-known author of books about grief, death and dying.

"It's just like a ripple effect," Kubler-Ross said. Those who stopped drinking "affect other people's lives...by what they are and how they behave....It works wonderfully all over the world. But it's lots of hard labor and lots of love."...

Many villages have tried to stem the violence and self-destruction by banning the sale and importation of alcohol. But that has not stopped the liquor flow. In large areas of Alaska, bootlegging is a thriving industry, and a bootlegged bottle of whiskey sells for as much as $100....

Jean McDonald, an alcohol counselor for the Kodiak Area Native Association, recalls arriving here and finding only two sober people in the village. "I turned around and went back to town because at that level of intoxication there's not much to be done," she said.

"A month never went by without us drinking," Annie Peterson said. "We couldn't wait until Friday so we could celebrate a weekend. We always found an excuse, any excuse, to party....We grow up with our parents drinking. And our children grow up drinking. It's a pattern...a way of life," she said.

Peterson and her husband, Nick, were among the heaviest drinkers in the village and often supplied booze to others. Now, they are ringleaders of the sobriety movement. During nearly 12 months of sobriety, they have built a new banya steam bath and a smokehouse outside their home, and launched an AA group that meets three times a week in the village community hall....

Gradually, other villagers began to take interest in the changes at the Peterson house. "They wondered why he [Nick] was so happy. He was not partying, but building the banya, doing family things now," Annie Peterson said. "We said if anyone has any questions, our house is open. People came in and talked."

By December, they established their AA group, and more than a dozen villagers were attending regularly.

In May, Canadian Indians from Alkali Lake arrived in Akhiok with a film documenting their own transformation from a village of 100 percent alcoholics to 98 percent sober. Afterward, they talked with villagers about the pain of alcoholism and how to begin healing the wounds....

The few people who still drink do so, for the most part, quietly, in their homes. "They're ashamed to walk around anymore,"...

Source: Bernton, H. (1988, August 28). After tragedies, Alaskan villagers work together to stay sober. *The Washington Post.*

Some well-known self-help groups similar to AA are listed in Exhibit 11-2. There are also groups for child abusers, exconvicts, widows and widowers, parents of twins, and parents without partners. Regardless of the specific purpose of the group, members help each other adjust and benefit from the encouragement and socialization at meetings. Computers have provided the newest contribution to self-help groups (see Exhibit 11-3, page 308).

Exercise 11-4
Imagine that an overweight friend asked you to join him in attending a meeting of his self-help group, "Blubber Be Gone." List three types of activities that you might expect to experience at the meeting.

a. _____

b. _____

c. _____

Please compare your list with the one given in the Feedback section.

COUNSELING OTHERS

Although you sometimes need time to yourself to mull over problems, often you really need someone to listen to you. Troubles seem to get worse when they are held inside. Finding a good listener can be a solution to simple adjustments and confusions. However, volunteering to help your friends by listening requires some caution. Sometimes your help is not wanted. It is usually best not to pressure a person. Simply make your friends aware that you care, are concerned, and want to help and understand their difficulties.

The Anonymous Proliferation

One of the grandaddies of the self-help movement is Alcoholics Anonymous, which this year celebrates its 50th anniversary. Founded in the United States by two alcoholics struggling to remain sober, the organization today boasts chapters in 115 countries—including its newest addition the Soviet Union.

Besides helping recovering alcoholics and their families through its sister organization, Al-Anon, AA has also become the model for numerous other self-help programs. The AA approach is based on a 12-step program in which participants learn to admit their powerlessness over a certain problem, be it alcohol or something else. They come to believe that there is a Power greater than themselves that can help restore them to sanity and they make a decision to turn themselves over to that Power.

Among the many groups patterned after AA are:

- Batterers Anonymous
- Cocaine Anonymous
- Debtors Anonymous
- Depressives Anonymous
- Divorce Anonymous
- Emotional Health Anonymous
- Emotions Anonymous
- Emphysema Anonymous
- Families Anonymous
- Fundamentalists Anonymous
- Gamblers Anonymous
- Homosexuals Anonymous
- Impotents Anonymous
- Marriage Anonymous

- Messies Anonymous
- Molestors Anonymous
- Narcotics Anonymous
- Neurotics Anonymous
- Overeaters Anonymous
- Parents Anonymous
- Pill Addicts Anonymous
- Prison Families Anonymous
- Rape Anonymous
- Sex Addicts Anonymous
- Sexaholics Anonymous
- Smokers Anonymous
- Survivors of Incest Anonymous
- Workaholics Anonymous

Source: Squires, S. (1988, May 17). The anonymous proliferation. *Washington Post Health.*

Once a friend begins discussing problems with you, keep relaxed and friendly. Try not to pass judgment. A young man whose date walked out on him does not need to be reminded that he made stupid remarks. You could be more helpful by showing your understanding with statements such as, "I can imagine how you must feel, I would have felt let down and upset, too." A little tact can remove some of the sting and pain. If you stress the young man's strong points, he will be better able to plan to avoid similar mishaps in the future.

Sometimes a friend sits you down to listen to an apparently simple problem. As the conversation continues the problem turns out to be severe. Although you should offer assurances that you respect privacy and will keep the conversation confidential, it is also best to recognize situations that you cannot handle competently. In such cases, recommend professional help! Information on professional help follows in the next section of this chapter.

Figure 11-1
Could this be another
self-help group to add
to the list?

Checkpoint

Use the following questions to check your understanding of this portion of the chapter. Choose and mark the one correct response to each question.

1. Before using one self-help technique, a physician should be consulted. Which technique?
   a. Biofeedback
   b. Smoking chair
   c. Anger control
   d. Cold turkey
2. What is the purpose of biofeedback?
   a. To control anger
   b. To increase self-control
   c. To eliminate bad habits
   d. To reduce hypertension
3. What is the first step in a self-control program to overcome a problem?
   a. Rewarding yourself
   b. Thinking of many possible ways to confront the problem
   c. Determining the type of events that produce the problem
   d. Controlling your arousal by taking deep breaths
4. What is the purpose of a smoking chair?
   a. To increase the pleasant associations with smoking
   b. To decrease the pleasant associations with smoking

For the Homebound, Computers Provide the Missing Uplink

The latest addition to self-help groups are computer "techies."

"People are using home computers, phoning into national computer networks and are actually able to meet 'on line,' " says Ed Madara, director of the New Jersey Self-Help Clearinghouse and a computer buff himself.

Self-help meetings regularly take place on the computer on such varied topics as alcoholism, smoking cessation and AIDS. There's a self-help computer network of Vietnam veterans. And the computer becomes the perfect meeting place for the home-bound, the sick, or people with disabilities who may otherwise have trouble getting around.

On the computer, "their disabilities disappear," says Madara.

One self-help group for the disabled "meets" Wednesday nights at 9:30 P.M. (EST) over CompuServe. Its founder is Georgia Griffith, a woman who is blind and deaf. Griffith works with a special high-speed printer that produces raised Braille characters. She can read the printout as quickly as a sighted person can read a computer screen, Madara says. If she's traveling, Griffith brings along a portable Braille computer.

Computer networks are also valuable for bringing together people with rare diseases who might not otherwise meet anyone else in their city—or even state—with the same illness. The computer, a modem and a phone line erase all distance. Madara describes how one individual put a message on a computer bulletin board asking for others who had the rare illness known as the Ehlers-Danlos syndrome, a genetic disease that affects the joints, the skin and can cause poor healing of wounds.

"She got four responses," Madara says. "A couple of the people had never talked to anyone else with the disease. Two people had lost family members with Ehlers-Danlos syndrome. They had died while giving birth." People with Ehlers-Danlos sometimes die from hemorrhaging.

Agoraphobics—people who fear going outside—are also good candidates for computer self-help networks. "Sometimes, having a meeting on a computer network can give agoraphobics the push they need to go outside their home to a meeting," says Madara.

Computerized networks can also provide a final—and important—link to the outside world for the terminally ill. One of Madara's friends developed stomach cancer and entered a hospice. The director of the hospice had a computer, and Madara's friend used it to keep in touch with dozens of people. When the man became too ill to use the director's desk computer, he turned to a laptop computer.

"He was in touch with people until the day before he died," says Madara. "He shared his fears and his feelings. Some of the people on the network had known him for several years, but had never met him or talked to him."

Source: Squires, S. (1988, May 17). For the homebound, computers provide the missing uplink. *Washington Post Health.*

    c. To help a person give up drinking

    d. To permit a person to quit using a cold-turkey method

5. Which of the following methods involves a form of behavior modification?

    a. Preparation

    b. Biofeedback

    c. Smoking chair

    d. Coping

6. Which of the following is the best example of a self-help group?

    a. Four pregnant unmarried teenage friends meet once a week to discuss their problems.

    b. Five middle-aged men sign up for a course in woodworking and carpentry.

    c. Six senior citizens purchase condominiums for the elderly in a nearby community.

    d. Seventy college students register for a psychology course required in their programs.

7. Assume your friend has just lost her job and has been crying for hours. You offer to help, but she does not want to talk about her problems. What should you do?

    a. Walk away and leave her alone.

    b. Tell her that her unwillingness to talk is probably the reason she lost her job.

    c. Insist that she talk to you, ask questions, and give her advice about finding another job.

    d. Tell her you are concerned about her, and suggest that she call you whenever she feels like discussing her problem.

Use the Checkpoint Answer Key to verify your responses. If you had any difficulty with a question, carefully reread the text. If you had little or no difficulty answering the questions or have resolved any problems that you might have had, you are ready to continue with the next portion of this chapter.

PROFESSIONAL HELP

Many problems cannot be cured or even helped by either self-help methods or a sympathetic, understanding listener. When people are upset they often lose their self-control and have difficulty communicating with others. In such cases, professional help is needed. As the article in Exhibit 11-4 reports, sympathetic nonprofessionals may help initially, but lasting success in treatment usually requires a trained psychotherapist.

"*Yes, dear, of course, dear, yes, dear . . . .*"

Figure 11-2
It appears she believes her problems will be resolved but he looks rather negative.

EXHIBIT 11-4

Therapy: Beyond "Warm Fuzziness"

How much of therapists' success with clients can be credited to their training and how much is the result of simple warmth and caring?

Finding answers by studying the one-on-one therapist-client relationship is abundantly complex but the task becomes daunting in the context of group therapy. Undeterred, Brigham Young University (BYU) psychologists Gary M. Burlingame and Sally H. Barlow gathered data from eight experimental therapy groups that met for 15 weekly sessions. Half the groups were run by therapists recommended by their peers as experts and half by nonprofessionals to whom BYU students said in a survey they most often turn for personal help.

Burlingame and Barlow suspected that the nonprofessionals' personalities alone could make them effective therapists. Results, in fact, showed that group members led by both professionals and nonprofessionals improved significantly more than a comparison group of people awaiting therapy.

However, an interesting twist with important implications for therapy showed up in the data. At the midpoint of the 15-week therapy series, members of the nonprofessionals' groups had improved significantly while those in the professionals' groups had actually deteriorated. By the end of therapy, those in the experts' groups had caught up with their counterparts in the nonexperts' groups. However, six months after the last group session, people led by nonexperts had gotten worse while those led by experts "maintained their gains and built on them," Burlingame says.

The researchers believe that the nonprofessionals' warmth and supportiveness elicited potent emotional experiences among their group members, but these leaders were not knowledgeable enough to channel the experiences very productively. "It seems to me that there's a limit to the helpfulness of warm fuzziness," Burlingame says. "As soon as it disappears, the clients [of nonprofessionals] appear to start getting worse."

While the nonprofessionals were supporting and nurturing their clients, the professionals were busy "pushing painful buttons," Barlow says, and their clients showed the wear and tear for a time. However, by helping group members make their pain work for them, the experts were able to begin a trend toward improvement that continued six months later.

Source: Bergin, S. (1988, April). Therapy: Beyond "warm fuzziness." *Psychology Today.*

An important factor in the success of psychotherapy is the client's belief that the emotional problems will be resolved (Prioleau, Murdock, & Brody, 1983).

Problems Requiring Professional Help

Simple emotional problems. Emotional problems are the simplest type of disorder that can profit from professional assistance. A person who is shy, has a poor self-image, or has difficulty adjusting to a marriage, children, a job, or a new situation will feel confused and disturbed. Most people who seek professional help have no deeper disturbances. Psychologists recommend that help be received during the early stages of a problem; it is important not to wait. Time often brings further complications. The likelihood of improvement for persons with emotional problems is good. The article in Exhibit 11-5 reminds us that everyone, including presidents, experiences instability in times of crises. Seeking help is a sign of good judgment rather than weakness.

EXHIBIT 11-5

311

GETTING HELP

The Politics of Psychotherapy

There Should Be No Stigma, Say Experts, in Seeking Counseling

One reason for grueling presidential campaigns is to reveal the fitness of the candidates and keep some modern psychopath like the Roman emperor Nero out of the Oval Office and his fiddle-playing finger off the nuclear button....

It's time to bury this shibboleth and eradicate the link between seeking psychiatric help and committing political suicide. The reality is that it's those who do not seek help who are more likely the ones headed for mental instability.

In fact, it's too bad previous presidents couldn't have had the opportunity to take advantage of today's mental health and social support services as well as scientists' better understanding of the biological underpinnings of many psychiatric disorders.

It's clear that the country has had many sick presidents, some physically, others mentally. But some of the sickest were also the greatest, such as...Abraham Lincoln, with his bouts of melancholia....

Too bad Polk couldn't have lived in the era of the employe assistance program and gotten a little psychological counseling on how to "let go" of his emotions and handle the job stress.

Another one-term president was Franklin Pierce, 1853–57, and he would have benefited from a stay at the Betty Ford Center. On the way to Washington, he and his wife watched in horror as their only son, 11, was killed in a railroad accident. She took to her room, seldom to reappear, to scribble notes to her lost boy; he took to the bottle and eventually died of cirrhosis of the liver.

Too bad there wasn't Alcoholics Anonymous around in those days or the support of other public figures to come forward and talk about substance abuse.

And what about Woodrow Wilson, the popular professorial president who saw the country through World War I? Much has been written about the strokes he suffered in his second term, the extent of his physical and mental disabilities and the cover-up of his incompetence by his physician and second wife....

On March 1, 1914, the first Mrs. Wilson collapsed in a faint in her room, probably from kidney failure. According to Kenneth R. Crispell and Carlos F. Gomez in "Hidden Illness in the White House," the White House physician Cary Grayson didn't want to alarm the president and so no kidney specialists were consulted until the very end. This conspiracy of silence allowed Wilson to deny to himself the severity of her illness despite what he was seeing before his own eyes.

Crispell and Gomez point out that in this psychological pressure cooker of denial, "Wilson may have misdirected his anger over his wife's illness at the Mexican dictator General Huerta."

Too bad Wilson couldn't have joined a spousal support group or at least have had the benefit of some reality-based guidance from the White House physician as his wife lay dying for six stressful months.

What history shows is that those presidents who did not find ways to gain psychological support during personal crises are the ones the electorate should worry about....In fact, a lot of voters would be relieved to know that in time of personal crisis—the loss of a family member, a serious physical illness or other traumatic event—a political leader had sought professional counseling to deal with the burden.

That's what ordinary folks do to cope. According to the American Psychological Association, one third of all families have at least one member who is or has been in therapy. The National Institute of Mental Health estimates that 15.5 million Americans undergo some form of psychotherapy every year.

Source: Trafford, A.
(1988, August 9). The
politics of
psychotherapy.
*Washington Post
Health.*

In addition, there's the burgeoning self-help movement, where an estimated 15 million people seek help from some 500,000 organizations ranging from Alcoholics and Pill Addicts Anonymous to Families of Persons with AIDS Support Group and New Beginnings, Inc., an organization for separated and divorced men and women....As Dr. Bryant L. Welch, a director of the American Psychological Association, puts it: "All people, including elected officials, no matter how healthy, are psychologically unstable during times of personal crisis.

"Often, such life crises can best be handled through competent psychological intervention. Left untreated, however, they can have unrecognized but seriously deleterious and insidious impacts on the objective decision-making capacity of the individual."

So where's the beef about a little psychotherapy for a politician?

The fact that it's made to look bad on an applicant's resume for the Oval Office betrays a gross misunderstanding not only of psychotherapy and mental illness but perhaps of the voters as well.

Mental disorders. People with the most severe problems are more likely to receive treatment than those with lesser disorders. Among schizophrenics 53 percent receive treatment, yet only 18 percent of alcohol and drug abusers are getting help (Shapiro et al., 1984). People with anxiety disorders and mood disorders are likely to recognize their problems and seek advice. However, unruly people, such as addicts and antisocial personalities, often deny their problems. Usually they are brought to treatment by others. Whether a person suffers from an anxiety disorder, a mood disorder, an addiction, a personality disorder, or schizophrenia, professional help will be beneficial.

Exercise 11-5

Read each of the following descriptions of people in need of professional help and indicate the type of problem(s) the person is likely to have.

a. This person denies any problems and was brought to therapy by his wife.

_____

b. This person lost her job and is having difficulty coping.

_____

c. This person has felt overwhelmingly sad and is seeking help.

_____

d. Fifty-three percent of people in this group receive help.

_____

Please turn to the Feedback section to check your answers.

Techniques in Individual Psychotherapy

Psychotherapists use a broad variety of methods to help individuals. Some therapists have been trained heavily in one particular technique and use that method exclusively. Others have had more diverse training and choose techniques that they consider appropriate and most beneficial for each case. They have been labeled "eclectic therapists" because they do not adhere to any one method. The most common forms of individual psychotherapy are psychoanalysis, humanistic counseling, rational-emotive therapy, and behavior therapy.

Psychoanalysis. A psychoanalyst is most often a psychiatrist, but occasionally a psychologist, who bases treatment on the theories of Sigmund Freud. Psychoanalysts believe that the most important aspects of your personality are buried deep in your unconscious, and consequently you are not aware of them. In a typical visit to a psychoanalyst you would be expected to rest comfortably on a couch and stare at a blank wall. Although not asleep, you are totally relaxed. You would then begin talking and say anything that comes into your mind without blocking or censoring anything. Random ideas would flow into each other, and the therapist would look for hidden unconscious meanings. Psychoanalysts also interpret dreams. Since you are fully relaxed when asleep, you are less likely to inhibit your thoughts and feelings. For psychoanalysts, dreams help to reveal the unconscious. Past experiences, particularly painful memories, must be uncovered for successful treatment. Some therapists resort to hypnosis. Psychoanalysis has been losing popularity. It requires more time than other techniques and is one of the most expensive forms of therapy.

psychoanalysis
Psychotherapy technique that involves uncovering the unconscious

Humanistic counseling. Did you notice the switch from the word "therapy" to the word "counseling"? One of the leading humanists, Carl Rogers, chose the word "counseling," and other humanistic psychologists agreed on the change. Humanists also prefer to call the person being helped a "client" rather than a "patient." The word "patient" implies helplessness, and *humanistic counseling* requires active, conscious participation by each client. The style of counseling used by Carl Rogers is labeled "client-centered" because the client actually sets the direction for the therapy and can talk about feelings without fear of criticism. The counselor acts almost as a mirror, reflecting the feelings and emotions of the client.

humanistic counseling
Psychotherapy approach that attempts to improve self-esteem and encourage personal growth

Client-centered counseling takes a positive approach. Counselors focus on what is right with a client rather than on what is wrong. A major goal is to increase self-esteem. A person with a good self-image can find new solutions to problems. Independence is strongly encouraged. The past is disregarded, and the client gains insights into present feelings. The counselor often paraphrases the client and shows understanding and caring.

For example, imagine that Chip Moods visits a client-centered therapist. He begins by expressing his irritation with his stern mother-in-law who is visiting too often. The counselor might reply, "You are upset because you feel your mother-in-law is around too much." Chip then continues, expressing his annoyance that his wife encourages her crabby mother's frequent calls. The counselor adds, "You feel angry with your spouse because she does not consider your feelings." Ideally, by the end of his sessions Chip will be better able to accept his feelings and resolve his problem.

Gestalt therapy and existential therapy also use humanistic approaches. Both stress the present rather than the past or future. As humanistic therapists, gestaltists and existentialists emphasize understanding your own feelings. However, each of these two therapies has a slightly different focus.

According to Perls (1973), the founder of gestalt therapy, gestalt therapists should be on the alert for phoniness. Your physical gestures and inner feelings

gestalt therapy Form of humanistic therapy that focuses on consistency between behaviors and inner feelings

existential therapy
Form of treatment
that focuses on free
will and the meaning
of life

rational-emotive therapy
Form of therapy that
helps people think
rationally and
eliminate their self-
defeating emotional
thoughts

behavior therapy
Psychotherapy that
uses techniques based
on learning principles

should match. For example, if you state that you are perfectly calm, while your voice quivers and your hands tremble, you are probably trying to cover your real feelings. A gestalt therapist would point out your physical shakes and allow you to reevaluate your true feelings.

The focus in *existential therapy,* according to Frankl (1955), is on the free will of each client. The therapist must help each person find meaning in life, develop values, and make responsible choices. There are no standardized procedures in existential therapy. Each therapy is a totally new experience and relationship.

Humanistic counseling requires far less time than psychoanalysis. Clients meet with counselors only once each week. In most cases, problems are resolved in less than six months.

Rational-emotive therapy. Ellis (1979), the founder of *rational-emotive therapy* (RET), claims that his technique is one of the briefer forms of individual therapy. Usually only a few sessions are required. In RET, unlike the humanistic therapies, the therapist is active and does most of the talking, particularly in the beginning. The goal of the therapist is to teach the client to think scientifically and rationally.

RET therapists assume people learn irrational and self-defeating propositions in their youth. For example, some people may assume that it will be disastrous if they fail in school or a horrible catastrophe if they are unpopular. As a result, they limit and restrict themselves and are unwilling to take chances. A young engineering student may refuse to sign up for a required course in drafting because she fears she will fail. Or a young man may dread asking women for dates because he is horror-stricken by the possibility of being refused. In RET, the therapist would teach them to reexamine their belief that one failure is a complete catastrophe. Clients are assigned homework; a shy young man may be told to strike up a conversation with a strange female before the next session. Even if he is unsuccessful, he can learn from his experience and hopefully realize that it is self-defeating not to continue trying.

RET is not for everyone. Ellis believes the approach is most profitable with clients who are above average in intelligence. The technique is clearly inappropriate for severe psychotics or anyone who has problems with thought patterns.

Behavior therapy. *Behavior therapy* is based on the principle of behavior modification described in Chapter 3. Appropriate behavior is rewarded, and inappropriate or undesirable behavior is ignored and not reinforced. Behavior modification has been used successfully in mental institutions. Each time a patient performs a chore, talks to a therapist, or behaves in any desirable way, he or she receives a token. Tokens may be used to purchase candy, desserts, additional recreation time, or any other items or activities that would be suitable rewards.

In severe cases rewards are given directly. For example, a patient who makes eye contact with the therapist might be given a stick of chewing gum or a piece of candy. Next the patient is rewarded for answering questions. This technique is often used as a first step to get a patient into some form of treatment.

Another form of behavior therapy, systematic desensitization, was described in Chapter 3. Systematic desensitization is a gradual method that has been successful in removing some fears and phobias. For example, a man afraid of heights might at first imagine he is on a balcony one story above the ground and listen to some relaxing, enchanting music. At each session he moves up another story until his phobia is overcome. The strategy is a step-by-step approach.

Exercise 11-6

Read each of the following descriptions, and specify whether each is an example of psychoanalysis, client-centered counseling, gestalt therapy, existential therapy, rational-emotive therapy, or behavior therapy.

a. Abe's therapist points out every move he makes. He comments whenever Abe crosses his feet, folds his arms, bites his lip, or scratches his head.

_____

b. Sarah is timid about selling things. Her therapist gave her homework. She must volunteer to work at an arts-and-crafts booth at her community center bazaar. _____

c. Judy's therapist interprets her dreams. She must try to relax and recall as much as she can. _____

d. Todd's therapist dwells on values. Todd is trying to unravel the real meaning of his life. _____

e. Bruce hopes to gradually overcome his fear of flying. Last week his therapist took him on board an airplane. Next week he will taxi down the runway in the same plane. Eventually he hopes to fly without fear. _____

_____

f. Jeanine does most of the talking in therapy, and her therapist is a good listener. He seems to really care about her feelings and shows immense understanding. _____

Check your answers in the Feedback section.

Results of individual psychotherapies. As yet, there is no solid evidence that any one technique in therapy is superior to all others. The individual skills of each therapist and the relationship between the therapist and patient or client seem to be more important factors. Most of the time psychotherapy has good results.

Checkpoint

Use the following questions to check your understanding of this portion of the chapter. For each of the two sets that follow, match each term on the left with the expression on the right that provides the best description.

8. _____ Schizophrenics

9. _____ Alcoholics and drug abusers

10. _____ Persons with anxiety disorders

11. _____ Addicts and antisocials

a. Likely to seek help themselves

b. More than half are treated

c. Are usually brought to therapy by someone else

d. Less than 20 percent are treated

"Well, if you must know, I have trouble making friends, fatso!"

Figure 11-3
Obviously, it is not always easy for therapists to develop good relationships with their clients.

12. _____ Psychoanalysis
13. _____ Humanistic counseling
14. _____ Client-centered counseling
15. _____ Gestalt therapy
16. _____ Existential therapy
17. _____ Rational-emotive therapy
18. _____ Behavior modification
19. _____ Systematic desensitization

a. Therapist points and gestures to help client evaluate true feelings
b. Focuses on past experiences and dreams
c. Used on mental patients to prepare them for other forms of therapy
d. A group of therapies that focus on the present and require active participation of clients
e. A gradual approach for overcoming phobias
f. Stresses free will and responsibility
g. Homework assignments help clients eliminate self-defeating thoughts
h. Counselor restates feelings of client and is accepting

Check your responses against the Checkpoint Answer Key at the end of the chapter. If you had difficulty with any question, reread the text. If you had little or no difficulty or have resolved any problems that you might have had, you are ready to continue with the final portion of this chapter.

Group Approaches to Psychotherapy

Group therapy became popular after World War II when a large number of American veterans needed help for emotional problems. Since then, it has steadily gained popularity. For certain people, group therapy is less expensive and has some unique advantages. Methods used may include any or a mixture

group therapy
Situation where a therapist directs a discussion in a group of usually six to twelve persons, so that they may learn and profit from communication within the group

of the many individual techniques. Some use humanistic approaches while others use rational-emotive therapy or behavioral methods. Usually six to twelve persons gather in an informal, comfortable seating arrangement. Members are carefully selected by the therapist. The group then talks openly about their ideas, their fears, and their troubles. The therapist directs the discussion and adds some insights and suggestions.

The group atmosphere helps individuals improve interpersonal relationships. Persons can share their thoughts, impressions, and experiences in a protected setting. Group techniques are particularly beneficial to people who are uncomfortable in social situations. As they learn appropriate roles for interacting with each other, they also become aware that others have similar problems. However, persons who have trouble telling their feelings to even only one person probably will not find the sessions useful.

Group therapy is particularly suitable for persons sharing similar troubles. Groups have been developed for persons who are recently divorced, bereaved, or suffering from the same illnesses. People in uncomfortable situations can learn from the experiences of their peers. People who are in institutions are usually involved in group therapy, since it helps them understand the problems of others in their institutional community.

Often members of a family are treated together. Family problems frequently stem from relationships between members rather than from the troubles of one person within the family. Even when only one member of the family suffers from emotional problems or a mental illness, the others must make adjustments. By working together in a group session, they can usually expose and resolve marital and family conflicts.

Group therapy is an important part of most drug treatment programs. Recovering addicts learn from hearing about each others' problems and reactions. (*Joel Gordon*)

Exercise 11-7

List four advantages of group therapy over individual therapy.

a. _____

b. _____

c. _____

d. _____

Please turn to the Feedback section to check your answers.

Medical Approaches to Therapy

The importance of medical and biological factors in mental problems has been debated. Nonetheless there is clear evidence that medical assistance can benefit psychotic patients, depressed persons, and even those with certain types of phobias. There are basically three medical approaches used in psychotherapy: drugs, electroshock, and psychosurgery. Although each of these techniques can bring relief to patients, they can sometimes also create added complications.

Drugs. For quite some time psychiatrists have prescribed mood-modifying or antipsychotic *drugs* for psychotic patients. The drugs have been used to calm patients and make them less fearful, hostile, and excitable. Although the drugs do not cure the patients' problems, they are helpful. Hospitals can allow more freedom among patients and can be less concerned about guarding and controlling patient behavior. However, these drugs are not without side effects. An added problem has arisen with the recent increase in psychotic persons being treated as outpatients. Studies have found that the added availability of antipsychotic drugs has led to many cases of overdose.

drug Chemical substance that causes physical, emotional, or behavioral changes

Another type of drug, an antidepressant, has been used for cases of depression. The purpose of these drugs is to stimulate and arouse patients who are feeling dejected and lethargic. Generally these drugs are slow to act and are only useful for short periods; prolonged use can cause deeper depression, fatigue, and weight gain. There has been some evidence that such drugs can be extremely helpful in the treatment of some phobias, although they do initially cause lightheadedness.

electroshock treatment (ECT) Physiological therapy that delivers an electric shock to the brain to induce a convulsion or coma and reduce depression by erasing memories

Electroshock treatment. In *electroshock treatment,* the patient is given an anesthetic. A brief electric pulse is then sent to certain areas in the frontal portion of the brain. The electric shock induces a convulsion, and memories are temporarily erased. During the recovery from the treatment, persons are less preoccupied with their previous problems. Although no one is certain of exactly what happens, electroshock treatment does seem to be beneficial to persons suffering from severe depression. However, this treatment has been controversial. Many patients suffer memory losses after ECT. But, some current research is finding that no structural brain damage occurs with this treatment (see Exhibit 11-6). In recent years, shock treatment has been used less, primarily because other types of therapy have been found to be equally effective in most cases.

EXHIBIT 11-6

319
GETTING HELP

An Inside Look at Electroshock

In a "before and after" study of the effects of electroshock therapy on the brain, relying for the first time on magnetic resonance imaging (MRI) technology, researchers found no changes in the brain structure of patients who had completed a course of the controversial treatment.

In addition, say psychiatrist C. Edward Coffey and his colleagues at Duke University Medical Center in Durham, N.C., patients with preexisting brain impairments, such as moderate shrinking of tissue causing enlargement of fluid-filled cavities in the brain, showed no worsening of their condition after electroshock, also known as electroconvulsive therapy (ECT).

The researchers examined nine patients with severe depression referred for their first course of ECT. Subjects received five to 11 ECT treatments, administered three times a week. MRI scans, which provide an accurate three-dimensional picture of structures throughout the brain, were taken before and several days after completion of the series of treatments.

Depression was significantly reduced in all but one of the patients after completing ECT, note the researchers in the June *American Journal of Psychiatry*. The exception was a woman who became markedly disoriented for about five days after treatment ended; she then became somewhat less depressed and was no longer suicidal. The other eight patients did not complain of persistent memory loss for events in the months preceding ECT, a common side effect of the treatment.

ECT critics charge the treatment has caused permanent brain damage in animals, but definitive studies of brain metabolism and tissue changes during and after electroshock have not been done (SN: 6/22/85, p. 389). Coffey and his co-workers say the initial MRI findings need to be confirmed in a larger patient sample followed for a longer time after treatment ends. Future studies, they add, should include patients who have previously undergone ECT.

Source: (1988, June 11). An inside look at electroshock. *Science News.*

Psychosurgery. About thirty years ago a type of brain surgery called a "prefrontal lobotomy" gained fame. When neurons in the frontal lobes of the brain were severed, a severely disturbed patient was freed from guilt, anxiety, and violent behavior. However, the patient also became totally disoriented and unmotivated and could not function normally. Consequently the technique has been little used in the past two decades.

Newer forms of *psychosurgery* are still in the experimental stage. Some research has been done on implanting electrodes in certain parts of the brain, believed to be "pleasure centers." The patient can use a control button to activate the electrode and bring on tranquil feelings. This form of surgery may benefit patients who cannot normally control their violence.

psychosurgery
Operations on the brain to treat mental disorders

Exercise 11-8
Read each of the following cases and indicate one advantage and one possible disadvantage in the type of medical therapy used.

a. Leslie, a patient suffering from schizophrenia, has responded well to treatment with antipsychotic drugs. She has been released from an institution and given a prescription for continued use of antipsychotic drugs.

Advantage: _____

Disadvantage: _____

b. Guy had suffered from severe depression for the past two years. Since taking antidepressant drugs he has found relief and has been able to return to work. He plans to take the drugs for the rest of his life.

Advantage: _____

Disadvantage: _____

c. Bobby has just had an electroshock treatment for his depression.

Advantage: _____

Disadvantage: _____

d. Vicky just read an article on a type of psychosurgery called a frontal lobotomy. She feels this will be an ideal treatment for her violent psychotic sister.

Advantage: _____

Disadvantage: _____

You may check your answers in the Feedback section.

COMMUNITY-HELP PROGRAMS

In 1963 Congress passed the Community Health Centers Act authorizing local communities to provide diverse services to prevent and treat mental problems. The services available in each community depend on the needs and interests of the people as well as the amount of funds available. Options include preventive approaches, outpatient services, and crisis management. In most communities diminishing funds have caused a decrease in services. The American Psychiatric Association has placed the blame on federal, state, and local governments (Lamb, 1984). Why not contact your own community mental health center to find out exactly which types of services are available?

Preventive Approaches

The purpose of a preventive approach is to keep emotional problems from occurring in the first place. Kessler and Albee (1975) outlined four possible ways to accomplish this goal: (1) improve child-rearing practices, (2) reduce stress, (3) improve communications, and (4) build control and self-esteem. Some communities have organized training programs for paraprofessionals—persons who have had limited previous instruction in psychology such as teachers, police officers, members of the clergy, or even bartenders and hairdressers. Although most have an associate's degree or a bachelor's degree, anyone with an interest in helping others can be trained to offer guidance in any or all of the four areas specified by Kessler and Albee. A study by Brown (1974) reported that paraprofessionals are often as effective as professionals in the area of prevention.

Among the preventive services offered by community mental health centers are workshops, infant and child care, biofeedback methods for stress control, and courses in assertiveness training (discussed in Chapter 13). Some communities have successfully used radio, television, and newspapers to reach additional people. There are undeniable advantages to preventive programs. Dodge and Rogers (1976) advised that communities with preventive facilities in their mental health centers had fewer admissions to psychiatric hospitals.

Outpatient Services

Most community mental health centers provide counseling and individual therapy. They strive to solve problems in early stages by working with children who are emotionally troubled or have alcohol or drug problems. Among the other outpatient services usually provided are family and marital counseling. Here, the focus is on resolving misunderstandings before they develop into disastrous problems. Some mental health centers focus on serving specific needs within the community such as abstaining from gambling (see Exhibit 11-7).

As a rule, community centers also provide outpatient care for former mental patients. To be sure, it is cheaper to look after patients who are living at home than to support staffs and institutional buildings. Some areas have halfway houses—temporary residences where people can readjust to living outside a mental institution. Patients receive psychotherapy and encourage one another to perform normal routines and work. Even after patients return to their homes, most continue to benefit from day care, work, and recreation at halfway houses. About 80 percent of former mental patients who resided at halfway houses have made successful adjustments. An impressive halfway house program is described in Exhibit 11-8.

Crises Management

Some problems are urgent and cannot wait. If you are in a state of panic and terror over an exam you must take tomorrow, an appointment with a therapist next week is of no help. Similarly, persons who are severely depressed and suicidal should not be kept waiting for assistance and support. Many commu-

EXHIBIT 11-7

The Gambler May Be Addicted

You gotta know when to hold 'em, know when to fold 'em—and if you're a compulsive gambler, you gotta learn how to walk away. That's what several new treatment centers are trying to teach compulsive, or pathological, gamblers....At a session on pathological gambling and its treatment, Robert M. Politzer and James S. Morrow of the Johns Hopkins University Compulsive Gambling Counseling Center defined the problem as a progressive behavior disorder in which an individual has an uncontrollable preoccupation with gambling and an urge to gamble. The typical client at their center owes between $15,000 and $80,000 in gambling debts, earns between $15,000 and $100,000 per year (when employed), is in the throes of job instability and is involved in or about to face court proceedings because of illegal attempts to get money....

John E. Davis Jr. of the Veterans Administration central office in Washington reviewed current developments in the treatment of pathological gambling. The field is still in an "adolescent stage," he says, but "growth has been rapid." Four public treatment centers and a number of private programs have been relatively successful in treating the problem with a variety of psychotherapeutic approaches. Seven states have introduced, or are planning to introduce, legislation that will start up treatment programs, and there is a move to establish a National Commission on Compulsive Gambling.

Source: (1980, September 20). The gambler may be addicted. *Science News.*

EXHIBIT 11-8

Source: (1980,
September 8). Halfway
houses for alcoholics:
A bootcamp approach
for middle-class
patients. *Time.*

Halfway Houses for Alcoholics

A Bootcamp Approach for Middle-Class Patients

More and more company health programs cover alcohol and drug detoxification programs. There are now scores of post-detox rehabilitation programs as well, but they can still be ruinously expensive. One that aims to break a patient's habit but not his bankbook is Georgia's Metro Atlanta Recovery Residences Inc., of MARRinc. Its fee: $125 a week. Begun in 1975 by Donnie D. Brown, then a rehabilitation counselor and therapist at the Georgia Mental Health Institute, the program runs seven Atlanta-area halfway homes for detoxed drinkers and drug addicts who are not yet ready to return to normal living. The residents are doctors, lawyers, ministers, professors, nurses, office managers.

MARRinc builds on techniques used in other programs but adds twists of its own. The residences are not isolated but located in neighborhoods. MARRinc looks for houses or apartments that can accommodate only five or so people. Explains Brown: "The limit is how many people can get around the dining-room table. The number is big enough to stir up a lot of different attitudes. It is also small enough to keep people from burying their feelings."

Classes and meetings occupy residents' free time. Formal therapy sessions, held three evenings a week by visiting counselors, allow residents to discuss problems. At one typical meeting, a resident being scolded for failing to clean a sticky kitchen floor tried to change the subject, prompting a housemate to snap: "I think this is the way you treat your wife when she confronts you. No wonder you drive her crazy." Notes Martin: "It forced the shirker to realize he doesn't face issues squarely."

Most residents rejoin the outside world after three months. But some stay as long as six months....Expulsion is automatic if a resident breaks the rule against using drugs or alcohol. But MARRinc does not intend to write these backsliders off forever. Says Martin: "Our goal is to open a house for people who have slipped."

---

nities have *hot lines,* telephones answered by trained volunteers or paraprofessionals who are available twenty-four hours a day, seven days a week. Persons with drug, alcohol, marital, grief, or other immediate adjustment problems can be given instant aid and comfort. Some college campuses maintain hot lines; not surprisingly they are usually busiest during final exam week!

Exercise 11-9

Imagine you have been elected to the board of directors of the community mental health center in Perfectown, U.S.A., a large prosperous community. Happily, Ben Evolant, a wealthy citizen, has just willed his entire fortune to be used for the improvement of community mental health programs. You must find ways to spend his money. Read the following description of existing programs in Perfectown, and suggest possible expansions and improvements in the three major areas listed below.

The Perfectown Mental Health center offers courses in stress management, self-improvement, and communication skills. All three courses are popular, and many citizens enroll. The center also operates a therapy program for children with emotional and/or school problems. The program is considered successful. Recently one of the three mental institutions in the state closed, and patients with minimal disorders were released. Former mental patients living in Perfectown must travel more than 50 miles for treatment.

a. Improvements in preventive approaches (2):

_____

_____

b. Improvements in outpatient services (3):

_____

_____

_____

c. Improvements in crises management (2):

_____

_____

Please compare your suggestions with those listed in the Feedback section.

SELECTING PROFESSIONAL THERAPISTS

When you are upset by problems, the task of deciding on the type of professional help needed can seem overwhelming. Indeed there are an enormous number of techniques, styles, and qualifications to consider. An important first step is to check with your physician. Although many problems have psychological causes, there may also be physical factors. For example, a headache could result from tension, but it could also be caused by a tumor, high blood pressure, or a visual disorder. Psychotherapy alone would not alleviate the problem.

If psychotherapy is needed, your family doctor is likely to be aware of the reputations and specializations of psychologists and psychiatrists in the community. If you do not have a family doctor or prefer not to use one in this way, a mental health clinic or a general hospital can usually provide a list of qualified professionals. As mentioned earlier in the chapter, specific techniques are less important than overall qualifications and skills. Most public libraries have directories of the American Psychiatric Association and the American Psychological Association that record the training and experience of each qualified therapist.

Checkpoint

Use the following questions to check your understanding of the final portion of this chapter. Indicate whether each statement is true or false.

20. _____ Group therapy is less expensive than individual therapy.

21. _____ Group therapy is particularly beneficial for severely psychotic patients who cannot communicate or even maintain eye contact with another person.

22. _____ Antipsychotic drugs are used to keep patients calm.

23. _____ Antidepressant drugs have been beneficial in the treatment of phobias.

24. _____ Electroshock treatment is the most popular and effective method of controlling depression.

25. _____ A television program on child care is an example of a preventive approach.

26. _____ A paraprofessional must have an M.D. or a Ph.D.

27. _____ Halfway houses can help former drug addicts, alcoholics, or patients from mental institutions.

28. _____ A suicide-prevention center is an example of a crisis-management program.

29. _____ It is generally advisable to check with a family doctor before beginning psychotherapy.

Check your responses against the Checkpoint Answer Key at the end of this chapter. If you had difficulty with any question, reread the text. If you had little or no difficulty answering the questions or have resolved problems that you might have had, you are ready to check yourself against the chapter inventory that follows.

CHAPTER INVENTORY

Use this list of objectives as a review checklist. You should be able to do each of the tasks outlined in the objectives and apply them to everyday examples. If you can, you may feel confident that you have mastered the material in this chapter.

1. Describe how biofeedback can be used to reduce stress.
2. Outline four steps to control anger, and suggest two possible methods for controlling bad habits.
3. Explain the purpose and give examples of self-help groups.
4. Recognize the cautions of counseling others.
5. Explain the importance of a trained therapist in a treatment program.
6. Distinguish between and describe the characteristics of simple emotional problems and mental disorders.
7. Explain the purpose and methods used in psychoanalysis, humanistic counseling, client-centered therapy, gestalt therapy, existential therapy, rational-emotive therapy, behavior therapy, and systematic desensitization.
8. Specify four advantages of group therapy.
9. Outline the advantages and limitations of drugs, electroshock, and psychosurgery.
10. List and give examples of three types of services that can be provided by community mental health centers.
11. Describe three possible methods for identifying qualified psychologists and psychiatrists.

Feedback

The correct answers to the exercises follow. If you did not answer an exercise correctly, review the preceding pages and return to the exercise to correctly complete it.

11-1. *a.* 5
     b. 2 or 3

      c. 6

      d. 1

      e. 4

      f. 2 or 3

11-2. *a.* Prepare himself by thinking about the type of situations and remarks that provoke his anger

      b. Think of ways to reply and handle himself

      c. Find ways to relax physically when he feels himself become agitated and upset

      d. Reward himself with something he enjoys whenever he handles a person calmly and successfully

11-3. The location of the chair sounds inconvenient and boring. It should remove some of the enjoyment of smoking.

11-4. *a.* Sharing successes and failures in dieting

      b. Encouraging and helping each other to continue dieting

      c. Socializing

11-5. *a.* Addiction or antisocial personality

      b. Simple emotional problem

      c. Mood disorder (depression)

      d. Schizophrenia

11-6. *a.* Gestalt therapy

      b. Rational-emotive therapy

      c. Psychoanalysis

      d. Existential therapy

      e. Behavior therapy

      f. Client-centered therapy

11-7. *a.* Cheaper

      b. Improves interpersonal relationships

      c. Allows participants to try out behaviors in a protected setting

      d. Allows learning from the experiences of others

11-8. *a.* Advantage: Leslie will probably be calmer and more controllable. Disadvantage: She could take an overdose or become overly dependent on the drug.

      b. Advantage: His depression is relieved by the drugs. Disadvantage: Prolonged use could worsen his depression and lethargy.

      c. Advantage: His unpleasant memories may be erased and his depression lessened. Disadvantage: There is no certainty about exactly what occurs during electroshock. There may be a danger.

      d. Advantage: Her sister would become less violent. Disadvantage: Her sister could never function as a normal person.

11-9. *a.* Preventive approaches: child-rearing course; training program for paraprofessionals (perhaps they could also expand into radio, television, and newspaper courses)

      b. Outpatient services: family and marital counseling; therapy program for mental patients; halfway houses

      c. Crises management: a suicide-prevention center; a hot-line telephone system

Checkpoint Answer Key

1. *a*	**9.** *d*	**17.** *g*	**25.** *true*
2. *d*	**10.** *a*	**18.** *c*	**26.** *false*
3. *c*	**11.** *c*	**19.** *e*	**27.** *true*
4. *b*	**12.** *b*	**20.** *true*	**28.** *true*
5. *d*	**13.** *d*	**21.** *false*	**29.** *true*
6. *a*	**14.** *h*	**22.** *true*	
7. *d*	**15.** *a*	**23.** *true*	
8. *b*	**16.** *f*	**24.** *false*	

CHAPTER 12

CHOOSING LIFESTYLES

There is only one kind of love, but it has a thousand guises.

La Rochefoucauld

Almost every newspaper has a section devoted to wedding announcements. There is also coverage on famous people who are living together or considering marriage or divorce. If a celebrity has a homosexual relationship, there is cause for headlines. Remember Boy George? People have a great curiosity about the lifestyles of others. Even if a recently divorced woman is only a casual acquaintance, people will wonder what caused the relationship to end, whether she has another lover, and if she will remarry.

Changes in lifestyles require adjustments that have a profound impact on the people involved. In this chapter you will learn more about sexual attitudes and choices. You will also consider the many adjustments that are encountered in sexual lifestyles. After considering the many environmental factors that contribute to learning sex roles, you will read about various forms of love. Next you will probe into the stages of development in heterosexual relationships. Adjustments to cohabitation, marriage, death of a spouse, divorce, and singleness will be examined. Finally you will briefly review findings on the causes of homosexuality.

ATTITUDES TOWARD SEX ROLES

The one thing you always remember about people is their sex. You might forget or not even notice their eye color, hair color, facial features, clothing, and jewelry. But you always notice and recall their sex. Obviously sex is more important than any other single characteristic.

Parental Influences on Sex Roles

Have you ever wondered when you first became aware of what sex you are? Psychologists have found that sex typing begins at birth. When parents are told that they have a son or a daughter, they have immediate feelings of what to expect from their child. Although it is impossible to detect sex differences in a covered or dressed baby, parents become annoyed if you think their infant son is a girl or vice versa. To avoid this type of irritation, baby girls are frequently dressed in pink and boys in blue. Similarly the baby's room is usually painted a sex-appropriate color and female or male toys are selected.

As children develop, sex-appropriate behaviors tend to be encouraged and *directly reinforced*. Girls who play with dolls receive smiles of approval. Behaviors deemed inappropriate for the child's sex are discouraged and given direct negative reinforcements. A boy who is unwilling to fight is called a sissy. Likewise, a girl who climbs trees is called a tomboy. Interestingly, it is more acceptable to be a tomboy than to be a sissy. Often children learn from watching other children. This type of observation is called "vicarious learning." Seeing a playmate ridiculed for being a sissy will discourage another boy from similar behavior.

vicarious learning Observing the positive and negative reinforcement of others

modeling Learning that occurs by observing and imitating others

Children also learn sex roles by imitating the behavior of the same-sex parent. This type of learning is called "modeling." Mothers who enjoy wearing frilly dresses and makeup are likely to see their little daughters dress similarly. Margaret Mead (1935) described a tribe in New Guinea with practices quite the opposite of traditional American sex roles. Among the Tchambuli tribe, men wore flowers and jewelry and tended to be dependent and flirtatious. Women worked at fishing and manufacturing and were expected to take the initiative in sex. Think about the sex roles of your parents. Undoubtedly your parents' notions had a strong influence on your early attitudes.

Parents have a strong influence on their children's sex roles. Girls tend to imitate their mothers' behaviors. (*Joel Gordon*)

Figure 12-1
If modeling occurs, the little girl may see her role as a future business executive.

"Gosh, Grandma, what a big office you have!"

But while parents influence their children's sex roles, children also influence their parents' sex roles. According to the research presented in Exhibit 12-1, the roles of both mothers and fathers are swayed by the sex of their child.

Exercise 12-1

Three methods of learning sex roles have been described: direct reinforcement (positive or negative), vicarious learning, and modeling. Read the following scenario and place the correct label on the line after each example.

Amanda's mother brought her into a day-care center for the first time. As the little 3-year-old girl walked over to a group of boys playing with trucks, her mother reminded her "only bad girls play with boys." **a.** (_____) When Amanda joined two other little girls, her mother sighed, "That's a good girl." **b.** (_____) The two girls were struggling and fighting over a toy telephone. The teacher intervened and scolded, "You are acting more like naughty boys than like nice little girls." Amanda put her hands behind her back and would not touch any toys. **c.** (_____) Concerned that she may have frightened Amanda, the teacher patted her on the head and stated, "You are a perfect little lady." **d.** (_____) Amanda then noticed her mother was seated in the back of the room with her legs crossed. She pulled up a chair and imitated the way her mother was sitting. **e.** (_____)

Please check your labels in the Feedback section.

EXHIBIT 12-1

Mellowing Dads

A father with two sons and no daughters wrestles with the boys on the living room rug while the dad down the street serves tea in tiny cups to his three smiling daughters. By adjusting their behavior to match their children's gender, the fathers' own sex-role orientation is changing.

We know that parents influence their children, but University of Missouri researchers Lawrence Ganong and Marilyn Coleman wanted to see if the sex of children can also influence parents. Using a questionnaire that measures both masculine and feminine behavior, the researchers tested 306 parents.

"Fathers who have sons are significantly less feminine than those who have daughters only," Ganong and Coleman say. That's not the same as saying that fathers without daughters are more masculine. Fathers of girls still retained their masculine side while picking up some positive feminine sensibilities to add to their parenting repertoire.

Mothers, too, are influenced by their child's gender. One might expect mothers of sons to become more masculine, but instead they become more feminine. What is happening?

"One explanation is that sons have a traditionalizing impact on parents' gender roles, with fathers becoming relatively more masculine than feminine and mothers relatively more feminine than masculine," the researchers write in *Journal of Family Issues* (Vol. 8, pp. 278–290).

Why is femininity influenced more than masculinity? Possibly because "parenting of both sons and daughters involves tasks that are nurturing, sensitive and emotional in nature," the researchers say. "Masculine attributes such as dominance, competitiveness and aggression are not a part of typical parenting schemas."

Source: Bozzi, V. (1988, June). Mellowing dads. *Psychology Today.*

Sex Differences

Aside from anatomy and hormones, how do males and females really differ? The existence of clearly inborn sex differences in abilities and personality has been a controversial topic. As reported by Begley and Carey (1979), there is considerable evidence that male hormones are related to aggressiveness in monkeys. However, none of these findings clearly indicate that differences in aggression can be linked only to hormones. The consensus among scientists is that both hormonal and environmental factors affect sex roles.

In addition to aggressiveness, a number of other differences between males and females have been described. Most of these differences relate to specific abilities. Boys have been found to have superior mechanical aptitudes, while girls have better fine motor coordination and verbal ability. Although there might be a genetic explanation for these differences, most can be explained by environmental factors. Boys are encouraged to play with trucks and mechanical toys. Girls, on the other hand, are presented with dolls to be dressed. Some studies have found that mothers tend to sing and talk more often to baby girls than to baby boys. This behavior could influence verbal ability.

There is evidence that training can change the differences in abilities observed in boys and girls. Changes in education have narrowed the gap between males and females in verbal, mathematical, and spatial skills (Deaux, 1985) (see Exhibit 12-2).

Most psychologists have found that sex differences are not large enough to predict skills and behavior (Hyde, 1981, 1984; Matlin, 1987).

Exercise 12-2

A psychologist reported that eighth-grade girls earn lower scores than eighth-grade boys on a mathematics aptitude test. A newspaper article concludes that there are innate differences in mathematical ability between males and females.

EXHIBIT 12-2

Women and Words

Think back to your school days: Remember how boys were supposed to be better at math, while girls excelled in English? Girls' superiority in verbal skills is a well-established "fact" in psychology, but this difference in intellectual ability is disappearing.

Psychologists Janet Shibley Hyde and Marcia C. Linn looked at 165 studies that measured verbal ability in more than one million people older than 5 (*Psychological Bulletin*, Vol. 104, No. 1).

Overall, 48 percent of men and boys scored above average on verbal ability tests, while some 52 percent of women and girls did so. "This discrepancy might have some practical applicability in success rates for cancer treatment," Hyde and Linn say, "but such a tiny difference in one area of intellectual ability does not translate into any meaningful implication."

These findings are congruent with other research showing decreasing sex differences in math and spatial skills, two other components of intellectual ability. "Decreased sex differences are partly due to a greater flexibility in gender roles," the researchers say. "Nowadays, boys and girls both engage in areas that were formerly thought of as closed." More women, for example, participate in advanced math classes and sports programs and receive more encouragement in these areas.

Source: Hall, H. (1988, July/August). Women and words. *Psychology Today.*

From what you have learned about factors that influence sex differences, specify why the author of the article may not have drawn a valid conclusion.

_____

_____

_____

Turn to the Feedback section to check your answer.

Modifying Traditional Attitudes toward Sex Roles

In the past forty years sex roles have become less rigid. Traditional ideas required men to be tough, aggressive, and independent. It was part of the male role to make decisions, strive for achievement, and work outside the home. On the other hand women were expected to be compassionate, understanding, gentle, tender, sensitive, and submissive. Female interests were to center on marriage, family, and the home. The article in Exhibit 12-3 describes some of the problems that were faced by women in the past, as well as some current concerns.

One major reason for changes in sex roles has been the increase in the percentage of women who work outside the home. Attitudes on the role of women in making decisions have also changed. Most women now feel they should have a voice in family decisions. However, researchers have found that when mothers work outside the home, their daughters' attitudes remain unaffected. Women who take jobs because they need money would often really prefer not to work. They tend to convey traditional attitudes about sex roles to their children. However, women who have stimulating, interesting jobs and enjoy their work are more likely to encourage less traditional and more liberated attitudes in their children.

Ickes and Barnes (1978) compared communications among male and female students with traditional views of sex roles and students with more flexible values. They found that students with traditional values did not look at each other, smile, gesture, or talk to each other as often as those who did not adhere to the traditional view. Further, the less traditional students were more relaxed and comfortable and enjoyed meeting members of the opposite sex.

Although initial meetings may be more comfortable when men and women have liberated attitudes toward their roles, a number of problems have been encountered by women who do not adhere to traditional values. An increasing number of women are complaining of sexual harassment at their jobs. Sexual harassment can range from being subjected to dirty jokes to sexual assault and rape. Some psychologists believe that sexual harassment has not really increased. Rather, liberated women are now more willing to admit the problems and complain (Dullea, 1980).

Married women who work outside the home often experience stress. Although they have careers, they usually maintain primary responsibility for the house and children. Trying to do everything well can create a stress labeled "superwoman's disease." One researcher recommended that women prepare themselves by considering the types of conflicts they may have to face (see Exhibit 12-4).

The liberation of women has also created a need for role changes in men. Many men have increased their involvement in both child care and household

EXHIBIT 12-3

333
CHOOSING
LIFESTYLES

Society Still Girdling Women's Dreams

Society must be restructured to incorporate "women's" values, and psychologists are part of that process, Betty Friedan told a packed audience at APA's annual convention here.

Friedan, whose book *The Feminine Mystique* was published 25 years ago, talked about "The problem that has no name: 25 years later." Younger women, she said, "don't realize how far we've come. I talk to undergraduates and they say to me 'I'm not a feminist, but I'm going to be an astronaut.' To get them to listen, I say 'How many of you have worn a girdle?'"

In response to laughter from the audience, Friedan said, "Some of you remember how it felt. You didn't ask why you wore it. Did it make you more attractive to men to look like a sausage?"

Continuing in a more serious vein, Friedan said she then tells young women, "How can I expect you to know what it felt like to wear a girdle here," she said, covering her eyes, "and here and here," she went on, pointing to her ears and mouth. "Even psychologists wore them."

Friedan was trained as a psychologist. She graduated from Smith in 1942 and was the first woman offered a psychology fellowship at the University of California–Berkeley. Intimidated by the connotations of "career-girl," she didn't accept the fellowship. Nevertheless, she did go to New York to work on a newspaper.

"I bought the feminine mystique hook, line and Freudian sinker," she said. "I really had wanted to be a psychologist, I had the general interest and commitment. I felt pangs whenever I looked at a psychology book."

She was fired "for being pregnant" and 15 years later, began secretly writing free-lance magazine articles at home "because women were not working outside the home."...

The problem, 25 years later, is that society is still polarized between male and female, that women have had to adopt the male model and reject their own feminine values of life and nurturing or attempt to be "superwomen," who combine high-powered careers with quality time for their children.

"Things are in chaos now, in transition," Friedan said, "and each woman is being made to feel it is her own cross to bear if she can't be the perfect clone of the male superman and the perfect clone of the feminine mystique."

Professional schedules are, for the most part, geared toward men with wives at home. Although most people feel women with small children shouldn't work outside the home fulltime, a majority also feels women shouldn't stay home fulltime. Yet part-time jobs and job sharing, parental leave and quality day care are nonexistent for most working mothers.

Friedan envisions a day when men and women will be freed from a strictly male/female model to embrace both assertiveness and tenderness, adventure and nurture, a day when children will benefit from growing up with two nurturing parents, a day when society does not demand an either/or choice, "but accepts lots of shades of gray, lots of flexibility.

"Where are we 25 years later?" she asked. "There are new problems, but they're so much more interesting."

Source: Denton, L. (1987, November). Society still girdling women's dreams. *APA Monitor.*

chores. An understanding of roles and sexual attitudes is critical in maintaining a lasting relationship.

Exercise 12-3

Indicate whether each of the following persons is likely to have a traditional or a flexible attitude toward sex roles.

EXHIBIT 12-4

Researchers Working on Cure for Superwoman's Disease

Natasha Josefowitz...business school professor, consultant and author, has developed a kind of self-help test designed to help women prepare for, and therefore overcome, severe stress associated with the dual-role crunch.

The questionnaire she developed is intended to both help women become aware of likely "dilemmas" and prepare to handle them. "How will you cope? There are no shoulds. Whichever way you answer, there is a cost and a benefit," Josefowitz says.

The more thought given to the problems she poses in the following test, however, the less chance of being caught in the bind afflicting women in the Stanford study.

Question: You're about to graduate from college and are offered a great job. Your fiance has an equally great opportunity elsewhere. What do you do?

(a) Move with him. (b) Take the job and postpone the wedding. (c) Ask him to relocate. (d) Take the job and cancel the wedding. (e) Try an alternative living arrangement such as a weekend marriage.

Question: It's a weekday morning and everyone is late: You're not going to be on work on time, the children have missed the school bus, the phone is ringing, breakfast is cooking, everyone is complaining. You:

(a) Sit down and yell. (b) Tell everyone to calm down and then delegate the work that needs to be done. (c) Leave for work and ask the family to cope without you, meaning your husband must take over.

Question: There are times in handling the mother, daughter, wife and friend roles you play that you will be needed by several important people at once. For example, on the same day:

Your lawyer husband has just lost a supremely important case and wants to talk to you about it; your daughter has been rejected by a longtime boyfriend and needs your support; you are in the middle of a vital project for your company, and your college friend calls with news she is getting a divorce.

How will you divide your time?

---

a. Claude informed his wife that he accepted a transfer in his job and their family would move to Liberia in two weeks.

_____

b. Marcia knows her mother hates her job, but their family needs the added income. _____

c. Greg, a college sophomore, feels as relaxed with females as with males.

_____

d. Thelma filed a complaint when her boss offered her a promotion if she would spend the night with him. _____

e. Mark intentionally stays at work longer so he will not have to concern himself with the children when he arrives home.

_____

Turn to the Feedback section to check your answers.

"*This time, you put on their coats,
and I'll go honk the horn.*"

CAPELINI

Figure 12-2
An example of
changing traditional
roles...

LOVING

Compared with poets, psychologists do a poor job of defining love. After surveying couples in love, Lindzey, Hall, and Thompson (1975) described the feeling as "an intense affection or liking." From your own experience you probably realize that love is not limited to adults of the opposite sex. As a child you undoubtedly felt love toward your mother and father and perhaps some grandparents. You might even have loved a cat or dog or other pet.

As an infant you experienced *selfish love:* You needed to be loved by your parents rather than to give love. Infants need to be held firmly and have the security of knowing they will receive care. As you grew older you began to experience more mature forms of love. *Mature love* includes understanding and caring for the welfare of another. Perhaps you had a sick or injured pet. Recall the pain you experienced in your concern for the animal.

Mature human love requires even more than understanding, caring, and empathy. It also includes respect. Your complete interest is in the happiness of another person. Mature love should not expect reciprocity. You can give love without receiving it in return. Indeed there is a risk in loving!

In Western culture, love brings feelings of possessiveness. If you love someone you have a feeling that the person belongs to you. This possessiveness tends to lead to jealousy. This attitude is not the same in all cultures. In some societies men offer their wives to strangers as a sign of hospitality. Interestingly, American men have been found to be more jealous than women. Completely possessive love is rare. But the next time you feel a twinge of jealously, think of Maslow's (1970) statement: "We can enjoy a painting without wanting to own it, a rosebush without wanting to pluck from it, a pretty baby without wanting to kidnap it, a bird without wanting to cage it, and also can one person admire and enjoy another in a nondoing or nongetting way.''

Checkpoint

Use the following questions to check your understanding of this portion of the chapter. Indicate whether each statement is true or false.

1. __T__ Parents are the first influence on attitudes toward sex roles.
2. __T__ Vicarious learning of sex roles requires observation of others.
3. __F__ Attitudes toward sex roles are inherited.
4. __F__ The sex of children does not influence their parents' sex roles.
5. __F__ There has been little change in attitude toward sex roles in the past forty years.
6. __F__ Women who are unhappy at work but need the money usually are flexible in their attitudes toward sex roles.
7. __T__ Male students with liberated attitudes toward sex roles are more relaxed when meeting women.
8. __T__ A woman who feels pressured and stressed by the responsibilities of both a family and a full-time job may be suffering from superwoman's disease.
9. __F__ Selfish love requires giving rather than receiving.
10. __F__ Mature love is always reciprocal.

Use the Checkpoint Answer Key to verify your responses. If you had any difficulty with a question, carefully reread the text. If you had little or no difficulty answering the questions or have resolved any problems that you might have had, you are ready to continue with the next portion of this chapter.

HETEROSEXUAL RELATIONSHIPS

Have you ever thought of the stages you go through when you begin a relationship with someone of the opposite sex? Gagnon and Greenblat (1978) described three stages. Although the order may vary, you can probably identify some of them in your own relationships. One stage involves meeting a person and feeling the person is desirable. This is called the ''attraction stage.'' Another stage occurs when an emotional closeness develops. This stage has been called ''emotional commitment.'' The third stage described by Gagnon and Greenblat involves ''sexual intimacy.'' These three stages may overlap and occur in any order. However, a complete heterosexual relationship will include all three stages.

Attraction

The process of socializing and pairing with the opposite sex usually begins in adolescence. Depending on the vogue of the times and the area, teenagers may choose gatherings, sports activities, dances, or dating as opportunities for meeting and selecting partners. You probably participated in several of these activities. What attracted you to someone else at an event? Often people find themselves attracted to persons who remind them of old acquaintances whom they liked or admired.

Probably the most important factor in attraction is *proximity*. You tend to develop relationships with people who live near you, attend school with you, or work with you (Zajonc, 1968, 1970). You also tend to be attracted to people with similar attitudes and personal characteristics. After surveying husbands and wives, Berelson and Steiner (1967) reported that people were attracted to partners of the same race, religion, education, social class, and even previous marital status. A divorced man is likely to be attracted to a divorcee, a widow will be attracted to a widower, and a forever single is most likely to find a person who never married appealing. If attitudes toward religion, drinking, and family size are similar, the attraction is apt to grow stronger. Not only does the attraction grow, but personalities and abilities also seem to grow more similar (see Exhibit 12-5).

Computer dating services are based on the notion that people with similar attitudes and backgrounds will find each other appealing. Usually a person is first asked to complete a questionnaire asking about a number of personal characteristics, attributes, and attitudes. Next a questionnaire about an ideal mate must be completed. The computer is used to match the questionnaires of males and females. Occasionally the system goes awry. Imagine the surprise of a college student who won a computer date with his sister! Apparently the computer was not programmed to rule out dates for persons with the same parents.

Perhaps by now you are concerned about the truth of that old adage, "Opposites attract." If indeed people with similar backgrounds and attitudes tend to find each other appealing, how can the adage still hold? There may be a kernel of truth in grandmother's maxim. Often people with a weakness will find themselves attracted to persons with a strength in the same area. For example, a shy man might find a friendly, talkative woman appealing. Her chatter can cover his shyness. Similarly, a woman who has trouble making decisions may find herself attracted to a decisive male who prefers to show his

Proximity is an important factor in attraction. Next-door neighbors are more likely to be friends than people who live at a distance. (*Stephanie Maze/Woodfin Camp*)

EXHIBIT 12-5

Birds of a Feather

Social scientists have long known that people tend to pick partners who are similar to themselves. Now it appears that the longer couples are married, the more likely they are to become like each other, eventually having the same thoughts, perceptions, and even math skills.

This is the conclusion of an ongoing study by K. Warner Schaie, a professor of human development, and his colleagues at Pennsylvania State University. The data, which come from a larger study tracking the mental ability of people as they age, indicate that wives are more likely to change than their husbands. Women who marry men brighter than themselves get smarter, and women who marry losers get worse, according to Schaie.

Ann Gruber-Baldini, a research associate of Schaie's, indicates, however, this finding may be a function of the age of the couples interviewed. All were married prior to 1970, and the men tended to be the primary or only breadwinners.

"The member of the couple leaving the home has more impact and influence," says Gruber-Baldini. "I would suspect it will become more mutual as more women enter the workplace."

Initial data indicate couples tend to quickly adopt each other's personality traits and intellectual capabilities during the first seven years of marriage, then level off for 7 to 14 years. As couples get older and after their children leave, they again become increasingly similar.

Couples will be surveyed again in 1991 as part of Schaie's larger study, called the Seattle Longitudinal Study, which has gathered data from 3,000 adult volunteers of all ages in Seattle every seven years since 1956.

Source: Schwartz, J. (1988, January). Birds of a feather. *Omni.*

Figure 12-3
Researchers say married couples grow more and more alike. They eventually adopt the same thoughts, perceptions, even math skills. (*Peter Miller/Photo Researchers*)

authority. However, although each couple may be opposite in their strengths and weaknesses, chances are they have similar backgrounds and attitudes on major issues.

Another old maxim on attraction has advised women to play hard to get. Here again, research (Malster et al., 1973) gives only limited support for the principle. Although playing hard to get may increase a woman's desirability, it often causes males to retreat. Men are likely to assume that the woman is simply not interested in them. However, a woman who gives the appearance of being hard to get but focuses her attention on the person she cares for is likely to improve her desirability with him. Lasting attraction requires interest. As the article in Exhibit 12-6 points out, this interest sometimes develops within ten minutes!

Exercise 12-4

Assume you have just accepted a job as a matchmaker at a dating bureau. The person you replaced left a list of recommended matches on your desk. Indicate whether you agree or disagree with each recommended match and specify your reason.

a. **Maurice L.** Male, 55 years old, divorced, three previous marriages, law degree from Harvard University, partner in law firm, atheist, wants to meet a younger woman, enjoys parties and drinking

and

Tanya M. Female, 20 years old, never married, high school graduate, clerk in department store, Mormon religion, likes older men, enjoys small gatherings with friends

EXHIBIT 12-6

Instant Intimacy

Most people view familiar gestures and intimate remarks as the private realm of close friends and couples. We're taught that such closeness develops gradually, but a recent study suggests that the behavior that distinguishes established couples and friends emerges early in relationships—perhaps in the first 10 minutes.

University of Mississippi psychologists Kelly E. Piner and John H. Berg wanted to learn whether those destined for close rather than casual relationships behave differently from the start. Their behavior, the researchers thought, depends on whether each individual in a pair believes that the other is both available and similar.

Piner and Berg took 30 steadily dating couples, paired some people with their own partners, some with others, and had them talk for 10 minutes about selected topics. They also paired 60 strangers together, telling them that their conversational partner was very similar or dissimilar to them.

Unacquainted pairs who believe themselves to be similar communicate remarkably like steadily dating couples, Piner and Berg reported at the annual meeting of the American Psychological Association. Conversely, pairs who believe themselves to be dissimilar communicate like unavailable people—those involved in steady dating relationships but conversing with another unavailable person.

The findings refute the notion that opposites attract and the view that "slow and steady" does it. Rather, says Berg, when it comes to coupling, the perception of similarity leads to more intimacy and familiarity. If that person is also available, the basis for closeness develops almost instantly.

Source: Simon, C. (1988, February). Instant intimacy. *Psychology Today.*

Agree/Disagree: _____

_____

b. **Jules Z.** Male, 48 years old, widower with three young children, operates a large laundry business, Jewish, seeking woman for permanent relationship (marriage)

and

Beta G. Female, 43 years old, widow with teenage daughter, employed as a beautician since death of her husband, Jewish, would like to find partner who will permit her to stay at home

Agree/Disagree: _____

_____

c. **Dwayne R.** Male, 22 years old, never married, senior at Academia University, English major, Catholic, rigorous studying does not give him time to meet females, wants to meet someone intelligent and stimulating

and

Mary M. Female, 21 years old, never married, junior at Academia University, astronomy major, history minor, Catholic, desires an acceptable male companion to escort her to college lectures and functions

Agree/Disagree: _____

_____

Please check your matchmaking abilities in the Feedback section.

Emotional Commitment

Emotional commitment occurs when people share their deepest feelings with others. If their feelings are not love, they at least experience the illusion of being in love. Most people expect to fall in love and commit themselves emotionally to another person. Think of the many love stories you have read and heard in poems, novels, films, and soap operas. Close relationships usually begin in high school. Larson et al. (1976) reported that 65 percent of white high school seniors and 77 percent of black high school seniors had gone steady while in high school. According to Gilligan (1982), young men tend to be threatened by these attachments while young women tend to feel safer and more secure.

There are many fantasies associated with emotional commitments. Storybook romances are often described as complete bliss and perfection. As a result, falling in love seems extremely desirable and wonderful. Have you ever heard the song "Falling in Love with Love"? Perhaps you have known someone who constantly claimed to be in love, but the object of the love could change from month to month, week to week, or even day to day. Somehow this love seems more an illusion than a stage in a deep relationship.

Transient love has been labeled "infatuation." Infatuation is usually a temporary state. Assume that Jennifer is learning sculpting from Edgar. Jennifer be-

infatuation Transient, temporary, selfish love

lieves that Edgar is perfect in every way. He is clearly the best-looking, most sensitive, intelligent, clever, artistic, and humorous person who ever existed. Jennifer cannot see any of Edgar's faults. Infatuation is a selfish love. Since Edgar is completely perfect, he could not possibly need Jennifer. She simply idolizes him. People who are infatuated usually cannot recognize the imperfections of the persons they adore.

Tennov (1979) introduced the term "limerance." Limerance is a total emotional commitment that gives the experience of falling or being "in love." A limerant man will go out of his way to drive by the apartment or house of a woman he loves, even if he knows she is not at home. He will also become jealous if she spends time talking with other men. Most of his waking hours are spent thinking about her, and he wants to be with her as much as possible. He wants to do everything he possibly can to help her and make her happy. In most relationships, limerance only lasts from eighteen months to three years. Only rarely does limerance last a lifetime. However, you can love a person without being limerant.

Often one person is more emotionally committed, or limerant, than the partner. As a result the committed person will make sacrifices to preserve the relationship. However, Rubenstein (1981) reported that the happiness of persons making sacrifices dwindles after eighteen months and their partners are even less satisfied as their relationship continues. For emotional commitment to endure happily, both partners need to work on communicating their feelings and continuing the relationship.

limerance Total emotional commitment that gives the experience of being or falling "in love"

Figure 12-4
Sounds as if he's limerant....

"Joyce, I'm so madly in love with you I can't eat, I can't sleep, I can't live without you. But that's not why I called."

Figure 12-5
Would you give this
relationship more than
eighteen months?

Exercise 12-5
In your own words, describe the key difference between infatuation and limerance.

_____

_____

_____

Please check your answer in the Feedback section.

Sexual Intimacy

Because of the increase in the number of pregnancies among unmarried teenagers, there has been a growing concern about adolescent sexual intimacy. A report from the House of Representatives Select Committee on Population stated that one-fifth of 13- and 14-year-old Americans have had sexual intercourse. Less than one-third of the sexually active teenagers ever used contraceptives. Every year one in every ten American teenage girls becomes pregnant (Dryfoos, 1985). The United States has one of the highest teenage birth rates in the Western world.

Premarital sex does not always result from a desire for intimacy. _Peer pressure_ seems to be an important factor. For young males sexual intercourse is often considered a way to prove their manliness. Young females believe that sexual intimacy will prove they are sexy and desirable. Several studies have found that attractive girls are less likely to have sexual experiences in high school. Young women with _poor self-images_ sometimes use sex as a method to feel better about themselves. Simon et al. (1972) reported that females who plan to attend college are less likely to have sexual intercourse during high school than females who do not plan to go to college. The most successful community programs for preventing teenage pregnancy have focused on improving self-esteem (Carrera, 1986).

Another important factor that increases the likelihood of premarital sex is *hostility*. For some young males and females having sex relations without caring about the person is a way to belittle the opposite sex. Girls who feel hostile toward their parents will sometimes have sexual relations primarily to punish their parents. They feel their parents will disapprove of their behavior and perhaps feel hurt or pained. The double standard of attitudes toward sex is fading. Teenagers hold similar standards for appropriate behavior for both sexes (Coles & Stokes, 1985).

Another changing trend has been an increased concern about the choice of sexual partners (Ehrenreich, Hess, & Jacobs, 1986). Fear of herpes and acquired immune deficiency syndrome (AIDS) have decreased the frequency of casual sex. While herpes is a bothersome condition, the AIDS virus is life-threatening. Initially AIDS was considered a disease of homosexual men and drug abusers using needles. However, the AIDS virus is now known to have been spread through heterosexual intercourse.

Emotional commitment and sexual intimacy do not always coexist. Sometimes one can lead to the other, but there are no guarantees. Marriages based on sex alone are rarely successful. Maslow (1970) strongly believed that sexual intimacy is more enjoyable and satisfying when accompanied by an emotional commitment.

Exercise 12-6

Janice, a 16-year-old, has just had sexual relations with Daryl, a boy who does not interest her. Specify three possible reasons for Janice's behavior.

a. _____

b. _____

c. _____

Turn to the Feedback section to check your responses.

Cohabitation

Some couples choose to *cohabit*, live together without marrying, during their developing relationship. Macklin (1972) surveyed students at a large university and described a variety of reasons for their cohabitation. Some couples wanted to try out their relationship before making a long-term commitment in marriage. Their cohabitation served as a trial marriage. Other couples simply did not believe in marriage. Among the other reasons listed were the need for a meaningful and convenient temporary relationship, avoiding loneliness, and sleeping with someone who cares about you.

Cohabitation is not limited to college students. It is becoming more common with all ages. Many elderly persons find it financially convenient to cohabit. According to the U.S. Census Bureau, the number of unmarried couples living together has more than doubled since 1970. Clayton and Voss (1977) interviewed males born between the years 1944 and 1954. Although only 5 percent of the men were cohabiting at the time of the survey, 18 percent had previously lived with a female for six months or longer. Results of the survey showed a high correlation between living with a woman and experimentation with lifestyles. Those who had cohabited were more likely to have "bummed around," studied ESP, astrology, or an Eastern religion, demonstrated for a cause, lived in a commune, or meditated.

Will living together improve the chances for a successful marriage? One Canadian study found that the odds of divorce were less among those who married after cohabiting than among those who had not lived together prior to marriage (Grant, 1988). However, results of an extensive survey in Sweden suggest that married couples who had cohabited are at a higher risk for divorce (see Exhibit 12-7).

Marriage and Adjustments

According to recent reports, 95 percent of all Americans are married or will get married at some point. But the divorce rate has increased. For the first time in history, marriages are as likely to end from divorce as from death of a spouse (Weitzman, 1986). But even most divorced persons eventually remarry. Many people marry while they are in love or in a state of limerance. Tennov (1979)

EXHIBIT 12-7

Marriage: Practice Makes Imperfect?

For many couples, living together seems like a good way to prepare for a successful marriage. Although a recent Canadian study found an advantage to living together before marriage (see Mind Openers, March 1988), it apparently does not hold true the world over.

Yale University sociologist Neil Bennett and colleagues found that cohabiting women were 80 percent more likely to separate or divorce than were women who had not lived with their spouses before marriage. The latest findings are based on an analysis of a Swedish survey of more than 4,000 previously or currently wedded women (*American Sociological Review*, Vol. 53, pp. 127–138).

In the first two years of marriage, women who had cohabited split from their husbands more than three times as often as women who had not lived with their mates before marriage. Within 10 years of marriage, nearly 20 percent of the cohabitors and 10 percent of those who did not cohabit had failed marriages.

Women who spent more than three years living with their future husbands were especially likely to divorce or separate. Long-term cohabitors, the researchers say, may be unsure about or ideologically opposed to marriage but tie the knot because of pressure from friends or relatives. Or, Bennett says, "couples who live together for long periods may be more accustomed to the nonconformity implicit in their relationships, and thus it might be easier for them to withstand the social repercussions of divorce."

Bennett and his colleagues believe the results of their analysis are applicable to couples in the United States. They cite other studies showing that differences between married and cohabiting couples are similar in both countries, with cohabitors being less likely to pool incomes, own joint property and share leisure activities.

"We are not saying that living together actually causes divorce," Bennett says. "What we are saying is that it appears that couples who live together premaritally are less committed to the values and interests typically associated with marriage and are more inclined to accept divorce."

Source: Hall, H. (1988, July/August). Marriage: Practice makes imperfect? *Psychology Today.*

found that marriages that begin with limerance tend to last longer. Some marry for security and convenience rather than for love.

Successful Marriages

Have you ever wondered what makes some marriages more successful than others? Psychologists have identified a number of general characteristics that correlate with lasting happy marriages. As described in Exhibit 12-8, commitment to the institution of marriage appears to be one of the most important conditions. Previous general adjustment and ability to maintain a good relationship with parents seem to be important factors. Children of happily married couples are more likely to have successful marriages. Although most people do not choose the year they plan to marry, age does make a difference. Marriages by persons under 21 are most likely to fail. The optimum age for successful marriages is 21 to 29 for women, and 24 to 29 for men. But, keep in mind that marriages by people of other ages can be successful. If you are over 29, do not despair; a happy marriage is still possible.

Choosing the right person to marry is crucial. Persons with the same attitudes and values will have fewer arguments. A computerized system called "Matesim" analyzes how a potential marriage might work out. The program includes questions in 180 areas, including goals, ambitions, attitudes toward life, job mobility, child discipline, and even television viewing habits. If the couple is in conflict in more than half the areas, the marriage could not be a predicted success (Rice, 1980).

Having had happily married parents, found the right person, and married at the optimum age, what else could be required for a successful marriage? Psychologists have specified a number of personality characteristics that correlate with successful marriages. If you are an emotionally stable person with high self-esteem, you are off to a good start.

A successful marriage requires tolerance and understanding between partners. The first years of marriage require many mutual adjustments. Partners sometimes test each other by trying out their old freedoms. A man might intentionally plan a ski weekend with his old buddies and leave his wife at home alone. Similarly a woman might circulate and flirt at a party to test her husband's reaction. Newly married couples need to consider the feelings of their spouses.

Communication is critical to successful marriages. Too often men and women believe they can change their spouses after the wedding. If they are unhappy about habits and attitudes, nothing will be said until after the honeymoon. Only rarely are such marriages successful. Compromises can only be reached when both partners are flexible and willing to be open about their feelings. Good listeners who want to improve themselves are the best marriage partners. Most sex problems in marriages stem from poor communication.

Changing Role Structure in Marriage

Because there is more uncertainty in male and female roles today, it has become difficult for husbands and wives to distinguish their personal responsibilities during their marriages. Although the freedom from traditional structures can lead to richer relationships, the uncertainty can also be a source of

EXHIBIT 12-8

Long-Married Couples Explain How They Stay Together

What makes one marriage last and another fall apart in a few years?

According to a study of couples married more than 20 years, the answer, not too surprisingly, is commitment. What's more surprising, however, is that it is not so much the partners' commitment to each other that counts, as their shared commitment to the institution of marriage.

Dr. David Fenell, a marriage and family therapist at the University of Colorado at Colorado Springs, presented his findings last month at the annual meeting of the American Association for Marriage and Family Therapy in Chicago. Fenell surveyed 150 couples married for an average of 29 years—to the same spouse.

He found that "a commitment to the institution of marriage," topped the list of essential characteristics that enabled a marriage to survive for decades. The couples said they felt that marriage itself was "an important ideal and concept."

First, Fenell and his colleagues developed a list of 70 characteristics that long-married couples said were crucial to making a marriage work. In addition, the couples identified critical issues that had tested their marriages—and been overcome—in order for their relationships to survive.

Fenell and his colleagues then took the characteristics and asked the 150 long-married couples to rank them in order of importance. Out of the list of 70 characteristics, six emerged in a distinct cluster as the most highly ranked by both husbands and wives.

After "commitment to marriage as an institution" came "commitment to the marriage partner," Fenell said, which included these qualities: loyalty and respect for the spouse, considering your husband or wife as your best friend, being able to forget and be forgiven when differences arise and the desire to please and support your partner.

The other most commonly reported characteristics of a strong marriage were (in descending order):

- Strong moral values.
- Desire to have children and to rear them well.
- Maintaining a good sexual relationship (including sexual fidelity) with your spouse.
- Spiritual commitment—be it faith in God or commitment to some other religious idea that is bigger than the relationship itself.

Asked to list the critical issues that had been the most important to overcome for their marriage to survive, the couples most often ranked establishing and maintaining a mutually satisfactory sexual relationship.

Other key areas of dispute that had to be overcome included:

- Disciplining and managing children. "Having different parenting styles can be a serious problem for a couple," Fenell says.

  "When the kids are older, it may create a situation for the couple to look at themselves and say, 'I wonder what I did that may have caused this problem or that problem in my children,'" Fenell says. "The relationship is strained. It's a time when the couple can either pull apart or be supportive of each other."

- The inability to recognize and deal with a spouse's thoughts and feelings. "It's a bit of a stereotype," Fenell said, "but men typically don't do as well with women's feelings as women would like."

- Having unrealistic expectations of a spouse.

- Taking the spouse for granted.

- Having financial disagreements.

- Not sharing important decisions.

- Not sharing enough common interests or activities.
- Loss of trust during some period in the relationship.

"If we can prepare couples to deal with these kinds of problems in marriage," Fenell said, "the big problem of long-term relationships lasting is really diminished."

Source: Squires, S. (1987, November 11). Long-married couples explain how they stay together. *Washington Post Health.*

frustration and anxiety. Many questions must be resolved. If the wife works, which chores should the husband assume responsibility for? Will there be children and who will care for them? How will the money be allocated? Interestingly, financial concerns have been the greatest single factor in divorce.

Psychologists and marriage counselors recommend that couples discuss and agree upon roles and responsibilities prior to the wedding. Even if roles are modified and changed during the course of a marriage, initial harmony helps the relationship last. Some couples draw up formal contracts agreeing on such mundane items as responsibility for ironing, housecleaning, and yard work, along with basic agreements on the distribution of money, amount of time for vacations, and future child care. Most couples do not sign contracts for their individual responsibilities, but hopefully they have an understanding

Figure 12-6
Hopefully this couple agreed on vacation plans....

about their general roles. Of course, contracts can be written and agreed upon anytime during a marriage.

Exercise 12-7

Read the following scenario. List eight factors that suggest a successful marriage and six factors that suggest an unsuccessful marriage.

Willy was 35 and Kelly was 26 when they decided to marry. Willy was limerant and in love with Kelly, but Kelly was marrying him only because her friends were married and she was feeling lonely. Both had graduated from college and had successful careers.

Willy's father had been married three times and his mother twice. Most of his childhood was spent moving to new homes, and he had little opportunity to maintain friendships. Other than Kelly, Willy had no close friends, just a few casual acquaintances.

Kelly's parents are happily married. She and her sister recently arranged a family reunion to help their parents celebrate their thirtieth anniversary. She strongly believes in the institution of marriage. Her family has always been close and spent holidays together.

Kelly and Willy met at a church picnic. Both had been attending the same church but went to services at different times. They became fast friends when they realized they both enjoyed jogging and science fiction. They both joked and laughed easily.

Kelly has been upset and concerned about Willy's tendency to drink too much. However, she has not mentioned this to him. She figures she can

Figure 12-7
Perhaps "poorer" was
not discussed.

GRIN & BEAR IT WAGNER

© 1987 North America Syndicate, Inc. All rights reserved.

"Whoa! Did you say POORER?"

change him after they are married. Although Kelly would like to have children as soon as possible, Willy feels they could purchase a magnificent sailboat if Kelly continued working and they did not need to support children. Kelly is certain he will change his mind after they are married.

a. Factors for a successful marriage: _____

_____

_____

_____

b. Factors for an unsuccessful marriage: _____

_____

_____

_____

Turn to the Feedback section to compare your lists.

Education for Marriage

Some psychologists have complained that more time is spent preparing people for a driver's license than for a marriage license. Although marriage gives opportunities for growth and happiness, it also requires many responsibilities. Preparation for making a decision to marry, accepting responsibilities, and communicating feelings has been minimal. As a result, expectations are often unrealistic. The changing roles of males and females have made marriages more complicated. Few are prepared for the stresses and strains of even the first years of marriage. If someone you know is planning to marry, suggest some reading and open communication.

Checkpoint

Use the following questions to check your understanding of this portion of the chapter. Choose and mark the one correct response to each question.

11. What is the first stage of a heterosexual relationship?
   a. Emotional commitment
   b. Attraction
   c. Sexual intimacy
   d. Any one of the above
12. With whom would you be most likely to develop a close relationship?
   a. A person who looks like you
   b. A person who lives near you
   c. A person from an interesting, exotic country
   d. A person more intelligent than you
13. Gerry was recently divorced. To whom is he most likely to be attracted?
   a. Nelly, a divorcee
   b. Sheila, a widow
   c. Deirdre, who never married
   d. Frances, a happily married woman

14. In what way is the saying "opposites attract" true?
    a. People with opposite attitudes are attracted to each other.
    b. People from different cultures are attracted to each other.
    c. People with opposite personal experiences in life are attracted to each other.
    d. People with personality strengths and weaknesses that complement each other are attracted.

15. Julia, a high school junior, is attracted to a boy in her class. According to psychological research, how can she attract his interest?
    a. Ignore him and play hard to get.
    b. Smother him with attention, phone calls, and gifts.
    c. Give the illusion of being hard to get with others but show interest in him.
    d. Act interested in everyone else but play hard to get with him.

16. Every time Ira comes home from a party he claims he just met the girl of his dreams. He has announced that he is in love eleven different times during the past month. What is Ira experiencing?
    a. Limerance
    b. Infatuation
    c. Emotional commitment
    d. Matesim

17. How long does limerance usually last?
    a. Less than one month
    b. Less than one year
    c. Less than three years
    d. A lifetime

18. Why has there been increased concern about adolescent sexual intimacy?
    a. There has been an increase in the number of pregnancies among unmarried teenagers.
    b. There have been increasing concerns about the double standard.
    c. The double standard has made adolescent girls feel immoral.
    d. Teenage girls who have sexual relations have strong emotional commitments to their partners.

19. According to surveys, which type of male is most likely to cohabit?
    a. One who is limerant
    b. One who is emotionally commited
    c. One who experiments with lifestyles
    d. One who never plans to marry

20. How are computers used in evaluating the success of potential marriages?
    a. Computers compare attitudes and values.
    b. Computers do family histories and check the happiness of the couple's parents.
    c. Computers analyze financial potential.
    d. Computers compare communication skills.

21. Which of the following is crucial for a successful marriage?
    a. Cohabitation prior to the wedding
    b. Communication of attitudes, goals, and responsibility

c. Limerance

d. A written marriage contract specifying responsibilities and duties of each partner

Use the Checkpoint Answer Key to verify your responses. If you had any difficulty with a question, carefully reread the text. If you have had little or no difficulty answering the questions or have resolved any problems that you might have had, you are ready to continue with the final portion of this chapter.

ENDING HETEROSEXUAL RELATIONSHIPS

Unless a couple dies simultaneously, all relationships must come to an end. Even though many couples use such expressions as "until death us do part" at wedding ceremonies, few consider how their marriage will actually end. There are only two choices: separation or death. The ending of a relationship is more than just a change in marital status. Adjustments are required in financial responsibility, social activities, sex life, and possibly even such daily routines as sleeping and eating habits. The situation is usually further complicated by legal problems such as separation and divorce agreements, wills, and insurance settlements.

Death of a Spouse

Few people think about or prepare for the death of their spouses. Even if the subject is brought up in conversation, most people will avoid further discussion. Since women are usually two to three years younger than their husbands and have a longer lifespan, there are about 4 times as many widows as widowers. Whether the death is sudden or follows a prolonged illness, the spouse will experience a period of grief lasting at least two to three months. Although friends and relatives can lend support and make the period less painful, the grief cannot be rushed.

Psychologists have described four stages of grief that follow the death of a spouse. Throughout the four stages there are mixed feelings of agitation, anger, guilt, and depression (Parkes, 1972). The stages may overlap but they usually occur in order.

Stage 1: shock The first stage is a period of confusion. The spouse cannot understand the emotions being experienced. If the death followed a long period of illness, the widow or widower will worry that the death may have been caused by negligence or mistakes. They will think of things they could have done to prevent the death or blame doctors for poor treatment. Alternative actions are dwelled on even if the death was sudden or accidental. The shock in this stage often delays open expressions of grief. However, the confusion of emotions leads to tears, sleepless nights, and a loss of appetite. Persons who normally drink or take sleeping pills are likely to take larger doses. Many widows and widowers wish for their own death.

Stage 2: protest During the second stage, bereaved spouses become easily irritated. A sense of unfairness is felt. They ask questions such as, "Why have I been left with all these responsibilities?'' There is anger about changes in lifestyle as well as paperwork and legal forms. Often there is no will or some confusion about the will. If there are financial burdens, the feelings of protest can become intense.

Stage 3: depression and withdrawal Daydreaming about the past dominates the third stage. There is a strong tendency to tears, and widows and widowers prefer not to talk to others or socialize. They prefer to be left alone with their memories. During this stage there is often a resurgence of guilt. Spouses think of things they might have done to have been better partners. The bereaved experience the many symptoms of depression described in Chapter 10. Support, warmth, and friendship from family and friends are crucial during this stage.

Stage 4: recovery Finally, the surviving spouse begins to function in a normal manner, completing routines and returning to work. Although performance is initially somewhat less than usual, going back to work usually helps a person feel more productive. Further, most working environments force some socializing, making it more difficult to remain depressed.

Exercise 12-8

Read the following descriptions and indicate the stage of bereavement for each widow and widower: shock, protest, depression and withdrawal, or recovery.

a. Jessica's husband died two weeks ago. She is furious that he never told her where he kept his insurance policies and securities. She feels he did not prepare her to handle family affairs and now has abandoned her. _____
_____ *Protest* _____

b. Kevin returned to work today after a two-month leave of absence to bury his wife and settle legal and family problems. He still feels numb and listless but was able to accomplish some work and go out to lunch with his buddies. _____ *Recovery* _____

c. Tom was exhausted from his wife's long illness. She suffered so much during her last days. Tom was hoping she would die to be spared further discomfort. When the doctor called him to tell him his wife had expired, Tom was certain her death was caused by his wishes. ___ *SHOCK* ____

d. Ursula's spouse died more than three months ago. Although friends have invited her to dinner, she refuses to go anywhere. She prefers to stay home and go through picture albums and letters that her husband had sent her. _____ *Depression & withdrawal* _____

e. When Albert heard his wife was killed in an automobile accident, he immediately poured himself a shot of whiskey. By the time his family arrived, he had consumed most of the bottle. He said he wanted to die, too. _____
_____ *SHOCK* _____

Please check your answers in the Feedback section.

Divorce

The divorce rate has been high and is steadily increasing. Presently more than one-third of marriages result in divorce. Many psychologists think the increased independence of women has been a leading factor in causing divorces. Hiller and Philliber (1978) found that working women with a positive self-concept and a sense of achievement are less dependent on their husbands for their own prestige. Since they do not need the emotional and economic support of their husbands, these women have become less willing to tolerate stresses in a marriage. On the other hand, men often have problems adjusting their roles to permit greater freedom for their wives and to take on more daily responsibilities in the home. According to Kelly (1982), the wife is more likely to decide to end the marriage.

Adjustments to Divorce

Divorce is sometimes the only solution for a miserable relationship, but unfortunately it is always accompanied by additional pain. Divorce creates a sense of failure that leads to feelings of guilt and depression in both partners. Many states now have no-fault divorce laws. In a no-fault divorce, both partners agree that their marriage has severe problems that they cannot overcome. Although this helps to eliminate the problem of blaming one partner, it does not fully remove the burden of guilt and depression felt by both husband and wife.

As pointed out in Chapter 10, the depression after divorce is even more severe and longer lasting than the depression that follows the death of a spouse. The divorced rarely receive sympathy and support from friends and relatives. While a bereaved spouse usually is allowed at least a one-week leave from work, a divorced person rarely takes more than a few hours. Some psychologists have suggested that ceremonies accompany divorces. The parted couple could vow to continue kindness and friendship toward each other and promise to support any children emotionally and financially. Friends and relatives would attend the ceremony and possibly a quiet reception would follow.

But a ceremony would be impossible for a group that suffers the greatest grief, the deserted. This is sometimes called "the poor man's divorce," since it is usually the woman who is abandoned. Since she is left with household bills and the economic responsibility of the children, desertion creates economic as well as emotional problems. Today, women as well as men are deserting their spouses. Desertion creates special problems. The forsaken mate has the burden of not knowing whether the spouse is alive, physically or mentally ill, or troubled. Only costly and often lengthy investigations can help.

Regardless of the method used in attaining a divorce, both partners must change their lifestyles. Divorced men often have problems performing household tasks. They feel a marked loss if they do not have custody of children. Hetherington et al. (1977) reported that divorced fathers work long hours, particularly if they have alimony payments. They also tend to sleep and eat poorly.

Women who have gained custody of their children often resent the father's freedom from responsibility. Many divorced wives see themselves as bogged down by household responsibilities while their husbands are allowed a carefree life. However, as Hetherington et al. (1977) reported, the fathers are far from happy. They become envious of their wives. They view their former spouses as fortunate, since they won the home and children. The result is often jealousy, bitterness, and hostility.

Divorced persons profit from support and encouragement from friends and relatives. Those who do not have close relationships to rely on can often be aided by counseling groups. Usually eight to ten recently divorced persons discuss their problems with a counselor. By listening to the troubles of others, people within the group feel less alone in their distress. They can also share their feelings and burdens with others. The benefits of group therapy are discussed in greater detail in Chapter 11.

Children of Divorced Parents

Divorce can be extremely painful for children. Often they feel responsible for the breakup of their parents' marriage and experience guilt. Since parents tend to argue about child rearing, children who have overheard arguments often assume that their misbehavior was the cause of the divorce. Children who have sided with one parent during an argument usually believe they have done the wrong thing. Some children are embarrassed by their parents' divorce. They believe that divorce is proof that their family has failed, and they fear others will pity them. As a result, they will try to keep the divorce a secret and refuse to discuss it with anyone. In communities where divorce is common, children usually suffer less embarrassment. A number of books and novels have been written about children whose parents' marriages have failed. Reading about the experiences and feelings of others helps children understand their own emotions and feelings.

After divorce children must adjust to separation from one parent. This adjustment is particularly difficult when parents continue to tear each other down. Although there have been many studies on the long-range effects of divorces on children, there are few clear conclusions. Bane (1976) acknowledged the initial guilt experienced by children but found no differences from children in intact families in social adjustment, school achievement, and susceptibility to delinquency. The article in Exhibit 12-9 indicates that boys usually suffer more than girls from divorce.

Hetherington (1972) reported that daughters of divorced parents who live with their mothers tend to have negative attitudes toward their fathers. These girls are also likely to have some difficulty relating appropriately to male peers and adults. According to Hetherington, they are prone to tenseness and promiscuity. As mentioned earlier in the chapter, having had divorced parents increases the likelihood that you will divorce someday.

Traditionally, mothers were usually awarded custody of their children. Currently, approximately 1 million children are in homes with a father only. As women have become more willing to relinquish their roles in child rearing, an increasing number of fathers have been assuming responsibilities for children. Joint custody is also gaining popularity. Children live with each parent for part of the year. When parents live near each other, children can visit in each home. As suggested in Exhibit 12-9, children in joint custody have fewer adjustment problems. As divorced persons begin their separate lives, the children from their previous marriage can create some awkward moments. Despite

EXHIBIT 12-9

Divorce Hurts Boys More, Studies Show

Boys generally suffer more from their parents' divorce than girls, especially if contact with fathers is limited, a cross-section of research on the long-term effects of divorce on children indicates.

"Boys in divorced families appear to be more exposed to conflict than girls," Joan Kelly, a psychologist with the Northern California Mediation Center, said during an invited address...

"Boys react more strongly to the diminished contact with the father than girls and desire more contacts," Kelly said. Mothers with custody of boys reported increased problems disciplining them. They often noted with frustration that their sons reminded them of their ex-husband, at whom they were angry. This may imply a double rejection for some of the boys, Kelly observed....

Traditional mother-custody arrangements, in which children visit their fathers every other weekend or four days per month, "has been found to create intense dissatisfaction among children, accompanied in many instances by profound feelings of deprivation and in some instances, reactive depression, particularly among young boys," Kelly observed.

Joint custody, in which a child spends at least 35 percent of the time with one parent, and the remaining time with the other parent, often lead[s] to more satisfied children and adults, Kelly said. Citing two studies comparing children in joint and sole custody, Kelly said "joint-custody boys were reported by mothers and teachers to have fewer emotional and behavioral problems than maternal-custody boys."

One study, in fact, found that boys in joint-custody arrangements did not differ from boys in happily married families on measures of self-esteem and overall adjustment. Boys in both groups "were significantly better adjusted than boys in sole custody or unhappily married families," Kelly reported. Joint-custody mothers also reported more respect for their former spouse's parenting abilities, and perceived their former spouses to be more supportive and understanding compared to maternal-custody mothers.

Kelly cautioned that most of the joint-custody studies were small, and larger studies would be helpful. She also qualified her remarks by warning against forming too many generalizations....

Source: Buie, J. (1988, January). Divorce hurts boys more, studies show. *APA Monitor.*

the many negative aspects of divorce, many psychologists feel that a broken home is better for children than a home of stress and conflict.

Exercise 12-9

Read the following scenario and describe how each underlined item is likely to *improve* adjustments to the divorce.

Nancy and John have decided that their marriage will never work. They argue constantly, and their relationship is miserable. They have decided on a (a) no-fault divorce. Nancy arranged for the (b) children of divorced friends to visit and chat with her youngsters; John purchased an interesting and appropriate novel for them. The divorcing couple explained to both children that (c) the failure of the marriage was their responsibility as adults. The children were not to feel any blame. Nancy and John then agreed to plan (d) a short ceremony and pledge their continued devotion to their children. Members of their immediate families and a few close friends would be invited. (e) Guests would be asked to lend their support and friendship to both the couple and their children during the difficult months following the divorce.

a. _____

_____

b. _____

_____

c. _____

_____

d. _____

_____

e. _____

_____

Please turn to the Feedback section to check your answers.

Singleness

Singleness may be temporary, transitional, or permanent. For some, singleness is only a waiting period for marriage or remarriage. Included among singles are four groups: people who never married but will eventually; people who never married and never will; the divorced; and the widowed. The majority of divorced persons eventually remarry; however, only about half of the widowed give up their singleness.

Only a small group remains single permanently. Included in this small group are persons who stay with their parents; brothers and sisters living together; people who live alone; and members of religious orders. Single persons are not necessarily isolated. Even those who live alone usually enjoy close relationships with friends, relatives, nieces, nephews, and children of friends. People who live by themselves tend to have more friends and are less likely to become irked than people who live with others.

There are some clear advantages to singleness. To be sure, a single person who lives alone has more personal independence. Traveling or changing jobs and locations do not require another opinion. It is easier for singles to maintain privacy and please themselves.

However, there are also some problems. Single persons have to be emotionally independent and not need a long-term relationship. You have undoubtedly heard single persons pressured with questions such as, "When are you getting married?" "Haven't you found anyone yet?" Facing these questions as well as such negative labels as "old maid" can be a chore!

Exercise 12-10
List two advantages and two disadvantages of remaining single.

a. Advantages: _____

_____

b. Disadvantages: _____

_____

Please compare your list with the one in the Feedback section.

HOMOSEXUALITY

Homosexuality is a lifestyle choice that involves intimate relationships between members of the same sex. Homosexuality is no longer considered a disorder. Hunt (1974) reported that 2 percent of the male population and 1 percent of the female population are homosexuals. The percent of homosexual people has remained constant over many years and appears to be similar in most cultures studied (Hyde, 1986).

The causes of homosexuality are controversial and not fully understood. It is known that male and female hormones are present in members of both sexes; but there is limited evidence that physical and genetic conditions alone can cause homosexuality. Among the possible causes explored are birth order, physique, and hormonal imbalance. Presumably everyone is a potential homosexual. Although there is some evidence that early family experiences could play a role in creating homosexual tendencies, research has had mixed results and therefore is not conclusive. Most psychologists believe that homosexuality results from an interaction of hormonal influences and situations in the environment.

Checkpoint

Use the following questions to check your understanding of the final portion of this chapter. Choose and mark the one correct response to each question.

22. Bill's wife was hospitalized four days ago following a heart attack. He has just been told that his wife died. Which of the following is likely to be his first reaction?
    a. Anger and resentment
    b. Confusion and shock
    c. Depression and guilt
    d. Protest and withdrawal
23. Imogene spends much of her time daydreaming about her deceased husband. Which stage of grief is she probably experiencing?
    a. Protest
    b. Shock
    c. Depression and withdrawal
    d. Recovery
24. According to psychologists, which of the following factors have contributed to the increase in the divorce rate?
    a. No-fault divorces
    b. Fewer children in marriages
    c. Changing male and female roles
    d. Books about divorce
25. Which of the following persons is likely to experience the most severe depression?
    a. A widow
    b. A divorcee

c. A single woman

d. A homosexual

26. Under which circumstance does divorce cause greatest grief?

(*a*) When a partner is deserted

b. When a no-fault divorce is filed

c. When there is a ceremony

d. When friends and relatives try to help

27. Last night 12-year-old Mark overheard his parents arguing violently about the amount of time he spent watching television. This morning Mark's mother told him she was moving out of the home and divorcing his father. How will Mark probably feel?

a. Furious with his mother

b. Furious with his father

(*c*) Guilty about causing the divorce

d. Relieved that there will be fewer arguments

28. Allison is upset and embarrassed about her parents' divorce. She does not want anyone to learn about it. Which of the following might help her?

a. Receiving sympathy and pity from others

b. Thinking about her own responsibility in causing the divorce

(*c*) Learning about the experiences of other children of divorced parents

d. Ignoring the problem

29. Which group of single persons is most likely to marry?

(*a.*) The divorced

b. The widowed

c. Members of religious orders

d. People who wish to live alone permanently

30. What conclusion can be reached concerning the cause of homosexuality?

a. Homosexuality is genetic.

b. Homosexuality is caused by an imbalance of hormones.

c. Homosexuality is caused by childhood experiences.

(*d.*) The causes of homosexuality are not fully understood.

Check your responses against the Checkpoint Answer Key at the end of the chapter. If you had difficulty with any question, reread the text. If you had little or no difficulty answering the questions or have resolved problems that you might have had, you are ready to check yourself against the chapter inventory that follows.

CHAPTER INVENTORY

Use this list of objectives as a review checklist. You should be able to do each of the tasks outlined in the objectives and apply them to everyday examples. If you can, you may feel confident that you have mastered the material in this chapter.

1. Specify and give examples of three ways parents can influence the sex roles of their children.

2. Discuss the difficulty in distinguishing between environmental and genetic influences on sex differences.

3. Differentiate traditional sex roles from the newer, more liberated attitudes.
4. Describe the effects of changed attitudes toward sex roles on lifestyles.
5. Identify the key differences between mature love and selfish love and between possessive love and nonpossessive love.
6. List and describe three stages in the development of heterosexual relationships.
7. Identify four factors that affect attraction.
8. Define and give examples of emotional commitment, infatuation, and limerance.
9. Specify three factors that influence the likelihood of premarital sex.
10. State reasons for cohabitation.
11. List three factors that correlate with successful marriages.
12. Describe personal characteristics required for a successful marriage, and identify pressures created by changing sex roles.
13. Explain the need for marriage education.
14. List and describe four stages of grief that follow the death of a spouse.
15. State one reason for the increasing divorce rate.
16. Describe the adjustments required after a divorce, and recognize the special problems associated with desertion.
17. Identify ways to improve adjustments to divorces.
18. Explain the problems confronting children of divorced parents.
19. Name the four groups of people described as singles.
20. List two advantages and two disadvantages of singleness.
21. Describe the lack of conclusive evidence on the causes of homosexuality.

Feedback

The correct answers to the exercises follow. If you did not answer an exercise correctly, review the preceding pages and return to the exercise to correctly complete it.

12-1. *a.* Direct reinforcement
b. Direct reinforcement
c. Vicarious learning
d. Direct reinforcement
e. Modeling

12-2. Since there are many environmental differences that could have influenced the scores, the author cannot be certain that the differences were innate. The types of games boys play could aid their mathematical skills. Similarly, teachers may have favored boys.

12-3. *a.* Traditional
b. Traditional
c. Flexible
d. Flexible
e. Traditional

12-4. *a.* Disagree: a 35-year difference in age; differences in marital status, education, religious attitudes, and social interests.
b. Agree: similar ages, marital status, and religion; needs seem to complement each other

  c. Agree: similar ages, marital status, education, religion, and academic interests

12-5. *Infatuation* is unrealistic and selfish. The loved person is perfect and does not need you. *Limerance* is realistic and involves an emotional commitment. You want to help the loved person as much as possible.

12-6. *a.* She has low self-esteem and wants to prove she is sexy and desirable.

  b. She wants to belittle males.

  c. She wants to aggravate her parents.

12-7. *a.* Factors for a successful marriage: Kelly is 26; Willy is limerant; Kelly believes in the institution of marriage; Kelly's parents are happily married; Kelly has close family relationships; Kelly and Willy attend same church; they have the same interests: sailing, jogging, and science fiction; both have a good sense of humor.

  b. Factors for an unsuccessful marriage: Willy is 35; Kelly is marrying for convenience; Willy's family is unstable; Kelly is not communicating her feelings about his drinking; they have different attitudes about children; Kelly is not communicating her feelings about children.

12-8. *a* .Protest

  b. Recovery

  c. Shock

  d. Depression and withdrawal

  e. Shock

12-9. *a.* Neither partner will be forced to bear the blame.

  b. The children will learn that they are not alone in their problems and feelings and will have a better understanding of what to expect.

  c. The children will feel less guilt.

  d. The children will feel less abandoned and will be better able to acknowledge the finality of the divorce.

  e. The divorced couple and their children will be able to share their problems with friends and relatives.

12-10. *a.* Advantages: personal independence; privacy

  b. Disadvantages: need to be emotionally independent; negative attitudes of other people

Checkpoint Answer Key

1. *true*	**9.** *false*	**17.** *c*	**25.** *b*
2. *true*	**10.** *false*	**18.** *a*	**26.** *a*
3. *false*	**11.** *d*	**19.** *c*	**27.** *c*
4. *false*	**12.** *b*	**20.** *a*	**28.** *c*
5. *false*	**13.** *a*	**21.** *b*	**29.** *a*
6. *false*	**14.** *d*	**22.** *b*	**30.** *d*
7. *true*	**15.** *c*	**23.** *c*	
8. *true*	**16.** *b*	**24.** *c*	

CHAPTER 13

COMMUNICATING

To have great poets, there must be great audiences, too.

Walt Whitman

LISTENING
   Listening Problems
   Improving Listening
VERBAL COMMUNICATION
   Improving Speaking Skills
   Improving Writing Skills
   Analyzing Verbal Expression
   Denotations and Connotations
   Transactional Analysis
   Assertiveness
NONVERBAL COMMUNICATION
   Artistic Forms and Symbols
   Appearance and Body Language
PATTERNS OF COMMUNICATION
   Networks
   Participation
   Self-Disclosure
   The Johari Window
   Hidden Agendas

Imagine the president of a packaging firm is overjoyed with the prospect of receiving a $10 million contract to enclose bubble gum in plastic wrappers. She feels she will be able to reward herself and her vice-president with hefty salary increases. She calls in the vice-president and announces, "The prospects for this contract look good. We may be able to raise our salaries enormously in a few months." The vice-president, believing the word "our" meant all managers, rushes to the shop foreman and reports, "Next month, when the new contract is signed, we will all get huge raises!" The shop foreman in turn believes "we" are all employees. He announces to his workers "Everyone is getting big raises next month!" Workers rush out and purchase new cars, computers, dishwashers, and jewelry, all based on a series of misinterpretations.

Although this imaginary tale seemed to end in catastrophe, far worse disasters have resulted from faulty communications. Good communication is a key to positive relationships, whether between spouses, family members, students and teachers, management and labor unions, races, or nations. When communication breaks down, the results can be divorces, failures, strikes, riots, or even wars.

The sequence of the first topics in this chapter will follow the order in which you learned to communicate. First you learned to listen, then to speak, and finally to write. After studying ways to improve each of these skills you will examine methods that psychologists have used to analyze communication. Next you will consider the various forms of communication without words. In the final portion of the chapter, patterns of communication will be compared.

LISTENING

Although you probably have no recollection of how you originally learned to communicate, your first step was to listen. As an infant you spent many months hearing the voices of others. You spoke not a single word and only made babbling sounds or cried. Eventually you learned the language by listening to others and associating their words with objects and actions. Even today an immense amount of information can only be acquired by listening. On the other hand, by not listening, significant data can be lost.

Listening Problems

Why do you not listen? Undoubtedly someone has complained to you, "You never listen to me!" or, "See, you should have listened!" One reason for not listening is *preoccupation*. You may be so anxious to speak yourself that you totally miss the content of other people's remarks. Or something may be bothering you—perhaps a family argument, a sick pet, an overdue bill, or a sore toe.

Being *turned off* is another reason for not listening. Emotional factors such as a dislike for a person's appearance or tone of voice could cause you to ignore statements. Whining children, nagging spouses, and scolding parents are often turn-offs. Similarly, monotonous voices and lecturers or preachers with thick foreign accents will usually have problems holding your attention. Undoubtedly some topics bore you. If you have no interest in botany, a lecture on the history of angiosperms will be an intellectual turn-off. Likewise if the lecturer used unfamiliar terms, your listening would diminish further. There

"...And how long do you want
to borrow this student?"

Figure 13-1
Cartoonists have long
capitalized on
misinterpretations and
communication
problems.

may also be a few topics that you would prefer to avoid for emotional reasons. Perhaps your mind would wander during discussions on cremation and cemetary plots.

Often people have set ideas and prefer not to hear anything contrary to their own thoughts. Rather than opening their minds to new suggestions, they become threatened and debate and argue. Have you ever tried to convince smokers that cigarettes are harmful? In spite of the evidence you presented, they probably turned you off and were not good listeners.

Improving Listening

Reik (1972) claims that "listening with a third ear" is the key to effective listening. Rather than just hearing words, the third ear listens and interprets feelings and meanings. The third ear focuses not only on what is being said but also on why and how the statements are made. To be sure, effective listening is not passive; rather, it is an active process that requires a concentrated effort. Psychologists have suggested several techniques to improve active listening.

Set a purpose for listening. Resolve to listen attentively. For example, if you know you must gain information from a boring lecture on soil tests in Greenland, decide beforehand that you will find out the composition of their dirt.

Resist distractions. Look directly at the speaker and avoid listening to other conversations or gazing out windows. In a classroom or lecture hall, seats in the front usually provide the least distraction, since you cannot see

"And now, from our news room
in Washington, here's Greg Barton and
George Miller with a completely revised version
of what the President just said."

Figure 13-2
No doubt, Barton and
Miller were listening
with their third ears.

your classmates fidget or make comments. If you are at a noisy party, try to find a quiet corner!

Listen openly and reserve judgment. Though you feel certain the speaker is a blockhead, give the person a chance. Even a clod can sometimes provide remarkable insights and information. Likewise a person may make some foolish statements initially but eventually may add important facts and opinions. If you follow the logic of speakers without interrupting, you will acquire a better understanding of their positions.

Paraphrase and ask questions. After a speaker is finished talking, wait before responding. Then summarize or rephrase the statement to be sure you understand. Also, ask any specific questions that might bother you. For example, suppose a man just mentioned a recipe for making beer bread, stating, "Just mix some beer, self-rising flour, and sugar. Throw it in a greased loaf pan and bake it at 350° for an hour." When his statement is completed, you should take a few seconds to envision the procedure. Then you might paraphrase: "Am I correct that there are only three ingredients, beer, self-rising flour, and sugar, and I bake it for an hour in a 350° oven?" You probably would also want to ask, "Just how much beer, flour, and sugar are needed?" Often speakers omit important details; by paraphrasing and asking questions you can be more certain that you understand the information being communicated.

There are many fringe benefits to being a good listener. In addition to learning and being able to make more accurate statements, you are also showing that you care about others. As a result, other people are more likely to listen to you. People who talk but refuse to listen are likely to discover that they have lost their audience.

Exercise 13-1

Read the following scenario, and in the space provided list four ways Ms. Slicker could improve her listening.

Ms. C. T. Slicker took her new sports car for an afternoon drive in the country. Soon lost, she pulled into a service and asked a mechanic for directions. As the mechanic began giving directions to the main road, Ms. Slicker began to wonder whether she had sufficient gas and began calculating the distance. She also checked the price of gasoline and pondered the possibility of getting to another filling station. The mechanic had a thick country twang and Ms. Slicker feared that she did not have accurate information. When the mechanic finished giving her directions, Ms. Slicker thanked her and drove off, hoping to find another service station.

a. _____

b. _____

c. _____

d. _____

You may compare your list with the one in the Feedback section.

VERBAL COMMUNICATION

In spite of the enormous technological advances in communication across greater distances, problems in interpreting and understanding messages still exist. Clearly, effective listening can improve understanding. However, better speaking and writing skills are also needed.

Improving Speaking Skills

Speaking is without a doubt the most frequently used method of communication. Brenner and Sigband (1973) reported that even in organizations where written messages are stressed, spoken communications were more common. More than two-thirds of the persons surveyed claimed at least 75 percent of their assignments were given by spoken orders from their bosses.

Speaking clearly requires more than pronouncing words distinctly. You must have a precise picture in your mind of exactly what you want to say. Then you must choose your words carefully, so your listener will hear an accurate statement. If you are giving a speech, you usually have some time for preparation. However, most oral communication requires spontaneous responses. These spontaneous responses often create uncertainty that leads to fear. The article in Exhibit 13-1 suggests that you practice facing these fears.

One way to improve the accuracy of everyday speech is to increase your vocabulary. Evans (1963) stressed the importance of having more control over the words you use. If you have a clear mental picture of what you want to say and a rich vocabulary, chances are you will be able to express yourself accurately, and

EXHIBIT 13-1

Speak Up!

What is it about speaking to a room full of people that makes our knees turn to jelly and our palms sweat? Dr. Dennis Becker, director of the Speech Improvement Company (which has offices in Brookline, Massachusetts and Providence, Rhode Island), says that most bad public speakers suffer from a stubborn, preconceived notion that there is a "right" and "wrong" way of speaking before an audience.

The numbing fear of looking foolish reduces executives who are dynamic and commanding off-stage to awkward text readers on-stage, adds Carolyn Dickson, president of VOICE-PRO Associates in Cleveland, Ohio. In the workplace, Dickson says, the executive "thinks quickly and is a firm decision maker." But standing before a group of people, that same executive turns to stone and reads the script in a monotone flat enough to put his own mother to sleep. "And the audience wonders, 'How did this guy become a CEO?' "

Sweaty-palmed speakers should first realize that without a doubt, they are going to make mistakes. But whether you trip your way to the podium or drop your notes all over the stage, Dickson says, your audience will forgive you *if* you handle the situation with aplomb. "The audience will forgive anything—even a fall off the stage—if the speaker treats his or her mistake with ease," she explains.

Learning to waltz through on-stage blunders when all you really want to do is dive under the nearest banquet table is certainly an acquired skill. In public speaking instruction classes, for example, teachers sometimes "frame" their students into botching up. Students must "go through the pain," Dickson says, noting that "Conquering a fear means the systematic step-by-step approach of facing that fear."

Each person is his own worse critic, though. And in lieu of formal coaching, public speaking experts advise that executives take inventory of their speaking skills by using a tape recorder or video camera. During the playback, recommends Becker, who also teaches presentation and sales skills at Harvard and MIT, ask yourself if you would be impressed or swayed by you as a speaker, or if you would instead flip through the program to see who's up next. Try to determine what you do or don't like about your delivery, and watch for annoying habits—for example, a consistently dropped *g* at the end of "ing" words. A critical study of yourself can reveal speaking strengths and weaknesses that might not be evident to you at the podium, especially over the din of your knocking knees. You might discover, for instance, that you need to smile more, or that the last joke bombed because you really are not funny.

The goal of effective public speaking, Dickson and Becker agree, is that "the person up there on stage should be the same person your colleagues know in the office."

Source: Handley, A. (1988, January). 8 resolutions for '88: Speak up! *USAIR*.

misunderstandings will be avoided. Persons who have difficulty organizing their thoughts and expressing themselves clearly can suffer bitter results.

Perhaps you are concerned that flaunting a big vocabulary might make you appear stuffy and condescending. Certainly a person who chooses words that are not likely to be understood is probably trying to appear superior. However, having a plentiful supply of precise and punchy words at your command can help you communicate with a variety of types of audiences. Interestingly, Armstrong (1973) found that professional persons can be impressed by phonies who are wordy (see Exhibit 13-2).

Another important aspect of speaking is holding the attention of your listeners. If you look someone directly in the eye, it is difficult for the person to ignore you. On the other hand, speakers who bury their heads in their notes as they read

EXHIBIT 13-2

367

COMMUNICATING

> ### Bafflegab Pays
>
> *"If you can't convince them, confuse them."* Simply put, this is the advice that J. Scott Armstrong, a marketing professor at the Wharton School, coolly gives his fellow academics these days. It is based on his studies confirming what he calls the Dr. Fox hypothesis: "An unintelligible communication from a legitimate source in the recipient's area of expertise will increase the recipient's rating of the author's competence."
>
> Dr. Myron L. Fox gave a celebrated one-hour talk, followed by a half-hour discussion period, on "Mathematical Game Theory as Applied to Physician Education." His audiences were professional groups, including psychologists, psychiatrists, social workers, and educators; afterward, on anonymous questionnaires, they said they found the lecture clear and stimulating.
>
> Fox, in short, was a smashing success. He was also a complete phony—a professional actor whom three researchers had told to make up a lecture of double-talk, patching raw material from a *Scientific American* article into nonsequiturs and contradictory statements interspersed with jokes and meaningless references to unrelated topics.

Source: Horn, J. C. (1980, May). Bafflegab pays. *Psychology Today.*

their speeches may find the audience has ignored their talks. An additional bonus of maintaining eye contact is learning the reaction of listeners. Frowns or puzzled expressions can inform you that you need to clarify your statements. Similarly smiles and nods of approval may permit you to give more details.

Face-to-face communication between two persons is usually the most effective. Political candidates have found that votes are most likely to be won by door-to-door campaigns. By meeting people individually, candidates can be sure they have the attention of each voter as well as learning their reactions and interests. In small communities residents are sometimes insulted if a candidate does not visit. But candidates for state and national offices can physically visit only a tiny percentage of their constituents.

Assuming that one-to-one communication is possible, how might a candidate best approach a voter? For that matter, how can anyone develop an effective conversation with someone else, whether a spouse, a teacher, a boss, or an intriguing person at a party? Psychologists have found that *open questions* are more conducive to improved conversation than *closed questions*. A closed question can be answered with a simple yes or no, where an open question requires a longer response. For example, "Do you like your job?" is a closed question. Once the person answers yes or no, the conversation is over. On the other hand if you asked, "What do you like about your job?" or "How could working conditions be improved?" an extended reply would be required. As a result you would learn more and could continue the conversation intelligently.

Exercise 13-2

In your own words describe how each of the following techniques can help you improve your speaking and conversing abilities.

a. Developing a clear mental picture of what you want to say:

_____

_____

b. Increasing your vocabulary: _____

_____

c. Using eye-to-eye contact: _____

_____

d. Asking open questions: _____

_____

Please turn to the Feedback section to check your answers.

Improving Writing Skills

Although written communication is not as popular as the spoken word, you certainly read and write a huge volume of messages. Consider the number of books, newspapers, and magazines sold—as well as the reports, letters, and even junk mail received each day—and you will realize the influence of written communication. Skill in writing has had an increased emphasis in the past few years. More employers are looking for people with writing ability. If you have had to complete a job application form with essay questions, chances are the employer wished to check your writing competence.

There is one clear advantage to writing rather than speaking: you have time to think, organize, and even rewrite if necessary. However, there are two distinct disadvantages: (1) You cannot use voice inflections or physical gestures, and (2) you usually do not receive immediate feedback from your audience. To overcome the first disadvantage, you must incorporate an emotional tone in your language. As in spoken communication, a rich vocabulary is an undeniable advantage.

The second problem is not difficult to overcome if you know the interest, the reading level, and the vocabulary of your audience. Usually writing that is short and simple is easiest to understand. Nonetheless, authors sometimes use words to impress others rather than to communicate effectively. Gilmer (1975) related an amusing episode:

> No doubt, most of us are sympathetic with the plumber who wrote the Bureau of Standards in Washington to say he had found that hydrochloric acid opened clogged drains in a hurry and asked if it was a good thing to use. The reply came back: "The efficacy of hydrochloric acid is indisputable, but the corrosive residue is incompatible with metallic permanence." The plumber replied that he was glad to know it was all right to use acid. The scientist showed the letter to his boss, who replied to the plumber: "We cannot assume responsibility for the production of toxic and noxious residue with hydrochloric acid and suggest you use an alternative procedure." The plumber thanked the Bureau and was glad they approved his use of acid. Finally, correspondence from Washington got through to the plumber: "Don't use hydrochloric acid. It eats the hell out of the pipes."

Checkpoint

Use the following questions to check your understanding of this portion of the chapter. Choose and mark the one correct response to each question.

1. How do infants learn to communicate?
    a. By using gestures
    b. By recognizing faces

c. By listening

d. By playing with objects

2. Ted is driving on a turnpike with his radio turned to a news station and blaring loudly. He is concerned about getting home before dark since the right front light of his car is not working. He checks his watch and the setting sun every few minutes. As he finally pulls into his driveway, Ted realizes he has not heard any news. What was his listening problem?

a. Overload

b. Preoccupation

c. Turn-off

d. Boredom

3. What does Reik mean by listening with a "third ear"?

a. Active listening and interpreting

b. Listening while also attending to distractions

c. Listening to two conversations at the same time

d. Using a hearing aid

4. If you want to listen attentively to a lecture, where is the best place to sit?

a. In a back corner

b. Directly in front of the speaker

c. Near a window

d. In the middle of the group

5. Assume your boss just finished describing a complicated assignment. As an active listener, what should you do?

a. Wait a few seconds, then paraphrase and ask questions.

b. Wait a few seconds, then criticize and give your judgment.

c. Immediately ask questions, then criticize.

d. Immediately criticize, then ask questions.

6. What is the single most frequently used method of communication?

a. Speaking

b. Writing

c. Gestures

d. Facial expressions

7. Gladys has written a ten-page speech to deliver to her basket-weaving club. Which of the following methods will help her hold the attention of the group?

a. Keeping her eyes on her notes

b. Looking straight ahead into space

c. Keeping her eyes downcast

d. Maintaining eye contact with the group

8. Which of the following is an example of an open question?

a. "Are you happy?"

b. "Am I late?"

c. "Why do you like me?"

d. "Are you drinking coffee?"

9. For effective communication, which of the following is the best rule for writers?

a. Impress others with big words.

b. Assume your audience is intellectual.

c. Keep your writing short and simple.

d. Avoid taking time for rewriting.

Check your responses against the Checkpoint Answer Key at the end of the chapter. If you had difficulty with any questions, reread the text. If you had little or no difficulty answering the questions or have resolved problems that you might have had, you are ready to continue with the next portion of this chapter.

Analyzing Verbal Expression

Having delved into listening, speaking, and writing, you may be wondering what else of importance is involved in communication. The actual words you choose can have a powerful impact. Likewise your attitude and intentions can convey messages to listeners. In this section of the chapter you will learn how psychologists have dissected language and conversations.

Denotations and Connotations

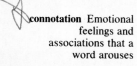

denotation Specific dictionary definition of a word

The *denotation* of a word is the dictionary definition. For example, Webster's New Collegiate Dictionary defines the word "father" as "a male parent." This definition is what the word denotes. The denotation of the word "communism" is "system [of social organization] in which goods are owned in common and are available to all as needed."

However, both the word "father" and the word "communism" have emotional overtones—meanings that are not in the dictionary. You may hear a man say "Don't give me an argument, I am your father!" He does not simply mean that he is a male parent. Or perhaps you have heard a politician claim that a vote for the opposition was a vote for communism. To be sure, the politician was not implying that his opponent shared property with the community. Rather, he probably was trying to associate his opponent with your negative feelings toward the word "communism." The feelings and emotions associated with words are called *connotations*.

connotation Emotional feelings and associations that a word arouses

You can experience some problems with denotations and connotations of words. Many words have more than one dictionary definition. Other words have been used in slang expressions and have taken on new meanings. Often you need to use the context to find the correct meaning. Suppose you were asked, "Would you like some grass?" Undoubtedly you would want to check on the speaker's definition of grass. If the speaker owned a golf course that was being replaced by a superhighway, you probably would be safe in assuming that you could improve your lawn. However, if the speaker seemed "spaced out," the other definition of grass was probably being used. Denotations are usually easier to discern than connotations, if you are familiar with definitions.

Among those interested in the connotations of words are employers. Even though a job may require the same tasks, changing the title can make a difference to a worker. For example, a job description may include activities such as dusting furniture, sweeping and vacuuming floors, scrubbing two bathrooms and a kitchen, and polishing silver. The title for the job could be "cleaning person," "maid," or "household technician." Clearly, the title "household technician" has more status and prestige than either "cleaning person" or "maid"; the connotations of household technician are more favorable. Consider the difference in your attitude toward being labeled "clerk-typist," "secretary," "executive secretary," and "administrative assistant." Yet all four titles can be used to describe the same tasks. Psychologists have even advised businesses that although the word "corporation" has more prestige, the word "company" is considered friendlier.

Another group intensely concerned about the connotations of words are advertisers. They seek words with both strong negative and strong positive emotional overtones. Whether the ad uses the word "grime," "bacteria," "congestion," "itch," "soreness," or "exhaustion," it is trying to draw out your negative feelings. Next the advertiser will offer a product that "cleanses," "relieves," "soothes," or "stimulates"—words with strong positive connotations.

Advertisers further capitalize on the connotations of words by means of voice inflections. A disgusted tone can make dirt and bacteria truly repulsive. Similarly, a low, comforting tone can make words such as "soothes" and "relieves" bring delight. Tone of voice can change both the denotation and connotation of words. A friend who sincerely states, "You really deserved that promotion" is delivering a different message than the person who makes the remark sarcastically. Yes, there may be truth to the old adage that it is not so much what you say, as the way you say it.

Exercise 13-3
What is the difference between the denotation and connotation of a word?

a. Denotation: _____

b. Connotation: _____

Exercise 13-4
Assume you want to find the real meaning of the word "mechanic."

a. How could you find the denotations? _____

b. How could you find the connotations? _____

Please turn to the Feedback section to check your answers.

Transactional Analysis

In *transactional analysis* (TA) rather than dissect the meaning of words, you examine everyday conversations or transactions between people. Any verbal interaction is considered a transaction. TA became popular about twenty years ago with the publication of two books, Berne's (1964) *Games People Play* and Harris's (1967) *I'm OK—You're OK*.

According to the theory behind TA, your personality has three aspects, a *child*, an *adult*, and a *parent*. When you converse with others, you can reflect any of these three aspects or states. By examining a verbal exchange, you can determine whether a person is speaking as a child, an adult, or a parent. There are some distinctive characteristics of each state.

The child. The child communicates spontaneously, with little or no forethought. Statements beginning with "I wish" and "I want" are typical of the child. The child is often frustrated and makes aggressive remarks, such as, "My brother can beat up your brother," "I am better than you," or "My car is bigger." Nonverbal behavior includes pouting, shouting, teasing, and laughing. Generally, the child

transactional analysis (TA) Method sometimes used in group therapy to examine verbal interactions between people

communicates selfish interests and attitudes. Listen to some conversations; you may be surprised at how often the child emerges from grown men and women.

The adult. The adult is rational, logical, and objective and makes decisions. Information is gathered by asking questions beginning with words like "who," "what," "when," "where," and "how." The adult is independent and can distinguish between opinions and facts. As a result many statements open with "I think" or "I understand" or "It is my opinion that." The preferred interaction is conversation between two adults.

The parent. Most people acquire some characteristics of their own parents and use them in their communication with others. Even such nonverbal behavior as frowns, pointing index fingers, and shaking fists can be traced to parents. The parent aspect of the personality is concerned with rules and can be either critical or protective. It emerges giving orders, stating rules, or approving or disapproving of ideas and behaviors. Parent remarks include "Hand me the paper," "Watch out for pickpockets!" "Perfect, keep up the good work," and "You have it all wrong."

Now imagine that two friends, Zeke and Lem, are conversing. Like everyone else, Zeke and Lem have three modes of speaking, a child (C), an adult (A), and a parent (P). As each talks, he addresses one of the three aspects of his friend's personality. For example, Zeke could speak at a C level to Lem: "I am taller than you." Lem then responds, "But I am stronger than you." The conversation could be illustrated as in Figure 13-3. A conversation on an A level might begin with Zeke inquiring, "How tall are you, Lem?" Lem might respond, "Last time I checked I was 6 feet 7 inches" (Figure 13-4).

Figure 13-3

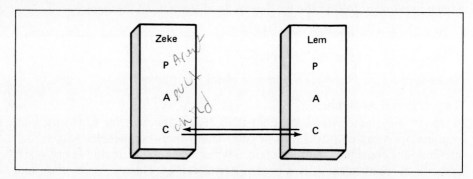

Figure 13-4

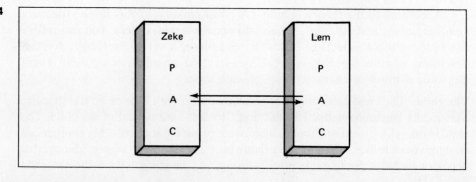

A P exchange would begin if Zeke shook his fist disapprovingly and said, "Whoever built this place was stupid!" and Lem then replied "He should have taken a course in ceiling heights." (Figure 13-5).

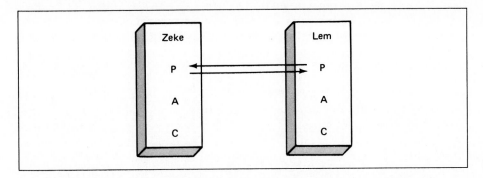

Figure 13-5

In all three of these exchanges Zeke and Lem were addressing each other as equals, first at a child level, next at an adult level, and finally at a parent level. As you probably realize, people do not always speak to each other on the same level. But even when people do not speak as equals, they can carry on a conversation that is compatible. For example, Susie may pout and complain, "I hate homework! I want to go out and play." Her mother reminds her, "You cannot go out until you finish your homework."

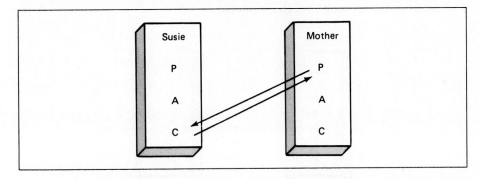

Figure 13-6

Or perhaps Susie again reflects her C by complaining, "I hate my new teacher." This time her mother's A emerges, and she inquires, "What is he like?"

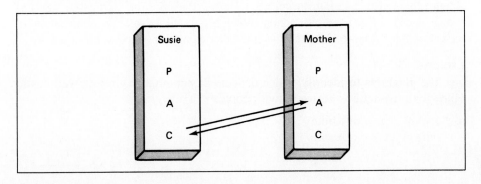

Figure 13-7

Possibly Susie would communicate on an A level and remark, "I don't understand why I cannot concentrate on my homework." Her mother's P instructs, "Turn off the television set."

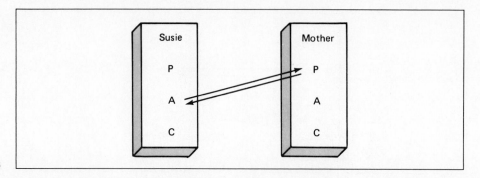

Figure 13-8

In each instance Susie's mother responded using the aspect of her personality that Susie had addressed. Since both Susie and her mother understood their roles, there was no problem in their communication.

Unfortunately, too often there are misunderstandings about roles. You address one aspect of a person, and he or she replies from another. For example, imagine Betsy and Trudy are both first-year high school students. Trudy feels they are equal, but Betsy believes she is more sophisticated than Trudy. Betsy inquires, "Isn't the history class interesting?" But Trudy answers, "You fool, it's the most boring subject in the school."

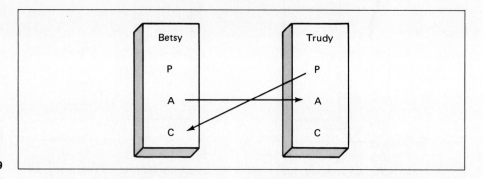

Figure 13-9

Trudy responded from her P aspect rather than her A, which was addressed. When a person responds from an aspect other than the one addressed, the exchange is called a crossed transaction. When illustrated, lines of communication intersect or cross. Figure 13-10 shows some other examples of crossed transactions.

Exercise 13-5

Use the diagrams to identify which aspects of personality are involved in the following transactions between two people.

a. "I want a new dirt bike."
"Dirt bikes are not safe."

P	P
A	A
C	C

Figure 13-10
Crossed transactions

b. "What is Jane's phone number?"
"I'm not sure. I'll look it up."

P	P
A	A
C	C

c. "Be sure to arrange the classroom chairs in a circle."
"No, they belong in rows."

P	P
A	A
C	C

Exercise 13-6

Of the transactions in Exercise 13-5

a. Which one is equal? ~~B~~ B
b. Which one is unequal, but compatible? A
c. Which one is crossed? C

Please turn to the Feedback section to check your responses.

Assertiveness

Assertiveness requires standing up for your own rights. Assertive behavior is not the same as aggressive behavior. When you act assertively, you respect the rights of others as well as your own individual rights. However, protecting your rights without offending others can be tricky. Psychologists suggest that

assertiveness Standing up for personal rights while respecting the rights of others

you act on your feelings. If you are upset, hurt, and depressed, or if you feel unfairly criticized, tell the appropriate person. It is usually best to state rather than act out your feelings. Stating "I feel furious" will help release anger. It is not necessary to pound a table or punch someone.

By stating your own feelings rather than attacking or accusing another person, you avoid making others become defensive. Gordon (1970) recommended using "I" statements instead of "you" statements. "I feel upset and hurt when you are unwilling to share toys with your brother" is preferable to "You selfish child, you never share things with your brother." To be assertive, it is not necessary to attack the character of other people. After stating your feelings, it is helpful to offer a positive suggestion. You might add, "If you let your brother play with the toy telephone, maybe he will share his truck with you."

Perhaps you have a spouse or a roommate who clutters your living space. This can be a ticklish situation, but with some effective assertiveness you can win. Rather than accuse the person of being sloppy, you might begin by reporting, "I feel depressed when I sit in a messy room." Next add a positive suggestion, such as, "If we put two bags in the corner, one for trash and one for dirty clothes, we will have more room to walk around." As suggested in Exhibit 13-3 the perfect ending is some good news. You could conclude the conversation with "You sure are fun to live with!"

Checkpoint

Use the following questions to check your understanding of this portion of the chapter. Choose and mark the one correct response to each question.

10. Which of the following is the denotation of the word "mother"?
   a. Sensitive and fair
   b. An authority

EXHIBIT 13-3

Your Foot's on Fire...Nice Shoes

Giving someone—particularly a friend or relative—bad news isn't easy. While some people may just blurt out the cold, hard truth, others try to soften it in some way, usually by adding some piece of good news or trying to induce a good mood in the recipient before letting the other shoe drop. But, ask Boston University psychologists Linda Marshall and Robert Kidd, "is there a good way to deliver bad news?"...

So, the researchers, in three separate experiments, offered subjects the choice of receiving bad or good news first. The results "clearly demonstrate that, given a choice, people prefer to hear bad news before good news," they report.

Based on theories suggested by social scientists in the mid-1960s, Marshall and Kidd offer two possible explanations for their findings: First, according to the "gain-loss hypothesis," people tend to like other people who they first view negatively, then come to view positively; second, according to the "adaptation-level theory," feelings are experienced as more pleasant or unpleasant "the greater the discrepancy or distance of the initial effect from the present one." In other words, the good news may seem all the better on the heels of bad news.

Source: (1980, April 26). Your foot's on fire...Nice shoes. *Science News.*

c. A female parent

d. A soft, friendly person

11. What is the connotation of a word?

    a. The dictionary definition

    b. The emotional associations

    c. The slang usage

    d. The transactional use

12. Which of the following factors can influence the connotation and denotation of words?

    a. Context and tone of voice

    b. Recognition and familiarity

    c. Recognition and context

    d. Context and familiarity

13. Which of the following techniques have been used to measure the connotations of words?

    a. Looking up words in a dictionary

    b. Checking associations on a questionnaire

    c. Analyzing transactions

    d. Using ''I'' statements rather than ''you'' statements

14. According to transactional analysis which of the following statements would be made by the C aspect of the personality?

    a. ''How are you?''

    b. ''Finish your dinner or no television.''

    c. ''Always wear a seat belt when riding in a car.''

    d. ''My family has more money than yours.''

15. ''Do you have change of a quarter?'' ''Let me check. Yes, here are two dimes and a nickel.'' How would you describe this transaction?

    a. Equal

    b. Unequal but compatible

    c. Unequal and incompatible

    d. Crossed

16. What is the best type of interaction in transactional analysis?

    a. P P   *b.* P$\rightleftarrows$P   *c.* P P   *d.* P P

       A A   A A   A A   A$\leftrightarrows$A

       C C   C C   C C   C C

17. Assume a neighbor borrowed Jim's chain saw three months ago. Jim wants to cut wood and notices that his neighbor has still not returned the saw. Which of the following would be the most desirable assertive behavior for Jim?

    a. Ignore the problem and cut the wood some other day.

    b. Borrow a chain saw from another neighbor.

    c. Tell his neighbor he is disappointed and ask that the saw be returned.

    d. Accuse the neighbor of being careless and inconsiderate and refuse to ever lend anything again.

Check your responses against the Checkpoint Answer Key at the end of the chapter. If you had difficulty with any question, reread the text. If you had little or no difficulty answering the questions or have resolved problems that you might have had, you are ready to continue with the final portion of this chapter.

NONVERBAL COMMUNICATION

Often people cannot find the words to describe their feelings or choose not to disclose information verbally. Anything that is communicated without the use of words is considered nonverbal communication. Whether you compose a symphony, yawn, wear a funny hat, stare into someone's eyes, or remain silent, you are sending a nonverbal message. Feelings and attitudes as well as information can be communicated by one or more of the nonverbal modes described in this section.

Artistic Forms and Symbols

Have you ever been moved by a symphony, religious music, or a popular tune? Perhaps it was the melody, the tone, or the rhythm that communicated a mood. To be sure, blues melodies have brought listeners to tears. Paintings, etchings, sculptures, and photographs have all been used to convey the feelings and attitudes of their originators. However, there is one problem with communicating through art forms: The original message is often misinterpreted.

Because there is no international language, efforts are being made to communicate essential information through picture symbols. Symbols that are easy to interpret have been chosen. Recently, the use of such symbols has become widespread. Poisons, restrooms, no-smoking areas, and highways now display international symbols.

Appearance and Body Language

Some aspects of your appearance and body language cannot be consciously controlled. For example, you cannot prevent yourself from blushing, flushing, quivering, or breaking out in goose bumps. Other aspects can be used purposely and deliberately. You can raise an eyebrow, slump, lower your eyes, spit, or wave your arms. There are no precise interpretations of such facial expressions and gestures. The meaning varies among cultures and individuals (see Chapter 8). If you have ever played a game of charades, you know the difficulties in deciphering body language.

Psychologists have found that body language sends a far stronger message than verbal language (see Exhibit 13-4). If you burst into tears saying, "Everything is fine," your friends will heed your tears rather than your words.

The clothing you wear can advise others of your mood, feelings, and attitudes. A woman who outfits herself in a tight, slinky, low-cut dress on a date is conveying a message to her companion, whether or not she realizes it. Similarly, a man who shows up at a formal party in tennis clothes is communicating an attitude. Advertisers of perfumes and after-shave colognes insist that their products will imply a message.

In addition to what you wear and how you stand, where you stand can communicate your attitude. Hall (1969) identified four types of personal zones or spaces.

Cartoon by John Brundidge

"It is customary, sir, that the jury's decision is given verbally."

Figure 13-11
Will juries use such
international symbols
in the future?

Figure 13-12
"Actions speak louder
than words."

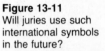

*"You folks holler if that's too much
air for you back there."*

EXHIBIT 13-4

Actions Speak Louder Than Words.

Common sense suggests that our impressions of people are shaped more by how they act than by what they say about themselves. But Brandeis University psychologist Teresa M. Amabile and her student Loren G. Kabat tested this idea by videotaping women while they deliberately acted either introverted or extroverted in conversations and while they described themselves as having one or the other personality trait.

Then, 160 students watched the videotapes and evaluated how "outgoing," "friendly," "shy" or "withdrawn" the women were. When the women's self-descriptions and actual behavior conflicted, the students usually gave more credence to behavior. In general, the students' judgments were influenced about 20 times more strongly by what the women did than by what they said about themselves.

Actions speak louder than words not only when we judge the character of adults but when we try to shape the character of children. Adults who want to encourage children to be generous should practice what they preach, according to psychologists James H. Bryan and Nancy Hodges Walbek of Northwestern University. These researchers awarded gift certificates to fourth-graders for playing a miniature bowling game and offered them a chance to put some of their winnings in a box "for the poor children" if they chose. The children had previously seen adults who either donated or didn't and who preached either generosity or selfishness. When the adults' actions didn't match their advice, the researchers found, the children were more likely to pay attention to the deeds than to the words.

Source: Kohn, A. (1988, April). "You know what they say...": Actions speak louder than words. *Psychology Today.*

Intimate distance (1 foot to body contact) This space is reserved for lovers, parents, children, and intimate friends. If a casual acquaintance came this close you would feel uncomfortable. Other than your dearest friends the only individuals usually permitted within this range are doctors, nurses, dentists, or other professionals responsible for your personal care. If you stand this close to another person, you are suggesting

Drawing by Anne Canevari Green

Figure 13-13
Distance zones

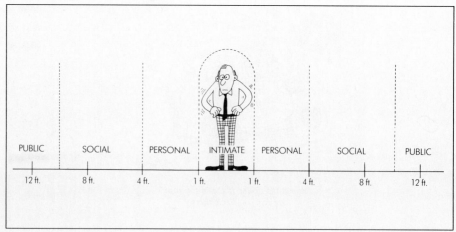

that you consider yourself an intimate friend or relative. One study found that happily married couples feel comfortable with each other within this distance. Troubled couples were too uneasy to come this close (see Exhibit 13-5).

Personal distance (1 to 4 feet) The actual size of this space can differ according to cultures. This space is primarily for personal conversations with your close friends. According to Fast (1970) most people believe this area belongs to them and any unwelcome person who enters violates their privacy. People are within reach and can touch each other, shake hands, or pat each other on the back.

Suppose you were sitting in an empty cafeteria and a stranger sat in a chair next to you, within your personal space. You would probably feel awkward. Have you ever noticed that people in crowded areas, such as elevators, trains, or buses, tend to avoid eye contact with each other and stare into space? They undoubtedly are ill at ease with the invasion of their personal space.

Social distance (4 to 10 feet) Social distance is used for impersonal business and casual conversations. Most likely, you have heard the expressions "Keep your distance" or "Stay at arm's length." Personal or intimate conversations at this distance would indeed be strange. People at interviews and business meetings usually sit or stand at a social distance.

Public distance (10 feet and beyond) If you are in a large lecture hall attending a town meeting or watching a play or a soccer game, communication is at public distance. At this distance, private behaviors or comments are inappropriate. It is even difficult to conduct business or an interview when the other person is so far away.

EXHIBIT 13-5

So Near and Yet So Far

When a wife complains that her husband seems "distant" it may literally be true. The emotional closeness of married couples can be measured, in inches, according to family therapist D. Russell Crane of Brigham Young University and colleagues.

The researchers tested 108 couples, asking partners to walk toward one another and stop when they got to a "comfortable conversation distance." After measuring the distance between them, the researchers gave each spouse several tests that tap marital intimacy, divorce potential and desire for change.

The greater the husbands' dissatisfaction with their marriage, the farther they stood from their wives, the researchers report (*Journal of Marital and Family Therapy*, Vol. 307, pp. 307–310). Or, to put it another way, the more emotional steps the husband had taken toward divorce, the fewer physical ones he would take to be near his wife.

The researchers also found that the average space between "distressed" couples (in which both were unhappy and had lots of unresolved conflict) was about 25 percent greater than that of "nondistressed" couples (both happy and low in conflict). The happy couples stood, on average, 11.4 inches apart; the unhappy ones stood 14.8 inches apart—but in their case, the inches felt like miles.

Source: Rosenfield, A. (1988, March). So near and yet so far. *Psychology Today.*

Exercise 13-7

Read each of the following descriptions of behaviors. From what you have learned about nonverbal communication, state the message that you think the individual is sending.

a. Jane was dressing for an interview. She pulled her long blond hair into a tight bun, borrowed her mother's pin-striped suit and her grandmother's oxfords. She filled her father's briefcase with file folders and took it along.

_____

b. After an argument with his wife, Andy painted an ugly portrait of her in blacks and grays. He hung it over her mirror.

_____

_____

c. Gretchen's boss patted her on the back and told her she was doing a great job. She immediately moved across the room from him. _____

_____

d. Tessie looked over the uncrowded beach. She put down her beach towel and sat about 3 feet away from an attractive young man. _____

_____

To check your interpretations, turn to the Feedback section.

PATTERNS OF COMMUNICATION

Whether the communication is verbal or nonverbal, there are basically only two patterns of communication, one-way and two-way. In *one-way communication*, the speaker speaks, the listener listens, and the communication is complete. The speaker does not receive any feedback from the listener. Mary talks to Bob and Bob listens but does not respond.

In *two-way communication*, the listener and speaker alternate roles; the result is a conversation. The speaker receives feedback from the listener. Mary speaks and Bob listens, then Bob gives his feedback while Mary listens. His feedback might include a question, a comment, an opinion, or his interpretation.

Both Leavitt (1951) and Tesch et al. (1972) studied the efficiency of one-way and two-way communications. One-way communication is faster but it is also less accurate. The speaker cannot be certain that the listener understands the message. One-way communication also protects power, since the speaker can be neither questioned nor criticized. Classrooms where the lecturer speaks and students take notes are orderly, quiet, and free of interruptions. However, the lecturer will not know whether the students understood his message until he receives some feedback. Unfortu-

one-way communication Speaker speaks and receives no feedback from the listener

two-way communication Speaker speaks and receives feedback from a listener, who then becomes a speaker

Figure 13-14 A one-way communication problem

nately for the students, the feedback may be in the form of a midterm or final exam.

In two-way communication the speaker receives immediate feedback. From the feedback, the speaker can decide if it is necessary to modify statements. Mistakes, inaccuracies, and oversights can be detected. If a lecturer is using jargon that students cannot understand, students will ask questions and the words can be defined. Because they can ask questions, listeners feel more sure of themselves in two-way communication. Problems can be alleviated immediately.

Two-way communication is clearly more accurate than one-way communication. Businesses are more successful when workers have a complete understanding of their jobs. Similarly, problems can be resolved as they arise rather than waiting for a union confrontation or a grievance procedure. However, there are two shortcomings: two-way communication takes more time, and the speaker is vulnerable to criticism.

Exercise 13-8

For each of the following situations, indicate whether one-way or two-way communication would be preferable.

a. _____ A newly appointed sergeant wants to assert his power over new soldiers.

b. _____ An accountant wants to be sure his clients understand how to keep financial records.

c. _____ An employer wants to avoid a strike.

d. _____ A businesswoman is in a hurry and wants to leave a message with her secretary.

network
Communication
involving more than
two people

e. _2_ A newly hired man wants to be certain that he understands his job requirements.

Please turn to the Feedback section to check your answers.

Networks

Whenever two-way communication involves more than two people, there must be a system or *network* for sending and receiving messages. Sometimes the network is formal, but more often it is informal and haphazard. Among the more popular informal networks is the *grapevine*. You spread the news or rumor to anyone you meet who might be interested. It often becomes difficult to identify the original source of the information. Hence the expression, "I heard it from the grapevine." Surprisingly, Davis's research (1973) found that the grapevine is both fast and efficient. He noted that 75 to 95 percent of grapevine information is correct.

Leavitt (1951) identified and studied four types of formal communication networks. He then experimented to determine the amount of accuracy and personal satisfaction that each type of network created.

Circle In a circle network, each person can communicate only with two other persons (see Figures 13-15 and 13-16). Information must then be relayed through the circle. No one person leads or coordinates. Each person in the circle is equal in power to the others.

Y arrangement According to their position on the Y arrangement, members can communicate with either one, two, or three other persons (see Figure 13-17). The person at the bottom and the two persons on the diagonals

Figure 13-15
Circle

Figure 13-16
An example of a circle
network

converse with only one other person. The person at the head of the line where the diagonals form a junction communicates with three others. This individual clearly has the most power. All others communicate with two people.

Wheel The person in the center of a wheel communicates with all others (see Figures 13-18 and 13-19). Persons along the rim of the wheel cannot converse with each other. All information must flow to and from the center. You may be more familiar with the wheel as an organization chart. The owner of a business communicates with the manager of each division.

Concom The concom arrangement is similar to a circle in that all members are equal (see Figure 13-20). However, in a concom arrangement individuals can communicate with three rather than two others.

By now you may be wondering about the consequences of using each of these different networks. Leavitt found that the most accurate network was the Y arrangement. Circle arrangements made the most mistakes, probably because no single person could coordinate a solution. However, members of circle networks were among the most satisfied. Members of circle and concom groups were more satisfied with their interactions. The most highly satisfied person within all groups was the person in the center of the wheel. The next most satisfied was the person at the top junction of the Y arrangement. Persons on the rim of the wheel proved to be least satisfied.

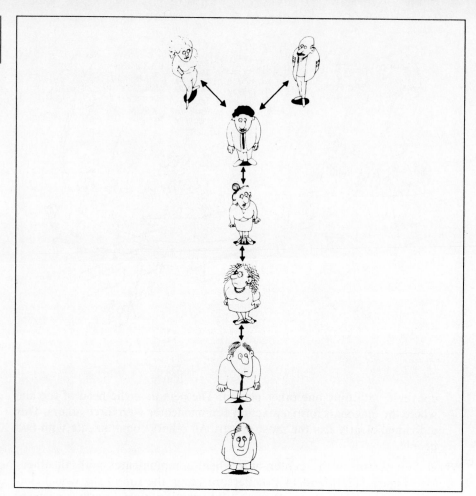

Figure 13-17
Y arrangement

Leavitt concluded that participation was a key to satisfaction. People were more content if they felt they shared in decisions.

Exercise 13-9

Illustrate each of the following communication networks. Specify whether the illustration demonstrates a circle, a Y arrangement, a wheel, or a con-com.

a. Carol is selling cosmetics. Money that she earns from orders is reported to Meg, and orders must be filled by Charlotte. Carol receives her first order and money from Ann. When Ann told Beth about her super new makeup, Beth gave money to Ann and asked her to place an order through Carol. Beth in turn told Jan about the new makeup, and Jan asked Beth to pass her money and order through Ann to Carol.

Figure 13-18
Wheel

Type of network: _____

Figure 13-19 Wheel organization chart

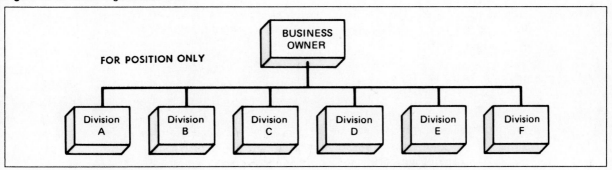

FOR POSITION ONLY

BUSINESS
OWNER

Division A

Division B

Division C

Division D

Division E

Division F

Figure 13-20
Concom

b. When Goldie inherited her fortune she hired a chauffeur to care for her three cars, a trainer to manage her stables and horses, a tax attorney to give her financial advice, a social secretary to handle her invitations, and a household technician to keep her home in good order.

Type of network: _____wheel_____

c. When the high school debating team prepares for a challenge with another school, Ted and John prepare some arguments. Then John goes over their presentation with Chris. Chris checks it with Scott. Scott contacts Paul for new ideas. Paul works with Len who gets back to Ted. Next, Ted works with Scott. Paul calls John and Len and Chris work together.

Type of network: _____ *Con Com* _____

Exercise 13-10
Of the networks described in Exercise 13-9

a. Which two persons would be most satisfied with their interactions? _____

_____ ~~Concord~~ _____

b. Who would be least happy? _____ ~~circled~~ _____

c. Which would be the most efficient? _____

Turn to the Feedback section to compare your illustrations and answers.

Participation

Leavitt's research clearly emphasized the importance of participation. People who were actively involved in a network were more satisfied with their interactions. Consequently, employers have developed a keen interest in increasing participation by improving both downward and upward communication.

Downward communication is the passing of messages from upper management down to workers. Messages may include goals, praise, comments on achievements, or criticisms and suggestions for improvement. Downward communication is usually direct. *Upward communication* can move in a number of patterns. Sometimes employees work upward through a line of managers. Other times there are opportunities for direct encounters with the top person, as in coffee-with-the-boss meetings. Individual workers are invited to comment and make suggestions openly.

Suggestion boxes, questionnaires, and open-door policies are all attempts at improving upward communications. However, often these techniques are not effective. Employees sometimes feel their suggestions are ignored. Thus it is considered best to reply to suggestions with reasons why the proposal was

downward communication Passing messages from upper management down to workers

upward communication Passing information from workers up to management

psychological size
Perceived importance
of a person

accepted or rejected. Unfortunately, according to Davis (1977), an open-door policy too often means the door is open for the manager to walk out.

Upward communication is sometimes difficult because of a problem labeled "psychological size." Bosses often seem overwhelmingly important. Talking with someone of great importance makes you feel anxious and small by comparison. The problem worsens if the boss must be addressed by an impressive title, such as "Your Honor" or "Professor." A professor who sits on a platform behind a lectern increases not only physical size but also psychological size. Upward communication becomes difficult and unlikely.

Perhaps you have been able to detect differences in attitudes toward upward communication by checking seating arrangements. Often the professor behind a lectern on a platform has little concern about the opinions of students. On the other hand, an instructor who arranges seats in a circle and sits among students is probably trying to encourage communication. Psychologists have found that circular formations encourage the most communication.

But back to the boss. What seating arrangement will reduce psychological size sufficiently to permit an employee to speak freely and easily? Sommer (1969) checked out some possibilities. To encourage communication, the best arrangement is across the corner of a desk. Next best is directly across a desk. The worst is side by side.

Some employers prefer to delegate upward-communication problems. Harriman (1974) reported that some organizations assign specific persons to work on upward communication. Employees can contact the persons anonymously by telephone or letter and discuss difficulties. The assigned person then works on the problems.

Figure 13-21
Ms. Ralston is
increasing Mr. Beck's
psychological size.

Exercise 13-11

Imagine you are the mayor of a small town. Newspapers give excellent coverage to your town meetings and members of the community are fully aware of town ordinances and changes. However, you are concerned because people do not attend your town meetings, and you are therefore not aware of their concerns and problems. List six techniques you could use to improve upward communication.

a. _____

b. _____

c. _____

d. _____

e. _____

f. _____

Compare your strategies with the ones listed in the Feedback section.

Self-Disclosure

Self-disclosure requires an ability to speak honestly and fully about yourself. When you disclose yourself, you show yourself and your feelings so that others can understand you. Jourard (1971) claims that self-disclosure is essential for effective communication. To be sure, there is a risk in self-disclosure. You must supply even embarrassing information and give others a chance to view your vulnerable self. If you are afraid of being rejected or ridiculed, you are not likely to provide such insights.

    However, there are also clear benefits. By self-disclosure you show that you trust the other person. This usually deepens a relationship. The other person is then more likely to develop trust in you and disclose private thoughts. The process is slow and gradual. As the relationship grows, each person reveals more. Disclosure steadily increases, and the result is a mutually intimate relationship.

self-disclosure
Speaking honestly and revealing true feelings to others

The Johari Window

One way of studying self-disclosure is with a *Johari window* (see Figure 13-22). Although it may have a strange name, the Johari window is simply a square

Johari window System of quadrants used in the study of self-disclosure

Figure 13-22
The Johari window

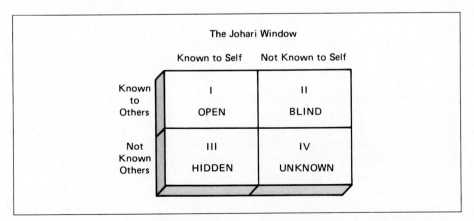

The Johari Window

	Known to Self	Not Known to Self
Known to Others	I OPEN	II BLIND
Not Known Others	III HIDDEN	IV UNKNOWN

with four quadrants. According to Luft (1970) the name was derived from a combination of the first names of its inventors, Joe Luft and Harry Ingham. Each quadrant of the Johari window describes an aspect in relationships between people.

Quadrant I: open. Quadrant I describes behavior that is known to both yourself and others. The color of your eyes, your sex, and other obvious physical information would be in this quadrant. Also included would be any information you wished to disclose to others. For example, suppose you scheduled a conference with your English instructor. The instructor knows nothing about you other than your appearance. If you open the conference by stating honestly, ''I feel nervous when I have to come for a conference,'' you immediately increase the size of quadrant I. Quadrant I reflects your self-disclosure.

Quadrant II: blind. In quadrant II lies information that is obvious to others but is concealed from yourself. It might include some annoying mannerisms. Perhaps you pace the floor or tap your foot or your pencils without realizing it. Many people are unaware that they constantly use words and expressions such as ''um,'' ''you know,'' or ''okay?'' However, everyone else is fully aware! Undoubtedly, you have seen people make complete fools of themselves. They may have thought they were extremely clever but observers shook their heads in disbelief. Or maybe you know people who cannot see that friends or relatives are manipulating them. In each of these cases, the individuals are blind to their own behavior.

Quadrant III: hidden. This quadrant describes information that is known to you but unknown to others. It may include such unimportant facts as the amount of coffee you drank yesterday or the brand of underwear you prefer. It will also include thoughts, feelings, and information that you are afraid to share because you fear embarrassment and ridicule. Most likely there are a few things that you are not proud of. You might hold back this information because you fear rejection.

Hidden information can complicate communication. Suppose three recreation workers, Peppy, Snaps, and Buddy, are setting up a schedule for their community center this month. Peppy wants to be sure she is free on her birthday but will not admit it to Snaps and Buddy. Although supposedly their agenda is to develop a practical schedule for the month, Peppy has a *hidden agenda,* or a special personal interest. She wants to schedule a day off on her birthday. As you might imagine, their meeting will probably last much longer than necessary. Peppy will reject any proposal that schedules her to work on her birthday.

Quadrant IV: unknown. In quadrant IV are your underlying motivations that are not known to anyone, even yourself. This quadrant is comprised primarily of unconscious feelings. For example, you might find yourself constantly arguing with your kid brother. You may not realize that you are really jealous of the attention he draws from your parents. He does not recognize your jealousy either and just sees you as a grouch.

The sizes of the quadrants in the Johari window change according to the type of relationship you are sharing with another person. Clearly you are more open with your lover or spouse and more hidden with casual acquaintances. Indeed, a casual acquaintance would probably be put off by your personal disclosures.

Exercise 13-12
Read each of the following descriptions of behavior and state in which quadrant of the Johari window each belongs.

a. A typing instructor constantly raps his fingers on his students' typewriters. He seems totally unaware of this behavior but it irritates his class. _____ *II Blind*

b. Dick had too much to drink last night. He has a severe headache but is smiling and acting cheerful. He fears people will think he has a drinking problem. _____ *III Hidden*

c. Mrs. Goode screamed, "I'm scared to death of these little creatures" when one of her second-grade students put his collection of frogs and worms on her desk. _____ *I Open*

d. An excellent actress always fears she will forget her lines. She has no reason for this fear and never has missed a line or a cue. _____ *IV Unknown*

Please turn to the Feedback section to check your answers.

Hidden Agendas
Quadrant III of the Johari window can create a barrier to effective communication. If someone has a *hidden agenda*, the conversation becomes overly lengthy. Other people become frustrated and conflicts can result. Bradford (1972) suggested watching for such clues to hidden agendas as increased tension or long discussions. If a hidden agenda is suspected, try to surface it with remarks such as, "Why is this problem taking so long? Perhaps we should discuss our feelings about it," or "Do you think we should discuss some other related problem?" It is usually best not to make others feel guilty about their hidden agendas. There will always be differences in opinions and perceptions.

hidden agenda
Important personal information that is not revealed to other members of a group

Checkpoint
Use the following questions to check your understanding of the final portion of this chapter. Indicate whether each statement is true or false.

18. __T__ Silence is a form of nonverbal communication.
19. __T__ If a stranger stood 2 feet away from you in an uncrowded area, you would feel uncomfortable.
20. __F__ Personal issues are usually discussed with people more than 4 feet away.
21. __T__ One-way communication is faster than two-way communication.

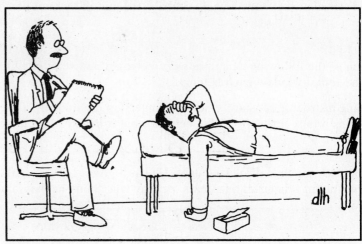

Cartoon by David Hanson

"I'm worried that if they do impose mandatory drug testing, the whole world is going to find out that I eat children's chewable vitamins!"

Figure 13-23
His hidden agenda
could interfere with a
discussion of
mandatory drug
testing.

22. __F__ One-way communication is more accurate than two-way communication.
23. __T__ In two-way communication the speaker is open to criticism.
24. __T__ The grapevine is an informal communication network.
25. __T__ A circle network has no leader.
26. __F__ In a Y arrangement network, everyone has equal power.
27. __F__ Members of wheel networks are most satisfied with their communications.
28. __F__ An increase in psychological size makes upward communication easier.
29. __T__ A suggestion box is an example of upward communication.
30. __F__ There is no risk to self-disclosure.
31. __T__ Self-disclosure builds trust.
32. __T__ Sizes of the quadrants in a Johari window can change.
33. __T__ Unconscious motives are included in quadrant II (blind) of a Johari window.
34. __F__ Hidden agendas usually shorten meetings.
35. __T__ It is best to try to surface hidden agendas.

Check your responses against the Checkpoint Answer Key at the end of the chapter. If you had difficulty with any question, reread the text. If you had little or no difficulty answering the questions or have resolved problems that you might have had, you are ready to check yourself against the chapter inventory that follows.

Use the list of objectives as a review checklist. You should be able to do each of the tasks outlined in the objective and apply them to everyday examples. If you can, you may feel confident that you have mastered the material in this chapter.

1. Describe the role of listening in communication.
2. Identify and provide examples of two types of listening problems.
3. List and discuss four ways to improve listening skills.
4. Identify and describe four ways to improve speaking skills.
5. Specify one advantage and two disadvantages to writing rather than speaking.
6. Differentiate between the denotation and connotations of words.
7. Describe the distinctive characteristics of the three states in transactional analysis: child, adult, and parent.
8. Define and provide examples of equal transactions, compatible transactions, and crossed transactions.
9. Distinguish between assertive and aggressive behavior.
10. Identify one limitation of art as a nonverbal form of communication.
11. Explain the role of appearance and body language in nonverbal communication.
12. List and describe four types of distance zones.
13. Compare the advantages and disadvantages of one-way and two-way communication.
14. Describe one type of informal communication network and four types of formal networks.
15. Distinguish between and provide examples of upward and downward communication.
16. List six possible ways to improve upward communication.
17. Define and explain the importance of self-disclosure.
18. Describe and provide examples for each quadrant of a Johari window.
19. Explain one method for bringing hidden agendas to the surface.

Feedback

The correct answers to the exercises follow. If you did not answer an exercise correctly, review the preceding pages and return to the exercise to correctly complete it.

13-1. *a.* Ms. Slicker should set a purpose for listening.
  b. She should avoid distractions while someone is talking. She should worry about the status of her gas gauge later.
  c. She should be more open-minded. Even though the mechanic has a twang, she might know her way around the countryside.
  d. She should ask questions if she feels she missed something. If she thinks she understood, she could paraphrase to be certain.
13-2. *a.* By thinking ahead, you can plan what you want to say.
  b. You will have greater control over the words you use and are more likely to be understood.
  c. You are more likely to hold the attention of listeners.
  d. You will get a more informative response.

13-3. *a.* The denotation is the dictionary definition.

   b. The connotation is the emotional association.

13-4. *a.* Look up "mechanic" in the dictionary.

   b. Hand out questionnaires asking people to measure the word on a number of dimensions.

13-5. *a.* P   P
          A   A
          C   C

   b. P   P
        A⇄A
        C   C

   c. P   P
        A   A
        C   C

13-6. *a.* A⇄A

   b. C⇄P

   c. P   P
        C   C

13-7. *a.* Jane is using her clothing and appearance to communicate that she is businesslike.

   b. Andy is using art to communicate his negative attitude toward his wife.

   c. Gretchen is telling her boss she does not want a personal relationship.

   d. Tessie is telling the young man she would like to have a personal conversation.

13-8. *a.* One-way

   b. Two-way

   c. Two-way

   d. One-way

   e. Two-way

13-9. *a.* Y arrangement (Figure 13-24)

   b. Wheel (Figure 13-25)

   c. Concom (Figure 13-26)

13-10. *a.* Carol and Goldie

   b. The chauffeur, the horse trainer, the tax attorney, the social secretary, and the household technician.

   c. The Y arrangement

13-11. *a.* Advertise "coffee with the mayor."

   b. Put up a suggestion box.

   c. Send out questionnaires.

   d. Announce an open-door policy and be available.

   e. Have people call you by your first name rather than "Your Honor" or "Mayor."

   f. Rearrange furniture to make it more conducive to communication.

13-12. *a.* Quadrant II: blind

   b. Quadrant III: hidden

   c. Quadrant I: open

   d. Quadrant IV: unknown

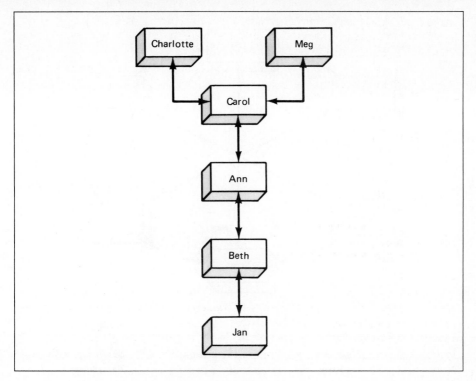

Figure 13-24
Y arrangement

Figure 13-25
Wheel

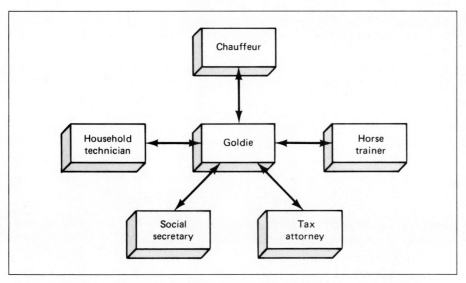

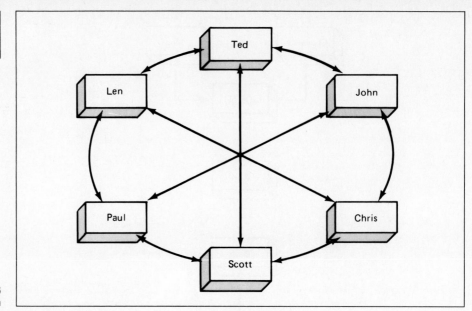

Figure 13-26
Concom

Checkpoint Answer Key

1. *c*	**10.** *c*	**19.** *true*	**28.** *false*
2. *b*	**11.** *b*	**20.** *false*	**29.** *true*
3. *a*	**12.** *a*	**21.** *true*	**30.** *false*
4. *b*	**13.** *b*	**22.** *false*	**31.** *true*
5. *a*	**14.** *d*	**23.** *true*	**32.** *true*
6. *a*	**15.** *a*	**24.** *true*	**33.** *false*
7. *d*	**16.** *d*	**25.** *true*	**34.** *false*
8. *c*	**17.** *c*	**26.** *false*	**35.** *true*
9. *c*	**18.** *true*	**27.** *false*	

CHAPTER 14

USING ATTITUDE THEORIES

A great many people think they are thinking when they are merely rearranging their prejudices.

William James

Have you ever been influenced by a television commercial? Try to analyze why your attitude was swayed by the ad. Why did you want to buy the product advertised? Perhaps it was endorsed by an expert. Or maybe some ordinary people like yourself claimed it was crackajack. Or you were impressed by some scientific research. Whether the product was a tennis racquet, mouthwash, plastic trash bags, or spaghetti sauce, the advertiser was probably using one of the many persuasion techniques found through research to influence people's attitudes. After reading this chapter you will be better able to examine the causes of people's attitudes and the inducements toward attitude change.

The chapter begins by differentiating between attitude, prejudice, and discrimination. Next, the causes of prejudice and positive or helping attitudes are explored. You will consider the many factors that influence people's attitudes toward each other. Finally, you will look at some methods that are used to persuade people and change their attitudes. Attention will focus on advertisements along with a brief description of brainwashing techniques.

ATTITUDES, PREJUDICE, AND DISCRIMINATION

To be sure, the three words in the heading are closely related. *Prejudice* is a type of *attitude*. *Discrimination* is the result of attitudes and can be caused by prejudice. But there are some clear distinctions in the meanings of the words. Next you will look at their meanings, along with some limitations in their relationships.

Attitudes

attitude Conviction based on beliefs, emotions, and behavior toward an object, person, or idea

Harrison (1976) identified three components in *attitudes:* beliefs, emotions, and behavior. Your *beliefs* are your basic values, or what you consider desirable and undesirable. Undoubtedly you have some stable underlying values. Perhaps you have strong convictions about freedom, independence, good health, close family relationships, money, or success. Any one of these values can influence many beliefs. For example, if good health is one of your important values, you probably believe people should eat nutritious foods, exercise, rest, and avoid alcohol and drugs. Similarly, if you value family relationships and success you will no doubt hold an assortment of beliefs that will promote better relationships within families and permit job advancement. Beliefs are the preferences that result from your values.

Emotions separate attitudes from opinions. Suppose a pollster asked a woman if she thought colleges should have book collections on earthquakes. She stops for a moment to think and replies, "Sure, why not." She then continues with her daily activities. She values education but does not have any emotional commitment about knowledge of earthquakes. If, on the other hand, she became upset about the lack of library books on earthquakes, her opinion would be developing into an attitude. Even if she felt annoyed that too many books on earthquakes were already available, she would be showing emotion. Feelings that accompany attitudes may be positive or negative, but they are never neutral.

Because attitudes are accompanied by emotions, there is almost always some form of *behavioral* result. You might simply speak out for or against an issue. If you feel more strongly, you might write a letter or contribute to a campaign. If you really have intense emotions, you might even run for public office. Even attitudes that do not bring on such noticeable actions have behavioral results. For example, suppose a man believes that a wealthy suburb is an ideal place to live. He loves the area but cannot afford any of the houses. Nonetheless, he spends some time daydreaming about his ideal home. His daydreaming is a behavior. Of course, if he ever inherits a fortune from a rich relative, you can probably guess how he will behave!

Exercise 14-1

Three components of attitudes have been described: *beliefs, emotions,* and *behavior*. Read the following scenario about a woman's attitude about abortion. In the space provided, identify signs of each of the three aspects of her attitude.

Adele feels that everyone should be entitled to personal freedom and total independence. Recently she has been arguing with friends who are members of the right-to-life movement. Adele contends that women should be permitted to decide for themselves whether or not they wish to bear a child. Disputes have become heated, and Adele once burst into tears when a friend called her a murderer. She feels angry that more women do not support her views.

a. Beliefs:_____

_____

_____

_____

b. Emotions: _____

_____

_____

_____

c. Behavior: _____

_____

_____

_____

The answers may be found in the Feedback section.

Prejudice

The word "prejudice" is derived from the Latin *praejudicium*, "a judgment based on previous experience." As the word was translated into English, it has come to mean a premature or snap judgment that is made before examining the facts. Today the meaning also usually includes a negative connotation.

prejudice Negative attitude based on a hasty judgment without facts

The negative attitude of prejudice is usually directed toward an out-group, people who are perceived to be different in some way. You may be prejudiced against people who are extremely overweight, or flashy dressers, or those who receive welfare checks. Most prejudices are against races, ethnic groups, religious minorities, and women.

History records several examples of racist prejudice. Racists believe that their group is superior to all others and therefore is entitled to special privileges. (An extreme example of racism is the attitude of German Nazis toward the Jewish people prior to World War II. Even in the United States, racism had been legalized through segregation laws.) Sexism refers to prejudice against women. Sexists maintain that women are inferior to men. A man who is sexist would feel extremely uncomfortable about working for a female boss and would not vote for a woman regardless of her abilities. Because prejudices, like all attitudes, are emotionally charged, they are difficult to change. In spite of information and evidence to the contrary, people stick to their old unjustified attitudes. Prejudices are acquired gradually and become a habitual way of thinking.

Perhaps by now you are looking around for those "awful" prejudiced people. You need not search far; everyone has some prejudices. For example, a woman may have a favorable attitude toward donating money to people who beg on street corners. She always has a coin for an outstretched hand. One day a man smelling of liquor asks for a handout. She has heard tales of alcoholics who ask for money to buy cheap wine and feels repulsed. She knows nothing about this particular man but is clearly biased against beggers with an aroma of alcohol. Her prejudice is based on an unjustified overgeneralization. But it is reasonable, in spite of her lack of sufficient evidence.

Exercise 14-2

In your own words describe the relationship between attitudes and prejudice.

_____

_____

_____

_____

You may check your reply in the Feedback section.

Discrimination

discrimination
Determining
differences and sorting
objects or people into
categories

Discrimination simply means deciphering differences or sorting items into categories. Undoubtedly you can discriminate between apples and peaches, adults and children, and males and females. Discrimination reflects an opinion but not necessarily a prejudice. For example, you probably differentiate between people whom you address by their first names and those whom you address by their titles and last names. A best friend would be shocked if you called him "Mr. Whoever" instead of "Joe" or "Harry." Similarly, unless your physician is a personal friend you probably call her "Doctor Whatsyourname" instead of "Jezabel" or "Tammy." Such discrimination is not related to negative attitudes.

Discrimination in hiring is inevitable. Jobs have qualifications, and an employer must distinguish among candidates who can do the job. A person who has completed courses and worked in data processing is probably a better candidate for a computer-programmer job than a person who studied wastewater treatment. Discrimination is clearly biased behavior, but it can be fair.

However, too often discrimination is unfair and stems strictly from prejudiced attitudes. A woman who chooses graduates of her alma mater over other job applicants is discriminating unfairly. Regardless of their education, experience, and abilities, graduates of other schools are not being considered. This form of discrimination has resulted not only in unequal hiring but also in unequal justice in the courts. Juries as well as judges have reflected prejudice and discrimination in their decisions. Prejudice is an attitude and discrimination is a behavior.

Have you ever served on a jury? If so, you are likely to be aware of the lengthy process involved in jury selection. Lawyers for both the prosecution and the defense ask extensive questions of all potential jurors. Both want to be certain that any discrimination will be in their favor. For example, assume a man is suing the owner of a poodle who bit his son. His lawyer would prefer a jury of parents who dislike dogs. The defense attorney would no doubt like to pick a jury of dog owners and humane society members who do not care for children. Each lawyer questions every potential juror and refuses to permit assignment of anyone who is likely to discriminate in an unfavorable way.

However, often people are either unaware of their prejudices or unwilling to admit to them. Bahr (1974) questioned white people about their attitudes toward American Indians. Although almost all stated that they wanted Indians to become part of the American culture, they did not want their children to have a close association with them.

What can be done to reduce unfair discrimination? Clearly this unfair behavior stems from prejudice. Although laws forbid discrimination based on sex, race, ethnic origin, or religion, prejudice and unfair behavior persist. An employer may unwillingly hire a person purely to conform with the law. The employer may then make unfair demands on the new employee. Legislation alone is not effective in removing discrimination caused by prejudice. Although the Civil Rights Act of 1964 guarantees equal employment opportunity, large differences in the salaries and job levels between men and women continue.

It is clear that laws alone cannot end unfair discrimination. One study (Langer, Bashner, & Chanowitz, 1985) attempted to teach sixth graders to use discrimination fairly. The researchers described this as *mindful discrimination*. They encouraged the sixth graders to be mindful by encouraging inventive thinking. The children discussed physical disabilities. They then decided whether specific disabilities would be an advantage or disadvantage in different situations. In one instance, the researchers showed the children pictures of two boys, one in a wheelchair and the other without a physical handicap. The students were then asked which boy they would prefer as a partner in checkers, soccer, and a wheelchair race. The researchers compared the responses of the trained children with another group of untrained sixth graders. The trained children made far more appropriate choices or discriminations. Perhaps future school programs will use these methods to increase ''mindful'' discrimination.

mindful discrimination Discrimination based on training and sound reasoning

reverse discrimination
Favoring a group that
elicits negative feelings

Occasionally people overreact to prejudices. They will bend over backwards to prove they are not prejudiced. As a result, they will discriminate in favor of a group they feel negatively about, or use *reverse discrimination*. For example, suppose a white man is prejudiced against black people. He often flies on business trips and prefers to work rather than converse with fellow passengers. On one trip a black man sits next to him. Although ordinarily he would not speak to the person next to him, he does not want the black man to think his silence is caused by prejudice. As a result, he starts a conversation. When people overreact to prejudice, they engage in behavior that they would not ordinarily.

Exercise 14-3
Discrimination can be caused by fair distinctions, prejudiced attitudes, or reverse discrimination. For each of the following examples, indicate which of these three factors is probably the cause of discrimination.

a. Nathan, a new student at college, does not want his fellow students to think he is prejudiced. Whenever he sees minority students in the cafeteria or at a library table he joins them, even though he prefers to eat and work alone.

_____

b. Lakefront Summer Camp will only hire swimming counselors who have passed a swimming test and have a lifesaving certificate. _____

_____

c. Arnold Livingston Cooper III does not want to have Jim Common accepted in his fraternity, since Jim's parents are not college graduates. _____

_____

d. Elvira refuses to hire any men. She claims men will not work well for a woman. _____

Exercise 14-4
Sometimes people who claim they are not prejudiced against a group will discriminate unfairly against them. Why might this occur? _____

_____

_____

To check your answers, please turn to the Feedback section.

FORMING ATTITUDES

Initially we all copy the attitudes of our parents. If your parents enjoyed jokes or fairy tales or books or intricate toys, you probably felt similarly. The location of your home and the school you attended were selected by your parents. Parents also choose the influences on their children. Many a mother and father have admonished their offspring to avoid playing with a rowdy child.

After parents select a school, their influence begins to decrease, while teachers and friends begin to contribute to the formation of attitudes. By adolescence, peers clearly become the most important influences on attitudes. Teenagers tend to assert their independence by rebelling against their parents' attitudes and clinging to the opinions of their friends. Newcomb (1963) studied the attitudes of Bennington College students over 25 years. Most students had come from families with conservative attitudes. The school faculty, however, had liberal attitudes and influenced the students. During their years at Bennington, students became more liberal and conformed to their faculty and peers. Newcomb found that over the 25-year period they stuck to their liberal attitudes. They did not revert to their parents' views.

Adolescents even conform in their attitudes toward clothing. Have you ever noticed their similarity in appearance? Adolescents feel more secure when they look alike. Zajonc (1968) concluded that people tend to have positive attitudes toward things and people who are familiar. The unfamiliar will be disliked. Perhaps this explains one reason for dressing in similar styles.

Exercise 14-5
In Figure 14-1, why might the sons have different attitudes than the fathers?

_____

_____

Turn to the Feedback section to check your response.

Figure 14-1

"Yeah, my son's the same kind of phony liberal—billions for
the Third World, zip for Chrysler."

First Impressions

Often first impressions are based on past experiences. If you are accustomed to talking with women in jeans, you will feel more comfortable with and probably like them. Similarly, if you meet someone who reminds you of an old buddy, he will probably make a good first impression. Have you ever met someone you instantly disliked? Think about some of the characteristics that have created positive and negative first impressions.

People often form strong first impressions for unusual reasons. A study reported by Horn (1980) found that waitresses could win heavier tips by wearing a flower in their hair. The study reported in Exhibit 14-1 noted that teachers rated tall boys and slim girls more favorably than short boys and heavy girls.

Checkpoint

Use the following questions to check your understanding of this portion of the chapter. Choose and mark the one correct response to each question.

1. According to Harrison, what are three essential ingredients in attitudes?
    a. Beliefs, prejudices, and values
    b. Values, emotions, and prejudices
    c. Beliefs, emotions, and behavior
    d. Beliefs, values, and convictions
2. The owner of a grocery store believes that shoplifters should be arrested or fined. What is this belief based on?
    a. A prejudice
    b. A basic value
    c. Racism
    d. An overgeneralization

EXHIBIT 14-1

A Sizable Advantage

People view tall men and slender women more favorably, giving them an edge in society, love and career. Now evidence suggests that such people may begin reaping these advantages as early as kindergarten.

Researchers had 18 teachers of 388 students in kindergarten through fourth grade rate each child's academic, athletic and social skills.

The teachers rated the larger boys higher on all counts, especially the older ones. At the end of the year they gave the bigger boys better grades.

For girls, however, bulkiness is taboo. Girls who weighed more were rated lower in academic, athletic and social skills, and teachers gave larger girls lower grades. As with boys, the effects were more pronounced for older girls.

"Teachers' attributions tend to reflect the cultural stereotypes that tallness is advantageous for males, whereas heaviness is disadvantageous for females," say psychologist Nancy Eisenberg of Arizona State University and her colleagues.

Physical size is said to be related to a child's mental development, but that would only explain why large boys do better, not girls. "Thus, a more plausible explanation is that teachers were influenced by stereotypes concerning males' physical size, and their expectations for large boys led them to give more attention and encouragement to these boys," the researchers conclude in *Sex Roles* (Vol. 15, pp. 667–681).

Source: Bozzi, V. (1988, February). A sizable advantage. *Psychology Today.*

3. How do attitudes differ from opinions?
    a. Attitudes involve emotions.
    b. Opinions involve emotions.
    c. Opinions are usually negative.
    d. Attitudes are usually negative.

4. Which of the following definitions best describes the current meaning of
   "prejudice"?
    a. A negative snap judgment that is not based on facts
    b. A positive or negative premature judgment
    c. A judgment based on previous experience
    d. A negative attitude toward other races
5. The owner of an apartment building claims that she has no prejudices
   against any groups. Yet she will not rent apartments to Jewish people. How
   can her behavior be explained?
    a. She may be unaware of her prejudices or unwilling to admit them.
    b. She is discriminating fairly and not showing prejudice.
    c. She is overreacting to her prejudices and showing reverse discrimina-
       tion.
    d. Her discriminating behavior is consistent with not being prejudiced.
6. Who was first to influence your attitudes?
    a. Your parents
    b. Your friends
    c. Your teachers
    d. Your brothers and sisters
7. Who is most likely to make the best first impression?
    a. A person who dresses differently
    b. A person who wears elaborate or dressy clothing
    c. A person who looks unfamiliar
    d. A person who looks familiar

Check your responses against the Checkpoint Answer Key at the end of the chapter. If you had difficulty with any question, reread the text. If you had little or no
difficulty answering the questions or have resolved problems that you might have
had, you are ready to continue with the next portion of this chapter.

Negative and Positive Attitudes

Since attitudes cannot be neutral (remember the emotion factor), your parents,
schools, and friends have instilled in you either positive or negative attitudes.
Your negative attitudes lead to disagreements, arguments, conflicts, or other
confrontations. Prejudice is a key factor in negative attitudes. On the other
hand, positive attitudes can induce you to assist other people, to be caring and
unselfish. Next you will consider the reasons behind prejudices (negative attitudes) and helping behavior (positive attitudes).

Forming Prejudices

Allport (1958) described two general sources of prejudice: personal concerns
and group conformity. *Personal concerns* include fears and worries about another group being a threat to you as an individual. *Group conformity* implies
that you go along with your peers in disliking an out-group, even though the

out-group is not a personal threat to you. Psychologists have studied the causes of prejudice in each of these categories.

Personal concerns. A prime cause of personal prejudice is the concern for *economic survival*. Assume you are working as a window washer at $5 an hour. An immigrant from Ugliopia is willing to complete your hourly tasks for only $4. You begin to develop a dislike for Ugliopians. They are a threat to you and can steal your job.

Bettelheim and Janowitz (1950) studied the attitudes of white, gentile World War II veterans. Veterans who did not obtain jobs as good as the ones they had before the war were more anti-Semitic and antiblack than veterans who found as good or better jobs. The minorities were blamed for taking jobs and opportunities away from others.

In large cities, *overcrowding* has been a cause of personal prejudice. If there has been an influx of Ugliopians and you cannot find a seat on the subway, are pushed off sidewalks, and never have a place to park your car, you are likely to blame the newcomers. The most recent immigrants are blamed for the overcrowding. In the United States during the early 1900s the Irish, Italians, and Jews were the victims of prejudice and discrimination. Later, blacks and Puerto Ricans were considered the culprits.

Figure 14-2
Ernie is likely to develop a prejudice toward elephants.

To Ernie's horror, and the ultimate disaster of all,
one more elephant tried to squeeze on.

Another cause of personal prejudice is *conflict and competition*. If you fear a group is threatening your life or the lives of your group, you will undoubtedly develop some very strong negative attitudes. Consider the attitudes of Americans toward the Japanese and German people during World War II. Iranians were unpopular during the hostage crisis of 1979–1980. Conflicts and battles clearly promote prejudice.

Groups that compete with each other generally develop prejudices against each other. Even when money or lives are not involved in the competition, strong negative attitudes can be generated. People who navigate sailboats are often irritated by owners of motorboats who do not give them the right-of-way or create unnecessary waves. Skippers of sailboats refer to motorboats as "stinkpots" and often consider their owners inferior. Similarly it is common for fraternity brothers and sorority sisters to have prejudiced attitudes against members of other fraternities and sororities. Consider the attitudes of Republican and Democratic activists toward each other!

Another cause of prejudice is *fear of the unknown*. Most people are comfortable in familiar situations with persons who are similar to themselves. A person who wears unusual native dress or has different cultural customs can seem a threat. Reasons for not associating are conjured up, and prejudices result. Studies have found that the attitudes of preschool children toward the elderly vary. Children who are unfamiliar with older people show clear prejudices. According to the article in Exhibit 14-2, physicians have developed prejudiced attitudes toward AIDS patients.

Individuals can derive personal satisfaction from their prejudices. Anger and hostility can be released. The target of prejudice becomes a *scapegoat* and

EXHIBIT 14-2

Phobic Physicians

An AIDS phobia may exist within the medical community and it could be affecting the way in which AIDS patients are treated, according to two recent studies by psychologist Jeffrey Kelly and his coworkers at the University of Mississippi.

In the first study, Kelly and colleagues presented one of four versions of a case report to 157 physicians from Ohio, Tennessee and Arizona, who, on average, had practiced for 20 years. The patient, "Mark," had the same symptoms in each version of the report, but he was identified as either an AIDS patient or a leukemia patient and as either a homosexual or a heterosexual.

Whether he was depicted as a homosexual or as a heterosexual, the AIDS patient was viewed by physicians as more responsible for his illness, more deserving of what happened to him, less deserving of sympathy and understanding, more dangerous to others and more deserving of quarantine than the leukemia patient was.

Physicians were also less willing to talk to an AIDS patient in comparison with the leukemia patient, attend a party with him or one where he prepared food, work in the same office, continue a past friendship, renew his apartment lease or allow their children to visit him.

Would a younger generation be more tolerant? Hardly. The researchers repeated the study with 119 second- and third-year students attending a Southern medical school. Not only did the students also judge the AIDS patient as more responsible and more deserving of his illness, they also thought he deserved to die more than the leukemia patient did.

Source: McCarthy, P. (1988, March). Phobic physicians. *Psychology Today.*

self-fulfilling prophecy
Making a prediction
and acting in a way to
ensure that it will
come true

is blamed for economic, social, and achievement problems. The prejudiced person can feel superior to the scapegoat. Because satisfaction accompanies personal prejudice, it is difficult to change. Further, as disclosed by Merton (1948) a *self-fulfilling prophecy* is also associated with prejudice. If you are prejudiced against a person, you will undoubtedly be unkind and unfair. The person in turn will respond in a negative way. This will convince you that your original attitude was accurate. A teacher who dislikes the young boys in her class might punish them unnecessarily. As a result they might become disrespectful toward her, perhaps using obscenities or making rude remarks. Their behavior would assure her that she was correct in assuming that little boys are rude and not to be trusted.

Exercise 14-6

Four possible causes of personal prejudice have been described: economic survival, overcrowding, conflict and competition, fear of the unknown. Read each of the following descriptions of prejudice and indicate the probable cause.

a. Mark is fed up with the increasing bumper-to-bumper traffic when he commutes to work. He is convinced it is caused by too many women working. He claims women are poor drivers, inefficient, and uncoordinated.

_____

b. The Hatfords were upset when a family from Saudi Arabia moved next door. They are afraid to talk with their new neighbors, who appear to be quite different.

_____

c. Nick's soccer team, the Kicks, lost to the Stops, 8–0. Nick claims all the team members of the Stops are rude and snobbish.

_____

d. The women's club of Biastown voted not to allow women to join until they have lived in Biastown for at least five years. They claimed they want to be sure of their members.

_____

e. Eliza quit her job to stay home and raise her children. When she decided to go back to work she had trouble finding a position at the same salary. She claims that incompetent black men and women are stealing jobs.

_____

Exercise 14-7

List two reasons why it is difficult to change personal prejudices.

a. _____

b. _____

You may find the correct answers in the Feedback section.

Group conformity. Often people change their beliefs to make them agree with the beliefs of a group. As mentioned earlier, adolescents will switch their attitudes to conform with their peers. Even if their parents were open-minded, a few prejudiced friends can convince youngsters to comply with their thinking. The out-group can even be former friends. But group conformity is not limited to adolescents. Adults also adopt the prejudices of their groups. A man who is promoted and now eats in the executive lounge may feel uncomfortable about bringing one of his former coworkers to dine with his new group. He may even shun his former buddies, since they are not accepted in his new social class.

Similarly, if your neighbors are upset about too many minorities moving into the community, you may begin to feel the pressure even if you are not prejudiced yourself. When selling your house, you might discourage minorities by pointing out the negative features. Chapter 15 covers the influence of groups on attitudes in more detail.

Exercise 14-8
Macho College, a traditional all-male school, began admitting women ten years ago. The alumni association maintains several college clubs throughout the country. None of these clubs admit women. A survey found that since women have been enrolled in the school, individual male students view the women as equals. Why might the prejudice persist in the alumni association?

_____

_____

_____

To check your response, turn to the Feedback section.

Helping Attitudes

Have you ever had car trouble and felt helpless? You may have raised the hood, flashed the blinkers, and wondered if someone—anyone—would come along and offer some assistance. Assuming you were not waving $10 at passers-by, the help you needed would stem from a person's altruism. *Altruism* is helping without expecting any reward or benefit. According to psychologists, whether or not you received altruistic help would depend on the following factors:

altruism Concern for others; helping others without expecting a reward or benefit

The number of observers. If you were on a crowded highway, your chances of getting help would decrease. Surprisingly, if cars went by you infrequently, you would have a better chance of someone stopping. A shocking murder case in Queens, New York, in 1964 sparked the interest of social psychologists concerned with altruism. A young woman, Kitty Genovese, was stabbed during an attack that lasted more than thirty minutes. More than thirty-eight neighbors in an apartment building admitted witnessing the struggle. Twice, people turned on lights and almost scared the attacker away. But he returned to murder her. Not one person called the police or tried to help the victim. Psychologists claim there is a "bystander effect"; the more people who witness a problem, the less likely that someone will interfere and help.

"Before we set out, there's this little matter of a waiver."

Figure 14-3
There seems to be a
limit to this boy scout's
altruism.

In an experiment on the bystander effect, Latané and Darley (1968) sent subjects into a room to complete a questionnaire. Supposedly, they were to fill in the forms while waiting for an interviewer. In one situation, subjects were alone in the room. Irregular bursts of smoke came out from under a door that led to another room. Fully 75 percent of the subjects reported the problem promptly. In a second experimental condition, a subject was sent to a room with two confederates (fake subjects assisting the experimenter). The confederates ignored the bursts of smoke initially. As it continued, they remained calm and apathetic and just brushed it away. Ten subjects were used individually with the confederates; only one reported the problem. In the third situation two subjects were sent to the questionnaire room. Thirty percent reported the smoke, but they took much longer than subjects who were alone.

In another experiment involving the bystander effect, Latané and Darley (1970) observed helping behavior among subjects who overheard another subject suffer a (fake) epileptic seizure. Each subject was assigned to a cubicle and seated in front of a microphone. The experimenter described the experimental conditions over an intercom. Subjects believed they simply were discussing adjustment problems with other students. One group of subjects believed they were communicating with only one other subject. Another group believed there were two others. A third group believed there were five subjects. In each situation, subjects believed a person in their communication network had epilepsy. A recording described epileptic problems; the voice began to choke, called for help, and expressed fears of dying. The subjects' reactions varied according to how many listeners they thought were present. All subjects who believed they were the only person to hear the seizure responded quickly. Subjects who believed another person overheard the seizure took longer and only 85 percent responded. When subjects thought four others were listening, they took more than 3 times longer and only 62 percent responded.

People seem to be reluctant to help if they believe others are available. Responsibility can be shared with the others. Each person looks to another and no one helps. Since no one is helping, one person does not want to appear different or foolish. The result is a bystander effect.

Location. Back to your car problem. Would you rather break down in the city or in the country? As you might have suspected, help is more likely in the country. Milgram (1970) and Korte and Kerr (1975) found that city dwellers are more indifferent and apathetic than rural residents. The general level of friendliness and socializing seems to be much higher when a country atmosphere is introduced, even in a city. Rubenstein (1981) reported that shoppers at a city farmers market are far more outgoing than those in a city supermarket.

Levine et al. (1976) concluded that city residents are less friendly and helpful because they are more vulnerable and threatened. Clearly there is more crime in cities. City people were less willing to let a stranger in their home than were people from small towns. Nonetheless, city residents were willing to assist strangers by making a phone call while the stranger waited outside.

Appearance. How you are dressed when your car breaks down could also make a difference. As mentioned earlier, people tend to be more trusting and accepting of someone who looks similar to them. A man with a button-down oxford shirt is more likely to be helped by another conservative than by the leader of a motorcycle gang. On the other hand, a young man in a leather jacket, boots, and a hard helmet will probably be assisted by a motorcycle gang rather than by an executive in a pin-striped suit.

Previous observations. If someone else had car problems on the highway and was receiving assistance, you would be more likely to find help. In a number of different studies psychologists have noted that people who see another person giving help are more likely to be altruistic themselves. In an interesting study by Macauley (1970), donations to a sidewalk Santa Claus and a Salvation Army kettle were observed. People who had seen another person making a donation were more likely to contribute.

Weather. Unfortunately, if you were standing out in the rain with your broken-down car, you would be less likely to receive any help. Although it is difficult to reason why, people are less altruistic on cloudy and rainy days. Apparently sunshine brings out the goodness and kindness in people.

Self-esteem. Suppose all the conditions for help were negative. Imagine you were in heavy city traffic on a cloudy day, dressed as Dracula on your way to a costume party. Several people had car problems, but no one was receiving help. Sound hopeless? A study by Michelini et al. (1975) offers some encouragement. They found that people with high self-esteem are more likely to help others, regardless of the situation. Take heart. In your moment of despair a person with a good self-image could come along and repair your car.

Exercise 14-9

In each of the following sets of cases, one person is more likely to receive help. Indicate which person has a better chance, and explain the reason for your choice.

a. Jim dropped his comb on a crowded sidewalk in the zoo.

or

Mitch's pen dropped out of his pocket while he was taking a closer look at a tulip at the flower show. There were only three other people at the tulip exhibition.

_____

_____

b. Gertrude falls and cuts her knee. She notices that Michelle, the president of the senior class and star of the soccer team, is coming along the walkway.

or

Naomi slips on a banana peel and her books are spread all over the grass. Eunice is out for a stroll on the green, trying to shake her depression.

_____

_____

c. Richard's umbrella blows inside out in a severe rainstorm.

or

Edward is having difficulty setting up his beach umbrella on a hot sunny day.

_____

_____

d. Cecilia cannot find a restaurant in Chicago.

or

Paula is having difficulty finding a hotel in Staple, New Mexico.

_____

_____

e. The entire ski patrol was out helping people who were skidding on the icy trails. Janice also skidded and was having trouble getting up.

or

Lots of fallen skiers were along the trails. People were skiing around them. Edith slipped and joined the ranks of the fallen.

_____

_____

f. Ben was letting his hair and beard grow for a part in a local play. He was wearing shabby old clothes, since he expected to paint sets and move equipment. When he realized he had forgotten his wallet, he decided to ask people coming out of office buildings if he could borrow change for a phone call.

or

Luke was wearing his school varsity football jacket when he realized he had left his car keys back in his locker. When he returned to the athletic building he realized that it was locked for the night. He decided to try to borrow taxi fare from some young men outside the building.

_____

_____

You may check your choices in the Feedback section.

Developing Altruistic Attitudes

To be sure, altruistic attitudes are extremely desirable. But with fears and personal concerns, people do not always behave in the best interest of others. Psychologists have found that altruistic behavior is present in young children. One study examined the altruistic behavior of children from six countries: India, Kenya, Mexico, Japan, the Philippines, and the United States (Whiting & Whiting, 1975). American children were the least altruistic. Societies where children had family responsibilities and strong respect for their parents had the most altruistic children.

Checkpoint

Use the following questions to check your understanding of this portion of the chapter. Choose and mark the one correct response to each question.

8. What types of attitudes can you have?
   a. Positive and neutral
   b. Neutral and negative
   c. Positive and negative
   d. Positive, negative, and neutral
9. Bettleheim and Janowitz found that veterans who could not find satisfactory jobs after World War II were more prejudiced than veterans who were content with their jobs. What was the likely cause of prejudice?
   a. Overcrowding
   b. Economic survival
   c. Fear of the unknown
   d. Group conformity

10. Personal prejudice can result from hostility. What is the target of this hostility called?
    a. A self-fulfilling prophet
    b. A conformist
    c. An altruist
    d. A scapegoat
11. You tend to treat people unfavorably if you are prejudiced against them. As a result they often behave badly toward you. What is this interaction called?
    a. Fear of the unknown
    b. Group conformity
    c. Self-fulfilling prophecy
    d. Altruism
12. A person who has no cause for personal prejudice often has biased attitudes against a group. Which of the following could contribute to this prejudice?
    a. Group conformity
    b. Altruism
    c. The bystander effect
    d. Weather
13. Henry saw a man drop a grocery bag on the sidewalk. Henry helped him pick up the products and offered to get a new bag for the man. Which term best describes Henry's attitude?
    a. Conformity
    b. Altruism
    c. Overcrowding
    d. Competition
14. What is a bystander effect?
    a. When many people view a problem, help is likely.
    b. When many people view a problem, help is unlikely.
    c. A city atmosphere encourages helping behavior.
    d. Bystanders with high self-esteem are unlikely to help.
15. Which type of weather seems to encourage helping behavior?
    a. Clouds
    b. Rain
    c. Sunshine
    d. Snow

Check your responses against the Checkpoint Answer Key at the end of the chapter. If you had difficulty with any questions, reread the text. If you had little or no difficulty answering the questions or have resolved problems that you might have had, you are ready to continue with the next portion of this chapter.

INFLUENCING AND CHANGING ATTITUDES

Whether your attitudes are good or bad (and you know they cannot be indifferent), they can be changed. Within a single day you probably shift and alter attitudes several times. Perhaps you want to go to a party but your friend prefers a movie. After your buddy provokes your interest in the film by listing the outstanding cast and discussing the intriguing plot, you become convinced the movie is a better idea. Or maybe you rarely read magazines. Your television blares an ad claiming people who read *Popularity* magazine are more successful and happier. You find yourself agreeing and calling their toll-free number to order a subscription.

Both the advertiser and your buddy were making deliberate attempts to change your attitudes. Such deliberate attempts constitute **persuasion**. As you probably suspect, some methods of persuasion are more effective than others. The type of person persuading you and the method being used can both influence whether or not you change your attitude.

Persuaders

The most crucial characteristics of a person who is trying to persuade others is **credibility** (Aronson et al., 1963). You must be able to trust the person and believe statements if you are to change your attitude. To be sure, an expert in a field has credibility. When Tracy Austin claims a brand of tennis shoes is durable and comfortable, people will believe her. Likewise, if a famous doctor recommends a particular brand of medication, he will be convincing.

Attractive people usually have more credibility than unattractive people. You may have noticed that magazine ads often show attractive men and women with products. Frequently the alluring people have nothing to do with the product. Their presence is expected to give the ad credibility. A study reported by Pecoraro (1981) concluded that jurors are more likely to believe attractive people, whether they are defendants or victims.

Even people who are neither experts nor overwhelmingly attractive will be believed if they are famous or well-known. You are more likely to be convinced by a statement from a familiar face than from one you have never seen before. You are also more likely to vote for a name you have heard. As a result, before an election, bumper stickers and posters with candidates' names are everywhere.

Have you ever noticed how famous people and experts seem down-to-earth in television advertisements? Several studies have shown you are more likely to be persuaded by a person who you believe is much like yourself. A person who is similar to you is more convincing. Because advertisers are attempting to appeal to average television viewers, a single ad may have several different types of people endorsing a product. A bar of soap will be proclaimed "terrific" by a toddler, a teenager, a working man, a housewife, a career woman, a fat man, and a senior citizen.

Persuasion is most effective when a listener thinks the speaker has nothing to gain from the attitude change. If a car dealer raves about the cars she sells, you might be skeptical. Clearly, she will profit if you buy one of her cars. However, if a woman who is not in the automobile business recommends a type of car, you are more likely to believe her. Walster and Festinger (1962) found that messages that are overheard are more convincing than ones spoken directly to you. When you overhear a conversation, you assume the message is not being directed at you. Thus, the person is not really trying to convince you. Commercials that show people who are supposedly unaware of the cameras are aimed at convincing viewers that they are witnessing and overhearing an actual conversation.

Exercise 14-10

List five characteristics that would make a person a successful persuader.

a. _____

b. _____

c. _____

d. _____

e. _____

You may compare your list to the answers in the Feedback section.

Persuasion Techniques

Suppose you wanted to convince people to sign up for a course in applied psychology. As a first step you could attempt to combine the characteristics of a successful persuader. You might have a famous, attractive, down-to-earth psychologist whisper loudly that applied psychology courses are super. But you may also want to consider some other strategies. As you are aware, people have reasons for not taking courses: insufficient time and money, work pressures, and other responsibilities. Should the psychologists present the opposite side of the argument as well? Research has shown that if the audience is well-informed and intelligent it is more likely to be persuaded if it hears a two-sided argument. If the audience is clearly opposed to your view, it is best to give its side first. For example, your famous psychologist may begin, "I know most people have many personal pressures and responsibilities and that money is tight. But if at all possible, they really would benefit from an applied psychology course. The course can actually help you reduce pressures and be more successful. Why I know one student who..." The many arguments in favor of the course could then be presented. The psychologist shot down the opposing argument before presenting the case. An audience that is leaning toward you may not need to hear the opposing view. Similarly, people of limited intelligence can become confused by a lengthy two-sided argument.

Psychologists and advertisers have discovered a number of specific techniques that effectively persuade people.

Emotional appeals. Television commercials often use emotional appeals. Some ads scare you into buying products, others make you feel homey, still others promise you popularity. Janis and Feshback (1953) experimented on the effects of scare tactics in changing attitudes. They divided subjects into two groups. The first group was given some mildly upsetting information. They were presented statistics on the relationship between poor oral hygiene and dental and gum problems. The second group was given more threatening and fear-arousing information. They were shown actual photographs of decayed teeth and diseased gums. Subjects in the first group improved their dental hygiene habits more than the people in the second group. The experimenters concluded that weak or moderate fear is more effective in changing attitudes than intense threats. No doubt you can recognize some mildly fearful ads. Commercials for deodorants, soaps, mouthwash, denture adhesive, tires, and batteries usually begin with someone suffering rejection or facing a problem.

Other emotional appeals have been pleasant. Products are sometimes associated with a warm, loving, old-fashioned, homey atmosphere. Recall commercials that refer to products that grandmother used to use. Whether cookies, breads, fruit punch, or spaghetti sauce, tracing the product to a family in the olden days brings added appeal. Indeed, if grandmother endorses it as tasting "homemade," sales will no doubt increase.

Another common emotional appeal is to a need for popularity. If you use a softener in your washing machine, everyone will thank you and appreciate you. This type of ad also insinuates that fabric softeners are important. Or you might prefer to gain your popularity by looking sexier in a certain brand of jeans. Then again, according to the ads, wearing the right perfume and purchasing the correct brand of sherry will also win intimate friendships.

Dissonance. Changing attitudes through *dissonance* was suggested by Festinger (1962). Festinger held that if you do the opposite of what you believe, you will become uncomfortable and tense. As a result of your tension, you will change your attitude. For example, suppose that you always believed that people who collect insects are rather strange. You find that an insect collection is required in your biology class. You spend several months collecting crawling creatures and pinning them in an old cigar box. Festinger claims that if you continue to behave in a way that is the opposite of your attitude, you will create a dissonance. Chances are you will change your attitude about insect collectors and recognize that there may be some reason and merits to their work. The study that is reported in Exhibit 14-3 found that people who were simply asked about whether or not they intended to vote, were, in fact, significantly more likely to do so.

McGuire (1961) found that people who agreed with logic in one situation would transfer the same reasoning to another situation. Dissonance and attitude change would result. Analogies were the method used. Again, advertisers have capitalized on the method. The commercial may begin with the statement that engines need oil or they will dry out and age prematurely. You are nodding your head in agreement. Next a picture of human skin is flashed. The ad continues warning you that skin that is not fed oil will also dry out and age. Even if you had not been keen on skin preparations, the motor analogy created a dissonance and there is a chance you will purchase the product.

In one instance, the analogy-dissonance method has been used to improve relationships between normal children and handicapped children. In trying to bring handicapped children into the mainstream of public schools, leaders found that normal children were fearful of the handicapped and had negative attitudes. A Washington, D.C., group began giving puppet shows about the handicapped. Each puppet represented a person with a different disability. One puppet was in a wheelchair, another was retarded, another was missing limbs. The children were encouraged to converse with the puppets and ask questions. Organizers of the shows found that normal children showed marked changes in attitudes after chatting with puppets. The analogy was made between the puppets and live children.

Foot in the door. Everyone is familiar with the image of a traveling salesman sticking his foot in a doorway so the person cannot close the door. The salesman's method is obvious. Psychologists have discovered several subtle

dissonance Discomfort that occurs from two inconsistent thoughts or beliefs

EXHIBIT 14-3

More Votes: Just Ask

Getting out the vote is no easy matter. Various schemes, such as keeping the polls open longer, declaring Election Day a holiday or holding it on Sunday, have been proposed or tried. University of Washington psychologist Anthony G. Greenwald and his coworkers wondered if merely asking people to predict whether they would vote would make them more likely to do so.

When people are asked whether they will perform some socially desirable act, contribute to charity, for example, they exaggerate their intention to do so. Studies suggest, however, that just asking the question makes people more likely to contribute than they would be if not asked to.

To test whether this can be applied to voting, the researchers conducted two studies just before the November 1984 election. In the first, the researchers phoned 62 students who were not registered one or two days prior to the Ohio deadline. The students were asked if they knew when the deadline was and where to register. About half were then thanked for their help, while the remaining students were asked if they intended to register.

When the researchers compared the actual registration rates between the two groups, they found that those who had been asked whether they would register were about 10 percent more likely to do so. This difference, however, was not statistically significant, they note in the *Journal of Applied Psychology* (Vol. 72, pp. 315–318).

The evening before Election Day, the researchers questioned other students about the location of their polling place and its hours. As in the first experiment, about half of the students were then thanked for their time, while the rest were asked whether they would vote.

This time there were real differences between the two groups of students; about 25 percent more voted from the group that were asked whether they planned to vote than those who were not asked.

Greenwald and colleagues say it is unclear why prior questioning obtained statistically significant results for voting but not for registration. But "in a large-scale application," they say, "even the weak effect [for registration] could be of great importance; and the effect observed [for voting] is certainly large enough to alter the outcome of an election."

Source: McCarthy, P. (1988, March). More votes: Just ask. *Psychology Today.*

ways to achieve the same purpose. Lanser (1973) observed that a salesperson can get you to agree on a number of unrelated things. Maybe the weather is getting colder, the cost of gasoline is increasing, skiing is a wonderful sport, or Hawaii is a beautiful vacation spot. Since you are in agreement on so many issues, you begin to feel that you both think alike. Next the salesperson pulls out a contract and gets you to agree to make a purchase.

Freedman and Fraser (1966) suggested that requests can be used similarly. A salesperson begins by making small requests such as, "Could I have just two or three minutes of your time?" "Would you take a second and look at this folder?" "May I ask you a few questions?" After you have been continually agreeing and complying, you are asked to sign a contract for a purchase.

Recently, psychologists have worked as court consultants for lawyers. They help lawyers construct strong opening statements that will set a framework. This helps lawyers get a foot in the door as they slide in their evidence (see Exhibit 14-4).

EXHIBIT 14-4

421

USING ATTITUDE
THEORIES

Trial Consultants' Job: Making the Facts Clear

Psychologists are going to court in growing numbers these days, not as witnesses, but to work with lawyers as trial consultants.

Gail Sutton-Barbere, who has been studying jury decision-making since writing her dissertation on the subject in 1977, said in a session at the Rocky Mountain Psychological Association meeting here this spring that 80 percent of the work she does at her firm, Trial Sciences in Albuquerque, centers on the clear presentation of evidence.

Attorneys are particularly interested in knowing whether a jury will understand evidence that is highly technical, she said.

Sutton-Barbere said she advises attorneys to carefully construct their opening and closing statements to give their presentations coherence.

In too many opening statements, she said, attorneys leave out the red flags that may help highlight upcoming issues in what could become hours of testimony.

After hearing a well-constructed opening, a jury knows what will be important, she said.

A good closing statement should repeat the opening and review the evidence that has been presented on each issue. The result is, Sutton-Barbere said, "a consistent framework."

"Go for the framework," she emphasized, "and slide the evidence in."

Sutton-Barbere uses simulated trials to predict how evidence is likely to be accepted by a jury. These simulations, which can be simple or elaborate, are abbreviated trials presented to a group of mock jurors in order to assess their reactions. Sutton-Barbere finds her mock jurors through ads in newspapers, from jury panels of trials already held, or sometimes through random phone calls.

The results of such simulations can help attorneys decide what evidence, presented in what manner, will be understood most clearly by a real jury.

"Sometimes an attorney has three or four legal issues to present," she says. For example, in a product liability case, the issues could include whether a manufacturer received a prior complaint about a product and therefore knew there was a problem; whether the product was designed defectively; or whether there was something about the warning label that did not effectively alert consumers to possible danger.

Psychologists, with their training in research, have a lot to add to an attorney's presentation, Sutton-Barbere says. Yet, she cautions, a psychologist is still "making giant leaps from research to actuality and must be comfortable doing this."

Attorneys are naturally interested in what the trial consultant can do to help them win a case. Sutton-Barbere said she tells them that "juries will do their best to be fair and to follow directions."

She said that while she has never been asked for ways to downplay certain evidence, she has been asked to offer advice on how to make the evidence less than clear and has turned those requests down.

Sutton-Barbere began her study of courtroom procedures by sitting through four or five trials and investing in some law books. "Working with attorneys has been an education," she added.

Studying juries and how they operate is vital for the psychologist interested in trail consulting, says Sutton-Barbere. "Attorneys don't feel they have a good grasp of how juries work."

Source: Landers, S. (1987, August). Trial consultants' job: Making the facts clear. *APA Monitor.*

reactance Strong resistance that results from receiving high-pressure persuasion and often causes a person to do the opposite of what is asked

Negative psychology. Have you ever been irritated by a high-pressure salesperson? Brehm (1966) claimed that if you get high-pressure treatment you will resist and try to assert your freedom and independence. He labeled this resistance and assertiveness "reactance." When salespeople suspect reactance, they often use negative psychology. A woman selling small economy cars might ask people browsing in the showroom, "Have you ever felt they are putting too much emphasis on economy in cars?" or "You probably are not concerned about mileage." Because most people are plagued with high-pressure sales pitches in junk mail, a home-improvement advertiser might realize they will read the first sentence of a flier and assert their independence by tossing it in the trash. Therefore, a negative approach would be a more effective weapon against their reactance. The letter might begin, "If you are wealthy and don't mind wasting thousands of dollars each year on home repairs, don't read any further."

Group pressure. Just as groups can pressure you into prejudiced attitudes, they can change and influence your attitudes each day. Groups and peers reinforce you when you conform. Bob Sober may prefer to go home directly after work. His coworkers chide him about being henpecked and suggest he join them for a few beers or shooters after work. When he shows up, they cheer and buy him drinks. As mentioned in the previous section of this chapter, adolescents are more susceptible to group pressure than any other age category.

Making implications. Whether intentional or not, many advertisements are misleading. Advertisers frequently use implications rather than facts. Implications avoid giving specific information. For example, the advertiser may claim a product "may help eliminate colds" or "fights blemishes." If you still have a cold and blemishes after careful use of the products, you cannot complain to the advertisers. The products may have been helping your cold and fighting your blemishes but without success.

Implications are often incomplete sentences. A claim may state "Cureyourills gives more relief." More relief than what? Or you may hear a claim, "Cleanup gives 30 percent more suds." More than what? Again the comparison is unclear. Perhaps it makes more suds than motor oil. Harris (1977) compared college students' reactions to asserted and implied claims in ads. The students heard phoney tape-recorded commercials that either made an assertion (a definite statement) or an implied claim. Students were then given test sentences and asked to mark them true or false. Exhibit 14-5 gives examples of an assertion, an implication, and a test sentence. There was no significant difference in the responses of students who heard implications and those who heard assertions: Students who heard implied statements were just as likely to mark the test sentence true. Harris also found that people who heard implied statements tend to remember the implications as facts.

Exercise 14-11

Read each of the following examples of persuasion attempts. Indicate the persuasive technique or techniques being used: emotional appeal, dissonance, foot in the door, negative psychology, group pressure, or making implications.

a. Oscar is serving jury duty. It is 3 A.M. and the rest of the jury is convinced the defendant is guilty. Oscar still thinks she may be innocent. Everyone

EXHIBIT 14-5

423

USING ATTITUDE
THEORIES

Assertions and Implications

Assertion: "In a survey of 500 doctors, over half reported that they recommended Knockout Capsules."

Implication: "In a survey of 500 doctors, over half reported that they recommended the ingredients in Knockout Capsules."

Test Sentence: (Answer true or false) "A majority of doctors in a survey recommended Knockout Capsules."

Source: Harris, R. J. (1977). Comprehension of pragmatic implications in advertising. *Journal of Applied Psychology, 62,* 603–608.

wants to go home. Jury members are yawning and ignoring Oscar's statements.

b. Mrs. Cash answers the telephone. The caller announces, "If you can answer this question, you can win a valuable prize. The question is, 'What color is a lemon?'" Mrs. Cash answers correctly. The caller then requests her name, occupation, salary, and the types of encyclopedias in her home. He then offers her, as a prize, a set of encyclopedias for only $850.

c. A radio ad begins, "Do you remember the lovely sweet smell of your grandmother's hands and the softness of her touch? For centuries family women

"This is recommended by four out of five commercials."

Figure 14-4
Is this an assertion or an implication?

have used Roses-in-Springtime hand cream. You too can prove you are a family woman! Roses-in-Springtime cream is twice as effective and lasts longer.''

---

d. Mr. Charity is trying to collect money for the Society for the Preservation of Old Timepieces. He meets his friend Sam and announces, ''Sam, you probably don't care much about history and changes that have taken place. Remember that lovely old Victorian mansion that was torn down for a high-rise apartment building? Some people were all worked up about destroying the past. They just get themselves in a panic. They're afraid to live in a crowded world of concrete. I'll bet you don't mind seeing the past crumble. So I won't even bother to ask you for a small donation to preserve old watches and clocks.''

You may check your answers in the Feedback section.

Propaganda and Brainwashing

If you are aware of the persuasion techniques that can be used, you will not be as susceptible to advertisements. Often advertisers intentionally mislead the public with emotional appeals, incorrect analogies, and implications. Information that is deliberately deceptive or erroneous is called ''propaganda.'' Although propaganda is usually associated with institutions and governments, an advertiser who deliberately distorts facts for selfish purposes is spreading propaganda.

propaganda
Information that is
deliberately deceptive
or erroneous

brainwashing
Dangerous technique
used in spreading
propaganda

A particularly vicious and dangerous use of propaganda is involved in *brainwashing,* a technique sometimes used by governments and religious cults. Schein et al. (1961) pointed out the method used in brainwashing. First a person is isolated so that old attitudes and beliefs will not be supported. The person is dependent on the attitude changers for food, drink, sleep, facilities, and other basic needs. Lacking sleep and food, the victim feels helpless. The propaganda program begins when the person is exhausted. Rewards of food, privileges, and praise are given when the victim cooperates and changes toward the desired attitude. Perhaps the most disastrous result of brainwashing occurred in Jonestown in 1978.

Checkpoint

Use the following questions to check your understanding of this portion of the chapter. Indicate whether each statement is true or false.

16. _____ Persuasion is a deliberate attempt to change an attitude.
17. _____ Unattractive people are more successful at persuasion than attractive people.
18. _____ Overheard conversations are more effective in changing attitudes than direct messages.
19. _____ Two-sided arguments are most effective on intelligent and informed people.
20. _____ If an audience seems to share your views, it is best to use only a one-sided argument.

The Jonestown
disaster is a tragic
example of
brainwashing. (*Frank
Johnston,* The
Washington Post,
1978)

21. _____ An advertiser who warns that perspiration odor can cause unpopularity is using a foot-in-the-door technique.

22. _____ Presenting intensely frightening information is the most effective method for changing attitudes.

23. _____ Dissonance occurs when your behavior is different from your attitude.

24. _____ Salespersons who have you agree with them on a number of unrelated matters are using dissonance.

25. _____ Reactance often occurs after a high-pressure sales pitch.

26. _____ Negative psychology is a method of dealing with reactance.

27. _____ Studies have shown that people clearly differentiate between assertions and implied statements in advertisements.

28. _____ "Seventy percent of children prefer Chewy chewing gum" is an example of an assertion.

29. _____ Propaganda is a deliberate attempt to change attitudes with false or deceptive information.

30. _____ Brainwashing is often used by advertisers.

Check your responses against the Checkpoint Answer Key at the end of the chapter. If you had difficulty with any question, reread the text. If you had little or no difficulty answering the questions or have resolved problems that you might have had, you are ready to check yourself against the chapter inventory that follows.

CHAPTER INVENTORY

Use this list of objectives as a review checklist. You should be able to do each of the tasks outlined in the objectives and apply them to everyday examples. If you can, you may feel confident that you have mastered the material in this chapter.

1. Define and differentiate among the terms ''attitude,'' ''prejudice,'' and ''discrimination.''
2. Specify three components of attitudes.
3. Define sexism and racism and provide examples of each.
4. Provide examples of three causes of discrimination.
5. Explain how attitudes develop.
6. Describe the role of first impressions.
7. List two general causes of prejudice.
8. Describe four personal concerns that can cause prejudice.
9. Define altruism and explain six factors that influence helping behavior.
10. Define persuasion and outline five characteristics of effective persuaders.
11. List and provide examples of six persuasion techniques.
12. Compare the usefulness of one-sided and two-sided arguments in persuasion.
13. Define and describe the applications of propaganda.
14. Outline the technique used in brainwashing.

Feedback

The correct answers to the exercises follow. If you did not answer an exercise correctly, review the preceding pages and return to the exercise to correctly complete it.

14-1. *a.* Beliefs: Adele values freedom and independence and has developed the belief that women should be permitted to decide whether or not they want abortions.
   b. Emotions: Adele must have had some feelings about the issue or she would not have begun arguing. Bursting into tears gives further evidence of her emotional involvement. Finally, her anger about the lack of support from other women is a clear indication that emotions accompany her opinions.
   c. Behavior: Adele's arguing and crying were both outward behaviors that resulted from her attitude toward abortion.

14-2. A prejudice is a type of attitude. Prejudice is based on a belief that is either not supported by facts or is contrary to facts. Prejudice is accompanied by negative emotions, whereas other attitudes can bring on either positive or negative feelings.

14-3. *a.* Reverse discrimination
   b. Fair distinctions
   c. Prejudiced attitudes
   d. Prejudiced attitudes

14-4. They may not be aware of their feelings, or they may be ashamed to admit their prejudices.

14-5. Parental influence on attitudes tends to lessen after adolescence. Possibly their sons attended liberal schools or had friends who had liberal attitudes. Peers have the strongest influence on attitude formation from adolescence on.

14-6. *a.* Overcrowding
   b. Fear of the unknown
   c. Conflict and competition
   d. Fear of the unknown
   e. Economic survival

14-7. *a.* Provides a scapegoat for anger and hostility; helps a person feel superior
   b. Self-fulfilling prophecy; prejudiced person becomes convinced of correctness

14-8. Although individual students may be open-minded about admitting women, their attitudes may change when they vote with a group. After graduating, male students become part of a new group—the alumni. The alumni club members have traditionally been males and group members tend to conform.

14-9. *a.* Mitch: The bystander effect suggests that the more people who witness a problem, the less likely anyone will help.
   b. Gertrude: People with high self-esteem are more likely to be altruistic. (A class officer and star athlete probably has higher self-esteem than a depressed person.)
   c. Edward: People are more willing to help on sunny days.
   d. Paula: People in the country tend to be more friendly and helpful than people in a city.
   e. Janice: People who have witnessed someone else being helpful are more likely to offer assistance themselves.
   f. Luke: People are more likely to help someone who is dressed similarly to them.

14-10. *a.* Being an expert
   b. Attractiveness
   c. Being famous or familiar
   d. Acting down-to-earth
   e. Speaking to someone else and being overheard

14-11. *a.* Group pressure
   b. Foot in the door
   c. Emotional appeal and making implications
   d. Negative psychology and dissonance

Checkpoint Answer Key

1. *c*	**9.** *b*	**17.** *false*	**25.** *true*
2. *b*	**10.** *d*	**18.** *true*	**26.** *true*
3. *a*	**11.** *c*	**19.** *true*	**27.** *false*
4. *a*	**12.** *a*	**20.** *true*	**28.** *false*
5. *a*	**13.** *b*	**21.** *false*	**29.** *true*
6. *a*	**14.** *b*	**22.** *false*	**30.** *false*
7. *d*	**15.** *c*	**23.** *true*	
8. *c*	**16.** *true*	**24.** *false*	

CHAPTER 15

WORKING WITH GROUPS

*There are two ways of spreading light: to be
The candle or the mirror that reflects it.*

Edith Wharton

Suppose you were chosen to work on a committee to select street names and street signs for a small-town community. The community is tightly knit, but committee members clash over the types of signs and street names that would be most suitable. Some want to retain the pastoral atmosphere, with wooden signposts and names like "Meadow Lane." Others prefer to modernize, with numbered streets and iridescent signs that will be visible at night. Within the committee, some people are leaning toward iridescent signs with pastoral names, while others prefer wooden posts with numbered streets. All seem rigid and unbending in their opinions.

What would you do to help the group agree? Think about how you usually behave in groups. Perhaps you like to generate new ideas, or maybe you just prefer to make jokes and help release tension. Within most groups there are both leaders and followers. If you tend to organize people's ideas and make suggestions about assignments, you are taking a leadership role. If you would rather do routine jobs and carry out orders carefully, you are clearly a follower. As you will learn in this chapter, being a leader or follower usually depends on the situation and the task set before a group. You may be a great leader in a group selecting faculty members for a college, but signposts for a small town do not turn on your leadership qualities.

In this chapter you will study the nature of leadership along with interactions and behaviors within groups. You will begin by considering the nature of groups and their goals. Some goals help groups stick together, while others seem to break up friendships and cause hostility. Next you will study factors that either aid or inhibit the productivity of groups. Finally you will examine leadership. Two possible types of leadership emphasis will be discussed. The techniques used by leaders will be related to the types of assumptions they can make. A brief summary on the pros and cons of groups will close the chapter.

THE NATURE OF GROUPS

Two or more people who interact or are aware of each other are a *group*. Usually, group members have a common goal. The students in your class probably share a goal of passing the course. Theatergoers standing in line all want to be admitted to the theater. A congregation gathered in a church probably is hoping for inspiration or a religious experience. Even people riding a bus form a group. Whether or not they interact, they are aware of each other and share a goal of being transported.

group Two or more people who interact or are aware of each other and share a common goal

Clearly every person must interact with groups. People need and rely on each other constantly. Some groups are formal and establish rules. Political parties and organizations such as the League of Women Voters, the United Fund, and labor unions are established for specific purposes. However, there are far more informal groups: your family, friends, coworkers, and any people you see, hear, or interact with during the course of a day.

Some groups have leaders while others do not. To be sure, audiences, crowds shopping, or people waiting for a train do not need a leader. But, orchestras, classes of students, and governments generally like to have someone in charge. Whether or not they have leaders, groups are dynamic; that is, they are constantly changing. As people interact with others, they change their attitudes and behaviors.

Exercise 15-1

Indicate which of the following are examples of groups.

a. _____ Two men are reupholstering a sofa.

b. _____ A mother is helping her two daughters with their homework.

c. _____ Three hundred people are watching a high school basketball game.

d. _____ A man is making phone calls to solicit money for a cancer fund.

e. _____ Five women are collecting trash to clean up a neighborhood.

f. _____ Two students are completing their project in a biology laboratory.

g. _____ Ten youngsters are practicing teamwork in soccer.

Please check your answers in the Feedback section.

Group Norms

group norms Rules of behavior for two or more people

Group norms are rules of behavior. The norm for a group of passengers in an elevator is to face the door without making eye contact or conversing with other passengers. Although there is no written rule, this is the proper way to behave in an elevator. If you faced the rear wall of the elevator and introduced yourself to each passenger, you would be breaking an informal, unwritten rule. There are many informal group norms. Hairstyles, clothing selection, and how and where to eat are usually not written but are rules that group members keep. Can you imagine combing your hair over your face, wearing pajamas, and facing your chair away from the table at a restaurant!

Some group norms are written and formalized. Laws, traffic regulations, and community housing restrictions are examples of written norms. Newly formed groups often want to be certain that members understand their purpose and rules. Many hours are spent drafting a constitution or bylaws to provide a

Figure 15-1
New York must have a group norm for walking pace.

"Could you walk a little faster, buddy? This is New York."

formal set of group norms. The bylaws may require members to wear funny hats, give unusual handshakes, or attend social functions.

If people want to continue as members of the group, they must accept and adhere to the norms, whether written or unwritten. Most likely, you are unaware of the many norms you comply with. You may have one group of friends that likes to study, another that is critical, and still another that jokes. In all probability, you study with the first group, criticize with the second, and clown with the third.

When you first join a group, you are usually uncertain of their norms. You want to be included but feel ill at ease because you have not determined the accepted behavior. New members usually appear quiet and aloof initially. In reality they are sizing up the group and trying to decipher the norms. Groups are accepting of people who adhere to their norms and tend to reject people who disregard them.

Exercise 15-2
Observe the informal norms of the group in the courtroom (Figure 15-2). What might Mr. Scrooge do to be accepted by the group and have a fair trial?

_____

_____

_____

_____

Please check your answer in the Feedback section.

Group Goals

Groups can have *cooperative* goals or *competitive* goals. Imagine your psychology instructor directed your class to work on a project together. The instructor plans to judge the completed project and decide whether the entire class should receive A, B, C, D, or F for their efforts. The class is working together toward the same goal: developing an excellent project. Each person has some responsibility in reaching the group goal. To be successful, class members must cooperate with each other. The instructor established a cooperative goal for the class.

Now suppose your psychology instructor wanted to set a competitive goal for the group. The instructor might announce an individual test and state that only one person in the class would receive an A grade. There would be two B's, three C's, and four D's; everyone else would fail. Everyone has the same goal: to receive an A on the test. However, each person hopes that others will be unsuccessful. In a competitive setting, each person's success results in someone else's failure. Only one person will receive the A.

When a group has a cooperative goal, people work together. When the goal is competitive, people work against one another. Crombag (1966) found that cooperative groups have better communication and their members are friendlier to each other. Deutsch (1968) found that cooperative groups were also more productive and generated better results. Cooperative group members contributed more diverse ideas, felt more pressure to achieve, and were

cooperative goal
Objective that a group works together to achieve

competitive goal
Objective that people in a group work against each other to achieve

Figure 15-2

more concerned about other members. Rivalry and opposition prevented members of competitive groups from exchanging ideas. However, competition is not without some benefits. It can create challenges, diminish boredom, and add interest.

No doubt you can think of many examples of cooperative and competitive goals. A campaign committee working to have their candidate elected has a cooperative goal. However, three candidates for the same office have a competitive goal. Teams present an example of both cooperative and competitive goals. Team members must cooperate among themselves but compete with other teams. For example, the Dallas Cowboys must cooperate to understand strategies and carry out plays. However, they clearly are competing when they play the Washington Redskins or the Philadelphia Eagles!

How can competitive teams be prompted to cooperate with each other? To be sure, there would be no fun and no advantage to cooperation between the Cowboys and the Redskins or the Yankees and the Red Sox. But cooperation among competing nations could reduce the likelihood of wars and save lives. There are clear advantages to reducing competition and hostility in some situations.

Sherif et al. (1961) studied cooperative and competitive goals among groups of 12-year-old boys. They divided the boys into two groups. Each group was sent to their own boy scout summer camp. The camps were actually operated by psychology experimenters. The psychologists selected counselors to observe and report on the boys. The experiment had three phases.

Phase 1: Cooperative goal development within groups. During the initial phase the experimenters suggested activities with a common cooperative goal for each group. The boys worked cooperatively at their own camps, fixing up swimming holes and building bridges. One group called themselves the Rattlers, the other the Eagles. Within each group the boys became friendly with each other and felt a spirit of belonging together.

Phase 2: Competitive goal development between groups. Next the experimenters arranged conflicts between the Eagles and the Rattlers. Sports competitions such as baseball games and tugs-of-war were scheduled. As expected, a strong sense of competition developed between the two groups. Hostilities led to name calling and arguments.

Phase 3: Cooperative goal development between groups. In the final stage of the experiment the psychologists attempted to reduce the hostility between the Rattlers and the Eagles. They brought the two groups together for

Football teams use both cooperative and competitive goals. Each team must work together to beat the opposing team. (*Cecile Brunswick/Peter Arnold, Inc.*)

meals, but this did not work. The groups remained hostile. Next they found a common enemy for the two groups, namely, a neighboring camp. Although the common enemy brought the groups closer, hostility still remained. Finally the experimenters had the two groups work together for a common goal on ventures similar to the tasks in phase 1. They arranged for a truck to break down at the bottom of a hill. The strength of both groups was needed to push the truck back up the hill. As a result of the cooperative activities, the boys from the two groups became closer to each other and hostility was reduced significantly.

Working toward a common goal is usually the best method to reduce hostility between groups. People realize they need each other to achieve their goal. The result is cooperation, better communication, and a friendlier attitude.

Exercise 15-3
Imagine a community has two local high schools. The two schools are openly competitive in both academics and sports. Recently their hostility toward each other has resulted in name calling, crank phone calls, and vandalism. You have been asked to help remedy the hostility. From what you learned about Sherif's experiment with the two boy scout camps, describe one technique that might help reduce the hostility.

_____

_____

_____

_____

Please turn to the Feedback section to check your answer.

Cohesiveness

cohesiveness Ability to stick together in a group

The *cohesiveness* of a group is its closeness or ability to stick together. Highly cohesive groups have a sense of identity. Their members stick close together, are loyal, and help each other. Shaw (1971) reported that people in cohesive groups are more likely to attend meetings and take an active role. They feel emotionally involved in the group, delight in group successes, and are upset by failures. The morale of cohesive groups is higher.

As you might have suspected, groups with cooperative goals are more cohesive than groups with competitive goals. Cohesiveness is further improved if the goals are precisely defined. Groups with clearly established norms also are more likely to be cohesive. Since members have an understanding of their expected behavior, they are more likely to participate.

Cohesiveness is desirable; it keeps a group together. Groups with low cohesiveness have difficulty with attendance at meetings. Members do not show up. If they do attend, they are often bored and fail to interact with each other.

Checkpoint

Use the following questions to check your understanding of this portion of the chapter. Choose and mark the one correct response to each question.

1. How many people are required to form a group?
   a. At least one
   b. At least two
   c. At least three
   d. At least five

2. Which of the following is an example of a formal group?
   a. A family of four
   b. Five friends at a cafeteria table
   c. A political committee of twenty
   d. Thirty people riding a public bus

3. Why are groups described as dynamic?
   a. They rarely have leaders.
   b. They are usually informal.
   c. They are usually competitive.
   d. They are constantly changing.

4. Why are new members of groups often quiet?
   a. Formal group norms do not permit them to speak.
   b. New members are learning both formal and informal norms.
   c. New members are usually more competitive than older members.
   d. New members are usually more cooperative than older members.

5. McEnroe and Lendl are playing for a singles tennis championship. How would you describe their goal?
   a. Cooperative
   b. Competitive
   c. Team
   d. Both cooperative and competitive

6. A group of competing wrestlers often quarrel and act hostile toward each other. Which of the following would best reduce their hostility?
   a. Spending more time together
   b. Competing with each other
   c. Finding a common enemy
   d. Working cooperatively on a job

7. Which of the following is characteristic of cohesive groups?
   a. Loyalty
   b. Competition
   c. Aloofness
   d. Poor attendance

Use the Checkpoint Answer Key at the end of the chapter to verify your responses. If you had any difficulty with a question, carefully reread the text. If you had little or no difficulty answering the questions or have resolved any problems that you might have had, you are ready to continue with the next portion of this chapter.

GROUP PRODUCTIVITY

Groups have clear advantages over individuals working alone. Information from individuals can be pooled, and insights can be gained from other members. In solving problems, groups make fewer errors than individuals. However, groups are not without limitations. A key disadvantage to groups is time. Although they are more accurate, groups take longer to solve problems and complete tasks.

The size of the group is an important factor in productivity. Research on small groups has concluded that five is an ideal size. Larger groups tend to become cumbersome and divide into factions. Also, quiet people are less likely to talk in a large group. Berelson and Steiner (1964) noted that groups with an odd number of members are more efficient than groups with an even number of members. Groups of four, six, or eight members are not as efficient as groups of five or seven. Psychologists have concluded that one reason five is ideal is because a minority of two people will feel free to discuss their opinions. Since only three can form a majority, they do not overpower the rest of the group.

Time constraints can also help group productivity. As the article in Exhibit 15-1 points out, groups that claim they need overtime are usually less efficient during regular hours. If groups are given realistic time limits, they can be more productive.

A number of other factors also influence the productivity of groups. Too much conformity and obedience can stifle new or original ideas. People in groups often give up their own beliefs to comply with others, even when they feel certain they are right. Similarly, people will obey rules and strong authorities against their own consciences.

EXHIBIT 15-1

Overtime Is Underproductive

Companies generally use overtime to deal with work that managers think cannot be finished during regular hours. A recent study, however, shows that overtime may, in fact, reward inefficiency.

For six months, Lloyd Baird, a professor of management at Boston University, and Philip Beccia, a researcher with the U.S. Office of Personnel Management, checked productivity at 42 district offices of a U.S. government agency where the work consisted of processing documents. The researchers defined productivity as a combination of how many documents each office processed each month and how many errors turned up when the offices checked their own processing for accuracy.

The slowest most error-prone offices generally used the most overtime. Even so, their total productivity—as the researchers defined it—was lower than that of the most efficient offices. (The researchers suspect that workers on overtime have already worked a regular day and are fatigued.) The least productive offices, moreover, hired the largest number of employees over the six months of the study, usually citing the fact that they were relying so heavily on overtime as evidence of their need for more staff.

"Offices needing overtime most should have the greatest hesitancy to use it," the researchers advise. "Before using overtime, they should critically analyze what is creating the need for it and correct whatever inefficiencies exist."

Being inefficient did not seem to please the employees, despite the overtime pay they received. Baird and Beccia asked 600 workers in the 42 offices how they liked their pay and their jobs and found that those in the least productive offices said they were the least satisfied.

Source: Rice, B. (1981, August). Management: Overtime is underproductive. *Psychology Today.*

Conformity

Suppose you walk up to join a line for a movie. There are about thirty people in the line, all facing the wrong way. Their backs are to the theater and cashier. What would you do? Would you go along with the group, or would you assert your independence by facing the usual direction?

To be sure, you would have some serious questions about why the group was facing the wrong way. But even if you thought the group was mistaken, you would probably go along with them rather than appear different. However, the next time you lined up for a movie you would revert back to your normal behavior and face the cashier.

Conformity and Compliance

Psychologists distinguish between compliance and conformity. Kelman (1958) explained that *conformity* requires people to accept the information and beliefs of a group. Because they accept the beliefs of the group, their behavior changes. However, sometimes people will change their behavior publicly to go along with a group, but privately maintain their own beliefs. They are demonstrating compliance. *Compliance* implies that the person is following the conventions of the group either for approval or to avoid embarrassment.

The most famous research on social pressure and compliance was performed by Asch (1956). Asch told subjects they were participating in an experiment on perception. Groups of seven students sat in a semicircle around an easel. Two large cards were presented on the easel for each trial. One card contained a standard line. The other card contained three lines, only one of which was equal to the standard (see Figure 15-4). Students were instructed to name which line was equal to the standard.

Although there were seven students in each group, only one was actually a subject. The other six were confederates, that is, persons helping the experimenter. They had been instructed to agree unanimously on correct and incorrect choices. The one genuine subject answered last and believed that the six confederates were also subjects. The confederates answered correctly for the

conformity Accepting the beliefs of a group and behaving accordingly

compliance Publicly behaving in accordance with a group while privately disagreeing with their beliefs

Figure 15-3

NOW SHOWING

TICKETS

CANEVARI

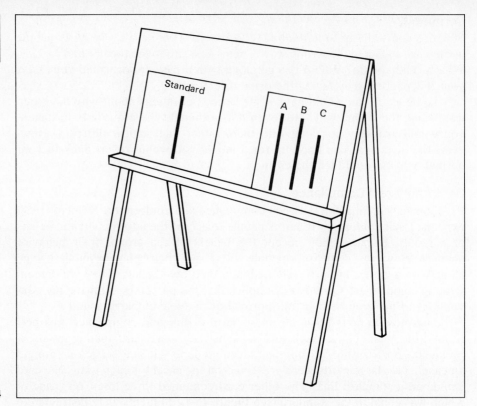

Figure 15-4

first few trials. Naturally, the subject agreed. But then the confederates began to agree on incorrect responses. The subject was in an awkward position. The correct answer seemed obvious; the subject had to decide whether to go along with the group or to stick with the correct response. Fully 37 percent of the subjects yielded to group pressure and gave incorrect responses.

After the experiment, compliant subjects were interviewed. They stated that they knew their responses were incorrect. They complied with the group so they would not look different. They could not believe that everyone else was wrong and that they were the only one who could see the correct answer.

Factors Affecting Conformity and Compliance

Why did some people refuse to go along with the incorrect responses of the group? Psychologists believe that group conformity and compliance are related to self-esteem. People with high self-esteem are less likely to follow a group when they believe the group is wrong. People with lower self-esteem are less sure of themselves. As a result, they are more likely to conform to pressure.

Overcrowded prisons provide an example of conformity to negative behavior (Footlick, 1981). Since many inmates were imprisoned for violent behavior, assaults, rape, and other violence become the norm. Persons jailed for nonviolent crimes sometimes become hardened criminals after a single jail sentence. As you might suspect, inmates at penitentiaries tend to have low self-esteem.

In addition to the self-esteem of the person being pressured by the group, certain conditions and characteristics of the group can affect the tendency to conform.

Size of the group. Gerald et al. (1968) found that the likelihood of conformity increases rapidly as the size of the group approaches five members, then increases at a slower pace as the group size approaches eight people. In a slightly different experiment on conformity, Milgram et al. (1969) had people stand on a sidewalk and stare up at the sixth-floor window of a building. The experimenters observed the percentage of passersby who conformed with the staring-upward behavior. When a group of five people gazed upward, 16 percent of the people passing by joined them. When the group size was fifteen people, 40 percent of the passersby conformed. Beyond this point, the size of the group no longer seemed to be a powerful influence on conformity.

Presence of another dissenter. Allen and Levine (1971) did a variation on Asch's experiment on compliance. Rather than have six confederates give an incorrect response, one dissented and agreed with the subject. However, this dissenter was wearing thick glasses and struggling to peer at the lines. But even with this minimal support, subjects showed less compliance and were more willing to stick with their independent judgments. Other research has also provided evidence that the presence of even one other dissenter makes nonconforming more comfortable and therefore more likely.

Public choices versus secret choices. If Asch had allowed his subjects to choose the correct line on a secret ballot, he might have had different results. Deutsch and Gerard (1955) found that subjects who had to express their opinions openly were more likely to conform with the group. A secret ballot spares you from the embarrassment of appearing different or strange to the other members of the group.

Exercise 15-4
In your own words explain why Asch's experiment studied compliance rather than conformity. _____

_____

_____

_____

_____

Exercise 15-5
Willy is participating in an experiment on group pressure. All other group members are confederates of the experimenter. The group will be asked to name the second president of the United States. A wrong answer, "Abraham Lincoln," will be given by the first member of the group. Others will conform. You are asked to decide whether Willy will comply with the wrong answer. List four factors you would like information on before making your decision.

a. _____

b. _____

c. _____

d. _____

Please turn to the Feedback section to check your responses.

Obedience

Obedience requires complying or conforming to rules or to the commands of an authority. No doubt from the time you were a child you practiced obedience. You submitted to orders from parents, teachers, baby-sitters, crossing guards, and any other adult who appeared to have authority. You may even have succumbed to obeying a neighborhood bully. You probably still are an obedient person. If you are driving along a highway and a police officer raises her hand ordering you to stop, you certainly would obey. But suppose the police officer ordered you to move forward, possibly harming other people. Would you do it?

Milgram (1963, 1974) experimented to learn whether people would be obedient, even if another person might be harmed as a result. Milgram advertised in a New Haven, Connecticut, newspaper, offering to pay men $4.50 to participate in a learning experiment. Forty men aged 20 to 50, from a variety of occupations and educational levels, were chosen as subjects for the experiment. Subjects were told the purpose of the experiment was to study the effects of punishment on memory.

In reality, the purpose was to see whether subjects would give increasingly higher levels of electric shocks to another person, following orders and urges from an experimenter. When each subject arrived for the experiment, he met with the experimenter and someone he believed was another subject. Actually the other person was a confederate of the experimenter. The experimenter explained that a learner and a teacher would be required. A fake drawing was set up so that the subject became the teacher, and the confederate the learner. The subject discovered that the learner was being strapped into a chair that appeared to be wired with electricity. The learner's electric chair was behind closed doors.

The subject was then instructed to sit in front of an electric-shock device. His goal was to have the learner memorize pairs of words. Whenever the learner made a mistake, the subject was to give an electric shock. Voltage level was to be increased with each error. Warnings appeared above fake switches on the electric-shock devices: 390 volts and above warned "Danger! severe shock"; 435 volts warned "xxx."

In the beginning of the experiment the learner answered correctly; then he made a few mistakes. At a planned point in the experiment the learner acted as if he was suffering from the shocks and began screaming out in pain. The experimenter urged the subject to continue increasing the levels of shock. Eventually the learner shrieked and pleaded that he wanted to quit. Again the experimenter directed the subject to continue. What would you have done?

Although Milgram's experiment did not really offer shocks to the "learners," the results did shock psychologists. All forty subjects went at least to the 300 voltage level of shocks. Only five refused to go above 300 volts. Twenty-six men, almost two-thirds of the subjects, went all the way to 450 volts, beyond the "danger" and "xxx" warnings.

The experiment was later repeated with undergraduate students and women and had similar results. In all situations, subjects were hesitant and unhappy but continued when encouraged. Milgram reported that they did show signs of stress. They bit their lips, sweated, trembled, stuttered, and laughed inappropriately. Nonetheless, they were obedient.

Milgram's study showed the power of authority and the limitations of individual freedom and choice. Subjects were willing to harm another person against their own conscience. The results of the experiment have been used to explain the willingness to follow harmful orders in Nazi Germany, Vietnam, and the Watergate scandal. Compliance is really widespread!

Exercise 15-6

Suppose you are driving along the highway and come upon an accident. The police officer in charge orders you to drive through the accident scene, inconveniencing many injured people. After reading the results of Milgram's experiment do you expect that you would be obedient? _____

_____

Please turn to the Feedback section to check your response.

Groupthink

Not only do conformity and obedience often lead to harm, they can also limit group productivity. A group that is constantly conforming will find itself in a rut. The members begin to think alike and neglect to look outside the group for ideas. Janis (1973) labeled this type of rut "groupthink." According to Janis, groupthink is more likely to occur in cohesive groups when no one wants to break up the cohesiveness. Members feel loyal to the group and do not want to raise controversial issues, even if they think the group is wrong. Everyone conforms and rubberstamps group ideas.

groupthink Conformity that keeps a group in a rut

Janis blames poor political decisions on groupthink. The lack of preparation for Pearl Harbor, the invasion of North Korea, the Vietnam war, the Bay

Figure 15-5
Does this group look likely to fall into a groupthink rut?

of Pigs invasion, and the Watergate scandal are his examples. The people working on these decisions were more concerned about being unanimous than about consulting outside experts and considering other alternatives. No member of the group was willing to express any doubts or criticisms.

What can be done to avoid a groupthink? How can a group get out of a rut? One technique that has been recommended is called "brainstorming." The goal in a brainstorming session is to generate different ideas and develop creative solutions to problems. Members are instructed to withhold criticism until the end of the session. First they are to let their imaginations stretch and be as creative as possible. Even seemingly outlandish ideas should be discussed. Suggestions can be mixed and combined. The session is freewheeling and spontaneous. Ideas are neither squelched nor criticized. Finally, at the end of the session, all ideas are evaluated.

Exercise 15-7

Polly Tish Chen is running for Congress. Her campaign committee has been mailing brochures and literature to her constituents. The committee is always unanimous in suggestions for her campaign. Committee members are close friends, respect each other, and rarely argue. Polly is falling behind her opponent in the polls. The committee met last night and unanimously agreed to increase the amount of brochures and literature they are mailing. Polly is concerned that her committee is in a rut and it may cost her the election. Describe what Polly might suggest to get some creative new ideas for her campaign.

_____

_____

_____

_____

Compare your suggestions to those in the Feedback section.

Risk Taking

Stoner (1961) found that groups are willing to take greater risks than individuals. He gave a number of risk-taking problems to individuals and to groups (see Exhibit 15-2). In each case the group chose a riskier solution. Stoner suggested that people in a group feel less responsible than they do as individuals. If the solution fails, no one person is responsible and each member feels less blame.

EXHIBIT 15-2

Source: Kogan, N. and Wallach, M. (1964). _Risk Taking_ New York: Holt Rinehart and Winston.

A Stoner Risk-Taking Problem

A college senior planning graduate work in chemistry may enter University X, where, because of rigorous standards, only a fraction of the graduate students manage to receive a Ph.D.; or he may enter University Y, which has a poorer reputation, but where almost every graduate student receives a Ph.D. What chance of success would you require before recommending that the student enter University X?

Suppose you were considering quitting your job and investing your savings in a small business. You have $5000. Two of your friends have the same savings and are willing to form a corporation with you. There are some definite risks in starting the business. If you fail, you cannot have your job back. Sitting by yourself, you may dwell on the risks and decide to stick with your job. However, if you meet with your friends you are more likely to go ahead with the new plan. Psychologists hold that most people are unwilling to admit not being as risky as others. Group pressure can cause risk taking.

Exercise 15-8
List two reasons why groups may be willing to take greater risks than individuals.

a. _____

_____

b. _____

_____

Check your reasons in the Feedback section.

Panic Behavior

Panic behavior occurs in a group when members are frightened and are competing for something scarce. Mintz (1951) concluded that panic results from a breakdown in cooperation. Imagine there is a fire in an old movie theater. There is only one exit, in the back of the theater. Who do you suppose would be more likely to panic, the people near the exit or the people up front? The people near the exit have little to fear; they know they can leave safely. However, the people up front will probably begin pushing if they fear they will burn before reaching the exit by waiting for their turn.

Riot behavior is an extension of panic behavior. Riots are usually based on fear and panic. But the panic is coupled with long-standing frustrations in addition to a triggering event. The article in Exhibit 15-3 reports a riot in a California prison. The riot resulted from a fear of losing privileges, coupled with continuous frustration over power losses. Lightning was the triggering event.

EXHIBIT 15-3

Riot over Lack of TV

Several hundred inmates in five units at the California Institution for Men vandalized their dormitories because they had no television and had to eat cold lunches during long power outages, a prison spokesman said.

When a lightning bolt knocked out electricity at the medium-security prison Friday night, for the second time in the day, many of the 375 prisoners in five open dormitories began a fire-setting, furniture-breaking, soap-throwing frenzy that lasted until 2:30 A.M., said spokesman Marvin Ryer.

No one was injured, and there was no damage estimate, he said.

Source: (1980, February 17). Riot over lack of TV. *Washington Post.*

What can possibly be done to prevent groups from panicking? A technique commonly used by airlines is to prepare ahead. If you have ever traveled by air, you are aware of the location of oxygen masks, flotation cushions, and emergency exits. Flight attendants spend a few minutes as the plane taxis on the runway explaining plans for an emergency. The technique is effective. People tend to be reasonable and orderly in airplane emergencies. Fortunately, panic behavior in disasters is becoming rare.

Checkpoint

Use the following questions to check your understanding of this portion of the chapter. Choose and mark the one correct response to each question.

8. Which of the following is a disadvantage of groups solving problems?
   a. Groups make more mistakes than an individual.
   b. Groups take more time than an individual.
   c. Groups have fewer insights than an individual.
   d. Groups cannot pool information.
9. Which size group is likely to be most productive?
   a. Three people
   b. Five people

Riots are not uncommon in Northern Ireland. In this scene, a funeral has uncovered long-standing anger and frustration. (*Bernard Bisson/Sygma*)

    c. Ten people

    d. Fourteen people

10. Which of the following terms best describes the behavior advocated by the expression "When in Rome, do as the Romans do"?

    a. Compliance

    b. Conformity

    c. Obedience

    d. Panic

11. How does conformity differ from compliance?

    a. Conformity does not require obedience to an authority.

    b. Conformity requires obedience to an authority.

    c. Conformity requires accepting the beliefs of a group.

    d. Conformity does not require accepting the beliefs of a group.

12. What did the results of Asch's experiment demonstrate?

    a. Perceptual ability changes when an individual joins a group.

    b. The perception of groups is a composite of the perceptions of individuals in the group.

    c. A person will go along with a group even when he or she feels certain the group is wrong.

    d. A person will go along with a group if he or she is rewarded.

13. Which of the following persons is most likely to conform or comply when pressured by a group?

    a. John, who has a poor self-concept

    b. Jim, who has a good self-concept

    c. Joe, who knows his best friend will always agree with him

    d. Jack, who knows the vote will be by secret ballot

14. Milgram showed that subjects would give electric shocks to a person even if they believed it could be harmful. Why were the subjects harming others?

    a. They wanted a reward.

    b. They feared punishment.

    c. They were pressured by a group.

    d. They were obedient to an authority.

15. Which of the following groups is suffering from groupthink?

    a. A group of women who are pooling all their savings on chances in the Irish Sweepstakes

    b. A group of men who always agree unanimously to the same solution

    c. A group of women who argue among themselves continuously

    d. A group of men who start a riot

16. What is the purpose of brainstorming?

    a. To help a group reach a unanimous decision

    b. To avoid panic behavior

    c. To develop creative new ideas

    d. To maintain obedience to an authority

17. In which situation would you probably be willing to take the greatest risks?

    a. Alone

    b. In a group

    c. With an authority

    d. With a confederate

18. Imagine you own an old wooden dance hall with only two exits. You want to be sure that people will not panic in the event of a fire. Which of the following techniques would be most effective?
    a. Station a police officer with a gun near the exit.
    b. Mark the exits with large signs.
    c. Schedule brainstorming sessions.
    d. Explain the emergency procedure at the beginning of each dance.

Use the Checkpoint Answer Key to verify your responses. If you had any difficulty with a question, carefully reread the text. If you had little or no difficulty answering the questions or have resolved any problems that you might have had, you are ready to continue with the next portion of the chapter.

LEADERSHIP

leader Person who gives guidance or direction to others and influences or changes their behavior

A *leader* is a person who gives guidance and direction to a group, influencing or changing people in the group. Some groups have a formal leader, a person elected or appointed to manage the group. A leader is perceived as an authority by the group. As you recall from the discussion of obedience in the previous section of this chapter, leaders can have a powerful influence on behavior. In corporations the names of formal leaders are listed on organization charts. But there are also informal leaders, people who emerge from groups and have a powerful influence on other members. Perhaps you have worked with a group where the formal leader was useless. Frequently, a member of the group will make up for the leader's inadequacy and provide some direction.

Although research has limited evidence of specific qualities found in leaders, there are some rather general characteristics. Surveys have found that most formal leaders are above average in height (Crenshaw, 1980). Shaw (1971) claimed leaders have enthusiasm, initiative, verbal ability, persistence, and sociability. Most leaders are intelligent, sincere, and have high self-esteem. The article excerpt in Exhibit 15-4 considers the qualities of military leaders.

EXHIBIT 15-4

Does Military Mentality Trigger War?

Brigadier generals in the U.S. Army are extremely smart, extremely well-educated, patriotic, competitive, decisive, practical, responsible and personally likeable, David Campbell has found. Yet he wonders if people like them throughout the world aren't largely responsible for war....

Campbell's description of military leaders' personality was based on 163 U.S. Army brigadier, or one-star, generals who have gone through a week-long leadership training course at the center in the past nine years. He compared results of those tests to data from some 100 high-level corporate executives and about 1000 mid-level workers who also attended the center.

The generals are "uncommonly well-educated," even compared to the thoroughly schooled comparative samples, he said. All the generals have college degrees, 88 percent have master's degrees, and 9 percent have a doctorate, while only 90 percent of the executives had college degrees and just one-third had graduate degrees.

The generals' average IQ on the Shipley Institute of Living Scale was 124, which is at the 95th percentile of the general population and higher than either of the comparative samples.

Behavior assessment exercises showed the generals to be more competitive than executives, although on tasks requiring cooperation, they rated about the same as executives.

On various psychological inventories, the generals ranked high in dominance, self-acceptance, achievement through conforming as well as through independence, and high responsibility and socialization. These latter factors, said Campbell, are where "the generals' sense of duty shows through."

Predictably, they scored extremely high in military interests, and also scored fairly high in liking adventure, being in charge, and in public speaking and law/politics. The generals scored lower on such scales as art, music, dramatics and the domestic arts.

"I have concluded, given the necessity for protecting ourselves from threats with military might, that the general officers that we have now are outstanding," he said.

"But a larger question is: Why do we need them? Why is the world a dangerous place?"...

Source: Bales, J. (1987, November). Does military mentality trigger war? *APA Monitor.*

Leadership Emphasis

Have you ever noticed that some groups have more than one informal leader? Often groups have two informal leaders or one formal and one informal leader. Each of the leaders has a different area of emphasis. Bales (1958) identified two types of leaders: task and socioemotional. A *task leader* presents new ideas and keeps the group working toward goals. A leader with a task orientation wants to get the job done efficiently. The emphasis will be on defining problems, collecting information, opinions, and suggestions, and evaluating and summarizing the group's work. Most formal leaders are assigned task roles. A leader with a *socioemotional* orientation is concerned about the personal and social needs of members of the group. The goal for this leader is group harmony and cohesiveness. Attempts are made to build an atmosphere of trust and friendliness. The leader is concerned about hurt feelings and soothes and comforts members. Praise is common and jokes are used to release tension. Japanese managers have been known to demonstrate a stronger leaning toward socioemotional emphasis than their American counterparts.

task leader
Person who keeps a group working toward a goal

socioemotional leader
Person who directs a group primarily according to the personal and social needs of the members

Exercise 15-9

Read each of the following descriptions and indicate whether each leader is formal or informal and task-oriented or socioemotionally oriented.

a. Ima Principal was appointed headmistress of a private school. She was aware of the problem with teacher turnover: Because of a limited budget, teachers left for higher-paying jobs at public schools. She is trying to keep teachers happy by having friendly gatherings and developing school spirit. She encourages them and gives them many privileges.

_____

_____

Figure 15-6
A leader with a clear
socioemotional
emphasis.

*"I don't think of us so much as 'the Board' as of a Walt,
a Phil, a Pete, a Flo, two Chucks, and a Moe."*

b. Bertha is one of four young women sharing an apartment in a large city. She was concerned about her roommates' disorganization in paying bills. She decided to take over by keeping records of the accounts and billing each woman every month.

_____

_____

c. When Harry Hatchet was appointed director of the Dreamy Day-Care Center, he vowed to get the center out of debt. He is holding weekly meetings to discuss improvements. Thus far he has fired five teachers because their enrollments declined and he felt they were unpopular. The remaining teachers are handling more children.

_____

_____

To check your answers turn to the Feedback section.

Assumptions of Leaders

theory X Belief that people are basically lazy and must be controlled and directed by management

McGregor (1960) claimed that leaders base their methods on assumptions they make about people. He divided assumptions into theory X and theory Y. *Theory X* is a pessimistic view of human nature. Managers who adhere to theory X believe that people are basically lazy and will avoid work and responsibility. These managers hold that individuals have selfish interests in their own security and do not care about the organization. People will avoid making decisions and prefer to be directed by others. As a result the manager who holds the assumptions of theory X will check on people's work and direct and control them. Because people dislike work, they must be directed, coerced, and threatened with punishment if they do not show effort.

On the other hand, *theory Y* holds a more positive set of assumptions about people. Theory Y assumes that people have a natural interest in work and are capable of directing their own behavior. Under proper conditions, people will seek responsibility, make decisions, and show imagination and creativity. A leader who believes the assumptions in theory Y will not threaten or pressure a group, but rather will allow them freedom.

theory Y Belief that people are naturally interested in work and can direct their own behavior

Leaders may choose the assumptions of either theory X or theory Y; the two are not compatible. Assume you are a manager of a secretarial staff and believe the assumptions of theory X. You probably would have employees sign in and out or punch a time clock. If they came in late or left early, you would dock money from their paychecks. Coffee breaks and lunch hours would also be monitored carefully. You probably would provide the secretaries with folders of sample letters to be sure they typed correctly. You also would edit their work for errors. As you might suspect, you would probably find that the members of the secretarial staff indeed conform to theory X: As you get tougher in handling them, they become even further entrenched in their theory X characteristics.

But the opposite is also true. If the same group of secretaries were managed assuming theory Y characteristics, they would probably work accordingly. If permitted to create original letters, they would. Likewise, they would edit and check their own work. Being motivated and finding the job interesting, they would be more likely to arrive on time and complete their day's work. So as a theory Y manager, you would also be convinced that your assumptions were correct.

Exercise 15-10
Read each of the following statements and indicate whether it is based on assumptions from theory X or from theory Y.

a. "Be sure to tell the carpenters to clean up when they are finished; otherwise they will probably leave a mess."

_____

b. "Always carry a map in a strange city. Taxi drivers will take you all over town just to make some fast money."

_____

c. "I always let my basketball team warm up by themselves. They know best which shots to practice."

_____

d. "Let the boy scout troop develop their own plan for cleaning up the neighborhood. Adults just get in their way."

_____

Please turn to the Feedback section.

Leadership Styles

Psychologists have identified three styles of leadership: authoritarian, democratic, and laissez-faire. Generally, authoritarian leaders are task-oriented and believe theory X assumptions about people. Laissez-faire leaders are more socially oriented and accept the assumptions of theory Y. Democratic leaders fall somewhere between these two extremes in both their orientation and their assumptions. In each of these styles, the leader accepts a different role.

authoritarian leader
Person who gives direct orders and is solely in charge of a group

Authoritarian. This style of leadership is also referred to as "autocratic." The leader is the sole person in charge of the group and has complete responsibility. Direct orders are given and are expected to be carried out by the group. The leader remains aloof from the rest of the group and is considered an expert.

democratic leader
Leader who expects group members to participate in decisions

Democratic. Democratic leaders expect group participation; hence this style is sometimes labeled "participative." The leader offers an overview or philosophy and sets objectives for the group. The group must then decide how best to implement the objectives. Group members draw on the expertise and experience of each other.

laissez-faire leader
Coordinator who gives a group free rein

Laissez-faire. In a laissez-faire style of leadership, the leader is more of a coordinator. The group has complete freedom and free rein. The laissez-faire leader acts as liaison with external groups but exerts no power or influence on the group.

Lewin (1943) compared these three styles of leadership as used with boys' clubs. Lewin formed three equal groups of boys with adult leaders using one of the three leadership styles. In the authoritarian group the leader made policies and instructed the boys but never socialized with them. The democratic leader held group discussions on policy and allowed the boys to choose their own work groups for projects. In the laissez-faire group, the leader provided information when it was requested but generally let group members do as they pleased.

The results of Lewin's experiment showed that the authoritarian leaders had smooth and well-organized groups. However, the members were unhappy and were hostile to each other. Members of the democratic groups liked their leaders and tried hard. The groups with laissez-faire leaders had very little constructive activity.

Although the results of Lewin's experiment seem to recommend a democratic style of leadership, there are situations where authoritarian and laissez-faire styles would be more appropriate. For example, if you were leading people out of a plane crash or a fire, you would hardly want to stop to take a vote. Giving direct authoritarian orders would be more realistic. Similarly, in professional areas, a laissez-faire system of leadership is suitable. Physicians, dentists, and college professors rarely need direction from a leader.

Most leaders maintain flexibility. Even the most authoritarian boss will permit employees to plan their own company picnic and decide on the date, the food, and entertainment. Similarly, a laissez-faire leader could recognize the potential chaos if a town permitted everyone to build houses, roads, office buildings, and high-rises wherever they wished.

Exercise 15-11

Imagine you have been assigned to lead a group in planting a vegetable garden on a 5-acre plot of land. Six people are assigned to your group. Describe what you would do as a leader if you used each of the three possible leadership styles.

a. Authoritarian: _____

_____

_____

_____

_____

b. Democratic: _____

_____

_____

_____

_____

c. Laissez-faire: _____

_____

_____

_____

_____

Compare your leadership plans with those listed in the Feedback section.

Leadership Strategies

Have you ever noticed the strategies used by your coworkers and bosses? Perhaps you have worked for a boss who constantly insisted on his own ideas and would persist until you agreed. Schmidt and Kipnis (1985) would label his approach "shotgun." The excerpt in Exhibit 15-5 lists six commonly used strategies and labels four general approaches.

Strategies may be successful or unsuccessful depending on whether you are a male or a female. Reason and logic are winning methods for men, but friendliness and passiveness are more likely to advance women. Interestingly, the use of the shotgun approach hinders men more than women.

Exercise 15-12

The article in Exhibit 15-5 identifies and describes six strategies: reason, assertiveness, friendliness, coalition, high authority, and bargaining. Four influence styles are also described. After reading the article, indicate which of the six strategies would probably be used by each of the following individuals.

a. Bill the Bystander _____

b. Irene the Ingratiator _____

EXHIBIT 15-5

The Perils of Persistence

Popular opinion holds that success at work depends upon continually pushing for what you want and refusing to take no for an answer. Fast-track people are often described as assertive, even brash, and always trying to influence others....

We have examined the consequences of different influence styles in the workplace, with a special look at the costs of using a persistent, assertive style. Our studies involved employees from hundreds of firms in industries ranging from manufacturing to financial services. The respondents fell into four categories: workers—composed of blue-collar and clerical workers—supervisors, sales representatives and chief executive officers (CEO's). All of them took a test we designed, called the Profiles of Organizational Influence Strategies (POIS), which looks at how frequently people influence their superiors using six strategies: Reason, Assertiveness, Friendliness, Coalition, Higher Authority, and Bargaining. (See "Different Ways of Getting Your Way," this article.)

In previous studies we found that people varied in their use of the six strategies. (See "The Language of Persuasion," *Psychology Today,* April 1985). In this study we were able to group people into four specific influence styles based on the ways in which they used the strategies:

• Shotguns These people refuse to take no for an answer. Shotguns use all six POIS strategies to get their way. When one strategy fails they shift to another.

• Tacticians They actively try to influence others, relying on reason and logic.

• Ingratiators They are also active in their persuasion, but they rely on ingratiation and flattery.

• Bystanders They seldom attempt to influence others but stand by watching the action, like wallflowers at a dance.

One of our goals was to see how different influence styles affected employees' performance evaluations. We asked employees' bosses, three-quarters of them men, to evaluate their employees' job performance and to describe their communication style. Since people who continually refuse to take no for an answer are often considered bothersome, our hunch was that employees who assertively attempted to influence their supervisors (Shotguns) would be viewed less favorably than those who were less strident. We also felt that women using the Shotgun style would have a particularly hard time with male superiors since conventional wisdom is that men don't like women telling them what to do.

As expected, Shotguns received low evaluations, but, much to our surprise, the men received slightly lower performance evaluations, on the average, from male superiors than the women did. Thus, assertive women are not disliked by their bosses any more than assertive men are.

Who did receive the best performance evaluations? Here the traditional sex-stereotype differences emerged. Male supervisors gave the highest ratings to male Tacticians, those who relied on reason and logic. In contrast, the women who received the highest evaluations were Ingratiators and Bystanders.

Why these differences in evaluation? When we asked superiors to describe their subordinates' communication styles, both female Ingratiators and male Tacticians were described as deferential and thoughtful. In other words, male superiors see men as thoughtful if they use reason and logic. Women are seen as thoughtful if they use friendliness and flattery, or are passive. The inevitable conclusion, it seems to us, is that men's ideas are valued and women's are not....

Different Ways of Getting Your Way

Reason	Explain the reason for your request. Write a detailed plan.
Assertiveness	Repeatedly remind. Confront face to face.
Friendliness	Make person feel important. Act humble and polite.
Coalition	Obtain support of coworkers. Obtain support of subordinates.
Higher Authority	Make a formal appeal to higher levels. Obtain the informal support of higher-ups.
Bargaining	Propose an exchange. Offer to help in exchange for what you want.

Source: Schmidt, S.M., & Kipnis, D. (1987, November). The perils of persistence. *Psychology Today.*

c. Shirley the Shotgun _____

d. Tim the Tactician _____

Please check your lists of strategies in the Feedback section at the end of this chapter.

THE PROS AND CONS OF GROUPS

Although groups are effective in reaching goals and providing helpful information, you probably have also been identifying some shortcomings. Buys (1978) outlined several negative influences of groups. Groups lose their sense of responsibility and tend to make risky and impulsive decisions. There is often a sense of conformity in groups, and members will go along with others even if they are wrong. Also, groups often encourage panic behavior. Since responsibility is shared, group members sometimes loaf, letting others do their work. This slowdown has been labeled "social loafing" (Latané, Williams, & Harkings, 1973). As the article in Exhibit 15-6 suggests, social loafing is common among cheerleaders.

social loafing
Tendency of individuals to exert less effort when they work together than when they work alone

   Harkins and Petty (1983) examined ways to make social loafing less likely. They suggested giving each group member a different important job so that each will have a strong sense of personal responsibility. Latané and associates called attention to the methods used by the Ohio State University football team. The coaches observe and score each play. They then compute the average performance score for each player. The scores are made public and high-scoring players are awarded honors at weekly luncheons. Outstanding players are rewarded with "buckeye" decals to wear on their helmets. Group members are recognized as individuals as well as cooperative group members. The Ohio State football team has become highly successful using this approach to avoid social loafing.

   In spite of their limitations, groups are here to stay!

EXHIBIT 15-6

Loafing in Groups

Go to any high-school football game and the people who seem to be working the hardest—the cheerleaders—are actually goofing off on the job.

Thanks to a noisy group of cheerleaders attending a camp at the University of North Carolina, researchers now know that social loafing exists even when people perform a task they enjoy and consider important. Social loafing means that people don't work as hard in a group as they do individually.

University of North Carolina psychologists Charles Hardy and Bibb Latane and other researchers have been studying social loafing for a decade to help businesses increase worker productivity. Previous experiments, however, tested only people engaged in activities that were of little intrinsic value to them. The girls were told they would be competing against one another and that the loudest would be recognized. Blindfolded and wearing earphones, the girls produced prodigious amounts of sound. But those who were told they were cheering with others made only 92 percent as much noise as those told they were cheering alone.

There tends to be a consistent drop of between 5 and 10 percent in effort, according to Latane, who says people are unaware of their social loafing.

"We did ask people in many experiments if they knew they were making less noise in groups, and most were not able to recognize it. Many claimed they were working harder. People seem to be utterly unaware that they are slacking off in groups," she says.

Source: Schwaz, J. (1987, March). Loafing in groups. *Omni.*

Checkpoint

Use the following questions to check your understanding of the final portion of the chapter. Indicate whether each statement is true or false.

19. _____ A formal leader is either elected or appointed.
20. _____ The name of an informal leader is likely to appear on a company's organization chart.
21. _____ Most leaders have a good self-concept.
22. _____ Formal leaders usually have a socioemotional emphasis.
23. _____ A leader with task emphasis is likely to joke to release tension.
24. _____ Theory X leaders are usually authoritarian.
25. _____ Leaders who believe theory X usually find out they are wrong.
26. _____ Laissez-faire leaders are task-oriented.
27. _____ Authoritarian leaders draw on the experience of group members.
28. _____ Democratic leadership is the most effective in all situations.
29. _____ The ingratiating approach is more successful for females than the shotgun approach.
30. _____ Groups can have negative influences.

Check your responses against the Checkpoint Answer Key at the end of the chapter. If you had difficulty with any question, reread the text. If you had little or no difficulty answering the questions or have resolved problems that you might have had, you are ready to check yourself against the chapter inventory that follows.

Use this list of objectives as a review checklist. You should be able to do each of the tasks outlined in the objectives and apply them to everyday examples. If you can, you may feel confident that you mastered the material in this chapter.

1. Define a group, and distinguish between formal and informal groups and group norms.
2. Explain why people new to a group often do not participate.
3. Differentiate between cooperative and competitive goals, and list their advantages and disadvantages.
4. Describe one method to reduce hostility among groups.
5. Define cohesiveness, and specify conditions that are conducive to its existence.
6. Discuss group size and time constraints as factors that affect group productivity.
7. Distinguish between conformity and compliance and describe one experiment on compliance.
8. Identify four factors that influence compliance.
9. Explain why Milgram's experiment showed the power of authority and the limitations of free choice.
10. List five factors that contribute to a groupthink, and describe a technique for avoiding group ruts.
11. State two reasons why groups take greater risks than individuals.
12. Identify the causes of panic behavior and riots, and describe a method to avoid panic behavior in groups.
13. Differentiate between formal and informal leaders and task-oriented and socioemotional leaders.
14. Explain the differences between theory X and theory Y.
15. Describe three styles of leadership, and relate them to the assumptions in theory X and theory Y.
16. Discuss the usefulness and application of the three leadership styles.
17. Describe six strategies and four approaches used by group leaders.
18. List two advantages and three disadvantages of groups.
19. Define social loafing and describe how it can be avoided.

Feedback

The correct answers to the exercises follow. If you did not answer an exercise correctly, review the preceding pages and return to the exercise to correctly complete it.

15-1. All seven are examples of groups. Two or more people are interacting or are aware of each other.

15-2. Mr. Scrooge should suggest a court recess. He might go home and put on a Santa Claus suit before returning. Groups reject people who disagree with them!

15-3. Activities that required the cooperation of students from both schools would help reduce hostilities. You might have suggested a community project, such as collecting money for the entire town, improving a local park, building a picnic area, or painting the town offices.

15-4. It is doubtful that subjects in Asch's experiment changed their behavior permanently. Those who did go along with the group admitted that their reason was to avoid embarrassment. They were aware of the correct response but were complying because of pressure from the group.

15-5. *a.* The level of Willy's self-esteem
   b. The size of the group
   c. Whether anyone else in the group will give a correct response
   d. Whether Willy can write his answer secretly

15-6. If you are like most of the subjects in Milgram's study, chances are you would obey the police officer. Undoubtedly it would bother you and you would show some signs of stress.

15-7. Polly needs to get her campaign committee out of their groupthink. She should suggest a brainstorming session. Members can mention any campaign suggestions they can conjure up, even if they seem ridiculous. At the end of the session, the committee could evaluate all the original ideas and perhaps find a more creative solution than more literature.

15-8. *a.* Group members can share the responsibility. If their risky decision fails, no one person will be blamed.
   b. Group members succumb to group pressure. No one wants to admit they are not as risky as the other members of the group.

15-9. *a.* Formal; socioemotional
   b. Informal; task-oriented
   c. Formal; task-oriented

15-10. *a.* Theory X
   b. Theory X
   c. Theory Y
   d. Theory Y

15-11. *a.* Authoritarian: Decide how and what you want planted in the garden. Draw a plan and purchase seeds. Assign group members specific tasks.
   b. Democratic: Discuss garden plans with the group. Allow members to choose vegetables and jobs they prefer. Members who wish can work together.
   c. Laissez-faire: Turn the group loose on the plot of land and let them do as they wish.

15-12. *a.* (None)
   b. Friendliness
   c. Reason, assertiveness, friendliness, coalition, higher authority, and bargaining
   d. Reason

Checkpoint Answer Key

1. *b*	**4.** *b*	**7.** *a*	**10.** *a*
2. *c*	**5.** *b*	**8.** *b*	**11.** *c*
3. *d*	**6.** *d*	**9.** *b*	**12.** *c*

13. *a*
14. *d*
15. *b*
16. *c*
17. *b*

18. *d*
19. *true*
20. *false*
21. *true*
22. *false*

23. *false*
24. *true*
25. *false*
26. *false*
27. *false*

28. *false*
29. *true*
30. *true*

CHAPTER 16

PLANNING CAREERS

*The human being is by nature active,
and when inactive begins to die*

Erich Fromm

Assume you are at a party. The host begins the introductions and tells you something about each person. You meet Maureen, a nurse's aide who assists retarded children, Clark, who picks grapes at a vineyard, Isaac, a chef and author of two cookbooks, and Joanne, a nuclear physicist. Based on their occupations, you probably form some first impressions. People are often identified with their jobs. Introductions are more likely to include information about occupations than other facts about people.

People are usually stereotyped according to their occupation: Nuclear physicists are expected to be intelligent; nurse's aides to retarded children are imagined to be patient and considerate. Indeed, a dumb nuclear physicist and an impatient nurse's aide would not be suited for their jobs. But there are also some unfair stereotypes. Clearly, it is wrong to assume that male hairdressers and ballet dancers are homosexual. Likewise, female executives are no less sensitive than female homemakers. But such stereotypes persist. Even within the harmony of a symphony orchestra, some rather negative job stereotypes endure, as shown in Exhibit 16-1.

Psychologists have evaluated successful people in occupations to determine their abilities and interests. In the first part of this chapter you will learn ways to use their findings to help you recognize the types of occupations that are likely to be suitable for you.

This chapter begins with a description of how to analyze yourself and some possible career choices to be sure that you select a job that suits your abilities, interests, and needs. Next, you will focus on how to get the job: letters of application, résumés, references, interviews, and follow-up letters. Factors involved in job satisfaction and decisions to change careers will also be discussed. Finally, you will consider the effects of unemployment and ways to use your leisure to prepare for retirement.

EXHIBIT 16-1

Stereo-phonic

It might come as a slight surprise to some people to find that within a nationally famous symphony orchestra based in Glasgow, where on the surface all appears to be sweetness and harmony, different groups of musicians have strongly stereotyped ideas about each other. In particular string players and brass players seemed to have very different views of each other.

BRASS (as seen by strings)
　　Slightly coarse and unrefined; heavy drinkers; less intelligent ("They're empty vessels. That's why they make the most noise"); loud-mouthed; play too loud ("They like to be in the limelight"); the clowns of the orchestra; "extroverts, big noises, that's why they like to play" brass instruments; don't practice sufficiently hard or conscientiously; unable to take anything seriously.

STRINGS (as seen by brass)
　　Like a flock of sheep; rather "precious"; oversensitive and touchy; seem to think they are "God's gift to music"; take the music, and themselves, too seriously; physically rather delicate; reluctant to do anything physically hard or tough, "in case they hurt their precious fingers."

Source: Davies, J. (1976, February 8). Stereo-phonic. *Washington Post.*

CHOOSING A CAREER

Psychologists describe a career as a set of experiences that permit you to use your abilities for profit. Profit is a crucial word in the definition of a career. A career for one person may be a leisure hobby for another. If you do needlework solely for pleasure, it is not a career. However, as soon as you sell an embroidered pillowcase or apron, you could be on the brink of starting your career.

Your choice of career is clearly among your most important decisions. The job you select will not only affect how you are introduced at parties, it will also affect your standard of living and financial security. Your friends and your status in the community will also be decided by your career choice. Likewise your own self-concept and sense of worth will be strongly affected by your work. Your career decision might also influence where you live. It would be difficult to be a farmer in downtown Chicago or a marine biologist in Bolivia.

Career decisions are not just a problem for high school and college students. Although early choices of a major may point to future career options, most people retrain, expand, and go into new areas during their lives. Many people change careers in their twenties, thirties, or forties. Some even begin new careers after they have retired.

Regardless of when career decisions are made they clearly have a crucial impact on your entire lifestyle. To be sure, you would not want to make such a decision in haste or under pressure. The best way to avoid being trapped into an unsuitable career is to take two steps: Analyze yourself, and analyze jobs. Hopefully, the result will be a career choice that satisfies your needs and interests.

Analyzing Yourself

Although it may seem bad taste to begin with the subject of money, to a large extent your career choice will be limited by the finances available to you. If you have wealthy parents or other relatives who are willing to invest in your future, or if you have accumulated your own fortune, your possible career choices will be limited only by your own abilities and interests. However, if you must borrow money or have only a small supply, you need to think about the costs of training programs and education. Institutions that offer scholarships and organizations that offer on-the-job training or tuition benefits deserve consideration. A college degree does not in itself offer better job opportunities. Successful careers also require ability and interest.

Assessing Abilities

The easiest way to determine your strengths and weaknesses is to recall your successes and failures. No doubt some school subjects seemed easy to you, while others were a dismal chore. If you always did well in biology classes but struggled through Spanish, you probably have more scientific ability than language ability. The only defect in this method is that your success in school subjects could also be influenced by teachers and classmates. For example, you may have had an excellent biology teacher and been in a class with friendly, outstanding students. The Spanish teacher, on the other hand, may

"Mrs. Beasley wants to borrow a cup of money."

Figure 16-1
Mrs. Beasley may be using a creative method to finance her education and training.

have been a misfit, and your Spanish classmates may have been poor students who joked and wasted classtime. However, if you studied science and Spanish with a variety of different teachers and students, you can be more certain of a correct assessment.

You might also recall abilities that friends and teachers noticed and commented on. Perhaps you have a clever writing style, or you are a skillful salesperson or an efficient organizer. Friends and instructors also notice weak points. Can you think of areas of criticism? If people consistently agree on your positive and negative qualities, they probably are reliable assessments.

Psychologists have developed tests to measure abilities. The three types of ability tests most commonly used for career counseling are intelligence tests, achievement tests, and aptitude tests. Intelligence tests, described in detail in Chapter 5, measure your general potential. *Achievement tests* assess the level of your past accomplishments, usually in academic subjects. *Aptitude tests* are designed to predict future achievements in specific areas. Aptitude tests have been devised to measure mechanical, artistic, musical, and literary ability, as well as potential in certain professions, such as medicine, law, education, and engineering. There are aptitude tests available to forecast your abilities in almost every career. Research has found that if people use their skills at work, they will develop a sense of competence that increases self-esteem.

achievement test Test designed to assess past accomplishments, usually in academic subjects

aptitude test Test designed to measure individual potential and to predict future achievements in a given area.

Figure 16-2
Do you suppose this
street painter took any
aptitude or
achievement tests?
(*Lee Betts.*)

Determining Values and Interests

Suppose a man has a beautiful bass voice. He also inherits a tremendous fortune. Several fine music colleges offer him scholarships, but he hates to sing and thinks music is a waste of time. He prefers working with animals. His values and interests would probably prevent his success in music. Even if he did accept one of the scholarships and pursued a career as a singer, he would undoubtedly be unhappy.

Before choosing a career course, it is wise to examine your values and interests. If you value the opinions of your family and friends, you most likely will want a job that pleases them. But you also want to please yourself. Do you prefer to work alone or in a group? Would you like a structured job, or would you rather manage and organize your work yourself? Oldham et al. (1976) reported that people with security needs usually prefer structured, routine jobs. Others with achievement needs enjoy controlling their own methods and techniques. You also want to consider the salary and status level you are seeking. Some people are interested in working for large corporations, while others find small companies preferable. Willingness to travel is yet another concern; many jobs require heavy travel commitments.

Travel requirements often present a particular problem for women. Although Crowley et al. (1973) found that women have the same concerns as men about their jobs, several other studies have reported that outside pressures can interfere with their achievements. Crowley noted that women are equally concerned with their personal growth on the job, opportunity for advancement, and intellectual challenge. However, in a paper presented to the American Psychological Association, Pines and Kafry (1977) highlighted the special concerns of women, pointing out their problems in balancing marital, parental, and work roles. Although men also share roles of spouses and parents, both Stafford et al. (1977) and Heckman et al. (1977) noted that most couples give the wife primary responsibility for household chores and child rearing. The findings of Mueller et al. (1977) will be no surprise: Women who have achieved high positions in their careers are more likely to remain single. Women need to consider their level of interest in family life before choosing a career. Many women decide to rear children first and then go to work. Others prefer to start their careers before choosing marriage. Still others are interested in careers that will be compatible with family life.

Just as tests are available to measure your abilities and aptitudes, psychologists have also developed inventories to check your values and interests. The purpose of these inventories is to help you sort out your interests and focus on your preferences and dislikes. The most commonly used *interest inventories* are the Strong-Campbell Interest Inventory for high school seniors and adults, the Kuder Preference Records for high school juniors, seniors, and adults, and the Vocational Interest Survey for students in grades 8 through 12. Although these tests have some usefulness in reflecting your interests, they have been widely criticized. Many psychologists believe interest inventories are not reliable: They only reflect how you felt at the time of testing. With additional education or new experiences, your interests will change. Matteson (1975) pointed out an additional limitation. People taking the tests are required to stretch their imaginations. Often they have had no experiences comparable to the test items. They must fantasize about what they would like to do, since they have never really tried it.

interest inventory Test designed to determine personal values, likes, and dislikes

Sorting your interests will help you determine whether or not you would enjoy a job. But keep in mind that interest alone does not indicate that you have the ability or are suited for a job. A man may be interested in interior design, but if he is color blind and lacks artistic ability, he will not get very far in his career.

Exercise 16-1
Read each of the following descriptions and indicate what steps each individual should take to improve his/her self-analysis in choosing a career.

a. Boyd, an 18-year-old high school senior, wants to be a dentist. He has an A average in school and a high score on his college aptitude tests. Results of an interest inventory suggested that he is fascinated by teeth and enjoys working with individual people. He is well organized and prefers to work at his own pace.

_____

_____

b. Hilda's mother is a policewoman and wants Hilda to join her on the force. Her mother emphasized that Hilda would receive excellent on-the-job training. Hilda feels it is best to do what her mother wants.

_____

_____

c. Grant likes to work in his own home. He decided that carpentry would be an excellent field for him, since he could set up a shop in his own basement.

_____

_____

_____

Please turn to the Feedback section to check your responses.

Analyzing Jobs

A prime concern in rating a job is opportunity. Not many people will become secretary general of the United Nations. Similarly, if you aspire to become the queen of Britain, it appears the job will be filled for quite some time. Even jobs that are currently plentiful may be eliminated in the future because of expansions in technology. Other positions are more stable. It is not likely that careers in cosmetics, funeral services, religion, or police science will ever become obsolete. However, the future for longshore workers, railroad ticket agents, toll collectors, and bookkeepers looks shaky.

Effects of Technology

In addition to eliminating some jobs, advances in technology will also cause changes in the nature of jobs. Factory work has become more fragmented as machines replace humans. Many jobs require workers to constantly update themselves. For example, twenty-five years ago computer programmers were expected to wire heavy plug boards to be inserted in the early computers. This aspect of their job has clearly been simplified, but anyone who did not update his or her training is out of work. The article in Exhibit 16-2 spells out some changes in detective jobs.

Current estimates suggest that within the next decade about 75 percent of all jobs will require some form of interaction with a computer. These estimates suggest that most people will need to retrain and become more knowledgeable

EXHIBIT 16-2

Source: Restak, R. M. (1980, March). Smart machines learn to see, talk, listen, even 'think' for us. _Smithsonian._

It Takes a Computer to Catch a Crook

In New York City a special police unit, CATCH (Computer-Assisted Terminal Criminal Hunt), is in operation to aid in the rapid identification of criminal suspects. The unit can selectively scan photographs and information on some 250,000 suspects arrested within the past three years. Initially, detectives question a crime victim about 56 descriptive features of the criminal. Answers are then fed into the system which correlates the identified characteristics. Finally, the computer prints out the photographs of the most likely suspects for the purpose of identification.

"Age?"

Figure 16-3
Could this be in our
future?

about computers. However, with improved technology new problems have been added. Many workers who must use video display terminals are complaining of physical disorders (see Exhibit 16-3).

Job Requirements

Once you have assured yourself that a job will still exist a few years hence, you will want to learn more about the job requirements and working conditions. First, you need to determine the skills and training required. Some jobs require good vision, good hearing, or strength. If you are considering a profession, you will need to have extensive schooling. Air-traffic controllers and management trainees usually have long periods of on-the-job training.

If you are satisfied with the training and skills required for a job, you are ready to check the working conditions. Whether you will be required to work indoors or outdoors, in a private office or an open area, or alone or with others are important considerations. Jobs requiring uniforms—for example, the military, nursing, and work with an airline—are sought by some and shunned by others. Working hours are another important factor. Some careers require shiftwork, others require evening hours, and still others require your availability twenty-four hours each day.

Where can you learn about job requirements and working conditions? The most widely used source is the *Occupational Outlook Handbook,** published by the U.S. Bureau of Labor Statistics and revised and updated every two

*Available at most libraries or may be ordered from the Superintendent of Documents, U.S. Government Printing Office, Washington, DC 20402.

EXHIBIT 16-3

VDT's on Trial

Do Video Display Terminals Pose a Health Hazard?

Two years ago, Virginia Wheaton was transcribing notes onto her video display terminal (VDT) when cramps began shooting through her arm. "It felt like my forearm was a set of gears and someone had stripped the gears," she recalls. The next day the pain was so intense she stopped typing. Two days later she couldn't even write with a pencil. Doctors diagnosed repetition strain injury—inflammation resulting from constantly moving a finger, limb or other body part. A tendon in Wheaton's elbow had become inflamed and pressed on a nerve, they said. During a seven-month leave of absence with worker's compensation from her job as an editor and reporter at the Bureau of National Affairs in Washington, D.C., she had surgery to move the injured nerve away from the irritating tendon. Today, her arm still cramps at times.

Wheaton is not alone. Many VDT workers have experienced illnesses or injuries that some researchers link to VDTs, says industrial engineer Michael J. Smith of the University of Wisconsin-Madison, who has surveyed VDT users throughout the United States and reviewed dozens of similar surveys. Researchers like Smith cannot explain entirely why the VDT, a labor-saving machine, should cause more harm than does an electric typewriter, but they have some possible answers. By obviating the need to change typing paper, dab on correction fluid or walk to the file cabinet, they say, VDTs prompt immobility and rigid postures that stress muscles and tendons and possibly lead to repetition strain injuries.

And repetition strain injury is only one complaint leveled against the terminals. Other accusations include backaches, facial rashes (SN:9/5/81, p. 150), eyestrain (SN: 8/29/81, p. 137), heart disease (SN: 2/2/85, p. 78), stress, even miscarriages (SN: 12/12/81, p. 377), and are increasing with the growing numbers of people using VDTs several hours or more daily. According to Beth O'Neil of the Center for Office Technology in Washington, D.C., 28 million people in the United States and Canada operate VDTs in their jobs and three-quarters of all jobs will involve VDTs by the end of the century....

While scientists, union officials and industry representatives continue to debate the VDT safety issue, workers like Virginia Wheaton await the verdict. Wheaton says she would like to see computer companies invest money toward finding the best seating arrangement, computer design and overall work conditions for VDT use. "I can no longer do reporting, which was my job," but further research, she says, may help others.

Source: Hendricks, M. (1988, September 10). VDTs on trial: Do video display terminals pose a health hazard? *Science News.*

years. More than 850 occupations are briefly and concisely described. Descriptions include the employment outlook, the type of work involved, qualifications, training, salary, working conditions, locations, advancement possibilities, and sources of additional information.

Another source is the *Dictionary of Occupational Titles,* * which is published by the U.S. Department of Labor and describes more than 22,000 jobs. Information includes aptitude requirements, physical demands, and the interests and traits of people currently working on the jobs.

Although these two volumes may provide some insights, it is preferable to get first-hand information. Most colleges have career centers with brochures and videotapes on different job groups. Interviewing people in jobs of interest to you would give you more specific information. If possible, try to spend a

*Available at most libraries or may be ordered from the Superintendent of Documents, U.S. Government Printing Office, Washington, DC 20402.

few days observing the work. Often what seems to be a glamorous or exciting career can be a dull routine on a day-to-day basis.

Exercise 16-2
Prepare a list of ten questions you would want answered in analyzing a job.

a. _____

b. _____

c. _____

d. _____

e. _____

f. _____

g. _____

h. _____

i. _____

j. _____

Compare your list with the one in the Feedback section.

Matching Jobs to People

Finding a suitable career is critical to both your success and your happiness. Only through an honest appraisal of yourself and each job is this possible. Often the stereotypes associated with jobs are incorrect. As the article in Exhibit 16-4 reports, only a small percentage of military pilots have "the right stuff" popularized in films. Careful job appraisal and self-analysis may seem tedious, but it is time well spent!

Checkpoint
Use the following questions to check your understanding of this portion of the chapter. Indicate whether each of the following questions is true or false.

1. _____ Leisure hobbies are examples of careers.
2. _____ Your self-concept is affected by your career choice.
3. _____ Career choices must be made before completing high school.
4. _____ Consistent success in school subjects can be an indicator of ability.
5. _____ Intelligence tests measure potential abilities.
6. _____ Aptitude tests cannot measure artistic abilities.
7. _____ Ability is more important than interest in choosing a career.
8. _____ People with achievement needs prefer routine jobs with close supervision.
9. _____ Female executives are more likely to be married and have families than single and childless.
10. _____ Interest inventories have been criticized because they only measure interests at the time of the testing.
11. _____ Interest is more important than ability in choosing a career.
12. _____ Improvements in technology will eliminate or change many jobs.

EXHIBIT 16-4

Flight Check

They're intelligent, courageous and hard-driven. They push themselves to the limit and somehow seem superior to mortal men. They're military pilots, and in the popular imagination they have "the right stuff." Now, new evidence lends some support to this myth and also pokes a few holes in its validity.

Air Force flight psychologists Paul D. Retzlaff and Michael Gilbertini administered a battery of personality tests to 350 men who entered the Air Force's Undergraduate Pilot Training Course at Reese Air Force Base in Texas. The pilots' scores were compared with those from a sample of college men (*Multivariate Behavioral Research,* Vol. 22, pp. 383–399).

The researchers say that pilots are a different breed from the others. Pilots are more dominant, achieving and competitive; more exhibitionistic, confident and self-possessed; and more likely to seek thrills and risks than the college students are. Although many of these traits are associated with leadership skills, the researchers also discovered that the pilots scored low on autonomy. The scientists note that while pilots must lead, they also must follow; they are expected to function as part of a team.

Retzlaff and Gibertini also discovered three distinct personality subtypes among the military pilots. One group epitomizes the "right stuff" stereotype, scoring high on such traits as aggression, dominance, impulsivity and playfulness.

The second, and by far largest group of pilots, tends to be as dominant as the first, but less aggressive and impulsive. Thrill-seeking and playfulness do not figure here.

The third cluster of pilots appear to have the "wrong stuff." Cautious, proper, conforming, polite and retiring, these pilots would probably rather follow than lead and are no more dominant than the sample of college students.

The authors say that based on their research, the "right stuff" personality is not necessarily a prerequisite for military aviators.

Source: Folkenberg, J. (1988, June). Flight check. *Psychology Today.*

13. _____ Salary is the most important consideration in selecting a job.
14. _____ The best way to learn about a career is to interview a person performing a job and observe the working conditions.
15. _____ Self-analysis and job analysis are crucial in choosing a career.

Use the Checkpoint Answer Key to verify your responses. If you had any difficulty with a question, carefully reread the text. If you had little or no difficulty answering the questions or have resolved any problems that you might have had, you are ready to continue with the next portion of this chapter.

APPLYING FOR JOBS

Assuming you have selected and prepared yourself for a career, your next step is to find a job. Inform your friends of your search; they might have a good lead. But if you already have a job and would rather your current employer not learn that you are job hunting, exercise some restraint in spreading the word. There are many sources that provide information on job options. You can check classified ads in newspapers, professional journals, and trade magazines. Or you can visit your school or college placement office, a state employment agency, or a private employment agency. Keep in mind that private agencies charge fees: Sometimes the employer pays, but often you are expected to forfeit some of your initial salary.

Once you have located a few opportunities, you are ready to send letters of application and résumés to prospective employers. Next, you must prepare yourself for interviews. Finally, you should follow up interviews with letters of appreciation. Each of these three steps must be performed properly to be sure you optimize your chances of winning the job you want.

Letters of Application

Letters of application should be short and factual. A letter addressed to a specific person is more likely to attract attention and be read. If you do not know anyone at a company, a quick phone call could determine the name of the person in charge of your area or the director of hiring. Exhibit 16-5 shows a sample outline of a letter of application.

A few cautions about application letters. Try to avoid sounding either hopeless and desperate or pompous and egotistical. Your letter will convey a first impression of you to a prospective employer. Also, avoid copying a form letter verbatim from a textbook. A letter that is written by you will be more informative. If possible, type the letter on plain white 8½ × 11-inch paper, and never send a machine-copied version.

Since a letter of application is brief, rarely more than one page, most of the information on your background should be recorded on your résumé. A résumé should accompany your letter of application and give full details about your education and experiences. The sample outline in Exhibit 16-6 provides guidelines for writing your résumé.

Brohard (1981) recommends *brainstorming* before writing a résumé. She claims the process requires several days of reflecting on your past accomplishments. During the brainstorming period, jot down every attainment you can recall—volunteer work, clubs, political work, courses, and extracurricular work. Then review your list and be sure to include everything relevant to the job you seek.

brainstorming
Technique for generating as many new and creative ideas as possible

Many organizations require you to complete their own application forms. It is wise to check dates beforehand to be certain that you are accurate. Some

EXHIBIT 16-5

Sample Outline for a Letter of Application

Name of Person (Employer)
Title
Name of Organization
City, State, Zip Code
Dear _____ :

Paragraph 1 State the name of the position for which you are applying and how you heard of the opening.

Paragraph 2 Indicate the reasons for your interest in the type of work, the employer, and the location.

Paragraph 3 Relate the information on your résumé to the job description. Point out how your experience and qualifications match the job.

Paragraph 4 Ask for an interview and indicate when you will be available or state when you will call for an appointment.

Sample Outline for Résumé

Name
Home address   Business address
Phone number   Business phone number

Job specification State concisely the type of job you desire.

Employment List previous relevant jobs in reverse chronological order, explaining precisely what you did on each job.

Education List schooling in reverse chronological order, and include any schooling that may have a bearing on the job you seek.

Special Skills Include equipment you have used and special skills you have acquired.

References Indicate that references will be furnished upon request.

applications require lengthy responses. Often the employer is evaluating not only your responses but also your ability to write, so be sure to check your spelling and sentence structure!

Application forms almost always request the names of references. As a courtesy and for your own protection, ask permission from any person you plan to use as a reference. Send a letter reminding the person being used as a reference about yourself. Former employers and teachers sometimes have difficulty recalling every worker and student. One or two facts might help jog their memories. Also mention a time when you will call to be certain you have their permission to use their names. The chances of receiving a positive reference will improve if you have permission.

Exercise 16-3
Assume Greg Loser asked you to read and criticize his letter of application. Comment on each of the areas listed below.

To whom it may concern:

I think you should know that I am an outstanding student and would be an exceptional asset to your company. I had the highest grade in my high school history classes and was the best bowler in my league. I am also very popular with everyone I meet. I would like to be an executive.

I know if you meet me you will probably want to hire me. I desperately need a job, since I have been out of work for three weeks. I cannot even afford food for my parakeet.

Here are some references: Professor Mercy, Mr. Hope, and Charity Love. Their addresses are in the phone directory. If they don't remember me, try Mr. Grinch, Ebenezer Grump, and B. Nasti.

I will be in town next week, and you could interview me on Tuesday or Wednesday. My phone number is (555) 123-4567. Please let me know if I can send or bring any additional information.

a. Addressee: _____

_____

b. Opening paragraph: _____

_____

c. Reference to résumé: _____

_____

d. Tone and attitude: _____

_____

e. References: _____

_____

f. Closing paragraph: _____

_____

Please check your critique in the Feedback section.

Types of Interviews

Most interviews take less than thirty minutes, but within the brief time period, opinions are formed and important decisions are made. There are as many types of interviews as there are interviewers. Each person puts some individual style into the exchange. However, most interviews can be categorized as either informal, standardized, or situational. There are distinct differences among these three types.

Informal interviews. An *informal interview* has no set agenda. The interview is either not planned at all or mapped out rather loosely. The employer and applicant converse and exchange questions and answers. Each applicant is asked to provide different information, according to the direction of the conversation. This technique is often used to size up applicants rather than to gather information. Comparing applicants is difficult, since each applicant may have been asked an entirely different set of questions.

informal interview
Verbal exchange without a specific structure or standard form

Standardized interviews. In a *standardized interview,* the employer asks every applicant the same prepared set of questions. The interviewer begins by attempting to put the applicant at ease with some informal conversation. Next the questioning begins with requests for specific details on work and educational experiences. A sample set of questions might be:

standardized interview
Personal exchange based on a prepared set of questions

- Why did you major in _____ ?
- Why did you leave your previous job?
- What did you enjoy most about your job?
- How do you feel about being pressured to meet deadlines?

Situational interviews. *Situational interviews* are usually limited to large organizations wishing to select people for upper-management jobs. Many of these organizations have assessment centers to handle their screening. The applicant is put in a specific situation, and the interviewer observes reactions. A rather

situational interview
Observation of an applicant in a specific situation set up by an interviewer

amusing type of situational interview is the *stress* interview. That is, it is amusing if you are not the applicant. The applicant might be seated in a chair with a broken leg. As the chair rocks and almost tumbles, the applicant is observed. Those applicants who survive the initial stress may then be handed a leaky coffee mug. The events that occur in a stress interview are limited only by the imagination of the interviewer.

in basket Situational
interview in which an
applicant must make
decisions based on
memos and notes
within a limited time

Another type of situational interview is the *in basket*. Here applicants must go through a series of memos, requests, and orders that they find in their in baskets. Time is limited and they must take action on them. Applicants are observed carefully, and notes are made on whether they are systematic or haphazard in approach. The observer also notes whether they perform tasks themselves or delegate some of the work. After the session each applicant must justify and explain the rationale for all actions taken.

leaderless group
Situational interview
in which several
applicants are
observed as they work
together to solve a
problem

The *leaderless group* is another type of situational interview. Six to twelve applicants are instructed to work together to solve a business problem. They are provided some initial information, and throughout the session the information is updated. Just when they are on the brink of an important decision, new information is sent in to wipe out their conclusions. Leadership and reactions to pressure are observed.

Exercise 16-4
Read each of the following descriptions of interviews, and indicate whether each is an example of an informal, standardized, stress, in-basket, or leaderless-group interview.

a. The interviewer handed Martin a pen and asked him to complete an application. The pen immediately broke. He was handed another pen and it also fell apart. A third pen spilled ink all over the application.

_____

b. When Jinx was applying for a job as a receptionist, her employer was cordial and friendly. They had a delightful chat about summer vacations, families, and football. At the end of the interview the employer shouted, "You're hired!" _____

c. Cloris was sent to a testing center for her interview. She was seated at a desk and told to handle the work in front of her. An interviewer sat across the room and observed her. _____

d. Chris felt at ease when his interviewer chatted with him about the weather last winter. Then the interviewer began reading a long list of questions.

_____

Please turn to the Feedback section to check your responses.

Preparing for Interviews
It is wise indeed to learn as much as possible about the company before your interview. You will appear more interested and ask better questions. As in other emotional situations, preparing ahead can spare you stress and anxiety. Make a checklist to be certain you remember to bring your résumé, a list of

references, and a list of questions for your potential employer. Put questions about salary and fringe benefits on the bottom of the list. Jot down some notes on why you want the job and why you feel you qualify. Be prepared to justify and expand on any items in your résumé.

To create the best impression, dress conservatively, preferably similar to the workers in the company. Of course, if you are being interviewed for a job in landscaping, you do not need to show up in mud-stained overalls. Practice a firm handshake; it will set a good tone. Show interest, stand properly, and avoid fidgeting. As the article in Exhibit 16-7 recommends, use moderation.

At the end of the interview, pull out the firm handshake again and thank your interviewer. Thank the secretary, receptionist, and anyone else who had a role in processing your application or scheduling the interview. If you hear nothing within ten days, you are entitled to call to determine whether the position has been filled.

Following Up on Applications

Immediately after the interview, send a thank-you note to your interviewer. You might restate your interest in the company and show appreciation for the time and information. Your note may make a difference if you are in a close race with other applicants. Also be sure to thank your references. Not only

EXHIBIT 16-7

Dressed for Excess

Their résumés may be perfect, their credentials impeccable, but job candidates still face a crucial test: the interview. Many job-seekers, wise to the ways of the working world, work as hard to appear competent, expert, interested and well groomed as they once did to get A's in school. These self-presentation tactics do earn high marks from employers, but only up to a point.

Psychologist Robert A. Baron recruited 73 undergraduate students to participate in a series of mock job interviews. Both men and women acted as interviewers; the job candidates were two women selected in advance by Baron. Candidates varied their behavior and demeanor by using or omitting positive nonverbal cues—smiling frequently, maintaining eye contact and leaning forward in an attitude of polite interest. Sometimes they also wore a modest but detectable amount of perfume.

After the interview, the students rated the job candidates' competence, potential and intelligence. The students also answered questions designed to test how well they remembered specific information about the candidates.

Baron found that it was possible to have "too much of a good thing." Each tactic—the perfume and the positive cues—helped candidates when they used them alone. But when used together, the tactics actually reduced ratings given by men, although not those given by women. At the same time, men also remembered less information about the candidates than women did.

One possible explanation for this pattern is that men reacted more negatively to these tactics because they found themselves distracted, which threatened their effectiveness as interviewers. Women, in contrast, were able to concentrate on the candidates' less superficial qualities.

"Such efforts by applicants to enhance their 'image' can readily go too far," Baron writes. "From a practical point of view...the best strategy for job applicants to follow appears to be one of careful moderation."

Source: Walton, S. (1987, August). Dressed for excess. *Psychology Today.*

does your appreciative note show courtesy, but you might need your references again.

Exercise 16-5
Assume you are being interviewed for a magnificent job next Monday. Prepare a checklist of at least five items that you want to remember.

a. _____

b. _____

c. _____

d. _____

e. _____

Please compare your list with the list in the Feedback section.

Holding a Job

After the application and interview process, most people are relieved to learn they have been hired. However, most organizations have a probation period. New employees are observed and reconsidered for a set period of time, usually between one week and six months. It is during this period that you must prove you can do the work. To perform any job well, you must organize time efficiently and set priorities.

Figure 16-4
The captain may have trouble holding this job.

"There'll be a slight delay—the captain got on the wrong airplane."

Use the following questions to check your understanding of this portion of the chapter. Choose and mark the one correct response to each question.

16. Which of the following agencies is most likely to charge you a fee for locating a job?
    a. College placement office
    b. State employment agency
    c. Private employment agency
    d. High school employment agency

17. Which of the following should accompany a letter of application?
    a. A thank-you note
    b. A résumé
    c. A fee
    d. A transcript

18. A young man is applying for a job at the Builtwell Hardware Company. The personnel director is Mr. Chain. How should the young man address his letter?
    a. ''Dear Builtwell Hardware Company:''
    b. ''Gentlemen:''
    c. ''Dear Personnel Director:''
    d. ''Dear Mr. Chain:''

19. How should a letter of application conclude?
    a. With a final plea about how you need the job
    b. With a request for an interview
    c. With a detailed description of your education
    d. With a summary copied from a text

20. Which of the following is an example of a situational interview?
    a. A leaderless group
    b. An informal interview
    c. A structured interview
    d. A formal interview

21. What advice would you give a friend who wanted to know how to dress for an interview?
    a. Wear clothing that will attract attention.
    b. Wear expensive clothes.
    c. Wear conservative clothes.
    d. Wear casual clothes.

Use the Checkpoint Answer Key to verify your responses. If you had any difficulty with a question, carefully reread the text. If you had little or no difficulty answering the questions or have resolved any problems that you might have had, you are ready to continue with the next portion of this chapter.

JOB SATISFACTION

Have you ever been unhappy about a job or a course in school? Perhaps you had a bad year in sixth grade or a boring part-time job for a cranky boss. To be sure, your unhappiness affected the work you were doing, but your dissatisfaction probably also affected your relationships off the job or out of school.

Iris and Barrett (1972) studied two groups of foremen. One group was happy and satisfied, the other unhappy and dissatisfied. Both groups were given a questionnaire to rate the importance of their jobs and a questionnaire on job and life satisfaction. They found that job satisfaction had a stronger influence on life satisfaction than life satisfaction had on job satisfaction. The impact of job satisfaction on life satisfaction was strongest for foremen who considered their jobs extremely important.

Both psychologists and corporations have been focusing more interest on the relationships between job satisfaction and life satisfaction. Many companies are now offering counseling services to their employees. Employees can discuss areas of dissatisfaction at work as well as personal matters that may be bothering them.

Lawler (1970) reported that more than 5000 articles have been published on job satisfaction. Most studies conclude that job satisfaction is relative to expectations and needs. People can be satisfied with some aspects of their work and dissatisfied with others.

Common Needs and Expectations

Resources and comfort. Working conditions are basic to job satisfaction or dissatisfaction. If you have a problem locating a parking space or must walk a half mile from the parking lot to your office, each day can get off to a poor start. Poor lighting, uncomfortable chairs, and noisy surroundings can all create dissatisfaction. Herzberg (1968) referred to such working conditions as "hygiene factors." Hygiene factors also include the availability of equipment, supplies, and help. If you must waste time waiting in line to use a copy machine or must work with a faulty printer, you could easily become irritated and unhappy. If you work in attractive surroundings, in a convenient location, at acceptable hours, with ample resources, these hygiene factors cannot create dissatisfaction. A ten-year study by Kohn and Schooler (1983) revealed that positive hygiene factors can increase self-esteem, job commitment, and motivation.

Challenge and stimulation. Although some individuals prefer the security of a routine job, most people seek some stimulation and challenge from their work. Dignity and pride are attached to achievements, and people search for ways to show some initiative. If a job becomes overly dull, you look for some stimulation. You might get yourself a cup of coffee, stroll over to the water fountain, or start up a social conversation with a coworker.

In the past two decades the level of education in the United States has increased markedly. Many people are overeducated for the jobs they perform (Rice, 1980). There are individual differences in needs for challenge. Some people are satisfied if they feel they are using their talents and their work is meaningful. Others have higher expectations and struggle for advancement.

Relations with coworkers. Work offers opportunities for socializing. Lasting, close relationships with coworkers can make a dismal job acceptable. However, productivity generally decreases. If you are dissatisfied with the challenge of your work and the general working conditions, you are likely to spend

The working conditions in this office most likely will create job dissatisfaction. (*Hazel Hankin*)

more time socializing than working. Nonetheless, there are some people who prefer to work among friends. If their coworkers are hostile or unfriendly, they will become dissatisfied with their jobs.

Escape. For some people, work is an escape from their homes. Some want to break loose from a tense family; others who live alone want to escape from their loneliness. By keeping busy, people can avoid facing unpleasant realities. If nothing else, a job can provide this escape, which is usually temporary.

Financial reward and security. Supposedly everyone has a price. What salary would you require to work in dreadful conditions? For some, money is more important than the nature of the work. Others will accept a lower salary if the job is stable and they can have a sense of security. Clearly, companies attempt to lure workers away from each other with offers of better salaries and fringe benefits. There probably has never been a perfect job that fulfilled every need and expectation described. But job satisfaction does not rely entirely on factors beyond your control. You can increase your satisfaction by focusing on positive aspects of an organization. If you are unhappy about an aspect of your work, try to criticize constructively. Describe problems to a person with authority and offer one or two possible solutions. Hopefully, you can help your job meet your needs.

Exercise 16-6
A psychologist and an architectural designer just completed individual surveys at a large corporation. The psychologist concluded that job satisfaction was low, and the architect claimed satisfaction was high.

Explain how the two professionals could come to such opposite conclusions.

_____

_____

_____

_____

_____

You may check your explanation in the Feedback section.

CHANGING CAREERS

Renwick and Lawler (1978) surveyed magazine readers and concluded that people do not give sufficient time to studying careers in their youth. Many just take jobs that are convenient. As a result, most people rethink and consider changing their careers sometime during their lives.

Some careers come to a natural end. Athletes must look for new jobs by middle age. Similarly, women who remained home to rear children find the children are off on their own careers.

After working on a job for a decade or more, people sometimes reach a dead end. They realize they cannot progress any further. Because of the limited opportunity for advancement or promotion, they consider changing careers. Janis and Wheeler (1978) suggested that people draw up a balance sheet on their alternatives and list the pros and cons of a career change. They suggested four categories for comparison:

• Gains and losses for yourself

• Gains and losses for important others (spouse, children, parents, etc.)

• Self-approval or disapproval

• Approval or disapproval of others

This type of exercise helps people recognize the features and drawbacks of both their present job and other potential jobs. A more interesting job for you may not be worth the sacrifice of making your family move and your children change schools. Likewise, you want to consider whether you need the respect of others for your work.

UNEMPLOYMENT

Because Western cultures value work, unemployment usually leads to guilt. Worse, people who are unemployed are not respected. Many stereotype the unemployed as lazy or parasitical. As a result, losing a job is traumatic. Several studies have found increased incidences of suicide, mental illness, alcoholism, and death from heart and kidney diseases among the unemployed.

For many persons, retirement is really unemployment. A surprising number of persons are being pushed into retirement (Selby, 1981). If not prepared, persons who are forced into retirement suffer from depression and illnesses

"Here's a nice 'Get well or find another
job' card from your boss."

Figure 16-5
Losing his job may
prevent him from
getting well.

similar to the unemployed. Many retired persons feel energetic and productive. Since they are unemployed, they must use their own imaginations and initiative. Returning to college, leisure activities, hobbies, and even a new career are all possibilities!

Exercise 16-7
Mr. Oldham is 70 years old. Although he is intelligent and energetic, his company retired him because of their mandatory retirement policy. Mr. Oldham felt the company was unfair, since he is more productive than most younger workers. He is rapidly becoming more depressed.

a. Why is Mr. Oldham likely to be depressed?

_____

_____

b. What do you recommend he do?

_____

_____

_____

Please turn to the Feedback section.

LEISURE

Not only are leisure activities essential in retirement, they are important throughout your life. Yankelovich (1978) reported that 80 percent of

Americans find more enjoyment in their leisure activities than in their work. Everyone needs relaxation and a change of pace to release tension. The amount of time spent in leisure activities usually increases as you age. Young couples with children have little free time to themselves. By middle age it is healthy to develop a hobby. Whether ceramics, bird watching, stamp collecting, painting, or playing computer games, the hobby can be carried into retirement. Free time that can be enjoyed is never depressing!

Checkpoint

Use the following questions to check your understanding of the final portion of this chapter. Indicate whether each of the following questions is true or false.

22. _____ There has been very little research on job satisfaction.
23. _____ According to Herzberg, hygiene factors include physical working conditions.
24. _____ People in dull jobs search for stimulation.
25. _____ Middle-aged managers have a strong need to socialize at work.
26. _____ People can be satisfied with some aspects of their work but dissatisfied with others.
27. _____ Few people change the careers that they originally chose.
28. _____ A balance sheet can be used to help make a decision about a career change.
29. _____ Unemployed people have fewer health problems.
30. _____ Developing a hobby can improve your adjustment to retirement.

Figure 16-6
Those who have read this text will never spend their leisure time here....

Check your responses against the Checkpoint Answer Key at the end of the chapter. If you had difficulty with any question, reread the text. If you had little or no difficulty answering the questions or have resolved any problems that you might have had, you are ready to check yourself against the chapter inventory that follows.

CHAPTER INVENTORY

Use this list of objectives as a review checklist. You should be able to do each of the tasks outlined in the objectives and apply them to everyday examples. If you can, you may feel confident that you have mastered the material in this chapter.

1. Discuss the importance of career decisions, and describe two basic steps required in making them.
2. List three considerations in analyzing yourself, and specify three ways to analyze your abilities.
3. Explain the special concerns of women in choosing a career.
4. Identify a technique used by psychologists to assess interests and needs.
5. List two general considerations in analyzing jobs.
6. Describe the probable impact of technology on jobs.
7. Identify three sources of information on the nature of jobs.
8. Identify ways to learn of possible job opportunities.
9. Write a letter of application, a résumé, and a request for a reference.
10. Recognize the importance of brainstorming before writing a résumé.
11. Distinguish among informal, standardized, and situational interviews.
12. Describe the procedure used in in-basket and leaderless-group interviews.
13. Prepare for an interview.
14. Recognize the relationship between job satisfaction and satisfaction in life.
15. Describe five aspects of job satisfaction.
16. State two reasons why people might decide to change careers.
17. Recognize the effects of unemployment and forced retirement on health.
18. Specify the importance of leisure activities while working and in retirement.

Feedback

The correct answers to the exercises follow. If you did not answer an exercise correctly, review the preceding pages and return to the exercise to correctly complete it.

16-1. *a.* Boyd had better check his bank account or find out if any friends, relatives, or institutions are willing to finance his education. (Equiping a dental office is an added expense.)

    b. Hilda needs to determine her own interests and abilities before making a career choice.

    c. Grant should find out if he has a talent for carpentry.

16-2. Your list should have included any ten of the following:

    Are there many openings for the job?

    Will the job be in demand in the future?

    Will continuous retraining be required?

    How will technology affect the nature of the work?

What skills and abilities are required?

What previous training is required?

Will there be lengthy training periods on the job?

Is most of the work performed indoors or outdoors?

Is travel required?

What are the office facilities like?

Is a uniform required?

What are the working hours?

Are there unpleasant or hazardous working conditions?

16-3. a. Greg should find out the name of the person who will be most interested in his letter.

b. The opening paragraph should tell more about the type of position he wants. "Executive" is too vague. Experience should appear on his résumé. The assets he mentions do not seem relevant.

c. What résumé? Greg should have a brainstorming session and enclose a résumé.

d. The tone and attitude sounds both puffed up and desperate. He should stick to relevant facts.

e. Greg needs to contact his references and obtain permission to use their names. He should also include addresses.

f. The closing paragraph is the best feature of the letter. He might suggest his interest in visiting the organization even if he cannot be interviewed.

16-4. a. Stress interview

b. Informal interview

c. In-basket interview

d. Standardized interview

16-5. Your list should include any five of the following:

Bring a résumé.

Bring a list of references.

Prepare a list of questions to ask at the interview.

Prepare notes on why you want the job and how you qualify.

Review résumé.

Have conservative clothes ready.

Practice shaking hands.

Thank everyone involved.

16-6. The architectural designer probably focused on resources and comfort, while the psychologist probably questioned employees on job stimulation, relations with coworkers, and possibly escape value of the job. It appears the physical setting is pleasant, but the work itself leaves much to be desired!

16-7. a. Mr. Oldham's retirement is really unemployment for him. He is showing a normal reaction to unemployment.

b. He could use his intelligence and energy in a productive way. Volunteer work, a hobby, or another job are possibilities.

Checkpoint Answer Key

1. false	**3.** false	**5.** true	**7.** false
2. true	**4.** true	**6.** false	**8.** false

9. *false*
10. *true*
11. *false*
12. *true*
13. *false*
14. *true*

15. *true*
16. *c*
17. *b*
18. *d*
19. *b*
20. *a*

21. *c*
22. *false*
23. *true*
24. *true*
25. *false*
26. *true*

27. *false*
28. *true*
29. *false*
30. *true*

GLOSSARY

achievement need Motivation to accomplish tasks and be a success.

achievement test Test designed to measure past accomplishments, usually in academic subjects.

affiliation need Motivation to associate and belong with other people and feel loved.

aggression Behavior that hurts or destroys another person, either verbally or physically, or both.

agoraphobia Most severe phobia, usually accompanied by panic attacks; an inability to go out of the house.

altruism Concern for others; helping others without expecting a reward or benefit.

Alzheimer's disease Organic brain disorder causing a gradual loss of memory, confusion, and general mental deterioration.

amnesia Loss of memory or memory gap that includes forgetting personal information that would normally be recalled.

amniocentesis Procedure involving the removal of fluid from the uterus of an expectant mother to detect possible disease or genetic defects.

anorexia nervosa Prolonged refusal to eat resulting in a severe weight loss.

antisocial personality Condition involving hurting others and breaking laws without guilt.

anxiety disorder A continuous state of tension, stress, and fearfulness.

applied psychology Approach involving practical uses of the study of behavior and thought.

approach-approach conflict Conflict that results from choosing between two desirable goals.

approach-avoidance conflict Conflict that results from weighing the positive and negative aspects of a single goal.

aptitude test Test designed to measure individual potential and to predict future achievements in a given area.

artificial intelligence   Computer programs that solve problems.

assertiveness   Standing up for personal rights while respecting the rights of others.

attitude   Conviction based on beliefs, emotions, and behavior toward an object, person, or idea.

authoritarian discipline   Regulating the behavior of others by rigid rules.

authoritarian leader   Person who gives direct orders and is solely in charge of a group.

avoidance-avoidance conflict   Conflict that results from being forced to choose between two undesirable goals.

behavior modification   Technique that uses principles of conditioning to reach a desirable goal.

behavior therapy   Psychotherapy that uses techniques based on learning principles.

behaviorism   Belief that psychology should be scientific and based on observable events.

biofeedback   Technique that provides information on heart rate and blood pressure so that a person can control these internal processes.

bipolar disorder   Mood disorder involving mood swings between depression and mania.

borderline personality   Personality disorder involving instability, confused self-image, and problems in relationships.

brainstorming   Technique for generating as many new and creative ideas as possible.

brainwashing   Dangerous technique used in spreading propaganda.

bulimia   Binge eating followed by laxatives or self-induced vomiting.

case study   In-depth study of one individual, usually including tests, biographical and family histories, and interviews.

catastrophize   Tendency to exaggerate things that may go wrong.

chunking   Grouping individual items together into units to increase short-term retention.

clairvoyance   Ability to perceive objects or events that are not within the reach of the senses.

classical conditioning   Form of learning based on pairing a stimulus that elicits a reflex or emotional response with a neutral stimulus, so that the neutral stimulus will eventually elicit the reflexive or emotional response.

cognition   Mental or thought process.

cognitive psychology   View that focuses on how the mind processes information.

cohesiveness   Ability to stick together in a group.

compensation   Healthy defense mechanism that allows persons who are inadequate in one area to turn to areas where they can excel.

competitive goal   Objective that people in a group work against each other to achieve.

compliance   Publicly behaving in accordance with a group while privately disagreeing with their beliefs.

compulsion   Repeated and pesistent behavior ritual that a person feels compelled to carry out to avoid disaster.

conformity   Accepting the beliefs of a group and behaving accordingly.

connotation   Emotional feelings and associations that a word arouses.

control group   Group of research participants that are the same as the experimental group with the exception of the variable being studied.

conversion disorder   Anxiety disorder characterized by a loss of sensation without any physical cause.

cooperative goal   Objective that a group works together to achieve.

corporal punishment   Inflicting bodily harm to decrease undesirable behavior.

correlation   Relationship between scores on two variables.

creativity   Ability to see things in a new way and come up with unusual solutions.

defense mechanisms   Variety of unconscious techniques used to avoid anxiety and protect self-esteem.

democratic approach   Method using explanations and reasoning for rules.

democratic leader   Leader who expects group members to participate in decisions.

denotation   Specific dictionary definition of a word.

depression   Mood disorder in which a person feels overwhelming sadness.

desensitization   Therapeutic approach that uses a gradual method of classical conditioning to remove fears.

discrimination   Determining differences and sorting objects or people into categories.

displacement   Redirection of feelings to a substitute person or object when the cause of the feelings is either an unacceptable or unavailable target.

dissonance   Discomfort that occurs from two inconsistent thoughts or beliefs.

downward communication   Passing messages from upper management down to workers.

drug   Chemical substance that causes physical, emotional, or behavioral changes.

dyslexia   Perceptual problem that results in reading problems; scrambled or confused message is sent to the brain.

eclectic view   Belief that psychology should select among appropriate findings of behavioral, gestalt, psychoanalytic, humanist, cognitive, and other views.

electroshock treatment (ECT)   Physiological therapy that delivers an electric shock to the brain to induce a convulsion or coma and reduce depression by erasing memories.

emetic   Substance that causes vomiting.

emotion   Feeling that arouses an individual to act or change.

emotional respondent   Emotion that is always elicited by a given stimulus and does not require learning; an emotional reflex.

existential therapy   Form of treatment that focuses on free will and the meaning of life.

experiment   Research technique using controls to find the causes of specific behaviors.

experimental group   Group that receives treatment being investigated in an experiment.

extinction   Weakening or diminishing of a response; removal of a positive reinforcer to decrease the likelihood of a behavior.

extrasensory perception (ESP)   Ability to perceive and/or influence objects without using external senses.

extrinsic motivation   Performing activities only for an outside or external reward.

fantasy   Defense mechanism that involves withdrawing to an imaginary world through daydreams.

flex-time   Program that permits employees to schedule their own hours of work.

free association   Following a sequence of associated spontaneous personal thoughts.

frustration   Feeling that results whenever you cannot reach a desired goal.

functional fixedness   Using objects only for their known purposes and being unable to think of other possible uses to solve problems.

gestalt   School of psychology that emphasizes patterns of organization in behavior.

gestalt therapy   Form of humanistic therapy that focuses on consistency between behaviors and inner feelings.

global demential amnesia   Type of amnesia characterized by an absent-mindedness about present events.

group   Two or more people who interact or are aware of each other and share a common goal.

group norms   Rules of behavior for two or more people.

group therapy   Situation in which a therapist directs a discussion in a group of usually six to twelve persons, so that they may learn and profit from communication within the group.

groupthink   Conformity that keeps a group in a rut.

halo effect   Bias that causes a person to overlook another person's specific deficiencies because of one favorable characteristic.

hidden agenda   Important personal information that is not revealed to other members of a group.

homeostasis   Ability of vital functions to maintain a stable condition.

hospice   Place for terminally ill patients where understanding, feelings, and dignity are primary concerns, along with health care.

humanistic counseling   Psychotherapy approach that attempts to improve self-esteem and encourage personal growth.

humanistic psychology   View that emphasizes the importance of self-direction and personal growth.

hypochondriasis   Anxiety disorder characterized by a total preoccupation with exaggerated health problems.

hypothesis   Educated guess that gives a tentative explanation and a basis for research.

hysterical amnesia   Amnesia that has no organic or physical cause; usually it occurs after a trauma and is temporary.

ideal self   Person's goal or dream self.

illusion   Misinterpretation or error in perception.

in basket   Situational interview in which an applicant must make decisions based on memos and notes within a limited time.

incentive   Reward that motivates behavior.

infatuation   Transient, temporary, selfish love.

informal interview   Verbal exchange without a specific structure or standard form.

intelligence   Ability to learn or adapt.

interest inventory   Test designed to determine personal values, likes, and dislikes.

interpretation   Inferring meaning from what is sensed by comparing it with previously stored information.

intrinsic motivation   Performing activities because they are rewarding and enjoyable in themselves.

Johari window   System of quadrants used in the study of self-disclosure.

laissez-faire leader   Coordinator who gives a group free rein.

Lamaze method   A preparation for active and conscious participation in the birth process.

leader   Person who gives guidance or direction to others and influences or changes their behavior.

leaderless group   Situational interview in which several applicants are observed as they work together to solve a problem.

learning   Relatively lasting changes in behavior that are caused by experience or practice.

Leboyer method   Childbirth method that attempts to minimize shock to the newborn infant.

life structure   The basic pattern of a person's life.

limerance   Total emotional commitment that gives the experience of being or falling "in love."

loci   A mnemonic device that associates locations along a familiar path with items to be remembered.

long-term memory   The third stage of memory; items remembered more than five minutes are likely to be stored there indefinitely.

management   Conditioning method that allows a person to choose alternatives of reward or punishment.

management by objectives (MBO)   System that requires managers to set goals and employees to develop their own strategies to accomplish the goals.

mental set   A limited view of possible solutions and a tendency to respond in the same way regardless of the problem.

mindful discrimination   Discrimination based on training and sound reasoning.

mnemonics   A method that gives meaning and organization to help memory.

modeling   Learning that occurs by observing and imitating others.

motivation   The needs and incentives that cause people to behave as they do.

multiple personality   A rare disorder in which a person has two or more distinct personalities, each becoming prominent at a different time.

negative correlation   When one variable increases, the other decreases.

negative reinforcement   Removal of an unpleasant stimulus to increase the likelihood of a behavior.

neonate   Newborn infant, usually less than two weeks old.

network   Communication involving more than two people.

normal curve   Bell-shaped frequency distribution.

observation   Research method that requires watching and recording behavior without interference or interpretation.

obsessions   Unwanted but persistent thoughts or ideas.

one-way communication   Speaker speaks and receives no feedback from the listener.

operant (instrumental) conditioning   Type of learning that occurs because of positive or negative reinforcements.

organic amnesia   Amnesia that has physiological causes.

parapsychology   Field of psychology that focuses on extrasensory perception.

peak experience   Brief sense of overwhelming total fulfillment that approximates self-actualization.

pegword   Method for improving memory, using a poem to attach mental image associations with items on a list that is to be retained.

perception   Process that combines both sensing and interpreting.

permissive approach   Method using little or no discipline.

personality disorder   Pattern of negative traits that cause distress and an inability to get along with others, but the traits are not viewed as abnormal by the person exhibiting them.

phobia   Intense, exaggerated, and unrealistic fear.

placebo   Inert substance or fake treatment often used on a control group in an experiment.

polygraph   Instrument commonly known as a lie detector that measures changes in heart beat, blood pressure, breathing, digestive activity, and electric resistance in the skin surface.

positive correlation   When one variable increases, the other also increases.

positive reinforcement   Rewards that increase the likelihood of a behavior.

post-traumatic stress   Anxiety disorder that causes a person to constantly re-experience a traumatic or shocking event.

power need   Motivation to dominate and rule others.

precognition   Ability to foresee future events.

predicate thinking   Nonlogical thought that unconsciously associates subjects of sentences that have the same predicates or endings.

prejudice   Negative attitude based on a hasty judgment without facts.

premise   Belief.

primacy effect   An explanation of why the first things learned are easier to remember.

proactive interference   Forgetting that occurs because of confusion with previously learned material.

projection   Defense mechanism based on guilt that involves accusing another of one's own weakness.

projective test   Personality test that uses ambiguous stimuli and is designed to measure unconscious feelings.

propaganda   Information that is deliberately deceptive or erroneous.

psychoanalysis   View that psychology should focus on unconscious feelings.

psychokinesis (PK)   Ability of the mind to manipulate physical objects without any physical contact.

psychological size   Perceived importance of a person.

psychology   Scientific study of human behavior and thought processes.

psychosurgery   Operations on the brain to treat mental disorders.

punishment   An unpleasant stimulus that decreases the liklihood of behavior.

rational-emotive therapy   Form of therapy that helps people think rationally and eliminate their self-defeating emotional thoughts.

rationalization   Defense mechanism that distorts truth to provide excuses for a situation that is unacceptable.

reactance   Strong resistance that results from receiving high-pressure persuasion and often causes a person to do the opposite of what is asked.

reaction formation   Defense mechanism that causes people to behave in a manner opposite to their unacceptable impulses.

recency effect   An explanation of why the last things learned are easier to remember.

reflex   Response that is always elicited after a given stimulus and does not require learning.

regression   Defense mechanism that involves the use of immature and child-like behaviors to cope with problems.

repression   Forgetting that is caused by unconscious blocking of thoughts that are threatening or frightening.

retroactive interference   Forgetting that occurs because of confusion with newly learned material.

reverse discrimination   Favoring a group that elicits negative feelings.

schizophrenia   Severe disturbance involving hallucinations, delusions, or thought disturbances.

script   Brief story that requires you to fill in information.

self-actualization   Highest need on Maslow's hierarchy; need to grow and fulfill potential.

self-concept   Collection of beliefs that a person has about his or her own self-image.

self-disclosure   Speaking honestly and revealing true feelings to others.

self-esteem   Personal regard that people have for their own worth.

self-fulfilling prophecy   Making a prediction and acting in a way to ensure that it will come true.

sensation Bringing stimuli from the outside world into the nervous system.

sensitivity training Form of group therapy that requires total honesty and trust among members.

sensory bombardment Overloading the senses with stimuli.

sensory deprivation Removal or reduction of sensory stimuli from the environment.

sensory register First stage of memory when information that is sensed is briefly recorded and rapidly decays if not passed along to short-term memory.

shaping Rewarding each behavior in a sequence that will eventually lead to a target behavior.

short-term memory The second stage of memory when information is stored for less than thirty seconds.

sibling rivalry Competition among brothers and sisters in a family.

situational interview Observation of an applicant in a specific situation set up by an interviewer.

social loafing Tendency of individuals to exert less effort when they work together than when they work alone.

socioemotional leader Person who directs a group primarily according to the personal and social needs of the members.

SQ3R Mnemonic for survey, question, read, recite, and review; a successful approach to studying.

standardized interview Personal exchange based on a prepared set of questions.

standardized test Test that has a uniform set of instructions for administration and scoring; the results can be compared with the scores of a larger population.

stress Tension caused by intense emotion.

sublimation Healthy defense mechanism that channels unacceptable impulses into positive, constructive areas.

subliminal Stimulus beneath a person's sensory threshold.

suppression Consciously and intentionally avoiding unpleasant thoughts and memories.

survey Poll to determine attitudes and behaviors of a group of people.

task leader Person who keeps a group working toward a goal.

telepathy Ability to understand what another person is thinking without the use of the senses; mind reading.

theory X Belief that people are basically lazy and must be controlled and directed by management.

theory Y Belief that people are naturally interested in work and can direct their own behavior.

threshold Smallest amount of stimuli that a person is aware of; stimulus a person can barely sense.

trace A memory impression stored in the brain.

transactional analysis (TA) Method sometimes used in group therapy to examine verbal interactions between people.

two-way communication Speaker speaks and receives feedback from a listener, who then becomes a speaker.

type-T personality   High thrill seeking.
type-t personality   Low thrill seeking.

unconscious   Motives, feelings, and impulses that are not in a person's awareness but nonetheless may influence the individual's behavior.

upward communication   Passing information from workers up to management.

vicarioius learning   Observing the positive and negative reinforcement of
others.

BIBLIOGRAPHY

Adams, A. J., & Stone, T. H. (1977). Satisfaction of need for achievement in work and leisure time activities. *Journal of Vocational Behavior, 11,* 174–181.

Albee, G. W. (1985, February). The answer is prevention. *Psychology Today,* pp. 60–64.

Allen, V. L., & Levine, J. M. (1971). Social support and conformity: The role of independent assessment of reality. *Journal of Experimental Social Psychology, 7,* 48–58.

Allport, G. (1958). *The nature of prejudice.* Garden City, N.Y.: Anchor/Doubleday.

Allport, G. (1961). *Pattern and growth in personality.* New York: Holt, Rinehart & Winston.

Angell, M. (1985). Disease as a reflection of the psyche. *New England Journal of Medicine, 312* (24), 1570–1572.

Aronson, E., Turner, J., & Carlsmith, M. (1963). Communicator credibility and communicator discrepancy as determinants of opinion change. *Journal of Abnormal and Social Psychology, 67,* 31–36.

Asch, S. E. (1956). Studies of independence and conformity: A minority of one against a unanimous majority. *Psychological Monographs, 70* (9, Whole No. 416).

Ashley, W. R., Harper, R. S., & Runyon, D. L. (1951). The perceived size of coins in normal and hypnotically induced economic states. *American Journal of Psychology, 64* (4), 564–572.

Averill, J. R. (1976). Emotion and anxiety: Social, cultural, biological and psychological determinants. In M. Zuckerman & C. Spielberger (Eds.), *Emotion and anxiety.* Hillsdale, N.J.: Lawrence Erlbaum Associates.

Bahr, H. M., & Chadwick, B. A. (1974). Conservatism, racial intolerance, and attitudes toward racial assimilation among whites and American Indians. *Journal of Social Psychology, 94,* 45–56.

Bales, R. F. (1958). Task roles and social roles in problem-solving groups. In E. E. Maccoby, T. M. Newcomb, & E. L. Hartley (Eds.), *Readings in social psychology.* New York: Holt, Rinehart & Winston.

Bandura, A. (1969). *Principles of behavior modification.* New York: Holt, Rinehart & Winston.

Bandura, A., Ross, D., & Ross, S. A. (1963). Imitation of film-mediated aggressive models. *Journal of Abnormal and Social Psychology, 66,* 3–11.

Bandura, A., & Walters, R. H. (1959). *Adolescent aggression.* New York: Ronald.

Bandura, A., & Walters, R. H. (1963). *Social learnings and personality development.* New York: Holt Rinehart.

Bane, M. J. (1976). Marital disruption and the lives of children. *Journal of Social Issues, 32,* 103–117.

Barron, F., & Harrington, D. M. (1981). Creativity, intelligence, and personality. *Annual Review of Psychology, 32,* 439–476.

Baumrind, D. (1967). Child care practices anteceding three patterns of preschool behavior. *Genetic Psychology Monograph, 75,* 43–88.

Baumrind, D. (1970). Socialization and instrumental competence in young children. *Young Children, 26* (2).

Beecher, H. K. (1959). *Measurement of subjective responses: Quantitative effects of drugs.* New York: Oxford University Press.

Beers, T. M., & Koroly, P. (1979). Cognitive strategies, expectancy and coping style in the control of pain. *Journal of Consulting and Clinical Psychology, 47,* 179–180.

Begley, S., & Carey, J. (1979, November 26). The sexual brain. *Newsweek.*

Bennet, W., & Gurin, J. (1982). *The dieter's dilemma: Eating less and weighing more.* New York: Basic Books.

Berelson, B., & Steiner, G. (1964). *Human behavior.* New York: Harcourt Brace Jovanovich.

Berkowitz, L. (1968). *Roots of aggression: A re-examination of the frustration-aggression hypothesis.* New York: Atherton.

Berne, E. (1961). *Transactional analysis in psychotherapy.* New York: Grove Press.

Berne, E. (1964). *Games people play.* New York: Grove Press.

Bettelheim, B., & Janowitz, M. (1950). *Dynamics of prejudice: A psychological and sociological study of veterans.* New York: Harper & Row.

Birnbaum, I. M., Parker, E. S., Hartley, J. T., & Noble, E. P. (1978). Alcohol and memory: Retrieval processes. *Journal of Verbal Learning and Verbal Behavior, 17,* 325–335.

Birns, B., Blank, M., & Bridger, W. H. (1966). The effectiveness of various soothing techniques on human neonates. *Psychosomatic Medicine, 28,* 316–322.

Bower, G. (1973, October). How to...uh...remember! *Psychology Today,* pp. 62–70.

Bradford, L. (1972). The case of the hidden agenda. *Group Development Selected Reading Series.* Washington, D.C.: National Training Laboratories.

Brazelton, T. B. (1970). Effects of prenatal drugs on the behavior of the neonate. *American Journal of Psychiatry, 126* (9), 95–100.

Brehm, J. W. (1966). *A theory of psychological reactance.* New York: Academic Press.

Brenner, M. H., & Sigband, N. B. (1973). Organizational communication: An analysis based on empirical data. *Academy of Management Journal,* p. 325.

Briscoe, C. W., & Smith, J. B. (1975). Depression in bereavement and divorce: Relationship to primary depressive illness, a study of 128 subjects. *Archives of General Psychiatry, 32,* 439–443.

Brohard, E. B. (1981). *The job application process.* Unpublished manuscript, Northern Virginia Community College.

Brown, W. F. (1974). Effectiveness of paraprofessionals: The evidence. *Personnel and Guidance Journal, 53* (4), 257–263.

Bugelski, B. R., & Alampay, D. A. (1961). Professor Ahman Oramouz. *Canadian Journal of Psychology, 15,* 206.

Buys, C. J. (1978). Humans would do better without groups. *Personality and Social Psychology Bulletin, 4,* 123–125.

Cangemi, J. (1974). Futuristics: A brief view of some aspects of the field of psychology circa the year 2000. *Psychology, 11* (1), 52–55.

Carrera, M. A. (1986, April 11). *Future directions in teen pregnancy prevention.* Talk presented to the annual meeting for the Scientific Study of Sex, Eastern Region.

Chambless, D. (1986). Fears and anxiety. In C. Tavris (Ed.), *Every woman's emotional well-being.* New York: Doubleday.

Chase, W. G., & Simon, H. A. (1973). The mind's eye in chess. In W. G. Chase (Ed.), *Visual information processing.* New York: Academic Press.

Clayton, R. R., & Voss, H. L. (1977). Shacking up: Cohabitation in the 1970's. *Journal of Marriage and the Family, 39* (2), 273–283.

Cohen, S., & Hoberman, H. M. (1983). Positive events and social support as buffers of life change stress. *Journal of Applied Social Psychology, 13,* 99–125.

Coleman, J. C. (1972). *Abnormal psychology and modern life.* Glenview, Ill.: Scott, Foresman.

Coles, R., & Stokes, G. (1985). *Sex and the American teenager.* New York: Harper & Row.

Coombs, B., Hales, D., & Williams, B. (1980). *An invitation to health.* Menlo Park, Calif.: Benjamin/Cummings.

Coopersmith, S. (1967). *The antecedents of self-esteem.* San Francisco: W. H. Freeman.

Crenshaw, A. (1980, February 24). "Big men" really are. *Washington Post.*

Cressen, R. (1978). Artistic quality of drawings and judges' evaluation of the DAP. *Journal of Personality Assessment, 42,* 597–603.

Crombag, H. F. (1966). Cooperation and competition in means-independent triads. *Journal of Personality and Social Psychology, 4,* 692–695.

Crowley, J. E., Levitin, T. E., & Quinn, R. P. (1973, March). Seven deadly half-truths about women. *Psychology Today,* pp. 94–96.

Crowne, D. P., & Marlowe, D. (1964). *The approval motive: Studies in evaluative dependence.* New York: Wiley.

Darley, C. F., Tinkleberg, J. R., Roth, W. T., Hollister, L. E., & Atkindon, R. C. (1973). Influence of marihuana on storage and retrieval processes in memory. *Memory and Cognition, 1,* 196–200.

Davis, K. (1973, July). The care and cultivation of the corporate grapevine. *Dun's.*

Davis, K. (1977). *Human behavior at work.* New York: McGraw-Hill.

Deci, E. L. (1971). Effects of externally mediated rewards on intrinsic motivation. *Journal of Personality and Social Psychology, 18,* 105–115.

Deci, E. L. (1975). *Intrinsic motivation.* New York: Plenum Press.

Deci, L. (1972, August). Work: Who does not like it and why. *Psychology Today,* pp. 56–68.

DeLongis, A., Coyne, J. C., Dakof, G., Folkman, S., & Lazarus, R. S. (1982). Relationship of daily hassles, uplifts, and major life events to health status. *Health Psychology, 1,* 119–136.

Deutsch, M. (1968). The effects of cooperation and competition upon group process. In D. Cartwright & A. Zander (Eds.), *Group dynamics: Research and theory.* New York: Harper & Row.

Deutsch, M., & Gerard, H. B. (1955). A study of normative and informational social influences upon individual judgment. *Journal of Abnormal and Social Psychology, 51,* 629–636.

Diagnostic and statistical manual of mental disorders. (DSM III-R). (1987). Washington, D. C.: American Psychiatric Association.

Disabling panic attacks (agoraphobia). How is agoraphobia treated? (1979, August). *Harvard Medical School Health Letter.*

Dodge, J. R., & Rogers, C. W. (1976). Is NIMH's dream coming true? Wyoming Centers reduce state hospital admissions. *Community Mental Health Journal, 12* (4), 399–404.

Drillien, C. M., & Ellis, R. W. B. (1964). *The growth and development of the prematurely born infant.* Baltimore: Williams & Wilkens.

Dryfoos, J. (1985). What the United States can learn about prevention of teenage pregnancy from other developed countries. *SIECUS Report,* XIV, 1–7.

Ehrenreich, B., Hess, E., & Jacobs, G. (1986). *Re-making love.* Garden City, N. Y.: Anchor/Doubleday.

Ekman, P. (1980). *The face of man.* New York: Garland STPM Press.

Ekman, P. (1982). Methods for measuring facial action. In P. Ekman & K. Scherer (Eds.), *Handbook of methods in non-verbal behavior research.* New York: Cambridge University Press.

Ekman, P., & Friesen, W. (1978). *FACS investigators guide*. Palo Alto, Calif.: Consulting Psychologists Press.

Ekman, P., Friesen, W., & Ancoli, S. (1980). Facial signs of emotional experience. *Journal of Personality and Social Psychology, 39*, 1125–1134.

Ellis, A. (1979). Rational emotive therapy. In R. Corsini (Ed.), *Current psychotherapies*. Itasca, Ill.: Peacock.

Engstrom, L., Geijerstam, G., Holmberg, N. G., & Uhrus, K. A. (1964). A prospective study of the relationship between psycho-social factors and the course of pregnancy and delivery. *Journal of Psychosomatic Research, 8*, 151–155.

Ennis, R. H. (1985). Critical thinking and the curriculum. *National Forum, 65* (1), 28–30.

Evans, B. (1963). *Word-a-day vocabulary builder*. New York: Random House.

Fantz, R. L. (1958). Pattern vision in young infants. *Psychological Record, 8*, 43–47.

Faraone, S. V., & Tsuang, M. T. (1985). Quantitative models of genetic transmission of schizophrenia. *Psychological Bulletin, 98* (1), 41–66.

Farley, F. (1986, May). The big T personality. *Psychology Today*.

Fast, J. (1970). *Body language*. New York: Pocket Books.

Festinger, L. (1962). Cognitive dissonance. *Scientific American, 207*, 93–98.

Footlick, J. K. (1981, March 23). Lock 'em up—but where? *Newsweek*.

Frankl, V. (1955). *The doctor and the soul*. New York: Knopf.

Freedman, J. (1978). *Happy people: What happiness is, who has it and why*. New York: Harcourt Brace Jovanovich.

Freedman, J., & Fraser, S. C. (1966). Compliance without pressure: The foot in the door technique. *Journal of Personality and Social Psychology, 4*, 195–202.

Freedman, M., & Rosenman, R. (1974). *Type A behavior and your heart*. New York: Knopf.

Gagnon, J. H., & Greenblat, C. S. (1978). *Life designs: Individuals, marriages and families*. Glenview, Ill.: Scott, Foresman.

Gardner, H. (1983). *Frames of mind: The theory of multiple intelligences*. New York: Basic Books.

Gardner, H. (1985). *Frames of mind*. New York: Basic Books.

Gelman, D., Carey, J., Gelman E., Melamud, P., Foote, D., Lubenow, G., & Contreras, J. (1981, May 18). Just how the sexes differ. *Newsweek*.

Gerard, H. B., Wilhemy, R. A., & Conelley, E. S. (1968). Conformity and group size. *Journal of Personality and Social Psychology, 8*, 79–82.

Gilligan, C. (1982). *In a different voice*. Cambridge, Mass.: Harvard University Press.

Gilmer, B. (1975). *Applied psychology: Adjustments in living and work*. New York: McGraw-Hill.

Ginott, H. G. (1969). *Between parent and child*. New York: Avon Books.

Glass, D. C. (1977). *Stress and coronary prone behavior*. Hillsdale, N.J.: Lawrence Erlbaum Associates.

Gold, P. W., Gwirtsman, H., Avgerinos, P. C., Nieman, L. K., Gallucci, W. T., Kaye, W., Jimerson, D., Ebert, M., Rittmaster, R., Loriaux, L., & Chrousos, G. P. (1986). Abnormal hypothalamic-pituitary-adrenal function in anorexia nervosa. *New England Journal of Medicine, 314*, 1335–1342.

Goldberger, L. (1982). Sensory deprivation and overload. In L. Goldberger & S. Breznitz (Eds.), *Handbook of stress: Theoretical and clinical aspects*. New York: Free Press.

Goleman, D. (1986, November 9). A different sort of IQ test. *New York Times*.

Gordon, T. (1970). *Parent effectiveness training*. New York: Peter Wyden.

Gould, R. (1975, August). Adult life stages: Growth toward self-tolerance. *Psychology Today*.

Grant, E. (1988, March). Marriage: Practice makes perfect? *Psychology Today*.

Greenberg, M., & Morris, N. (1974). Engrossment: The newborn's impact upon the father. *American Journal of Orthopsychiatry, 44* (4), 520–531.

Gurman, A. S., & Kniskern, D. P. (1976). Research on marital and family therapy. In S. L. Garfield and D. E. Bergin (Eds.), *Handbook of psychotherapy and behavior change*. New York: Wiley.

Gyllenhammer, P. G. (1977). How Volvo adapts work to people. *Harvard Business Review, 55,* 102–105.

Haire, D. (1972). The cultural warping of childbirth. *International Childbirth Association News,* p. *35.*

Hall, E. T. (1969). *The hidden dimension.* Garden City, N.Y.: Anchor/Doubleday.

Harkins, S. G., & Petty, R. E. (1983). Social context effects in persuasion. In P. Paulus (Ed.), *Basic group processes.* New York: Springer-Verlag.

Harriman, B. (1974). Up and down the communication ladder. *Harvard Business Review, 52,* 147–148.

Harris, R. J. (1977). Comprehension of pragmatic implications in advertising. *Journal of Applied Psychology, 62,* 603–608.

Harris, T. A. (1967). *I'm OK—you're OK.* New York: Harper & Row.

Harrison, A. A. (1976). *Individuals and groups.* Monterey, Calif.: Brooks/Cole.

Hart, K. J., & Ollendick, T. H. (1985). Prevalence of bulimia in working and university women. *American Journal of Psychiatry, 142* (7), 851–854.

Hartley, D., Roback, H., & Abramowitz, S. (1976). Deterioration effects in encounter groups. *American Psychologist, 31,* 247–255.

Harvard Medical School Mental Health Letter (1986, February). Suicide, Part I and II. *2* (8), 1–4.

Heckman, N. A., Bryson, R., & Bryson, J. B. (1977). Problems of professional couples: A content analysis. *Journal of Marriage and the Family, 39* (2), 323–330.

Herzberg, F. (1968, March). Motivation morale. *Psychology Today,* pp. 42–45.

Hetherington, E. M. (1972). The effect of father absence on personality development in adolescent daughters. *Developmental Psychology, 7,* 313–326.

Hetherington, E. M., Cox, M., & Cox, R. (1977, April) Divorced fathers. *Psychology Today,* p. 42.

Hettlinger, R. F. (1975). *Human sexuality: A psychosocial perspective.* Belmont, Calif.: Wadsworth.

Hill, W. F. (1985). *Learning: A survey of psychological interpretations* (4th ed.). New York: Harper & Row.

Hiller, D. V., & Philliber, W. W. (1978). The derivation of status benefits from occupational attainments of working wives. *Journal of Marriage and the Family, 40* (1), 63–68.

Holmes, T. H., & Rahe, R. H. (1967). The social readjustment rating scale. *Journal of Psychosomatic Research, 2,* 213–218.

Holtzman, W. H. (1975). New developments in the Holtzman Inkblot Technique. In P. McReynolds (Ed.), *Advances in psychological assessment* (Vol. 3). San Francisco: Jossey-Bass.

Horn, J. C. (1980, June). Dining: What tips tippers to tip. *Psychology Today,* p. 32.

Horn, P., et al. (1973, October). The phony Doctor Fox. *Psychology Today,* pp. 19–20.

Horner, M. (1969, March). Women's will to fail. *Psychology Today,* pp. 36–38.

Hunt, M. (1974). *Sexual behavior in the 1970's.* Chicago: Playboy Press.

Huston, T., Ruggiero, M., Conner, R., & Geis, G. (1981). Bystander intervention into crime: A study based on naturally occurring episodes. *Social Psychology Quarterly, 44,* 14–23.

Hyde, J. S. (1981). How large are cognitive gender differences? *American Psychologist, 36* (8), 892–901.

Hyde, J. S. (1984). How large are gender differences in aggression? A developmental meta-analysis. *Developmental Psychology, 20,* 722–736.

Hyde, J. S. (1986). *Understanding human sexuality* (3rd ed.). New York: McGraw-Hill.

Ickes, W., & Barnes, R. (1978). Boys and girls together and alienated: On enacting stereotyped sex roles in mixed sex dyads. *Journal of Personality and Social Psychology, 36* (7), 669–683.

Iris, B., & Barrett, G. (1972). Some relationships between job and life satisfaction. *Journal of Applied Psychology, 56* (4), 301–304.

Ismail, A. H., & Gruber, J. J. (1967). *Integrated development: Motor aptitude and intellectual performance*. Columbus, Ohio: Charles E. Merrill.

Janis, I. L. (1973). *Victims of groupthink: A psychological study of foreign policy discussion and fiascos*. Boston: Houghton Mifflin.

Janis, I. L., & Feshbach, S. (1953). Effects of fear-arousing communications. *Journal of Abnormal and Social Psychology, 48,* 78–92.

Janis, I. L., & Wheeler, D. (1978, May). Thinking clearly about career choices. *Psychology Today,* pp. 67–68.

Johnson, W. G. (1971). Some applications of Homme's covariant control therapy: Two case reports. *Behavior Therapy, 2,* 240–248.

Jourard, S. (1971). *Self-disclosure*. New York: Wiley-Interscience.

Jourard, S. (1971). *The transparent self*. New York: Van Nostrand Reinhold.

Kalish, R. A., & Reynolds, D. K. (1976). *Death and ethnicity: A psychocultural study*. Los Angeles: University of Southern California Press.

Kaminoff, R. D., & Proshansky, H. M. (1982). Stress as a consequence of the urban physical environment. In L. Goldberger & S. Breznitz (Eds.), *Handbook of stress: Theoretical and clinical aspects*. New York: Free Press.

Kanner, A. D., Coyne, J. C., Schaefer, C., & Lazarus, R. (1981). Comparison of two modes of stress measurement: Daily hassles and uplifts versus major life events. *Journal of Behavioral Medicine, 4,* 1–39.

Kastenbaum, R., & Costa, P. T. (1977). Psychological perspective on death. *Annual Review of Psychology, 28,* 225–249.

Kelly, J. B. (1982). Divorce: The adult perspective. In B. Wolman (Ed.), *Handbook of developmental psychology*. Englewood Cliffs, N.J.: Prentice-Hall.

Kelman, H. C. (1958). Compliance, identification and internalization: Three processes of attitude change. *Journal of Conflict Resolution, 2,* 51–60.

Kessler, M., & Albee, G. W. (1975). Primary prevention. *Annual Review of Psychology, 26,* 557–592.

Keys, A. B., Brozek, J., Henschel, A., Michelson, O., & Taylor, H. L. (1950). *The biology of human starvation* (Vol. 2). Minneapolis: University of Minnesota Press.

King, K., Balswick, J. O., & Robinson, I. E. (1977). The continuing premarital sexual revolution among college females. *Journal of Marriage and the Family, 39,* 455–459.

Klatzky, R. L. (1975). *Human memory: Structures and processes*. San Francisco: Freeman.

Klatzky, R. L. (1980). *Human memory: Structures and processes* (2nd ed.). San Francisco: Freeman.

Koch, K. (1977). *I never told anybody*. New York: Random House.

Kohlberg, L. (1969). Stage and sequence: The cognitive developmental approach to socialization. In D. A. Goslin (Ed.), *Handbook of socialization theory and research*. Chicago: Rand McNally.

Kohlberg, L. (1976). Moral stages and moralization. In T. Lickona (Ed.), *Moral development and behavior*. New York: Holt, Rinehart & Winston.

Kohn, M., & Schooler, C. (1983). *Work and personality*. Norwood, N.J.: Ablex.

Korte, C., & Kerr, N. (1975). Response to altruistic opportunities in urban and nonurban settings. *Journal of Social Psychology, 95,* 183–184.

Kübler-Ross, E. (1969). *On death and dying*. New York: Macmillan.

Lamb, H. R. (1984). *Homeless mentally ill*. Washington, D.C.: American Psychiatric Association.

Lamb, M. (1979). Paternal influences and the father's role: A personal perspective. *American Psychologist, 34* (10), 938–943.

Langer, E. J., Bashner, R. S., & Chanowitz, B. (1985). Decreasing prejudice by increasing discrimination. *Journal of Personality and Social Psychology, 49* (1), 113–120.

Langer, E. J., & Dweck, C. S. (1973). *Personal politics: The psychology of making it*. Englewood Cliffs, N.J.: Prentice-Hall.

Lapp, D. (1987). *Don't forget! Easy exercises for a better memory at any age*. New York: McGraw-Hill.

Larson, D. L., Spreitzer, E. A., & Snyder, E. E. (1976). Social factors in the frequency of romantic involvement among adolescents. *Adolescence, 11,* 7–12.

Latané, B., & Darley, J. M. (1968). Group inhibition of bystander intervention. *Journal of Personality and Social Psychology, 10,* 215–221.

Latané, B., & Darley, J. M. (1970). *The unresponsive bystander: Why doesn't he help?* New York: Appleton-Century-Crofts.

Latané, B., Williams, K., & Harkins, S. (1979). Many hands make light work: The causes and consequences of social loafing. *Journal of Personality and Social Psychology, 37,* 822–832.

Lawler, E. E. (1970). Job attitudes and employee motivation: Theory, research and practice. *Personnel Psychology, 23,* 223–237.

Leavitt, H. J. (1951). Some effects of certain communication patterns on group performance. *Journal of Abnormal and Social Psychology, 46,* 38–50.

Leboyer, F. (1975). *Birth without violence.* New York: Random House.

Levanway, R. W. (1955). The effect of stress on expressing attitudes toward self and others. *Journal of Abnormal and Social Psychology, 50,* 225–226.

Levine, M. E., Villena, J., Altman, D., & Nadien, M. (1976). Trust of a stranger: An urban/small town comparison. *Journal of Psychology, 92,* 113–116.

Levinson, D. (1986). A conception of adult development. *American Psychologist, 41* (1), 3–13.

Levinson, D. J., Darrow, C. N., Klein, E. B., Levinson, M. H., & McKee, B. (1978). *The seasons of a man's life.* New York: Knopf.

Lewin, K. (1935). *A dynamic theory of personality.* K. E. Zener & D. K. Adams (Trans.). New York: McGraw-Hill.

Lewin, K., Lippitt, R., & White, R. (1943). Patterns of aggressive behavior in experimentally created social climates. *Journal of Social Psychology, 10,* 271–299.

Lindzey, G., Hall, C., & Thompson, R. (1975). *Psychology.* New York: Worth.

Loftus, E. F. (1975). Leading questions and the eyewitness report. *Cognitive Psychology, 1,* 560–572.

Loftus, E. F., Miller, D. G., & Burns, H. J. (1978). Semantic integration of verbal information into visual memory. *Journal of Experimental Psychology: Human Learning and Memory, 4,* 19–31.

Luft, J. (1970). *Group process: An introduction to group dynamics.* Palo Alto, Calif.: National Press Books.

Lynn, D. (1974). *The father: His role in child development.* Monterey, Calif.: Brooks/Cole.

Macauley, J. R. (1970). A shill for Santa Claus. In J. Macauley & L. Berkowitz (Eds.), *Altruism and helping behaviors: Social psychological studies of some antecedents and consequences.* New York: Academic Press.

Maccoby, E. E., & Jacklin, C. N. (1974). *The psychology of sex differences.* Stanford, Calif.: Stanford University Press.

Macklin, E. D. (1972). Heterosexual cohabitation among unmarried college students. *Family Coordinator, 21,* 463–472.

Madigan, C. O., & Elwood, A. (1984). *Brainstorms and thunderbolts.* New York: Macmillan.

Mahoney, M. J. (1971). The self-management of covert behavior: A case study. *Behavior Therapy, 2,* 575–578.

Maier, S. F., & Laudenslager, M. (1985, August). Stress and health: Exploring the links. *Psychology Today,* pp. 44–45.

Marcus, M. G. (1976, May). The power of a name. *Psychology Today,* pp. 75–76.

Marion, R. W., Wiznia, A. A., Hutcheon, G., & Rubinstein, A. (1986). Human T-cell lymphotropic virus Type III (HTLV-III) embryopathy. *American Journal of Diseases of Children, 140* (7), 638–640.

Martin, R. A., & Lefcourt, H. M. (1983). Sense of humor as a moderator of the relation between stressors and moods. *Journal of Personality and Social Psychology, 45,* 1313–1324.

Maslow, A. H. (1970). *Motivation and personality.* New York: Harper & Row.

Mason, R. A. (1985). Artificial intelligence: Promise, myth, and reality. *Library Journal, 110* (7), 56–57.

Mathews, K., Helmreich, R., Beane, J., & Lucker, W. (1981). Making it in academic psychology: Demographic and personality correlates of attainment. *Journal of Personality and Social Psychology, 39,* 896.

Matlin, M. M. (1987). *The psychology of women.* New York: Holt, Rinehart & Winston.

Matteson, D. R. (1975). *Adolescence today: Sex roles and the search for identity.* Homewood, Ill.: Dorsey Press.

Mayer, R. E. (1983). *Thinking, problem solving, cognition.* New York: W. H. Freeman.

McClelland, D. C. (1961). *The achieving society.* Princeton, N.J.: Van Nostrand.

McGaugh, J. L. (1970). Time-dependent processes in memory storage. In J. L. McGaugh & M. J. Herz (Eds.), *Controversial issues of memory trace.* New York: Atherton.

McGaugh, J. L. (1983). Preserving the presence of the past: Hormonal influences on memory storage. *American Psychologist, 38,* 161–174.

McGregor, D. (1960). *The human side of enterprise.* New York: McGraw-Hill.

McGuire, W. J. (1961). Resistance to counter-persuasion conferred by active and passive prior refutation of the same alternative counter-arguments. *Journal of Abnormal and Social Psychology, 63,* 326–332.

Mead, M. (1935). *Sex and temperament in three primitive societies.* New York: Morrow.

Menninger, K. (1938). *Man against himself.* New York: Harcourt Brace Jovanovich.

Merton, R. (1948). The self-fulfilling prophecy. *Antioch Review, 8,* 193–210.

Milgram, S. (1963). Behavior study of obedience. *Journal of Abnormal and Social Psychology, 67,* 371–378.

Milgram, S. (1970). The experience of living in cities. *Science, 167,* 1461–1468.

Milgram, S. (1974). *Obedience to authority.* New York: Harper & Row.

Milgram, S., Beckman, L., & Berkowitz, L. (1969). Note on the drawing power of crowds of different size. *Journal of Personality and Social Psychology, 13,* 79–82.

Miller, G. (1969). On turning psychology over to the unwashed. American Psychological Association Paper.

Miller, M. E., Adesso, V. J., Fleming, J. P., Gino, A., & Lauerman, R. (1978). Effects of alcohol on the storage and retrieval processes of heavy social drinkers. *Journal of Experimental Psychology: Human Learning and Memory, 4,* 246–255.

Mintz, A. (1951). Non-adaptive group behavior. *Journal of Abnormal and Social Psychology, 46,* 150–159.

Monahan, K. D., & Shaver, P. (1974). Interpsychic versus cultural explanations of the "fear of success" motive. *Journal of Personality and Social Psychology, 29,* 60–64.

Moreno, J. L. (1953). *Who shall survive?* New York: Beacon House.

Morris, D., Collett, P., & O'Shaughnessy, M. (1979). *Gestures.* New York: Stein & Day.

Mueller, C. W., & Campbell, B. G. (1977). Female occupational achievement and marital status: A research note. *Journal of Marriage and the Family, 39* (3), 587–593.

Mussen, P. H., Conger, J. J., & Kagan, J. (1978). *Child Development and Personality.* New York: Harper & Row.

Myers, D. G. (1980). *The inflated self.* New York: Seabury Press.

Nahas, G. G. (1979). *Keep off the grass.* Elmsford, N.Y.: Pergamon Press.

Nathan, P. E., & O'Brien, J. S. (1971). An experimental analysis of the behavior of alcoholics and nonalcoholics during prolonged experimental drinking: A necessary precursor of behavior therapy? *Behavior Therapy, 2,* 455–476.

Nathan, P. E., O'Brien, J. S., & Lowenstein, I. M. (1971). Operant studies of chronic alcoholism: Interaction of alcohol and alcoholics. In P. J. Creaven & M. K. Roach (Eds.), *Biological aspects of alcohol.* Austin: University of Texas Press.

National Center for Health Statistics. (1986). Maternal weight gain and the outcome of pregnancy, United States, 1986. *Vital statistics* (Series 21, No. 44, DHHS Pub. No. 86-1922), Washington, D.C.: U.S. Government Printing Office.

National Institute on Alcohol Abuse and Alcoholism (NIAAA) (1981). *Fourth special report to the U.S. Congress on alcohol and health.* Washington, D.C.: U.S. Government Printing Office.

National Institute on Alcohol Abuse and Alcoholism (NIAAA) (1982). *Alcohol and Health Monograph Nos. 1,2,3,4.* Washington, D.C.: Department of Health and Human Services.

National Institute of Health (1984). *Drugs and insomnia.* NIH consensus development statement, *4* (10). Washington, D.C.: U.S. Government Printing Office.

Nemy, E. (1973, April 16). Suicide now no. 2 cause of deaths among young. *New York Times*, p. 1.

Neugarten, B. (1980, April). In E. Hall (Interviewer), Acting one's age: New rules for the old. *Psychology Today*, pp. 66–80.

Newcomb, T. (1963). Persistance and regression of changed attitudes: Long-range studies. *Journal of Social Studies, 19,* 3–14.

Nidetch, J. (1962). *The story of weight watchers.* New York: New American Library.

Nolan, J. D. (1968). Self-control procedures in the modification of smoking behaviors. *Journal of Consulting and Clinical Psychology, 32,* 92–93.

Nord, W. (1970). Improving attendance through rewards. *Personnel Administration, 33,* 37–41.

Norton, A. J., & Glick, P. C. (1976). Marital instability: Past, present and future. *The Journal of Social Issues, 32,* 5–20.

Novaco, R. W. (1975). *Anger control: The development and evaluation of an experimental treatment.* Lexington, Mass.: Heath, Lexington Books.

Oldham, G., Hackman, J. R., & Pearce, J. F. (1976). Conditions under which employees respond positively to enriched work. *Journal of Applied Psychology, 61* (4), 395–403.

Olshan, N. H. (1980). *Power over your pain without drugs.* New York: Rawson, Wade.

Osgood, C. E. (1957). A behavioristic analysis of perception and language as cognitive phenomena. In *Contemporary approaches to cognition.* Cambridge, Mass.: Harvard University Press.

Parker, E. S., Birnbaum, I. M., & Noble, E. P. (1976). Alcohol and memory: Storage and state dependency. *Journal of Verbal Learning and Verbal Behavior, 15,* 691–702.

Parkes, C. M. (1972). *Bereavement: Studies of grief in adult life.* New York: International Universities Press.

Paul, R. W. (1984, September). Critical thinking: Fundamental to education for a free society. *Educational Leadership.*

Pearlin, L., & Schooler, C. (1978). The structure of coping. *Journal of Health and Social Behavior, 19,* 2–21.

Pecoraro, T. (1981, October). Beauty I: Jurors go easy on handsome rapists and homely victims. *Psychology Today.*

Perls, F. S. (1973). *The gestalt therapy and ex-witness to therapy.* Palo Alto, Calif.: Science & Behavior Books.

Petersen, R. C. (1984). Marijuana overview. In M. D. Glantz (Ed.), *Correlates and consequences of marijuana use* (DHHS Pub No. ADM84-1276). Washington, D.C.: U.S. Government Printing Office.

Phares, E. J. (1976). *Locus of control in personality.* Morristown, N.J.: General Learning Press.

Piaget, J. (1952). *The origins of intelligence in children.* New York: International Universities Press.

Pick, H. I., & Pick, A. D. (1970). Sensory and perceptual development. In P. H. Mussen (Ed.), *Carmichael's manual of child psychology* (Vol. 1). New York: Wiley.

Pines, A., & Kafry, D. (1977). *Burn-out and life tedium in three generations of professional women.* American Psychological Association Paper.

Plateris, A. (1978). *Divorce and divorce rates, United States vital health statistics* (Series 21, No. 29, National Center for Health Statistics) Washington, D.C.: U.S. Government Printing Office.

Pogrebin, L. C. (1980, June 30). Celebrating ourselves. *Bottom Line Personal.*

Polivy, J., & Herman, C. (1985). Dieting and binging: A causal analysis. *American Psychologist, 40,* 193–201.

Prioleau, L., Murdock, M., & Brody, N. (1983). An analysis of psychotherapy versus placebo studies. *Behavioral and Brain Sciences, 6,* 275–285.

Pyke, S. W., & Kahill, S. P. (1983, Winter). Sex differences in characteristics presumed relevant to professional productivity. *Psychology of Women Quarterly, 8,* 189–192.

Raudsepp, E. (1980, July). More creative gamesmanship. *Psychology Today,* pp. 71–76.

Reik, T. (1972). *Listening with the third ear.* New York: Pyramid Publications.

Relman, A. S. (1982). Marijuana and health. *New England Journal of Medicine, 306* (10), 603–604.

Renne, K. S. (1970). Correlates of dissatisfaction in marriage. *Journal of Marriage and the Family, 32,* 54–67.

Renwick, P., & Lawler, E. (1978, May). What you really want from your job. *Psychology Today,* pp. 58–66.

Rice, B. (1980, January). Dear Miss C-3PO. *Psychology Today.*

Rice, B. (1980, July). Work: Education for restlessness. *Psychology Today.*

Robins, L. N., Helzer, J. E., Weissman, M. M., Orvalschel, H., Greenberg, E., Burke, J. D., & Regier, D. A. (1984). Lifetime prevalence of specific psychiatric disorders in three sites. *Archives of General Psychiatry, 41,* 949–958.

Rogers, C. (1970). *Carl Rogers on encounter groups.* New York: Harper & Row.

Rogers, D. (1972). *Adolescence: A psychological perspective.* Monterey, Calif.: Brooks/Cole.

Rorschach, H. (1942). *Psychodiagnostics: A diagnostic test based on perception.* New York: Grune & Stratton.

Rosenbaum, B. (1980, September 22). Self-esteem gets the job done. *Chemical Engineering.*

Rotter, J. B. (1966). Generalized expectancies for internal vs. external control of reinforcement. *Psychological Monographs, 80* (Whole No. 609).

Rubenstein, C. (1981, January). Relationships: Martyrdom's brief glow. *Psychology Today,* p. 82.

Rubenstein, C. (1981, July). Alienation in supermarkets. *Psychology Today*

Sass, L. (1982, August 22). The borderline personality. The *New York Times Magazine,* pp. 12–15, 66–67.

Schacter, D. L. (1986). Amnesia and crime: How much do we really know? *American Psychologist, 41,* 286–295.

Schank, R., & Abelson, R. (1983). Scripts, plans and knowledge. In R. Mayer, *Thinking, problem solving, cognition.* New York: W. H. Freeman.

Schank, R. C., & Hunter, L. (1985). The quest to understand thinking. *BYTE, 10* (4), 143–155.

Schein, E. H., Schneier, I., & Barker, C. H. (1961). *Coercive persuasion.* New York: Norton.

Schmeck, H. (1988, July 23). Research hints at link to Alzheimer's disease. *New York Times.*

Schmidt, S. M., & Kipnis, D. (1985, April). The language of persuasion. *Psychology Today.*

Selby, H. (1987, March). Work: Retiring from unemployment. *Psychology Today.*

Seligman, M. E. P. (1974, January). Submissive death: Giving up on life. *Psychology Today,* pp. 80–85.

Shapiro, S., Skinner, E. A., Kessler, L. G., Von Korff, M., German, P. S., Tischler, G. L., Leaf, P. J., Benham, L., Cottler, L., & Regier, D. A. (1984). Utilization of health and mental services. *Archives of General Psychiatry, 41* (10), 971–978.

Shaver, P., & O'Connor, C. (1986). Problems in perspective. In C. Tavris (Ed.), *Every woman's emotional well-being.* New York: Doubleday.

Shaw, M. E. (1971). *Group dynamics.* New York: McGraw-Hill.

Sheehy, G. (1976). *Passages: Predictable crises of adult life.* New York: Dutton.

Shekelle, R. B., Raynor, W. J., Ostfield, A. M., Garron, D. C., Beliauskas, L. A., Lin, S. C., Malizia, C., & Paul, O. (1981). Psychological depression and 17-year risk of death from cancer. *Psychosomatic Medicine, 43* (2), 117–125.

Sherif, M., Harvey, O. J., White, B. J., Hood, W. R., & Sherif, C. W. (1961). *Intergroup conflict and cooperation: The robbers' cave experiment.* Norman, Okla.: Institute of Group Relations, University of Oklahoma.

Sherman, L. M., & Berk, R. A. (1984). The specific deterrent effects of arrest for domestic assault. *American Sociological Review, 49,* 261–271.

Simon, W., Berger, A. S., & Gagnon, J. H. (1972). Beyond anxiety and fantasy: The coital experiences of college youth. *Journal of Youth and Adolescence, 1* (3), 203–221.

Sirpola, E. M. (1935). A study of some effects of preparatory set. *Psychological Monographs, 46* (Whole No. 210).

Sklar, L., & Anirman, H. (1951). Stress and cancer. *Psychological Bulletin, 89,* 369–406.

Sommer, R. (1969). *Personal space.* Englewood Cliffs, N.J.: Prentice-Hall.

Spitz, R. (1965). *The first year of life.* New York: International University Press.

Stafford, R., Backman, E., & Dibona, P. (1977). The division of labor among cohabiting and married couples. *Journal of Marriage and the Family, 39* (11), 40–47.

Stein, R. (1988, July 22). Study suggests virus is involved in at least some Alzheimer's cases. *Philadelphia Inquirer.*

Sternberg, R. J. (1984). *Beyond IQ: A triarchic theory of human intelligence.* New York: Cambridge University Press.

Stoner, J. A. F. (1961). A comparison of individual and group decisions involving risk. Unpublished master's thesis, MIT, Cambridge, Mass.

Stuart, R. B., & Davis, B. (1972). *Slim chance in a fat world.* Champaign, Ill.: Research Press Company.

Taylor, S., Lichman, R., & Wood, J. (1984). Attribution, beliefs about control and adjustment to breast cancer. *Journal of Personality and Social Psychology, 46,* 489–502.

Tennov, D. (1979). *Love and limerance.* Briarcliff Manor, N.Y.: Stein & Day.

Tesch, F., Lansky, L. M., & Lundgren, D. C. (1972). The exchange of information: One-way versus two-way communication. *Journal of Applied Behavioral Science, 8,* 4.

Thigpen, C. H., & Cleckley, H. (1954). *The three faces of Eve.* New York: McGraw-Hill.

Thorndike, P. W. (1977). Cognitive structures in comprehension and memory of narrative discourse. *Cognitive Psychology, 9,* 77–110.

Tyhurst, J. S. (1951). Individual reactions to community disaster. *American Journal of Psychiatry, 10,* 746–769.

U.S. Census Bureau. (1979). *Perspectives on American husbands and wives.* Washington, D.C.: U.S. Government Printing Office.

Vokey, J. R., & Read, J. D. (1985). Subliminal messages: Between the devil and the media. *American Psychologist, 40,* 1231–1239.

Wagner, R. K., & Sternberg, R. J. (1985). Practical intelligence in real-world pursuits: The role of tacit knowledge. *Journal of Personality and Social Psychology, 49* (20), 436–458.

Walster, E., & Festinger, L. (1962). The effectiveness of "overheard" persuasive communications. *Journal of Abnormal and Social Psychology, 65,* 395–402.

Walster, E., Walster, G. W., Piliavin, J., & Schmidt, L. (1973). "Playing hard to get": Understanding an elusive phenomenon. *Journal of Personality and Social Psychology, 26,* 113–121.

Warner, R. (1986, June). Hard times and schizophrenia. *Psychology Today.*

Weisman, A. D. (1972). *On dying and denying: A psychiatric study of terminality.* New York: Behavioral Publications.

Weitzman, L. (1986). *The divorce revolution.* New York: Free Press.

Wetzel, C. D., Janowsky, D. S., & Clopton, P. L. (1982). Remote memory during marijuana intoxication. *Psychopharmacology, 76,* 278–281.

Williams, A. F. (1966). Social drinking, anxiety and depression. *Journal of Personality and Social Psychology, 3,* 689–693.

Wolfe, J. M. (1983). Hidden visual processes. *Scientific American, 218* (2), 94–103.

Wylie, R. C. (1957). Some relationships between defensiveness and self-concept discrepencies. *Journal of Personality, 25,* 600–617.

Yankelovich, D. (1978, May). The new psychological contract at work. *Psychology Today,* p. 4.

Zajonc, R. (1968). Attitudinal effects of mere exposure. *Journal of Personality and Social Psychology, 9,* 1–27.

ACKNOWLEDGMENTS

For permission to use copyrighted materials, the author is indebted to the following:

Chapter 1

Page 2   Quotation from George Miller. Reprinted by permission of George Miller.

Page 3   Exhibit 1-1. Copyright 1987 by the American Psychological Association. Reprinted by permission.

Page 6   Figure 1-2. Reprinted with special permission of NAS, Inc.

Page 7–9   Exhibit 1-2. Adapted from the University of Colorado, School of Liberal Arts catalog with permission from the University of Colorado, Psychology Department.

Page 14   Figure 1-3. Reprinted from *The Saturday Evening Post* © 1987 BFL&MS, Inc.

Page 16   Figure 1-4. Reprinted from *The Saturday Evening Post* © 1987 BFL&MS, Inc.

Page 18   Exhibit 1-4. Reprinted with permission from *The Arlington Journal* .

Page 19   Exhibit 1-5. Reprinted with permission from *Psychology Today* Magazine. Copyright © 1988 (P. T. Partners, L.P.).

Page 19   Figure 1-7. Drawing by Drucker, © 1987 *The New Yorker* Magazine, Inc.

Page 21   Exhibit 1-6. Reprinted with permission from *Psychology Today* Magazine. Copyright © 1981 (P. T. Partners, L.P.).

Page 23   Exhibit 1-8. Reprinted with permission from *Psychology Today* Magazine. Copyright © 1987 (P. T. Partners, L.P.).

Chapter 2

Page 32   Exhibit 2-1. Reproduced with permission of *The Washington Post*.

Page 32   Exhibit 2-2. Reproduced with permission of Parade Publications, Inc.

Page 35   Figure 2-2. Used by permission of Don Bousquet.

Page 36   Figure 2-4. Reprinted from *The Saturday Evening Post* © 1987 BFL&MS, Inc.

Page 36   Figure 2-5. Drawing by Vietor, © 1988 *The New Yorker* Magazine, Inc.

Page 40   Exhibit 2-3. Reprinted from *The Saturday Evening Post* © 1988 BFL&MS, Inc.

Page 41   Figure 2-6. Copyright 1961 Canadian Psychological Association. Reprinted by permission.

Page 43   Exhibit 2-4. Reprinted with permission from *Psychology Today* Magazine. Copyright © 1987 (P. T. Partners, L.P.).

Page 45   Figure 2-8. Reprinted with permission from the University of Illinois Press, copyright © 1951.

Page 52   Exhibit 2-5. Copyright 1987 by *OMNI* Magazine and reprinted with the permission of Omni Publications International, Ltd.

Page 53   Exhibit 2-6. Reprinted with permission from *Psychology Today* Magazine. Copyright © 1987 (P. T. Partners, L.P.).

Page 56   Exhibit 2-7. Copyright 1988 by *OMNI* Magazine and reprinted with the permission of Omni Publications International, Ltd.

Chapter 3

Page 65   Figure 3-2. Reprinted from *The Saturday Evening Post* © 1987 BFL&MS, Inc.

Page 72   Exhibit 3-1. Reprinted with permission from *Science News,* the weekly newsmagazine of science, copyright 1978 by Science Service, Inc.

Page 73   Exhibit 3-2. Copyright 1987 by *OMNI* Magazine and reprinted with the permission of Omni Publications International, Ltd.

Page 75   Figure 3-7. Reprinted with special permission of King Features Syndicate, Ltd.

Page 80   Exhibit 3-3. Copyright 1987 by the American Psychological Association. Reprinted by permission.

Page 85   Figure 3-8. Reprinted courtesy *OMNI* Magazine © 1989.

Chapter 4

Page 96   Exhibit 4-1. Reprinted with permission from *Psychology Today* Magazine. Copyright © 1988 (P. T. Partners, L.P.).

Page 101   Figure 4-3. Drawing by W. Miller, © 1987 *The New Yorker* Magazine, Inc.

Page 105   Exhibit 4-2. Reprinted with permission from *Psychology Today* Magazine. Copyright © 1987 (P. T. Partners, L.P.).

Page 110   Exhibit 4-3. Reprinted with permission from *Psychology Today* Magazine. Copyright © 1988 (P. T. Partners, L.P.).

Page 115   Exhibit 4-4. Copyright 1988 by *OMNI* Magazine and reprinted with the permission of Omni Publications International, Ltd.

Pages 121 and 122   Exhibit 4-5. Reprinted with the permission of Jill York Miller.

Chapter 5

Page 128   Figure 5-1. Reprinted from *The Saturday Evening Post* © 1987 BFL&MS, Inc.

Page 131   Exhibit 5-1. Reprinted from *The Saturday Evening Post* © 1987 BFL&MS, Inc.

Page 132   Figure 5-2. Reprinted from *The Saturday Evening Post* © 1980 BFL&MS, Inc.

Page 133   Exhibit 5-2. Copyright © 1980 by Eugene Raudsepp. From *More Creative Growth Games* published by Perigee Books. Used by permission.

Page 134   Figure 5-3. *Herman* © 1987 Universal Press Syndicate. Reprinted with permission. All rights reserved.

Page 136   Exhibit 5-3. Reprinted with permission from *Science News,* the weekly newsmagazine of science, copyright 1987 by Science Service, Inc.

Page 137 Exhibit 5-5. Reprinted from *The Saturday Evening Post* © 1987 BFL&MS, Inc.

Page 139 Exhibit 5-4. Reprinted with permission from *Science News,* the weekly newsmagazine of science, copyright 1987 by Science Service, Inc.

Page 141 Exhibit 5-6. Reprinted with permission from McGraw-Hill Book Company © 1988.

Page 145 Exhibit 5-7. Reprinted with permission from *Psychology Today* Magazine. Copyright © 1987.

Pages 146 and 147 Exhibit 5-8. Copyright © 1986 by the New York Times Company. Reprinted by permission.

Page 147 Exhibit 5-9. Reprinted with permission from *Science News,* the weekly newsmagazine of science, copyright 1988 by Science Service, Inc.

Chapter 6

Page 155 Exhibit 6-1. Reprinted with permission from *Psychology Today* Magazine. Copyright © 1988 (P. T. Partners, L.P.).

Page 159 Exhibit 6-2. Copyright 1988 Time, Inc. Reprinted by permission.

Page 160 Exhibit 6-3. Reprinted with permission from *Science News,* the weekly newsmagazine of science, copyright 1980 by Science Service, Inc.

Page 164 Figure 6-1. Reprinted from *The Saturday Evening Post* © 1980 BFL&MS, Inc.

Page 166 Figure 6-3. Reprinted from *The Saturday Evening Post* © 1988 BFL&MS, Inc.

Page 168 Exhibit 6-4. Reprinted with permission from *Psychology Today* Magazine. Copyright © 1988 (P. T. Partners, L.P.).

Page 169 Exhibit 6-5. From *How to Eat Like a Child* by Delia Ephron. Reprinted by permission of Viking Penguin, Inc.

Page 170 Exhibit 6-6. Reprinted with permission from *Psychology Today* Magazine. Copyright © 1987 (P. T. Partners, L.P.).

Page 173 Figure 6-4. Drawing by M. Twohy, © 1987 *The New Yorker* Magazine, Inc.

Page 178 Poem by Mary Zaharjko. Reprinted from *I Never Told Anybody* by K. Koch © 1977 with permission from Random House, Inc.

Page 180 Exhibit 6-8. Copyright 1987 by the American Psychological Association. Reprinted by permission.

Chapter 7

Page 187 Figure 7-1. Reprinted by permission of NEA, Inc.

Page 189 Figure 7-2. Reprinted from *The Saturday Evening Post* © 1988 BFL&MS, Inc.

Page 194 Figure 7-4. Drawing by Mort Gerberg, © 1987 *The New Yorker* Magazine, Inc.

Pages 196 and 197 Exhibits 7-1, 7-2. Reprinted with permission from Marilyn Machlowitz © 1980.

Page 198 Figure 7-5. Reprinted from *The Saturday Evening Post* © 1988 BFL&MS, Inc.

Page 202 Exhibit 7-3. Copyright 1981 Time, Inc. All rights reserved. Reprinted by permission from *Time*.

Page 205 Exhibit 7-4. Reprinted with permission from *Psychology Today* Magazine. Copyright © 1988 (P. T. Partners, L.P.).

Page 205 Exhibit 7-5. Reprinted by permission of *The Harvard Business Review*. Excerpt from "Must Success Cost So Much?" by Fernando Bartolome and Paul A. Lee Evans (March–April 1980). Copyright © 1980 by the President and Fellows of Harvard College; all rights reserved.

Chapter 8

Page 215 Exhibit 8-1. Reprinted with permission from *Science News*, the weekly newsmagazine of science, copyright 1988 by Science Service, Inc.

Page 217 Exhibit 8-2. Reprinted with permission from *Psychology Today* Magazine. Copyright © 1987 (P. T. Partners, L.P.).

Page 218 Figure 8-2. Reprinted from *The Saturday Evening Post* © 1988 BFL&MS, Inc.

Page 221 Exhibit 8-3. Reprinted from the *Washington Star*, copyright reserved.

Page 227 Exhibit 8-4. Reprinted with permission from *Psychology Today* Magazine. Copyright © 1980 (P. T. Partners, L.P.).

Page 229 Figure 8-6. Reprinted from *The Saturday Evening Post* © 1954 BFL&MS, Inc.

Page 232 Exhibit 8-5. Reprinted with permission from *Journal of Psychosomatic Research, 3* Thomas H. Holmes and Richard H. Rahe, ''The Social Readjustment Rating Scale,'' copyright 1967, Pergamon Press, Ltd. and with permission of Thomas H. Holmes.

Page 234 Exhibit 8-6. Adapted with permission from Plenum Press copyright, 1981.

Page 235 Figure 8-7. Drawing by Mankoff, © 1987 *The New Yorker* Magazine, Inc.

Page 236 Exhibit 8-7. Reprinted with permission from *Science News*, the weekly newsmagazine of science, copyright 1987 by Science Service, Inc.

Page 237 Exhibit 8-8. Reprinted with permission from *Psychology Today* Magazine. Copyright © 1987 (P. T. Partners, L.P.).

Page 238 `Figure 8-8. Reprinted from *The Saturday Evening Post* © 1987 BFL&MS, Inc.

Page 239 Exhibit 8-9. Reprinted with permission from *Psychology Today* Magazine. Copyright © 1988 (P. T. Partners, L.P.).

Chapter 9

Page 244 Figure 9-1. Drawing by C. Barsotti, © 1980 *The New Yorker* Magazine, Inc.

Page 246 Figure 9-2. Reprinted with permission from *Psychology Today* Magazine. Copyright © 1988 (P. T. Partners, L.P.).

Page 247 Figure 9-3. Drawing by D. Reilly, © 1987 *The New Yorker* Magazine, Inc.

Page 248 Exhibit 9-1. Rosenbaum, B. L. ''Self Esteem Gets the Job Done,'' © 1980. Reproduced by permission of McGraw-Hill Book Company.

Page 251 Figure 9-4. Reprinted from *The Saturday Evening Post* © 1979 BFL&MS, Inc.

Page 252 Figure 9-5. Reprinted from *The Saturday Evening Post* © 1987 BFL&MS, Inc.

Page 253 Figure 9-6. Reprinted by permission of NEA, Inc.

Page 260 Exhibit 9-2. Reprinted by permission of *Psychology Today* Magazine. Copyright © 1988 (P. T. Partners, L.P.).

Page 261 Exhibit 9-3. Reprinted with permission of Jane Brody.

Pages 261 and 262 Exhibit 9-4. Reprinted with permission from *Science News*, the weekly newsmagazine of science, copyright 1978 by Science Service, Inc.

Pages 265 and 266 Exhibit 9-5. Copyright 1987 by the American Psychological Association. Reprinted by permission.

Page 267 Exhibit 9-6. Reprinted from *USAir Magazine*, Pace Communications, Inc., Greensboro, North Carolina, with permission from Ann Handley.

Chapter 10

Page 274 Exhibit 10-1. Reprinted with permission from *Psychology Today* Magazine. Copyright © 1988 (P. T. Partners, L.P.).

Page 276   Exhibit 10-2. Reprinted with permission from *Science News,* the weekly newsmagazine of science, copyright 1988 by Science Service, Inc.

Page 277   Figure 10-1. *Tank McNamara* © 1988 Universal Press Syndicate. Reprinted with permission. All rights reserved.

Page 278   Exhibit 10-3. Reprinted with permission from *Science News,* the weekly newsmagazine of science, copyright 1988 by Science Service, Inc.

Page 280   Figure 10-2. Reprinted courtesy *OMNI* Magazine © 1987.

Page 281   Figure 10-3. Reprinted from *The Saturday Evening Post* © 1987 BFL&MS, Inc.

Page 282   Exhibit 10-4. Reprinted with permission from *Psychology Today* Magazine. Copyright © 1988 (P. T. Partners, L.P.).

Page 284   Figure 10-4. Reprinted courtesy *OMNI* Magazine © 1987.

Pages 285 and 286   Exhibits 10-5, 10-6. Copyright 1987 by *Newsweek,* Inc. All rights reserved. Reprinted by permission.

Page 288   Exhibit 10-7. Reprinted with permission from *Science News,* the weekly newsmagazine of science, copyright 1987 by Science Service, Inc.

Page 289   Exhibit 10-8. Reprinted with permission from *The Washington Post* © 1988.

Page 290   Exhibit 10-9. Reprinted with permission from *Science News,* the weekly newsmagazine of science, copyright 1988 by Science Service, Inc.

Page 292   Figure 10-5. Drawing by Ross, © 1987 *The New Yorker* Magazine, Inc.

Page 294   Figure 10-6. Reprinted from *The Saturday Evening Post* © 1979 BFL&MS, Inc.

Page 295   Exhibit 10-10. Reprinted with permission from *Psychology Today* Magazine. Copyright © 1988 (P. T. Partners, L.P.).

Page 296   Exhibit 10-11. Reprinted with permission from *Science News,* the weekly newsmagazine of science, copyright 1987 by Science Service, Inc.

Chapter 11

Page 300   *Down on Me* (Janis Joplin), quotation used by permission of Slow Dancing Music, Inc., c/o BSA. All rights reserved.

Page 300   *Yesterday* (John Lennon and Paul McCartney) © 1965 Northern Songs Limited. All rights for the U.S.A., Mexico, and the Philippines controlled by Maclen Music, Inc., c/o ATV Music Corp. Used by permission. All rights reserved.

Pages 304 and 305   Exhibit 11-1. Reprinted with permission from *The Washington Post* © 1988.

Page 306   Exhibit 11-2. Reprinted with permission from *The Washington Post* © 1988.

Page 307   Figure 11-1. Reprinted courtesy *OMNI* Magazine © 1988.

Page 308   Exhibit 11-3. Reprinted with permission from *The Washington Post* © 1988.

Page 309   Figure 11-2. Reprinted from *The Saturday Evening Post* © 1988 BFL&MS, Inc.

Page 310   Exhibit 11-4. Reprinted with permission from *Psychology Today* Magazine. Copyright © 1988 (P. T. Partners, L.P.).

Pages 311–312   Exhibit 11-5. Reprinted with permission from *The Washington Post* © 1988.

Page 316   Figure 11-3. Reprinted courtesy of Hoest and *Parade Magazine* © 1989.

Page 319   Exhibit 11-6. Reprinted with permission from *Science News,* the weekly newsmagazine of science, copyright 1988 by Science Service, Inc.

Page 321   Exhibit 11-7. Reprinted with permission from *Science News,* the weekly newsmagazine of science, copyright 1980 by Science Service, Inc.

Page 322   Exhibit 11-8. Copyright 1980, Time, Inc. Reprinted by permission.

Chapter 12

Page 329   Figure 12-1. Drawing by Ross, © 1987 *The New Yorker* Magazine, Inc.

Page 330   Exhibit 12-1. Reprinted with permission from *Psychology Today* Magazine. Copyright © 1988 (P. T. Partners, L.P.).

Page 331   Exhibit 12-2. Reprinted with permission from *Psychology Today* Magazine. Copyright © 1988 (P. T. Partners, L.P.).

Page 333   Exhibit 12-3. Copyright 1987 by the American Psychological Association. Reprinted by permission.

Page 334   Exhibit 12-4. Reprinted from *The Washington Star,* copyright reserved.

Page 335   Figure 12-2. Reprinted from *The Saturday Evening Post* © 1988 BFL&MS, Inc.

Page 338   Exhibit 12-5. Copyright 1988 by *OMNI* Magazine and reprinted with the permission of Omni Publication International, Ltd.

Page 339   Exhibit 12-6. Reprinted with permission from *Psychology Today* Magazine. Copyright © 1988 (P. T. Partners, L.P.).

Page 341   Figure 12-4. Drawing by Bernard Schoenbaum, © 1988 *The New Yorker* Magazine, Inc.

Page 342   Figure 12-5. Drawing by Ziegler, © 1987 *The New Yorker* Magazine, Inc.

Page 344   Exhibit 12-7. Reprinted with permission from *Psychology Today* Magazine. Copyright © 1988 (P. T. Partners, L.P.).

Pages 346 and 347   Exhibit 12-8. Reprinted with permission from *The Washington Post* © 1987.

Page 347   Figure 12-6. Reprinted from *The Saturday Evening Post* © 1987 BFL&MS, Inc.

Page 348   Figure 12-7. Reprinted with special permission of NAS, Inc.

Page 355   Exhibit 12-9. Copyright 1988 by the American Psychological Association. Reprinted by permission.

Chapter 13

Page 363   Figure 13-1. Reprinted from *The Saturday Evening Post* © 1987 BFL&MS, Inc.

Page 364   Figure 13-2. Reprinted from *The Saturday Evening Post* © 1987 BFL&MS, Inc.

Page 366   Exhibit 13-1. Reprinted from *USAir Magazine,* Pace Communications, Inc., Greensboro, North Carolina, with permission from Ann Handley.

Page 367   Exhibit 13-2. Reprinted with permission from *Psychology Today* Magazine. Copyright © 1980 (P. T. Partners, L.P.).

Page 376   Exhibit 13-3. Reprinted with permission from *Science News,* the weekly newsmagazine of science, copyright 1980 by Science Service, Inc.

Page 379   Figure 13-11. Reprinted from APA Monitor, 1988.

Page 379   Figure 13-12. Reprinted from *The Saturday Evening Post* © 1988 BFL&MS, Inc.

Page 380   Exhibit 13-4. © 1988 by Alfie Kohn. Reprinted by permission of the author.

Page 381   Exhibit 13-5. Reprinted with permission from *Psychology Today* Magazine. Copyright © 1988 (P. T. Partners, L.P.).

Page 383   Figure 13-14. Reprinted courtesy *OMNI* Magazine © 1987.

Page 390   Figure 13-21. Drawing by Leo Cullum, © 1987 *The New Yorker* Magazine, Inc.

Page 391   Figure 13-22. From *Group Processes: An Introduction to Group Dynamics* by Joseph Luft by permission of Mayfield Publishing Company, Copyright © 1963, 1970 by Joseph Luft.

Page 394   Figure 13-23. Reprinted by permission of David Hanson.

Chapter 14

Page 405   Figure 14-1. Drawing by Donald Reilly, © 1980 *The New Yorker* Magazine, Inc.

Page 406   Exhibit 14-1. Reprinted with permission from *Psychology Today* Magazine. Copyright © 1988 (P. T. Partners, L.P.).

Page 408   Figure 14-2. *The Far Side* © 1987 Universal Press Syndicate. Reprinted with permission. All rights reserved.

Page 409   Exhibit 14-2. Reprinted with permission from *Psychology Today* Magazine. Copyright © 1988 (P. T. Partners, L.P.).

Page 412   Figure 14-3. Drawing by Brian Savage, © 1987 *The New Yorker* Magazine, Inc.

Page 420   Exhibit 14-3. Reprinted with permission from *Psychology Today* Magazine. Copyright © 1988 (P. T. Partners, L.P.).

Page 421   Exhibit 14-4. Copyright 1987 by the American Psychological Association. Reprinted by permission.

Page 423   Figure 14-4. Reprinted from *The Saturday Evening Post* © 1988 BFL&MS, Inc.

Chapter 15

Page 430   Figure 15-1. Drawing by M. Stevens, © 1987 *The New Yorker* Magazine, Inc.

Page 432   Figure 15-2. Drawing by Chas. Addams, © 1980 *The New Yorker* Magazine, Inc.

Page 436   Exhibit 15-1. Reprinted with permission from *Psychology Today* Magazine. Copyright © 1981 (P. T. Partners, L.P.).

Page 441   Figure 15-5. Reprinted courtesy *OMNI* Magazine © 1989.

Page 442   Exhibit 15-2. From N. Kogan and M. Wallach, *Risk Taking,* Holt Rinehart and Winston, 1964. Reprinted by permission of Holt Rinehart and Winston.

Page 443   Exhibit 15-3. © 1980 by *The Washington Post.* Reprinted by permission.

Pages 446 and 447   Exhibit 15-4. Copyright 1987 by the American Psychological Association. Reprinted by permission.

Page 448   Figure 15-6. Drawing by D. Reilly, © 1987 *The New Yorker* Magazine, Inc.

Pages 452 and 453   Exhibit 15-5. Reprinted with permission from *Psychology Today* Magazine. Copyright © 1987 (P. T. Partners, L.P.).

Page 454   Exhibit 15-6. Copyright 1987 by *OMNI* Magazine and reprinted with the permission of Omni Publications International, Ltd.

Chapter 16

Page 459   Exhibit 16-1. Reprinted with permission from John B. Davies.

Page 461   Figure 16-1. Drawing by Booth, © 1987 *The New Yorker* Magazine, Inc.

Page 464   Exhibit 16-2. Reprinted with permission from *Smithsonian* © 1980.

Page 465   Figure 16-3. Reprinted courtesy *OMNI* Magazine © 1985.

Page 466   Exhibit 16-3. Reprinted with permission from *Science News,* the weekly newsmagazine of science, copyright 1988 by Science Service, Inc.

Page 468   Exhibit 16-4. Reprinted with permission from *Psychology Today* Magazine. Copyright © 1988 (P. T. Partners, L.P.).

Page 473   Exhibit 16-7. Reprinted with permission from *Psychology Today* Magazine. Copyright © 1987 (P. T. Partners, L.P.).

Page 474   Figure 16-4. Reprinted from *The Saturday Evening Post* © 1987 BFL&MS, Inc.

Page 479   Figure 16-5. Reprinted from *The Saturday Evening Post* © 1987 BFL&MS, Inc.

Page 480   Figure 16-6. Drawing by Handelsman, © 1980 *The New Yorker* Magazine, Inc.

INDEX